D0633627

SHORT STORIES
for Students

Advisors

Jayne M. Burton is a teacher of English, a member of the Delta Kappa Gamma International Society for Key Women Educators, and currently a master's degree candidate in the Interdisciplinary Study of Curriculum and Instruction and English at Angelo State University.

Mary Beth Maggio teaches seventh grade language arts in Schaumburg, Illinois.

Tom Shilts is the youth librarian at the Okemos branch of Capital Area District Library in Okemos, Michigan. He holds an MSLS degree from Clarion University of Pennsylvania and an MA in U.S. History from the University of North Dakota.

Amy Spade Silverman has taught at independent schools in California, Texas, Michigan, and New York. She holds a bachelor of arts degree from the University of Michigan and a master of fine arts degree from the University of Houston. She is a member of the National Council of Teachers of English and Teachers and Writers. She is an exam reader for Advanced Placement Literature and Composition. She is also a poet, published in *North American Review*, *Nimrod*, and *Michigan Quarterly Review*, among others.

Mary Turner holds a BS in Secondary Education from East Texas State University and a Master of Education from Western Kentucky University. She teaches English 7 and AP English 12 literature and composition at SBEC in Southaven, Mississippi.

Brian Woerner teaches English at Troy High School in Troy, Ohio. He is also a Program Associate of the Ohio Writing Project at Miami University.

SHORT STORIES *for Students*

Presenting Analysis, Context, and Criticism on Commonly Studied Short Stories

VOLUME 34

Sara Constantakis, Project Editor

Foreword by Thomas E. Barden

GALE
CENGAGE Learning

Detroit • New York • San Francisco • New Haven, Conn • Waterville, Maine • London

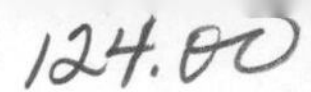

Short Stories for Students, Volume 34

Project Editor: Sara Constantakis

Rights Acquisition and Management: Margaret Chamberlain-Gaston

Composition: Evi Abou-El-Seoud

Manufacturing: Rhonda A. Dover

Imaging: John Watkins

Product Design: Pamela A. E. Galbreath, Jennifer Wahi

Content Conversion: Katrina Coach

Product Manager: Meggin Condino

For product information and technology assistance, contact us at
Gale Customer Support, 1-800-877-4253.
For permission to use material from this text or product,
submit all requests online at **www.cengage.com/permissions.**
Further permissions questions can be emailed to
permissionrequest@cengage.com

Gale
27500 Drake Rd.
Farmington Hills, MI, 48331-3535

ISBN-13: 978-1-4144-8583-6
ISBN-10: 1-4144-8583-2

ISSN 1092-7735

This title is also available as an e-book.
ISBN-13: 978-1-4144-8234-7
ISBN-10: 1-4144-8234-5
Contact your Gale, a part of Cengage Learning sales representative for ordering information.

Printed in Mexico
1 2 3 4 5 6 7 15 14 13 12 11

Table of Contents

Why Study Literature At All?

Short Stories for Students is designed to provide readers with information and discussion about a wide range of important contemporary and historical works of short fiction, and it does that job very well. However, I want to use this guest foreword to address a question that it does *not* take up. It is a fundamental question that is often ignored in high school and college English classes as well as research texts, and one that causes frustration among students at all levels, namely why study literature at all? Isn't it enough to read a story, enjoy it, and go about one's business? My answer (to be expected from a literary professional, I suppose) is no. It is not enough. It is a start; but it is not enough. Here's why.

First, literature is the only part of the educational curriculum that deals directly with the actual world of lived experience. The philosopher Edmund Husserl used the apt German term *die Lebenswelt*, "the living world," to denote this realm. All the other content areas of the modern American educational system avoid the subjective, present reality of everyday life. Science (both the natural and the social varieties) objectifies, the fine arts create and/or perform, history reconstructs. Only literary study persists in posing those questions we all asked before our schooling taught us to give up on them. Only literature gives credibility to personal perceptions, feelings, dreams, and the "stream of consciousness" that is our inner voice. Literature wonders about infinity, wonders why God permits evil, wonders what will happen to us after we die. Literature admits that we get our hearts broken, that people sometimes cheat and get away with it, that the world is a strange and probably incomprehensible place. Literature, in other words, takes on all the big and small issues of what it means to be human. So my first answer is that of the humanist we should read literature and study it and take it seriously because it enriches us as human beings. We develop our moral imagination, our capacity to sympathize with other people, and our ability to understand our existence through the experience of fiction.

My second answer is more practical. By studying literature we can learn how to explore and analyze texts. Fiction may be about *die Lebenswelt*, but it is a construct of words put together in a certain order by an artist using the medium of language. By examining and studying those constructions, we can learn about language as a medium. We can become more sophisticated about word associations and connotations, about the manipulation of symbols, and about style and atmosphere. We can grasp how ambiguous language is and how important context and texture is to meaning. In our first encounter with a work of literature, of course, we are not supposed to catch all of these things. We are spellbound, just as the writer wanted us to be. It is as serious students of the writer's art that we begin to see how the tricks are done.

Seeing the tricks, which is another way of saying "developing analytical and close reading skills," is important above and beyond its intrinsic literary educational value. These skills transfer to other fields and enhance critical thinking of any kind. Understanding how language is used to construct texts is powerful knowledge. It makes engineers better problem solvers, lawyers better advocates and courtroom practitioners, politicians better rhetoricians, marketing and advertising agents better sellers, and citizens more aware consumers as well as better participants in democracy. This last point is especially important, because rhetorical skill works both ways when we learn how language is manipulated in the making of texts the result is that we become less susceptible when language is used to manipulate us.

My third reason is related to the second. When we begin to see literature as created artifacts of language, we become more sensitive to good writing in general. We get a stronger sense of the importance of individual words, even the sounds of words and word combinations. We begin to understand Mark Twain's delicious proverb "The difference between the right word and the almost right word is the difference between lightning and a lightning bug." Getting beyond the "enjoyment only" stage of literature gets us closer to becoming makers of word art ourselves. I am not saying that studying fiction will turn every student into a Faulkner or a Shakespeare. But it will make us more adaptable and effective writers, even if our art form ends up being the office memo or the corporate annual report.

Studying short stories, then, can help students become better readers, better writers, and even better human beings. But I want to close with a warning. If your study and exploration of the craft, history, context, symbolism, or anything else about a story starts to rob it of the magic you felt when you first read it, it is time to stop. Take a break, study another subject, shoot some hoops, or go for a run. Love of reading is too important to be ruined by school. The early twentieth century writer Willa Cather, in her novel *My Antonia*, has her narrator Jack Burden tell a story that he and Antonia heard from two old Russian immigrants when they were teenagers. These immigrants, Pavel and Peter, told about an incident from their youth back in Russia that the narrator could recall in vivid detail thirty years later. It was a harrowing story of a wedding party starting home in sleds and being chased by starving wolves. Hundreds of wolves attacked the group's sleds one by one as they sped across the snow trying to reach their village. In a horrible revelation, the old Russians revealed that the groom eventually threw his own bride to the wolves to save himself. There was even a hint that one of the old immigrants might have been the groom mentioned in the story. Cather has her narrator conclude with his feelings about the story. "We did not tell Pavel's secret to anyone, but guarded it jealously as if the wolves of the Ukraine had gathered that night long ago, and the wedding party had been sacrificed, just to give us a painful and peculiar pleasure." That feeling, that painful and peculiar pleasure, is the most important thing about literature. Study and research should enhance that feeling and never be allowed to overwhelm it.

Thomas E. Barden
Professor of English and Director of Graduate English Studies, The University of Toledo

Introduction

Purpose of the Book

The purpose of *Short Stories for Students* (*SSfS*) is to provide readers with a guide to understanding, enjoying, and studying short stories by giving them easy access to information about the work. Part of Gale's "For Students" Literature line, *SSfS* is specifically designed to meet the curricular needs of high school and undergraduate college students and their teachers, as well as the interests of general readers and researchers considering specific short fiction. While each volume contains entries on "classic" stories frequently studied in classrooms, there are also entries containing hard-to-find information on contemporary stories, including works by multicultural, international, and women writers.

The information covered in each entry includes an introduction to the story and the story's author; a plot summary, to help readers unravel and understand the events in the work; descriptions of important characters, including explanation of a given character's role in the narrative as well as discussion about that character's relationship to other characters in the story; analysis of important themes in the story; and an explanation of important literary techniques and movements as they are demonstrated in the work.

In addition to this material, which helps the readers analyze the story itself, students are also provided with important information on the literary and historical background informing each work. This includes a historical context essay, a box comparing the time or place the story was written to modern Western culture, a critical overview essay, and excerpts from critical essays on the story or author. A unique feature of *SSfS* is a specially commissioned critical essay on each story, targeted toward the student reader.

To further help today's student in studying and enjoying each story, information on audiobooks and other media adaptations is provided (if available), as well as reading suggestions for works of fiction and nonfiction on similar themes and topics. Classroom aids include ideas for research papers and lists of critical and reference sources that provide additional material on the work.

Selection Criteria

The titles for each volume of *SSfS* were selected by surveying numerous sources on teaching literature and analyzing course curricula for various school districts. Some of the sources surveyed include: literature anthologies, *Reading Lists for College-Bound Students: The Books Most Recommended by America's Top Colleges*; Teaching the Short Story: A Guide to Using Stories from around the World, by the National Council of Teachers of English (NCTE); and "A Study of High School Literature Anthologies," conducted by Arthur Applebee at the Center for the Learning and Teaching of Literature and sponsored by the National Endowment for the Arts and the Office of Educational Research and Improvement.

Input was also solicited from our advisory board, as well as educators from various areas. From these discussions, it was determined that each volume should have a mix of "classic" stories (those works commonly taught in literature classes) and contemporary stories for which information is often hard to find. Because of the interest in expanding the canon of literature, an emphasis was also placed on including works by international, multicultural, and women authors. Our advisory board members—educational professionals—helped pare down the list for each volume. Works not selected for the present volume were noted as possibilities for future volumes. As always, the editor welcomes suggestions for titles to be included in future volumes.

How Each Entry Is Organized

Each entry, or chapter, in *SSfS* focuses on one story. Each entry heading lists the title of the story, the author's name, and the date of the story's publication. The following elements are contained in each entry:

Introduction: a brief overview of the story which provides information about its first appearance, its literary standing, any controversies surrounding the work, and major conflicts or themes within the work.

Author Biography: this section includes basic facts about the author's life, and focuses on events and times in the author's life that may have inspired the story in question.

Plot Summary: a description of the events in the story. Lengthy summaries are broken down with subheads.

Characters: an alphabetical listing of the characters who appear in the story. Each character name is followed by a brief to an extensive description of the character's role in the story, as well as discussion of the character's actions, relationships, and possible motivation.

Characters are listed alphabetically by last name. If a character is unnamed—for instance, the narrator in "The Eatonville Anthology"—the character is listed as "The Narrator" and alphabetized as "Narrator." If a character's first name is the only one given, the name will appear alphabetically by that name.

Themes: a thorough overview of how the topics, themes, and issues are addressed within the story. Each theme discussed appears in a separate subhead.

Style: this section addresses important style elements of the story, such as setting, point of view, and narration; important literary devices used, such as imagery, foreshadowing, symbolism; and, if applicable, genres to which the work might have belonged, such as Gothicism or Romanticism. Literary terms are explained within the entry, but can also be found in the Glossary.

Historical Context: this section outlines the social, political, and cultural climate in which the author lived and the work was created. This section may include descriptions of related historical events, pertinent aspects of daily life in the culture, and the artistic and literary sensibilities of the time in which the work was written. If the story is historical in nature, information regarding the time in which the story is set is also included. Long sections are broken down with helpful subheads.

Critical Overview: this section provides background on the critical reputation of the author and the story, including bannings or any other public controversies surrounding the work. For older works, this section may include a history of how the story was first received and how perceptions of it may have changed over the years; for more recent works, direct quotes from early reviews may also be included.

Criticism: an essay commissioned by *SSfS* which specifically deals with the story and is written specifically for the student audience, as well as excerpts from previously published criticism on the work (if available).

Sources: an alphabetical list of critical material used in compiling the entry, with bibliographical information.

Further Reading: an alphabetical list of other critical sources which may prove useful for the student. Includes full bibliographical information and a brief annotation.

Suggested Search Terms: a list of search terms and phrases to jumpstart students' further information seeking. Terms include not just titles and author names but also terms and topics related to the historical and literary context of the works.

In addition, each entry contains the following highlighted sections, set apart from the main text as sidebars:

Media Adaptations: if available, a list of audiobooks and important film and television adaptations of the story, including source information. The list also includes stage adaptations, musical adaptations, etc.

Topics for Further Study: a list of potential study questions or research topics dealing with the story. This section includes questions related to other disciplines the student may be studying, such as American history, world history, science, math, government, business, geography, economics, psychology, etc.

Compare and Contrast: an "at-a-glance" comparison of the cultural and historical differences between the author's time and culture and late twentieth century or early twenty-first century Western culture. This box includes pertinent parallels between the major scientific, political, and cultural movements of the time or place the story was written, the time or place the story was set (if a historical work), and modern Western culture. Works written after 1990 may not have this box.

What Do I Read Next?: a list of works that might give a reader points of entry into a classic work (e.g., YA or multicultural titles) and/or complement the featured story or serve as a contrast to it. This includes works by the same author and others, works from various genres, YA works, and works from various cultures and eras.

Other Features

SSfS includes "Why Study Literature At All?," a foreword by Thomas E. Barden, Professor of English and Director of Graduate English Studies at the University of Toledo. This essay provides a number of very fundamental reasons for studying literature and, therefore, reasons why a book such as *SSfS*, designed to facilitate the study of literture, is useful.

A Cumulative Author/Title Index lists the authors and titles covered in each volume of the *SSfS* series.

A Cumulative Nationality/Ethnicity Index breaks down the authors and titles covered in each volume of the *SSfS* series by nationality and ethnicity.

A Subject/Theme Index, specific to each volume, provides easy reference for users who may be studying a particular subject or theme rather than a single work. Significant subjects from events to broad themes are included.

Each entry may include illustrations, including photo of the author, stills from film adaptations (if available), maps, and/or photos of key historical events.

Citing Short Stories for Students

When writing papers, students who quote directly from any volume of *SSfS* may use the following general forms to document their source. These examples are based on MLA style; teachers may request that students adhere to a different style, thus, the following examples may be adapted as needed.

When citing text from *SSfS* that is not attributed to a particular author (for example, the Themes, Style, Historical Context sections, etc.), the following format may be used:

> "The Celebrated Jumping Frog of Calavaras County." *Short Stories for Students*. Ed. Kathleen Wilson. Vol. 1. Detroit: Gale, 1997. 19–20.

When quoting the specially commissioned essay from *SSfS* (usually the first essay under the Criticism subhead), the following format may be used:

> Korb, Rena. Critical Essay on "Children of the Sea." *Short Stories for Students*. Ed. Kathleen Wilson. Vol. 1. Detroit: Gale, 1997. 39–42.

When quoting a journal or newspaper essay that is reprinted in a volume of *SSfS*, the following form may be used:

> Schmidt, Paul. "The Deadpan on Simon Wheeler." *Southwest Review* 41.3 (Summer, 1956): 270–77. Excerpted and reprinted in *Short Stories for Students*. Vol. 1. Ed. Kathleen Wilson. Detroit: Gale, 1997. 29–31.

When quoting material from a book that is reprinted in a volume of *SSfS*, the following form may be used:

> Bell-Villada, Gene H. "The Master of Short Forms." *García Márquez: The Man and His Work*. University of North Carolina Press, 1990. 119–36. Excerpted and reprinted in *Short Stories for Students*. Vol. 1. Ed. Kathleen Wilson. Detroit: Gale, 1997. 89–90.

We Welcome Your Suggestions

The editorial staff of *Short Stories for Students* welcomes your comments and ideas. Readers who wish to suggest short stories to appear in future volumes, or who have other suggestions, are cordially invited to contact the editor. You may contact the editor via E-mail at: **ForStudents Editors@cengage.com.** Or write to the editor at:

Editor, *Short Stories for Students*
Gale
27500 Drake Road
Farmington Hills, MI 48331-3535

Literary Chronology

1809: Edgar Allan Poe is born on January 19 in Boston, Massachusetts.

1841: Edgar Allan Poe's "The Murders in the Rue Morgue" is published in *Graham's Magazine.*

1849: Edgar Allan Poe dies of unknown causes on October 7 in Baltimore, Maryland.

1866: Herbert George Wells is born on September 21 in Bromley, England.

1871: Stephen Crane is born on November 1 in Newark, New Jersey.

1882: Virginia Woolf is born on January 25 in London, England.

1889: Conrad Potter Aiken is born on August 5 in Savannah, Georgia.

1890: Agatha Christie is born on September 15, in Torquay, Devon, England.

1898: Stephen Crane's "The Blue Hotel" is published in *Collier's* magazine. The next year it is published in *The Monster and Other Stories.*

1900: Stephen Crane dies of tuberculosis on June 5 at a sanatorium in Germany.

1903: Frank O'Connor is born on September 17 in Cork, Ireland.

1904: H. G. Wells's "The Country of the Blind" is published in the *Strand* magazine.

1915: Julio Cortázar is born on August 26 in Brussels, Belgium.

1928: Agatha Christie's "Wasps' Nest" is published in the London *Daily Mail.* In 1961, it is published in *Double Sin and Other Stories.*

1930: Grace Ogot is born on May 15 in Asembo, Kenya.

1934: Conrad Aiken is awarded the Pulitzer Prize for Poetry for *Selected Poems.*

1934: Conrad Aiken's "Impulse" is published in *Among the Lost People.*

1936: Lucille Clifton is born on June 27 in Depew, New York.

1939: Frank O'Connor's "First Confession" is published in *Harper's Bazaar.*

1941: Virginia Woolf commits suicide on March 28 near the town of Rodwell, in Sussex, England.

1946: H. G. Wells dies on August 13 in London, England.

1948: T. Coraghessan Boyle is born Thomas John Boyle on December 2 in Peekskill, New York.

1952: Judith Ortiz Cofer is born on February 24 in Hormigueros, Puerto Rico.

1955: Gish Jen is born on August 12 in Long Island, New York.

1956: Julio Cortázar's "The Night Face Up" is published in Spanish as "La noche boca arriba." It is published in English in 1967 in *Blow Up and Other Stories.*

1966: Frank O'Connor dies of a heart attack on March 10 in Dublin, Ireland.

1968: Grace Ogot's "The Rain Came" is published in *Land Without Thunder*.

1973: Conrad Aiken dies on August 17 in Savannah, Georgia.

1976: Agatha Christie dies on January 12 at her home in Cholsey, England.

1979: Lucille Clifton's *The Lucky Stone* is published.

1982: T. Coraghessan Boyle's "Greasy Lake" is published in the *Paris Review*.

1982: Virginia Woolf's "The Widow and the Parrot" is published in *Redbook Magazine*.

1983: Gish Jen's "The White Umbrella" is published in the *Yale Review*.

1984: Julio Cortázar dies of leukemia and heart disease on February 14 in Paris, France.

1995: Judith Ortiz Cofer's short story "An Hour with Abuelo" is published in *An Island Like You: Stories of the Barrio*.

2010: Lucille Clifton dies of cancer-related illness on February 13 in Baltimore, Maryland.

Acknowledgements

The editors wish to thank the copyright holders of the excerpted criticism included in this volume and the permissions managers of many book and magazine publishing companies for assisting us in securing reproduction rights. We are also grateful to the staffs of the Detroit Public Library, the Library of Congress, the University of Detroit Mercy Library, Wayne State University Purdy/Kresge Library Complex, and the University of Michigan Libraries for making their resources available to us. Following is a list of the copyright holders who have granted us permission to reproduce material in this volume of *SSfS*. Every effort has been made to trace copyright, but if omissions have been made, please let us know.

COPYRIGHTED EXCERPTS IN *SSfS*, VOLUME 34, WERE REPRODUCED FROM THE FOLLOWING PERIODICALS:

Alif: Journal of Comparative Poetics, no. 27, 2007. Reproduced by permission.—***American Literary Realism***, v. 25, no. 2, Fall, 1994. Reproduced by permission.—***American Literature***, v. 47, no. 2. Copyright, 1975, Copyright ©Duke University Press. All rights reserved. Reproduced by permission of the publisher.—***Antigonish Review***, no. 57, Spring, 1984. Reproduced by permission.—***Biography***, v. 19, no. 2, Spring, 1996. Reproduced by permission.—***Booklist***, v. 91, no. 12, February 15, 1995. Reproduced by permission.—***Books Abroad***, v. 50, no. 3, Summer, 1976. Reproduced by permission.—***Christianity and Literature***, v. 54, no. 2, Winter, 2005. Reproduced by permission.—***Claremont Quarterly***, v. 9, no. 2, Winter, 1962. Reproduced by permission.—***Clues***, v. 25, no. 1, Fall, 2006. Reproduced by permission.—***Horizon***, v. 27, no. 9, November, 1984. Reproduced by permission of the author.—***Horn Book***, v. 71, July/August, 1995; v. 71, September/October, 1995. Copyright ©2010 by The Horn Book, Inc., a wholly owned subsidiary of Media Source, Inc. No redistribution permitted. All reproduced by permission.—***Interactions***, v. 15, no. 2, Fall, 2006. Reproduced by permission.—***International Fiction Review***, v. 34, nos. 1 & 2, January, 2007. Reproduced by permission.—***International Journal on World Peace***, v. 19, no. 1, 2002. Reproduced by permission.—***Journal of the Short Story in English***, no. 40, Spring, 2003. Reproduced by permission.—***Literature and Medicine***, v. 18, no. 1, 1999. Reproduced by permission.—***MELUS***, v. 26, no. 2, 2001. Reproduced by permission.—***Modern Fiction Studies***, v. 3, no. 2, Summer, 1957. Reproduced by permission.—***Notes on Contemporary Literature***, v. 39, no. 4, September, 2009. Reproduced by permission.—***Publishers Weekly***, v. 242, no. 16, April 17, 1995. Copyright ©1995 by PWXYZ, LLC. Reproduced by permission.—***Review of Contemporary Fiction***, v. 19, no. 3, 1999. Reproduced by permission. —***Southern Literary Journal***, v. 34, no. 2, Spring, 2002. Copyright © 2002 by the University of North Carolina Press. Reproduced by permission.—***Southern Review***, v. 41, Spring, 2006. Reproduced by permission.—***Studies in American Fiction***, 23:2, (1995). ©1995 Northeastern University. Reprinted with permission of The Johns Hopkins University Press.—***Studies in Short Fiction***, v. 8, winter, 1971; v. 31, Spring, 1994. Copyright ©1971, 1994 by *Studies in Short Fiction*. All reproduced by permission.—***Times Literary Supplement***, v. 13, January 31, 1986. Reproduced by permission.—***Twentieth Century Literature***, v. 36, Fall, 1990. Copyright ©1990, Hofstra University Press. Reproduced by permission.—***Wellsian***, no. 14, Summer, 1991. Reproduced by permission.—***Women's Review of Books***, v. 19, no. 5, February, 2002. Reproduced by permission.

COPYRIGHTED EXCERPTS IN *SSfS*, VOLUME 34, WERE REPRODUCED FROM THE FOLLOWING BOOKS:

John Conder. From "Stephen Crane and the Necessary Fiction," in ***Naturalism in American Fiction: The Classic Phase***, Copyright ©1984 University Press of Kentucky. Reproduced by permission.—Paul Gleason. From "T. C. Boyle's Short Fiction: An Overview from 'Descent of Man' to 'Tooth and Claw'," in ***Understanding T. C. Boyle***, Copyright ©2009 University of South Carolina Press. Reproduced by permission.—Florence Stratton. From "Men Fall Apart: Grace Ogot's Novels and Short Stories," in ***Contemporary African Literature and the Politics of Gender***, Routledge, 1994. Reproduced by permission of Taylor & Francis Books UK.

Contributors

Bryan Aubrey: Aubrey holds a Ph.D. in English. Entries on "The Night Face Up" and "The White Umbrella." Original essays on "The Night Face Up" and "The White Umbrella."

Kristy Blackmon: Blackmon is a poet, writer, and critic of literature from Dallas, Texas. Entry on "Impulse." Original essay on "Impulse."

Catherine Dominic: Dominic is a novelist and a freelance writer and editor. Entries on "The Murders in the Rue Morgue" and "The Widow and the Parrot." Original essays on "The Murders in the Rue Morgue" and "The Widow and the Parrot."

Diane Andrews Henningfeld: Henningfeld is a professor emerita of English who writes widely on literary topics and current events for educational publications. Entry on "An Hour with Abuelo." Original essay on "An Hour with Abuelo."

Michael Allen Holmes: Holmes is a writer and editor. Entries on *The Lucky Stone* and "The Rain Came." Original essays on *The Lucky Stone* and "The Rain Came."

David Kelly: Kelly is an instructor of creative writing and literature. Entry on "Greasy Lake." Original essay on "Greasy Lake."

Michael J. O'Neal: O'Neal holds a Ph.D. in English. Entries on "The Blue Hotel" and "First Confession." Original essays on "The Blue Hotel" and "First Confession."

April Paris: Paris is a freelance writer who has an extensive background working with literature and educational materials. Entry on "Wasps' Nest." Original essay on "Wasps' Nest."

Rebecca Valentine: Valentine is an award-winning writer with an emphasis on literature and history. Entry on "Good Country People." Original essay on "Good Country People."

Kathleen Wilson: Wilson is a writer and editor of many books on literature. Entry on "The Country of the Blind." Original essay on "The Country of the Blind."

The Blue Hotel

STEPHEN CRANE

1898

"The Blue Hotel," by American author Stephen Crane, is a relatively long short story, almost a novella (or short novel) that tells of a fatal encounter in a saloon in 1890s Nebraska. The story was first published in two parts in *Collier's Weekly* magazine on November 26 and December 3, 1898, and was later included in Crane's 1899 collection *The Monster, and Other Stories*. Three other magazine publishers had rejected the story, and *Collier's* agreed to publish only a shortened version of it. Someone on the magazine's staff, though, mislaid the alternate version, so the full version was published.

"The Blue Hotel" bears many similarities to contemporary novels that were set in the Old West, complete with saloons, gunslingers, gamblers, and a general sense of danger and threat. "The Blue Hotel," along with most of Crane's work, is regarded as an example of a type of nineteenth-century realism called naturalism. Naturalism can be described as a literary form that takes a harsh view of the human condition. The naturalist writers strove for objectivity and frankness. They were not afraid to deal with characters from the lower social orders who were victims of their environment. They took the position that the world can be amoral and people have no free will. They also tended to conceive that religious beliefs were illusory and that a person's destiny was likely to be that of a miserable life followed by an obscure death. Crane has been highly regarded for his vivid imagery, his use of irony, and his ability to puncture the illusions of his characters.

Stephen Crane
(The Library of Congress)

AUTHOR BIOGRAPHY

Stephen Crane was born on November 1, 1871, in Newark, New Jersey. His father was a Methodist minister in Newark, and his mother was a crusader in the temperance movement (which discouraged people from drinking alcohol). Both parents believed fervently in the existence of a benevolent God, in human free will, and in the importance of humanity in the universe—beliefs that Crane would come to reject. Crane's original ambition was to be a soldier, and to that end he attended a military preparatory school, but he withdrew in 1890 to attend Lafayette College, where he studied mining and engineering. Later he transferred to Syracuse University, in New York, where he played on the university baseball team. During this period he began writing his first short stories while also working as a correspondent for the *New York World* newspaper, run by famed newspaper publisher Joseph Pulitzer. He left Syracuse without a degree and moved to New York City, where he associated with bohemian artists and found work as a freelance journalist.

The slums of New York City provided Crane with background material for his first novel, *Maggie: A Girl of the Streets*, published in 1893—a novel that was shocking in its time for its depiction of squalor and immorality and that is considered the first American naturalist novel. The book was so shocking that he had to publish it at his own expense. In 1895 he published his first volume of poetry, *The Black Riders*, and the novel for which he is best known, *The Red Badge of Courage*. It was this novel that brought him fame internationally.

The remaining years of his short life were filled with travel and activity. He spent time in the American West, Florida, and Cuba as a roving correspondent for a newspaper syndicate. He joined a gun-running expedition that gave rise to his best-known short story, "The Open Boat." He moved to England, where he became friends with such famed authors as Joseph Conrad and Henry James. During this period he lived an extravagant life, forcing him to earn money by doing editorial work, as well as by continuing to write fiction. Despite his poor health, he returned to Cuba as a correspondent for the New York *World* during the Spanish-American War. In 1899 he returned to England, but he had contracted tuberculosis. He went to a sanitorium in Germany to find a cure, but he died in Germany on June 5, 1900, at just twenty-eight years of age.

PLOT SUMMARY

Section I

"The Blue Hotel" is set in a Nebraska prairie town called Fort Romper. The hotel where most of the action takes place is called the Palace Hotel, a somewhat ironic name given that the building is something of an eyesore. It is painted "a light blue, a shade that is on the legs of a kind of heron, causing the bird to declare its position against any background." The hotel's proprietor is Pat Scully, an Irishman who makes it a practice each morning to meet trains at the station to persuade travelers to stay at his hotel.

One snowy morning, Scully encounters three men: the Swede; Bill, a "tall bronzed cowboy"; and Mr. Blanc, a "little silent man from the East" who is generally called the Easterner. Scully entices them to stay at the hotel. As they enter, the narrator mentions the presence of Scully's son, Johnnie, who is playing cards and quarreling with an old farmer. Scully breaks up the card game and then allows the three newcomers to wash and

MEDIA ADAPTATIONS

- "The Blue Hotel" was performed as a radio play adapted by E. Jack Neuman, episode 185 in the series *Escape*, on May 24, 1953, although no known recording of the episode exists. The radio broadcast was recreated in 1977 on the program *Something's Happening* out of Los Angeles. The performance was directed by David L. Krebs. In this adaptation, Mr. Blanc (the Easterner) functions as a narrator.
- "The Blue Hotel" was adapted by Harry Mark Petrakis as a short film by American Short Story Theater in 1974, directed by Jan Kadar. David Warner plays the Swede, Rex Everhart is Scully, and James Keach is Johnnie. Running time is 55 minutes.
- "The Blue Hotel" was adapted for the stage by Michael Trocchia, with original music by The Shakes. In 2009, the band released a CD called *The Blue Hotel* under the label Towndowner, with original music composed in conjunction with the world premier of Trocchia's play.

relax. The Swede remains silent, although later at dinner he volunteers that he is from New York, where he has worked as a tailor for ten years.

Section II

After "dinner" (lunch), the men return to the front room, where Johnnie challenges the farmer to a game of cards. The farmer agrees, and the cowboy and the Easterner watch, while the Swede sits near the window. Again Johnnie and the farmer quarrel, prompting a new card game, with the cowboy volunteering to be Johnnie's partner and the Swede agreeing to be the Easterner's partner. Throughout, the Swede acts strangely, punctuating periods of silence with strange laughter. When he finally speaks, he asks questions that suggest that his view of the West has been influenced by fictional accounts of gunslingers and shootings. The men are drinking, and as the Swede gets drunk, he becomes more and more antagonistic and thinks that everyone is against him. As part of his drunken bravado, he predicts that before he leaves the hotel, someone is going to kill him. After Scully enters, the Swede again insists that someone is going to kill him and threatens to leave the hotel. Scully blames his son for antagonizing the Swede.

Section III

The Swede is in his room packing his valise to leave. Scully appears and refuses to accept payment from the Swede. Scully engages the Swede in conversation with a view to keeping him at the hotel. He tells the Swede a little about his family, including Carrie, who has died, and Michael, who works as a lawyer in Lincoln, Nebraska. He then pulls out from under the bed a bottle of whisky rolled up in a coat and offers a drink to the Swede. The Swede takes a drink but watches Scully with anger and distrust.

Section IV

This section returns to the men at the card table, who discuss the Swede and his strange behavior. Mr. Blanc believes that the Swede is frightened from having read dime novels (inexpensive, sensational novels) about the Old West. As the men are talking, Scully and the Swede return to the room. The five characters arrange themselves around the wood-burning stove and converse. Suddenly, the Swede announces that he is thirsty and leaves the room to get a drink.

Section V

By suppertime at six o'clock, the Swede is drunk, and he "domineered the whole feast, and he gave it the appearance of a cruel bacchanal" (drunken revelry). The men finish supper and adjourn to the card room, where the Swede insists on another game. Scully, meanwhile, reads the newspaper until he hears the Swede accuse Johnnie of cheating. The men push the Swede away from Johnnie, who denies that he was cheating. After further accusations of cheating, Johnnie challenges the Swede to a fight. Scully agrees to allow the fight to go forward.

Section VI

Outside, in the snow and cold, the Swede insists that all the men are against him and will "pitch" on him (betray him). The Swede and Johnnie face off and trade blows; Scully and Mr. Blanc remain largely silent as the cowboy urges Johnnie on. Johnnie lands a blow that sends the Swede sprawling, but not before the Swede lands a blow that weakens Johnnie. Johnnie is winded, and Scully stops the fight. The men return inside, where Johnnie's mother and sisters tend to him, and the mother scolds Scully for allowing the fight to occur.

Section VII

The cowboy had been especially eager to see Johnnie vanquish the Swede and expresses the wish to fight the Swede himself. The Swede enters the room, and he and the cowboy trade insults. Scully, insulted by the Swede, expresses his own dislike of the visitor, and he and the cowboy share their desire to teach the Swede a lesson.

Section VIII

The Swede leaves the hotel and wanders through the streets of the town until he finds a saloon, where he again becomes drunk, all the while intimidating the other men in the saloon, including two prominent local business merchants, a district attorney, and a professional gambler. The men refuse to drink with the Swede, who becomes increasingly belligerent at their refusal. The Swede grabs the gambler by the throat and is dragging him from his chair when the gambler pulls a knife and stabs him. The gambler wipes his knife on a towel and leaves.

Section IX

The final section takes place months later. The cowboy and the Easterner are at a small ranch near the Dakota line. The Easterner arrives with newspapers and tells the cowboy that the gambler was sentenced to three years in prison. In response, the cowboy asserts that the Swede got what was coming to him. The cowboy believes that the Swede would still be alive if he had not falsely accused Johnnie of cheating, but the Easterner astounds the cowboy by insisting that Johnnie was in fact cheating. The Easterner then berates himself for not standing up and backing the Swede's accusations. He says "We are all in it! . . . Every sin is the result of a collaboration. We, five of us, have collaborated in the murder of this Swede." The story closes with the cowboy puzzled by this "mysterious theory" and denying that he had any hand in the Swede's death.

CHARACTERS

Mr. Blanc (the Easterner)

Mr. Blanc, one of the guests at the Palace Hotel, is generally referred to as "the Easterner." He is described as a "little silent man" who does not exhibit the boisterousness of, for example, the cowboy. He generally remains quiet and goes along with the wishes of others. He does, however, share insights on occasion. He tells the others at one point that he believes the Swede is afraid: "He's clear frightened out of his boots." He goes on to say, "it seems to me this man has been reading dime-novels, and he thinks he's right out in the middle of it—the shootin' and stabbin' and all."

During the fight between Johnnie and the Swede, the Easterner is described as "nervous," and later he tries to stop the fight. The Easterner plays a major role in the final section of the story, when he informs the cowboy that the gambler was sentenced to prison for stabbing the Swede. He then articulates a theme of the story when he says to the cowboy that all of the men in the Palace Hotel had been complicit in the Swede's death and that the gambler's actions were merely "a culmination, the apex of a human movement."

The Cowboy (Bill)

Although he has a name, Bill is referred to consistently as simply the cowboy. He is staying at the hotel on his way to a ranch near the Dakota line. He is somewhat boisterous, referred to as a "board-whacker" from his habit of playing high-ranking cards "with a glowing air of prowess and pride" and smacking them down. Unlike the Easterner, he seems oblivious to the tensions around him. He does, however, come to share the general dislike of the Swede. During the fight between Johnnie and the Swede, he cheers Johnnie on and later wishes that he could beat the Swede himself.

In the story's final section, the cowboy has arrived at his ranch, along with the Easterner, who informs him from the newspaper that the gambler has been sentenced to prison for killing the Swede. When the Easterner reveals to the cowboy that Johnnie actually did cheat at cards and tries to explain how all the men at the Palace Hotel were complicit in the Swede's death, the cowboy is "injured and rebellious" and responds, "Well, I didn't do anythin', did I?" suggesting an inability to digest Mr. Blanc's theory about the experience.

The Gambler

A man referred to as a professional gambler is one of a group of men the Swede encounters in a saloon after he departs the Palace Hotel. He is described as a man of "quiet dignity," one of "candor and gentleness." He is thought to have a wife and children and to lead an exemplary home life. He is called a "thieving card-player," yet at the same time he "was so generous, so just, so moral, that, in a contest, he could have put to flight the consciences of nine-tenths of Romper." In his encounter with the Swede, he refuses to drink with the man. When the Swede attacks him, the gambler draws a knife and stabs the Swede to death. Later, through the Easterner, the reader learns that the gambler was sentenced to three years in prison for his role in the Swede's death.

Henry

After the Swede leaves the Palace Hotel, he enters a saloon where a bartender referred to as Henry serves him.

Johnnie Scully

Johnnie is Pat Scully's son. Johnnie is a quarrelsome young man. When the reader first encounters him, he is quarreling with an old farmer during a card game. When the Swede accuses him of cheating at cards, Johnnie becomes highly defensive and refutes the accusation. He loudly proclaims his innocence, both of cheating and of antagonizing the Swede. He challenges the Swede to a fight, but he is bested by his opponent and has to concede the fight. Throughout, Johnnie is portrayed as a hot-tempered, immature young man, and in the final section, it is revealed that he was in fact cheating at cards and that the Swede's accusations were true.

Mrs. Scully

Mrs. Scully, Pat Scully's wife and Johnnie's mother, appears briefly in the story to tend to Johnnie's injuries and scold her husband for allowing the fight between Johnnie and the Swede to go forward.

Pat Scully

Pat Scully is the proprietor of the Palace Hotel in Fort Romper, Nebraska. When he greets passengers getting off the train to persuade them to stay at his hotel, he is described as "nimble and merry and kindly." He is an Irishman, but his patterns of speech are said to mix an Irish brogue with Western expressions. His son is Johnnie, and after conflict between Johnnie and the Swede erupts, Scully tries to smooth matters over. Nevertheless, he allows his son to fight the Swede after the Swede accuses Johnnie of cheating at cards. In many respects, Scully seems unaware of the undercurrents of resentment and animosity among the men staying with him until the Swede becomes insulting to him personally. At that point he hints at a wish to have beaten the Swede himself.

The Swede

The Swede is the most mysterious character in the story. He is described as "shaky and quick-eyed," as though he looks on everyone with suspicion. Initially he is silent and withdrawn and seems to think that Fort Romper is part of the Wild West of legend, where people are regularly shot and stabbed in fights. As he drinks, he becomes increasingly aggressive and belligerent. He has a look of cunning and seems to regard those around him as treacherous. He expresses the belief that before he leaves the hotel, someone is going to kill him. He accuses Johnnie—correctly as it turns out—of cheating at cards, and the two of them fight over the accusation. Later, the Swede leaves the hotel and enters a saloon, where he becomes drunk. When a group of men in the saloon refuse to drink with him, he again becomes belligerent and demands loudly that they join him. He is particularly insulted by the refusal of an unnamed gambler in the group, and after he seizes the gambler by the throat and tries to pull him out of his chair, the gambler pulls a knife and stabs him to death.

THEMES

Western United States

In some respects, "The Blue Hotel" is an example of western literature, specifically the depiction of the Old West of cowboys, gunslingers, gamblers, and saloons—stock features of novels and stories about the Old West and the western frontier. At the same time, Crane seems to parody the literature of the West. He sets a group of characters in a small western town, although Nebraska at the time could be thought of as a kind of borderland between the more settled and civilized East and the "Wild West" of places like Wyoming, Montana, and Arizona. Thus, he is able to bring into conflict the values of these regions of the country, as suggested by his inclusion of a character called the Easterner (who might be thought of as a "city

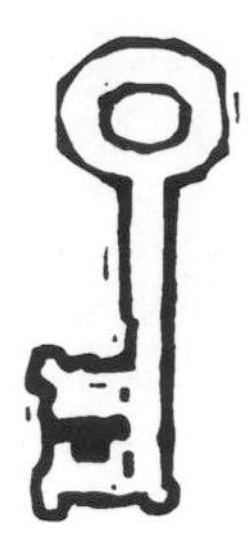

TOPICS FOR FURTHER STUDY

- Conduct an Internet search for photos of small prairie towns in the late nineteenth century, preferably in Nebraska or one of the other plains states. Locate photos of a hotel, a saloon, a train station, a Pullman railroad car, and the surrounding environment. Create a slideshow of the pictures to present while narrating voice-over excerpts from the short story.
- Prepare an interactive time line showing the history of the railroads, particularly those that would have passed through a small Nebraska town such as Fort Romper. In connection with the time line, prepare a brief essay or oral presentation that explains how the railroad contributed to the settlement and development of such a place.
- During the story, the characters play a card game called High-Five. Conduct research to learn about the game and how it is played. With three other participants, demonstrate how the game was played to the rest of your class.
- Nat Love (who pronounced his first name "Nate") was an African American cowboy who acquired the nickname Deadwood Dick for his exploits. He recounted the adventures of his life in the West in an autobiography, *Life and Adventures of Nat Love*, written in 1907. Locate a copy of Love's autobiography (available as a free e-book at Project Gutenberg) and prepare a brief oral presentation explaining how his book contributes to historians' understanding of the role of African Americans on the western frontier.
- Locate another short story or novel about the Old West set roughly during this time period. One possibility is Jack Schaefer's young-adult novel *Shane*. Another is Owen Wister's 1902 book *The Virginian: Horseman of the Plains*. Write an analysis comparing the book you have selected with "The Blue Hotel," focusing on the nature of the characters and how Crane uses the devices of traditional western fiction for his own purposes.

slicker") and one called the cowboy, described as tall and "bronzed."

By introducing the Swede into the mix, Crane is able to explore the relations among the characters. Unlike in many novels and stories of the Old West, here the stereotypical distinction between good and evil—the "good cowboy" in the white hat and the "bad cowboy" in the black hat—is muddled. The Swede is belligerent and antagonistic, like many "bad guys" in western novels. He loses his life in large part because of these personality flaws; yet Crane does not include a "good guy" who brings justice to the frontier. Only the Easterner, who tends to observe the action rather than participate in it, is able to bring perspective to the events by seeing the Swede's death not as the result of a stereotypical confrontation between good and evil but as the result of the circumstances in which he was placed. Although readers will tend not to regard the Swede as in any way admirable, in the end it turns out that he was right—Johnnie was in fact cheating during the card game. Thus, although "The Blue Hotel" incorporates some of the elements of traditional western literature and its depictions of the West, Crane turns away from the commonplace "good versus evil" theme characteristic of much of this literature.

Masculinity

The ambience of "The Blue Hotel" is perpetually masculine. Only briefly do female characters—Mrs. Scully and her daughters—appear. In this environment, characters often feel forced to engage in male bravado, a boyishness hinted at by the name of the town, Fort Romper (a *romper* was a one-piece garment children at the time wore to play in). They gamble, drink heavily, and quarrel. The central conflict is between Johnnie and the Swede. The Swede accuses Johnnie of cheating at cards; Johnnie insistently denies that he is cheating. The pair trade insults, and eventually they come to physical blows.

The other men share Johnnie's dislike of the Swede. At one point the cowboy says, "I'd like to git him by the neck and ha-ammer him . . . hammer that there Dutchman until he couldn't tell himself from a dead coyote!" (The cowboy inexplicably thinks that the Swede is Dutch.) Later, when the gambler is introduced, the reader is told that "in the strictly masculine part of the town's life he had come to be explicitly trusted and admired." With this type of male swagger dominating the action, it seems inevitable that the Swede, who winds up in a saloon, would drink heavily, engage in bluster and bravado with the other men in the saloon, and pick a fight that leads to his death.

The cowboy represents the "Old West."
(sad / Shutterstock.com)

Naturalism

Naturalism was a literary movement that was prominent in the late nineteenth and early twentieth centuries. Some American naturalists included Hamlin Garland, Frank Norris, Jack London, and Stephen Crane. Naturalism was an extension of realism and could be described as realism taken to a kind of extreme. The naturalists strove for the faithful representation of reality. They tended to avoid moral judgments on their characters. The naturalists took a deterministic view of life, presenting characters as victims of their heredity and/or their environment; less emphasis was placed on the characters' moral or rational qualities. People were often regarded as helpless victims either of instinct or of external forces, which is one of the reasons that emphasis is given less to personal names and more to designations such as cowboy, Easterner, or gambler.

In "The Blue Hotel," the Swede is not judged, nor does the author try to explain why he is the way he is. Similarly, the other characters are presented with little or no comment. As a blustery winter storm rages outside, the characters are simply thrown together into a volatile mix. There is little sense of moral judgment, for although the Swede is not a likable character, he is correct in his belief that Johnnie was cheating at cards; had Johnnie not cheated, or had the Easterner, who knew that Johnnie cheated, spoken up, it is highly likely that the Swede would not have left the hotel and met his fate at the saloon. As a naturalist, Crane allows characters to appear and events to happen. The death of the Swede was the result, in part, of his own inner drives but also the result of his environment—in this case, the refusal or inability of the men at the hotel to expose Johnnie.

STYLE

Point of View

The point of view of "The Blue Hotel" is third-person omniscient. This means that the story is narrated in the third person and that the narrative voice is "all knowing," able to see into the characters' minds and comment broadly on the action. For example, the narrator comments with regard to the hotel near the story's beginning, "With this opulence and splendor, these creeds, classes, egotisms, that streamed through Romper on the rails day after day, they had no color in common." That said, the narrative voice of "The Blue Hotel" restricts commentary on the characters largely to external clues. The narrative voice reports dialogue and actions that indicate the nature of the characters. The narrator never engages in extended commentary on the action, nor does the narrator comment on the moral or social significance of the characters' behavior.

Setting

The setting for "The Blue Hotel" is a small Nebraska town, presumably during the 1890s. The town is called Fort Romper—like many towns in the West, named after a military fort established to protect western pioneers and settlers. The season is winter, with falling snow and gusts of wind. The landscape is therefore colorless and nondescript. The only element of color in the setting is the hotel, painted blue. Thus, the hotel stands out in its environment and becomes the focal point for the action. The reader is told that in this regard it differs from the "brown-reds and the subdivisions of the dark greens of the East."

The purpose of this setting is to isolate the characters. The reader has little sense of other people or other activities in the town. People arrive at the town and the hotel out of the gray landscape, interact, and then leave. Thus, Crane creates a kind of microcosm, or "little world," in which he places his characters, allows them to behave in certain ways with certain consequences, and then abandons them to the town. Only later, in section IX, does the action move away from Fort Romper to the cowboy's ranch. Time has passed, allowing perspective on the events of the story to emerge.

Protagonist and Antagonist

In a typical novel, story, or play, the central character is called the protagonist, the character who is the focus of the action, the work's themes, and its development. Generally positioned against the protagonist is an antagonist, a character who opposes the protagonist and thus precipitates the conflict that forms the core of the story. In a typical western story, the protagonist is the "good guy," often a mysterious stranger who metes out justice to "bad guys" (gunslingers, greedy ranchers, corrupt lawmen), the antagonists. "The Blue Hotel," however, experiments with this typical structure. The Swede eventually becomes the central protagonist, although the narration never comments on him and his motivations. He simply exists as he is. At the same time, the Swede is given the role of antagonist, for he is the character who sparks the story's conflict; in this way, he shares the role of antagonist with Johnnie, although the narration never comments on Johnnie's motivations or explains why he is the way he is.

In a larger sense, then, the characters do not act with the type of purpose a reader might find in, for example, a tragedy by Shakespeare with a clearly defined protagonist and antagonist. In a larger sense, Crane adopts the naturalist perspective that the terms protagonist and antagonist are meaningless, for the words imply purpose and motivation. Rather, Crane sees the world, at least in this story, as a stark, gray landscape in which each individual takes on a role based on inexplicable inner drives. When the Easterner concludes at the end of the story that everyone in the hotel was complicit in the Swede's death, he suggests a vision in which people are intertwined with their social environment.

HISTORICAL CONTEXT

Survival on the Plains

"The Blue Hotel" makes no specific reference to historical events. However, the time period is clearly the late nineteenth century, and the setting is a small town in Nebraska. Crane wrote the story after his own experiences traveling in the American West in 1895, and his earliest biographer reports that Crane actually saw a blue hotel on the plains and witnessed a saloon fight. During this time, Crane worked as a roving correspondent for a newspaper syndicate. One of his newspaper stories, dated February 22, 1895, was from a small Nebraska town called Eddyville and titled "Nebraska's Bitter Fight for Life." Although "The Blue Hotel" does not directly refer to the conditions Crane reported in his newspaper story, a comparison of the fictional story with the real-life story suggests that "The Blue Hotel" reflected Crane's experience with a severe drought that affected portions of Nebraska in the 1890s.

Crane reports in the article that the people were "engaged in a bitter and deadly fight for existence." He notes that previously, the "bounteous prolific prairies" and towns "were alive with the commerce of an industrious and hopeful

COMPARE & CONTRAST

- **1890s:** The total population of Nebraska is just over a million people.

  Today: The total population of Nebraska as of 2009 is estimated at just under 1.8 million.

- **1890s:** The Central Pacific Railroad is one of the main rail arteries that run through Nebraska and that link the state with the eastern half of the United States. Omaha, Nebraska, is a major rail hub, particularly for the shipment of cattle for slaughter.

  Today: The nation places less emphasis on rail transportation, particularly for passengers (as opposed to cargo). Many rail stations in Nebraska are now defunct, but many of the buildings survive and are listed on the National Register of Historic Places.

- **1890s:** Railroad passengers routinely disembark and stay at centrally located hotels, where they interact with each other by playing cards, conversing, and drinking, often in the absence of anything else to do. It is unusual for women to travel alone and stay at one of these hotels.

  Today: With more transportation options, people stay at a variety of hotels and motels, where they are unlikely to interact with each other except in passing. Women routinely travel alone for business and pleasure.

community." However, conditions changed with "the scream of a wind hot as an oven's fury." He writes that the country died "in the rage of the wind." He notes that "in a few weeks this prosperous and garden-like country was brought to a condition of despair." Many people were driven away, but "then came the struggle of the ones who stood fast. They were soon driven to bay by nature, now the pitiless enemy." Then winter came: "The chill and tempest of the inevitable winter had gathered in the north and swept down upon the devastated country. The prairies turned bleak and desolate." Later he writes that "Over the wide white expanses of prairie, the icy winds from the north shriek, whirling high sheets of snow and enveloping the house in white clouds of it." Crane concludes his newspaper story by saying that the people "depend upon their endurance, their capacity to help each other, and their steadfast and unyielding courage."

It is easy to see how this experience could have provided the germ of "The Blue Hotel." The story is set in winter, and frequent references are made to the snow and pounding wind. The landscape in which the story is set is bleak and colorless. In particular, Crane takes the naturalist view that nature is a "pitiless enemy" and that people are products of their environment and natural forces they can neither understand nor control.

The Temperance Movement

Nebraska was the scene of at least two social developments during the years surrounding the events depicted in "The Blue Hotel." One was the rise of the temperance movement. Many people came to believe that drinking was a major social ill, one that caused people to lose jobs, neglect their families, and turn to crime—or simply bring about crime, as with the events that lead to the gambler stabbing the Swede in Crane's short story. In 1886, a political party called the Prohibition Party was organized in Nebraska, and although the party was never able to elect candidates to office, it continued to call for the prohibition of alcohol as part of a movement that would lead to the nation's Prohibition era in the 1920s.

The Populist Movement

The second significant social development in the late nineteenth century related to the discontent of farmers and ranchers. As Crane noted in "Nebraska's Bitter Fight for Life," farmers and ranchers faced droughts as well as severe winters and summer tornadoes, which made life on the

A pair of kings in a poker game
(Tony Mathews / Shutterstock.com)

plains a bitter struggle for many Nebraskans. Prices for agricultural products during this period were low, while shipping costs were high, in large part because the railroads were able to fix artificially high rates. Additionally, farmers had to go into debt to buy farm implements, seed, outbuildings, and the like. Financial discontent led to the formation of radical political organizations calling for agricultural reform in opposition to the eastern banks and "moneymen" who profited by the work of western farmers and ranchers. This activism grew into the populist movement, and the Populist Party was able to elect its candidate as governor of Nebraska in 1894.

CRITICAL OVERVIEW

Critics were initially somewhat unkind to "The Blue Hotel." In a review in *Book Buyer* in April 1900, the story is dismissed in one sentence as dealing "with a rather shop-worn subject." A contributor to *Athenaeum*, in a review dated March 16, 1901, calls the entire volume in which the story appeared (*The Monster, and Other Stories*) "somewhat disappointing" and says that the tales leave the reader "untouched." Referring specifically to "The Blue Hotel," the reviewer calls it a "brilliant fulguration, [something that has the quality of flashing like lightning] but still a bolt from the blue." A contributor to *Academy*, however, praised the story. In a review dated March 16, 1901, the reviewer calls "The Blue Hotel" an "excellent piece of work," and says that it has "a very peculiar knowledge of human nature in every line," and later refers to it as "an amazing story." Commenting generally on Crane's work, H. G. Wells, writing for the *North American Review* in August 1900, says that Crane's untimely death "robs English literature of an interesting and significant figure."

Modern critics have taken a largely favorable view of "The Blue Hotel." Daniel Weiss, in an essay titled "The Blue Hotel," calls the story "the finest thing Crane created." Michael W. Schaefer, in *A Reader's Guide to the Short Stories of Stephen Crane*, states, "Critics have generally been lavish in their praise of this story, regarding it as one of Crane's best and, in many cases, one of the best short stories in the entire American canon."

Thomas A. Gullason, in "Stephen Crane's Short Stories: The Blue Hotel," calls the story "the darkest of Crane's tragedies" and praises Crane for his ability to "foreshadow the coming events and help to establish the various moods of the story." Many critics have focused on "The Blue Hotel" as a western story. Robert Glen Deamer, in "Stephen Crane and the Western Myth," argues that "The Blue Hotel" is not a western story and concludes that "the hellishness—the cowardice, the fear, the cheating, the hypocrisy, the greed, the violence—of this story is the product not of the West but of the civilization of which Scully is so enthusiastic a proponent."

CRITICISM

Michael J. O'Neal

O'Neal holds a Ph.D. in English. In the following essay, he examines Crane's selection of "The Blue Hotel" as the title of his short story.

In selecting a title for a short story, or any literary work, an author is making decisions about at least two matters. One has to do with how much the author wants to reveal about the content of the work. Some famous titles are neutral and point directly at the work's content. *The Adventures of Huckleberry Finn*, for example, is strictly informative; the reader expects to find a central character named Huckleberry Finn engaged in a series of adventures. The other decision, not unrelated to the first, has to do with what the author wants as the focus or central image of the work. In such classics as *The Scarlet Letter* by Nathaniel Hawthorne, *The Grapes of Wrath* by John Steinbeck, or *Moby-Dick* by Herman Melville, the reader does not immediately know the subject of the work, although the subjects become readily apparent early on. By choosing such titles, the authors make clear the central focus of their imaginative vision. The scarlet letter is an emblem for the alienation of the central character, Hester Prynne, from her New England Puritan community; the grapes of wrath are a metaphor for the hardships of dust-bowl fugitives; and Moby Dick is the name of a whale that dominates not only the physical action but also the psychological drives and obsessions of Captain Ahab, who is determined to hunt the whale down and kill it.

So the question arises, why did Crane choose to call his story "The Blue Hotel"? The title calls

> "THE RESULT IS THAT THE FOCUS OF THE STORY IS PLACE RATHER THAN PEOPLE, AT LEAST INITIALLY, AND INDEED THIS FOCUS ON SETTING SEEMS TO HAVE BEEN AN IMPORTANT ONE FOR CRANE."

attention to the color its owner, Pat Scully, painted it, but the story could just as well have been titled with the hotel's actual name, the Palace Hotel—and the irony of the word *palace* would have been appropriate, for the hotel is by no means a palace. Clearly the author for some reason wants the reader to bear in mind the hotel's color as the action unfolds. Further, the story focuses on the interactions of a group of men. These interactions lead to conflict, and the story reaches its climax with the killing of the protagonist, the Swede. In a kind of coda or afterword to the events of the story, the Easterner comments to the cowboy on the significance of the events in which they were involved. On this basis, readers could imagine a host of titles that might, at first glance, seem more appropriate or more informative: "The Swede," "A Killing in Fort Romper," "The Death of a Stranger," and numerous other titles that Crane might have imagined. Why, then, "The Blue Hotel"?

No one can reconstruct the thought processes that lead an author to select a title. Perhaps Crane merely dashed the title off as an afterthought. However, a careful, concise writer such as Crane would have been unlikely to attach a title to any story without consideration. For one thing, Crane indicates the significance of the color blue in the story's opening paragraph. The reader is told that the shade of the hotel is that of a species of heron, whose color causes it "to declare its position against any background." The hotel is said to be "always screaming and howling in a way that made the dazzling winter landscape of Nebraska seem only a gray swampish hush." Any traveler who alights at the train station is almost obligated to pass the Palace Hotel and notice it because it stands out against the "low clap-board houses which composed Fort Romper"—houses the reader imagines as

WHAT DO I READ NEXT?

- Crane is the author of the frequently anthologized short story "The Open Boat" (1897). The story is in many ways similar to "The Blue Hotel" in that it throws together a group of mostly unnamed men in a bleak, colorless environment over which they have little control. "The Open Boat" is widely available; it can be found, for example, in *The Works of Stephen Crane*, Vol. 5, *Tales of Adventure*, edited by Fredson Bowers and published in 1970.
- Crane's novel *The Red Badge of Courage*, set in the Civil War, was published in 1895. The novel's battle scenes are so realistic that many readers assumed that the author had fought in the war. The novel focuses on the experiences of a private, Henry Fleming, and depicts war not as a clash of high ideals but as an indication of a world with no moral absolutes, one that is indifferent to human suffering.
- Hamlin Garland was an American author who wrote numerous short stories about the prairie frontier, what today is called the Midwest. Like those of Crane, Garland's stories adopt the conventions of the naturalist school. "The Return of a Private" (1890), one of his most frequently anthologized stories, begins, like "The Blue Hotel," with a group of men disembarking from a train in a small midwestern town. The story is widely available online.
- Written nearly a half century after Crane's story, Ann Petry's *The Street* (1946) is regarded as a novel in the naturalist tradition, examining the troubled lives of African Americans in 1940s Harlem (a neighborhood in New York City).
- In 1893, Frederick Jackson Turner published an influential essay, "The Significance of the Frontier in American History." In 1920, he published an expanded exploration of the topic in a collection of essays titled *The Frontier in American History*. For many historians and others, Turner defined American conceptions of the frontier and how the frontier shaped American thinking.
- Beginning in 1932, Laura Ingalls Wilder published a series of books collectively referred to as the "Little House" books. Two of these novels, *The Long Winter* (1940) and *Little Town on the Prairie* (1941), took place in the West around the time when "The Blue Hotel" is set. Compared with Crane's fiction, these novels for young adults present a very different picture of life in the prairie states during the late nineteenth century.
- Willa Cather is the author of a trilogy of novels set on the American plains in the nineteenth century. *O Pioneers!* (1913) tells the story of Swedish immigrants to a small Nebraska town. Later books in the trilogy include *The Song of the Lark* (1915), which moves the action to Colorado, and *My Ántonia* (1918), which returns to the immigrant experience in small-town Nebraska.

---

unattractive and probably unpainted. The narration goes on to say that the "creeds, classes, egotisms, that streamed through Romper on the rails day after day, they had no color in common," suggesting that when people stay at the hotel, no matter what their beliefs or social class, they acquire something in common.

The result is that the focus of the story is place rather than people, at least initially, and indeed this focus on setting seems to have been an important one for Crane. His first novel, *Maggie: A Girl of the Streets*, focuses the reader's attention not only on a character but also on her location, and to emphasize the point, a further subtitle, "A Story of New York," informs the reader that the novel is as much about place as it is about Maggie. The focus of Crane's short story "The Open Boat" is on the physical placement of the characters in a small boat at sea rather than on the characters themselves. "The Bride Comes to Yellow Sky," another frequently anthologized Crane short story, shifts the focus from the bride and her husband to their destination.

Therefore, a further question is why Crane seems, in the title of this story, to be channeling the reader's attention to place rather than characters. To answer that question, it is necessary to return to the literary movement of which Crane is an important exemplar: naturalism. During the post–Civil War era, a number of forces in American life converged to create the kind of literature Crane and others wrote. Industrialism was beginning to triumph over agrarianism (farming). Cities were growing, and they were home to large and growing numbers of poor and unskilled workers, particularly immigrants. The tempo of life accelerated. Railroad systems made people more mobile. It was an age of steam and iron, of petroleum and electricity. From 1870 to 1890, the U.S. population doubled.

Increased democratization meant that a new generation of writers came not from genteel, aristocratic, Ivy League backgrounds but rather from the middle class, and many of the new writers—Mark Twain is a key example—got their fingers inky from practicing the trade of journalism rather than writing literary essays for highbrow New England journals. They were determined to reflect in their writing the realities of life, which sometimes meant they had to depict squalor, misery, and violence. They wanted truth, and one way they accomplished this was through the use of dialect and the depiction of the sights and sounds and smells of the nation's regions, including the Great Plains. Another way was to dismiss soothing moral truths. They wanted frankness and objectivity. They also wanted to depict characters who were products of, and often victims of, both their heredity and their environment and thus had little free will.

"The Blue Hotel" contains named characters, principally Pat Scully and his son, Johnnie, but the other characters go largely without names: the cowboy, the gambler, the Swede, and the Easterner. Even the Easterner's name, Mr. Blanc, suggests a lack of strong identity. It is as though they are defined by a role rather than their individuality—a technique Crane used to good effect in "The Open Boat," where the characters include the cook, the captain, the correspondent, and the oiler (although the oiler is given the name Billie). At the blue hotel, placed in the context of a stark, colorless landscape, one made more colorless by the snow, in a small, nondescript town, the characters converge with little explanation and little sense of particular purpose. They are simply *there*, and the blueness of the hotel, making it stand out from its surroundings, forces the reader to think of the characters as a small, isolated community, a microcosm, with no *before* and little *after*.

The narration never tries to explain the Swede; it does not explore Johnnie's background and upbringing or try to explain why he cheated at cards. It does not explain the behavior of the cowboy, the gambler, or the Easterner. All are driven by forces they do not understand. The central conflict of the story, that between Johnnie and the Swede, is lifted entirely out of any kind of defining context. What brings the characters together is not a sequence of events defined by character, but accident. They all simply wind up at the same location, a blue hotel that stands out in the middle of nowhere, where their drives and personalities create a volatile mix that leads to conflict and violent, reasonless death. The result is a bleak view of the human condition, a view that is a defining characteristic of the naturalist movement.

Source: Michael J. O'Neal, Critical Essay on "The Blue Hotel," in *Short Stories for Students*, Gale, Cengage Learning, 2012.

John Feaster

In the following excerpt, Feaster proposes a less cosmic reading of "The Blue Hotel" by looking at it through a specific cultural context.

Critical commentary on Stephen Crane's "The Blue Hotel" during the past four decades provides an instructive example of the general dominance of interpretive critical methods that regard literary works, in the words of Jerome J. McGann, as "modeling rather than mirroring forms." From this dominant a-historical (and at times rigidly antihistorical) viewpoint, literary works "do not point to a prior, authorizing reality (whether 'realist' or 'idealist'), they themselves *constitute*—in both the active and the passive senses—what must be taken as reality (both 'in fact' and 'in ideals')." Readings of Crane's provocative story of course differ widely in interpretive details; what they also share widely, however,

Cowboy, Easterner, and Swede gamble in the saloon.
(grynold / Shutterstock.com)

is a strenuous formalist insistence that somehow it needs rescuing from the taint of "mere" referentiality.

With the exception of a very few readings that have treated it as a story concerned largely with the passing of the Old West, the trend in interpretation of "The Blue Hotel," consistent with what McGann has observed about interpretive strategies in general, has been to regard the story in rarified symbolic terms—as a "model" of reality, not a "mirror," in which universal man plays out his destiny in a placeless and timeless context devoid of any "authorizing" historical circumstance. When the work is regarded as having any mirroring function at all, what it reflects (consider Bruce L. Grenberg's references to Crane's "religious and philosophical values," for example) is approvingly regarded as transcending the trivially historical through achievement of some cosmic level of significance. While such readings may bring the story more in line with the "isolative sensibility" (the phrase is Daniel G. Hoffman's) of Crane's poetry, they ignore certain of the universalizing versus particularizing distinctions inherent in the whole question of genre, isolate the story from other of Crane's works (fictional as well as journalistic) which, I will argue, are related intentionally, and, above all, dissociate the story from its specific and clarifying social ground. What I will argue, on the contrary, is that the issues of first order importance in "The Blue Hotel" are not cosmic but cultural, and as such are definable with reference to the complex social and economic factors, and accompanying ideology, that shaped the evolving frontier culture in which the story is set and of which Crane had exact "historical" experience. Whatever the cosmic implications of the story, and I would suggest that they are peripheral and slight, they cannot be wrenched free from these containing and shaping objective as well as subjective circumstances. Crane was hardly unique in his fascination with the western experience and its effects on the development of American character and moral identity. For Crane, as for others of his time, the Old West may have been dead, but this hardly lessened his interest in it as a site of alleged human progress.

"THE WORLD OF 'THE BLUE HOTEL,' MICROCOSMIC IN A SOCIO-CULTURAL SENSE, PROVIDES AN IDEOLOGICALLY RICH ETHNOGRAPHIC PORTRAIT OF A CULTURE CAUGHT AT A SIGNIFICANT MOMENT OF SOCIAL AND ECONOMIC DEVELOPMENT AND, ULTIMATELY, OF MORAL FAILURE."

I

"The Blue Hotel" was first published in 1898, just five years after Frederick Jackson Turner delivered his famous address on the "Significance of the Frontier in American History" before the American Historical Association meeting at the Columbian Exposition in Chicago. That the Exposition was being held in Chicago at all, as Larzer Ziff observes, was a tacit acknowledgement that by the 1890s the center of commercial energy in the United States had shifted dramatically to the west. "Those who came to see the Exposition would also see Chicago," Ziff writes, "and that young city, if it had no past to display, was at least equipped to give visitors a glimpse into the future and show them how things were done in a wide-awake commercial fashion." Turner's purpose was to explain the whole complex process of social evolution involved in the civilizing of the American people and their institutions, to explain, in more specific terms, how the "complexity of city life" had evolved from "the primitive economic and political conditions of the frontier." As Crane would be just five years later, Turner was concerned (somewhat more optimistically than Crane) with the process by which American society evolved from "savagery" to "civilization." For Crane, the process was far from complete.

The phenomenon of the Western frontier, according to Turner, has made our experience peculiarly American. For Turner, the development of that frontier was not accomplished by a simple process whereby the civilized was extended into and displaced the uncivilized. This may have been true of the Eastern experience, which occurred in a relatively limited geographical area, but such a theory hardly explains the complexity of social development in such large areas as those involved in the American West. According to Turner's thesis, settlement of these vast areas was characterized by successive returns to primitive conditions along an advancing frontier line. This meant that different stages in the evolution of social, political, and economic organization could be seen at any one time on the leeward side of that advancing line. Moreover, "as successive terminal moraines result from successive glaciations, so each frontier leaves its traces behind it, and when it becomes a settled area the region still partakes of the frontier characteristics." A place like Nebraska, for example, would still possess certain displaced frontier characteristics even when it had ceased to be front-line frontier.

Turner's theory was meant to explain, and did so in idealistic and at times even poetic terms, the relationship between the American character and the harsh environment that had shaped it. But however eloquent Turner might have been in his description of the American character and the environmental press in which it developed, it is clear that his ideas were rooted very firmly in the practical realities of political economy. Indeed Turner's vaunted Individualism, as his biographer, Ray A. Billington, has pointed out, must be understood more as economic individualism than as some kind of ideal or heroic "distinctiveness." As Billington somewhat trenchantly observes, "individualism in its distinctly American usage does not apply to the non-economic world," a world in which, as a matter of fact, Americans tend to be decidedly conformist. "The legend of frontier individualism," Billington goes on to say, "rested on what people thought should be true, rather than what was true. The West was in truth an area where cooperation was just as essential as in the more thickly settled East." The inevitable conflict between an unrestrained individualism and the more complex cooperative needs of a settled society, as John Cawelti has shown in his *Adventure, Mystery, and Romance*, was a central feature in the development of the western formula. In a somewhat modified form, I will suggest, this conflict is equally central to the evolution of social organization depicted in "The Blue Hotel." Of particular relevance in this context is that, for Turner, social evolution meant economic (even, more basically, commercial) evolution, development from a primitive hunting society up through various stages of trading, ranching, farming, to an urban manufacturing society, the highest form of social and economic organization, and precisely the kind of organization, according to Scully, that Fort Romper is well on its way to achieving.

Without attempting to show the utterly improbable, that "The Blue Hotel" is in any sense "influenced" by Turner's thesis, however influential that thesis in fact turned out to be, I nonetheless want to suggest that, like Turner, Crane is similarly concerned with fundamental issues of cultural evolution involved in development of the American West. Unlike the more idealistic Turner, however, the ironic Crane provides not only cultural description but cultural critique as well. The world of "The Blue Hotel," microcosmic in a socio-cultural sense, provides an ideologically rich ethnographic portrait of a culture caught at a significant moment of social and economic development and, ultimately, of moral failure.

II

Stephen Crane's only direct experience of Nebraska was acquired during a brief tour of the West, Southwest, and Mexico in the spring of 1895 sponsored by the Bacheller, Johnson, and Bacheller newspaper syndicate. What made Nebraska newsworthy at this particular time was a severe drought in the north central area of the state that had begun in the summer of 1894 and by the time of his visit, as Crane would eventually write, had brought "this prosperous and garden-like country" to a "condition of despair." During the years between the passage of the Homestead Act of 1862 and the late 1880s, the plains states had experienced an unparalleled boom, made possible, as it was then becoming apparent, by a period of uncharacteristically generous rainfall. In the period alone between 1880 and 1890, the population of Nebraska had increased by 134% (from 452,402 to 1,058,910), but by the time of Crane's arrival in February of 1895, a process of exodus eastward had begun that was not to reverse itself until after 1897 when a period of relative prosperity returned—but by which time, of course, Crane was living in Ravensbrook, England, far away from the scene where a set of lasting impressions of economic devastation had been formed. "In the single year of 1891," according to John D. Hicks, "no less than eighteen thousand prairie schooners crossed from the Nebraska to the Iowa side of the Missouri River in full retreat from the hopeless hard times," with the eventual result that "from one-third to one-half of the counties in Kansas, Nebraska, and South Dakota had a smaller population in 1900 than in 1890."

When Crane arrived in Lincoln in February of 1895, as Joseph Katz writes in his Introduction to *Stephen Crane in the West and Mexico*, he arrived unsuspectingly "in the midst of a Situation." If the region were to survive economically, then the kind of Eastern capital investment that had flowed westward so plentifully during the prosperous 1870s and 80s would have to continue. But, as Katz points out, "Nebraska business interests feared that Eastern investors would shy away from a state that lived so perilous a relationship with nature." Although Crane's fame was somewhat limited in 1895, his arrival was nonetheless heralded by Nebraska newspapers as an opportunity for Eastern readers to acquire a "true" conception of conditions in the drought-stricken area. "Mr. Crane's newspapers have asked him," the Nebraska *State Journal* reported (in an article that Crane in fact clipped for his scrapbook), "to get the truth, whether his articles are sensational or not, and for that reason his investigations will doubtless be welcomed by the business interests of Nebraska."

In his resulting report, "Nebraska's Bitter Fight for Life," Crane does in fact emphasize that "the grievous condition is confined to a comparatively narrow section of the western part of the state," and quotes freely then-governor Silas A. Holcomb, who in an interview with Crane described incipient irrigation projects that would return Nebraska to conditions "'safe and profitable for agriculture,'" and assured Crane that "in a year or two her barns will be overflowing" ("Nebraska's Bitter Fight," 13). To some extent, given the burden placed on him by certain "interests" to "get the truth," Crane must have felt compelled to enter into this suspiciously optimistic rhetorical defense of Nebraska as a safe place for capital investment. And while Crane did attempt to counter "extraordinary reports which have plastered the entire state as a place of woe" ("Nebraska's Bitter Fight," 12), his overall account of conditions is decidedly bleak.

The "business interests of Nebraska," as a consequence, could hardly have been entirely pleased by Crane's imaginative portrayal (somewhat sensational after all) of the onset of the drought in the summer of 1894:

> From the southern horizon came the scream of a wind hot as an oven's fury. Its valor was great in the presence of the sun. It came when the burning disc appeared in the east and it weakened

> when the blood-red, molten mass vanished in the west. From day to day, it raged like a pestilence. The leaves of corn and of trees turned yellow and sapless like leather. For a time they stood the blasts in the agony of futile resistance. The farmers helpless, with no weapon against this terrible and inscrutable wrath of nature, were spectators at the strangling of their hopes, their ambitions, all that they could look to from their labor. ("Nebraska's Bitter Fight," 4)

Nor would those business interests have been much pleased by Crane's account of the subsequent winter of 1894–95, one of the harshest in memory, which he experienced first-hand and therefore gave a sense of impressive immediacy, writing from an Eddyville rooming house where "the temperature of the room which is the writer's bedroom is precisely one and a half degrees below zero":

> Meanwhile, the chill and the tempest of the inevitable winter had gathered in the north and swept down upon the devastated country. The prairies turned bleak and desolate.
>
> The wind was a direct counter-part of the summer. It came down like wolves of ice. And then was the time that from this district came that first wail, half impotent rage, half despair. The men went to feed the starving cattle in their tiny allowances of clothes that enabled the wind to turn their bodies red and then blue with cold. The women shivered in the houses where fuel was as scarce as flour, and where flour was sometimes as scarce as diamonds. ("Nebraska's Bitter Fight," 6)

It was during Crane's journey by rail from Lincoln to Eddyville, according to Thomas Beer, that at "a dreary junction town" in Dawson County he chanced to see the light blue hotel that was to serve as the germ of "The Blue Hotel." "In a hotel painted so loathsomely," Beer suggests, "some dire action must take place and, after four years, he made it seem so." Of Eddyville itself, very likely one of the small towns later to serve as a partial model for Fort Romper, Crane reports: "Approaching it over the prairie, one sees a row of little houses, blocked upon the sky. Most of them are one storied. Some of the stores have little square false-fronts. The buildings straggle at irregular intervals along the street and a little board side-walk connects them. On all sides stretches the wind-swept prairie." "This town was once a live little place," Crane writes of Eddyville, "where the keepers of the three or four stores did a thriving trade." What he saw when he arrived there, however, was "as inanimate as a corpse," a place where "in the rears of stores, a few men, perhaps, sit listlessly by the stoves" ("Nebraska's Bitter Fight," 9–10).

What Crane saw in Eddyville was a scene of economic depredation brought about by a set of unfortunate natural conditions, not malevolent cosmic ones; and when he finally set about writing "The Blue Hotel," these conditions along with their practical economic implications could hardly have been far from his mind—and all of this associated with that memorable blue hotel. But Crane's conceptions of the "true conditions" of the West had been formed in some measure even before he arrived in Eddyville. His journey there from Lincoln had been delayed by his much-reported "arrest" (more likely only a brief detention, as Bernice Slote has suggested) on unspecified charges for interfering in a barroom fight in a Lincoln hotel the night before his departure for Eddyville. As Beer recounts this episode, Crane pushed himself between "a very tall man" who was "pounding a rather small one." "'But thus I offended a local custom,'" Crane wrote of the encounter. "'These men fought each other every night. Their friends expected it and I was a darned nuisance with my Eastern scruples and all that. So first everybody cursed me fully and then they took me off to a judge who told me that I was an imbecile and let me go. . . .'"

This episode, actually more reminiscent of the staged confrontations between Jack Potter and Scratchy Wilson in "The Bride Comes to Yellow Sky" than of the grim and savage encounter between the Swede and Johnnie in "The Blue Hotel," must have impressed Crane with the peculiarities of local custom on the Western frontier, especially as it pertained to the display, and the containment, of human violence. His consistent vision of the West, in the group of Western stories he wrote between the summer of 1897 and late 1899, is of a place where the inclination to violence is never far from erupting to the surface, though as a matter of carefully calculated public policy that particular feature of Western reality is generally suppressed by a not disinterested citizenry. And as I am about to suggest, this is exactly the social reality that Crane depicts in "The Blue Hotel." . . .

Source: John Feaster, "Violence and the Ideology of Capitalism: A Reconsideration of Crane's 'The Blue Hotel,'" in *American Literary Realism*, Vol. 25, No. 2, Fall 1994, pp. 74–94.

John J. Conder

In the following excerpt, Conder outlines Stephen Crane's naturalistic vision in "The Blue Hotel."

. . . Why, then, if there is no clear moral axis in the first seven sections, does Crane introduce moral perspectives in the last two? The apparently moral perspectives of the narrator in section viii and of the Easterner in ix seem more like deliberately planned additions to the story to impale the reader on the horns of what can be called the Hobbesian dilemma: man is free and can be judged morally, but his acts of the will are caused, a fact that undercuts the premise on which moral judgment is based—that under the same conditions individuals could behave other than as they do.

It is Crane's emphasis on types, on what he early in the story refers to as "creeds, classes, [and] egotisms," that initially challenges that premise. The story shows that an individual's character type is one of the conditions governing behavior, a fact that makes nonsense of the idea that under the same conditions a character could act other than as he does. Perhaps so, but then he would be a different character! And as the story develops, one sees the challenge to this premise strengthened, for another dimension of character that acts as cause emerges: its elemental nature. The story presents character as type defined by class or creed and character as animallike in its egotism. Indeed, in this story, these two aspects of character become inseparable, and this twin emphasis resolutely turns the Hobbesian definition of liberty ("the absence of all the impediments to action that are not contained in the nature and intrinsical quality of the agent") into a deterministic vision.

In order to see that both aspects of character operate as conditions that govern behavior, the reader must be aware of how thoroughly Crane blurs the distinction between the human and the nonhuman worlds. He does this primarily by presenting the story as though it were a scientific experiment, the subject of which is human responses. The unusual color of the hotel, blue, suggests its role as a laboratory where the experimental scientist blends the "creeds, classes, egotisms, that streamed through Romper on the rails day after day." Those, like the Easterner, who came from "the brown-reds and the subdivisions of the dark greens of the East" had "no color in common" with the "opulence and splendor" of the hotel—or so the reader is told. But Crane's

> "SEEN IN THE LIVED MOMENT OF ACTION, HENCE, THE STORY CONTAINS A PSYCHOLOGICAL DETERMINISM DEPENDENT ON CHARACTER TYPE."

naturalistic vision manipulates color to show that even a sophisticated Easterner is, finally, a part of nature and can be viewed as such in a laboratory.

The first hint of this comes from the particular colors that this color-conscious author chooses to emphasize in his story. The East is equated with brown-red and dark green; the West, with blue. Red, green, and blue-violet are primary colors—not the pigment primaries of the painter, to be sure, but the light primaries of the physicist, more appropriate to the perspective of the narrator as that of a detached scientist. To understand the narrator's "scientific findings," however, the reader must ignore Crane's choice of *brown*-red and his omission of violet as the tone of his blue. Eastern subdivisions, after all, are not fire-engine red, and it would be awkward to call the story "The Blue-Violet Hotel." Granting Crane this privilege, the reader can see that Crane deliberately reduces regions and the particular "creeds, classes, egotisms" that they breed to color; he blends together in the hotel not the subtractive primaries of the painter, which combine to produce black, but the additive primaries of the physicist—red, green, and blue—whose blending produces white. So the characters do, after all, share a "color in common." White, furthermore, is the color (really noncolor) of the snowstorm, and so blending these character-colors together equates all of them with the world of physical nature—even the Easterner, despite his civilized veneer. Crane, indeed, emphasizes the sophisticated Easterner's association with physical nature. His name is Blanc, French for white. And Mont Blanc, the highest peak in the Alps, is eternally covered with glaciers and snow, a fact that inspired Coleridge and Shelley and very likely Crane as well.

But the story is named "The *Blue* Hotel," and Crane gives equal emphasis to that color to make the point that man is a part of nature. The hotel's color seems to set it apart not just from the world of the East but, by its sharp contrast to the white of the snowstorm, from the world of physical nature as well. But the blue is also associated with physical nature, for it covers the snow with its "unearthly satin"; thus, the human creation—the hotel—and nature share a common color, suggesting that the division between the two worlds of man and nature is tenuous at best. Furthermore, people grow blue when they are cold and, though the hotel is supposed to protect them from this condition, it is in this very blue hotel that temperaments so commingle as to force them into the world of nature that will make them blue.

Crane's use of color, then, partly translates into a philosophical meaning akin to Ishmael's final speculations in the chapter "The Whiteness of the Whale" in *Moby-Dick* (chapter 42). Colors may distinguish one type of man from another type, and they indeed seem to separate man from the world of nature, which is snow-white-colorless. But in fact the human world represented by color is part of the continuum of nature because the whiteness of nature contains all colors—if the mixing of the colors produces white, the colors are *in* the white. Or, as Ishmael puts it, whiteness is not just "the visible absence of color" but is "at the same time the concrete of all colors." Hence, nature and man are one, not two, in "The Blue Hotel."

If the usual distinctions between the human and nonhuman worlds ultimately collapse, then one can legitimately examine human responses as a biologist examines the responses of birds or bullocks. And Crane's narrator does exactly that. His investigation shows that character operates as condition in *both* its social and its animal dimensions. In other words, the narrator's angle of vision is Hobbesian, and that angle of vision issues in a Hobbesian view of freedom because it views man's civilized self, with its "freedom," in the same way that it views man's animal nature. Initially the emphasis falls on character type—that is, social type—as one important condition that causes certain emotional responses and leads to certain characteristic actions.

He introduces the Swede's first paranoid response, one that has its conditions: his foreignness, the locale, and his familiarity with the clichés of dime novels. And that paranoid response acts as the condition sparking the initial responses of others, differing types responding in different ways to one condition. Thus, the action that unfolds in the opening sections seems perfectly reasonable—"reasonable" in the sense of explicable and plausible rather than rational. Each character seems to have good reason to behave as he does, given his respective type. But by the end of section vii the reader can perceive that beneath the different types a common "savagery" emerges, though the expression of that violent emotional response again varies with the character type. That is, some people are more civilized than others and require greater external provocation before becoming like their fellow animals—before becoming, that is, creatures of instinct and emotion rather than creatures of a social class. Section vii ends with the cowboy and Scully vying in expressions of frustration as they repeat how they would like to kill the Swede, though Scully's stronger ethical sense prevents the cowboy from taking him on. The Easterner does not participate in section vii's verbal orgy, but he is hardly exempt from the emotional responses there expressed. For that section's marked emphasis on savage responses prepares for the final and most important response in the story, the Easterner's in section ix. It is there that his place in nature, and so in Crane's laboratory experiment, becomes apparent.

The Easterner's "fog of mysterious theory" seems to proceed naturally from the reasoned and reflective character type assigned him earlier, a type in marked contrast to others in the work. But the cowboy's protestations against the Easterner's assertion, "The Swede might not have been killed if everything had been square," "reduced him [the Easterner] to rage." He is no more exempt from frustration than the cowboy, as the following words indicate: "'You're a fool!' cried the Easterner *viciously*" (emphasis provided). He is enraged by the cowboy's obtuseness, and his rage proceeds from a sense of guilt generated by a knowledge of the conclusion of his encounter with the Swede. This "fog of mysterious theory," then, hardly possesses a rational base, and in his desire to relieve himself of the anguish of guilt, the Easterner dilutes it by imposing it on four others as well. It would be logical, of course, to blame the Swede, too; indeed, the whole community, which supported the "unfortunate gambler" whose action of killing the Swede is "the apex of a human movement." But such logic would only be for one not caught in the throes of guilt. Where everyone is guilty, no one is, and the Easterner's guilt feelings are too intense to allow for their complete dissipation. But their very intensity also demands that they be shared. Hence, though he observes that "usually there are from a dozen to forty women really involved in every murder" (a comment that suggests that guilt can be widely distributed to the point where the concept becomes meaningless), he acknowledges his own felt guilt by implicating himself and just four others in the killing.

Seen in the lived moment of action, hence, the story contains a psychological determinism dependent on character type. Psychic states determine not just the obvious emotional responses of a simple cowboy who shrieks "Kill him" during the fight but also the apparently reasoned concluding observations of the sophisticated Easterner. But viewing events in retrospect, the reader is forced to the determinism that is part of the Easterner's theory, that historical determinism which describes every sin as the "apex of a human movement," a determinism that is the natural complement of the psychological; for indeed any present moment is "the apex of a human movement" in a past in which men's behavior is a function of conditions then prevailing.

These two ways of witnessing the action show that the Easterner both is and is not Crane's spokesman. The moral aspect of his theory is false because it involves only five men as collaborators in a "sin." But because his theory embraces both the moral and the deterministic, thereby reducing "sin" to a "result," "the apex of a human movement," his theory in broad outline does indeed represent the story's preferred philosophical vision. For the Easterner forces the reader to think in two sets of opposed terms, and so does Crane, who structures his story to embody a classic modern vision expressed by the Easterner, the Hobbesian paradox that undoes liberty with causation. That human movement whose apex is the Swede's death may be the result of characters performing "freely-willed" actions, but each action is reducible to conditions over which the character has no control. This paradox is the source of richness in "The Blue Hotel" and moves it resolutely in the direction of determinism. More important, the clear surfacing of the Hobbesian paradox in this, one of Crane's late works, suggests that his earlier works contain a dual vision that is responsible for such thoroughly incompatible interpretations of them.

Source: John J. Conder, "Stephen Crane and the Necessary Fiction," in *Naturalism in American Fiction: The Classic Phase*, University Press of Kentucky, 1984, pp. 22–42.

James Trammel Cox

In the following excerpt, Cox offers an analysis of "The Blue Hotel" that illustrates that Stephen Crane was a symbolist, rather than a naturalist.

The limitations of labels are less apparent when the term, like *naturalism*, has clearly definable boundaries than when it suffers from an excess of meaning, as in the much discussed omnibus *romanticism*. But they are no less real, and no less critically inhibiting. In the case of *naturalism* I would say this is particularly true, and as it has been applied to the fiction of Stephen Crane the effect has been to encourage a view and a lethargy which Crane hardly deserves. R. W. Stallman is almost alone in perceiving a fundamental difference in the fictional method of Crane and that of other naturalists in American fiction; and the value of his work in the eyes of many of the critics of American literature has been obscured by the set features, like a comic mask, of French naturalism. As articulated by Zola in *Le roman expérimental*, it is a central doctrine that "*le naturalisme, je le dis encore, consiste uniquement dans la méthode expérimentale, dans l'observation et l'expérience appliquees à la littérature*" and that "*la méthode atteint la forme elle-même.*" And it is this linkage of form and matter, uncritically accepted since the 1870's as an unalterable constituent of literary naturalism, that is at the root of our failure to recognize significant distinctions between our own naturalists, such as Dreiser or Norris or Crane. We are too quick to assume that any determinist not only has a certain familiar body of ideas but employs a certain method in the presentation of these ideas, that, of course, of the reporter or mere recorder of life.

With Crane this assumption has indeed been qualified to the extent of recognizing a difference, quantitatively at least, in the cumulation of detail, between Crane, say, and Dreiser. Further, a tendency to render much of his material visually, together with an exaggeration of his well-known haste in composition, has combined to demand some sort of qualification of Crane's naturalism; but all too frequently this qualification appears only in the equally half-safe addition of the adjective *impressionistic*, while the underlying assumption remains that Crane as a literary naturalist is also a literalist. Emotional perhaps, eclectic perhaps, Crane, a sort of cub "reporter" lives on.

"SUPPORT FOR THIS VIEW OF THE FUNCTION OF THE STOVE IS ABUNDANTLY EVIDENT, AS SUGGESTED ABOVE, IN THE WAY CRANE RELATES THE CONTRAST CLUSTERS WHITE-RED, FEAR-ANGER, AND SNOW-FIRE."

It is consequently my purpose in the following analysis of "The Blue Hotel" to establish first of all that Crane's fictional method is that of the symbolist rather than the naturalist in that he carefully selects his details not as pieces of evidence in a one-dimensional report on man but as connotatively associated parts of an elaborately contrived symbolic substructure. Secondly, I am concerned to arrive at what this substructure means. More briefly, I hope to demonstrate the extent to which Stephen Crane is and is not a naturalist, in the abused sense of the term.

The total conceit, which it seems to me "The Blue Hotel" essentially is, fantastically extended and elaborately interwoven, will perhaps emerge with greater clarity if we begin somewhat undramatically at the symbolic center of the story. This I take to be the stove, with the rest of the story, like the room and the hotel itself, "merely [its] proper temple." Crane centers our attention upon it immediately upon the entry of Scully with his guests "through the portals of the blue hotel." For the room which they enter is described as "merely a proper temple for an enormous stove, which, in the centre, was humming with godlike violence. At various points on its surface the iron had become luminous and glowed yellow from the heat." While tonally a little grandiose as literal description, the language used here in this picture of the stove takes on considerable significance when we have noted more than twenty instances in which man is metaphorically shown to "embrace [this] glowing iron." For instance, the cowboy is referred to as "bronzed." Scully's cap is said to cause "his two red ears to stick out stiffly, as if they were made of tin." Also "The cowboy and the Easterner burnished themselves fiery red with this water, until it seemed to be some kind of metal polish." The picture of Scully's daughter has the "hue of lead." The Swede's eyes and Johnnie's cross "like blades," and again "the two warriors ever sought each other in glances that were at once hot and steely." At the fight the Easterner is pictured as "hopping up and down like a mechanical toy." Scully is the "iron-nerved master of the ceremony." The fight is described as presenting "no more detail than a swiftly revolving wheel," and aside from this picture of the fight as a wheel the Swede is described at supper as having "fizzed like a firewheel." *Wheel* as a verb is also used four times. After the first knock-down the fighters are "actuated by a new caution as they advanced toward collision." The Swede is pictured as "breathing like an engine." And when Johnnie is ready to fight again Scully doesn't tell the cowboy to get out of the way but to "'git out of the road.'"

What these indiscriminantly mechanical and/or metallic references have to do with the stove will become increasingly evident when we have gone on to the first group of symbolically related contrasts, white-red, snow-fire, and fear-anger. For the present, however, the purpose of these equations, to identify man with the stove, is suggested more specifically in the two pictures below, first, of the Easterner and then of Scully. For when the fight is over and the group has come back inside, the Easterner "rushed to the stove. He was so profoundly chilled that he almost dared to embrace the glowing iron." And when Scully follows the Swede upstairs to dissuade him from leaving, it would seem that he *has* embraced the glowing iron—in the sense of enclosed within—: "Scully's wrinkled visage showed grimly in the light of the small lamp he carried. This yellow effulgence, streaming upward, coloured only his prominent features, and left his eyes, for instance, mysterious shadow. He resembled a murderer." For this "murderer's" visage is the same color as that of the surface of the stove, yellow; and it would thus seem to be the stove, "humming with godlike violence," which Crane has in mind as the "engine of life" in the summarizing passage below wherein the indirect statement and the direct meet: "The conceit of man was explained by this storm to be the very engine of life—." Or, philosophically stated, man's inner nature is egocentric, and it is this egocentrism in contact with environment which creates the storm or fundamental conflict relationship between man and his environment.

Thus by the use of the color yellow for its surface and the central position of the stove, spatially and imagistically, together with the supporting figures of speech equating man and metal, Crane in the symbol of the stove sets up a definition of man's inner nature as burning with elemental aggressions, "humming with godlike violence."

Support for this view of the function of the stove is abundantly evident, as suggested above, in the way Crane relates the contrast clusters white-red, fear-anger, and snow-fire. First let us note three occasions in which whiteness is associated with fear. ". . . it seemed to the Swede that he was formidably menaced. He shivered and turned white near the corners of his mouth." Again when the Swede resolves to leave the room because of his fearful conviction that he is going to be killed, he is described as "the whitefaced man." Similarly, the alarmed Easterner, as the Swede later thrusts his fist into Johnnie's face during the card game, is described as having grown "pallid." As instances of what is often called *natural symbolism*, these repetitions are hardly adequate to establish white as a part of a contrived symbolic structure, but as the contrasting association of red with anger emerges in the material to come and a conflict relationship is insisted upon between the two, it becomes evident that these associations do have such a function. For instance in the first scuffle, Johnnie is pictured with "his red face appearing over his father's shoulder." And the Swede, whose actions on a narrative level exemplify the extremes suggested here, is pictured so: "Upon the Swede's deathly pale cheeks were two spots brightly crimson." The same slightly ludicrous image is repeated during the fight, significantly, I think, attached to the other characters as well as the Swede: "Occasionally a face, as if illumined by a flash of light, would shine out ghastly and marked with pink spots." Again it is not without ironic finality when the gambler "wiped his knife on one of the towels that hung beneath the bar rail," leaving inevitably the red stain of blood on the white towel.

In these instances the associations involve color alone and the connection between this material and the symbolic significance of the stove is hardly apparent, but with the addition of snow and fire to white and red, as linked to fear and anger, the connection becomes not only clear but meaningful in the same terms that the stove is meaningful. For instance, in the Swede's first flush of defiance as he raises Scully's bottle to his lips, he looks at Scully with a glance "burning with hatred." After supper as the Swede claps Scully on his sore shoulder, Johnnie expects his father to "flame out" over the matter. Later when the Swede thrusts his first into Johnnie's face his eyes are "blazing orbs." And the room, after this scuffle, is said to be "lighted with anger." The corresponding contrast, linking snow with white and fear, may also be seen in this line: "A gatepost like a still man with a blanched face stood aghast amid this profligate fury." And the ultimate fusion of these two together in imagery that is loaded with dramatic tension is especially apparent in the passages following: "When the party rounded the corner they were fairly blinded by the pelting of the snow. It burned their faces like fire." Also the earth, in the crucial paragraph mentioned above containing the reference to the "engine of life," is described as a "fire-smitten, ice-locked . . . bulb." And in front of the saloon when the Swede reaches the town "an indomitable red light was burning, and the snowflakes were made blood-colour as they flew through the circumscribed territory of the lamp's shining." Thus symbolically through the fire, fear and anger are brought into relationship with the stove, so that we may now see it—or man—as burning not only with elemental aggressions but also with elemental fears and the stove with its yellow surface as the same sort of tension-bursting symbol as that of its opposite, the snow that "burned . . . like fire. . . . "

Source: James Trammel Cox, "Stephen Crane as Symbolic Naturalist: An Analysis of 'The Blue Hotel,'" in *Modern Fiction Studies*, Vol. 3, No. 2, Summer 1957, pp. 147–58.

SOURCES

Crane, Stephen, "Nebraska's Bitter Fight for Life," in *Stephen Crane: Prose and Poetry*, Library of America, 1984, pp. 688–99.

———, "The Blue Hotel," in *Anthology of American Literature*, Vol. II: *Realism to the Present*, 2nd ed., edited by George McMichael, Macmillan, 1980, pp. 767–85.

Deamer, Robert Glen, "Stephen Crane and the Western Myth," in *A Reader's Guide to the Short Stories of Stephen Crane*, edited by Michael W. Schaefer, G. K. Hall, 1996, p. 21; originally published in *Western American Literature*, Vol. 7, Summer 1972, p. 122.

Gullason, Thomas A., "Stephen Crane's Short Stories: The Blue Hotel," in *A Reader's Guide to the Short Stories of Stephen Crane*, edited by Michael W. Schaefer, G. K. Hall, 1996, p. 20; originally published in *Stephen Crane's*

Career: Perspectives and Evaluations, edited by Thomas A. Gullason, New York University Press, 1972.

McMichael, George, ed., *Anthology of American Literature*, Vol. II: *Realism to the Present*, 2nd ed., Macmillan, 1980, pp. 2, 746.

"Nebraska QuickFacts," in *U.S. Census Bureau*, http://quickfacts.census.gov/qfd/states/31000.html (accessed February 28, 2011).

"The Records Project," in *Nebraska Census Record Information Online*, http://recordsproject.com/census/nebraska.asp (accessed February 28, 2011).

Review of *The Monster, and Other Stories*, in *Stephen Crane: The Critical Heritage*, edited by Richard M. Weatherford, Routledge and Kegan Paul, 1973, pp. 263–64; originally published in *Academy*, March 16, 1901, p. 230.

Review of *The Monster, and Other Stories*, in *Stephen Crane: The Critical Heritage*, edited by Richard M. Weatherford, Routledge and Kegan Paul, 1973, pp. 262–63; originally published in *Athenaeum*, March 16, 1901, p. 334.

Review of *The Monster, and Other Stories*, in *Stephen Crane: The Critical Heritage*, edited by Richard M. Weatherford, Routledge and Kegan Paul, 1973, p. 262; originally published in *Book Buyer*, April 1900, p. 244.

Schaefer, Michael W., *A Reader's Guide to the Short Stories of Stephen Crane*, G. K. Hall, 1996, pp. 10–12.

Weiss, Daniel, "The Blue Hotel," in *Stephen Crane*, edited by Harold Bloom, Chelsea House, 1987, p. 49; originally published in *The Critic Agonistes: Psychology, Myth and the Art of Fiction*, edited by Erica Solomon and Stephen Arkin, University of Washington Press, 1985.

Wells, H. G., "An English Standpoint," in *Stephen Crane: The Critical Heritage*, edited by Richard M. Weatherford, Routledge and Kegan Paul, 1973, p. 267; originally published in *North American Review*, August 1900, pp. 233–42.

FURTHER READING

Fishkin, Shelley Fisher, *From Fact to Fiction: Journalism and Imaginative Writing in America*, Oxford University Press, 1988.

> Fishkin begins by noting that many American authors from the late nineteenth century onward, including Crane, began their careers as journalists and explores why these authors turned to imaginative writing. She examines attitudes toward fiction and journalism and the way authors have converted fact into fiction (or poetry).

Luebke, Frederick C., *Nebraska: An Illustrated History*, University of Nebraska Press, 1995.

> Students interested in the history of Nebraska, the setting for "The Blue Hotel," will find in Luebke's book discussion of important elements of Nebraska history, all supplemented with numerous illustrations. In particular, Luebke's examination of the history of the railroads in Nebraska and the state's immigrant experience would be relevant to an understanding of Crane and his observations about the state.

Smith, Christopher, ed., *American Realism*, Greenhaven Press, 2000.

> This volume, suitable for high-school students, is a collection of essays about the realist movement in American literature, including the emergence of the naturalist movement. One group of essays defines realism. A second group discusses the rise of naturalism and its outgrowth from scientific views of society. Additional sections contain essays about race, class, and gender in the realist movement and about images of the frontier and small towns in realist literature.

Sorrentino, Paul M., *Student Companion to Stephen Crane*, Greenwood Press, 2005.

> This book, written principally for high-school students by the founder of the Stephen Crane Society and its journal, contains information about Crane's family and includes critical commentaries and discussions of writings. Students can find information not only about Crane's novels and poetry but also about his short stories and sketches.

SUGGESTED SEARCH TERMS

American frontier

American plains

journalism AND American fiction

naturalism

Nebraska history

Old West

railroads AND late nineteenth century

realism

Stephen Crane

Stephen Crane AND The Blue Hotel

The Country of the Blind

H. G. WELLS

1904

H. G. Wells's story "The Country of the Blind" was first published in the April 1904 issue of the *Strand Magazine* and later appeared in his 1911 collection *The Country of the Blind, and Other Stories*. It examines the adage "In the country of the blind, the one-eyed man is king" through the adventures of Nunez, a South American mountain climber, who discovers an isolated community high in the Ecuadorian Andes whose members have all been blind for fifteen generations. His quest for power and glory is derailed by the villagers' belief that his talk about being able to see is nothing more than a mental defect that must be corrected. The story illustrates Wells's belief that forward-thinking individuals are usually dismissed by backward societies to their own detriment.

Wells published two versions of "The Country of the Blind." By far the most popular is the original 1904 version, in which Nunez escapes the village and dies of exposure trying to make his way back to civilization. In the lesser-known version, published as a limited-edition volume by Golden Cockerel Press in 1939, Nunez tries in vain to save the villagers from an impending avalanche that only he can see coming. The only survivor besides Nunez is the blind woman he loves, Medina-saroté. While the subtexts of the two versions are completely opposite, the story remains one of the best-known and well-regarded tales of physical disability in the literary canon. Wells considered "The Country of the

H. G. Wells

Blind" one of his best stories, although he had little regard for the genre of the short story, which he believed was an antiquated literary form that had run its course by the time he published his collection in 1911.

AUTHOR BIOGRAPHY

Herbert George Wells was born on September 21, 1866, in Bromley, England. His lower-middle-class parents struggled to support their four children, and Bertie, as young Wells was known, suffered an early education in false starts and dead ends. From 1880 to 1883 he served unhappily as an apprentice in the fabric trade, but in 1884, he received a scholarship to study biology at the Normal School of Science in London. He joined the school's debating society and plunged headfirst into an exploration of politics and society, becoming an advocate for socialism and an enthusiastic member of the reform-minded Fabian Society.

Wells, who had always enjoyed literature, began writing both fiction and nonfiction in the *Science School Journal,* which he helped found at the college. In 1887, he published an early version of his first novella, *The Time Machine*, in the journal. Nevertheless, he soon lost his scholarship and was left penniless, and he did not receive a college diploma until he graduated from the University of London in 1889. Shortly thereafter, he became a teacher and married a cousin, Isabel Mary Wells.

Meanwhile, his literary output grew enormously. He published numerous critical essays as well as stories, novels, treatises on world history, and political commentaries, at a rate that far surpassed the most prolific writers of the day. Most of his short stories, including "The Country of the Blind," were published before 1910, and after 1911, when he published the collection *The Country of the Blind, and Other Stories*, he considered the genre passé and never returned to it. Wells dubbed his earliest novels "scientific romances" and considered them lesser works in his oeuvre. In fact, these novels, which include *The Time Machine* (1895), *The Island of Doctor Moreau* (1896), *The Invisible Man* (1897), *The War of the Worlds* (1897), and *The First Men in the Moon* (1901), launched the science-fiction genre and proved to be his most enduring literary legacy, universally acknowledged for their prescient view of the future and deft portrayal of the intersection of science and human nature. These works predicted the rise of the automobile and suburbia, the European Union, and the sexual revolution. The dangers of radioactive decay are featured in his novels *Tono-Bungay* (1909) and *The World Set Free* (1914), which foreshadowed the development of the nuclear bomb by decades. *The Shape of Things to Come* (1933) predicted the rise of fascism and World War II.

As a freethinker and socialist, Wells was interested in the concept of utopia, which figures prominently in the "The Country of the Blind." He warned against the possibility of a world war long before his contemporaries could see it coming, and in 1917 he joined the committee that researched the potential founding of the League of Nations, the forerunner of the modern United Nations. Though controversial in his time for his views on race, sex, women's equality and suffrage, free love, and politics, he believed in working toward a more just world that would be achieved partly through education. Toward that end, he envisioned a permanent encyclopedia of world knowledge accessible freely to all people, which he dubbed the World Brain.

Wells had two sons with his second wife, Amy Catherine Robbins, and two other children born out of wedlock. Anthony West, his son with the journalist and feminist Rebecca West, became a writer himself and portrayed his lonely childhood in his biography of his father, *H. G. Wells: Aspects of a Life* (1984). Wells had numerous affairs with other women, including controversial American birth-control activist Margaret Sanger. Many of Wells's stories and novellas have been adapted for film, the most notable being *The Time Machine* and *The War of the Worlds*. Wells died on August 13, 1946, in London, England.

PLOT SUMMARY

"The Country of the Blind" opens with a prologue of sorts describing how the isolated mountain community originated. A band of Peruvians seeking refuge from Spanish invaders settles high in the Ecuadorian Andes, in a hospitable, verdant valley where they farm and raise llamas. Soon they become afflicted with a disease that causes them to slowly go blind. The older generation loses its sight, while a new generation is born blind. Believing this is punishment for failing to thank the gods for their new home, the community elects a member to travel down to the lower world, find a cheap religious idol, and bring it back. Half-blind already, the man stumbles down to civilization clutching what little silver the villagers could scrape together. While he is gone, an avalanche seals the valley off from the rest of the world. When he reaches the city, no one believes the man's fantastic tale. He loses his sight completely, falls ill, and dies working in the mines. His story fuels the myth of "the Country of the Blind." Fifteen generations pass; the villagers adapt to life in their hospitable valley but lose all knowledge of their past. They come to believe that their small valley constitutes the entire world, which is capped above them by a dome made of smooth, solid rock. They have no concept of sight, but they have developed extraordinarily refined senses of smell, hearing, and touch. They work in the coolness of the night and sleep during the heat of the day.

The action of the story commences with the introduction of Nunez, a mountain climber from Quito, Ecuador, whose love of adventure has taken him far and wide in South America. He is leading a group of British climbers on an expedition to conquer Parascotopetl, a peak known as "the Matterhorn of the Andes." The group makes camp on a precarious ledge at the base of the final ascent, whereupon Nunez silently and suddenly falls off the cliff. The British climbers see his footprints in the snow the following morning. Assuming his fall was fatal, they do not even attempt a rescue.

Nunez does not die, though. Miraculously, his thousand-foot tumble deposits him in a bank of soft snow; he finds himself bruised and disoriented but otherwise uninjured. In the daylight, he digs his way out and observes a village far off

MEDIA ADAPTATIONS

- John Dunkel adapted "The Country of the Blind" for an episode of the radio show *Escape* that aired on November 26, 1947, starring Paul Frees as Nunez. The broadcast can be downloaded from the *Escape and Suspense!* Web site (http://www.escape-suspense.com). In this version of the story, Nunez escapes from the village and makes his way back to Bogotá to tell his story. The adaptation was broadcast two additional times, on June 20, 1948, and March 20, 1949, both with Berry Kroeger playing Nunez.
- Frank Gabrielsen adapted the story for the teleplay *The Richest Man in Bogota*, a June 1962 production of *The DuPont Show of the Week*. Lee Marvin starred as Nunez.
- Ekaterina Obraztsova wrote and directed a short animated adaptation called *The Land of the Blind*, which was released by the Russian company Soyuzmultifilm in 1995.
- Frank Higgins's stage adaptation of "The Country of the Blind" was produced at the Coterie Theater in Kansas City, Missouri, in 2006, and focused on the story's theme of what it means to be disabled.

in the valley below, surrounded by a lush meadow in bloom with beautiful flowers. The strange mud houses have no windows and, with no care given to color, look as if they were built by blind men. He notices other peculiarities as he gets closer. The crop fields are extraordinarily tidy, and a wall encircles the entire village. The wall is punctuated at regular intervals with holes that irrigate the crops with melting snow from the mountains. The water is distributed via a series of chest-high aqueducts that lead to neat channels in the fields. Paths radiate out on a central axis, each lined with stone curbs in a manner that reminds Nunez of an urban landscape. The villagers' huts are lined up in perfect symmetry on a very clean street.

Most of the villagers are resting, but three are carrying pails balanced on poles across their shoulders. Nunez calls out to them and waves wildly. They appear to hear him but not see him. Frustrated, he makes his way to a door in the wall that rings the village. When they still cannot see him, he slowly comes to understand he has found the legendary Country of the Blind. He is seized with excitement and delusions of grandeur. "In the Country of the Blind the One-eyed Man is King," he repeats to himself.

The three men approach cautiously, frightened by the intruder. Their eye sockets are closed and shrunken, as if they have no eyes at all. One of the men comments—in an archaic form of Spanish—that Nunez must be a newly formed man or a spirit. Nunez cordially introduces himself, stating that he is from Bogota, a big city "where men can see." The villagers do not understand the words *see* and *sight*. They reach out their hands and feel his face gently; they are puzzled by the bulging, fluttering protuberances on his face and dislike his coarse hair. They decide to lead him to their elders. Nunez objects to being led by the hand, saying he can see, yet he immediately stumbles over one of their pails. They theorize that he is a newly formed man, still imperfect and with much to learn.

In the village, the people crowd around, observing Nunez with all their remaining senses. He repeats that he comes from Bogota, but no one understands—they think it is his name and begin to call him that. They thrust him into a pitch-black cabin, whereupon he stumbles over a seated elder and accidentally strikes several people as he falls down. The elders take his clumsiness to mean that he is newly formed, along with his strange words about "darkness" and "the outside world." He tries in vain to convince them of who he is and where he comes from, but he finally gives up, believing that "much of their imagination had shriveled with their eyes." He listens to their tales of how the world was formed from a hollow in the rocks and how time is divided into warm and cold. The elders tell Nunez that he must be patient and try hard to understand their wisdom in order to transform his unformed mind to be as wise as they are.

They bring him food and tell him to get some sleep, but he remains awake, resolving to "bring them to reason." He hatches a plan to demonstrate how his sense of sight sets him apart—he will hide from them. But his plan backfires; no matter how quiet he is, they can hear his footsteps. They think he is acting like a child by walking on the grass and wonder why he cannot "hear the path." They repeatedly tell him he has much to learn, while Nunez staunchly believes it is they who have much to learn. He tells them that in a country of blind people, the one-eyed man should be king. Their only response is to ask what *blind* means. Becoming their leader is proving more difficult than he thought. For several days he decides to play it safe. He learns their customs and manners. He is irritated by working at night and resolves to change that fact as soon as he can.

Meanwhile, he observes that the village is a happy place. The people work hard, but not oppressively so. The children are happy, and their environment has been regulated to such a degree that getting around poses no problem for anyone. Their hearing is acute enough to "hear and judge the slightest gesture of a man a dozen paces away." Their sense of smell is as keen as a dog's. They tend to their llamas confidently.

Still, he tries to convince them of the wonders of sight. They defend their view of the universe adamantly, declaring his talk of an outside world to be "wicked." Nunez becomes so exasperated at their refusal to acknowledge his superiority that he raises his spade with the intent to kill one of them; instantly, he realizes that killing a blind man would be unjust. Spade in hand, Nunez flees in anguish as "he began to realize that you cannot even fight happily with creatures who stand upon a different mental basis to yourself."

The villagers chase after him to the village wall and implore him to drop the spade and get off the grass. He is taunted by the refrain that echoes in his head: "In the Country of the Blind the One-eyed Man is King." Trapped as they surround him, he hits one with the spade to escape. He runs through the town panic-stricken and escapes through the door in the village wall, whereupon he realizes that "his *coup d'etat* [had come] to an end."

After two nights outside the wall, he is cold and hungry, and he realizes he must live on the blind people's terms. He returns to the village and admits that his anger was the result of having been newly made. He tells them he no longer believes he can see. They are gladdened by his change of heart, forgive his violent outburst, and accept him back into the fold. They nurse him back to health and assign him to some of their most taxing chores as a way of making amends. The blind philosophers continue to educate him on their beliefs and ways.

He becomes one of them; the world beyond the Country of the Blind fades into the realm of myth for him. His master, Yacob, regards him as somewhat exasperating but mostly harmless. Nunez falls in love with Yacob's youngest daughter, Medina-saroté. The blind consider her ugly; her long eyelashes are thought to be a deformity. But what they consider ugly, Nunez finds beautiful. Medina-saroté, whose deformity limits her options, returns Nunez's affections. She is, however, made uncomfortable by his occasional remarks about sight and the outside world, which she considers a product of his imagination. Eventually, Nunez asks Yacob if he can marry Medina-saroté.

Opposition to the marriage is great. Nunez, still known as Bogota by the villagers, is regarded as an idiot of sorts. Medina-saroté's sisters believe he brings shame on the family. The men believe he will corrupt their race. But Yacob is eventually swayed by his daughter's tears. The community decides that he will be an acceptable husband only if he submits to an operation to remove his eyeballs. The orbs, they reason, are diseased and the cause of his madness; removal is the only cure. "Thank Heaven for science!" Yacob exclaims, agreeing to the solution.

Nunez, too, agrees to the operation for Medina-saroté's sake. He does not wish to give up the ability to see all the beautiful things in the world—the mountains, the trees, and Medina-saroté herself—but he acquiesces to her argument that it is their only chance for leading a normal, happy life. He is sleepless and restless for the next week. On the day before the operation, Nunez witnesses "the morning like an angel in golden armour, marching down the steeps." The sight is so beautiful that he walks through the door in the city's wall to drink in its grandeur one last time. He becomes overwhelmed with utter desolation that he will soon be separated from this world. Staring at the towering mountains, he thinks of all the wonders of the world he has seen. Then he spots what he believes is a manageable route up the mountain and through the pass to the other side.

Gazing upon the Country of the Blind, he sees it anew as a "pit of sin." Medina-saroté, though he loves her, seems insignificant. He turns away from the village and begins his ascent. He climbs until sunset finds him bruised and bloody, but happy. The Country of the Blind is hazy in his mind already, whereas the magnificence of the mountains is tangible, colorful, and beautiful. Nunez, lying still on his back and gazing up at the cold stars above, dies.

CHARACTERS

Medina-saroté

Medina-saroté is the youngest of Yacob's three daughters. The villagers consider her deformed because of her long eyelashes and misshapen eye sockets, but Nunez finds her beautiful precisely because of them. Medina-saroté is grateful for Nunez's attention, as she is shy and appears to believe that she is ugly. She bonds with Nunez partly because of her status as a fellow outsider. She is discriminated against because of her deformity, and this discrimination makes her more sympathetic to his claims. She is the only villager who will even listen to Nunez talk about being able to see, though it goes against everything she knows and makes her uncomfortable. She genuinely falls in love with him but considers his stories about "sight" and the outside world figments of his imagination or disease. She desperately wants to marry Nunez and begs her father for permission. When her father's permission becomes contingent upon Nunez having his eyes removed, she begs him to undergo the surgery.

In Wells's 1939 alternate ending to the story, Medina-saroté allows Nunez to rescue her as an avalanche destroys the Country of the Blind. Her ability to trust in his self-professed gift of sight results in her being the only survivor. The two escape the isolated valley and return to civilization. For the rest of her days she refuses to have an operation that could restore her sight. She desires to know Nunez only through her sense of touch; she believes the "gift" of sight must be a terrible burden. In essence, Medina-saroté accepts the larger world on her own terms, being comfortable with how she was born and believing that those who can see are the ones who are disabled.

Nunez

Nunez is a mountain climber who discovers the legendary Country of the Blind while leading an expedition of British climbers through the Andes. He is motivated by his refrained belief, "In the Country of the Blind the One-eyed Man is King." He believes that his ability to see makes him superior to the blind people and that in the natural order of things, he will easily become their leader. Thus, Nunez is opportunistic, arrogant, and exploitative, but his plan is not well thought out. He plans to start working during the day and sleeping at night, but how else he intends to wield power as their leader is unclear.

He is a lover of nature and an adventurer by trade; his profession as a mountain guide is a testament to his physical strength, love of freedom, and sense of wanderlust. He believes that the villagers are provincial and backward because of their isolation from the world at large and that their blindness makes them doubly so. He sees himself as a cultural savior, as evidenced from his pronouncement that he comes from "the great city Bogota." Initially, he is ethnocentric, having no respect for the blind villagers' culture or heightened senses of hearing and smell, although he does admire their urbanized landscape.

Despite his arrogance, Nunez is a man of reason and feeling. He exhibits pity by refusing to kill a blind man with a spade, and he appears genuinely contrite when he apologizes for hitting a villager shortly after that. His love for Medina-saroté conveys his humanity and passion, as does his initial agreement to sacrifice his ability to see for the woman he loves. Although for a time he compromises in order to live peacefully in the Country of the Blind, his love of freedom and nature eventually take precedence. Refusing to succumb to an inflexible culture that cannot adapt to its changing environment, Nunez chooses a slim chance at freedom—which ultimately proves fatal—over compromising his beliefs for the sake of familial happiness and stasis.

Philosopher

The philosopher, also called a doctor and a medicine-man, is a village elder in the Country of the Blind. It is he who proposes a solution that will allow Nunez to live in harmony in their world. Nunez's "deformed" eyes are an irritant, and their presence is making him mentally ill. They must be removed—a solution that appeals to almost everyone.

Yacob

Yacob is a town elder and Medina-saroté's father. He steadfastly clings to his traditions and obstinate, erroneous beliefs despite Nunez's explanation of the visual world. When Nunez abandons his goal of becoming king of the blind, Yacob becomes Nunez's master. He gives Nunez physically challenging tasks as part of his education and rehabilitation but is otherwise kind to him. Others continue to regard Nunez suspiciously, but Yacob sees him as a harmless, mostly well-intentioned buffoon and humors him. When Medina-saroté pleads with her father to let her marry Nunez, Yacob initially refuses. When the philosopher decides that the marriage would be allowed if Nunez consents to an operation to remove his supposedly diseased eyeballs, Yacob remarks, "Thank Heaven for science!" Wells intended this remark to be ironic, for there is nothing scientific about the Country of the Blind. They are, in fact, blind to reason and science.

THEMES

Power

The story's central refrain, "In the Country of the Blind the One-eyed Man is King," underscores its main theme: power. Nunez, being a two-eyed, seeing man, believes he is innately superior to the blind people of the valley. Their disability, once made known to them, will pave the way for him to take over as their leader. The blind are "fools," he tells himself, although it never crosses his mind that their remaining senses might be sharper than his. As king, however, what he would do with his power is unclear. His desire for power, then, is one of convenience and opportunity rather than strategy.

TOPICS FOR FURTHER STUDY

- Write a short scene in which Nunez tries to convince Medina-saroté of the beauty she is missing by not being able to see, while Medina-saroté tries to convince Nunez that being able to see is a terrible burden. Record video of two students acting out the scene and upload it to your school's Web site for teachers, parents, and other students to see and discuss.
- Using the Web site *The Blind Photographer* (http://www.theblindphotographer.com) as a source of information and ideas, explore an environment without your sense of sight. Wearing a blindfold, take a series of ten digital photographs. Then, take ten more photographs of the same environment with your eyes open. Using Flickr or PowerPoint, create a slide show for the class in which you explain why you took each picture and what you wanted to convey through each. Also explain how the two groups of photographs differ, and which group you like better and why.
- Use a map-making software program intended for gaming, such as Dundjinni, to create a colorful visual representation of the Country of the Blind using Wells's detailed descriptions. Include the huts, the irrigation system, the wall around the village, the grassy areas, the grazing area for the llamas, the paths, and the surrounding mountains. Include other details that Wells does not mention but that you think might be pertinent, such as a kitchen, a laundry area, or a communal gathering spot.
- In the 1939 alternate ending to the story, Medina-saroté escapes with Nunez but believes that sight "must be a terrible burden." Research recent medical advances in helping blind people to see. Draw a diagram to explain how a bionic retina and/or other visual prosthetics work, explaining who benefits most from such devices and why. Write a five-hundred-word medical history of a member of the Country of the Blind and give a prognosis as to whether a visual prosthetic would help him or her.
- Research one of the ethnic groups previously known as pygmies, such as the Aka in Congo or the Negrito in Southeast Asia, and write a five-paragraph paper stating their similarities to and differences from the people in the Country of the Blind. What is the reason for their short stature? Do their physical characteristics give them advantages not instantly obvious to an outsider? And finally, has the group ever been subjected to a situation like that of the villagers in this story? If so, who was the outsider? Did the events support or refute the adage "In the country of the blind, the one-eyed man is king"?
- *Helen's Eyes: A Photobiography of Annie Sullivan, Helen Keller's Teacher* (2008), by Marfe Ferguson Delano, is a young-adult book that depicts the obstacles that Sullivan overcame as a destitute, abandoned, legally blind youth to change the public's perception of blind people in the United States. Using the free software available at http://www.gliffy.com and the information provided in the book, construct a time line featuring twenty major events in Sullivan's life. Also mark the 1904 publication of "The Country of the Blind" on the time line. Conclude your project with a paragraph on how you think Sullivan would have responded to Wells's story and how she would respond to the idea that "in the country of the blind, the one-eyed man is king."

Nunez believes that the blind will easily be swayed by reason, but when they "believe and understand nothing whatever he told them," it is "a thing quite outside his expectation." Eventually, after trying to demonstrate the superiority of his eyesight, he realizes that "you cannot even fight happily with creatures who stand upon a different mental basis to yourself."

A power struggle ensues in which Nunez tries to convince the villagers of his natural superiority, while they try to bend him to their will. Nunez cannot believe how "little they know they've been insulting their heaven-sent king and master," while the villagers believe that "Nunez must have been specially created to learn and serve the wisdom they had acquired." The power struggle culminates in the episode with the spade, wherein Nunez realizes he cannot kill a blind man and escapes outside the village wall. After two days without food, the people of the Country of the Blind emerge victorious in the power struggle. Nunez succumbs to them, rather than they succumbing to him. He begs to be let back in and admits that he is, as they had thought, "newly made." His "*coup d'etat* came to an end."

Xenophobia

Xenophobia is an irrational fear of people from other countries, which perfectly characterizes the attitude of the Country of the Blind. Xenophobes do not accept, much less welcome, deviations from their norm. No matter how much Nunez tries to explain the glory of being able to see and how he has come from *out* of the greater world rather than simply arriving *into* theirs, the blind people refuse to alter their worldview to accommodate this new information. Their rigid belief system leaves no room for doubt: Their valley encompasses the entire world, and it is covered by a smooth, dome-shaped rock. Nunez's strange talk about "sight" and the beauty of the mountains, sky, and sunset is considered "wicked" by the blind. He remarks that their "imagination had shrivelled with their eyes." While the blind people pity Nunez for being an imbecile rather than fear him, their staunch insistence that he cease and desist all talk about the outside world constitutes a form of xenophobia.

Nunez's will to power is no match for the community's xenophobia. After the episode with the spade, he returns to the village and admits that he cannot see. They regard his violent outburst as "proof of his general idiocy and inferiority." So strong is their belief system and their indoctrination during his convalescence that he almost "doubted whether indeed he was not the victim of hallucination in not seeing" the smooth stone dome said to constitute the lid of the universe.

In a xenophobic society, an outsider can never truly be accepted as part of the group, and so it is for Nunez. When he falls in love with Medina-saroté and wants to marry her, the villagers strongly object because he is "an idiot, incompetent thing below the permissible level of a man," despite having lived and worked side-by-side with them for some length of time. Marriage is possible only if he consents to becoming one of them in body as well as mind by having his eyes removed. Only then will he become, in the words of the village doctor, "a quite admirable citizen."

Freedom

Nunez is a man of the world. He is familiar with cities like Quito, Ecuador, and Bogotá, Colombia, and has "been down to the sea and had seen the world." He prizes the freedom that comes from being an adventurer; he announces his arrival to the people in the valley with a shout and "gesticulate[s] with freedom." Realizing he has discovered the fabled Country of the Blind, Nunez is seized by "a sense of great and rather enviable adventure." He tries to retain his freedom and individuality but finds it impossible to prevail against the blind people's xenophobia. He stolidly maintains his right to freedom by stating, "I'm going to do what I like in this valley.... I'm going to do what I like and go where I like!"

Eventually, Nunez willingly curtails his freedom to live in peace with them, toiling away and remaining silent about his ability to see. He falls in love with Medina-saroté and contemplates a happy existence conforming to their world, even if it means rejecting freedom and sacrificing his treasured eyesight. In meditation just hours before succumbing to the knife, Nunez realizes that their attempt to rein him in makes the valley "a pit of sin." He turns away from the village, which represents submission, and toward the majestic mountains that signal the way toward "that great free world he was parted from." He longs to see the city again, to take a river journey and gaze up forever at the blue sky. The sky perhaps more than anything represents freedom to Nunez, while the blind people's stone dome represents confinement. Finally, when he is considering his freedom, Medina-saroté "had become small and remote."

Ultimately, Nunez chooses freedom—with fatal consequences—over the stultifying world of the blind. As he lies dying, he smiles, "as if he were

The villagers did not believe that Nunez could see the rock slide coming. (Shannon Heryet / Shutterstock.com)

satisfied merely to have escaped from the valley of the Blind."

STYLE

Parable

A parable is a story that uses an analogy to illustrate a moral lesson. "The Country of the Blind" illustrates the adage "In the country of the blind, the one-eyed man is king." Or rather, Wells illustrates that this moral lesson is false in presenting a man gifted with perfect vision who stumbles onto a blind community that has no knowledge or understanding of vision. The man believes he will easily become king, yet the blind people's rigid beliefs prove so powerful that it is they who become king over him. The analogy in this case is fairly straightforward: Nunez is the one-eyed man; the blind villagers are the country of the blind. The parable works on its most straightforward, basic level, and also on a more nuanced metaphorical level. Wells, a proponent of socialism as well as a staunch believer in intellectual reasoning, shows that reason, represented by the nature-loving, adventure-seeking Nunez, cannot overcome the ignorance of a population that adheres blindly to superstition and tradition even when faced with proof to the contrary.

Parables, though not as fantastical as fables, frequently take place in distant, unnamed realms that exist beyond the reach of civilization, and such is the case with "The Country of the Blind." Realism is suspended for artistic effect. Thus, Wells has Nunez plummet off a mountain in a fall that no mortal could survive only to discover a population completely devoid of sight—a situation that Wells, with his wealth of scientific knowledge, renders believable but which is nothing more than speculative fiction. The idyllic mountain valley, in which the inhabitants know nothing of snow or rain, sounds as beautiful as it does implausible. Nevertheless, it brings to mind other legendary places that would have been familiar to Wells and his readers, such as Shangri-La, a mythical land in the Tibetan Himalayas, or El Dorado, the mythical city of gold purported to be in the Andes. Interestingly, the sky-high mountain valley of the blind does bear some resemblance to Machu Picchu, the lost Incan city built 8,000 feet above sea level in the Peruvian Andes and made known to the outside world several years after Wells published his story.

Symbolism

The most important symbol in "The Country of the Blind" is blindness itself. Although it is a literal condition of the valley community, it is also a symbol of their inability to see anything that they do not want to see. They are blind to the idea that they might not know everything, and they are blind to the beauty of the world (which mystifies Nunez the most), but most of all they are blind to anything they find threatening. They have formed their worldview based upon their knowledge of their isolated valley; when evidence appears to contradict their worldview in the form of Nunez, they hold steadfast in their blind conviction that he is a lunatic and must be reformed.

Mountains are another symbol in the story. They represent both a physical and a spiritual barrier between the Country of the Blind and the rest of the world. As a mountaineer, Nunez enjoys conquering barriers. He intends to conquer the attitude of the blind people just as he conquers mountaintops. Yet when Nunez tells the blind people about the mountains, they refuse to acknowledge their existence. How can they deny the existence of something as immovable and hard to ignore as a mountain? In this sense, the mountains symbolize the villagers' ignorance—a gargantuan divide between their beliefs and reality. But they have also constructed their own barrier, the village wall, and refuse to contemplate any evidence for life outside their arbitrary boundary.

Prologue

"The Country of the Blind" begins with a prologue, an opening passage that establishes the circumstances for the main events of a story. A prologue often takes place many years before the action of a story and explains how the situation came to be. For a short story, Wells's two-page prologue represents a substantial part of the narrative, though it is not set apart from the main action of the story. It begins with the description of the remote mountain valley in the Andes that becomes the home of the blind and ends with the statement "this is the story of that man." Between those paragraphs is the tale of how the community began to lose its sight, how they sent an ambassador down to the lower country to procure an idol to reverse the course of the disease, and how his fantastic tale gave rise to the legend of the Country of the Blind.

By inserting all this information into a prologue, Wells can focus the action of the story on the events that illustrate the adage. The reader already knows why the blind are blind, how long they have been like that, and how they got there. Wells can thus keep the narrative going at a steady clip without having to interrupt events with these details. The prologue also functions as a mental barrier between reality and the mythical land in which the parable is set. The reader is drawn into the world slowly, through several paragraphs of description and background events that mimic Nunez's long, slow climb up the mountain, each step taking him further away from civilization. By the time Nunez's interactions with the blind commence, we have been mentally climbing that mountain with him in delving into the lengthy prologue.

HISTORICAL CONTEXT

Mountaineering and Exploration

Around the turn of the twentieth century, when Wells wrote "The Country of the Blind," mountaineering was a popular sport among the wealthy in Great Britain and other European countries. The sport originated in the first half of the nineteenth century when legions of adventurers set about to climb the Alps. The golden age of Alpinism was the brief era between the ascent of the Wetterhorn in 1854 and the ascent of the Matterhorn in 1865. Many of these early mountaineers were scientists, such as John Tyndall, who conducted field experiments during their climbs. This golden age gave rise to accepted climbing practices and the profession of the guide as someone who accompanies groups on climbs. Great Britain's Alpine Club was established in 1857 as a gentlemen's adventure organization. By 1900, the highest peaks in the Alps had been conquered, and many countries had their own Alpine Clubs, whose members shared stories, equipment, and techniques. Wells published his story in the brief span between the first ascent of the highest peak in the Andes (when Matthias Zurbriggen climbed Aconcagua in 1897) and that of the highest peak in North America (when Hudson Stuck climbed Mt. McKinley in 1913).

COMPARE & CONTRAST

- **1904:** Sir William Martin Conway is president of Great Britain's Alpine Club and is the first to climb several peaks in the Bolivian Andes.

  Today: Eleven-year-old Matthew Moniz of Boulder, Colorado, sets the record as the youngest person to reach the summit of Aconcagua, the highest mountain in the Andes, which he reaches on December 16, 2008.

- **1904:** The ruins of Machu Picchu, the "Lost City of the Incas," built in 1450 CE in the Peruvian Andes eight thousand feet above sea level, are reportedly spotted by a British engineer from a distant mountaintop. However, they are not officially discovered by outsiders until 1911, when Hiram Bingham is guided to the ruins by locals.

  Today: Machu Picchu is a UNESCO World Heritage site and the most frequently visited site in Peru, welcoming roughly four hundred thousand visitors annually.

- **1904:** Helen Keller becomes the first deaf and blind person to receive a college degree when she graduates cum laude from Radcliffe College.

  Today: Advances in medical science, particularly in the use of stem cells, give rise to new procedures to restore sight to people blinded by macular degeneration and other diseases.

- **1904:** Bogotá, Colombia, with a population of roughly one hundred thousand people, is known as the Athens of South America for its many libraries and universities.

  Today: Bogotá is the most populous city in the country and is one of the largest in Latin America, with a metropolitan population of 8.6 million people.

The Rucksack Club was founded in Manchester, England, in 1902, the same year as the American Alpine Club was founded. The Rucksack Club was intended for anyone interested in walking tours, cave exploration, and mountain climbing in Great Britain and elsewhere. Its members pioneered several mountain-rescue techniques. The American Alpine Club was founded by Charles Ernest Fay as a nonprofit organization and remains the country's leading mountain-climbing organization, with focuses on environmental preservation and scientific advancement. It was also in 1902 that K2, the second highest mountain in the world, in the Himalayas, was attempted by the Eckenstein-Crowley expedition. Oscar Eckenstein, a mountaineer, and Aleister Crowley, a famed occultist, reached twenty-two thousand feet before they turned back. By the 1950s, all the major peaks of the world had been conquered, and the great era of exploration shifted into an industry for professionals and amateur adventurers.

Fabian Society and Socialism

The Fabian Society, named in honor of the Roman general Quintus Fabius Maximus, was founded on January 4, 1884, in London as a socialist political organization that decried Britain's imperialistic advances around the world. Wells joined around 1904 at the suggestion of its members, which included the writers George Bernard Shaw, Edith Nesbit, and Leonard and Virginia Woolf. At its heart were the economic ideas of Sidney and Beatrice Webb, scholars who later founded the London School of Economics. The society sought to address what they perceived as social injustices by advocating for a minimum wage, universal health care, a national education system, and collective bargaining and labor unions.

Once a member, Wells sought to change the group's focus from intellectual discussion to lobbying and advocating openly for social change. The other members resisted, and Wells resigned from the group in 1908 but continued to favor a

Nunez fell down a mountain in the Ecuadorian Andes. (*XuRa | Shutterstock.com*)

form of socialism that relied on the governance of educated, intelligent, thoughtful people. Toward that end, several years later he traveled to Russia and met with Vladimir Lenin to discuss their ideas for the Russian Revolution. Shaw, still a member of the Fabian Society, became an outspoken critic of Wells. Readers of "The Country of the Blind" can see Wells's reformist nature at work in his tale of a mountain climber who pressures an isolated population to see the truth about the world around them, but to little avail. As of 2011, the Fabian Society had more than seven thousand members in Great Britain, and it has maintained a close relationship with the Labour Party.

CRITICAL OVERVIEW

"The Country of the Blind" is considered one of Wells's best short stories for its parable-like culture clash between a freethinking man and a closed society whose happiness depends on conformity. Nunez's inability to convince the blind people of his ability to see is a "parable on intolerance" and an "eloquent assertion of the invincibility of the human spirit," according to John R. Hammond in *An H. G. Wells Companion: A Guide to the Novels, Romances and Short Stories*. Richard Hauer Costa remarks in his biography *H. G. Wells* that "of all his vast array of works, this story best states H. G. Wells's philosophical position in terms of the techniques of the literary artist." Jack Williamson, in *H. G. Wells: Critic of Progress,* notes that the story is "one of Wells' finest stories, and perhaps his most mature and sophisticated survey of the universal conflict of self against society." Hermann Weiand, in an essay published in *Insight II: Analyses of Modern British Literature*, considers the story "profoundly pessimistic in outlook" and "strongly didactic." Alfred C. Ward characterizes the plot as "the uncommon man's revolt against the tyranny of the common man" in *Aspects of the Modern Short Story*.

Wells expert Bernard Bergonzi, in *The Early H. G. Wells: A Study of the Scientific Romances*, calls the story a "magnificent example of Wells's mythopoeic genius" and explains Nunez as not a king among the blind, but rather as "the open mind among conformists, a free spirit in a bourgeois world." Subjected to techniques resembling brainwashing as practiced by totalitarian regimes, Bergonzi explains, Nunez, having been exposed to the elements for two days and now starving, admits that he cannot see, though his eyesight is perfectly fine. His spirit has been crushed by conformists; playing along with their game becomes a matter of survival. Thus, Nunez's "free, active and intelligent spirit," Bergonzi states, is what makes the valley inhabitants regard him from their closed world as "an inferior being" who is "systematically ridiculed and humiliated."

Two critics have theorized that the story takes place solely in Nunez's head as he lies dying from his fall down the mountain, a theory that is "corroborated by Wells's grammatical insertion of ellipses throughout the text" writes Jodie R. Gaudet in the *Explicator*. Theo Steinmann, writing in *Studies in Short Fiction,* believes that the story is a rare example of literary premortem consciousness, similar to that in Ambrose Bierce's "An Occurrence at Owl Creek Bridge." Steinmann cites as his primary evidence the position of Nunez's body and the cold stars he sees both after his fall and at the end of the story; in between, "the reader is taken into the unknown realm between life and death."

Another Wells expert, Patrick Parrinder, wrote extensively about Wells's alternate endings for the story in *Science-Fiction Studies,* having examined three manuscript versions housed at the Wells Collection at the University of Illinois. The earliest version has Nunez returning to the village for the surgery. Combined with the other two endings—one in which Nunez dies and one in which he and Medina-saroté escape—they present "Wells's radical uncertainty both as to the appropriate fate for Núñez and as to the significance of that fate and the explicitness with which it should be presented," Parrinder states.

CRITICISM

Kathleen Wilson

Wilson is a writer and editor of many books on literature. In the following essay, she examines how Wells's supposedly dystopian view of "The Country of the Blind" is in fact more utopian than the author intended.

"NUNEZ SIZES UP THE SITUATION AND CONFIDENTLY EXPECTS, 'IN THE COUNTRY OF THE BLIND THE ONE-EYED MAN IS KING.' HOWEVER, WELLS'S PURPOSE IN THIS STORY IS TO DISPROVE THAT VERY NOTION."

H. G. Wells's 1904 short story "The Country of the Blind" tells of an isolated mountain community whose members have been completely blind for fifteen generations, long enough for them to have no cultural memory of sight or even the concept of vision. Into their bucolic village drops—literally—Nunez, a mountaineer from Quito, Ecuador, who has tumbled off a nearby peak while guiding a tour of Englishmen to the top of Parascotopetl. Nunez sizes up the situation and confidently expects, "In the Country of the Blind the One-eyed Man is King." However, Wells's purpose in this story is to disprove that very notion.

The blind have adapted remarkably well to their environment. Their verdant valley is circumscribed by a stone wall, and curbed paths efficiently get them where they need to go. In the absence of snow and rain in their temperate climate, they have devised a clever series of canals to irrigate their crops with the snow melt from the surrounding Andean peaks. They raise llamas on the pasture just outside the village walls. Their senses of hearing and smell have stepped in to fill the void left by the atrophy of their eyes. By any account, they have adapted magnificently.

Yet their Achilles' heel is their recalcitrance as to integrating new knowledge into their worldview. Their cosmogony holds that the universe consists solely of their valley—nothing beyond their perception exists, not even the surrounding mountains. This small universe, formed long ago out of a hollow in the rock, is covered, they believe, by a smooth stone dome roughly sixty feet above their heads. The fluttering forms that Nunez knows as birds are known to the blind as angels. This sheltered and isolated high-altitude dale is, for all intents and purposes, a utopia—an ideal society—at least until the uninvited mountaineer arrives on the scene.

WHAT DO I READ NEXT?

- A revised version of "The Country of the Blind" is contained in *The Complete Short Stories of H. G. Wells* (1998), edited by John Hammond. This 1939 version is identical to the 1904 story except for the last two pages, in which Nunez and Medina-saroté barely escape the village as it is destroyed by an avalanche.
- *A Modern Utopia* (1905) is Wells's fictional philosophical treatise based partly on the work of the ancient Greek philosopher Plato. Inspired by a mountain-climbing trip to the Alps and his Fabian beliefs, the work outlines Wells's recipe for a happy society based on socialist beliefs as practiced by an educated populace dedicated to goodwill for all.
- *H. G. Wells: Another Kind of Life* (2010), by Michael Sherborne, is a recent biography that recounts Wells's colorful life, including his many affairs with famous and controversial women and his unconventional political beliefs. Throughout it all, he remained a prolific writer with an opinion on everything.
- "Harrison Bergeron" (1961) is a science-fiction story by Kurt Vonnegut, Jr., about the United States in the future. Society is presented as a dystopia, a nightmare land that is the opposite of a utopia. All citizens are required to be handicapped in various ways so that everyone remains equal. It is included in Vonnegut's collection *Welcome to the Monkey House* (1968). It is a humorous satire regarding the popular misunderstandings of socialism and communism among the American public.
- D. H. Lawrence's "The Woman Who Rode Away" (1924) is a "lost race" story written by a contemporary of Wells's. A bored American wife and mother, enthralled by tales of the Chilchui Indians who live in mountains of Mexico, embarks on a solo expedition in search of adventure. She is taken in by the mysterious tribe and ultimately sacrificed in a religious ceremony. It can be found in the collection *The Woman Who Rode Away, and Other Stories* (1928).
- Stephen Kuusisto's *Planet of the Blind* (1998) is the memoir of a man who was born with only residual sight in one eye and whose attempt to live as a sighted person led to misery. Only when he begins to live his life as a blind person, adapting to a guide dog and a white cane, does he find happiness. Ultimately, he envisions a "planet of the blind" that favors the world of touch and other senses. His follow-up volume *Eavesdropping: A Memoir of Blindness and Listening* (2006) continues his story.
- *Three Cups of Tea: One Man's Mission to Promote Peace One School at a Time*, by Greg Mortenson and David Oliver Relin (2007, young-adult edition), is the story of Mortenson, an American mountain climber who becomes lost and almost dies trying to climb K2 in the Himalayas. He is rescued by the residents of an isolated, impoverished Muslim village in Pakistan, who painstakingly nurse him back to health. Over the course of many years, he repays his debt by building schools for them in an area so remote that the Pakistani government does not provide them services.

Nunez, with his nonsensical talk about *sight* and *blindness*, disrupts the villagers' carefully constructed worldview. They surmise that he is "newly formed" and thus not possessed of a fully developed intellect. A power struggle ensues, with Nunez insisting that he should be the king of the blind, and the blind insisting there is no such thing as sight. Their utopian world crushes Nunez's sense of rationality and his sense of adventure, stranding him in a dystopia where the price he must pay for complete acceptance is the removal of his eyes. In the Country of the

Blind, the one-eyed man (or two-eyed, in this case) is a threat to the social order and must be forced to conform. Wells's view of his own creation is harsh. His parable supposedly illustrates how a rigid, insular belief system is a danger to freedom, truth, and reason. This belief system is represented by the Country of the Blind, a dystopia.

"The Country of the Blind" is not as overtly a work of dystopian fiction as Wells's novel *A Modern Utopia*, which was published in 1905, just a year after the story. Both, however, were influenced by his interest in alpine mountain climbing (which he used to great effect in "Little Mother up the Mörderberg" [1910], which serves as a humorous counterpoint to "The Country of the Blind") and his intense but short-lived involvement with the politically socialist Fabian Society. His later works, including *The Sleeper Awakes* (1910) and *Men Like Gods* (1923), are more nuanced examinations of the utopian/dystopian construct, but "The Country of the Blind" served as his opening volley on the subject.

But first, what is a utopia? The term was coined by Sir Thomas More in his 1516 book *Utopia*, which depicts a peaceful, agrarian New World island nation that lives communally, enjoying a short workday, religious freedom, and the assistance of two slaves per household. The term itself is derived from the near homophones *eutopia*, meaning "good place," and *outopia*, meaning "no place." But the idea of a smoothly functioning earthly paradise extends back into antiquity—the biblical Garden of Eden is one example—is present at the foundation of Western literature with Plato's *Republic* (ca. 380 BCE), an account of a land ruled by benevolent philosopher-kings, and is featured prominently in Virgil's *Eclogues* (ca. 42 BCE), set in the idyllic, bucolic land of Arcadia.

While artistic license allows for all kinds of utopias, a careful observer can divine several shared characteristics among those posited. (1) A utopian society favors equality and the participation of all its citizens. (Perceptions of who may be a citizen have changed since More's time.) Everyone engages in meaningful work and contributes to the community's economic well-being while pursuing personal fulfillment. (2) A utopian society has little or no discrimination, poverty, violence, or abuse of power. (3) A utopian society lives in harmony with its environment, does not exploit natural resources beyond what is sustainable, and uses technology wisely.

The Country of the Blind fits this general description quite well. It is situated in a protected valley that is "irrigated with extraordinary care." The villagers' houses stand "in a continuous row on either side of a central street of astonishing cleanness." Nunez observes that their life includes "all the elements of virtue and happiness.... They [have] days and seasons of rest; they [make] much music and singing, and there [is] love among them, and little children." Moreover, they have no inkling about their disability; Nunez remarks how "it was marvellous with what confidence and precision they went about their ordered world." So far, utopia.

Conversely, what is a dystopia? The literal definition, in Greek, is "bad place." The term entered the lexicon quite a bit later than its counterpart, via an 1868 speech by John Stuart Mill given before the House of Commons that criticized Irish land policy. As a literary device, the term arose with the publication of Aldous Huxley's science-fiction novel *Brave New World* (1932), which was written partly in response to Wells's own *Men Like Gods* and which attained a position in the Western literary canon many years after its first publication. Before Huxley, however, Wells introduced a dystopia in *The Time Machine* (1895), as did Jack London in *The Iron Heel* (1908). Huxley and those who followed used the concept of a dystopia to satirize existing societal injustices. Dystopias frequently appear in science fiction as futuristic societies in which good intentions have been twisted into policies by which repressive regimes seek to keep their people powerless and ignorant.

Dystopian societies often present themselves as utopias. Totalitarian regimes coerce submission by propaganda. In *Brave New World*, Huxley satirizes rapid industrialization through his depiction of a World State that worships Henry Ford instead of God. George Orwell's *Nineteen Eighty-Four* (1948) presents a society in a perpetual state of war and a regime that enforces totalitarianism through the Ministry of Truth and Big Brother. Since these early examples, dystopian literature has become as varied and colorful as a bouquet of menacing flowers. Lois Lowry's Newbery Award-winning *The Giver* (1993) presents a society in which everyone is rendered color-blind as part of its official policy of Sameness. In Kurt Vonnegut's "Harrison

Bergeron," everyone is made handicapped to ensure that no one excels.

So does "The Country of the Blind" represent a utopia or a dystopia? Wells intends it to be a dystopian representation of the nefarious consequences of conformity, but it does not read that way. The Country of the Blind exhibits far more traits of a utopia than a dystopia, thus rendering much of Wells's argument ineffective. Perhaps this is why he labored over a new ending more than thirty years after its initial publication.

The Country of the Blind shares few, if any, of the common traits of a dystopia. Yes, the pressure to conform to the society's beliefs leads to Nunez's violent outburst (striking a man with a spade) and eventual acquiescence. However, the blind successfully prevent him from taking over as their "king." Power is held by the village elders, who show no inclination toward repression or oppression of anyone in their community (other than a slight pity toward Medina-saroté because her eyelashes are perceived as a deformity).

Nunez is never forced to stay in the Country of the Blind. In fact he begs to come back, and when he is ill "they nursed him kindly." He is never forcibly held, nor is he shunned. All he must do is deny his ability to see. Then, although he is not an equal, he is invited to participate in their society. He is even allowed to fall in love. Their request that he have his eyes removed comes about only because he wants to marry Medina-saroté. That is their condition, take it or leave it. Nunez is given a choice, something that does not usually happen in a dystopia. Eventually, he exercises his right to leave. No one stops him.

Thus, rather than illustrating the destructive nature of societies whose rigid beliefs do not bend to science and rationality, Wells's "The Country of the Blind" shows a well-functioning society that easily shrugs off imperial intentions by outsiders. That is a utopia, not a dystopia, even if Nunez considers the little town "a pit of sin."

It is also a reflection of an author who "viewed mankind darkly," writes Richard Hauer Costa in *H. G. Wells*, and "as a giant struggling in an evolutionary whirl to achieve a millennium of happiness and beauty, but always forced back into some sealed-off country of the blind." John Huntington, in *The Logic of Fantasy: H. G. Wells and Science Fiction*, concurs with this view: "Nunez's dream of kingship is a selfish fantasy that both ignores the happiness the blind people enjoy and condescends to the adjustment they have made."

Hermann Weiand, in an essay in *Insight II: Analyses of Modern British Literature*, sides with Wells's dim view of humanity when he describes the story's blind as a people who "look upon their modest and scanty life as the only possible mode of existence, and upon their termite world as the crown of creation," [making] "them unspeakably grotesque and absurd." Yet it is ludicrous to describe a peaceful people who have survived for fifteen generations without sight as "unspeakably grotesque" simply because their creation myth explains the world only as they perceive it. How long did it take the Roman Catholic Church to accept that the earth is round and that it is not the center of the universe? Weiand is hyperbolic; Huntington is much more reasonable when he concludes of Nunez that "in the tradition of European imperialism, he aims to exploit a culture he does not appreciate." When viewed this way, Nunez is an interloper, the early-twentieth-century literary equivalent of the Ugly American, lumbering into a foreign culture as a self-professed hero.

Perhaps Wells recognized the flaws in his community. Clearly, something about the story created an ambivalence that was troubling enough for him to publish a revised version in 1939 in which the "pit of sin" is destroyed by an avalanche. Such is the blind dystopians' punishment for not allowing themselves to be saved by Nunez's warning. But this end is still not convincing. Their punishment elicits sympathy because it seems disproportionate to their crime of ideological stubbornness.

Ultimately, Wells's two endings may signify an inability to integrate his socialist ideas into a cohesive whole. He believed in socialism, but he also believed in freedom. Huntington concludes that "The Country of the Blind" demonstrates these "conflicting imperatives": "society's traditions and scientific expectations are oppressive, but to demand kingly freedoms is selfish and involves a misunderstanding of the adaptive virtues of social organization." Such is the problem with Nunez. He has stumbled upon a utopia that he perceives as a dystopia. "In the Country of the Blind the One-eyed Man is King," he tells himself, a rational thought for someone whose vain quest is to be the first to scale Parascotopetl. The winner-take-all approach may work for getting to the mountaintop, but to sustain life in a valley

"THE AUTHOR HAS ADDED ABOUT 3000 WORDS IN THE REVISED VERSION, THUS INCREASING THE STORY'S ORIGINAL LENGTH BY APPROXIMATELY ONE-THIRD. THE DIFFERENCE LIES SOLELY IN THE ENDING."

amidst the clouds a cooperative spirit goes much further. The blind people's inability to believe Nunez's strange proclamation that he can see is nothing more than the very human trait of self-preservation. Even if that trait engenders mild hostility, it remains a far cry from being dystopian.

Source: Kathleen Wilson, Critical Essay on "The Country of the Blind," in *Short Stories for Students*, Gale, Cengage Learning, 2012.

A. Langley Searles

In the following essay, Searles examines the two different versions of "The Country of the Blind."

Although H. G. Wells' short fantasy "The Country of the Blind" has been reprinted frequently since its original appearance early in the century, few readers are apparently aware of the fact that there are two different versions of the story extant. It is almost universally remembered in its first form, which saw print originally in the April 1904 number of the English *Strand Magazine*, and which has since been included in *The Door in the Wall, and Other Stories* (1911), *The Country of the Blind, and Other Stories* (1911) and *The Short Stories of H. G. Wells* (1927).

In this version, one Núñez—an expert mountain-climber and guide—enters an isolated Andean valley which has been completely cut off from outer civilization for fifteen generations. The ancestors of the present inhabitants had suffered from a rare malady that caused them gradually to lose their sight—a loss of faculty which proved to be hereditary, for their children were also born blind. Yet so gradual was this process that over a period of decades the people managed to evolve an existence that was not dependent on seeing for its continuance. And as generations were born, lived, and died the other four senses managed to sustain the civilization of the group. The old concepts of reality were changed; traditions were weighed, and molded to fit seemingly more rational concepts; the very universe, to these blind people, shrank to the area of their tiny valley, a hollow between all but unscalable rocky cliffs. And at the time Núñez arrives, the very names for all things connected with sight have faded from the language.

Núñez remembers that "in the country of the blind the one-eyed man is king," but soon discovers that this aphorism is not valid. With their highly-developed sense of hearing and keen dog-like sense of smell the inhabitants have him always at their mercy; and since they regard his talk of "seeing" as a symptom of insanity he is kept under strict surveillance. In the end, not wishing to continue at hard manual labor for subsistence to the end of his days, Núñez abandons the Country of the Blind and Medina-saroté, a girl there who has come to love him, and manages to climb out of the valley by the same dangerously precipitous way he entered it.

In 1939 Wells revised the story extensively. This revised version was published in a limited edition by the well-known Golden Cockerel Press of London. Only 280 numbered copies were printed, which makes the volume virtually unobtainable as far as the average collector is concerned. This is indeed unfortunate, for along with the new version is also included the original one, and both are embellished with numerous engravings by Clifford Web. Luckily, however, the tale has been reprinted in its 1939 form in two other volumes: *The College Survey of English Literature* (1942), edited by B. J. Whiting and others, and *Masterpieces of Science Fiction* (1967), edited by Sam Moskowitz.

The author has added about 3000 words in the revised version, thus increasing the story's original length by approximately one-third. The difference lies solely in the ending. Here, instead of abandoning Medina-saroté and her people, Núñez at this point in the narration suddenly notices that a great section of the precipices surrounding the valley has developed a serious fault-line since his arrival. This can mean only one thing: the ultimate collapse of a portion of the rock into the Country of the Blind, which would of course cause its complete destruction. All attempts to warn the people prove useless; they regard his excitement over this imminent danger as a final proof of incurable insanity, and in the end, their patience exhausted, drive him from the village. Soon the overhanging rocks do indeed slide down into the valley, and in the final moments Núñez and Medina-saroté win through to freedom by climbing out the newly-created rift.

After several days of wandering the two are found by native hunters in a condition of near-starvation, and brought back to civilization. They marry, and settle in Quito with Núñez' people, Núñez himself becoming a prosperous tradesman. The couple have four children, all of whom are able to see. Though happy with her husband and loved by her children, Medina-saroté after many years still thinks of her former peaceful life with regret, silently mourning its irrevocable loss. Steadfastly she refuses to consult oculists who might remedy her blindness. A conversation with the narrator's wife reveals her attitude:

> "I have no use for your colors or your stars," said Medina-saroté. . . .
> "But after all that has happened! Don't you want to see Núñez; see what he is like?"
> "But I know what he is like and seeing him might put us apart. He would not be so near to me. The loveliness of *your* world is a complicated and fearful loveliness and mine is simple and near. I had rather Núñez saw for me - because he knows nothing of fear."
> "But the *beauty*!" cried my wife.
> "It may be beautiful," said Medina-saroté, "but it must be very terrible to *see*."

In his introduction to the Golden Cockerel Press edition of *The Country of the Blind* Wells gives his reasons for rewriting the original story in this new form:

> The essential idea . . . remains the same throughout, but the value attached to vision changes profoundly. It has been changed because there has been a change in the atmosphere of life about us. In 1904 the stress is upon the spiritual isolation of those who see more keenly than their fellows and the tragedy of their incommunicable appreciation of life. The visionary dies, a worthless outcast, finding no other escape from his gift but death, and the blind world goes on, invincibly self-satisfied and secure. But in the later story vision becomes something altogether more tragic; it is no longer a story of disregarded loveliness and release; the visionary sees destruction sweeping down upon the whole blind world he has come to endure and even to love; he sees it plain, and he can do nothing to save it from its fate.

Regardless of whether or not the reader agrees with Wells that changing world conditions have necessitated a change in this story's outlook, he will probably regret that such a change was actually made. Firstly, all allegorical purpose aside, that quality of insulation that made the original so memorable is completely lost. In the first version Wells draws his circle and wisely remains within it to cover the ground thoroughly and completely. But in the second, with the expansion of the locale from the small isolated valley to the larger canvas of the outside world, the author cannot—and does not—succeed in working up the area properly. The result is a certain lack of convincingness that is unmistakable. Even granting his wish to change "the value attached to vision" Wells obviously need not have violated the insulation of his setting in order to accomplish this.

Secondly—all allegorical considerations once more aside—this new ending lacks the fundamental originality the first version possesses. Such a dénouement, with its conventional satisfaction of public demand for consummation of love-interest (and a tacked-on love-interest at that), is precisely what modern hack "pulpists" would resort to. Not even the native Wellsian story-telling ability can dissipate this impression.

The style of Wells' writing, however, remains unchanged; he had lost little or nothing in the third-of-a-century interim in which "The Country of the Blind" remained untouched. Always he remains an excellent story-teller.

And because Wells is such a good story-teller it is regrettable that in later years he attempted the metamorphosis to the preacher and philosopher. He will always be remembered for the incisive and vigorous creative power that lent life to his original imaginative ideas in such fine works as *The War of the Worlds* and *The Time Machine*, as well as the "pure" fantasy of shorter tales like "The Magic Shop" and "A Dream of Armageddon." Yet as a philosopher and a preacher Wells will probably not be remembered, because his abilities in these fields are not outstanding. We tolerate Wells the preacher because he is one with Wells the story-teller—but if some kind of schizophrenic split could effect a physical separation of the two there is no doubt which Wellsian twin we would choose.

In "The Country of the Blind" this combination is both good and bad: good, since the story may be read and enjoyed and judged as excellent without thought or reference to the allegory which underlies it; and bad, since because of this very fact the allegory is obviously both extraneous and unnecessary. And, it may be added, ineffective: for if a reader cannot perceive easily at first reading what Wells is allegorically driving at, the author might as well have abandoned this ulterior motif to begin with.

One further comment on the 1939 version of "The Country of the Blind" may be appended. In the introduction quoted on the previous page Wells mentions "the tragedy of their incommunicable appreciation of life" concerning those who "see more keenly than their fellows." Yet we note in the second version that the girl Medina-saroté, who has been taken from the valley, later on realizes the existence of something beyond her senses and her conception of the world. She has learned to speak of "seeing," and uses the words of sight in a manner that shows she has some vague, empirical idea of their meaning. Yet she shrinks fearfully from the opportunity to realize their full significance that surgery offers.

This is important, for it furnishes a deeper insight into Wells' philosophy. He always regarded Stupidity as the monarch of the world, and always, too, held forth that transformation of the earth into a near-utopia could be accomplished if the scientist-intellectual type were in control—in fact his confidence in this cure-all by dint of a generation's repetition became so cocksure that it is almost wearisome. And now the reader is indirectly made cognizant of what Wells considers to be the chief reason why his scheme has not as yet been tried: the people themselves fear it. Because of their stupidity they not only do not at present understand it, but they are afraid to allow themselves to be led by those who do. And thus the tragedy that visits upon the Country of the Blind is nothing less than a measure of punishment, an allegorical lashing which Wells feels the world of reality richly deserves.

Source: A. Langley Searles, "Concerning 'The Country of the Blind,'" in *Wellsian*, No. 14, Summer 1991, pp. 29–33.

SOURCES

"Algunos Datos Historicos," in *Revista Credencial Historica*, Vol. 133, 2001, http://www.banrep.gov.co/blaavirtual/revistas/credencial/enero2001/colmundo.htm (accessed March 17, 2011).

Armour, Philip, "Boulder Boy, 11, to Attempt 14 Colorado 14ers in 14 Days," in *Colorado Daily*, July 5, 2009, http://www.coloradodaily.com/outdoor-recreation/ci_12963717#axzz1Gse2rTKz (accessed March 17, 2011).

Bergonzi, Bernard, *The Early H. G. Wells: A Study of the Scientific Romances*, University of Toronto Press, 1961, pp. 77–85.

Clark, Ronald, *The Victorian Mountaineers*, Batsford, 1953, pp. 78–90, 101–109, 207–215.

Conefrey, Mick, and Tim Jordan, "On High: The Quirky Preacher Who First Conquered America's Mightiest Peak," in *American Enterprise*, Vol. 13, No. 7, October/November 2002, pp. 36–39.

Conway, Sir Martin, *Mountain Memories: A Pilgrimage of Romance*, Cassell, 1920, pp. 228–45.

Costa, Richard Hauer, *H. G. Wells*, Twayne Publishers, 1967, pp. 61–63.

Delano, Marfe Ferguson, *Helen's Eyes: A Photobiography of Annie Sullivan, Helen Keller's Teacher*, National Geographic Children's Books, 2008.

Dettmar, Kevin J. H., "H. G. Wells," in *Dictionary of Literary Biography*, Vol. 156, *British Short-Fiction Writers, 1880–1914: The Romantic Tradition*, edited by William F. Naufftus, Gale Research, 1996, pp. 375–96.

Eisner, Peter, "Who Discovered Machu Picchu?" in *Smithsonian*, March 2009, http://www.smithsonianmag.com/history-archaeology/Binghams-List-In-Dispute.html (accessed March 17, 2011).

Gaudet, Jodie R., "Wells's 'The Country of the Blind,'" in *Explicator*, Vol. 59, No. 4, Summer 2001, p. 195.

Hammond, John R., *An H. G. Wells Companion: A Guide to the Novels, Romances and Short Stories*, Macmillan, 1979, p. 72.

Hennessy, Hannah, "Row Erupts over Peru's Tourist Treasure," in *BBC News*, December 27, 2003, http://news.bbc.co.uk/2/hi/americas/3335315.stm (accessed March 17, 2011).

Huntington, John, *The Logic of Fantasy: H. G. Wells and Science Fiction*, Columbia University Press, 1982, pp. 126–29.

Huxley, Aldous, *Brave New World*, Doubleday, 1932.

"Join the Fabian Society," in *Fabian Society*, http://www.fabians.org.uk/ (accessed March 17, 2011).

Kristoff, Nicholas D., "As the World Intrudes, Pygmies Feel Endangered," in *New York Times*, June 16, 1997.

London, Jack, *The Iron Heel*, Macmillan, 1907.

Lowry, Lois, *The Giver*, Houghton Mifflin, 1993.

Orwell, George, *Nineteen Eighty-Four*, Harcourt, 1949.

Parrinder, Patrick, "Wells's Cancelled Endings for 'The Country of the Blind,'" in *Science-Fiction Studies*, Vol. 17, No. 1, March 1990, pp. 71–76.

Pease, Edward, *The History of the Fabian Society*, Echo Library, 2006, pp. 98–110.

Sivan, Kfir, and Iris Darel-Shinar, *The Blind Photographer*, http://www.theblindphotographer.com/ (accessed March 17, 2011).

Steinmann, Theo, "The Second Death of Nunez in 'The Country of the Blind,'" in *Studies in Short Fiction*, Vol. 9, No. 2, Spring 1972, pp. 157–63.

Templeton, Sarah-Kate, "Blind to Be Cured with Stem Cells," in *Sunday Times* (London, England), April 19, 2009, http://www.timesonline.co.uk/tol/news/uk/health/article6122757.ece (accessed March 17, 2011).

Ward, Alfred C., "H. G. Wells: 'The Country of the Blind,'" in *Aspects of the Modern Short Story: English and American*, University of London Press, 1924, p. 144.

Weiand, Hermann, "The Country of the Blind," in *Insight II: Analyses of Modern British Literature*, edited by John V. Hagopian and Martin Dolch, Hirschgraben-Verlag, 1965, p. 353.

Wells, H. G., "The Country of the Blind," in *The Complete Short Stories of H. G. Wells*, edited by John Hammond, Phoenix Giant, 1998, pp. 629–48, 846–60.

———, *Men Like Gods*, Macmillan, 1923.

———, *Russia in the Shadows*, Hodder & Stoughton, 1920, p. 1.

———, *The Time Machine*, Holt, 1895.

———, *When the Sleeper Awakes*, Harper, 1899.

Williamson, Jack, *H. G. Wells: Critic of Progress*, Mirage Press, 1973, pp. 88–94.

FURTHER READING

Blankenship, Judy, *Cañar: A Year in the Highlands of Ecuador*, University of Texas Press, 2005.

Blankenship is a journalist and author who spent several years in an isolated mountain community in Ecuador, documenting the local customs and ceremonies, many of which survive from pre-Columbian times.

Hintz, Carrie, and Elaine Ostry, eds., *Utopian and Dystopian Writing for Children and Young Adults*, Taylor & Francis, 2003.

This collection of essays includes a study of Wells's dystopia in *The Island of Doctor Moreau* and an essay on dystopia by Lois Lowry, author of *The Giver*. Other essays consider the ways utopian and dystopian societies are presented through classic and modern works geared toward young adults.

McDermott, Ray, and Herve Varenne, "Culture as Disability," in *Anthropology and Education Quarterly*, Vol. 26, 1995, pp. 323–48.

This lengthy essay uses "The Country of the Blind" as a springboard for a discussion on how disability is viewed in modern times. The authors believe that disabilities are a cultural fabrication; the blind in the valley refuse to believe there is anything wrong with them, but other cultures insist that those who are blind do have something wrong with them. Nunez could not convince the people they were blind because they had no concept of disability.

Parrinder, Patrick, ed., *H. G. Wells: The Critical Heritage*, Routledge & Kegan Paul, 1972.

This collection of Wells criticism covers all of the author's major works.

Sherborne, Michael, *H. G. Wells: Another Kind of Life*, Peter Owen, 2010.

Sherborne is the former editor of the *Wellsian* and chair of the H. G. Wells Society. This book delves into the many controversies of the writer's life, including allegations that he was racist and sexist and his high-profile disagreements with George Orwell, Henry James, and other notable figures.

Wells, H. G., *H. G. Wells in Love: Postscript to an Experiment in Autobiography*, Faber, 2009.

This volume reveals Wells's candid thoughts regarding his numerous affairs; it was not published until well after his death. Detailing his private life beginning in the 1930s, it covers his second marriage and his affair with the much younger author Rebecca West.

SUGGESTED SEARCH TERMS

H. G. Wells

The Country of the Blind AND Wells

blind

power

mountaineer

mountain climbing

Andes

Ecuador

lost world

utopia AND Wells

dystopia AND Wells

Quito

Bogotá

First Confession

FRANK O'CONNOR

1939

"First Confession," a comic short story by Irish writer Frank O'Connor, was first published in *Harper's Bazaar* in March 1939. An earlier version of the story, "Repentance," was published in 1935, but the story was extensively revised for publication in 1939. O'Connor, as was his habit, made further minor revisions to the story for publication in his *Collected Stories* in 1946 and again for his collection *Traveller's Samples* in 1951. The 1951 version, representing O'Connor's final intentions, is the one usually reprinted, but the core of the story was written during the 1930s.

Although the setting is unspecified, the story clearly takes place in Ireland, possibly Cork. The story is a first-person account, one that is in many respects autobiographical, of the experiences of Jackie, a precocious Catholic boy who has to make his first confession before he can receive his first Communion. Plagued by his irascible grandmother and his vindictive, treacherous sister Nora, Jackie tries to navigate his way through this rite of passage to a more mature understanding of spiritual matters and the role of religion in his life. O'Connor incorporates many elements of highly traditional Catholicism in a way that gently pokes fun at them while recognizing that religious belief is a matter to be taken seriously. At the core of the story is Jackie's confession to a priest that he had plotted to kill his grandmother, though readers know from the tone of the story that he would never have actually committed such a deed.

Frank O'Connor *(CBS via Getty Images)*

AUTHOR BIOGRAPHY

Frank O'Connor was the pseudonym of Michael O'Donovan. O'Connor, a prolific writer of short stories constructed around the details of Irish life, was born on September 17, 1903, in Cork, Ireland, where he grew up in poverty. His father, a day laborer, was frequently drunk and berated the young boy for his unmanly interest in books; his mother, though, knew that her son could escape poverty only by acquiring an education, so she supported his efforts in that direction. He attended school only until age twelve, but he continued his education afterward by reading widely. During the Irish War of Independence of 1920–1921, O'Connor supported the Republicans in their fight for independence from England, and he was arrested and held in jail in 1923–1924. The events surrounding the Irish revolt, as well as his own disillusionment with the cruelty of the Irish Republican Army, shaped his first two books, *Guests of the Nation* (1931), a collection of short stories, and *The Big Fellow: Michael Collins and the Irish Revolution* (1937), a study of Irish Republican Army leader Michael Collins.

After he was released from prison, O'Connor worked as a librarian. He grew close to Irish poet William Butler Yeats, and the two formed the Irish Academy of Letters with the purpose of resisting censorship. During the 1930s, O'Connor was especially prolific as a writer. In 1932, he published his first novel, *The Saint and Mary Kate*, and his first translations of Gaelic literature, *The Wild Bird's Nest*. More collections of short stories followed, including *Bones of Contention* in 1936. His first collection of poetry, *Three Old Brothers*, was also published in 1936. In 1937 he turned to drama with *In the Train*, followed a year later by *Moses' Rock*, both written for the Abbey Theatre in Dublin, where he served as director from 1935 to 1939. *Crab Apple Jelly*, published in 1944, was another collection of short stories. During the 1940s and early 1950s, O'Connor came to the attention of censors, who banned as indecent his novel *Dutch Interior* (1940); *The Midnight Court* (1945), which was a translation of Brian Merriman's *Cúirt an Mheán-Oíche*; and two collections of short stories, *The Common Chord* (1947) and *Traveller's Samples* (1951), which includes "First Confession." Many of his short stories during these years were first published in the *New Yorker*.

In 1951, O'Connor was invited to lecture in the United States. He accepted various teaching posts at American universities until he suffered a stroke in 1961. He returned to Ireland, where he continued to write and teach until he died of a heart attack in Dublin on March 10, 1966.

PLOT SUMMARY

"First Confession" is narrated in the first person by Jackie, an Irish lad who begins by saying that "all the trouble began" when his grandmother, his father's mother, came to live with Jackie's family. The grandmother is described as slovenly and given to drinking, but Nora, Jackie's older sister, is said to suck up to the old woman in exchange for a weekly allowance. Jackie is of an age when he is expected to perform his first confession and first Communion. (In traditional Roman Catholicism, these two events are linked; a person cannot receive Communion at mass while in a state of sin, so anyone receiving Communion for the first time must make a confession to a priest.)

To prepare for these events, Jackie receives instruction from an older woman named Mrs. Ryan, of whom he thinks, "Hell had the first place in her heart." Mrs. Ryan's view of religion is one of fire and brimstone, and she is obsessed with the sufferings that sinners will endure in hell. She also tells a story of a man who made a "bad confession," that is, one that did not report all of his sins. Jackie is frightened about making

MEDIA ADAPTATIONS

- In 1969, the British television series *Thirty-Minute Theatre* broadcast a television adaptation of "First Confession," directed by Roderick Graham, adapted by Nicholas Bethell, and featuring Jack Wild as Jackie, Eddie Byrne as the priest, Pippy Duncalfe as Nora, and Sheila Manahan as Gran.
- "First Confession" is included on an audio CD titled *Selected Shorts: Family Matters*, produced by Symphony Space in 2007. The story is read by Malachy McCourt.

his first confession. On the day when he is supposed to make his confession, Jackie feigns a toothache and does not go to school. Mrs. Ryan sends home a note instructing Jackie to make his confession by himself on Saturday. Nora, a constant source of torment to Jackie, accompanies him to church.

At the church, Jackie describes his anguish about making his first confession. Nora, depicted as a religious hypocrite, precedes Jackie into the confessional (a small enclosed booth where the priest hears confessions through a screen so that the penitent and the priest do not see each other). Jackie finds the shelf where he would normally place his folded hands to be too high, so he climbs up onto it, to the consternation of the priest. Jackie falls and tumbles out of the confessional into the church's aisle. Nora, who is waiting for Jackie, responds with typical scorn and strikes her brother. The priest has exited the confessional and immediately comes to Jackie's defense, and Jackie feels an instant bond with the priest. The two return to the confessional and the priest hears Jackie's confession—and is astonished to learn that Jackie "had it all arranged to kill my grandmother." Jackie also confesses to once having tried to kill Nora with a bread knife. It is clear that the priest does not take Jackie's confession literally—he knows Jackie would never have committed such an act but that he feels guilty about his dislike for his grandmother. The priest soothes Jackie and accompanies him outside into the churchyard.

There, Jackie encounters Nora, who becomes angry when she learns of the light penance Jackie has been given. (Traditionally, the priest assigns a penance, usually consisting of the recitation of prayers such as the Hail Mary, a commonly recited prayer to the mother of Jesus.) She is also angry that the priest has given Jackie a bullseye, a type of candy. Nora is disgusted, and the story closes with her saying "'Tis no advantage to anybody trying to be good. I might just as well be a sinner like you."

CHARACTERS

Gran

Gran is Jackie's paternal grandmother. She is described as "a real old country woman and quite unsuited to the life in town." Jackie says that "she had a fat, wrinkled old face," and he is troubled by the fact that she "went round the house in bare feet." She drinks porter (a type of ale) and uses snuff (powdered tobacco that is inhaled), which mortifies Jackie and his mother. Jackie is troubled in his conscience because he thinks that he hatched a plan to kill Gran.

Jackie

Jackie is a seven-year-old boy living in Ireland who is about to make his first confession and receive his first Communion. He makes it clear that he intensely dislikes his grandmother, who has come to live with Jackie and his family. Jackie, a precocious boy, prepares for his first confession and feels guilty for having probably broken all of the Ten Commandments—more specifically, he planned to kill his grandmother and tried to stab his sister with a bread knife. He finally makes his first confession to a priest who treats him with kindness and understanding.

Nora

Nora is Jackie's sister. Nora sucks up to Gran in exchange for a penny every Friday. She torments her younger brother and tattles on him. At one point, Jackie says that Nora "became the raging malicious devil she really was." The priest calls her a "vixen." When Jackie exits the church with the priest, Nora is waiting for him with a "very sour puss" and is "mad jealous because a priest had never come out of the church with her." Nora is a religious hypocrite; she practices the outward forms of Catholicism but is an unkind person.

Priest

The unnamed priest who hears Jackie's confession is depicted as a highly sympathetic character. He seems to have instantly sensed Jackie's fears, and the reader recognizes that the priest sees the humor in Jackie's guilt over his purported plan to kill his grandmother. When Jackie says that the priest "said nothing for quite a while," the reader infers that the priest is stifling laughter. Rather than scolding Jackie, the priest talks to him, and Jackie concludes that "he was the most entertaining character I'd ever met in the religious line."

Mrs. Ryan

Mrs. Ryan gives Jackie and his schoolmates instruction as they prepare for their first confession and first Communion. She is about the same age as Gran and is described as "well-to-do." In teaching the children about their religion, she emphasizes the torments of hell that sinners will suffer. Jackie says, "She may have mentioned the other place [heaven] as well, but that could only have been by accident." To impress on the children their obligation to make a good confession, she tells a grim and uncanny story about a man who made a bad confession.

THEMES

Irish Culture

In 1922, Ireland was partitioned into the Irish Free State and Northern Ireland. The Irish Free State was the predecessor of today's Republic of Ireland. This portion of Ireland (in contrast to Northern Ireland) was and remains overwhelmingly Catholic, and in many senses Catholicism defines Irish culture. Because the Irish Free State, which lasted until 1937, was impoverished, the Catholic Church assumed many of the functions that normally would fall to government. Chief among these was education. Virtually all students, like Jackie, would have received a Catholic education. They would also have regularly attended Sunday Mass, received Communion, and made confession. The parish priest, like the priest in "First Confession," would likely have known nearly all of his parishioners personally, and he would have wielded great influence in the community. Catholicism was not a matter of mere Sunday worship, nor was it a set of religious beliefs that people kept private; it was, for many, an inseparable part of being Irish.

Hypocrisy

Perhaps the chief theme of "First Confession" is religious hypocrisy, as represented by the character of Jackie's sister, Nora. Nora does not in any sense represent the spirit of Christianity. Although she practices the outward forms of Catholicism, she is vindictive and spiteful. Jackie, the far more sympathetic character, calls his sister a "raging malicious devil." Nora's character is revealed in the scene when she accompanies Jackie to church on Saturday to make his confession. Jackie says, "She held my hand as we went down the hill, smiling sadly and saying how sorry she was for me, as if she were bringing me to the hospital for an operation." When they get to the churchyard and presumably out of sight of others, with a "yelp of triumph" she hurls him through the church door and says, "And I hope he'll give you the penitential psalms, you dirty little caffler." (Here she refers to the priest assigning penance; "penitential psalms" refers to various sections of the biblical book of Psalms, with the implication that reciting them all would be a severe penance. *Caffler* is Irish slang for a "rogue" or "impudent person.") Nora's religious hypocrisy is emphasized in the story's final line, when she tells her brother, "'Tis no advantage to anybody trying to be good. I might just as well be a sinner like you."

Sibling Relations

Closely related to the theme of hypocrisy is that of sibling relations. Much of the conflict of the story derives from the relationship between Jackie and his sister, Nora. Jackie makes clear his contempt for Nora when, early on, he points out that Nora "sucked up" to Gran in exchange for a weekly penny. When Gran cooks dinner, Jackie refuses to eat it; Nora tries to make him and pretends "to be very indignant"—but then Jackie adds parenthetically, "she wasn't, of course, but she knew Mother saw through her, so she sided with Gran." Throughout the story, Nora hovers around Jackie, taunting him and calling him names. When Jackie falls out of the confessional box, Nora has no sympathy for him. Rather, she says, "I might have known you'd disgrace me," and she gives Jackie "a clip across the ear." The troubled sibling relationship in this family is used as a structural device to illustrate the theme of religious hypocrisy.

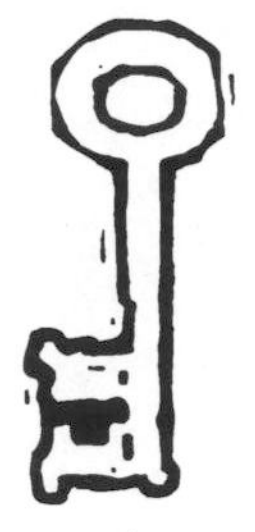

TOPICS FOR FURTHER STUDY

- Conduct research using online and print resources on traditional Roman Catholic practices and beliefs with regard to making a confession and receiving Communion for the first time, remembering that some of these practices have changed since O'Connor's youth, as the Catholic Church has become more liberal. Prepare an oral presentation for your class in which you explain these practices and beliefs in detail.
- Conduct online and print research to find images of Irish towns, such as Cork, from the early part of the twentieth century. Prepare a digital presentation in which you display these images to your classmates, and be prepared to explain how the natural and urban environment might have shaped the outlook of someone like O'Connor.
- Although Jackie is still quite young, his first confession (and first Communion) can be seen as a coming-of-age ritual in the Catholic Church, as well as in the Irish community of which he is a part. Prepare a chart that lists coming-of-age rituals in other cultures and faiths. You might, for example, include quinceañera for Hispanic girls, bar mitzvah and bat mitzvah for Jewish youths, or a Confucian ceremony called *gwallye* for Korean youths. Be prepared to explain these rituals, what they mean to the participants, and why they are considered part of a young person's coming of age.
- A well-known young-adult novel that deals with religious themes is Judy Blume's 1970 book *Are You There God? It's Me, Margaret.* The novel deals with Margaret's struggle to find religious belief, and it includes a scene in which she enters a church and a confessional booth. Prepare an essay or blog post in which you compare and contrast the nature of the religious growth that Margaret and Jackie undergo.
- Use online and print sources to research the development of Irish nationalism during the early decades of the twentieth century and how that development might have influenced someone like O'Connor. Provide your classmates with a "cast of characters," listing the chief figures in the movement and the roles they played. Have your classmates act out their roles in a debate-style forum.

STYLE

Conflict

On one level, the conflict that propels "First Confession" forward is that between Jackie and his hypocritical sister Nora—and thus between genuine religion and Nora's false piety. That conflict, however, never plays out and is never resolved in any way. The reader pictures the two characters continuing to grate on each other in the future. The more fundamental conflict of the short story has to do with Jackie and his attitudes toward traditional religion, as well as his attitudes toward himself. Jackie has grown up in a community in which great emphasis is placed on traditional religious practices. He, like his classmates, is required to attend classes designed to prepare him for his first confession and, in the process, to undergo an examination of his conscience to identify his sins. He then is required to confess those sins to a priest, who will impose on him a penance and grant him absolution from God.

Jackie, though, is only seven years old. Most readers would regard his "sins" as rather minor—the failings to which any person is liable. In reality, he seems to the reader like a thoughtful, caring boy. When he makes his first confession, he assumes that he is up against a theology based on a wrathful God and that the Catholic Church as an institution is an instrument of that

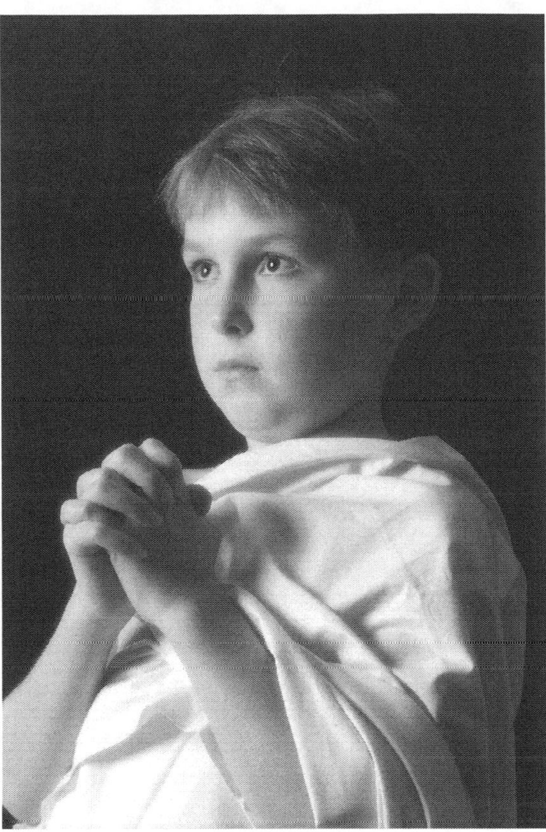

Jackie prepares for his first communion. *(Leah-Anne Thompson / Shutterstock.com)*

wrath. He is surprised when he discovers that the priest to whom he makes his confession is kindly and understanding. The priest does not judge him or make him feel as though he is a sinner or a bad person. Although the narrative makes no comment on the outcome of Jackie's confession, the reader infers from his contact with the priest that Jackie emerges from the experience with a firmer sense of the role of religion in his life. That role is not one of judgment and condemnation, as it is for Mrs. Ryan, nor is it a matter or outward forms and ritual, as it is for Nora. Rather, religion has a healing function. It puts people right not only with God but with themselves. Jackie, then, recognizes that religion is not a matter of dogma and external piety but rather an inner state—something that people like Nora, the reader suspects, will never understand.

Point of View

"First Confession" is told from a first-person point of view; that is, the story is narrated by one of the characters, who refers to himself as "I" or "me" and is involved in the story's events. In some fiction, the first-person narrator is largely an observer and reporter; in others, like "First Confession," the narrator is the central character. O'Connor's story skillfully handles the problem of having the story narrated by a child who may or may not fully comprehend the events in which he is involved. Jackie is telling the story from his perspective as a young boy. But for readers to understand the themes of the story, they have to bring a more adult perspective and make inferences from the details Jackie reports. Thus, when Jackie is making his confession, he tells the priest that his grandmother drinks porter. The priest responds with an "Oh, my!" and Jackie comments that he "could see he was impressed." Jackie goes on to tell the priest that his grandmother takes snuff. The priest responds, "That's a bad case, sure enough, Jackie." When Jackie confesses his "plan" to kill his grandmother, the priest asks, "And what would you do with the body?" These and other comments by the priest suggest to the more adult reader that the priest is amused by Jackie's confession. He tells Jackie, "you're a terrible child," but it is clear that the priest does not think so at all and that he is sympathetic toward Jackie. In this way, O'Connor is able to merge the point of view of the child with the more mature perspective of an adult reader.

Comedy

"First Confession" is very much a comic story. The comedy derives primarily from point of view and the interaction between Jackie's perspective as a child and the adult perspective of the reader, as well as that of the priest. This interaction plays out in virtually every line and scene in the story. For example, when Jackie is waiting his turn to go to confession in the church, he watches a penitent who is also waiting and who seems disturbed by his sinfulness. Jackie reflects, "I wondered had he a grandmother too. Only a grandmother could account for a fellow behaving in that heartbroken way." Jackie goes on to think, "But he was better off than I, for he at least could go and confess his sins; while I would make a bad confession and then die in the night and be continually coming back and burning people's furniture" (referring to the story told to him by Mrs. Ryan). The comedy of the story becomes almost slapstick when Jackie tries to climb onto the small shelf in the confessional booth, a shelf on which the penitent would normally just place his or her hands. Jackie tries to keep his grip on molding at the top of the box,

COMPARE & CONTRAST

- **1930s:** Catholics are required to attend Mass every Sunday (and on various holy days, such as Christmas) and receive Communion; traditionally, Catholics are required to go to confession at least once a year, but most traditional Catholics go to confession much more often.

  Today: Catholicism tends to be less rigid in its requirements. Many Catholics do not attend Mass every week, and many no longer go to confession; confession is now referred to as the sacrament of penance or the sacrament of reconciliation.

- **1930s:** Ireland is a relatively poor country trying to find its way in the world in the wake of its recent independence.

  Today: Ireland is a relatively thriving country, although the nation faces a severe debt crisis as part of a widespread recession in Europe and the United States.

- **1930s:** Ireland is an unstable country politically, where violence threatens because of religious differences between the Catholic Republic of Ireland and Protestant Northern Ireland; much of the violence in ensuing decades is centered in Northern Ireland.

  Today: Ireland, after centuries of disorder, is relatively peaceful after the signing of the Belfast Agreement by Northern Ireland and Great Britain on April 10, 1998.

but he loses his grip and tumbles out of the booth into the aisle of the church. The comic elements of the story serve multiple purposes: they paint Jackie as a sympathetic character, a young boy trying to come to terms with his conscience; they underline the hypocrisy of Nora; and they present the reader with an amusing picture of religious observances.

HISTORICAL CONTEXT

"First Confession" makes no reference to historical events. It was written, however, in the context of developments in the Irish Free State. For centuries, Ireland and England had been at odds with one another over the issue of Ireland's status. Early in the twentieth century, Irish nationalists under the banner of the Irish Republican Army gained power and rose in revolt against England. The political party that represented the nationalists was called Sinn Féin, a name that means "ourselves" or "we ourselves." One of the most prominent nationalists during this period was Michael Collins. A chief event in the Irish revolt was the Easter Rising, which occurred during Easter week in late April 1916. During this uprising, Irish nationalists tried to overthrow the British government in Dublin. The uprising failed, and its leaders were arrested and executed. Some of the conflict abated during World War I, and Ireland joined with Great Britain to defeat the Central Powers (principally Germany and Austria-Hungary). But conflict resumed after the war and continued until the signing of the Anglo-Irish Treaty of 1921, a treaty that was as much a ceasefire as a lasting peace agreement. Under the terms of the treaty, Ireland was partitioned. Northern Ireland, largely Protestant, became a separate political entity that chose to remain part of the United Kingdom. The remainder of the country became the Irish Free State, later called the Republic of Ireland. It proclaimed its independence, though it strove for full Irish unity. Under the terms of the treaty, the Republic of Ireland was a self-governing dominion; in this way, it held the same status as, for example, Canada and Australia. It was part of the British Empire but governed its own affairs. The Anglo-Irish Treaty, however, did not end the fighting. Civil war broke out between supporters of the treaty and its opponents, and the fighting continued for another two years.

Jackie must take confession before his first communion. *(Lagui / Shutterstock.com)*

During his early adulthood, O'Connor fought on the side of the Irish nationalists. After the war of independence, he experienced firsthand the struggles of the new republic. During the 1920s and 1930s, two issues dominated Irish politics. One had to do with the constitutional status of the new nation and its relationship with Britain. The other had to do with the partitioning of the country. During these years, resentment against the British government grew, as Britain and the Irish government refused to adjust the border with Northern Ireland. The leader of the Irish government, Eamon de Valera, who had opposed the Anglo-Irish Treaty, became popular by abolishing the oath of loyalty to Britain. He also discontinued the practice of paying Britain for the use of Irish lands. His policies prompted a trade war with Britain, which ended in 1938, the year before "First Confession" was published.

Also important to the historical context of "First Confession" is Irish Catholicism. Catholicism has historically played a major role in Irish culture, particularly in the Republic of Ireland. This fervent Catholicism has given rise to numerous folk traditions and practices. For example, relics of the saints are thought to have curative powers. Processions in honor of local saints are commonplace. Devotion to the Virgin Mary, the mother of Christ, is deep-rooted, and Catholics make pilgrimages to shrines throughout Ireland. The Catholic Church has exercised considerable control over institutions such as schools and hospitals. It has also influenced political decisions; for example, Ireland strongly opposes divorce and abortion, and during O'Connor's lifetime, censorship of publications was commonplace.

CRITICAL OVERVIEW

O'Connor wrote an immense number of short stories, many of which appeared in various collections after they were first published, usually in a magazine or journal. As such, critics have tended to comment on his work taken as a whole, with less emphasis on particular short stories. Thus, for example, William James Smith, writing in *Commonweal*, says that O'Connor's "stories are as unassuming and as effortless as across-the-bar or over-the-back-fence gossip.... This effort has resulted in a superbly clean and lean style." Gary T. Davenport, in "Frank O'Connor and the Comedy of Revolution," calls O'Connor "an authority on the short story and one of the century's foremost practitioners of the genre." Writing for the London *Times Literary Supplement*, Patricia Craig concludes, "Honesty of expression, rather than realism, is O'Connor's objective, and this he achieves in an impressive number of stories. And always, his craftsmanship is unfaltering and his showmanship assured." William Trevor, reviewing O'Connor's *Collected Stories*, offers this praise:

> In almost all the stories in this excellently balanced collection O'Connor's people explode from the page. The nice are here, and the nasty; the gentle, the generous, the mean, the absurd, those rich in dignity, those with a shred of it.

Deborah Averill comments approvingly on the stories' "atmosphere of warm intimacy" and says that

> the tone of the stories is conversational, animated and evocative, embodying O'Connor's own energetic vitality. It is intended to elicit an immediate emotional response from the reader. The language and idiom come directly from the situation.... His easy, confident fluency creates a deceptive impression of casual off-handedness.

One critic who comments specifically on "First Confession" is William Tomory in *Frank O'Connor*. He calls "First Confession" "one of the finest comic stories written by O'Connor." The story's underlying theme "is deftly worked into the story in the opposing characterizations of Nora and Jackie." Tomory goes on to say that "O'Connor's ability to recreate the emotions of childhood in all their intensity is remarkable." He adds that "as in most of the juvenile stories, the narratorial voice exhibits a flexibility that captures the speech and the thought patterns of a child while providing the unified interpretation of experience characteristic of an adult."

CRITICISM

Michael J. O'Neal

O'Neal holds a Ph.D. in English. In the following essay, he examines the nature and effect of the revisions O'Connor made to "First Confession."

Frank O'Connor had a reputation as an incurable tinkerer with his writing. Some of his short stories went through literally dozens of drafts. Even after he had sent the "finished" version of a story to a publisher, he often continued to work on it. Many of these later revisions were minor changes in wording to, for example, sharpen a line of dialogue. "First Confession" is unusual because it exists in four different published versions. The last version, published in 1951 in *Traveller's Samples*, is the version that is anthologized today. O'Connor published the first version of this story under the title "Repentance" in 1935; in that version, the protagonist is named Micky. The author revised the story for publication in 1939 under the title "First Confession," then continued to revise it for publication in a 1946 collection of his stories and again for publication in 1951. By comparing the 1935 version with the 1951 version, readers can get a firm sense of how O'Connor practiced the craft of writing fiction and how he revised his tale to make it one of his best. The comparison also offers insight into the craft of fiction writing in general. Three passages stand out in showing the development of O'Connor's craft.

In "Repentance," the character of Mrs. Ryan is a "horrid old devil of a woman" who tries to impress upon her charges the torments of hell in this way:

> "Hell," she intoned, "is a school from which you will never get out. Never! Three o'clock will come, half-past three, four, but no devil will say 'School is over.'" She chuckled grimly, and, leaning with one hand on the back of her chair, she poked her finger at one after the other of them. "And it won't be any use holding up your hands then and saying, 'Please may I go home now?'"

Notice, first, that "Repentance" is narrated in the third person ("one after the other of them"). In "First Confession," O'Connor changes the narration to first person, allowing the reader greater insight into Jackie's state of mind. The first-person narration also allows for an ironic, and often poignant, contrast between Jackie's childlike perspective and the reader's more adult perspective. In "First Confession," Mrs. Ryan tells a very different story about a man who made a bad confession and disappeared, leaving "only a smell of burning timber." Jackie goes on to say that "this story made a shocking impression on me." The story told by the "horrid old woman" in "Repentance" is flat and not very interesting. The story in "First Confession" is far more dramatic and far more in keeping with a traditional "fire and brimstone" conception of hell. Jackie's comment on Mrs. Ryan's story is comic in its simplicity, and thus more effective and engaging. And by making

WHAT DO I READ NEXT?

- O'Connor's "Guests of the Nation" (1931), his first published short story and one that is still frequently anthologized, draws on the author's experiences during the Irish War of Independence. It tells the story of two British prisoners held at a rural cottage. They befriend their captors, the woman of the house, and members of the local community as they help with chores, play cards, and debate theology and politics. It can be found in *Guests of the Nation*, published by Dufour Editions in 1999.
- "First Confession" almost demands comparison with "Innocence" (1948), a story by another great Irish short-story writer, Sean O'Faolain (with whom O'Connor established a literary journal, the *Bell*, in 1940). This story, too, deals with a young boy who makes a confession, although it does so from an adult's perspective forty years later.
- Tomás Rivera is the author of a novel, ... *Y no se lo tragó la sierra* (... *And the Earth Did Not Devour Him*), first published in a bilingual edition in 1971. The novel consists of interrelated stories, one of which is titled "First Communion." The story is about a Hispanic adolescent and his initiation into Catholicism and adult society.
- James Joyce is one of the most acclaimed Irish writers. His collection of short stories *The Dubliners* (1914) provides readers with portraits of Irish life in the early twentieth century. Like O'Connor, Joyce drew on everyday experiences of the middle class and small moments of illumination. The story "Grace" involves the efforts of a pair of men to convert another man to Catholicism, inviting him to attend a confessional retreat. The story relies for its humor and irony on the characters' superficial understanding of the church and its beliefs.
- Carmel McCaffery's *In Search of Ireland's Heroes* (2007) uses narrative and original sources to present portraits of Ireland's heroes through the centuries—heroes both famous and hardly known. The book is written and compiled to some degree from a Catholic perspective, giving the reader understanding of the role of Catholicism in Irish history and in the development of Irish nationalism.
- Olive Ann Burns's *Cold Sassy Tree* (1984) is a comic coming-of-age novel for young adults set in Georgia in 1906 and 1907. It is told in the first person from the point of view of Will Tweedy, who is fourteen years old when the novel's action begins. Like "First Confession," it involves a grandparent. It centers on the scandal caused when Will's grandfather and mentor suddenly marries a much younger woman just weeks after the death of his first wife. Will examines the nature and source of prejudice, ponders the role of God in the lives of individuals, and develops a more mature, adult perspective on life.
- *Of Water and the Spirit* (1994) is an autobiography by Malidoma Patrice Somé, an elder in the Dagara tribe of west-central Africa. He describes his early life at a French Catholic boarding school. The students here, like Jackie, were taught to fear the wrath of a "temperamental God." The core of the book covers his month-long initiation into Dagara religious views, addressing his anxieties and uncertainties.

Mrs. Ryan a well-to-do woman from an affluent neighborhood, O'Connor avoids creating the impression that Jackie thinks that every elderly woman is "horrid." She is respectable, and it is Jackie's struggle with religious respectability that is the heart of the story.

Perhaps one of the best examples of a revision that sharpened the story is the scene in

> "IN 'FIRST CONFESSION,' 'MAGIC' HAPPENS IN THE MOMENT OF TELLING, NOT YEARS LATER."

which the protagonist makes his confession to the priest. In "Repentance," the confession is reported in narrative form, again in the third person:

> Micky had to explain what sort of woman his grandmother was, that she drank porter, took snuff and went about the house in her bare feet. It was all made infinitely easier because the priest never once took his eyes off Micky's face, and at every few words interrupted with a sympathetic "Tut-tut!" or "Well! Well!" As he seemed to be so interested and understanding, Micky thought he might as well tell him the whole thing; how he had planned to come behind her while she was eating a meal of potatoes and hit her over the head with a hatchet. The priest thought a knife would have been better, as there would be a danger that the old woman would scream. Micky admitted that he hadn't thought of that, but this wasn't quite true, as he had thought of it vaguely, but had rejected it because he couldn't imagine himself running a knife into her.

This passage merits close comparison with the corresponding passage in "First Confession." A number of changes are immediately apparent. Again, "Repentance" is narrated in the third person, while "First Confession" is in the first person. Additionally, the passage in "Repentance" is entirely in narrative form; the reader is told what the characters said, and the overall effect is slightly flat. Furthermore, the passage in "Repentance" falls just short of achieving the comic effects of "First Confession." Micky's confession to the priest almost comes across as serious and almost gives the impression that Micky is in fact driven by evil demons and could have actually killed his grandmother. Put simply, the passage is not particularly funny, nor does it exploit the ironic contrast between the protagonist's perception of his thoughts and the priest's perception of the confession he is hearing. Comedy is implied when the reader is told that "The priest thought a knife would have been better," but again, the comedy is not exploited because the reader is simply told that this is what he said.

In contrast, "First Confession," perhaps reflecting O'Connor's interest in the theater at this time, uses dialogue to portray the interaction between Jackie and the priest.

> "Father," I said, feeling I might as well get it over while I had him in a good humor, "I had it all arranged to kill my grandmother."
> He seemed a bit shaken by that, all right, because he said nothing for quite a while.
> "My goodness," he said at last, "that'd be a shocking thing to do. What put that into your head?"
> "Father," I said, feeling very sorry for myself, "she's an awful woman."
> "Is she?" he asked. "What way is she awful?"
> "She takes porter, father."

Most readers would agree that this version of the confession is far more accomplished. By having Jackie tell his own story, "First Confession" creates greater immediacy. When Jackie reports that the priest "said nothing for quite a while," the reader is allowed to infer that he is stifling laughter; in this way, the ironic contrast between Jackie's perspective and that of the priest is sharpened and given greater effect. The priest's statement that killing the grandmother would "be a shocking thing to do" contributes to the comic effect by using understatement. When Jackie reports that his grandmother is awful because she drinks porter, the effect of this line is termed *bathos*: an abrupt descent from sublime, elevated, or important ideas (or language) to the trivial and ridiculous. Sometimes bathos can be unintentional, but often writers use it for comic effect. Jackie confesses to a wish to commit murder, and when asked why, he responds by saying that his intended victim drinks ale. The reader can imagine a theatrical audience bursting into laughter at the bathos of Jackie's response to the priest.

A final example concerns the ending of the stories. Here is the outcome of "Repentance":

> For three years Micky went to confession to him every Saturday. Then one day it all came back to him, he grew hot and cold by turns, and afterwards he went to that priest no more. When he saw him in the street he ran miles to avoid him. As he died some years later they never spoke again. But one night in a Paris hotel Micky remembered it all, and it was as if tears were falling in his mind, and then it seemed as if window or door were suddenly opened and magic caught him by the hair.

Of course, "First Confession" ends with Jackie's exit from the church and a final encounter with Nora. Nothing is said about Jackie's future; the reader is left to infer what that future might be. The passage from "Repentance," though, makes a labored and not very successful attempt to give

Jackie's teacher makes him fear he has violated all ten commandments. (Lena Grottling / Shutterstock.com)

significance to the events of the story. Micky gains perspective and insight only years later when, unaccountably, he is in a hotel in Paris—as if to imply that the sophisticated French capital will provide him with insight lacking in a small Irish town. The reader is simply told that "magic caught him by the hair," but this again represents a labored effort to give significance to the events of the story. "First Confession," in contrast, does not have to labor to make the events significant. The reader can grasp the significance of the events in the telling of them through the central character. In "First Confession," "magic" happens in the moment of telling, not years later. It is this ability to make magic happen in the moment that makes Frank O'Connor one of the best short-story writers in the English tradition.

Source: Michael J. O'Neal, Critical Essay on "First Confession," in *Short Stories for Students*, Gale, Cengage Learning, 2012.

Bogdan B. Atanasov

In the following excerpt, Atanasov illustrates how "Guests of the Nation" can be used as an example of friendship that succeeds despite diversity.

Modern literature can carry messages related to peace through the magic of words that transport the reader into weighty life and death situations. The author uses Frank O'Connor's short story "Guests of the Nation" as a sounding-board for ideas on friendship and strife between characters of different ethnic and religious origins.

In the short story two English prisoners of two Irish guards become treated as guests as a friendship develops and the hosts face the anguish of killing their guests in the name of a higher national purpose.

The themes of the short story are analyzed with the views of Martin Luther King, Vlacav Havel, G. K. Chesterton and several other modern thinkers and activists for peace.

Modern literature can effectively carry a didactic message as well as ever. It can deal with the weightiest existential questions. Literature matters mainly because of its bold and honest satire and the beauty of its art, the magic of words. If literature in its written form is virtually non-existent for the preponderant majority of the population on Earth, at least for a large and, for the present, significant segment thereof, it is of vital importance and can have enormous cultural and social impact.

Frank O'Connor deserves the highest esteem for infusing the dozen pages of his Guests of the Nation with ideas of such great substance and power that one cannot help being overcome with grief when the inevitability of the tragic sacrifice of the two Englishmen becomes evident; the bitter irony of it is that they were sacrificed on the altar of Triumphant National Glory, the irony of ironies being that this is not the gallant sacrifice of a life on the battlefield that leaders have inculcated since hosts began ravaging their neighbors' lands, but a heinous execution of two English hostages in retaliation for the British Army's equally, or rather doubly, execrable execution of four Irish hostages. Through these reciprocal assassinations carried out outside the theater of war, Frank O'Connor explodes the fatuous myth of death crowning the soldier with everlasting military honor and he shows it up for what it truly is—a glorification of institutionalized homicide in the name of the prevailing isms.

Like the mythical Prometheus, O'Connor brings the heavenly fire of moral philosophy down to a work of high literature that is not beyond the understanding of the ordinary man. That is sheer genius.

The importance of Frank O'Connor's writing for people of the twenty-first century, and particularly for the young, cannot be rated too highly, especially if we believe that literature, as a part of the cultural milieu, can enlighten our way of thinking and so may help in the resolution of some of our most pressing moral, social and political

"HE SEEMS TO FEEL THAT IN THE ORGANIZED GROUP AN INDIVIDUAL IS FORCED TO RELINQUISH HIS OR HER RELIGIOUS FAITH, HIS ESSENTIAL HUMANITY, HIS HUMILITY AND RESPONSIBILITY BEFORE GOD."

problems. This gripping short story impresses itself upon the minds of all students, but, from my teaching experience, I am aware that for students from post-totalitarian Eastern Europe it does so with a kind of acuity and relevance that cannot compare to its perception in the West with the exception of Ireland. That can be explained with the ethnic and religious tensions, which have existed for centuries in these parts and seem to have escalated sharply since the late 80s, as the media have been informing us profusely. The net effect is that our sympathy threshold has risen and we are hardly touched any more by the gruesome newsworthy and filmworthy atrocities we see on the TV screen with predictable regularity. When quality fiction depicts a scene or a character, it does so with a greater depth of reasoning and emotion and in greater relief because of the very nature of the word which can shift from the concrete to the abstract or metaphorical in a split second, and can go into the furthest recesses of any consciousness or constellation. So literature is managing to hold its own against the onslaught of the moving image and we feel sure that it will continue to make an impact on the progress of ideas in our world.

For whatever reason a writer may be writing, and whatever kind of literature he or she may be producing, all writers are children of their times and they will be writing for their contemporaries and it may be that they wish to stand up for or destroy a certain cause. I believe that such is the case in "Guests of the Nation." The issue here is: will men-at-arms act according to moral norms or will they become automatons and therefore plead innocence. If there is moral responsibility, where does the buck start and where does it stop? Does it go all the way up to the top of the pile, or is responsibility shared?

I feel his answer is that we are all answerable to God, wherever we place ourselves and others in our ridiculous, meaningless hierarchies; absurd because they are figments of the imagination in the minds of people, tribes, nations, races, religious denominations, government institutions, social classes, income-bracket groups, professional divisions and every other imaginable division of inferiority and superiority.

So in this short story, Frank O'Connor sets out to analyze the faculties of the human heart and mind functioning in unusual circumstances—under the extreme conditions of armed conflict between a foreign occupying army and a local insurgency: Englishmen versus Irishmen, the former fighting for King and Empire, the latter fighting for an independent Irish republic. Frank O'Connor, a one-time member of the Irish Republican Army, places his characters in an uncharacteristic situation for combatants; he takes them out of the heat of the fighting. When bullets are zipping through the air, it would take a superhuman mind to ponder the possibility of fraternizing with the enemy while the enemy soldiers are firing at you and your buddies and you are naturally trying to stay alive simply by keeping up your fire. Human, all too human! So O'Connor plants his characters in a remote farmhouse far from the distracting sound of the firing and the high probability of becoming a statistic on the casualty lists and there two young and patriotic Irishmen have to kill time while keeping watch over two curious and curiously different from one another English POWs. Yet the idea of killing John Bull's stooges never even crosses the minds of the Irish rebels or the crotchety old crone. These decent and friendly English "prisoners" start being treated by their decent and friendly Irish "guards" as guests, and gradually the guards become hospitable hosts, though all four of them are more like boarders on vacation at the old widow's farmhouse. (Here we might profitably digress into the amazing etymology of 'host': Latin hostis originally meant 'stranger, foreigner' but later developed the negative meaning of 'foreign enemy'; in Old French we see hoste meaning 'guest, host' hence the ambiguous senses of 'guest' and 'enemy' and then 'army'—a multitude of enemies; the derivative 'hostage' hovers in this story, at least etymologically, between these pairs of discrepant meanings.)

So the practical problem for this chummy group is how to provide a more enjoyable time for the guests and the answer is quite simple—do what young men in these parts would be doing in peace time: playing cards, going out to village dances, flirting with the lasses; being helpful about the house is pleasurable only to Belcher, the timid, silent giant of an Englishman. Why drinking is not mentioned seems a bit of a wonder. Still, despite the blithe process of acculturation and the frivolity of certain situations, the impending doom of the two strangers looms over them throughout the story. As the plot thickens, the moral dilemma emerges. The natural instincts of these good people, with the exceptions of those who are in charge the troubled Jeremiah Donovan, the group leader, and Feeney, the local intelligence officer, are pushing them away from a retaliatory execution, from what the rank and file would regard as an assassination, as the murder of not just fellow humans, but of friends, of "chums" as the adopted English idiom goes. This openness of the more friendly Irish to typical English parlance is yet another sign of friendly acceptance of the other. We gradually come to understand that the two belligerent sides are confronted with the same moral problems: Can POWs be used as hostages? Does loyalty to your own people make it your patriotic duty to murder a helpless unarmed prisoner in cold blood? For one murdered hostage are we duty-bound to retaliate with the shooting of one of theirs or even go several better? What kind of person is it that has the heart to pull the trigger on a prisoner, or rather, a prisoner-friend? Does it entail a superhuman effort to befriend one's future assassin? Did Belcher scale a spiritual Jacob's ladder? Wasn't even Hawkins just a few rungs below him? Wasn't their disbelief in evil and their belief in the greater power of friendship what made them walk to the bog so meekly, like lambs to the slaughter?

In "Guests of the Nation," O'Connor sees his set of characters as a microcosm, a social web of interrelations and feedback, where he seems to have faith in the individual, but very little in the individual acting as a member of an organization. He seems to feel that in the organized group an individual is forced to relinquish his or her religious faith, his essential humanity, his humility and responsibility before God. After the deed, the reluctant killers stand stunned by the horror and mental anguish of having taken the life of persons they knew personally, persons they had become friendly with, persons they had chatted and joked and disputed with and had fun playing cards and going to dances with. They were persons they had enjoyed life with and they were compelled to take those lives on the terrible and irrevocable orders from a commander whose powers to work evil on Earth are ridiculously puny by comparison with God's omnipotence. O'Connor ends his story letting his humane and inhumane characters go their separate ways and the former return to the farmhouse and contemplate their part in the evil action—the old woman and Noble pray on their knees, while the narrator merely stands at the door and looks up at the faint light of the "bloody stars" and he feels "very small and very lost and lonely like a child astray in the snow."

But through the tragic ending, the author seems to be suggesting that though such general folly is possible only because we are living in a primitive and benighted era, each individual can still choose to act morally, can still choose to oppose evil, can still choose to help his brothers and sisters "on the other side," even in times of conflict, be it "ethnic" or "religious."

Source: Bogdan B. Atanasov, "Friendship and Strife in Frank O'Connor's 'Guests of the Nation,'" in *International Journal on World Peace*, Vol. 19, No. 1, 2002, p. 75.

M. Longley

In the following interview, Longley and O'Connor discuss writing and Ireland, among other subjects.

The white slip of cardboard was inscribed "O'Connor—O'Donovan." I pressed the button and the mysterious box which looked like a small radio spoke in a charming American accent, "Yes?" One's name sounds even more peculiar spoken into midair toward a box in reply to someone invisible—in that brief situation it seems the only thing (and a very flimsy thing at that) by which one is to be judged. I was directed toward the lift. "And we're on the second floor."

I heaved upward, the lift opened, and to my surprise I found myself at once in the O'Connors' flat. "Come in!"—the familiar American accent, Mrs. O'Connor's—and I negotiated the two sets of lift doors. Frank O'Connor appeared from a room.

"What on earth's that?," he asked suspiciously, pointing at my right hand.

"A tape recorder—the editor's bright idea," I apologised. In my confusion I headed for one of the bedrooms but was successfully deflected by Mrs. O'Connor into the living room.

"Shall I plug the thing in?"

"Yes, go ahead—anywhere you like."

I shifted a chair, eyed a gramophone, and fiddled around for a few minutes to discover the plugs did not fit.

"I CAN MANAGE THE MECHANICS OF WRITING EASILY ENOUGH BUT I LIKE TO GET THE ESSENCE, THE SPIRIT OF A STORY DOWN IN ABOUT FOUR HOURS—IN ANY OLD RIGAMAROLE (I'VE GOT TO CATCH IT LIKE A POEM). AND THEN I POLISH ENDLESSLY."

"The plugs don't fit," I said, relieved to be rid of my demanding partner.

"Ah, well," said Frank O'Connor, also relieved, I suspected. "You'll be much better writing it out of your head. Will you have a sherry?"

Sherries poured, cigarettes lit, and the interview began.

Interviewer: What would you say were the sources of your imagination? (Pause) It's a corny question I know.

O'Connor: The sources of my imagination? It is a difficult question.

I suppose anything could engage my imagination. It could be a poem or a folk song or a character that starts me off. Anything.

Int.: Do you still get inspiration from Dublin?

O'C.: Well, I don't find Dublin invigorating any more, although of course I'm closer to my material. The literary atmosphere of this city is one in which every young writer is chopped down as soon as he makes an appearance and shows signs of talent. That is one of the reasons why I went all out to praise Gerry Simpson's play. This must be about the only city in the world where a writer could be destroyed. There's such violence and ignorance here. The writer is up against a terrible middle-class hatred.

Int.: Do you find childhood an especially rewarding subject to write?

O'C.: Not especially rewarding. It's material like anything else.

Int.: Do you enjoy the effort of remembering the distant past?

O'C.: The remembering is not an effort. I find it just comes— . . .

Int.: Which do you prefer, autobiography or short stories?

O'C.: I prefer short stories. You are more like God when you're writing stories and controlling the characters.

Int.: Have you enjoyed appearing on television?

O'C.: Oh I love being on television—and the radio. It is a pleasant change not to be writing. But I loathe public speaking. Television, in spite of the cameras, is more like conversation. There is one person to talk to.

Int.: On the Monitor programme you talked about the mental age of cities, estimating Cork's at 17, Dublin's at 25. Why are you still in Dublin?

O'C.: (with determined sideways flash of eyes in direction of interviewer) I'm here to try and raise the mental age. Every artist should attempt this. There are risks of course. Forrest Reid killed himself by staying in Belfast all his life.

Int.: Do your enjoy Reid's work?

O'C.: Oh yes, he's very fine—within his limitations. His two autobiographical books, *Apostate* and *Private Road*, are especially good. Yes, he is outstanding on childhood. And he was an interesting link with writers like Forster and De la Mare.

Int.: And what about the North?

O'C.: I'm very fond of Belfast. I have a lot of friends there. I'm fond of the whole of the North really—in fact at one time I was tempted to live there. Still artists in Ulster are a beleaguered minority. Yes, they are forced into rather frantic cultural cliques.

Int.: Did you enjoy working in American universities?

O'C.: Very much. I was involved in creative writing classes, which I found excellent in practice. Writing can be taught just like painting or music. Presuming the material, the talent, is there, these classes probably cut two years off a young writer's apprenticeship. The American student enjoys absolute freedom and he can change courses quite easily. Each academic year begins with ten days' shopping when the students hunt around for the courses and lectures which appeal to them most. I found American students very rewarding—and the country too. But then, I like most countries I visit.

Int.: A friend of mine said that he found the Americans extraordinarily generous but lacking in any real, deep sympathies.

O'C.: You just can't make these sweeping generalisations. Right enough, there is a change of atmosphere as you go from country to country but you mustn't generalise on it. The Americans realise that their own grandparents were probably immigrants and as a result they are very gentle with foreigners. Stalin stated that there were no such things as races, only phases of civilisation. Quite a good remark coming from an old scoundrel like that!

Int.: When were you first published?

O'C.: Russell was the first to publish me. I was seventeen when I got a poem into the *Sunday Independent*—and a terrible poem it was too. After the Civil War I wrote for the *Insiz Statesinan*. Russell and Yeats encouraged me. I am still excited by getting into print, but if afterward I discover the stuff is bad I feel like committing suicide. Yes, I was pleased to be published by Penguins. I'm always glad to appear in cheap paperback editions. People in Ireland can't afford expensive books. I have a second volume of short stories coming out in the future sometime. There has been a delay because the printers have messed it up. I'm quite pleased with it.

Int.: Do you regret not having been to a university?

O'C.: I don't think a university does anybody any harm. It gives one a certain discipline.

Int.: Would you say it was bad for writing that so many writers now—especially in the States—are academics?

O'C.: You just have to find a way to buy your time. You have got to sell yourself in order to buy those three or six free months per year in which you do your writing. And I would just as soon sell myself to an American university as to a newspaper or any other institution.

Int.: How do your feel about your lectureship at Trinity?

O'C.: Trinity is an Irish university with Irish problems. In American universities there is a much larger element of disengagement. I feel there is much more at stake in lecturing at Trinity—I am engage[d] before I begin.

Int.: How much pleasure do you get from translating?

O'C.: A great deal. Translation is a kind of literary criticism. In my classes I give parody and translation central places—they are the best ways of commenting on literature. As for myself I translate because a certain poem has given me a kick and I want to convey that kick. It doesn't matter if I fake my results so long as I convey the excitement I felt. A translation is a poem about a response.... It is like any other poem.

Int.: Do you write any original poetry yourself now?

O'C.: No. I stopped writing poetry when I stopped being able to remember long screeds of poetry off by heart. You see your head has got to be full of it. I couldn't remember poets like Betjeman or Frost now.

Int.: Did you know Frost?

O'C.: Yes, I can remember the two of us fighting like cats over the ways Yeats read his poetry. I was all for it and Frost violently against. He wrote some bawdy poems which have never been published of course. There was a marvelously blasphemous one about the Blessed Virgin. Frost was disgusted that so many young poets were being converted, Auden an Anglican, Allen Tate a Roman Catholic. "They haven't the courage of their sins," he used to say. Yes, he was a very great poet.

Int.: There is a lot of literary activity in Dublin just now. How real would you say this is?

O'C.: There are half a dozen good poets writing in Dublin at the moment. But as I said earlier young talent here runs the risk of being killed before it begins. A great deal of the new liveliness is due to Liam Miller of the Dolmen Press. It gives me great pleasure to see a young writer like Kinsella making an international reputation for himself—

Int.: I find his poetry very difficult—

O'C.: Well, it's very scholarly, of course.

Int.: What about Montague?

O'C.: I don't get the same pleasure from his work as from Kinsella's. He's a tough Northern Irishman!

Int.: Are you a fast writer?

O'C.: Very fast. I hate to write a story over a period of even two days because then I lose the mood. I write my stories as though they were lyrics. I can manage the mechanics of writing easily enough but I like to get the essence, the spirit of a story down in about four hours—in any old rigamarole (I've got to catch it like a poem). And then I polish endlessly. In my latest book there are stories I have rewritten fifty times. I go back to my stories even after publication and read and reread them until I sense what's wrong. Once I know a story is as perfect as I can make it I never look at it again. Yes, these processes are purely intuitive. I would say that I have a slow mind, and I like to feel my way.

Int.: Have you written any novels?

O'C.: Two novels—both of them awful. It's not my metier. You see I would call myself a spoiled poet. I write my stories, as I've suggested, as a lyric poet would write his poems—I have to grasp all my ideas in one big movement, I am a violent, emotional man, and novels require meditation and a more plodding day-to-day kind of energy.

Int.: You resemble Schubert in this respect. He was great at conceiving and perfecting single brilliant ideas, but poor at putting different ideas together—greater as a songwriter than as a symphonist.

O'C.: Yes, there's some truth in that. Beethoven is the supreme architect for me.

Int.: Do you like music?

O'C.: I adore it. Ireland has produced many writers and singer, but there is not the necessary machinery nor the tradition here to produce composers. It's rare to find two intellectuals together in any Irish town, so what chance have you of encountering a string quartet?

Int: Who is your favorite composer?

O'C.: Mozart, I suppose. After Beethoven.

Int.: I have just become acquainted with Beethoven's last string quartets—

O'C.: Oh, marvelous music!

Int.: I found them immediately exciting, and yet some people would warn you off them as sacred ground not to be explored until you have prepared yourself with years of listening.

O'C.: That's nonsense of course. His C-sharp minor quartet was almost the first thing to hit me between the eyes.

Int.: Is that the one that goes . . . (Hums out of tune)?

O'C.: Well, the slow movement goes (Hums out of tune). I used to write stories around music. There was one, I remember, called "Michael's Wife" which I wrote with the slow movement of Beethoven's Seventh Symphony in mind. That's a very beautiful piece of music—it used to haunt me while I was in gaol—that and the Mozart A-minor violin concerto.

Int.: Who are your favorite modern poets?

O'C.: Well, I'm not so well up on modern poetry. Frost of course (and I heard them dismiss him in the States as "that agricultural poet." Yes it was England who discovered him when he was about forty. There was a lot of bitterness in Frost). And I like Betjeman too. A born poet—he couldn't stop talking poetry for more than four or five minutes at a time. He was working over here during the last war—he is an enchanting character.

Int.: Do you enjoy writing?

O'C.: I love writing—it's the only thing really. There are tough patches of course. But I can never understand those writers who say they don't enjoy their work.

Source: M. Longley, "Frank O'Connor: An Interview," in *Twentieth Century Literature*, Vol. 36, No. 3, Fall 1990, pp. 269–74.

SOURCES

Averill, Deborah, "Human Contact in the Short Stories," in *Contemporary Literary Criticism*, Vol. 14, Gale Research, 1980, pp. 395–96; originally published in *Michael/Frank: Studies on Frank O'Connor*, edited by Maurice Sheehy, Knopf, 1969, pp. 28–37.

Craig, Patricia, "Vagrant Stories," in *Contemporary Literary Criticism*, Vol. 23, Gale Research, 1980, p. 331; originally published in *Times Literary Supplement* (London, England), July 31, 1981, p. 873.

Davenport, Gary T., "Frank O'Connor and the Comedy of Revolution," in *Contemporary Literary Criticism*, Vol. 23, Gale Research, 1980, p. 326; originally published in *Éire-Ireland*, Vol. 8, No. 2, 1973, p. 108.

Hopkinson, Michael, "Irish Free State/Republic," in *Oxford Companion to British History*, edited by John Cannon, 2002.

O'Connor, Frank, "First Confession," in *Collected Stories*, edited by Richard Ellmann, Knopf, 1981.

Smith, William James, "Calm, Wise Stories of the Human Comedy," in *Contemporary Literary Criticism*, Vol. 23, Gale Research, 1980, p. 326; originally published in *Commonweal*, October 25, 1957, pp. 101–102.

Steinman, Michael A., *Frank O'Connor at Work*, Syracuse University Press, 1990, pp. 25–36.

Tomory, William, *Frank O'Connor*, Twayne Publishers, 1980, p. 126.

Trevor, William, "Frank O'Connor: The Way of a Storyteller," in *Contemporary Literary Criticism*, Vol. 23, Gale Research, 1980, p. 331; originally published in *Washington Post Book World*, September 13, 1981, p. 2.

FURTHER READING

Cahill, Susan, ed., *For the Love of Ireland: A Literary Companion for Readers and Travelers*, Ballantine Books, 2001.

Although it is nominally a travel book, in reality this volume is a literary exploration of Ireland. The editor provides excerpts from the works of more than forty Irish writers, including O'Connor, along with information about the places in which those works are set. The book is written for readers interested in Irish culture and how that culture is reflected in Irish literature.

McKeon, James, *Frank O'Connor: A Life*, Mainstream Publishing, 1998.

McKeon's biography of O'Connor is briefer than more scholarly biographies and more likely to be of interest to the general reader. McKeon places particular emphasis on the misery of O'Connor's poverty-stricken boyhood and how that experience influenced the course of his life.

Regan, Stephan, *Irish Writing: An Anthology of Irish Writing in English, 1789–1939*, Oxford University Press, 2008.

This volume includes Irish literature from the late eighteenth century to the early years of the nation's political independence. It includes a wide selection of fiction, poetry, and drama. It also includes such documents as speeches, letters, memoirs, songs, travel writings, and essays, many of which are difficult to find elsewhere.

Townshend, Charles, *Ireland: The Twentieth Century*, Hodder Arnold, 1999.

Readers interested in twentieth-century Irish history and the events that shaped O'Connor's early life might start with this volume. It traces the course of the Irish independence movement and includes discussion of both northern and southern Ireland. The book's intended audience includes readers who are approaching modern Irish history for the first time.

SUGGESTED SEARCH TERMS

Anglo-Irish Treaty 1921

Catholic AND sacrament AND confession

censorship AND Ireland

Frank O'Connor

Frank O'Connor AND First Confession

Irish AND Catholicism

Irish Free State

Irish nationalism

Irish AND short story

Irish War of Independence

modern Irish fiction

Good Country People

FLANNERY O'CONNOR

1955

Flannery O'Connor's "Good Country People" is one of the most widely anthologized short stories in the American canon, even after more than fifty years since its first publication. Initially included in the 1955 collection *A Good Man Is Hard to Find*, the story was republished in 1971 in the posthumously published *The Complete Stories*. The latter compilation won the 1972 National Book Award for Fiction.

O'Connor herself considered "Good Country People" to be one of her finest short stories. Richard Giannone, in *Flannery O'Connor and the Mystery of Love*, reports that in a letter to Robert Giroux, her editor, she wrote that "Good Country People" would anchor the rest of the stories included in *A Good Man Is Hard to Find*, as it was a "very hot story" that would "set the whole collection on its feet."

The story contains all the hallmarks of classic O'Connor fiction. Set in the American South, "Good Country People" explores themes of faith, good and evil, and grace through irony and symbolism using a gothic style that O'Connor preferred to think of as grotesqueness. Her stories, including "Good Country People," were typically humorous, although hers was a dark humor commonly lost on the average reader, who could not always see through the violence wrought by corrupt characters to O'Connor's moral messages. As quoted by J. B. Cheaney in "Radical Orthodoxy: The Fiction of Flannery O'Connor,"

Flannery O'Connor (AP Images)

Giroux once explained that her critics often "recognized her power but missed her point."

AUTHOR BIOGRAPHY

Born on March 25, 1925, Mary Flannery O'Connor was the only child of Edward O'Connor, Jr., and his wife, Regina Cline. The couple doted on their daughter and raised her in a devoutly Catholic home in Georgia. When she was twelve years old, O'Connor and her family moved to Atlanta, but within months, she and her mother returned to their home in Milledgeville. Edward was diagnosed with lupus, a disorder that causes the immune system to attack healthy cells and tissues, and died just weeks before his daughter's sixteenth birthday in 1941.

That same year, O'Connor graduated from high school and enrolled at Georgia State College for Women, where she served as art editor for her school's newspaper and edited the campus literary magazine. O'Connor graduated with a degree in social science in 1945. That was the year she dropped her first name and applied to the University of Iowa's graduate journalism program, where she was accepted into the Writers' Workshop master of fine arts program.

O'Connor sold her first short story, "The Geranium," to *Accent* magazine and subsequently won the Rinehart-Iowa Fiction Award. She left Iowa in 1947 with her degree and headed to Sarasota Springs, New York, where she worked on her first novel, *Wise Blood.* During this time, she met Robert Giroux, who would one day become her editor, and the translator Robert Fitzgerald and his wife, Sally. The Fitzgeralds would remain lifelong friends.

O'Connor moved in with the Fitzgeralds in their apartment in Ridgefield, Connecticut, after a brief stay in New York City. While living with the Fitzgeralds, O'Connor wrote and published three more short stories and made great progress on her novel. In late 1950, the writer's health began to decline, and she became critically ill on a trip home to Milledgeville. At the young age of twenty-five, O'Connor was diagnosed with lupus, the same disease that killed her father. She spent most of the following year in Atlanta, undergoing blood transfusions and experimental treatments with the drug ACTH to combat her illness. In 1951, she returned home to live with her mother. The women moved onto a dairy farm that O'Connor's mother had inherited in 1947. O'Connor would live out the rest of her life on the farm, which she renamed Andalusia.

In 1952, O'Connor completed and published *Wise Blood.* Her life at Andalusia was not an unhappy one; she and her mother ate regularly in town and had scores of visitors to the farm. The ACTH made O'Connor's lupus symptoms bearable but left her bones in such fragile condition that she was forced to walk with crutches beginning in 1953. Although travel was difficult, she did manage to range the lecture circuit among regional colleges, and she even made the journey overseas to France and Rome.

O'Connor published her first short-story collection, *A Good Man Is Hard to Find,* in 1955. "Good Country People" was included in that compilation. In 1960, she published a second novel,

The Violent Bear It Away. The author published her final work, an introduction to *A Memoir of Mary Ann*, a book which she also edited, in 1961. On August 3, 1964, at thirty nine years old, O'Connor died from complications of lupus. She was buried next to her father in the Milledgeville Memory Hill Cemetery.

Several other works of O'Connor's have been published posthumously, the most significant one being *The Complete Stories* (1971). She was awarded the National Book Award for Fiction in 1972 for that title. Regina Cline O'Connor donated the bulk of her daughter's manuscripts and letters to Georgia College & State University, which now acts as the principal repository for her works.

MEDIA ADAPTATIONS

- "Good Country People," adapted as a film by Jeff Jackson and distributed by Taos Land and Film Company, was released in 1976. Shot in 16 mm film, this brief movie (32 minutes) stars Shirley Slater, a friend of O'Connor's, as Hulga.

PLOT SUMMARY

"Good Country People" opens with a vivid description of Mrs. Freeman and her inability to see any character flaws in herself. A woman who can never be brought to admit she is wrong, she instead will change the subject or become distracted with something else. This opening scene also introduces Mrs. Hopewell, the owner of the Georgia tenant farm. Although Mrs. Freeman and her husband are tenants on the farm, the two women have developed a mutual appreciation of each other's company, at least, if not a true friendship.

Mrs. Freeman and Mrs. Hopewell spend an inordinate amount of time talking about Mrs. Freeman's two teenage daughters, Glynese and Carramae. When they are not talking about those girls, they are exchanging clichés. Mrs. Hopewell, who had had many tenants on her farm in bygone years, had chosen the Freemans carefully. Despite a warning from another farmer who had hired them that Mrs. Freeman was extremely nosy, Mrs. Hopewell hired them because she felt that, deep down, they were good country people, much like herself. That was four years before, and the two women have spent their mornings together ever since.

More than anything, the ladies boost each other's egos with gentle compliments and by being in general agreement on their barely developed philosophies on life, embodied in platitudes such as "everybody is different" and "it takes all kinds to make the world." These inane conversations drive Mrs. Hopewell's daughter, Joy, crazy. Joy is a thirty-two-year-old woman who holds a doctorate in philosophy but lives on the farm with her mother. She had her leg blown off in a hunting accident when she was ten and has walked with an artificial leg ever since. In addition to the prosthesis, she has poor eyesight, for which she wears corrective lenses, and a heart condition that has set her life expectancy at a maximum of forty-five years. Despite her age, Joy dresses in shabby clothes that make her look like a child.

Years ago, Joy changed her name legally to Hulga. Her mother is certain she chose the name for being the ugliest in any language. Mrs. Hopewell refuses to use the new name and continues to call her daughter Joy. Determined to overcome her disfigurement, Hulga has earned her doctorate, but to her mother's dismay, she does not use her degree for any practical profession; it does not sound impressive to Mrs. Hopewell to simply tell people her daughter is a philosopher. Despite the fact that Hulga worked hard to achieve a high level of education, in an era when girls primarily went to college to have a good time and find a husband, Mrs. Hopewell takes no pride in her daughter's accomplishment.

Hulga embraces the philosophy of nihilism, which holds that all beliefs and values are baseless and that nothing can be known or communicated; life is without purpose, and nothing matters because in the end, there will only be nothing. This idea mortifies Mrs. Hopewell, and she is sure her daughter's unhappiness could be remedied if only she would smile and act pleasant. Hulga barely tolerates her mother on most days.

Enter Manley Pointer, a nineteen-year-old traveling Bible salesman. Because the boy is hatless and disheveled, Mrs. Hopewell concludes that he comes from poverty. He seems eager to please, however, and that wins Mrs. Hopewell over, as does his ability to make her feel infinitely superior to him in terms of intelligence and common sense. She can see his admiration as he looks around her parlor and notices the shining silverware displayed in the sideboards, and it is then that she decides he has never seen so grand a place.

Though doing his best to sell Mrs. Hopewell a Bible, Manley does not have much hope of getting her to part with her money. He confesses, "Not many people want to buy one nowadays and besides, I know I'm real simple.... I'm just a country boy. People like you don't like to fool with country people like me!" Much of Manley's dialogue ends with an exclamation point; he is eager to appear gullible and humble. His approach works because Mrs. Hopewell cannot spew out clichés fast enough in response: "Good country people are the salt of the earth! Besides, we all have different ways of doing, it takes all kinds to make the world go 'round. That's life!" Manley understands that he has managed to worm his way into his host's good graces, and soon he is accepting her invitation to dinner. Hulga, who has been standing behind the kitchen door, groans and instructs her mother to get rid of the boy and serve dinner. She cannot believe that her mother is so foolish as to take in this stranger and allow him to sit at the table.

As the meal progresses, Hulga steals an initial glance at the strange dinner guest but then completely ignores him as he provides detailed accounts of his childhood as well as his future plans to conduct missions overseas, where he can bring Christianity to the damned. After two hours, even Mrs. Hopewell has had enough, and she instructs Manley to go. He obeys and sets off down the road, where he finds and speaks with Hulga. They make plans to meet the next morning.

In the morning, Mrs. Freeman and Mrs. Hopewell are talking in the kitchen. Mrs. Hopewell tells Mrs. Freeman about Manley Pointer: "Lord... he bored me to death but he was so sincere and genuine and I couldn't be rude to him. He was just good country people, you know." Mrs. Hopewell believes she is good at reading people and judging their character.

Hulga thinks over her conversation with the salesman from the day before, when he had asked if they could meet for a date at 10 a.m. Hulga had lain in bed half the night imagining the date and how it would progress. For now, she stands in the kitchen, lost in her thoughts of yesterday when Manley stopped in front of her and turned to stare directly at her. Nearly a minute passed before he said anything, and when he did, it was a bizarre question: "You ever ate a chicken that was two days old?" Hulga quickly answered yes.

Manley and Hulga begin walking, and he mentions her wooden leg. Although Hulga is taken aback by his boldness, he assures her that he finds her sweet. When he tells her he finds her glasses attractive and likes girls who wear them, Hulga begins to loosen up a bit. It is then that he asks her to meet him on Saturday at 10 a.m. for a picnic. Hulga lies in bed the whole night, imagining various seduction scenes. She thinks that he would be ashamed if he allowed himself to be seduced but that she would be able to use her superior intelligence to teach him something from the experience.

Hulga and Manley meet as planned, and she notices he is carrying his valise of Bibles. When she asks why he has brought it, he tells her one can never know when one will have use for a Bible. Almost immediately, Manley becomes preoccupied with Hulga's leg and wants to know where it joins with her actual flesh. Although Hulga is offended by the question, Manley quickly recovers and explains that he just thinks she is brave. During their stroll to the barn, Manley and Hulga share a kiss that is far from earth-shattering for Hulga, and eventually they discuss topics she finds interesting. When he asks if she has been saved (by accepting Jesus Christ as her savior), she replies that she does not believe in God, and Manley is clearly impressed. They continue to talk until they reach the barn, where they climb into the hayloft.

Once settled against a hay bale in the loft, Manley kisses Hulga. At first she does not respond, but then she returns his kisses with affectionate ones of her own. Within minutes, Manley insists that Hulga tell him she loves him. This is another opportunity for her to flaunt her knowledge, and she claims she can see through people rather than just into them.

While kissing on the hayloft floor, the two converse breathlessly. Manley seems determined to hear Hulga say she loves him, and after telling him that all people are damned, she admits that, in a way, she does love him. At that point, he lets her go and tells her to prove it by showing him how her wooden leg attaches to her real leg. He whispers this into her ear, like a lover whispers secrets. Hulga, though she believes that her shame about her leg has been removed by years of education, is aghast at his request. No one but she ever touches the artificial limb. It is, for the physically and emotionally crippled Hulga, her life source.

When she refuses his request, Manley acts hurt and angry. He explains that the leg is what sets her apart and makes her special. Hulga, naively believing Manley to be truly innocent, surrenders to his request and shows him how to take off and reattach the leg. He does it once himself, then removes it again and takes it from her. Already he had removed her glasses, leaving her with little sight. By placing her leg out of her reach, Manley also takes away her mobility. Hulga panics as he forcefully pushes her down into the hay and begins to kiss her more passionately. She finally pushes him off of her and demands that he give her the leg.

Instead, Manley pulls the valise toward him and opens it to reveal its contents: a deck of pornographic playing cards, a flask of whiskey, and a box of condoms. Also inside are two Bibles. He offers Hulga a drink from the flask but she refuses. When Hulga again requests that he give her back the wooden leg, Manley loses his temper and mocks her. In a rage as she realizes how easily she was misled, Hulga screams that Manley is a hypocrite who professes to be a Christian but whose behavior betrays that faith. Manley righteously informs his victim that he does not have to believe in Christianity just because he sells Bibles.

At that point, he places the wooden leg inside the valise. He slams the lid shut and descends through the hole to the barn floor below. No longer giving any pretense of admiration or awe, the salesman informs Hulga that he once got a woman's glass eye the same way he got her leg. Right before he disappears completely through the hole, Manley sneers at Hulga and tells her that he does not believe she is special or exceptionally smart, because he has believed in nothing his entire life. With that, he is gone.

Mrs. Hopewell and Mrs. Freeman see Manley in the distance walking toward the highway and decide he must have been selling Bibles to the Negroes who live in the backwoods. Mrs. Hopewell remarks on the salesman's simplicity while Mrs. Freeman decides that not everyone can be so simple-minded.

CHARACTERS

Carramae Freeman

Carramae is one of Mrs. Freeman's two daughters. Just fifteen years old, she is married and pregnant. One of the highlights of her mother's day is reporting to Mrs. Hopewell how many times Carramae has vomited from morning sickness that day. She does not appear in the story but instead is shown only through the gossip exchanged by Mrs. Freeman and Mrs. Hopewell.

Glynese Freeman

Glynese is Mrs. Freeman's eighteen-year-old daughter. A redhead, she has many admirers. One night on a date, the boy she was with gave her a chiropractic adjustment, claiming it would get rid of the sty in her eye. The next morning, the sty had vanished. Like her sister, Glynese is introduced into the story only in the conversations between Mrs. Freeman and Mrs. Hopewell.

Mrs. Freeman

Mrs. Freeman is the tenant wife on Mrs. Hopewell's farm. Although her husband is a hard worker, Mrs. Freeman does little more than chatter and gossip. A former employer tells Mrs. Hopewell, "She's got to be into everything.... If she don't get there before the dust settles, you can bet she's dead, that's all." Although Mrs. Freeman thinks highly of herself in terms of her morals and intelligence, she is in reality a simple country woman who cannot see beyond the nose on her face.

Mrs. Hopewell

Mrs. Hopewell is the divorced mother of Hulga and the employer of Mrs. Freeman and her husband. Like Mrs. Freeman, Mrs. Hopewell is full of herself, yet in reality she is merely a simple country woman whose knowledge extends barely beyond trite clichés and local gossip. Mrs. Hopewell has many favorite sayings, each more banal than the last. She prides herself on her solid common sense and ability to read people, yet she lacks both of these assets. To Mrs. Hopewell,

Mrs. Freeman was "good country people" and much more reputable than the "trash" who had previously lived on her farm.

The greatest hope—and disappointment—of Mrs. Hopewell's life is her thirty-two-year-old daughter, Joy. Joy had her leg blown off in a hunting accident at the age of ten, and the event changed her outlook on life forever. Mrs. Hopewell had dreamed of a fulfilling life for her daughter, and "it tore her heart to think instead of the poor stout girl in her thirties who had never danced a step or had any *normal* good times." Although she wants to love her daughter, the reader is made aware that doing so is almost beyond her abilities. She abhors the sound Joy makes when clumping into the kitchen each morning and hates her refusal to be decent to others—especially her own mother—even more. Mrs. Hopewell does not understand her daughter, believing that "there was nothing wrong with her face that a pleasant expression wouldn't help. Mrs. Hopewell said that people who looked on the bright side of things would be beautiful even if they were not."

The irony in Mrs. Hopewell's character lies in the fact that she is so focused on finding faults in others that she completely fails to see any in herself. Therefore, while she admits to lacking patience, she fulfills what she perceives as her Christian duty to sit with Manley Pointer for hours and listen to him drone on and on about his sorrowful (and, unbeknownst to her, completely fabricated) life story. She is a woman sure of who she is and completely unaware of what she is not.

Hulga Hopewell

Born with the name Joy Hopewell, Hulga legally changed her first name when she turned twenty-one. The name, she felt, suited her and the physical disfigurement that had come to define, in her subconscious, who and what she was. She chose the ugliest name she could think of and claimed it as her own.

Hulga lost her leg in a hunting accident when she was ten years old, and her life was forever altered by the resulting damage to her self-image. Despite the fact that she is a learned woman with a doctorate in philosophy, Hulga lives at home with her mother and goes "about all day in a six-year-old skirt and a yellow sweat shirt with a faded cowboy on a horse embossed on it." With bad eyesight and a heart condition as well as a wooden leg, Hulga turns her back on her own physical condition and instead focuses on developing her mind; yet the life she leads is one of bitterness, for she considers herself far superior intellectually to everyone she knows and deems them unworthy of her time or attention.

As Hulga studied philosophy, she came to embrace nihilism, which holds that all beliefs and values are baseless and that nothing can be known or communicated. It is not a lack of faith but a faith in the lack of anything. Hulga uses this philosophy to protect herself from further pain and humiliation. Her wooden leg, the heart condition that will surely shorten her lifespan, the loneliness of her cloistered life—none of these things matter if she believes there is no purpose to life, that nothingness is the ultimate goal.

So armed with a faith born of intellect rather than the heart, Hulga approaches life with a narcissistic attitude and a deep-seated desire to be seen and accepted for who she really is. When her mother asks her to join her on a walk, but only if she can behave pleasantly, Hulga replies, "If you want me, here I am—LIKE I AM." The ironic aspect of Hulga is that although she cannot tolerate not being accepted for who she is, she herself has never fully accepted herself for who she is either. Instead, she has hidden behind her intellect and neglected every other aspect of her personal development.

Hulga meets her match in Manley Pointer. Hulga judges him to be an unsophisticated country boy, and her mistake costs her dearly. Manley's own nihilistic tendencies are far more deeply ingrained than Hulga's, and when he steals her leg as well as her dignity, she realizes that she has been duped by someone far more clever than she. She shares her first kiss with a man so insensitive and contemptuous that what should have been a special moment in her life becomes part of a terrible memory. He even tricks her into saying that she loves him, and she has the haughtiness to behave as if such emotion did not matter: "We are all damned ... but some of us have taken off our blindfolds and see that there's nothing to see. It's a kind of salvation." As she watches him walk away from the scene of her debasement, Hulga realizes that it had taken someone with a genuine lack of faith to make her understand that when one believes in nothing, nothing is what one has.

Joy Hopewell

See Hulga Hopewell

Manley Pointer

Manley Pointer is a traveling Bible salesman who tricks all of the women on the farm into believing he is nothing more than a simple, devout Christian boy who has dedicated his young life to sharing the gospel of Christ. In fact, Manley is exactly the opposite of what he appears to be. Everything about him, right down to his name, is false, created for the purpose of trickery and manipulation.

Manley chooses his victims carefully and depends on their trusting and simple ways to allow him into their homes and lives. When he first appears on the scene, it is apparent that he is poor, because he has no hat. Men of class in those days wore hats. Manley is gaunt, and his dirty hair hangs down across his face. With his first words, it is apparent he is manipulating Mrs. Hopewell into thinking she is smarter than he. He calls her Mrs. Cedars, and when she corrects him, he pretends to be puzzled. Manley's lack of sincerity is hinted at by the way that everything he says ends with an exclamation point. He wants badly to appear jovial and cheerful. By acting like a country bumpkin, he makes his way into Mrs. Hopewell's home—literally falling through the door, valise first—without even being asked. As he looks around the room, he lets Mrs. Hopewell believe he is admiring her silver place settings when in reality he is playing to her vanity by acting intimidated and dumb.

Manley continues this behavior with Hulga as he plays on her low self-esteem and insecurities. While she believes in her superiority, he is one step ahead of her, figuring how to best encourage her feelings. When she admits her atheism, he whistles in apparent admiration and amazement. When she gets upset at a comment he makes about her wooden leg, he quickly reassures her that he likes it because it is what sets her apart from others. Manley clearly sees what Hulga needs—ego strokes, compliments, the appearance of being impressed—and he gives her all of it.

In return, he takes what he wants—first, her glasses, leaving her nearly sightless. This loss of sight is ironic, given that she already cannot see things clearly for all her knowledge. He also takes her wooden leg. The artificial leg is Hulga's life preserver; it defines who she is and sets limits on who she can potentially be. For all her professed atheism and lack of faith, Manley's own nihilism makes Hulga realize that her faith in nothing is a facade.

THEMES

Faith

O'Connor exhaustively explored the theme of faith in everything she wrote. She was nearly consumed with the idea of maintaining faith toward the goal of redemption—a concept she called "Christian realism"—and in her mind, redemption could be achieved only through suffering. This led the author to create and develop what she referred to as Christ-haunted characters. In "Good Country People," the Christ-haunted character is Hulga, and it is through her choices and behavior that the theme of faith is explored.

Hulga lacks faith in anything. Unlike her mother or the other "good country people" in the story, she does not believe in God. She does not believe in herself, for that matter. She has studied existentialism and nihilism, schools of philosophy that deny the existence of unified, objective truths and do not coincide with the teachings of Christianity. In an extremely simplified explanation, nihilism is the belief that nothing has meaning and nothing can be known. Hulga very clearly states that this is where her faith lies: "I don't have illusions. I'm one of those people who see *through* to nothing." However, she believes in the power of science to prove or at least confirm all meaningful statements and concepts, and so while Hulga believes she has faith in nothing, she is actually a logical positivist. This is in keeping with the fact that she has a doctorate in philosophy. Hulga replaced any faith she may have once had in God or a higher power with a faith in empirical (measurable and provable) knowledge, and she did so the moment her leg was shot off at age ten.

Manley Pointer, on the other hand, is most definitely a nihilist. His belief in the purposelessness of life and the power of nothingness has turned him into a corrupt, empty human being. Whereas Hulga eventually arrived at her positivism (which, really, is not what she embraces at her core but rather a philosophy she uses to help her deal with her crippling disfigurement), Pointer claims to have been a nihilist all along. Right before he climbs down the ladder of the hayloft with Hulga's leg, he tells her, "You ain't so smart. I been believing in nothing ever since I was born!"

O'Connor made both of her main characters flawed in the sense that they have no spiritual, specifically Christian, faith. Hulga's faith only in what she can prove or confirm through science

TOPICS FOR FURTHER STUDY

- Research music genres popular in the Deep South during the 1950s. Divide "Good Country People" into scenes of your choice and set each scene to music using music-writing software such as Garage Band that allows you to record and/or burn music onto a CD. Write a brief description of each song selection, making sure to include the song title and why you chose it. Bring your soundtrack to class and be prepared to present your selections.
- Every character in a story comes into the plot with a personal history of experience that makes one the way one is. Manley Pointer is a pivotal character and one with obvious and deep-seated personality traits. How did he become so deceptive and corrupt? What happened to him in his past to cause his personality to develop as it has? Write a short story that gives a glimpse into his past and helps readers understand his motivations in "Good Country People." Read your story to the class, or post it on your blog site and invite classmates to review it.
- Using computer-aided design or other graphics software, design and create a book cover for "Good Country People." Another option is to illustrate a favorite scene from the story.
- Using the Internet, research southern literature, a genre that exhibits specific traits. Apply this template to "Good Country People," and using Gliffy or another computer software program accessible to you, create a visual aid to help explain exactly what makes this short story an ideal example of southern literature. Be sure to provide evidence from the story to support your claims.
- Research O'Connor's life on Andalusia, her family farm. Compare your findings to the circumstances depicted in "Good Country People." Write an essay in which you cite specific instances of descriptions or activities from the story that may have been inspired or influenced by O'Connor's actual life.
- Read Vera and Bill Cleaver's award-winning young-adult novel *Where the Lilies Bloom*, another well-known example of southern fiction. Compare and contrast the novel with "Good Country People." What similarities exist in terms of setting, characters, and literary style? How do these elements differ between the two pieces of literature? Develop a multimedia presentation that illustrates your findings.

turns out to leave her in a desperate situation. She can neither see (as Manley took her glasses and put them out of reach) or move (as she is stuck in the hayloft without her leg). As soon as Hulga chose to value education of the mind over the inherent belief in her heart, she doomed herself. Manley Pointer was a lost soul from birth because his life lacked meaning. At the end of the story, only Hulga is redeemed, through her suffering and loss. The reader is given no hope that Manley Pointer will ever shed his nihilism.

Knowledge

The theme of knowledge—specifically, its nature and value—is explored primarily using the same two characters as with the theme of faith. Early in the story, it is clear that Mrs. Hopewell is not proud of her daughter's quest for knowledge: "The girl had taken the Ph.D. in philosophy and this left Mrs. Hopewell at a complete loss." The mother considers this study of philosophy confusing, perhaps even frightening. When she comes upon a book Hulga has been reading and in which she underlined a passage, the words "worked on Mrs Hopewell like some evil incantation in gibberish. She shut the book quickly and went out of the room as if she were having a chill."

Hulga herself uses her knowledge like a shroud to hide behind. In her own estimation,

Hulga's faith is at the crux of her problems. (alphaspirit / Shutterstock.com)

her degree and continuous study of philosophy makes her superior to the "good country people" among whom she lives. Her contempt for them is evident in nearly everything she says. Having grown up with poor eyesight, a physical disfigurement, and a weak heart, Hulga feels inferior to everyone else. The one thing she could do to boost her own sense of self-esteem was to nurture her mind and lord it over others, the people she considers simple and stupid.

Even in the hayloft scene, Hulga's smugness is evident, as she believes herself to be smarter and more worldly than the manipulative Manley Pointer. He soon rids her of that notion, and she is left in the loft helpless and empty. For all her vast and deep knowledge, she was outwitted by a country bumpkin and thus left to feel inferior once again. O'Connor uses Hulga to subtly suggest to the reader that knowledge for the sake of itself is useless, but when combined with faith, it may allow for an enriching life.

Both Mrs. Hopewell and Mrs. Freeman also contribute to the theme of knowledge. Both are simple country women, yet each believes herself to be supremely wise. Within the opening paragraph, the reader learns that Mrs. Freeman has just two expressions, forward and reverse. She never veers sideways because she so seldom needs to retract a statement. Mrs. Hopewell does not fare any better, because it seems most of her conversation is riddled with idioms like "it takes all kinds to make the world."

Both women, nonetheless, judge themselves to be of noteworthy intelligence and quick-witted. Mrs. Freeman says of herself, "I've always been quick. It's some that are quicker than others." Mrs. Hopewell's bloated self-image drives her daughter crazy as the women sit at the kitchen table exchanging idle banter. When Hulga can take it no longer, she jumps up in a rage and exclaims, "Woman! do you ever look inside? Do you ever look inside and see what you are *not*? God!" While O'Connor clearly wants the reader to question the value of too much knowledge untempered by faith, she also seems to criticize the concept of going through life without enough knowledge.

STYLE

Southern Gothic Literature

Although O'Connor preferred her work to be labeled "southern grotesque," the grotesque is actually a feature of the southern gothic subgenre. Southern gothic typically involves stories featuring deeply flawed characters, so much so that readers may find them simultaneously revolting and riveting. In the case of "Good Country People," Manley Pointer fits that description. He is a cruel sort of man, inclined to act aroused by physical deformities resulting in prostheses such as wooden legs and glass eyeballs. Masquerading as a devout Christian whose only goal is to spread the gospel, he is in reality a deceitful, despicable man. Southern gothic fiction also usually includes stereotypical figures like the falsely self-righteous, such as Mrs. Hopewell and Mrs. Freeman.

The grotesque also shows itself in the form of graphic violence or physical disfigurement, as in the case of Hulga. O'Connor's fiction tends to make the grotesque even more obvious because she often involves it in some sort of shocking twist of events. In "Good Country People," Hulga has a wooden leg. That in itself is not grotesque but merely unfortunate. What makes the scene grotesque is the seductive way in which Manley Pointer removes the artificial limb and then reattaches it, his "face and his voice . . . entirely reverent." As Hulga removes and replaces the wooden leg and then Manley follows suit, it is almost as if the two are engaged in sexual intercourse. While Hulga is imagining running away with the salesman and letting him take the leg off nightly, he is murmuring and becoming more forceful with her physically. Then he pulls out his valise, which once housed another woman's glass eye—a souvenir of a previous seduction—and now has a flask of whiskey, a deck of pornographic playing cards, and a box of condoms. It suddenly dawns on Hulga that this warped scene was something he created regularly, or at least whenever he could find a willing victim.

Irony

Most readers familiar with O'Connor's writing associate her name with irony, the technique of indicating—through plot development or character—an attitude or intention that is the exact opposite of what is actually stated or implied. "Good Country People" abounds with examples of irony. Characters' names, for instance, are ironic. Mrs. Freeman is not free at all, but a worker on a tenant farm. Nor is Mrs. Hopewell hopeful; she is distraught over her daughter's choices, behavior, and attitude. Joy is not joyful, and so she becomes Hulga. And Manley Pointer? The name Manley suggests he possesses the qualities of a man—virulent, chivalrous, virtuous—yet he is none of these.

O'Connor employs irony in her development of Hulga, upon whom she bestows a wealth of esoteric knowledge but virtually no real wisdom. She is by far the most intelligent character in the story, and yet she is the one who is the most severely manipulated and deceived. It is she who suffers and must ultimately find redemption.

Irony is also at play in the final scene with Mrs. Freeman and Mrs. Hopewell. Both women are digging up onions in the back pasture when they see Manley Pointer emerge from the woods in the direction of the highway. Mrs. Hopewell remarks that he is the "nice dull young man" who tried to sell her a Bible. "He was so simple," she says. "But I guess the world would be better off if we were all that simple." Mrs. Freeman gives her friend's comment a moment's thought and replies, "Some can't be that simple. I know I never could." However, there they are, two women who hold themselves in such high esteem, completely ignorant of what went on right under their noses.

Humor

Upon first reading "Good Country People," it is easy to miss O'Connor's dark humor. There is so much going on under the surface of this seemingly simple story, but the humor is there. O'Connor herself has been quoted as believing that the comic and the terrible may well be two sides of the same coin; to her mind, they are forever linked. The astute reader recognizes the author's humorous style in the first page of the story, as the two simple country women idly chat and gossip back and forth. So completely full of their own sense of morality and good Christian values—not to mention their belief in the superiority of their wisdom—the two cannot possibly be taken seriously by the reader.

Joy, who is much easier to relate to when thought of as the uglier-sounding Hulga because of her bleak and negative outlook on life, is treated with humor of a sarcastic nature. When she overhears her mother talking with Manley Pointer and the discussion turns to country people, who are the salt of the earth, Hulga cannot be bothered to be polite: "Get rid of the salt of the earth . . . and let's eat," she tells her mother. O'Connor again relies on a sense of the absurd when she has Manley ask Hulga if she has ever eaten a two-day-old chick. Without hesitation, Hulga answers in the affirmative. Regardless of the era or the region or the circumstances, no one is likely to eat a two-day-old chicken. It is an absurd question, and one the salesman perhaps asks solely to gauge just how full of herself Hulga is.

Manley himself is treated with humor, foreshadowing that he is not who he seems to be. When he is first invited into Mrs. Hopewell's home, he is literally jerked forward into the parlor by the weight of his valise. This is a scene of slapstick comedy. Add to that the humor found in the fact that even though Mrs. Hopewell never likes to be made to look foolish, she is tricked into inviting Manley to stay for dinner. Already one can clearly see how manipulative he is, and Mrs. Hopewell "was sorry the instant she heard herself" offer the invitation.

Even the final scene, in the hayloft, is treated with dark humor despite the seriousness of its redemptive outcome. This is the scene where irony and gothicism meet head on to tackle the themes of faith and knowledge. Manley Pointer becomes forceful physically with Hulga, and it is evident that he is somehow aroused by her disfigurement. As the scene plays out, one can imagine it visually, and there is a comic effect to it, but with a very dark kind of humor that complements O'Connor's southern gothic style.

HISTORICAL CONTEXT

The South as the Bible Belt

Even in the twenty-first century, America's southern states (and, less commonly, a handful of midwestern states) are collectively known as the Bible Belt because of the region's fervently religious inhabitants. According to Joseph M. Flora in his article in *The Companion to Southern Literature: Themes, Genre, Places, People, Movements, and Motifs*, the term was first used by journalist and social commentator H. L. Mencken in the 1920s. Mencken used the term negatively, comparing the Bible Belt to forms of discomfort and "lynching" (execution without due process of law, a common crime committed against African Americans in the South through the 1960s). It is a term still being used in the twenty-first century.

This is not to say that everyone who lives in the South is devoutly religious, but some of the more fundamentalist denominations of Christianity, such as Baptist and Pentecostal, have their roots in the South. In the South of the 1950s, church was the primary place of fellowship and community, especially in rural regions. There were no recreation centers, and schools were not nearly the social hubs they are today. To make friends or even to build business contacts, one had to belong to a congregation. In short, belonging to a church implied a person was trustworthy.

Even today, religion is a cornerstone of southern society. According to the *Insider's Guide to Memphis*, that city alone is home to an estimated five thousand houses of worship. When talking about Memphians, the guide's author, Rebecca Finlayson, writes that "their religion is such a fundamental part of their lives they have difficulty imagining someone who's not religious at all or who embraces another form of worship."

The Rise of Consumerism

Until World War II, America was largely an agrarian society. That is, the economy relied heavily on agricultural production. Rural America was the country's heartland, a label still used in the twenty-first century. The 1950s saw the rise of consumerism, and seemingly overnight, the dynamics of the economy allowed for more income and more leisure time in which to spend it. Technological advances allowed average American families to own washing machines, vacuum cleaners, and other conveniences that freed up one's time. Material possessions took on new importance as mass marketing became the rage and advertising reached new levels. What was once a want became a need, as consumers were convinced they had to have the latest and best in order to maintain their quality of life. This economic prosperity created a

COMPARE & CONTRAST

- **1950s:** According to the Lupus Foundation of America, half of all patients die within five years of a lupus diagnosis because there is no treatment available.

  Today: Ninety-five percent of lupus patients live more than ten years after their diagnosis, and the vast majority live normal life spans.

- **1950s:** Door-to-door selling has a rich history in rural America, and traveling salesmen are a common sight in the South. Nicknamed "Yankee peddlers," these men travel from town to town—selling everything from perfume to hardware to sewing supplies. This is the first form of direct marketing.

  Today: Door-to-door selling is no longer a common practice and has even been outlawed in many areas. A more acceptable form of this sort of direct selling is the home party, such as those hosted by cosmetic and kitchen-supply companies. Alternative methods of shopping such as the Internet and mail order have eclipsed door-to-door selling.

- **1950s:** Atheism (the denial of the existence of any god) is nearly synonymous in the American mind with communism. Communism is perceived as a major threat to America's social and cultural foundation. Paranoia reaches a new height when Senator Joseph McCarthy begins conducting veritable witch hunts in an effort to weed out communists living in the United States. In fact, according to Stephen Bates in a *Society* magazine article, McCarthy warns in 1950 that the "final, all-out battle" will be between "communistic atheism and Christianity." Atheism, therefore, is often viewed as responsible for much of the evil and ills of the world, right alongside communism.

  Today: Although there are more self-proclaimed atheists in America than there were in the 1950s, a 2006 poll conducted by the University of Minnesota reveals that atheists are the most distrusted of all minorities. Atheism is perceived to be associated with immorality, elitism, and criminal behavior. Interestingly, the poll also indicates that respondents with higher levels of education and those living on the east and west coasts are more tolerant and accepting of atheism. Despite progress in attaining rights for gays and lesbians, immigrants, and other minorities, atheists continue to be identified as a threat to the American way of life.

societal and cultural attitude in the more metropolitan areas that was not easily or readily accepted by those living in rural areas whose way of life was now being questioned and even threatened. This chasm helped fuel the rustic notion that people who lived outside the rural regions were not genuine or morally respectable. From a 1950s farmer's perspective, life was being turned upside down, and one was wise to trust only one's own kind.

Women and Higher Education

In the 1950s, society's attitude toward women in college was sexist: college was a great place for a girl to find a husband. According to an *American Experience* program titled "The Pill" on PBS.org, "the dominant theme promoted in the culture and media at the time was that a husband was far more important for a young woman than a college degree." Women were expected to get married right out of high school or at least during college, and if they failed to do so by their mid-twenties, they were considered old maids.

Although exact numbers and statistics on women's enrollment in college in the 1950s are difficult at best to come by, the *Digest of Education Statistics* indicates that 31.6 percent of all students enrolled in college in 1950 were women.

Hulga is abandoned in the hayloft. (Losevsky Pavel / Shutterstock.com)

Compare that with 57.2 percent in 2007. Experts noticed the upward trend in the 1990s, and it has not changed through the first decade of the twenty-first century. A 2010 *USA Today* article written by Scott Jaschik announced that for the first time in history, more women than men (50.4 percent) earned doctoral degrees in the 2008–2009 school year.

CRITICAL OVERVIEW

"Good Country People" was originally published as one of a collection of short stories in 1955. Although criticism about specific aspects of the story has been written, most of the criticism of O'Connor's work is focused on her output as a whole rather than on individual stories or novels. This is the case because O'Connor was a specific type of writer. She did not write with varying styles and on different topics but rather infused the same techniques and themes into everything she wrote. The surprise was not in what she was going to write about but in how she would present it.

Indeed, the author considered it her duty to shock readers. In his critical essay "Grace and the Grotesque: Flannery O'Connor on the Page and on the Screen," writer Jon M. Sweeney quotes O'Connor as remarking,

> When you can assume that your audience holds the same beliefs you do, you can relax a little and use more normal ways of talking to it; when you have to assume that it does not, then you have to make your vision apparent by shock—to the hard of hearing you shout, and for the almost blind you draw large and startling figures.

Often compared to such great writers as Nathaniel Hawthorne and Fyodor Dostoevsky, O'Connor possessed a unique voice and remarkable talent with which to present it. She was a Catholic writer whose worldview was developed through a fervent religious doctrine, one that, it seems, was not always understood, much less appreciated, by critics (hence, her need to make her vision apparent via shock). However, her story collection *A Good Man Is Hard to Find* was published to much acclaim. It was this collection that cemented her reputation as a southern gothic writer, although the author herself preferred the term 'southern grotesque."

Her stories rarely revolve around likable characters, and each is almost without exception what O'Connor, quoted by Brad Gooch in a *New York Times* article, called a "freak," either physically or emotionally, sometimes both. Despite the author's fervent Catholicism, the majority of her characters are Protestant, and the American South she depicts in her fiction is much more than local color. Her respect for the mystery of life, rooted in her religious beliefs, informed everything she ever wrote. "The writer's gaze has to extend beyond the surface, beyond mere problems until it touches that realm of mystery that is the concern of prophets," O'Connor once said, as quoted in a 1966 essay that originally appeared in *Atlanta* magazine.

It has been widely speculated that much of what is explored and revealed in "Good Country People" is a reflection of O'Connor's own life. The story's main female character, Hulga, is disfigured and in ill health, much like O'Connor was for most of her adult life. Hulga has a brief yet torrid affair with a traveling Bible salesman, and the author herself experienced a similar relationship with a traveling textbook salesman named Erik Langkjaer.

In letters to friends and Langkjaer himself, which are made available by Sally Fitzgerald in her book *The Habit of Being: Letters of Flannery O'Connor* and are explored by Mark Bosco in the *Southern Review*, it becomes apparent that there are indeed similarities between O'Connor's fictional plot and her actual life experience. Those letters, especially the ones written to Langkjaer, reveal a more passionate and emotional O'Connor than one might imagine from her fictional writing. When Langkjaer returned to his native Denmark in 1954 because he felt he did not fit into American society, O'Connor became lonesome and wrote to him:

> You wonder how anybody can be happy in his home as long as there is one person without one. I never thought of this so much until I began to know you and your situation and I will never quite have a home again on account of it.

To that letter she added a postscript: "I feel like if you were here we could talk about a million years without stopping."

Whatever the influence, "Good Country People" exemplified O'Connor's writing at its finest, and it was part of the 1971 posthumously published collection that won the National Book Award for Fiction in 1972.

CRITICISM

Rebecca Valentine

Valentine is an award-winning writer specializing in literature and history. In the following essay, she examines the role of nonverbal traits in understanding the depth of characters in Flannery O'Connor's "Good Country People."

Much has been written about Flannery O'Connor's literary style. Her name is associated with irony and the southern gothic subgenre, and critics have had a wonderful time dissecting her literary body from a religious—Catholic—perspective. She is famous for her exploration of a handful of themes, which she returns to repeatedly, somehow without repeating herself. Loyal O'Connor fans glory in the idea that the author develops characters with deep and penetrating flaws. Beautiful people have no place in the O'Connor canon. Because there is so much of the obvious to praise and admire in her writing, O'Connor's deft usage of nonverbal traits in her character development is often overshadowed, yet it is the very thing that gives her extraordinary characters believability.

O'Connor recognized the importance of nonverbal traits and clues in good literature. One of her most oft-cited quotes refers to her attitude toward her reading audience. If it could not be assumed that the audience was in agreement with the writers' personal perspective, it was essential to draw them in by making things clear. In her essay "The Fiction Writer and His Country," published in the 1969 collection *Mystery and Manners* and referred to by Stephen R. Portch in his book *Literature's Silent Language: Nonverbal Communication*, O'Connor states, "To the hard of hearing you shout, and for the almost blind you draw large and startling figures."

To do this effectively, O'Connor understood there have to be both obvious and subtle clues to understanding characters, at least the memorable, three-dimensional characters. Some of her stock characters, such as Mrs. Freeman and Mrs. Hopewell, could be fully understood through their dialogue alone. Shallow and superficial, there is no deeper meaning or life of the mind for these characters, and so they did not need further treatment. The personalities they embody as the story opens

WHAT DO I READ NEXT?

- O'Connor's first novel, *Wise Blood* (1952), is a dark comedy, a satire of America's secular (nonreligious) culture and values. With its graphic violence and unlikable characters, the novel shocked many readers of the era. Its serious religious overtones may prove challenging for the average reader to wade through to find the true meaning of the message behind the madness.
- Zora Neale Hurston wrote southern fiction of a different flavor, and in 1937 she gave the world *Their Eyes Were Watching God,* a novel set in Florida with main characters who are primarily African American. The novel was controversial in its day because it did not depict these characters in relation to white characters, though neither did the author ignore race relations. Instead, she gave her characters a home and dared to give them lives of their own.
- Kate Chopin was a southern writer who preceded O'Connor. Chopin's stories, of which "The Awakening" is the most widely known and anthologized, were scandalous in part because of their overt sexuality. Published beginning in 1899, Chopin was a woman writer ahead of her time. *The Awakening, and Selected Stories of Kate Chopin* was republished in 2004 in a volume that includes contemporary criticism of these classic texts.
- Patricia Yeager's 2000 book *Dirt and Desire: Reconstructing Southern Women's Writing, 1930–1990* reinterprets classical texts written by southern women to reveal that, regardless of race, southern women were preoccupied with the grotesque, gender politics, and the world of physical labor. The writers included span from O'Connor to Eudora Welty to Harper Lee to Zora Neale Hurston, with several more in between.
- Historian James C. Cobb's treatise on southern identity charts the tumultuous waters of American southern culture. *Away Down South: A History of Southern Identity* (2007) provides insight as to how southerners see themselves and their region. This volume would be valuable to both the student and the casual reader.
- *To Kill a Mockingbird* was published in 1960 to the highest praises, and author Harper Lee never published another novel. Set in Georgia, the story challenges notions of race, family, and common decency as it portrays a South where justice is not always served. This novel remains one of the most widely read books in high schools across America.

---

will remain unchanged throughout; their fate includes no evolution or epiphany. They come to us as mindless supporting characters, and we leave them mumbling in the onion field, oblivious to their own blinding personal limitations.

O'Connor herself valued the nonverbal. Portch points out that in one of her *Mystery and Manners* essays, the writer criticizes stories lacking in nonverbal traits: "Characters have no distinctive speech to reveal themselves with; and sometimes they have no really distinctive features." O'Connor took to heart the idea that characters needed distinctive features, and she gave the readers as much in "Good Country People" via Hulga and Manley Pointer. To be certain, both characters reveal themselves through their dialogue, but O'Connor so subtly crafted their nonverbal traits that one must almost read the story specifically in search of them to appreciate both their abundance and their effectiveness.

O'Connor's skill with this kind of nonverbal characterization is exemplified by Hulga. Her speech reveals her to be sarcastic, quick-witted, educated. Unlike the other characters in the story, Hulga uses correct grammar and is obviously well educated. Based solely on these observations, a reader might judge her to be worldly

"BECAUSE THERE IS SO MUCH OF THE OBVIOUS TO PRAISE AND ADMIRE IN HER WRITING, O'CONNOR'S DEFT USAGE OF NONVERBAL TRAITS IN HER CHARACTER DEVELOPMENT IS OFTEN OVERSHADOWED, YET IT IS THE VERY THING THAT GIVES HER EXTRAORDINARY CHARACTERS BELIEVABILITY."

and confident, but her nonverbal traits provide clues as to the true personality of Hulga.

When first we meet Hulga, we are told that she has learned to "tolerate Mrs. Freeman" and that she finds the sisters Glynese and Carramae "useful" when they are able to keep her mother's attention occupied and thus not focused on Hulga. When Mrs. Freeman dares to call Hulga by her legal name rather than her given name of Joy, Hulga "scowl[s]" and her face "redden[s]" with contempt. Each of these cues tells the reader that Hulga values other people only in the way that they can serve her. She is quick to anger whenever she feels her personal space has been invaded.

O'Connor lets us know that Hulga needs to feel superior to others even if those others are unaware of her elevated intelligence. Hulga considers her choice of ugly name as her "highest creative act," and "one of her major triumphs" is that her choice has kept her mother from finding any satisfaction or fulfillment in the fact that she had named her only daughter "Joy." Hulga's "greater" triumph, however, was that she was actually able to transform herself—her looks, attitude, outlook, behavior, and mannerisms—into "Hulga."

Every morning, Hulga "stumped" into the kitchen, even though she was perfectly capable of walking without making noise. What victory would there be in that, when she could start her mother's day with an "ugly-sounding" gait and thus remind her that though a new day had dawned, there was no hope in it? Mrs. Hopewell saw in her daughter the sad reality that every day, she grew more and more to fit her chosen name. She was "bloated, rude, and squint-eyed," characteristics of someone for whom the world holds no happiness.

When Manley Pointer enters the story and sits at the table with Hulga and Mrs. Hopewell, Hulga expresses her disinterest not with words but by glancing at him upon introduction and then pointedly ignoring him for the rest of the meal. When he addresses her, she pretends not to hear him, and when dinner is over, she further spurns him by clearing the table and leaving altogether. When finally the two do converse, Hulga looks at him "stonily." She answers his questions in a "flat voice" and stands "blank and solid and silent." Whether or not she is speaking to Manley, she makes it absolutely clear that she is barely allowing him to be in her presence.

Later, as she lies in bed fantasizing about seducing the salesman, she considers herself in possession of "true genius" so powerful that it can communicate even with Manley's "inferior mind." Hulga thinks so highly of herself that she believes she can actually transform Manley's expected remorse at having surrendered to her intoxicating sexuality "into a deeper understanding of life." She imagines she can erase his shame and give it back as "something useful." This entire scene is verbally silent, yet it screams of Hulga's grandiose self-image and bloated sense of power and influence.

Hulga's slovenliness is illuminated when she chooses to wear a dirty white shirt to her picnic with Manley. "As an afterthought," she rubs Vapex on the collar of the shirt in lieu of applying perfume. Vapex was the 1950s version of Vicks VapoRub and emitted a strong eucalyptus smell associated with illness. These are not the choices of a woman who takes pride in her appearance or who deems herself worthy of even the most basic steps of hygiene. For all of Hulga's caustic verbal emphasis on her superiority over others, her silent behaviors speak much more loudly as to how she truly views herself.

As things heat up between Manley and Hulga and they share a kiss, her reaction is one of "amusement" and "pity." Whereas a woman's first kiss is commonly believed to be a milestone event, Hulga was "pleased to discover that it was an unexceptional experience and all a matter of the mind's control." So guarded and cerebral is our heroine that she is completely unable to experience true connection with another human being. While the two are embracing in the hayloft and Hulga begins to return Manley's kisses,

A Georgia chicken farm *(Paul Brennan / Shutterstock.com)*

her mind "never stopped or lost itself for a second to her feelings." Rather than lament this fact, Hulga holds onto it like a child clings to his security blanket. It comforts and soothes her.

Hulga is "as sensitive [of her leg] as a peacock about his tail." She cares for it "as someone else would his soul." This tells the reader that Hulga has projected onto that wooden leg every last ounce of her self-identity. It has become for her, symbolically, her soul, her faith, her *self*. When Manley steals it from her and leaves her prostrate on the hayloft floor, he in essence destroys the Hulga that Joy gave herself to all those years ago. It is up to Hulga to decide what to do from there—whether to let the maudlin event define her or to seek in it a sense of redemption and a chance to begin anew.

O'Connor suffused Manley Pointer, the story's other main character, with similar telltale nonverbal traits. Before he even utters a single word, we know that Manley is a "gaunt hatless youth," which is to say he is poor and underfed. He has to brace himself against the weight of his Bible-filled valise, and though cheerful of voice, he seems "on the point of collapse." Although not ugly, he is dressed in bright blue and yellow, a color combination that invokes amusement more than respect. Surely this is not a man of whom to be suspicious, but one who is unassuming and perhaps even simple.

O'Connor describes Manley alternately as "sparkling," "pleasant," "jerking," and "earnest" as he enters Mrs. Hopewell's parlor. When he wants to convince her to buy a Bible, Manley "twists his hands" and speaks "softly." He makes all the right moves, displays all the necessary convincing mannerisms to manipulate Mrs. Hopewell. Even if he had never spoken, she would have judged him to be nothing more than good country people.

When Manley first meets up with Hulga on the road outside the Hopewell house, he gazes at her with a curious fascination, "like a child watching a new fantastic animal at the zoo." He giggles nervously and feels triumphant when he manages to engage her in conversation. Hulga notices how his face reddens with embarrassment and how his gaze becomes one of admiration, while "his smiles came in succession like waves breaking on the surface of a little lake." Manley has his moves down pat. By the end of the story, we know he has done this before, and he is incredibly suave in how he communicates with Hulga not through words but with body language and mannerisms.

These early nonverbal traits of his are in direct contrast with those he exhibits in the hayloft, once he has tricked Hulga. What was just moments earlier a look of admiration becomes a look that was "irritated but dogged." As he rolls up Hulga's pant leg to reveal the wooden prosthesis, his face and voice are "reverent," and as he removes and attaches the leg himself, he takes on a "delighted child's face." But once Manley has successfully relieved Hulga of her leg and claimed it as his own prize, he takes on a "lofty indignant tone." He "slam[s] the lid shut and snatche[s] up the valise." The last image—blurry though it must be without her glasses—Hulga has of her pseudo-lover is one of "his blue figure struggling successfully" away from her. Manley is the victor, and Hulga is the victim.

Flannery O'Connor was considered by many critics to be the master of the short story of her generation. It is the hallmark of someone who does her job well that it is made to look easy. Only upon close reading of "Good Country People" are we made fully aware of just how subtly O'Connor crafted and breathed life into her characters, not only through obvious dialogue but in simply making them all too human.

Source: Rebecca Valentine, Critical Essay on "Good Country People," in *Short Stories for Students*, Gale, Cengage Learning, 2012.

Rachel Pietka

In the following essay, Pietka analyzes how O'Connor illustrates both nihilism and humanism in the characters of "Good Country People."

Mrs. Hopewell and Hulga, the bickering mother and daughter in Flannery O'Connor's "Good Country People," are united by their interest in the legendary category of people for which the story is named. Mrs. Hopewell tells a Bible salesman that "good country people are the salt of the earth!" and Hulga responds to this sentiment with "Get rid of the salt of the earth" (*A Good Man is Hard to Find and Other Stories* [Orlando: Harcourt, 1955]). While the simplicity of good country people keeps Mrs. Hopewell optimistic about the world, Hulga, the nihilist, bases her identity on her self-aggrandized superiority to them. However, when she finds herself deceived by Manley in the dramatic role reversal of her final scene, she learns, traumatically, that belief in good country people is an illusion, as is nihilism. Manley shatters both Mrs. Hopewell's and Hulga's belief systems, and by doing so he becomes a vehicle of grace through which Hulga is prepared for salvation.

While O'Connor responds emphatically to the destructiveness of nihilism through Manley's humiliation of Hulga, the humanist beliefs that Mrs. Hopewell demonstrates are disputed in a more subtle manner. Mrs. Hopewell's religion is an ambiguous moral code that she feels good country people abide by. She says "people who looked on the bright side of things would be beautiful even if they were not" and she lives by her sayings, "Nothing is perfect," "that is life!" and "well, other people have their opinions too." What ultimately exposes Mrs. Hopewell's profane belief in the goodness of humanity is her statement that equates good country people to "the salt of the earth," a biblical reference to early followers of Christ. Commentator Donald A. Hagner writes that the metaphor refers to "something that is vitally important to the world in the religious sense" (Matthew 1–13 [Dallas: World Books, 1993]: 99). Mrs. Hopewell's usage of this phrase maintains that good country people are indispensable, though her need of them is not based on a religious deficiency, but a desire for morality. Her lack of interest in the specifics of Christianity is revealed in the same scene, as the narrator tells us that Mrs. Hopewell lies to Manley when she tells him her Bible is beside her bed: "It was not the truth. It was in the attic somewhere."

Hulga, however, is the only character "privileged" by enlightenment, which occurs as a result of her victimization at the hands of Manley. Her experience with him in the barn opens her to redemption, for O'Connor points Hulga to God and away from nihilism by causing her to experience a kind of conversion with the ideals bound to betray her. Though she had determined to maintain her superiority over Manley, she promptly forgets about her nihilistic beliefs and is captivated by the illusion of intimacy she experiences with him. She makes herself completely vulnerable to Manley by allowing him to see her wooden leg, the most private part of her: "No one ever touched it but her. She took care of it as someone else would his soul." When she concedes to let him take it on and off, the language recalls a typical Christian conversion experience. She feels that Manley "had touched the truth about her" and when she gives him permission, "it was like surrendering to him completely. It was like losing her own life and finding it again, miraculously, in his." She has the correct experience with the wrong entity, as is made clear in the exchange between Manley and Mrs. Hopewell when he echoes the words of Jesus: "whosoever will lose his life for my sake shall find it" (Mt. 16:25 KJV). Having already discarded nihilism in order to fall in love with Manley, Hulga retreats to the safety of good country people when his guile becomes evident. But this belief that Hulga appeals to is also shattered. When Manley leaves Hulga speechless in the barn, she is in a fractured state, which is absolutely necessary in order for her to be prepared for a "true" conversion that she should find in God.

It is significant that Mrs. Hopewell, for all the scrutiny of her beliefs, is not brought to a moment of redemption as Hulga is. The values she taught Hulga are challenged in this story, though she remains oblivious while Hulga is confronted with their falsity. The story is framed by the presence of Mrs. Freeman, the original example of a good country person. Though Mrs. Hopewell accepts Mrs. Freeman's flaws, such as her officiousness, her belief is grounded in an innate sense of morality that accounts for her trust in Manley and others she considers to be like him. This perspective contradicts the doctrine of original sin, which Hulga learns as she stammers, "Aren't you [. . .] aren't you just good country people?" in her final scene.

Country people may exist, but not as Mrs. Hopewell believes. Manley's perfidy speaks to the hollowness of belief in the goodness of humanity and so the ending lines reinforce the idea of original sin as Mrs. Freeman admits her own inability to be good: "Some can't be that simple [. . .]! I know I never could." These lines are nevertheless ironic, as O'Connor intimates the complicated task of challenging this belief system. Though Mrs. Hopewell and Mrs. Freeman are aware of their own shortcomings, they both watch Manley leave the woods and admire his simplicity directly after he has violated Hulga. The nihilist in disguise as good country people acts as the unlikely catalyst for Hulga's enlightenment, but Mrs. Hopewell and

THAT O'CONNOR DID IN FACT INTENTIONALLY WITHHOLD THE STORY FROM HIM—WHILE SHE HAD SENT NUMEROUS OTHERS FOR HIM TO READ—POINTS TO HER PERHAPS UNEASY AWARENESS OF THE EXTENT TO WHICH IT WAS ROOTED IN HER FEELINGS FOR HIM."

Mrs. Freeman are left in the dark. At the end of this story, the belief in nihilism has been eliminated, though Mrs. Hopewell's brand of humanism remains. "Good Country People" therefore closes with two unfortunately deceived women whose situation proclaims the perpetual infection of the world with false ideals.

Source: Rachel Pietka, "'Good Country People' Unmasked: Hulga's Journey to Salvation," in *Notes on Contemporary Literature*, Vol. 39, No. 4, September 2009, p. 2.

Mark Bosco

In the following excerpt, Bosco draws autobiographical parallels between O'Connor and the character of Hulga in "Good Country People," based on the suggestion that the character Manley Pointer represents Erik Langkjaer, a man O'Connor dated prior to writing the story.

> What would you make out about me just from reading "Good Country People"? Plenty, but not the whole story.
>
> —Flannery O'Connor, *The Habit of Being*

The year 2004 marked the fortieth anniversary of Flannery O'Connor's death from kidney failure brought on from her years of fighting the effects of lupus, in midcentury a debilitating disease and difficult to survive. The intervening time since her death has seen an explosion of critical and popular enthusiasm for her work, so much so that in 1988 she achieved canonical status in American arts and letters with the publication of her *Collected Works* by the Library of America. In the fall of 2003 an international symposium, the fifth of its kind, was held in O'Connor's hometown of Milledgeville, Georgia. It brought together over two hundred scholars and enthusiasts, including novelists, poets, and other artists who have acknowledged O'Connor's influence on their work.

Readers have been fascinated by this very private woman's stories, as well as by her life. Much of what is known about O'Connor's personal life is revealed in Sally Fitzgerald's award-winning edition of the writer's letters to friends and admirers, *The Habit of Being* (1979). These letters reveal the intelligence, wit, and religious sensibility of a writer proud of both her southern heritage and her Roman Catholic faith. Arranged chronologically, the letters give a sense of O'Connor's personal development as an artist and offer insight into her personality. What they do not provide, however, is an account of romantic interest in her life. Many critics have assumed that her physical condition, compromised after the onset of lupus in her twenties, precluded her forming—even hoping to form—deep attachments with men.

"Good Country People" (1955), one of O'Connor's most successful and most anthologized stories, centers on the maimed Joy Hopewell, fitted with a wooden leg as the result of a childhood accident. She has officially changed her name to Hulga to reflect the ugliness she feels about life and to spite her mother. Hulga, who has a doctorate in philosophy and displays a disdain for her mother's southern, Christian manners, lives as an aloof recluse on the family farm. One day she has an encounter with a disarming Bible salesman named Manley Pointer, a rustic Lothario who is attracted to this lonely intellectual, in part because he senses an unspoken kinship between her exotic beliefs and his own charlatanism. Surprised by Hulga's declaration of her atheism, he reckons that she is a woman who has thrown off the Bible-belt conventions of the South. They share a brief kiss on a walk in the country, a walk that ends in a secluded loft in a barn. Once there, Manley Pointer continues his amorous maneuvers and seems chagrined when Hulga resists. He asks her to take off her artificial leg to prove that she loves him, and she guardedly agrees. But when Hulga quickly discovers that Manley professed a naïve Christian faith just to get his way with her, he malevolently grabs her wooden leg, stuffs it into his suitcase, and leaves her stranded in the loft. With a sense of brutal revelation, she watches from the window the charlatan's "blue figure struggling successfully over the green speckled lake."

How art mediates life is a question of general interest in postmodern culture, and "Good Country People" has often made O'Connor fans wonder whether there is any connection between the author's own life and the creation of this story. Parallels abound between O'Connor's history and Hulga's: O'Connor was incapacitated by lupus, which forced her to leave the intellectual and cultural reaches of New York City and return to the South; there she was cared for by her mother on their family farm. A close reading of O'Connor's collected letters reveals in the writer's personality a bit of Hulga's ornery side. O'Connor comes through as a very complex woman who, with great intelligence, is aware of her own vices and virtues. Given these connections between O'Connor and Hulga, it's reasonable to wonder if someone in O'Connor's life served as the basis for the character of Manley Pointer in "Good Country People."

Several letters in *The Habit of Being* provide hints of O'Connor's emotional involvement with at least one man in her life. The most striking is her assertion in 1955 to Elizabeth Hester (known simply as "A" in the published correspondence) that she "used to go with" the nephew of Helene Iswolsky, a Dane named Erik Langkjaer. Another strong statement about experience with love is found in another letter to Hester dated August 24, 1956, and concerns the motivation for "Good Country People." O'Connor's letter responded to Hester's declaration that the character of Joy/Hulga seems very autobiographical, as if there were indeed an ugly, "Hulga" part of the author exposed in the story. O'Connor was most insistent in her response:

> Where do you get the idea that Hulga's need to worship comes to flower in "GCP" ["Good Country People"]? Or that she never had any faith at any time, or never loved anybody before?... Nothing comes to flower here except her realization in the end that she ain't so smart. It's not said that she had never had any faith, but it is implied that her fine education has got rid of it for her, that purity has been overridden by pride of intellect through her fine education. Further, it's not said that she has never loved anybody, only that she's never been kissed by anybody, a very different thing. And of course I've thrown you off myself by informing you that Hulga is like me... but you cannot read a story from what you get from a letter.... That my stories scream to you that I have never consented to be in love with anyone is merely to prove that they are screaming an historical inaccuracy. I have God help me consented to this frequently.

With all due respect to O'Connor's own caveat against "reading a story from what you get from a letter," O'Connor's unpublished correspondence with Erik Langkjaer shows that the creation of "Good Country People" follows on the heels of her last, powerful experience of romance. Her letters, in particular, reveal that this unrequited love was a likely source of inspiration for this story.

What is already known publicly of Erik Langkjaer in connection with Flannery O'Connor was derived first from four obscure references in *The Habit of Being*. Additionally, O'Connor's biographers, Sally Fitzgerald and more recently Jean Cash, have brought to light further information about the relationship. Langkjaer worked as a college textbook salesman for Harcourt, Brace and traveled throughout the South during the 1952–1954 academic school terms. Danish on his father's side and Russian on his mother's, Langkjaer had graduated from Princeton and finished two years of graduate studies in philosophy at Fordham University before he decided to begin a career in publishing. Cash quotes Helen Greene, O'Connor's former history professor at Georgia College in Milledgeville, who is said to have introduced Mr. Langkjaer to O'Connor: "Flannery took him all over the county. I think she really liked him a lot... [but] he wasn't Roman Catholic." He visited her frequently, driving one hundred miles or so out of his way on weekends in order to spend time with O'Connor at Andalusia, the family's farm. To her consternation, however, he decided to return to Denmark, and in the course of the next year she began corresponding with him. In April 1955 he wrote O'Connor announcing his engagement to a Danish woman. Though it was a painful revelation for O'Connor, she continued corresponding with him. Her last letter to him is dated February 26, 1958.

In a 1997 article in the *Georgia Review*, Sally Fitzgerald focused on the significance of this friendship in the development of O'Connor's vocation as a writer. She mentions the importance of the Langkjaer relationship to O'Connor's emotional life, "the last, and most seriously painful, instance in which the old pattern of unrequited love was to reappear." Having located Langkjaer in Denmark, Fitzgerald interviewed him for her biography of O'Connor; Langkjaer, in turn, shared with her the twelve letters that O'Connor had sent him after he departed from the South. Fitzgerald noted a qualitative difference in these letters, which reveal a depth of feeling seen nowhere else in O'Connor's correspondence. She quotes a handwritten postscript in one such letter to Langkjaer as indicative of O'Connor's feelings for the young Dane: "I think that if you were here, we could talk for about a million years." The poignancy of this revelation lies in its timing, for her letter to Langkjaer was sent shortly before the arrival of his own letter to her announcing his engagement to marry. O'Connor, Fitzgerald notes, instantly withdrew into her customary reserve, and the letters sent to Langkjaer thenceforward were warm but very correct in their southern manners.

..."Good Country People" was written by O'Connor while the fateful letters were still in transit, and she quickly had it added to her forthcoming volume of stories, *A Good Man Is Hard to Find* (1955). On February 26, 1955, a few months before the book was published, O'Connor wrote to her editor, Robert Giroux: "I have just written a story called 'Good Country People' that Allen [Tate] and Caroline [Gordon] both say is the best thing I have written and should be in this collection." She also informed Sally and Robert Fitzgerald on April 1, "I wrote a very hot story at the last minute called 'Good Country People.'" And she told Elizabeth Hester a year later, "I wrote 'GCP' in about four days, the shortest I have ever written anything in, just sat down and wrote it."

Just how "hot" this story was in the aftermath of her bitter disappointment with Langkjaer is evident in the many significant parallels between the O'Connor-Langkjaer relationship, on one hand, and the imaginative portrayal of Joy/Hulga Hopewell and Manley Pointer, on the other. Though Langkjaer admits that the tone of the story strays far from that of his relationship with O'Connor, there is a level of correspondence that suggests that O'Connor may have drawn on her own recent experience in imagining this story. Like Manley Pointer, Langkjaer was at that time a traveling salesman, in his own way a "displaced" person with no fixed abode. In the story, Manley tells Mrs. Hopewell that he is from "out in the country around Willohobie, not even from a place, just from near a place." And in the O'Hare interview Langkjaer discloses that O'Connor had often thought of him in the same terms: "she felt that I was very much like a displaced person, a displaced person as a character in one of her short stories, that I was the child of divorced parents, that I had come to the U.S., that I was now traveling somewhat rootlessly in the South, and that I had all these religious concerns and problems."

More interestingly, Langkjaer carried around what he called his "bible," a term that Harcourt, Brace used to describe the folder containing the tables of contents that would be presented to professors whom he visited throughout the South. On his sojourns to the O'Connor farm the two of them would often joke about his being a Bible salesman. Langkjaer remarks, "It amused her very much that something that was not a bible should have been called a bible." Manley Pointer's "profession" is a clear instance of O'Connor's creatively deploying a memory, though turning it to a darkly ironic use. Manley's "bible" is definitely something else: merely a covered box containing his pornographic playing cards, flask of whiskey, and his blue box of condoms.

A final obvious comparison between O'Connor's experience with Langkjaer and Hulga's with the Bible salesman that can be drawn concerns the manner by which each was courted and then suddenly dropped: just as Langkjaer initiated the car outings with O'Connor in order to spend some time out from under the watchful eye of Mrs. O'Connor, so Manley takes the same initiative in the story, inviting Joy/Hulga to take a picnic with him the following day. And with similar suddenness, Langkjaer departs from O'Connor's life quite dramatically across the ocean for Denmark, while Manley is seen departing "over the green speckled lake."

Yet by far the most striking revelation of O'Connor's artistic use of her own recent experience comes during the moment in the story when Manley Pointer kisses Joy/Hulga at the edge of the wood. O'Connor describes Hulga's reaction in a famous passage from the story:

> The kiss, which had more pressure than feeling behind it, produced that extra surge of adrenalin in the girl that enables one to carry a packed trunk out of a burning house, but in her, the power went at once to her brain. Even before he released her, her mind, clear and detached and ironic anyway, was regarding him from a great distance, with amusement but with pity. She had never been kissed before and she was pleased to discover that it was an unexceptional experience and all a matter of the mind's control. Some people might enjoy drain water if they were told it was vodka. When the boy, looking expectant but uncertain, pushed her gently away, she turned and walked on, saying nothing as if such business, for her, were common enough.

It is a brilliant piece of descriptive writing that has the feel of genuine experience, revealing a complex and clumsy reaction to a kiss.

Though O'Connor the artist was quick to deny an autobiographical basis for the kissing scene in her letter to Elizabeth Hester, it is fair to question if this kiss represents anything other than O'Connor's own experience. For his part, Langkjaer provides a frankly detailed and deeply moving account of a similar kiss with O'Connor. It occurred on his last visit to Andalusia, fifty years ago, not long before his decision to leave for Denmark. Langkjaer recalls that he had invited O'Connor for a ride in the countryside and she accepted. He describes what ensued as if it took place yesterday.

> As we drove along I parked the car and I may not have been in love, but I was very much aware that she was a woman, and so I felt that I'd like to kiss her, which I did, and I mean it wasn't as if I caught her by surprise. She had been surprised that I suggested the kiss, but she was certainly prepared to accept it. Now as it happened, as our lips touched I had a feeling that her mouth lacked a resilience, it was as if she had no real muscle tension in her mouth, a result being that my own lips touched her teeth rather than her lips, and this I must admit gave me an unhappy feeling of a sort of *memento mori*, and so the kissing stopped. And shortly after that two people turned up from a parked car nearby, poked their heads in as, you know, probably someone is apt to do to find out what's going on in another parked car where they see a man and a woman, and I don't know that there was much of an exchange of any sort, but they withdrew hastily, and Flannery found this rather enjoyable.... I was not by any means a Don Juan, but in my late twenties I had of course kissed other girls, and there had been this firm response, which was totally lacking in Flannery. So it's true that I had a feeling of kissing a skeleton, and in that sense it was a shocking, a shocking experience, and it was something that reminded me of her being gravely ill.

Langkjaer is uncertain whether O'Connor realized that the kiss had not been a success, but his memory of it stresses how the reality of her illness overwhelmed his own attraction to her in that moment.

But it is O'Connor's experience that is artistically reworked in the story. The supposedly detached and ironic Hulga, whose "mind... never stopped or lost itself for a second to her feelings," is at the same time passionately kissing Manley "as if she were trying to draw all the breath out of him." She is enraptured by the moment—certainly filled with more "Joy" than "Hulga" for the first time in the story. It moves her to surrender her wooden limb to this amorous imposter. It is fair to wonder if such a rush of adrenaline was part of O'Connor's feelings for Langkjaer, and if the car rides, and this fateful kiss, were calculated risks that she too was taking. Joy/Hulga's illusion of herself as a seducing nihilist is undercut by Manley's deception and flight from her; so, too, is O'Connor's illusion of romance shaken by Langkjaer's departure for Denmark.

Langkjaer himself provides evidence to corroborate how closely drawn Joy/Hulga is to O'Connor. If he was not completely sure at the time that O'Connor had fallen in love with him, he nonetheless sensed the strong feelings she had for him and knew that they shared intimate conversations. Langkjaer reads the following line from Hulga's point of view as a very personal declaration by O'Connor about her feelings for him: "This boy, with an instinct that came from beyond wisdom, had touched the truth about her.... It was like surrendering to him completely. It was like losing her own life and finding it again, miraculously, in his." Hulga surrenders the emotionally cautious, reticent, perhaps "wooden" part of her that was so essential to her sense of identity, and in its place discovers in her feelings for him the "Joy" part of herself, a more complex and emotionally engaged person. Langkjaer sees O'Connor in the same light: proud of her intellectual and artistic sense of herself, but cautiously willing to surrender her emotions and cede to a passionate moment. O'Connor's letters to Langkjaer illustrate this same kind of emotional yielding; despite the young Dane's absence, they make it painfully clear how much hope O'Connor had placed in his return to her and the South.

Though it would be wrong to argue from the evidence that "Good Country People" is simply autobiography, writing the story clearly served as a creative channel for O'Connor to come to terms with these decisive movements in her inner life. But if one reads the trajectory of the story as an imaginative literary negotiation of the real-life association, then one has to contend with the imperfect congruence between Manley Pointer's spiteful final act toward Hulga and O'Connor's presumed judgment of her last rendezvous with Langkjaer. The story presents such disappointment as a devilish betrayal. When Hulga is first asked to show the Bible salesman her wooden leg, she utters a sharp cry because "no one ever touched it but her. She took care of it as someone else would his soul, in private and almost with her own eyes turned away." Yet, she does allow him to take off the leg, and in consequence, she feels exposed. As Manley places it out of her reach and kisses her again, Hulga vacillates between a romantic vision of running away with him and the acute fear of her now defenseless state. The story hinges on whether Manley will accept the leg with the right intention, the one that Joy/Hulga deeply hopes for and desires. Only after he divulges the tawdry items from his valise is it clear that her leg is to be yet another one of his sexual trophies, like the glass eye of a previous conquest about whom he boasts.

Langkjaer himself wonders whether O'Connor actually thought of herself as a trophy, another feather in a young man's cap. In the interview he ponders:

> Flannery may have felt that I was, that she was, in a sense, another trophy, or to put it maybe even more starkly, a kind of another scalp. Of course this wasn't at all the way that I saw the relationship. But in the story he gets the leg from the Hulga part of Joy and she feels that in surrendering this leg voluntarily that in the end she has really given herself completely to the Bible salesman.... Nonetheless, she must have felt this, she must have felt not that I took advantage of her, but that in some sense, in some ultimate sense she was not being treated any differently than the girls I had met previously.

Langkjaer claims that the depth of her feeling for him—and the degree of exposure she felt—was not at all clear to him at that time because she was such a reticent person. Many years after her death, Langkjaer remembers being startled on first reading in *The Habit of Being* O'Connor's claim to Betty Hester that she had "gone with" him: "I must say, to my own surprise I read that she felt that she had gone steady with me, that she felt that strongly about our relationship." He then began rereading O'Connor's twenty-five-year-old letters in this new light, and it became clear to him that when O'Connor started writing him shortly after his return to Denmark, she had, in effect, given herself to him:

> I did recognize of course the fact that she wanted to see me and she encouraged me to visit her as often as possible, the fact that she wanted to go on these rides, the fact that she surrendered herself sufficiently enough to allow me to kiss her. I realized of course that she had become very fond of me, else she

> wouldn't have done that otherwise, especially as she was "a good Catholic"; but still I didn't realize at the time how much it all meant to her, and I only discovered this through the subsequent correspondence.

Upon reading "Good Country People" after it was published in *A Good Man Is Hard to Find*, Langkjaer wrote O'Connor a letter, offering his own assessment of the story and the perceptible autobiographical references in it, asking specifically if she identified her Bible salesman with him. He expressed shock that she might have perceived his actions as deceptive in the way Manley Pointer is deceptive with Hulga. O'Connor's eighth letter to him is her reply, both an admonishment and a word of assurance:

> April 29, 1956
>
> I am highly taken with the thought of your seeing yourself as the Bible salesman. Dear boy, remove this delusion from your head at once. And if you think the story is also my spiritual autobiography, remove that one too. As a matter of fact, I wrote that one not too long after your departure and wanted to send you a copy but decided that the better part of tact would be to desist. Your contribution to it was largely in the matter of properties. Never let it be said that I don't make the most of experience and information, no matter how meager. But as to the main pattern of that story, it is one of deceit which is something I certainly never connect with you.

On this point, real life and art diverge, for O'Connor assured Langkjaer that if he was a source for the story, in no way did she feel that he had anything to do with deception. Langkjaer remembers discussing with Sally Fitzgerald the timing of the story's creation. Fitzgerald told him that when O'Connor claimed in her letter that she had composed the story "not too long after" his departure, it was to make sure that he understood that it was written long before she had learned of his engagement and was not in any way a settling of scores. However elastic the term "not too long after" might be, the story was actually written in February 1955, more than half a year after Langkjaer had left. That O'Connor did in fact intentionally withhold the story from him—while she had sent numerous others for him to read—points to her perhaps uneasy awareness of the extent to which it was rooted in her feelings for him.

Writing a story more autobiographical than autobiography, with "Good Country People" O'Connor wrestled her way out of an emotional, even artistic crisis. Fitzgerald claimed that the concluded liaison with Langkjaer "forced [O'Connor] to face the inescapable likelihood that her destiny was not to include any bond of human love closer than that of friendship." Indeed, after Langkjaer moved out of the South and thus out of her life, it would seem O'Connor reconciled herself both to the physical restrictions caused by lupus and to the interpersonal limitations imposed by social perceptions of the disease—both burdens having been perhaps greater then than they would be today. She came likewise to see that her proper calling was to be single and single-mindedly focused on her craft. O'Connor took great pleasure in writing the story: a creative way to come to terms with the romantic upheavals she had felt and the ability to see beyond her own disappointment. Langkjaer concurs, for he thinks that O'Connor discovered that her unspoken and unrealized hope for romance was very much her own wooden leg: "her sense of rejection broke her heart but in hindsight she benefited from it. That was her own wooden leg... she had a sense that this was her final chance. And she accepted it as her destiny, as one has to when one has a limitation." In consenting to love Langkjaer and seeing that love not returned, O'Connor hung onto this metaphorical "wooden leg" for the second and last time. But Langkjaer ends his interview noting, "Looking back I feel sorry that things did not work out the way she had wanted them to. That we might have had a meeting of minds, but not a meeting of hearts."

Source: Mark Bosco, "Consenting to Love: Autobiographical Roots of 'Good Country People,'" in *Southern Review*, Vol. 41, No. 2, Spring 2005, pp. 283–95.

SOURCES

"American Experience: The Pill," in *PBS.org*, http://www.pbs.org/wgbh/amex/pill/peopleevents/p_mrs.html (accessed March 24, 2011).

Bates, Stephen, "'Godless Communism' and Its Legacies," in *Society*, March/April 2004, pp. 29–33.

Bosco, Mark, "Consenting to Love: Autobiographical Roots of 'Good Country People,'" in *Southern Review*, Spring 2005, pp. 283–95.

Cheaney, J. B., "Radical Orthodoxy: The Fiction of Flannery O'Connor," in *World and I*, Vol. 16, May 2001, p. 255.

Edgell, Penny, "Atheists Identified as America's Most Distrusted Minority, According to New U of M Study," in *UM News*, March 28, 2006, http://www1.umn.edu/news/

news-releases/2006/UR_RELEASE_MIG_2816.html (accessed March 21, 2011).

Finlayson, Rebecca, *The Insider's Guide to Memphis*, Morris Book Publishing, 2009, p. 283.

Fitzgerald, Sally, ed., *The Habit of Being: Letters of Flannery O'Connor*, Farrar, Straus and Giroux, 1988, pp. 75–76.

Flora, Joseph M., "Bible Belt," in *The Companion to Southern Literature: Themes, Genre, Places, People, Movements, and Motifs*, edited by Joseph M. Flora, Lucinda Hardwick MacKethan, and Todd W. Taylor, Louisiana State University Press, 2002, pp. 99–100.

Giannone, Richard, *Flannery O'Connor and the Mystery of Love*, Fordham University Press, 1999, p. 61.

Gooch, Brad, "Flannery O'Connor," in *New York Times*, http://topics.nytimes.com/top/reference/timestopics/people/o/flannery_oconnor/index.html (accessed March 7, 2011).

Jaschik, Scott, "For First Time, More Women Than Men Earn Ph.D.," in *USA Today*, September 14, 2010, http://www.usatoday.com/news/education/2010-09-15-women phd14_st_N.htm# (accessed March 24, 2011).

"(Mary) Flannery O'Connor (1925–1964), A Brief Biographical Sketch," in *Timberlane Books*, www.timberla nebooks.com/foc.pdf (accessed March 20, 2011).

"O'Connor Country," in *Comforts of Home: The Flannery O'Connor Repository*, http://mediaspecialist.org/occountry.html (accessed March 7, 2011); originally published in *Atlanta*, December 1966.

O'Connor, Flannery, "Good Country People," in *The Complete Stories*, Farrar, Straus and Giroux, 1971, pp. 271–91.

Oliver, Kate, "O'Connor's 'Good Country People,'" in *Explicator*, Vol. 62, No. 4, Summer 2004, pp. 233–37.

Portch, Stephen R., "Visual Flannery," in *Literature's Silent Language: Nonverbal Communication*, Peter Lang, 1985, pp. 117, 135.

Roubenoff, Ronnen, "Chat Transcript for Dr. Ronnen Roubenoff, November 14, 2007," in Lupus Foundation of America, http://www.lupus.org/webmodules/webarticles net/templates/new_donate.aspx?articleid = 1333&zoneid = 6 (accessed March 21, 2011).

Sparrow, Stephen, "Stamping Out Joy: The Fallacy of Certainty in 'Good Country People,'" in *Comforts of Home: The Flannery O'Connor Repository*, http://media specialist.org/ssstamping.html (accessed March 7, 2011).

Sweeney, Jon M., "Grace and the Grotesque: Flannery O'Connor on the Page and on the Screen," in *America*, June 22, 2009, pp. 27–32.

"Table 188: Total Fall Enrollment in Degree-Granting Institutions, by Attendance Status, Sex of Student, and Control of Institution: Selected Years, 1947 through 2007," in *Digest of Education Statistics*, National Center for Educational Statistics Web site, http://nces.ed.gov/programs/digest/d08/tables/dt08_188.asp (accessed March 24, 2011).

Yin, Dan, "The Irony Revealed by the Characters' Names in *Good Country People*," in *US-China Foreign Language*, Vol. 4, No. 3, March 2006, pp. 37–39.

FURTHER READING

Anderson, Jon W., and William B. Friend, eds., *The Culture of Bible Belt Catholics*, Paulist Press, 1995.

Anderson provides thoughtful insight into the similarities that link Bible Belt Catholics to their northern brethren as well as their differences.

Gooch, Brad, *Flannery: A Life of Flannery O'Connor*, Back Bay Books, 2010.

Gooch's biography provides a detailed account of the eccentric writer's life, with information gleaned from family, friends, letters, and myriad other documents.

Hawthorne, Nathaniel, *Hawthorne's Short Stories*, Vintage, 2011.

Hawthorne is the writer with whom critics have most often compared O'Connor, and this collection of short stories contains some of his most powerful and timeless writing. Hawthorne deftly uses symbolism and allegory throughout his stories, much like O'Connor.

Ketchin, Susan, *The Christ-Haunted Landscape: Faith and Doubt in Southern Fiction*, University Press of Mississippi, 1994.

Ketchin explores how religion has affected twelve major southern fiction writers and their literary output.

Magee, Rosemary M., *Conversations with Flannery O'Connor*, University Press of Mississippi, 1987.

O'Connor had a lot to say about her own writing, and in this volume readers gain insight into intended messages as well as the author's interpretation of her stories and their characters.

McCullers, Carson, *Collected Stories of Carson McCullers*, Mariner Books, 1998.

McCullers was a contemporary of O'Connor's and another southern grotesque writer. It was no secret that the two authors had little respect for one another. This collection of short stories provides readers with another taste—with a different emphasis and literary style—of southern fiction of the 1950s.

Weaks, Mary Louise, and Carolyn Perry, eds., *Southern Women's Writing, Colonial to Contemporary*, University Press of Florida, 1995.

Weaks and Perry, both college English professors, have compiled a collection of short stories that provides a time line of the evolution of women's southern literature. Thirty-four white and African American writers are showcased, and their stories illustrate how the women are bound and yet divided by race, social status, and even gender bias.

SUGGESTED SEARCH TERMS

Flannery O'Connor

Good Country People

Flannery O'Connor AND irony

regional AND fiction

southern AND literature

Flannery O'Connor AND biography

Good Country People AND themes

Flannery O'Connor AND southern gothic

Good Country People AND Flannery O'Connor

Greasy Lake

T.C. BOYLE

1982

"Greasy Lake" is an early short story by T. C. Boyle, one of America's most prolific and respected writers. It was published first in the *Paris Review* in 1982 and then in Boyle's second collection of short fiction, *Greasy Lake, and Other Stories*, published by Viking Press in 1985. "Greasy Lake" can also be found in the 1998 volume *T. C. BoyleStories*, which combines new stories with the best from the author's career.

Told with humor and frequent cultural references, the story concerns an unnamed narrator and his friends, young men recently out of high school, who struggle to see themselves as "bad characters." They drink, smoke, and take drugs, driving aimlessly until all hours of the night in a borrowed car, looking for trouble.

At Greasy Lake, they find the trouble they sought. A brutal fight, an attempted rape and murder, and the discovery of a bloated, unidentified corpse make the protagonists question their thirst for danger. Boyle tells the tale in a way that shows exactly what it means to be young and filled with the belief that danger and power are the same thing.

AUTHOR BIOGRAPHY

Boyle was born in Peekskill, New York, on December 2, 1948. Born Thomas John Boyle, he officially changed his middle name at the

T. C. Boyle *(AP Images)*

age of 17 to Coraghessan, an approximation of the surname of one of his Irish ancestors. Boyle's mother was a secretary, and his father was a janitor. He graduated from Lakeland High School in Shrub Oak, New York, in 1964 and from the State University of New York at Potsdam with degrees in English and history in 1968. After graduating, Boyle returned to teach for four years at Lakeland High School before being accepted into the prestigious Writers' Workshop program at the University of Iowa, graduating with a master of fine arts degree in 1975. He stayed at the University of Iowa and received his Ph.D. in English literature in 1977. He won a National Endowment for the Arts award that year and began his long association with the University of Southern California, in Los Angeles, where he was teaching as of 2011.

Boyle's first collection, *Descent of Man, and Other Stories*, was published in 1979. In 1986, he was recruited to establish the writing program for the University of Southern California. In the ensuing years, he published eight collections of short fiction and twelve novels. His works often incorporate historical themes, weaving actual people from history into the narrative along with his own fictional creations. His most popular novels are 1993's *The Road to Wellville*, which was adapted the following year as a film by director Alan Parker; *The Tortilla Curtain* (1995), about the tension surrounding immigration along the Texas-Mexico border; and *World's End*, which won the 1988 PEN/Faulkner Award. His short fiction has appeared in the *New Yorker*, *Harper's*, *Playboy*, and *Esquire*, as well as numerous literary quarterlies. The anthology *T. C. Boyle Stories* was awarded the 1999 PEN/Malamud Award for Short Fiction.

Since the 1990s, Boyle has published under the name T. C. Boyle, dropping "Coraghessan." He published the novel *When the Killing's Done* in 2011.

PLOT SUMMARY

Following the title is a quotation from Bruce Springsteen's song "Spirit in the Night," which gave Boyle the title "Greasy Lake." Neither Springsteen nor Boyle has specified the location of the song or the story; although the name is fictional, the song lyric implies that it could have been Lake Shenandoah, which is near Route 88 in Lakewood, New Jersey.

The story begins by establishing a nostalgic mood about what it was like to be a young man in a time "when it was good to be bad." Cultural references suggest a time frame in the 1970s, but the period is deliberately vague.

The story takes place one night when the nineteen-year-old narrator and his friends Digby and Jeff, looking for trouble and unable to find it, drive around in the car the narrator has borrowed from his mother. They end up at Greasy Lake at two in the morning. In the parking lot they see a motorcycle and a blue 1957 Chevy, which they think belongs to their friend Tony Lovett. Assuming that Tony is in the car with a girl, they decide it would be funny to harass and interrupt them. Leaving their car, the narrator, who has been drinking and taking drugs all evening, drops his keys, which he likens to "Westmoreland's decision to dig in at Khe Sanh," a famous tactical mistake in a 1968 battle in the Vietnam War.

The car turns out to not be Tony's, though, and the man who emerges from it, later referred to as Bobbie, is actually as mean as the three friends are pretending to be. He fights them

MEDIA ADAPTATIONS

- In 1988, director Damian Harris produced a 30-minute adaptation of "Greasy Lake," starring Eric Stoltz as the narrator (named "T.C." for the film) and James Spader as Digby. Tom Waits does the narration. The film played the American Film Institute festival at the time of its release, but it is not currently available. However, it was released with three other short films on a 1990 videocassette called *The Discovery Program*, volume 1, distributed by JCI Video and available in some libraries.

one by one and is beating them badly when the narrator remembers that he keeps a tire iron under the seat of his car "because bad characters always kept tire irons under the driver's seat, for just such an occasion as this." As the other two fight the stranger, the narrator comes up behind him and hits him on the head with the tire iron.

Bobbie, the attacker, falls immediately to the ground and appears dead. The young woman he was with emerges from the car, wearing just her underwear and a man's shirt. She screams at the narrator, Digby, and Jeff, calling them animals. Instead of running away, the three grab for her. In a primal frenzy, they rip apart her clothes and start opening their own pants.

Before they rape her, however, another car pulls into the parking lot, its headlights illuminating the scene. The narrator and his friends scatter. The narrator dives into Greasy Lake. He tries to keep silent in the waist-deep water, hearing male voices try to calm the girl. He plans to swim away from the situation, but something floats up against him, and it takes him just a few seconds to realize that the floating object is a decaying corpse.

Shocked, he jumps from the water and lets out a shout. The girl and the men who had just arrived in the car become aware of his presence nearby. She cries that he is one of "them," the men who tried to rape her, and her rescuers are enraged. The narrator then hears Bobbie's voice and is filled with joy and relief to realize that Bobbie was only knocked unconscious, not killed.

All of the men in the parking lot turn vicious. First they shout for the narrator, Digby, and Jeff to come out and fight. When there is no response, they attack the narrator's car. They break the windows and lights and throw garbage in it. They find the tire iron in the grass and use it to bang dents into the car's body.

Eventually, the girl becomes bored, and she encourages Bobbie to leave. They climb into his '57 Chevy and drive off. The two men who came to her rescue, whom the narrator describes as "blond types, in fraternity jackets," become aware that not only are they exposed and vulnerable to the unknown toughs who knocked Bobbie unconscious, but they are also themselves committing a crime in vandalizing the car. They jump into their car and leave as well.

After a short wait, the narrator comes out to the parking lot. Digby and Jeff arrive almost immediately. They realize that the car will still run, and in the first gleam of sunrise, the narrator spots his car keys.

Before they drive off, however, another car arrives at Greasy Lake. Two young women get out and walk to the abandoned motorcycle, calling someone named Al. As one of them approaches the narrator, he can see that she is stumbling, hardly able to walk. She asks if any of the boys knows where Al is. The narrator assumes that Al is the body in the lake, but he says nothing.

The girl takes out some pills and offers to share them, referring to the narrator, Digby, and Jeff, who look like they have been fighting, as "bad characters." Her gesture has the narrator on the verge of crying, and Digby politely declines the offer. They climb into the battered car and drive away. Looking back, the narrator sees the sun rising over Greasy Lake and the stoned girl holding her hands outstretched toward him.

CHARACTERS

Blond Boys

Two young men, presumably near the narrator's age, arrive in a car and interrupt the rape that the protagonist and his friends are about to commit. They drive a Trans Am, a fashionable sports car. The narrator describes them as "blond types," as if they might not actually be blond but rather have the good looks and social position that are popularly associated with blondness. When they arrive, the would-be rapists have already fled, but the blond boys join Bobbie in attacking the narrator's car. When Bobbie leaves, though, they falter, as if the excitement of destruction has given way to the fear that they might be vulnerable to attack, and then the fear that they might be held legally responsible for what has happened. Like the narrator and his friends, they are capable of animalistic rage but are also frightened when they become self-conscious.

Bobbie

Throughout most of the story, the man who emerges from the '57 Chevy to fight with the narrator and his friends is referred to as "this bad greasy character." Near the end, the girl he is with, tired of all of the violence and wanting to go home, calls him "Bobbie."

Bobbie presents an image of the sort of man—a "man of action"—that the narrator and his friends want to emulate. He is wearing working-class clothes: dirty, greasy jeans and engineer boots with steel toes, drawing a contrast to their comparatively pampered lives as students living with their families. As soon as he is provoked, he jumps into action, attacking them and managing to fight off all three by himself. It is a shock, then, when he becomes completely, instantly disabled when the narrator hits him in the heat of the fight. He immediately goes from seeming indestructible to soiling his pants. When he revives, he uses the tire iron that knocked him out to take out his anger on the narrator's mother's car.

Digby

Digby is one of the narrator's friends. Like the narrator, he seems to be from a stable, middle-class background and to be using drugs and alcohol as a form of rebellion. Another form of rebellion is the gold star earring that he wears (earrings for men being much less common, and less accepted, in the 1970s than in later decades). Digby attends Cornell University, a prestigious Ivy League school, indicating that he is in reality quite different from the drinking, brawling "bad character" that he aspires to be.

Digby shows more initiative than his friends. It is his idea to harass the car that he thinks belongs to their friend Tony Lovett. He is the one to suggest that they get into the damaged Bel Air and go home, and then he is the one to talk to the women who approach the car wanting to party.

Drugged Girl

At the end of the story, a drugged young woman and her friend Sarah arrive at Greasy Lake looking for Al, the owner of the motorcycle. The drugged girl tries to engage in conversation with the narrator, Digby, and Jeff. She is high; her words are slurred, and she is hardly able to walk.

She likes them because they seem to be "bad characters" who have been fighting, and she offers to share her drugs with them. She admires drug use but is unaware of how unstable she looks, and she admires violence, although her friend Al is probably floating dead in the water. The narrator wants to get away from her as soon as he can.

At the end of the story, the narrator looks back to see her outlined by the rising sun over Greasy Lake, simultaneously slouching and reaching out, an image of the allure and tawdriness of the partying lifestyle.

Fox

The woman parked with Bobbie in the '57 Chevy at Greasy Lake is not given a name in the story, but Boyle's narrator refers to her several times as "the fox," indicating her attractive sexuality. When the trouble begins, she stays in the car, emerging only when it appears that the narrator and his friends have killed her boyfriend. When Bobbie falls to the ground, she faces his attackers, more concerned about him than with her own well-being. While the narrator may have been intimidated by her under other circumstances, he is keyed up from fighting, and the hormonal increase from violence turns to sexual violence against her as he and his two friends attack her.

After Bobbie awakens and has attacked the narrator's car for a while, the "fox" tells him that it is time to leave. For a brief moment after he was felled she acted out emotionally, but she does not have the anger or thirst for revenge that he has.

Jeff

Jeff, one of the narrator's friends, is an accomplice in his trouble at Greasy Lake. He is either too shy or too under the influence of alcohol and drugs to have an active role in this episode. He has no speaking lines, following the narrator and

Digby in their actions. Early in the story, the narrator notes that Jeff is leaning out of the car and vomiting while they are on the way to Greasy Lake, and for the rest of the story he does nothing that could be considered independent action.

Like his friends, Jeff is a student. He has aspirations, though they are vague and unlikely. He would like to be a painter and a musician, and at the same time he imagines himself running a head shop to sell drug paraphernalia. Tellingly, though, he has done nothing toward attaining these dreams: he imagines them being more important than his education, but he is still in school.

Narrator

The narrator of this story is a nineteen-year-old who is concerned with his image. Though he lives with his parents and drives his mother's car, he would like to imagine himself as a bad, dangerous person. He goes out with his friends, drinking and doing drugs, trying to convince himself that he is some sort of criminal, but his actions never lead to anything interesting.

During the incident at Greasy Lake he achieves his desire to be a "bad character." The situation starts off as a misunderstanding, as he and his friends think they are playing a prank on a friend. Things escalate to a fight, in which he is kicked and bruised and has a tooth chipped. He knocks the other man out with a tire iron, leading the narrator to believe he has committed murder. Instead of fleeing, though, in his excitement, he and his friends attack a woman and try to sexually assault her. Discovered in that act by an approaching car, he realizes the shame of being caught. He tries to escape into Greasy Lake but is stopped when he encounters a decaying corpse floating in the water.

The encounter with the corpse causes the narrator to see himself in a new light. He is aware of the potential for lasting consequences, and he worries about what story he will use to explain the damage to his mother's car. When some women, older than him, approach him and his friends as the "bad characters" and partiers they wanted to be, the narrator finds himself disgusted with his own tough-guy fantasy, unable to respond because he is nearly in tears.

Sarah

Sarah is one of the two women who show up late in the story in a Mustang. She does not talk or approach the battered car that the narrator and his friends are in, staying in the distance.

THEMES

Coming of Age

The nineteen-year-old boys in this story find themselves poised between childhood and adulthood, leaning toward the latter. They rely on their parents for transportation, food, and shelter, but they do what they can to break free of their parents' influence by dressing in denim and leather (considered rebellious at the time), driving recklessly, drinking, taking drugs, and reading intellectual authors. Although they try to pose as "dangerous" or "bad" men, their boyishness shows through in the way that they decide to harass their friend Tony when he is romantically engaged by the lake—to them, sex is something to long for but is also something to giggle about.

The lake itself is an apt metaphor for coming of age: its ancient roots predate the modern developments that have been built up around it, giving it a natural purity that Boyle describes as "primeval," but age has polluted it. When the narrator thinks he has murdered someone, he jumps into the water but is unable to submerse himself in it; similarly, he tests a wild, irresponsible lifestyle but at the end of the story is unable to fully embrace it.

In the end, the three young men find themselves faced with a situation that would have been a dream to them at the beginning of the story: an older woman offers them drugs and the possibility of sex. The events of the evening, however, have frightened them, so they retreat back into the security of childhood, politely declining her offer and going back to the safety of their parents' homes.

Primitivism

For almost half of the story, the situation described is not very remarkable, detailing the adventures of three boys who travel around looking for trouble and eventually find it in the form of a fight. In the heat of their battle, however, the situation becomes deadly serious, as the swing of a tire iron causes such an

TOPICS FOR FURTHER STUDY

- In a letter to the *New York Times Book Review*, Boyle noted that this story is not about characters from Bruce Springsteen's "Spirit in the Night" but that the story is "a kind of riff on the song, a free take on its glorious spirit." Choose a song that you like and write a short story that evokes its mood and setting. You may choose to create an audio version of your story with the song as background music.
- Describe the procedural steps that would be used by the police to investigate the death of the body found in Greasy Lake. Explain how evidence should be handled and how potential witnesses could be found and questioned. Create a flow chart that could be used by an investigator to complete all steps.
- Read Charles Benoit's young-adult novel *You*, published in 2010, about a fifteen-year-old who finds himself drawn into gang life to escape a sense of ordinariness. *You* is written in the second person, that is, using "you" in its narration, an unusual choice for fiction. Rewrite a scene from Benoit's novel in the way that Boyle would write it, then rewrite a scene from "Greasy Lake" to match the style of *You*. Present both to your class with a discussion of which style you think is more effective for this kind of story and why.
- This story draws attention to the types of cars driven by the various characters. Update the cars to modern times, explaining what each character would be driving and why you think so. Research the technical specifications of the cars in the story, and present them to your class side-by-side in a chart with the technical specifications of the modern cars. Include pictures to support your claims about each car's significance.
- Write a blog chronicling a week in the life of the narrator, Digby, or Jeff, spanning the time before and after the event at the lake. Make up some incidents that are not in the story. Illustrate your work with pictures (such as a demolished car) that you find on the Internet. When you present this blog to your class, explain which details of his life this character would or would not write about and why you think that.
- Make a video documentary about a legendary Greasy Lake-type hangout for young adults near where you live. Interview people about their feelings about the place, including people who have never been there as well as people who have. Edit your footage into a short film using video-editing software, and make sure the finished product explains to audiences whether you think the place deserves its reputation or not.

immediate, serious collapse of their opponent that the narrator is certain he has committed murder.

Murder is such a fundamental violation of all social laws that the narrator and his friends immediately revert to a primitive state. Moments before, they were three mild, mischievous students looking for some excitement (though they imagined themselves tougher than that), but once the threshold of murder is crossed, they have no more social filters. When the girl from the car emerges she calls them "animals," and when they see that she is only partially dressed they attack her with what the narrator calls "purest primal badness." They are "disassociated from humanity and civilization," he explains, with "the first of the Ur-crimes behind us, the second in progress." ("Ur-" is a German-derived prefix meaning "original.") They are prevented from raping her only when the light of the approaching car brings their actions into the open, making them self-conscious about who they are and what they are doing.

Greasy Lake got its nickname from the pollution within it. (Stéphane Bidouze / Shutterstock.com)

Guilt

To some extent, it is basic self-preservation that drives the narrator and his friends to scatter when the headlights of the Trans Am catch them assaulting the woman. They do not want to be caught and punished, but they also become instantly aware that what they are doing is wrong: as the narrator describes it, "The headlights came at me like accusing fingers."

To the narrator, the destruction of his mother's car is a lasting reminder of his guilt. If the night's events could be left behind on the shores of Greasy Lake, he might be able to forget the trouble he has caused, since the man he almost killed is alive and the woman he almost raped has driven off into anonymity. He might eventually return to his search for danger. The physical damage, though, forces him to think about the lasting effects of the action. He cannot think of a plausible alibi to give his parents that does not give away his secret behavior.

Unable to reconcile his partying life with his home life anymore, the narrator loses his interest in dangerous nighttime activity. Asked to "party" in the sunlight, he refuses, aware of the potential for destruction within him, waiting to be released.

STYLE

Anonymous Narrator

Boyle does not give the narrator of this story a name. Other characters are also unnamed, but it is natural that their names would not come up in the situations described. The two blond boys in the Trans Am are far away from the narrator when he observes them, involved in destroying a car and unlikely to identify each other in any incriminating way. The girl from the '57 Chevy, "the fox," is never spoken to directly in the story. The woman at the end who wants to party with them refers to her friend as "Sarah," but her own name never comes up. The tough young man who fights with all of them is known only as "the bad greasy character" and variations on that term until the girl he is with calls him "Bobbie" as she is imploring him to leave.

Digby and Jeff have ample opportunities to call the narrator by name at the beginning or end of the story. By withholding the narrator's name, Boyle makes him noticeably obscure. This does not necessarily make it any easier for readers to put themselves in his position, since readers throughout history have been able to see the world from the perspective of first-person narrators whose names are given, such as "Ishmael" or "Holden." It does, however, offer psychological insight into the speaker. It shows him to be the sort of person who cares almost exclusively about events outside of himself, rather than himself or his own ideas. The absence of a name for this character corresponds with the tone of this story, which is so distant from the narrator's inner thoughts that readers often have to guess at why he does the things he does.

Dark Comedy

Dark comedy seems to be a contradiction in terms, since comedy and laughter are typically associated with good feelings and happiness, lightness rather than darkness. However, there is a type of comedy that draws on life's tragic absurdity, often incorporating elements of the macabre (the strange or uncanny) to contrast expectations with cold, brutal reality. As Lawrence Mintz puts it in his review of Wes Gehring's *American Dark Comedy: Beyond Satire*, dark comedy, or black humor, is common to the human condition and "can be traced back to cynical and ironic views of life, particularly the comic potential of juxtaposing violence and the grotesque with a refusal to take them seriously or to be unduly saddened by them." That which is comic, in other words, should not be confused with the merely humorous. In this view, "Greasy Lake," a simple story of a young man and his friends who unexpectedly fall into bad circumstances, can be considered dark comedy. The key to this is the story's tone, which is, in Mintz's words, "cynical and ironic," refusing to give weight to even the most serious developments.

Boyle's comic view of the world shows through in the horrifying touches that make a bad situation increasingly terrible. The first is the apparent death of Bobbie: another writer might have allowed the narrator to hurt Bobbie badly with the tire iron, but Boyle shuts down the excitement of the fight by having Bobbie collapse instantly. Boyle immediately changes tone again, as the protagonist shakes off his shock and guilt and turns into a potential rapist within a matter of a few lines of text.

Even the shocking discovery of a rotting body in the lake can be seen as comic because none of the characters, or the reader, has any personal bond with this anonymous person. The only person who might care about his death is the woman at the end of the story, who gives up her search for Al quickly. Ironically, the drugs that she has loaded herself up with do not make her a sinister, criminal character, as they might in another context, but instead help her retain her innocent perspective, resulting in more comic juxtaposition.

HISTORICAL CONTEXT

Postmodernism

Several critics have identified Boyle's writing style as postmodern, although what they mean by that seems to vary from one critic to another. It is the very nature of the word to be inexact, malleable, and adaptable to different situations.

The term *postmodernism* is indeed difficult to define even for those who freely use it in literary criticism. It came into use, as the term implies, to describe a response to the modernist movement, which prevailed in the arts from around 1910 through the end of World War II in 1945. Modernism encouraged artists to seek new forms to express their ideas, bringing a new awareness of the relationship between how something is said and what is being said. In literature, the clearest example of this is poetry's move away from traditional line, rhythm, and stanzas and toward free verse, which allowed poets to raise readers' curiosity about the relationship between form and content. While the term "postmodern" had been in use since the nineteenth century, primarily in the field of philosophy, it came to be applied to the arts, such as literature, film, music, and architecture, only in the last half of the twentieth century.

The main characteristic of postmodernist literature is the relationship between the author and the work's subject. Starting in the 1960s, there was a trend in American fiction toward stories that showed an awareness of being told as stories. This awareness blurred the lines between author, reader, and story, making all three partners on a shared adventure. This shift reflected the general trend throughout the arts to

COMPARE & CONTRAST

- **1980s:** The first oil shortage of the mid-1970s creates nostalgia for the car culture that grew up in the postwar era, when driving around was considered to be a cheap, nearly free, way to spend an entire evening. This nostalgia persists and is still a factor when this story is written.

  Today: Although people still identify themselves with their cars, rising oil prices and awareness of pollution encourage people to drive less.

- **1980s:** Many nineteen-year-old students live at home while attending college, as the characters in this story do, but the trend is to view college as an opportunity to move away from family and start a new life.

  Today: More and more young adults are forced by economic conditions to stay in their parents' homes after high school or to move back in after college.

- **1980s:** Suburban teens struggle to break away from mainstream culture to assert their "badness."

  Today: Interactive games provide young adults with ways of tapping into their violent and antisocial urges in a virtual way.

- **1980s:** About 45 percent of high school graduates enroll in college. The narrator of this story and his friends are in the minority.

  Today: College enrollment has grown steadily each year since this story, peaking with more than 70 percent of those graduating high school in 2009 attending a postsecondary institution.

- **1980s:** Abandoned bodies of water like Greasy Lake are attractive to criminals and polluters because they are not well supervised. The Environmental Protection Agency starts designating hazardous waste sites under the Superfund statute in 1980.

  Today: Authorities are more aware of the dangers of having public waters polluted, and more money is spent on measures like gates and video surveillance to control criminal activities.

---

view an artistic work in context instead of as an independent entity.

Boyle's stories, particularly his earlier works, are often categorized as postmodern because of the playful way that he acknowledges the storytelling process. Other fiction writers, such as John Barth, Italo Calvino, and Donald Barthelme, openly address readers in their works, a practice not used in Boyle's fiction. He was, however, known to reflect on the action of the story while staying in the narrative voice, as he does frequently in "Greasy Lake," making his anonymous young narrator show an improbable awareness of his philosophical situation.

One aspect of Boyle's work that is particularly identified as "postmodern" is the openness of his work to interpretation. A story like "Greasy Lake" does not steer readers toward a moral or message, forcing them instead to participate in finding its meaning. The reader's past experience is a significant part of the overall meaning. Postmodern fiction often offers readers a new, unfamiliar experience that intentionally takes them out of their comfort zone, forcing them to reconsider what fiction is. By that standard, this story is fairly traditional: its characters are defined and its action proceeds in chronological order. But the surprising, surreal twists that are common in Boyle's work challenge tradition, in a sense rewriting the rules and challenging readers who were comfortable with the styles modernist writers had developed.

Seventies Hedonist Culture

The 1970s are often considered a culturally quiet period, lacking the danger of other decades that

The boys hang out at the lake at night. (*Michael G. Mill / Shutterstock.com*)

saw major wars or cultural revolutions. One reason for this was the fact that the 1960s had brought so much change. The sixties began with growing racial tension, as the civil rights movement sought to capitalize on recent gains; demonstrations led to escalating violence as two key voices of the movement, Malcolm X and Martin Luther King, Jr., were assassinated in 1965 and 1968. Following the civil rights movement's drive for racial equality led other groups to assert their rights to live freely as equals among the mainstream, and movements arose to fight for the rights of gays, women, American Indians, and the handicapped, to name a few.

The civil rights movement was embraced by the antiwar movement, which grew along with America's military involvement in Vietnam in the early 1960s. The war had opponents across the social spectrum, but its most vocal opponents were organized on college campuses. A generation of young people grew up in the 1960s fighting against war and social injustice. In the course of breaking down social boundaries, they experimented with drugs and rejected social rules against sexual activity.

By the 1970s, however, the social passion of the youth culture had dimmed. The revolutionary stance that had fought against the mainstream had become the mainstream: rock music became the defining factor in the music industry, President Nixon was run from office, and American troops were withdrawn from Vietnam without a victory. Other aspects of social change proved more dispiriting, however, as racial and gender harmony made only modest gains. The enthusiasm of the 1960s gave way to the disillusionment of the 1970s.

As the revolutionary spirit faded away, however, the hedonistic spirit of the 1960s remained. Marijuana, which had become common on college campuses throughout the sixties, became obtainable in cities, suburbs, and rural areas. By the end of the seventies, the established distribution routes that had moved marijuana throughout the country helped bring cocaine to the same consumers. While there was no financial incentive for promoting social revolution, there was great incentive for keeping drugs distributed. The other most prominent remnant of the upheaval of the sixties was the increase in sexual activity. Ken Goffman (who writes about culture under the name R. U. Serious), in *Counter Culture through the Ages*, quotes Gary Herman's 1983 book *Rock and Roll Babylon* as identifying sexual freedom as the defining characteristic of the seventies:

"Liberation became personal liberation, freedom from oppression became freedom from sexual oppression, the democratic urge toward equality and freedom of association became an individualistic quest for guiltless promiscuity." The boys in "Greasy Lake" may seem like any other adolescents in their quest to forget their bland lives through sex and drugs, but they are particularly a product of their time.

CRITICAL OVERVIEW

"Greasy Lake" was the title story of Boyle's second collection of short stories, published in 1985. Grove Koger of *Library Journal* calls that collection "a lively and varied volume for most short story collections." Larry McCaffery, reviewing the collection in the *New York Times Book Review*, expresses his admiration for Boyle's short fiction, which shows a range of style and "a convincing and disturbing critique" of American consumer culture. Though McCaffery felt that Boyle did his best work in his novels (he had published two by that time), the critic does note, in the end, that "despite some unevenness in execution, the stories in *Greasy Lake* display a vibrant sensibility fully engaged with American society—and with the wonder and joy that defiantly remain a part of our culture as well."

In the decades since this story was published, Boyle's reputation as one of America's preeminent writers has grown. By the time his collection *T. C. Boyle Stories*, which gathered his best stories from his other four collections, was published, he was well known in literary circles as a writer whose imagination promised readers an entertaining and thought-provoking time. James Knudson reviewed that book, the winner of the prestigious PEN/Malamud Award for 1999, in *World Literature Today*. Knudson notes that the stories, spanning twenty years of the author's life, are organized in the book thematically, not chronologically, and he points out that "it is indicative of the author's skill that there is little or no discernable difference in quality between the earliest stories and the latest." Addressing a common concern that Boyle's highly amusing fiction is more about showmanship than about actual literary talent, Knudson concludes that "the reader who looks deeper into *T. C. Boyle Stories* will find that Boyle, at his best, 'makes art' of the highest order and that even his most interesting stories 'weave a web of mystery.'"

Boyle still publishes short fiction frequently, and he has practically been a household name since the back-to-back publication of his two best-known novels, *The Road to Wellville* in 1993 and *The Tortilla Curtain* in 1995. He has published eight novels since then, as well as four more collections of short stories, all to critical acclaim.

CRITICISM

David Kelly

David Kelly is an instructor of creative writing and literature. In the following essay, he argues that the character who does not appear in the story, Al, is crucial for establishing the story's tone and ultimate message.

T. C. Boyle's short story "Greasy Lake," like much of his work that balances serious themes and a comic strain, is notable for riding a precarious balance between the obvious, the hidden, and the unknowable. On the obvious side, Boyle tells a fairly clear-cut story about three boys—nineteen-year-olds, actually, but boys at heart—who go out one night, as they do every night, in search of an experience or two that will affirm that they are rugged individuals, or "bad characters." In traditional short-story fashion, these boys end up finding more than they bargained for. Fueled by alcohol, marijuana, and an excess of greasy fast food, they get into a fight and appear to commit murder, and then, when the veil of civilization that has enshrouded their sheltered lives is lifted, they turn to sexual assault. Interrupted in that, they know shame. In the end, they have to drive home with their shame marked by their very conspicuous demolished car. The basic coming-of-age story is tinged, however, with elements that Boyle never gives an explanation for. There is the corpse that is never explained; the narrator comes across it floating in Greasy Lake and leaves it behind in the water. Later, some girls come looking for someone named "Al," but the narrator never mentions the dead body to her. He drives away with his friends, leaving readers wondering what kind of a world this is, where a dead body could so easily be forgotten.

The dead man in the water must be the girls' Al, as the narrator assumes. Since the story never conclusively says so, other interpretations are possible, but none of the options makes as

WHAT DO I READ NEXT?

- American poet William Stafford wrote about the same theme, the young man's attraction to danger, in his poem "Fifteen," which concerns a fifteen-year-old adolescent who finds a running motorcycle in the bushes beside a road and briefly considers the thrill of climbing aboard and riding off on it. Originally published in 1962, this poem, a popular selection for young-adult readers, is included in *The Darkness Around Us Is Deep: Selected Poems of William Stafford*, published in 1994.
- Raymond Carver is a short-story writer and Boyle's contemporary. His short story "Tell the Women We're Going" imagines two high school friends who grow up into confining marriages. Seeking to recapture their youth, they follow two young women into the woods and assault them. Carver's chilling story is collected in the Library of America's *Raymond Carver: Collected Stories*, edited by William Stull and Maureen Carroll and published in 2009.
- "Where Are You Going, Where Have You Been?" is a frequently anthologized short story by Joyce Carol Oates. First published in 1967, it concerns a young girl who, like the narrator of Boyle's story, wants to expand beyond the boredom of her family life and ends up facing danger. It is included in Oates's 2007 collection *High Lonesome: New and Selected Stories, 1966–2006*.
- Nigerian poet and novelist Ben Okri drew international acclaim with his 1992 novel *The Famished Road*, about a narrator who is a "spirit child," with connections to the supernatural world, and his observations of the violence and corruption in his village.
- Paul Goodman's 1962 sociological study *Growing Up Absurd* was considered a breakthrough work in understanding the disaffected generation of teens that used cars and drugs to rebel against sedate suburban life in the 1950s. Many of Goodman's cultural references in that book are outdated, but Goodman's enduring observations about how education affects the young identity can be found in the 2011 publication *The Paul Goodman Reader*, edited by Taylor Stroher.
- Many of T. Coraghessan Boyle's novels incorporate historical elements into their plots. His 1987 novel *World's End* takes place in a setting similar to that of "Greasy Lake," the New York Hudson River valley. The twenty-year-old protagonist tells the story of his own life and the lives of his parents in the 1940s and of ancestors going back to the founding of the land.

---

much sense as the most basic logic: Al's motorcycle is present, Al is missing, and the floating corpse has no other attachments: he either arrived with people who left him, or walked out to the isolated lake, or arrived on the motorcycle. Reading the dead man as Al twists a few loose ends together, but it does not actually explain why a dead person belongs here. To explain that, readers have to promote Al's existence beyond being just one element within the story and instead read him as the focus of the story.

This is, after all, a story about different degrees of "badness," and Al is, or was, the baddest character of them all. Boyle establishes different levels of badness that readers can understand by identifying characters with the vehicles they drive. For instance, the narrator and his friends are out on the prowl in a Chevy Bel Air, a respectable suburban vehicle that they work to make threatening: "When we wheeled our parents' whining station wagons out into the street," he says in the prelude to the action, "we left a patch of rubber a half a block long." Badder than them are the two boys who interrupt their attack of the girl, who join in on the destruction of the Bel Air because their chivalric

AL HAD APPARENTLY POSSESSED EVERYTHING THAT THE NARRATOR, DIGBY, AND JEFF HAD BEEN SEARCHING FOR THAT NIGHT."

sense of honor has been offended by what they have heard (and also, apparently, because they just like destruction): they drive a Trans Am, a respectable muscle car for a high-school tough. The best car of all in this gearhead world is the '57 Chevy driven by Bobbie, the "bad, greasy character" who throws himself into a bloody fight with three strangers just because they have annoyed him. Anyone unfamiliar with the legendary status of the '57 Chevy can take some sense of its special esteem from the fact that it is referred to by year; the young men of this culture of course already know.

Bobbie may have the most prestigious car, but Al's motorcycle implies a different kind of badness, one sprung naturally from danger and self-sufficiency. When the narrator first considers the motorcycle, though, he does not think of it that way. The first time he sees it, he assumes it belongs to "some junkie half-wit biker"; later, when he connects the corpse in the lake and the bike, he determines it must be "a bad older character come to this," unaware of how ironic such a statement is in a story that begins with the declaration that "it was good to be bad." The dead man is a biker, probably a drug dealer, but in the narrator's eyes he is dead and alone, unlike Bobbie, who has a woman. The narrator knows nothing about the body in the lake, but it is obviously someone who has been forgotten.

Al's relevance changes in the last scene when the two girls who arrive in a Mustang—itself a respectable gearhead car—come looking for him. It turns out that the dead man has friends who care, who know his name, and his friends are women, which means that they hold the promise of sex. This rounds out his image of a bad character, along with the good ride, drugs, and liquor. Al had apparently possessed everything that the narrator, Digby, and Jeff had been searching for that night. He had been even cooler than Bobbie, whom they nearly supplanted in an oedipal way by killing him and taking his girl for their own. The glassy-eyed woman who arrives at the end admires the torn-up look they have gotten from fighting, offers them unidentified drugs that are much stronger than the marijuana they are accustomed to, and then openly invites them to join her and her friend. The absence of Al presents them with the opportunity to become the new kings of badness. And yet, they decline.

One level of this story has been fulfilled as soon as the narrator crawls out of the lake and surveys the damage to his mother's car, realizing the dangerous consequences of being the dangerous characters they originally aspired to be. It could be that their newfound awareness of consequences is what makes the narrator decide to not take up with Al's female friends—he knows what the party life has done to Al, even though Digby and Jeff do not. His personal experience with the dead man, though, leads him beyond fear, which is only a temporary inhibitor of bad behavior. In the space of perhaps an hour, he has come to a point where he no longer needs to be bad, but he can still be a little nostalgic about who he was when the story began.

In the rising sun, life at the lake is not about fun and the excitement of danger; it is about exhaustion, glassy-eyed lack of focus, and, ultimately, death. The narrator knows this, but he does not tell it to anyone. He does not tell Digby and Jeff what he saw, and he does not tell the older woman in stiletto heels what he knows about Al's fate. For one thing, what he thinks he has seen is never confirmed. Boyle treats the body in the lake like a private hallucination, like something the narrator might not have really seen at all. What he does see is the sham of a woman to whom he might have been attracted in the night but who now looks addled. He realizes that she admires him for looking bad when he knows he is only frightened and beaten. Daylight dissolves the pretenses surrounding badness, and the very idea of death, whether real or imagined, drives it home.

Telling his friends about Al would intensify the fear in Digby and Jeff, but that hardly seems necessary. Telling the drugged woman that Al is dead might lead her to her own revelation, make her turn from the bad life, too, but he chooses to not do that. He lets her continue believing that fast cars, fights, and drugs are fun. It is too late for him to unknow what he already knows, but he does approve of her faith that badness will someday

The '57 Chevy does not contain their friends.
(Kim D. French / Shutterstock.com)

make her life better. When he looks back to her in the story's last line, she is reaching out her hands. The door to the bad life is always open to him because he has left it open, even though readers can guess that he will never go back.

A coming-of-age story requires its protagonist to change. The violent events of the evening do change the narrator of "Greasy Lake," and the discovery of a corpse in the filthy lake seems to merely intensify the sense of danger. In the end, though, Boyle gives the corpse a name and a little bit of personality. The narrator does not reject his former values entirely: through Al, he comes to accept them in the way that one would accept a wrong, misguided friend.

Source: David Kelly, Critical Essay on "Greasy Lake," in *Short Stories for Students*, Gale, Cengage Learning, 2012.

Paul Gleason

In the following excerpt, Gleason reflects on the social issues represented by the stories in the Greasy Lake *collection.*

T. C. Boyle has published around one hundred and fifty short stories in literary magazines and eight collections of short fiction in just over a quarter century of writing. He is one of American short fiction's most wide-ranging and adventurous writers. His short fiction consists of political satires ("Ike and Nina" and "The New Moon Party"), takeoffs on and sequels to the works of other writers such as Ernest Hemingway ("Me Cago en la Leche [Robert Jordan in Nicaragua]") and Nikolai Gogol ("The Overcoat II"), autobiographical meditations on small-town America and alcoholic parents ("If the River Was Whiskey" and "Rara Avis"), yarns of romance and sex ("Modern Love" and "Without a Hero"), tales of environmentalism and ecology ("Whales Weep" and "Rapture of the Deep"), comic riffs on American pop culture ("The Hit Man" and "All Shook Up"), and sports writing ("56–0" and "The Hector Quesadilla Story"). To these stories Boyle's two most recent collections, *After the Plague* (2001) and *Tooth and Claw* (2005), append a postapocalyptic analysis of American society ("After the Plague"), complex commentaries on romantic relationships ("She Wasn't Soft" and "Tooth and Claw"), and disturbing studies of controversial American social issues such as drug use and abortion ("Killing Babies" and "Up against the Wall")....

GREASY LAKE AND OTHER STORIES (1985)

First published in 1985, Boyle's second collection of short fiction was *Greasy Lake and Other Stories*. In the six years between *Descent of Man* and *Greasy Lake*, Boyle had published his first two novels, *Water Music* (1981) and *Budding Prospects* (1984). *Greasy Lake* most resembles *Budding Prospects*, which satirizes capitalism in its presentation of the adventures of a team of aging California hippies who try to grow an illegal crop of marijuana for profit. Like *Budding Prospects*, the stories collected in *Greasy Lake* explore social issues, such as artificial insemination, the treatment of the elderly, environmentalism, and the relationship between political promises and political actions.

"Greasy Lake," the title story of the collection, takes the same postmodern approach that Boyle employs in "Descent of Man": it refers to another text in its title, in this case Bruce Springsteen's 1973 song "Spirit in the Night." "Spirit in the Night" celebrates and romanticizes Greasy Lake as an escape from the constraints of conventional American life and as a place where drug use and sex lead to spiritual enlightenment.

Boyle begins his "Greasy Lake" with an epigraph taken from Springsteen's song that indicates the location of Greasy Lake: "It's about a mile down on the dark side of Route 88." His story portrays the dark side of thinking that rebellious drug use and sex result in spiritual enlightenment. For Boyle the first line of the story is, as usual, instrumental in setting up the story's theme: "There was a time when courtesy and winning ways went out of style, when it was good to be bad, when you cultivated decadence like a taste." The narrator of the story immediately establishes himself as an older man reflecting on the vanished days of his youth, when being a social rebel was acceptable. He and his friends, Digby and Jeff, strike "elaborate poses to show that [they] didn't give a shit about anything," but they are really just mild-mannered college students who enjoy the monetary support of their parents.

The toughness of the narrator and his friends is put to the test when they visit Greasy Lake one night. Already drunk and stoned by the time they reach the lake, they see what they think is the car of their friend Tony Lovett but soon learn that the car actually belongs to a "very bad character in greasy jeans and engineer boots" who is making out with his girlfriend. After the narrator ends the ensuing fight by hitting the bad character, Bobby, in the head with a tire iron, he and his friends attempt to rape the girlfriend but are interrupted by an approaching car. The narrator flees to the woods, where he wades into a pond and discovers a decaying corpse.

Not Springsteen's place of mystical escape, Boyle's Greasy Lake is a site of violence and death. The narrator's comparison between his and his friends' decision to approach Bobby's car and "Westmoreland's decision to dig in at Khe Sanh" links the events that transpire at Greasy Lake to the conflict in Vietnam, which many Americans opposed on moral and political grounds. As college students, Digby, Jeff, and the narrator are not eligible for the draft, so the narrator's comparison highlights their personal immaturity, which does not allow them to recognize their status as economically privileged members of society. Unlike many of their poorer contemporaries who have to fight in the jungles of Vietnam, the narrator and his friends have the privilege of constructing themselves as "bad" characters. As Michael Walker has argued, the friends "are unwitting soldiers in a Vietnam of their own making, out of their depth." When Boyle's narrator finds the corpse in the pond in the woods, the reader realizes the mortality and animality that connect all humans and morally condemns the narrator and his friends for their violent actions.

"All Shook Up," another story from the *Greasy Lake* collection, is the story of an unsuccessful Elvis Presley impersonator, and like "Greasy Lake," it explores the relationship between appearance and identity. Patrick, the twenty-nine-year-old narrator of the story, is a high-school guidance counselor whose wife, Judy, has recently left him. When twenty-year-old Cindy Greco and her twenty-one-year-old husband, Joey, move into the house next door, Patrick immediately notices from Joey's voice and appearance that he is an Elvis impersonator and later agrees to visit their house for dinner. Patrick's musical interests do not include Elvis: "By the time I gave up pellet guns and minibikes and began listening to rock and roll, it was the Doors, Stones, and Hendrix, and Elvis was already degenerating into a caricature of himself." His condescending attitude toward Joey arises from his opinion that by impersonating Elvis, Joey makes a caricature out of a caricature. Patrick's underlying assumption is that musicians such as the Doors, the Rolling Stones, and Jimi Hendrix are more authentic and complex than Elvis Presley.

Boyle uses the rhetoric of authenticity to indicate the ways in which Patrick himself is just as much of an impersonator as Joey. Patrick's job as a high-school guidance counselor affords him the opportunity of giving advice to many attractive and pregnant girls. Patrick admits that he is attracted to these girls, but his position as an authority in the school prevents him from acting on his desires. When Patrick begins an affair with the much younger Cindy, however, the reader sees that his ethics do not impede his sexual desire for much younger women, that he only requires a convenient social situation, like the invitation to dinner. By the conclusion of the story, when Patrick accepts his wife's offer to return home without telling her about the affair, the reader comprehends his unethical nature, hypocritical self-absorption, and immaturity. Patrick does not want the responsibility of caring for Cindy and her baby when Joey offers them to him at the end of the story. Patrick's posturing with Cindy and his wife has greater and more lasting consequences than Joey's more benign Elvis impersonation. Even though "All Shook Up," with Joey's amusing Elvis impersonations, is more comic than "Greasy Lake," it nonetheless critiques the dark behavior of its protagonist.

...Despite being complex, intriguing, and often extremely funny and provocative on their own terms, Boyle's short stories in many cases also serve as texts in which he first approaches key themes he later explores in more depth in his novels. For instance, "Descent of Man," one of his first stories, introduces the theme of a so-called enlightened humanity's essential irrationality, which *Water Music*, his first novel, explores with greater penetration. "If the River Was Whiskey" demonstrates the autobiographical bent that also characterizes *World's End*; "Filthy with Things" includes a chief character, Susan Certaine, whose megalomania and skewed idealism parallel similar traits in Dr. John Harvey Kellogg in *The Road to Wellville* and Dr. Alfred Kinsey in *The Inner Circle*; and "After the Plague" is a postapocalyptic tale of viral devastation that precedes the environmental disaster in *A Friend of the Earth*. In using his best short stories as "workshops" in which he develops thematic ideas for his novels, Boyle creates a series of exciting intertextual relationships that allow the reader to consider his key issues—American history, the social ramifications of idealism and science, environmentalism, illegal immigration, racism, and the role of popular culture in the formation of identity—from many disparate angles and perspectives.

Source: Paul Gleason, "T. C. Boyle's Short Fiction: An Overview from *Descent of Man* to *Tooth and Claw*," in *Understanding T. C. Boyle*, University of South Carolina Press, 2009, pp. 12–34.

Michael Walker

In the following essay, Walker offers an overview of "Greasy Lake" and characterizes Boyle's fiction as "inventive" but lacking an ethical dimension.

In her essay, "Notes Toward a Dreampolitik," Joan Didion describes the funeral of a motorcycle outlaw portrayed in *The Wild Angels*, the 1966 "classic exploitation bike movie" starring Peter Fonda. After the gang has raped and murdered while destroying a small town, "they stand at the grave, and, uncertain how to mark the moment, Peter Fonda shrugs. 'Nothing to say,' he says." Didion finds in this remark the existential myth of the outlaw embracing man's fate, a myth that suits both the motorcycle gang and the film's teenage audience. The adult audience, including Didion herself, sees in this remark the moral emptiness of these fallen angels; for them, there is nothing to be learned from human experience; there is nothing to say. The film bothers to say this: art, even schlock, has the habit of revealing something about the essence of human life, bad or good.

When we look around at contemporary fiction, though, we notice that this habit of revelation is missing. Because T. Coraghessan Boyle's story "Greasy Lake" has recently been presented in X. J. Kennedy's fifth edition of his literature anthology, *Literature* (along with stories by John Updike, James Joyce, and Katherine Anne Porter), comparisons are bound to occur. Although this is not the place for a survey of Boyle's work, a brief overview of "Greasy Lake" may serve as an introduction to his short fiction and to a major theme in it: the failure of moral nerve that has become a commonplace in contemporary fiction.

"THROUGH THIS COMPARISON, BOYLE HAS DRAWN THE ATTENTION OF THE READER TO A THORNY MORAL PROBLEM, ONE THAT HAS RECENTLY ACHIEVED NATIONAL ATTENTION: HOW DO WE RESPOND TO THE MORAL DECISIONS—PERSONAL AND NATIONAL—BROUGHT ABOUT BY VIETNAM?"

If *postmodern* means anything (and there is increasing evidence that, like *political*, it doesn't), it refers not only to the oft-noted element of self-consciousness or "intertextuality," but more importantly to a Fonda-like shrug and the admission, "nothing to say." We are all accustomed to the ubiquitous breaking of the proscenium that is the hallmark of "clever" mass-produced art. From Robbe-Grillet to *Roseanne*, the wink into the mirror has become habitual, almost a nervous tic. But while the conservative art forms that practice this "hey, ma, no hands" approach to post-modernity hold fast to some sort of "family values," the avant-garde of postmodern fiction, because it is in the grip of a self-image that transcends anything so banal as beliefs, is necessarily limited to parody. It attempts satire, but because it lacks any moral standards, its exaggeration and self-absorption can only serve as frenetic substitutes for a moral point of view.

Before postmodernism and its resulting habits put a stranglehold on fiction, one of the most common practices of the twentieth-century short story was presenting the sudden insight of a character under pressure. Any number of stories that make up the core of a traditional course in short fiction—and that make up most anthologies—could serve as examples: "The Death of Ivan Ilyich," "A & P," "Araby,"

"The Jilting of Granny Weatherall." At the moment of emotional climax, the usually unwilling protagonist encounters a sudden Joycean epiphany, a new awareness of the reality of human existence. The titles I cited, of course, are good examples of this practice; like any facet of fiction, revelation can be handled well or ill and we are all familiar with stories that have banal or stupid morals tacked on willy-nilly.

Contemporary fiction has, to a great degree, avoided this last problem by avoiding revelation altogether. In these worlds of fiction, there is nothing to be learned, nothing to be revealed; there is only the endless circuit of plot and character, the zanier, the more discordant, the more violent the better. Boyle's fiction, though, goes further to parody the revelatory nature of fiction itself. Characters in Boyle's first two collections, *Descent of Man* and *Greasy Lake & Other Stories*, are frequently put in a position to understand the world around them and then to act according to this new understanding; but each time they ignore the knowledge, fumble the opportunity, or avoid the entire situation. This is not noticeable in Boyle's first collection, *Descent of Man*, because the stories tend toward farce, or the medieval genre *fabliau*. They are divorced from revelation not only by their lack of morality but also by their lack of realism. They read as if one of Boyle's major influences were Woody Allen's early essays. The work of his second collection, though, and the third, *If the River Was Whiskey*, strikes an uneasy balance; it is as though Boyle desperately wants to become a writer of realistic fiction with all it entails, but can't bring himself to do it.

"Greasy Lake" is an excellent example of a story that includes many conventions of the revelatory tale but draws back at every opportunity of displaying any true revelation in the characters in such a way that the story parodies the belief in revelation itself. The story is told by an older narrator describing himself as a pampered adolescent who considers himself and his friends "bad" characters who "cultivated decadence like a taste." Throughout the story, the naïveté of the adolescent and his two friends Digby and Jeff is mocked by the ironic, amused, and detached tone of the narrator. Insofar as narrative technique is concerned, the story is strictly modernist, and models could be found almost anywhere: Joyce's *Dubliners* and *Portrait of the Artist as a Young Man* come to mind instantly. When the three friends go searching for the heart of darkness at Greasy Lake, the small-town mecca of adolescents in search of thrills, they find themselves in more trouble than they had anticipated. Arriving at the lake, they mistake a parked car for a friend's, and begin annoying its occupants. Unfortunately for the three, they disturb a truly bad character engaged with his girlfriend. The character ("Bobby") emerges from the car and takes on all three. The bad companions are getting the worst of the battle when the narrator hits Bobby on the head with a tire iron.

The three friends, adrenalin pumping, are suddenly accosted by Bobby's "fox," who emerges screaming from the car. The bad characters attempt to rape her, but are interrupted by another car swinging into the parking lot (the occupants of which are later seen to be two blond fraternity brothers). The three companions—convinced as they are that Bobby is dead—run into the woods before determining who the new visitors are, and the college students decide to avenge the woman's honor. While hiding in the shallows of the lake, the protagonist encounters a "nasty little epiphany"—the floating corpse of a dead biker, whose motorcycle is parked in the lot.

After their car is destroyed by the recovered Bobby and the two fraternity men, the three emerge from the woods at daybreak. Two women who drive up in a Mustang ask them if they've seen "Al," whose motorcycle is parked nearby. The women, apparently stoned, offer drugs to the three friends, who refuse. They drive off, the narrator noting that "The girl was still standing there, watching us, her shoulders slumped, hand outstretched."

We could easily confuse "Greasy Lake" with a story of revelation. All the traditional requirements for that subgenre have been met. Taken from almost any angle, the story presents many possibilities of knowledge and understanding that the 19-year-old protagonist could have gained as a result of his experience. The setting establishes this for us: the passage of the protagonist from water to land, and from night to morning, parallels his passage from ignorance to knowledge, from chaos to order, from naïveté to understanding. The action establishes the same concept: the protagonist compares for himself the depth of his own miseries to those of the dead biker: "Then I thought of the dead man. He was probably the only person on the planet worse off than I was.... My car was wrecked; he was dead." The narrative style itself—the older narrator looking back on his youthful ignorance and bravado with an ironic detachment—leads us to expect the awareness of truth dawning upon the adolescent. This story could be special-ordered for an introduction-to-fiction anthology. Kennedy himself, in the "Questions" at the end of the story, asks "How does the heroes' encounter with the two girls at the end of the story differ from their earlier encounter with the girl from the blue Chevy? How do you account for the difference?"; a question urging the student to find a revelation in the story.

But if we look at "Greasy Lake" as a story of revelation, we miss Boyle's parody of that subgenre and misunderstand what postmodern fiction does and does not offer us. Boyle knows his business, and these well-worn elements of revelation are not in the story accidentally. If we compare his story with John Updike's "A & P," we will see where and to what effect Boyle's story shrugs and admits of nothing to say. In "A & P," one of the most widely anthologized and commonly taught of the revelation-style stories, John Updike hands us the character's revelation on a plate. When his narrator, Sammy, a clerk in an A & P store, rebels against oppression (his boss's insensitive criticism of three girls in bathing suits), he realizes that such defiance will neither protect the oppressed nor win him reward from those he defends, but also realizes that his action reflects his deepest character: "... my stomach kind of fell and I felt how hard the world was going to be on me hereafter."

What is the difference between these two stories? By means of both style and silence, Boyle denies the possibility of his character's learning anything from the experience.

Boyle's style is breathless, fast-paced, and outrageous in its use of description and comparisons. Metaphors and similes come thick and fast on the shores of Greasy Lake, and Boyle never contents himself with one when he can offer two or three. The comparisons, for their abundance, are neither aimless nor without purpose; they enable us to see the referent from strategic points of view. When the three adolescents rush into the lake after being interrupted in their attempted rape, the narrator says, "Behind me, the girl's screams rose in intensity, disconsolate, incriminating, the screams of the Sabine women, the Christian martyrs, Anne Frank dragged from the garret." The metaphors here are well-chosen, presenting the reader with the various aspects of the situation: pagan rape, spiritual defiance, and political/religious oppression. They also keep a logical and emotional rhythm, increasing in intensity and culminating with one of the most emotion-laden icons of the twentieth century. When the narrator touches the floating corpse of Al the biker, he notes that "it gave like a rubber duck, it gave like flesh." Once again, the pattern of similes works well and logically: the reference to a bath toy carries us from a child's response to a sickening awareness.

I present this to demonstrate, however briefly, Boyle's skill in establishing mood and purpose by means of figurative language. A comparison Boyle makes between the protagonist's losing his car keys and the Vietnam war establishes such a great similarity between the protagonist and the narrator that we cannot see any change in the two between the time of the episode at Greasy Lake and the time of telling the story. Ironic or not, the same penchant for exaggeration in the 19-year-old remains in the narrator. When the companions see the car they mistakenly believe belongs to a friend, they rush out of their own in order to harass him. But the narrator's youthful self makes a grave mistake:

> In the excitement, leaping from the car with the gin in one hand and a roach clip in the other, I spilled [the car keys] in the grass—in the dark, rank mysterious nighttime grass of Greasy Lake.... I stopped there by the open door, peering vaguely into the night that puddled up round my feet.

The metaphor of water in the images of "spilling" car keys and the night "puddling" bring to our minds the fluidity of the universe of Greasy Lake. This is an inchoate world, the world of the night, in which solidity, form, and definition are lost.

This fluidity is the basis of another, more important comparison: "This [loss of the car keys] was a tactical error, as damaging and irreversible in its way as Westmoreland's decision to dig in at Khe Sanh." We can take this link between the tactical errors at Greasy Lake and Vietnam either of two ways: first, we can laugh it off as an obviously overblown and almost clownish comparison between a wartime tragedy and the foolishness of a drunken 19-year-old. If we do that, though, we are assuming that Boyle is still in his *fabliau* phase and we ignore the logical and emotional grammar of his style.

A second interpretation leads us further into the mind of Boyle's fiction: by means of these two comparisons (the night bubbling up and the loss of the keys as Khe Sanh) Greasy Lake becomes a nightmarish swamp, the crucible of a forming consciousness, as it was for the United States.

As in most of Boyle's fiction, the narrator of this story is not only as old as Boyle is himself, but has much the same background. Boyle, born in 1948, would have been 19 in 1967, the trough of the United States' involvement in Vietnam. None of his characters, though, are soldiers; those who do mention the politics of that time have always been deferred from the armed forces, usually as students. The protagonist of "Greasy Lake," like the narrator, is separated from Vietnam and all it stood for; but because of this comparison, Greasy Lake becomes his own rice paddy, his own moral quagmire.

Through this comparison, Boyle has drawn the attention of the reader to a thorny moral problem, one that has recently achieved national attention: how do we respond to the moral decisions—personal and national—brought about by Vietnam? During the 1992 presidential campaign, Bill Clinton encountered criticism over the possibly questionable means he used to avoid military service. Clinton and his team spent much of the campaign creating a version of himself as a young man in search of moral ground; his final decision was to reject the war, to separate himself from that quagmire. Unfortunately, it was a far-reaching swamp that sucked down many who wanted nothing to do with it. The attempts of this and other public figures in the '90s to recreate their selves of 25 years ago mirror Boyle's narration and life. Born Thomas John Boyle, he took "Coraghessan" as a middle name when he started college. This practice of reforming oneself, reinventing the past, taking Gatsby's doomed words "Can't change the past? Of course you can" as a way of life, is not new; but Vietnam and the issues that surrounded it have made the issue of great importance. When Bill Clinton refers to his hometown as Hope, Arkansas, when it is actually Hot Springs, or when he claims to have experimented with marijuana without inhaling, and when Hillary Rodham Clinton drops her middle name during the presidential campaign, we may see these actions as both perfectly obvious political gambits and as part of an ongoing attempt by a generation to avoid or alter its past.

At the time Boyle's character is searching for his car keys in the grass around Greasy Lake, thousands of his peers were encountering genuinely bad characters in the swamps of Vietnam. Boyle's narrator has consciously alerted us to this, but that moral awareness finds no answering chord in the character. Moral blindness is common in the revelation stories "Greasy Lake" parodies, but we expect that such moral and psychological blindness will be replaced by sight as a result of the action of the story. This does not happen in "Greasy Lake"; the 19-year-old does not pick up the message. . . .

Source: Michael Walker, "Boyle's 'Greasy Lake' and the Moral Failure of Postmodernism," in *Studies in Short Fiction*, Vol. 31, No. 2, Spring 1994, pp. 247–55.

Neville Shack

In the following review, Shack commends Boyle's tone and method in the short stories in Greasy Lake.

T. Coraghessan Boyle's new collection of stories displays an impressive craftsmanship. His method, seamless and well-turned, gives him great scope for working the right tone of flippancy into his burlesques, as well as pathos into his personal diagnoses. There is never a hint of sentimentality about his depictions of losers in trouble. People are left alone with their own visions, sometimes ridiculous because of their stupidity; self-awareness being in shorter supply than luck.

> These are stories—mostly set in America—about fecklessness and fiasco, cushioned in the best sense by a prose style that is alternately staccato and verbose. So the satire is fine, even when some of the descriptive detail is glutinous.

"Ike and Nina" posits a love affair between President Eisenhower and Mrs. Khrushchev, hilariously proof against the seething enmity of the Cold War. The narrator, Paderewski, a minor functionary in the White House with special responsibility for discreet assignations, tries to tell the tale as dispassionately as possible. He marvels at the intense emotions felt by the two protagonists during the Khrushchevs' visit to America. Circumstances couldn't be more bathetic, given the backdrop of a grand state occasion, particularly when Paderewski is charged with the task of secretly chauffeuring the couple around the streets of Washington. The whole notion of a private face behind glaringly public events is being sent up—"I alone knew by how tenuous a thread hung the balance of world peace." This solemn manner unfailingly produces comedy through deadpan documentation.

Boyle's skill at imaginative dramatization of a clichéd Western view of life in Moscow itself is demonstrated in "The Overcoat II." The small ambitions of a small conformist, Akaky, seem to be extended fantastically when he acquires a stylish coat. Every received tabloid opinion about the grinding tedium of Russian life finds its way in here, third-hand impressions turned into wicked fancies on the page. So there are lengthy food queues, shabby clothes and all the patient sufferings of an exemplary citizen of the Soviet Union who inhabits a room which is stated, quite factually, to be perhaps half a size larger than the one that drove Raskolnikov to murder. The satire in this piece does more than simply poke fun at bullying Russian officialdom and its hypocritical view of Western consumer culture. The irreverence is seasoned, the caricature absurd but not extravagantly so.

Boyle often dwells on images which are then etched on the sensibility and made vital. "Whales Weep" takes one man's very amateurish and short-lived interest in the giant mammal of the deeps; his own tacky sentiments and the scale of his world-weariness are dwarfed, as you would expect, by contact with Leviathan itself. The nerve-ends of Boyle's prose sting at the encounter. "Stones in My Passway, Hellhound on My Trail" is a rendering of episodes in the doomed life of the legendary bluesman, Robert Johnson. Here the whole mood is built up out of a composite of powerful fragments, dream-like pictures and everyday ones in alternation. "Greasy Lake," the title story, centres on a fairly godforsaken place, fit for nothing more than a violent set-to and heaps of detritus. The correlatives in this diseased landscape are masterfully exploited, while the general grotesque effect is registered in the first-person narrative; all-too immediate experience through the pores of the skin.

In "Rupert Beersley and the Beggar Master of Sivani-Hoota," Boyle sportively cracks the mould of a sub-genre of Anglo-Indian detective stories. The numerous children of an Indian ruler are disappearing one by one, and the bumbling Beersley is brought in to solve the mystery. Almost predictably, he loses himself down alleyways of self-indulgent speculation. The lampooning works so well—and this is true of the whole volume—because the foibles of an essentially asinine figure are exaggerated to just the right degree. Boyle can also find plenty of straightforward lively entertainment in playing about with trifles, making them graphic, but still managing to tune everything to the demands of a constructive riotousness.

Source: Neville Shack, "Fecklessness and Fiasco," in *Times Literary Supplement* (London, England), Vol. 13, January 31, 1986, p. 112.

SOURCES

Boyle, T. Coraghessan, "Up to Greasy Lake," in *New York Times Book Review*, February 27, 2000, p. 4.

———, "Greasy Lake," in *T. C. Boyle Stories*, Penguin, 1998, pp. 261–68.

Goffman, Ken, and Dan Joy, *Counter Culture through the Ages*, Villard Books, 2004, p. 315.

Hart, Kevin, *Postmodernism: A Beginner's Guide*, Oneworld, 2004, pp. 1–5.

Knudson, James, Review of *T. C. Boyle Stories*, in *World Literature Today*, Vol. 74, No. 3, Summer 2000, pp. 591–92.

Koger, Grove, Review of *Greasy Lake, and Other Stories*, in *Library Journal*, Vol. 111, No. 9, May 15, 1985, p. 77.

McCaffery, Larry, "Lusty Dreamers in the Suburban Jungle," in *New York Times Book Review*, June 9, 1985, p. 15.

Mintz, Lawrence, Review of *American Dark Comedy: Beyond Satire*, in *Journal of Popular Film and Television*, Vol. 25, No. 2, 1997, p. 91.

Rampell, Catherine, "College Enrollment Rate at Record High," in *New York Times*, April 28, 2010, http://economix.blogs.nytimes.com/2010/04/28/college-enrollment-rate-at-record-high/ (accessed March 25, 2011).

"T. Coraghessan Boyle Biography and Notes," in *Biblio.com*, http://www.biblio.com/t-coraghessan-boyle~104531~author (accessed March 23, 2011).

Utley, Sandye, "Biographical Information," in *All about T. Coraghessan Boyle Resource Center*, April 29, 2001, http://www.tcboyle.net/bio.html (accessed March 23, 2011).

———, "Greasy Lake," in *All about T. Coraghessan Boyle Resource Center*, April 29, 2001, http://www.tcboyle.net/greasy.html (accessed March 23, 2011).

Wood, Tim, "Postmodernism in the Literary Arts," in *Beginning Postmodernism*, Manchester University Press, 1999, pp. 49–59.

FURTHER READING

Boyle, T. C., *T. C. Boyle Stories*, Viking, 1998.
This seventy story collection gathers twenty-five years of Boyle's short fiction, along with seven new short stories. The collection won the

PEN/Malamud Award for Short Fiction in 1999.

Gleason, Paul, *Understanding T. C. Boyle*, University of South Carolina Press, 2009.

This rare book-length study of Boyle's writing offers an overview spanning from his early works to recent publications.

Leland, John, *Hip: The History*, Ecco, 2005.

Leland traces the detached, ironical stance that characters like those in "Greasy Lake" have worked to convey throughout American history, from slavery and the New England transcendentalists to the rock sensibilities seen in the story to the computer culture of today.

Lyons, Bonnie, and Bill Oliver, "T. Coraghessan Boyle: Entertainments and Provocations," in *Passion and Craft: Conversations with Notable Writers*, University of Illinois Press, 1998, pp. 42–59.

In this interview, Boyle reveals some of the ideas that inspire his writing and the different functions he assigns to short stories and novels. The conversation often returns to Boyle's view that writers should view themselves as entertainers while still avoiding triteness and sentimentality.

SUGGESTED SEARCH TERMS

Boyle AND Greasy Lake

Boyle AND Springsteen

Greasy Lake AND coming of age

Greasy Lake AND drug use

T. C. Boyle AND interviews

teenagers AND 1970s

T. Coraghessan Boyle AND early stories

T. Coraghessan Boyle AND adolescence

T. C. Boyle AND postmodernism

1980s fiction

An Hour with Abuelo

JUDITH ORTIZ COFER

1995

Judith Ortiz Cofer's short story "An Hour with Abuelo," is the story of Arturo's visit with his elderly grandfather in a nursing home near Paterson, New Jersey. Arturo is a teenage Puerto Rican American who is in a hurry to achieve everything he wants in life. Over the course of the story, he learns something about patience, life's obstacles, life's triumphs, and the value of his grandfather's experience. "An Hour with Abuelo," like many of Cofer's stories, explores the divide between younger, American-born people of Puerto Rican descent and older, Puerto Rican-born adults living in America. Drawing on her own bilingual, bicultural childhood, Cofer imparts her characters with lifelike voices and wit.

"An Hour with Abuelo" first appeared in Cofer's short-story collection *An Island Like You: Stories of the Barrio*, published in 1995 by Orchard Publishing and also by Penguin in their Puffin Books series. In 2009, Scholastic reissued the collection. Upon its publication, *An Island Like You* was named an American Library Association Best Book for Young Adults and the *School Library Journal* Best Book of the Year. The American Library Association also awarded the Pura Belpré Award to *An Island Like You.*

AUTHOR BIOGRAPHY

Cofer was born as Judith Ortiz on February 24, 1952, in Hormingueros, Puerto Rico, to Jésus Ortiz

Arthur remembers time with his abuelo. *(Monkey Business Images / Shutterstock.com)*

Lugo and Fanny Morot Ortiz. Her father was in the U.S. Navy and assigned to the Brooklyn Navy Yard. He moved the family to Paterson, New Jersey, when Ortiz was a small child. This community forms the backdrop to many of her stories.

Although the family lived in Paterson, Ortiz's mother took her children back to Puerto Rico for a portion of every year, and they would stay with Ortiz's grandmother. In an interview with Nikki Grimes, the writer recalled, "For the first 15 years of my life, we moved back and forth from Paterson, New Jersey to the island, so I grew up truly bilingual and bicultural."

Although Ortiz's mother valued her Puerto Rican heritage, her father believed that it was important that the family be fully integrated in to U.S. culture. Jody Sather and Lauren Curtright, in a biography appearing on the University of Minnesota's Voices from the Gap Web site, report that the author's father "didn't want them to have the limited choices that he perceived himself to have been faced with as a boy coming into adulthood."

Although Ortiz attended primary school in Puerto Rico, most of her education was in the United States. She attended a private Catholic school from sixth through tenth grades. The family then moved to Augusta, Georgia, where she finished high school. She also went to Augusta College, where she earned a bachelor of arts degree in English in 1974. Upon marrying Charles John Cofer in 1972, she took Cofer as her last name. She earned a master of arts degree in English at Florida Atlantic University in 1977, and she also studied at Oxford University, in England. In the years that followed her graduation, Cofer was a bilingual teacher in public schools before teaching English and composition at a number of community colleges. She subsequently began teaching at the University of Georgia and has served as the Regents' and Franklin Professor of English and Creative Writing.

Cofer published *Latin Women Pray*, a three-act play, in 1980. In 1981, she won a fellowship to attend the prestigious Bread Loaf Writers' Conference; she worked for Bread Loaf for several ensuing summers. During her time there, she produced poetry chapbooks.

She turned her attention to fiction later in the 1980s, and in 1989, her first novel, *In the Line of the Sun*, appeared to critical praise. The book was nominated for a Pulitzer Prize. She followed this success with her first memoir, *Silent Dancing: A Partial Remembrance of a Puerto Rican Childhood*, published in 1990, another highly praised and honored book.

Cofer has also explored the short-story genre, producing *The Latin Deli* in 1993 and *An Island Like You* in 1995. "An Hour with Abuelo" is included in the latter book. In the years since 1995, Cofer has produced a steady stream of critically acclaimed and popularly well received novels, short stories, poems, and essays, including a young-adult novel, *The Meaning of Consuelo* (2004); a book of essays, *Woman in Front of the Sun: On Becoming a Writer* (2000); and a collection of poems and stories, *A Love Story Beginning in Spanish* (2005), among many others.

In addition to the Pulitzer Prize nomination Cofer received for *In the Line of the Sun*, she has garnered a host of other awards and honors, including the 1998 Paterson Book Prize for *The Year of Revolution: New and Selected Stories and Poems*; an Anisfield Wolf Book Award for *The*

Latin Deli: Prose and Poetry; and *Fanfare's* Best Book of the Year for *An Island Like You*. This book also won the American Library Association's Reforma Pura Belpré Medal. Cofer has continued to be a vibrant teacher and an active writer. As of the early 2010s, she and her husband lived in Georgia with their daughter, Tanya.

PLOT SUMMARY

Arturo, a young Puerto Rican American, does not want to visit his *abuelo*, or grandfather, in a nursing home. He says that he has too much to do and there is not much summer vacation left. In addition, he does not like going to the nursing home. The smell of the place disgusts him. He manages only to visit briefly at Christmas time, but now when his mother pleads with him to spend just one hour with Abuelo, Arturo gives in. She drops him at the home, saying she will return in one hour.

Arturo's spirits fall as soon as he walks in the door. People in wheelchairs line the hall. He goes to Abuelo's room and finds him writing in a notebook. Arturo asks him if he is writing the story of his life, intending his remark as a joke. However, Abuelo informs Arturo that that is exactly what he is doing.

Arturo recalls that his mother has told him that Abuelo had originally been a teacher in Puerto Rico but had lost his job after World War II. Abuelo then became a farmer. Arturo's mother believes that this was a waste of a fine mind; nonetheless, her attitude is "*Así es la vida*," a Spanish expression meaning "Such is life" or "That's the way life is." Arturo thinks that it is stupid that adults "accept whatever crap is thrown at them because 'that's the way things are.'" He says he will always go after his goals.

Arturo notices that when Abuelo talks to him, his eyes are bright and his mind is sharp even though his body is very old and wrinkled. When Abuelo offers to read the story of his life to Arturo, Arturo agrees.

Abuelo says that he "loved words from the beginning of [his] life." Although there were not many books available, his mother read them over and over to him. She taught him how to read and write, and Abuelo developed a lifelong love for books and writing. His mother sent Abuelo to high school; he was the only one in his family to go.

He began teaching in his village right after high school graduation with books sent to him by the government. Although he was still poor, he felt rich because of the books. Abuelo said that it was a wonderful time for him. He taught the children of the village to read and write poetry and plays, and sometimes they would put on shows for the parents.

Soon, however, the United States went to war. Because Puerto Rico was a commonwealth of the United States, all men of a certain age who lived there were subject to the military draft. Abuelo asked to be deferred because he was the only teacher in his village. Nevertheless, he was drafted.

Once in the army, he told his sergeant that he could teach farm boys how to read so that they could be better soldiers. The sergeant thought he was a smart aleck, and instead of being assigned teaching duties, he was assigned bathroom duty. For the entire war, he worked as a janitor cleaning toilets.

After the war, when he returned to Puerto Rico, he discovered that only people with college degrees could teach in public school. Because his parents were sick and he was the only one of his brothers and sisters who could help them, he became a farmer. He got married and raised a family. He taught all of his children to read and write.

Abuelo closes his story at this point. He tells Arturo that the name of his book is *Así es la vida*. Then Abuelo falls silent for a long time, and Arturo does not know what to say. He liked the story, but he does not like the title. He thinks Abuelo could have been a teacher if he had tried harder. He struggles with his own thoughts and with his Spanish, wanting to talk to Abuelo about how he does not intend to let life get in the way of what he wants to do.

At this moment, however, an old woman in a pink jogging suit comes into the room and begins talking to Abuelo. She flirts with him and reminds him that today is poetry-reading day. He has promised to read his poems to the people there. Abuelo seems to come alive. His voice becomes stronger, and he instructs Arturo to get the wheelchair out of the closet. He asks Arturo to give him a notebook with the words *Poemas de Arturo* written on the front cover.

Arturo intends to wheel his grandfather to the rec room, but the elder sends him away, saying his time is over. Arturo watches the lady in the pink jogging suit wheel Abuelo away and thinks, "I can't help but think that my abuelo has been timing *me*." The idea makes him laugh, and he goes to find his mother.

CHARACTERS

Abuelo

Abuelo is Arturo's grandfather. (*Abuelo* is the Spanish word for grandfather.) His name is also Arturo. Although he now lives in a nursing home near or in Paterson, New Jersey, he is originally from Puerto Rico. Abuelo is very old, with wrinkled brown skin. Although he is very elderly, he is still sharp—as if while his body is giving out, his mind remains clear.

Abuelo grew up in a large, very poor family. His mother, however, was educated and owned a few books. With these books, she taught the children of the family to read. She also taught them how to write, using slates and chalk. Abuelo developed a love of reading and writing very early, and he was an intelligent young man. His mother managed to send him to high school; he was the only one among his siblings who had this advantage. After graduation, he returned to his village and began to teach school. He felt honored and wealthy in this position. Although he had very little money, he had many books sent to him by the government. Because he valued books and learning so much, he was very happy in his position.

When World War II broke out, he was drafted into the army, despite his appeal to the governor of Puerto Rico. He wanted to remain to teach the children of his village, since they would grow up ignorant without a teacher. In the army, he was forced to clean latrines. This was his job for the entire war, as a punishment for his offer to teach his fellow soldiers how to read and write.

After the war, he was unable to return to teaching because he lacked a college degree and found himself turning to farming in order to support his parents, his new wife, and their growing family. He taught all of his children to read and write and instilled a love of learning in them. Thus, although he was no longer formally a teacher, he fulfilled the role of teacher for his family.

When he grew old, there was no one in Puerto Rico to care for him, so his grown children brought him to the United States so that he could live in a nursing home near them. In the nursing home, he writes his life story, a story he calls *Así es la vida*, or "Such Is Life." He also writes many poems.

In the nursing home, the other residents seem to look up to him. They look forward to hearing his stories and his poems. One of the residents, an elderly woman in a pink jogging suit, seems to be infatuated with Abuelo.

Abuelo demonstrates throughout "An Hour with Abuelo" that he is a man of great intelligence, compassion, and honor. Throughout his life, he has recognized his duty, to both his country and his family, even when that duty has gotten in the way of pursuing his real loves, literature and teaching. Now that he is old, he returns to what he loves best, reading and writing. He is also an educator: he teaches Arturo about life and duty, and he enlightens the residents of the nursing home through poetry.

Arturo

Arturo is a young high-school student. He lives with his family in Paterson, New Jersey. His family is from Puerto Rico, although Arturo is American born. Readers know from the first paragraph that Arturo is quite intelligent and also ambitious. He has a pile of books he wants to read so that he can pass a test and get into advanced-placement English classes in the fall. He says that he is "going stupid in some of [his] classes," suggesting that he does not feel challenged by the intellectual level of his current curriculum. Thus, he demonstrates that he is willing to work hard for what he wants and that he sees education as a worthy goal.

He is also a young man in a hurry. The days of his summer vacation are slipping by him, and he does not want to waste any of the time he should spend reading going to see his grandfather. In addition, as the story unfolds, it becomes obvious that he thinks one should get whatever one wants in the present, if one is willing to work hard enough for it. He does not understand why adults, including his mother and Abuelo, take what life hands them rather than reaching out and grabbing what they want. He believes that there is nothing one cannot accomplish if one works hard enough for it and if one refuses to compromise. Because of his hurry, Arturo resents the hour he has to spend with his grandfather. He glances at his watch, a gesture he immediately realizes is rude.

It seems clear in the beginning of the story that Arturo has never been close to his grandfather, despite being his namesake. He initially refers to him as "the abuelo," distancing himself from the old man. In addition, he does not like visiting him because the nursing home smells bad. When he goes to visit at Christmas, he reads magazines rather than trying to talk to Abuelo.

It also seems clear that he has never worked at getting to know his grandfather as a person. Arturo knows that Abuelo was a teacher in Puerto Rico who later became a farmer but does not know the details. Indeed, he seems to dismiss his grandfather as an individual because he believes that Abuelo has not worked for what he most wants out of life but rather has blindly accepted what fate has dealt him.

In addition, Arturo does not seem to value elderly people. He fails to recognize that even though a person is old, he or she can still be productive and intelligent. When he looks at the residents of the nursing home, all he sees are people in wheelchairs at the end of their lives. When he sees his grandfather writing in a book, he makes a joke, which suggests that he does not think his grandfather has anything worthwhile to say. When he sees the woman in the pink jogging suit, he makes fun of her in his mind, calling her "the world's oldest marathoner." It does not occur to him that such a thing could be true.

Over the course of the story, Arturo comes to know his grandfather better and begins to respect the elderly. His grandfather's story touches him. In addition, he suddenly realizes that his grandfather has a life of his own, apart from his family. Abuelo has friends and is well respected among his peers. Although Arturo initially thought that he was doing his grandfather a favor by coming to spend an hour with him, he realizes that it is Abuelo who has done the favor by spending an hour with him. Although Arturo still has much to learn about life, Abuelo has taught him an important lesson.

Lady in the Pink Jogging Suit

The unnamed lady in the pink jogging suit is Abuelo's friend at the nursing home. She comes to bring Abuelo to the recreation room for a poetry reading near the end of the story. Although Arturo thinks she looks funny in her jogging suit and tennis shoes, the woman is young in her actions and movements. She pushes Abuelo down the hall with ease, going faster than Arturo believes they should.

Mother

Arturo's mother wants him to visit Abuelo. She tells him that Abuelo does not have much more time to live. She also tells Arturo about her father being a teacher in Puerto Rico and how he had to become a farmer later. This is a waste of a good mind, she says. Arturo's mother nags at him to visit Abuelo until he gives in.

Although the picture of the mother is not entirely positive through Arturo's eyes, the reader can form a different picture of the woman through clues in the text. When she drops Arturo off at the nursing home, she gets choked up and thanks her son for agreeing to the visit. This demonstrates her love of her father and her son, and her grief over her father's impending death. In addition, his mother has lived up to her responsibility to her father by bringing him to the United States after the death of her mother. She has arranged the best care she can manage for him. Arturo's mother is in all likelihood a positive influence on the young man, instructing him in duty and familial responsibility as well as encouraging him in his studies.

THEMES

Aging

In "An Hour with Abuelo," Cofer provides two perspectives on the theme of aging. In the first place, readers see the theme of aging through Arturo's eyes. As a young man, his response to his aging grandfather is somewhat callous; he reports that the doctors say his *abuelo* "doesn't have too long to go now" and then immediately says that he does not have much time left in his summer vacation. Arturo seems to think that the fact that his summer vacation is about to end is somehow equivalent to his grandfather's life quickly drawing to a close.

Arturo also makes clear that he dislikes visiting his grandfather because he hates "the old people's home." The home smells bad to Arturo and makes him nauseous. Inside the home, Arturo mentions that the orderlies line up the nursing home residents in the hall in their wheelchairs. He clearly feels sorry for them, as evidenced by his comment that the orderlies do not even look at the people in the chairs, but the old people also make him feel uncomfortable. "I walk

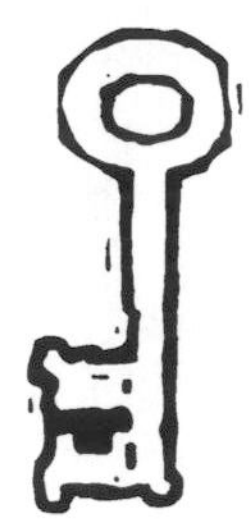

TOPICS FOR FURTHER STUDY

- Read Virginia Driving Hawk Sneve's young-adult short story "The Medicine Bag." Think about how its main character and Arturo in "An Hour with Abuelo" are alike and different, specifically in the ways they relate to their grandfathers. Write an essay or create an expanded Venn diagram in which you compare and contrast what the main characters learn over the course of the story.
- With a small group of classmates, research the customs and culture of Puerto Rico both in the library and on the Internet. What is life like in Puerto Rico? What kinds of foods do Puerto Ricans eat? What kinds of music do they enjoy? Plan a celebration for your class featuring Puerto Rican food, music, poetry, and art. Decorate your classroom with pictures and illustrations of Puerto Rico.
- Prepare a list of questions about the early life of one of your grandparents. Interview your grandparent in person, on the phone, or using Skype. (If your grandparents are no longer alive or not available to you, choose another older relative or family friend to interview.) Where did your grandparent grow up? What language did he or she speak? What were some of the important events of his or her life? Using the information you learn, write a short story featuring your grandparent as the main character.
- Write a play based on "An Hour with Abuelo." With a small group of classmates, rehearse and perform your play. Using a video camera, record your presentation and upload it to YouTube so that you can share your play with other students in your school.
- What are the ways that elderly people in the United States are cared for? Use personal experience, the Internet, and the library to research this topic. With the permission of your parents and your teacher, organize a trip to an assisted-living facility or nursing home to visit with some of the residents. What are some of the advantages and disadvantages of such places? Use computer software such as Inspiration 9 to help you keep track of your information and create a presentation for the rest of your class about care of the elderly in the United States.

fast to room 10, Abuelo's 'suite,'" he says. Tellingly, he is no better than the orderlies who do not look at the residents; he does not look at them either, nor does he smile or greet them. Arturo attempts to make the elderly people invisible. Throughout the story, Arturo's comments about the people living in the nursing home demonstrate his lack of sympathy for and understanding of the elderly. His attitude toward aging is a negative one.

The second perspective used by Cofer to tackle the theme of aging is that of Abuelo. By the end of the story, it is clear that Abuelo is still a person to be reckoned with, someone who still has a great deal to teach the world. Cofer demonstrates that, despite being confined to a wheelchair, Abuelo is able to live his life and help other people. He does not depend on his young grandson for company or to give his life meaning. Cofer's characterization of Abuelo demonstrates to readers that aging is not necessarily a negative process but rather is an opportunity for someone to finally realize his or her life's dreams.

"An Hour with Abuelo," then, suggests that the impatience of youth has much to learn from the wisdom of age. Although Arturo initially believes that he is making a great sacrifice to spend an hour with Abuelo, he finally learns that it is his Abuelo who has made time for him.

Fate and Free Will

Así es la vida is a Spanish expression meaning "Such is life," or "That is the way life is." Arturo

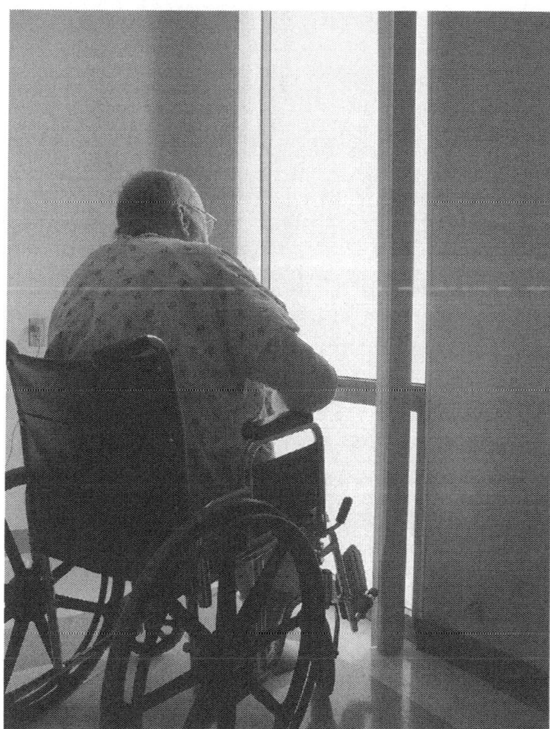

Arthur's abuelo wanted visitors at the nursing home. *(Amanda Haddox / Shutterstock.com)*

hates the phrase; he is impatient with adults who use the phrase to explain how things turn out the way they do. In Arturo's mind, people who use this phrase believe they have no power to affect how their lives turn out.

Arturo believes in free will. He states openly that he will go after what he wants, no matter what life puts in his way. This attitude suggests that he believes that his life is of his own making and that nothing is predetermined or fated. Arturo's worldview is that hard work on the part of an individual in pursuit of a worthy goal will always lead to success.

Arturo's attitude is naive and simplistic. His life in the United States, attending a high school where he can take advanced-placement classes, has been largely made possible by the sacrifices of his grandfather. He has not faced the poverty or problems that his grandfather faced as a young person in Puerto Rico. Although it is admirable that Arturo is committed to his goals and intends to succeed, his lack of patience with people who have had to forgo their dreams in order to put food on the table is immature. Moreover, he has not lived long enough to know that although one may not be able to reach a goal quickly, it does not mean that it will not be met at all.

One of the ways that Cofer demonstrates Arturo's growth in the story is to depict his growing awareness that his grandfather never gave up on his love of learning and teaching. Indeed, one of the most important life lessons Arturo takes from his hour with Abuelo is this: a door may close when a person is young, through no fault of his or her own, but the door may open again, much later.

STYLE

Voice

One of the most difficult tasks a writer faces is establishing distinctive voices for each of his or her characters. A writer creates a voice for a character through word choice, syntax (also called word order), grammar, and punctuation. When a writer is successful in creating a voice for a character, the reader can almost hear that character speaking as he or she reads.

In "An Hour with Abuelo," Cofer has given herself an additional factor to consider. Arturo is not only the main character but is also a first-person narrator. That is, the entire story is told through his eyes and voice. However, because the middle section is entirely Abuelo's story, she must insert Abuelo's voice into Arturo's narration. That she is able to do so successfully speaks to Cofer's talent as a writer. In addition, although Arturo's mother only has a few lines in the story, Cofer manages to create a distinctive voice for her as well.

Cofer establishes Arturo's voice as that of an ambitious, intelligent, and impatient teenager. He uses informal American dialect, unlike his mother or his *abuelo*. For example, Arturo says, "I'm going stupid in some of my classes." This is a colloquial (familiar or informal) expression. He says that the nursing home smells bad, "like industrial-strength ammonia and other stuff I won't mention." The use of the word "stuff" is also indicative of the informal speech of a young person. Likewise, Arturo uses contractions such as "I'm" and "could've." Again, contraction use is common in informal speech, but it contrasts with the way his mother and his *abuelo* speak.

Arturo contributes to the reader's understanding of Abuelo's voice. He describes his grandfather's voice as slow and says, "He speaks what my mother calls book English. He taught himself from a dictionary, and his words sound stiff, as if he's sounding them out in his head before he says them." Abuelo's language is formal: he uses correct and precise words in every instance. While his vocabulary is refined, it is also not overly academic or difficult to understand. The rhythm of his story is created not only by his word choice but also by his sentence structure and length. It sounds as if he is telling a story aloud, with all the rhythms a storyteller would use to create drama and poignancy in his work, particularly a storyteller whose first language is not English. Being completely proper, Abuelo's English is not colloquial, the way Arturo's is.

Arturo's mother speaks only briefly in the story, with just fourteen words in her own voice and a few more lines reported through Arturo. Of her fourteen words, four of them are in Spanish. She uses the Spanish in the first case to emphasize what she has said in English: "Just one hour, *una hora*, is all I'm asking of you, son." In the second case, when she thanks Arturo for giving in to her request to visit his grandfather, all she says is "*Gracias, hijo*," that is, "Thank you, son." The implication is that she resorts to Spanish when she is overcome with emotion. Like her father, Arturo's mother speaks English as a second language, although her English is not as formal as her father's. Arturo, on the other hand, speaks English as a native speaker.

The story uses the voices of its characters to show how an American is made. Arturo's ideas and language are of the United States, whereas his grandfather and mother still cling in many ways to Puerto Rico in their voices. Through his interaction with his grandfather, however, Arturo learns to honor his heritage as well as look forward to achieving the American dream.

Epiphany

In literature as in life, an epiphany is a moment when someone has a sudden revelation or understanding about the truth of a situation or a person. In the case of Arturo, he reaches an epiphany in the last paragraphs of the story. The epiphany is precipitated by his grandfather's reaction when he tries to wheel him to the rec room: "I start to push him toward the rec room, but he shakes his finger at me. 'Arturo, look at your watch now. I believe your time is over.' He gives me a wicked smile."

For Arturo, who before had been glancing at his watch because he did not want to be at the nursing home and was timing the hour he had promised to spend with his grandfather, Abuelo's comment is shocking. Until this moment, Arturo believed that he was doing his grandfather a favor by sacrificing one of his precious summer vacation hours to visit with him. However, his grandfather's wicked smile forces him to quickly reverse his thinking: "I look at my watch and the hour *is* up, to the minute. I can't help but think that my abuelo has been timing *me.*" This revelation changes the way that Arturo feels about his grandfather and about his visit.

Further, although Arturo finds it funny that his grandfather has been timing him, there is also a serious implication. Abuelo's remaining hours are far fewer than Arturo's; that he has been willing to grant Arturo his full attention for an hour is a far more valuable gift than Arturo perhaps realizes.

HISTORICAL CONTEXT

Puerto Rico

Puerto Rico is an island in the Caribbean Sea. In 1493, Christopher Columbus landed on the island during his second voyage. According to Clara E. Rodríguez in her article "Puerto Ricans: Immigrants and Migrants," this was the first contact of the Taino indigenous population with Europeans. Spain quickly colonized the island because it was a rich source of gold and silver, although both the mines and the Taino people whom the Spanish enslaved to work the mines soon wore out. However, because the island was also important strategically to Spain, they maintained tight control.

During the nineteenth century, Puerto Rico grew rapidly with immigration from a variety of countries and was considered an important trade center. In 1898, the United States engaged in war with Spain and consequently invaded Puerto Rico. Rodríguez notes that an independence movement within Puerto Rico helped the United States defeat the Spanish because the people hoped to be granted independence. This was not forthcoming, however; the United States designated Puerto Rico a commonwealth. Ironically, Puerto Rico had more autonomy under the Spanish than under the Americans.

COMPARE & CONTRAST

- **1990s:** According to the 2000 census, during the 1990s, the elderly population of the United States is about 35 million.

  Today: According to the U.S. Census Bureau, the elderly population of the United States is estimated at just over 40 million.

- **1990s:** While Puerto Rican immigrants tend to live in East Coast U.S. cities such as New York, the Puerto Rican population begins to spread across the United States.

  Today: Puerto Rican Americans live in every state, contributing to their communities and culture.

- **1990s:** Cofer publishes poetry, novels, essays, and short-story collections, including *An Island Like You: Stories of the Barrio* and *The Latin Deli: Telling the Lives of Barrio Women.*

  Today: Cofer remains an active writer and teacher, publishing the poems of *A Love Story Beginning in Spanish* in 2005 and *Lessons from a Writer's Life: Readings and Resources for Teachers and Students* in 2011.

- **1990s:** More than 22 million people of Hispanic heritage live in the United States, according to the 1990 census.

  Today: Over 35 million people of Hispanic heritage live in the United States in 2000. Projections based on the 2010 census suggest that over 47 million people of Hispanic heritage presently live in the United States.

Puerto Rico has remained a commonwealth of the United States since 1898. In 1917, Puerto Ricans were granted U.S. citizenship. During World War II, Puerto Rican men were subjected to the military draft and served the United States well. In 1952, the year of Cofer's birth, Puerto Rico established a constitution authorizing the commonwealth to manage its own internal affairs. Although Puerto Rico has one commissioner who sits in the U.S. House of Representatives, he or she has no voting powers. Neither do the citizens of Puerto Rico have the right to vote in U.S. presidential elections.

There has long been a history of Puerto Ricans immigrating to the United States, particularly to New York City. Rodríguez classifies the immigration of Puerto Ricans into three broad categories. The first arrived in New York between 1900 and 1945 and settled in areas of New York such as Brooklyn and *el Barrio* in East Harlem. The second phase is called Puerto Rico's "Great Migration," which occurred between 1946 and 1964. It was during the Great Migration that Cofer's family came to the United States. At this time, Puerto Rican enclaves were established in Connecticut, New Jersey, and Illinois, although most immigrants remained in New York City. The last period began in 1965 and continues to the present. Puerto Ricans have dispersed across the country during this last wave.

Most immigration to the United States has been driven by job and income considerations. When wages are high and unemployment low in the United States, Puerto Ricans come to the mainland. In times such as the 1970s, during an economic recession in America, more people returned to Puerto Rico than immigrated to the mainland.

The CIA World Factbook reports that Puerto Rico has one of the strongest economies in the Caribbean. There is a growing industrial segment as well as traditional agricultural interests. Tourism is a growing industry.

Puerto Rico and Literature

According to Pamela Gray, writing in "The Poetry Heritage of Puerto Rico," "Puerto Ricans call themselves *Boricua*, a distinct and unique people with a heritage that values song and verse as one

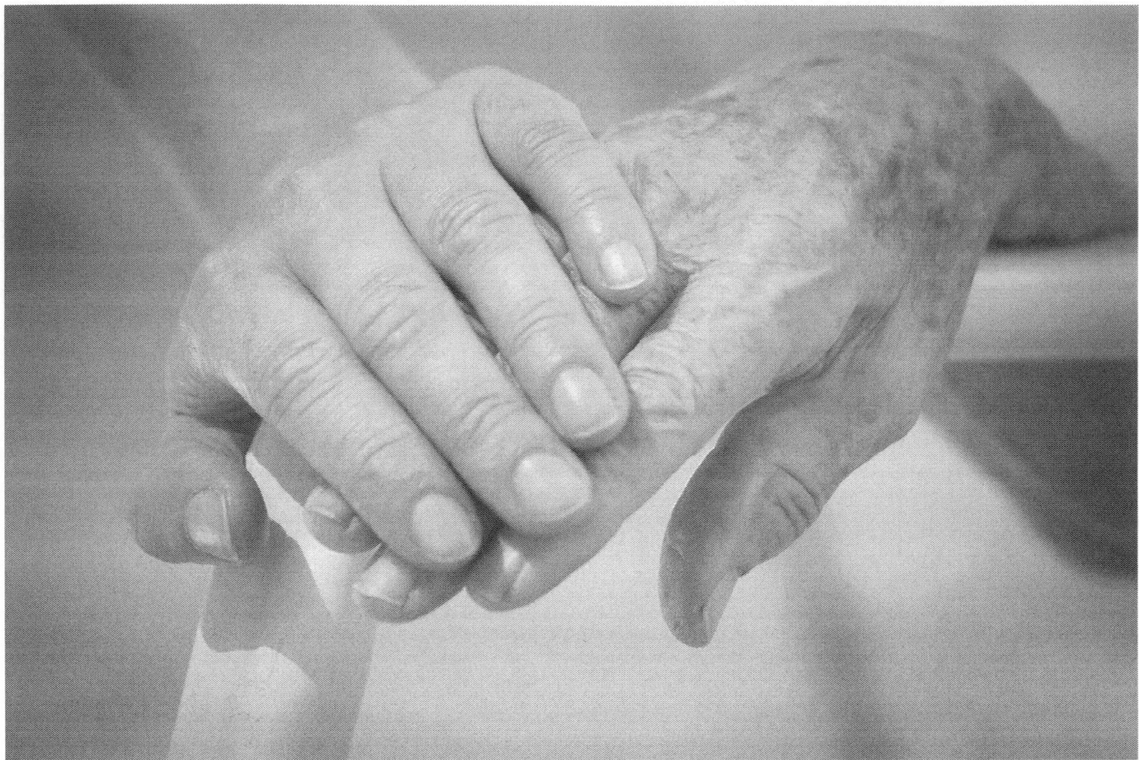

Arthur and his abuelo bond over memories. (tepic / Shutterstock.com)

of the cultural pillars." The island was a crossroads where many cultures and people met (and sometimes collided), each providing their own influence on what has come to be a rich literary milieu.

Gray discusses the Spanish roots of Puerto Rican literature as well as the African influence brought about by the large-scale importation of African slaves to work on the agricultural plantations of the island. The languages of these peoples, along with Portuguese, melded together to form a particular dialect that finds resonance in poetic creation.

Later, when many Puerto Ricans emigrated to the United States, they took with them their love of language and writing. Abuelo in Cofer's short story "An Hour with Abuelo" demonstrates such deep love of words and poetry. The writings of these immigrants were then influenced by English and the social milieu in which they found themselves, largely in New York City.

Beginning in the early 1970s, a group of Puerto Rican writers living in New York City began to meet together in the home of poet Miguel Algarín, a college professor, according to the history found on the Nuyorican Poets Café Web site. Originally a derisive term used by Puerto Ricans to describe those who had left the island and settled in New York, this avant-garde group of writers claimed the label for themselves. After a few years and the publication of an anthology of Nuyorican poetry, the group grew too large to meet in someone's home. Algarín established the Nuyorican Poets Café in an old Irish pub in New York. The movement continued to grow from that time, offering readings and poetry slams. Most of the writers participating in this movement are of Puerto Rican birth or descent and live in or near New York City. Much of their work focuses on the experience of living within two language and two cultures.

Cofer has remarked, in an interview with Rafael Ocasio in the *Kenyon Review*, that although she reads and supports Nuyorican writers, she is not heavily influenced by them. She stated,

> They do not exactly speak to me and for me in the sense that the *Nuyorican* school is specific to that area. Although I lived in Paterson, it is not the same as living in New York City, in the *barrios*.

In another interview, this one with Carmen Delores Hernández, Cofer stated,

> There all kinds of Puerto Rican writing. We don't have to consider ourselves Nuyorican in order to write. Puerto Rican writing does not come only out of Spanish Harlem. That is a colorful part of our heritage, but it's not the only part.

Thus, the literature growing out of the Puerto Rican experience, both on the island and on the mainland, continues to evolve, accounting for the many facets of Puerto Rican literary experience in many different kinds of settings.

CRITICAL OVERVIEW

Cofer is a critically acclaimed poet, essayist, novelist, and short-story writer. Many critics focus on both Cofer's highly developed sense of craft and her position as a Latina woman. In the introduction to an interview with Cofer appearing in *Meridians*, Margaret Crumpton writes that her "method of combining prose and poetry places Cofer at the forefront of a contemporary movement that is expanding and redefining literary genres." Crumpton further notes,

> Most of Cofer's works portray the tensions of characters who move between cultures.... Her respect for the language, religion, and culture of her parents is evident in her writing, even when she portrays the need to resist the confines of heritage.

Likewise, Edna Acosta-Belen, in the introduction to her interview with Cofer appearing in the journal *MELUS*, writes,

> Judith Ortiz Cofer joins [Latina writers] in telling her visions about straddling between the Puerto Rican culture of her parents and ancestors and a U.S. culture often blinded by its own prejudices and undiscerning capacity to acknowledge its own pluralistic nature.

In addition, in "Attempting Perfection: An Interview with Judith Ortiz Cofer," appearing in the book *Latina Writers*, Renee H. Shea notes that "readers look to Cofer for her honest explorations into what it means to be bilingual and bicultural."

Suzanne Bost, writing in *MELUS*, examines the notion of multicultural identity and *mestizaje* in Cofer's writing. *Mestizaje,* Bost explains, "is the Latin American term for the racial and cultural mixture that was produced by the conquest of the so-called 'New World.'" Rafael Ocasio, in an essay in *Callaloo*, on the other hand, discusses Cofer's independence from the Nuyorican style of Puerto Rican American writing. He asserts that "her work builds on the concept of *puertorriqueñidad* [Puerto Ricanness] within mainstream English constructions."

An Island Like You: Stories of the Barrio, Cofer's 1995 short-story collection that includes "An Hour with Abuelo," received strong and positive reviews at the time of its publication. Rudine Sims Bishop, writing in *Horn Book* magazine, calls the book "the best of the new anthologies." She continues, "Cofer's writing is lively and the characters memorable.... The voices in these stories ring true, as do the stories themselves." Hazel Rochman, writing in *Booklist*, concurs that the voices Cofer creates for her characters are at the heart of the stories. Rochman states that "the contemporary teenage voices are candid, funny, weary, and irreverent in these stories about immigrant kids caught between their Puerto Rican families and the pull and push of the American dream."

Likewise, a contributor to *Publishers Weekly* comments that the stories of *An Island Like You* are "consistently sparkling" and "pungently recreate the atmosphere of a Puerto Rican barrio in Paterson, N.J." Finally, a brief review for the Cooperative Children's Book Center of the University of Wisconsin summarizes the appeal of Cofer's stories: "The range of experience which Cofer brilliantly illuminates through the singular lives of her adolescent characters reveals truths that are sometimes comforting, sometimes startling, but always dancing on the edge of enlightenment."

CRITICISM

Diane Andrews Henningfeld

Henningfeld is a professor emerita of English who writes widely on literary topics and current events for educational publications. In the following essay, she examines the ways Cofer uses irony to move Arturo, the young protagonist, to greater understanding of his grandfather and of life.

"An Hour with Abuelo" is a story that demonstrates the growth in understanding of a young man through his hour-long visit with his elderly grandfather in a nursing home near Paterson, New Jersey. Arturo, the young man, is ambitious, impatient, and sure that he can wrest from life

WHAT DO I READ NEXT?

- *Riding Low on the Streets of Gold: Latino Literature for Young Adults* (2004), edited by Judith Ortiz Cofer, is a collection of poems and stories about the experience of growing up in two languages and cultures. Some of the poems are in Spanish with English translations.
- Cofer's memoir *Silent Dancing: A Partial Remembrance of a Puerto Rican Childhood* (1995) recalls the author's childhood, which was divided between Paterson, New Jersey, and Puerto Rico.
- Linda Tagliagerro's *Puerto Rico in Pictures* (2003) is a volume in the "Visual Geography" series. The book provides an excellent young-adult overview of the island's history, geography, economy, and culture.
- Virginia Driving Hawk Sneve is a Lakota storyteller who was raised on a Sioux reservation. The stories in her collection *Grandpa Was a Cowboy and an Indian, and Other Short Stories* (2000), many of which feature children and young adults, mix history and folklore, bringing Native American traditions to life.
- *The House on Mango Street*, Sandra Cisneros's 1984 novel, is about a young Mexican American girl living in Chicago who must travel with her family to Mexico to see her grandmother. It is an excellent choice for students interested in Latino culture and experience.
- Esmeralda Santiago's 1993 memoir *When I Was Puerto Rican* traces the writer's childhood in a large family living in both Puerto Rico and New York.

whatever he sets his mind to. Over the course of the story, he begins to question his own naive notions about his grandfather and life itself. Cofer accomplishes this movement through her deft use of irony.

> "ULTIMATELY, IT IS ARTURO'S HUMOROUS APPRECIATION OF THE IRONY OF HIS VISIT THAT INDICATES HOW MUCH HE HAS LEARNED FROM HIS HOUR WITH ABUELO. HIS LAUGHTER SUGGESTS THAT HE IS ABLE TO SEE BOTH HIS OWN MISTAKEN BELIEFS AS WELL AS HIS GRANDFATHER'S WISDOM."

Irony is defined in the *Bedford Glossary of Critical and Literary Terms* as:

> A contradiction or incongruity between appearance or expectation and reality. This disparity may be manifested in a variety of ways. A discrepancy may exist between what someone says and what he or she actually means, between what someone expects to happen and what really does happen, or between what appears to be true and actually is true.

In the first case, then, irony is simply a verbal device. When someone says, "What a lovely day!" when it is pouring down rain, the person is being ironic. In "An Hour with Abuelo," Arturo uses verbal irony a number of times. First, when he asks Abuelo if he is writing the story of his life, he does not mean what he says. He believes that he is making a joke. He uses irony a second time when he calls the lady in the pink jogging suit "the world's oldest marathoner." Again, he does not mean this literally; rather, he is making fun of the elderly lady's attire.

There are also examples in the story where there is a discrepancy between what Arturo expects to happen and what really does happen. As noted above, Arturo is ironic when he asks his grandfather if he is writing the story of his life. However, when Abuelo replies that that is exactly what he is doing, irony takes another form. Arturo does not expect Abuelo's response. The joke, it appears, is on Arturo.

The most important form of irony in the story, however, is the discrepancy between what Arturo believes to be true and what he discovers really is true. There are many examples of this throughout the story. First, when Arturo arrives at the nursing home, he has an opinion of what old people are like, particularly the residents of the nursing home who sit in their wheelchairs in the hall. He rushes past them, presumably so he will not have to see them, speak to them, or acknowledge that they are there. For Arturo, the elderly do not count, have no value, and ought to be invisible. Cofer, however, has different ideas she wants readers to take from the story. Elfreida Abbe quotes Cofer in the *Writer*:

> There are people in the world who are considered beneath notice. I would like for there not to be invisible people. Good writing teaches you that everyone has an inner life. From the president of the United States to the woman who comes in and empties the trash can in the classroom.

It is not difficult to extend this thought to the elderly residents of Abuelo's nursing home. Thus, Arturo's dismissal of the nursing-home residents is ironically undercut by his experience with his still-sharp grandfather and the lady in the pink jogging suit. The story his grandfather tells about his life brings the old man into sharp focus for the boy; Arturo sees for the first time that his grandfather has a rich inner life. Additionally, the lady in the pink jogging suit defies all of Arturo's expectations of what an elderly lady should be like. She is flirtatious and capable of pushing Abuelo's wheelchair at a high rate of speed. (And her matching pink jogging suit and shoes makes it very difficult for her to fade into invisibility!)

Arturo also believes that his grandfather is very different from him, although they share the same name. Underlying this belief is his grandfather's use of the expression "*Así es la vida*," or "Such is life." Arturo believes that adults who use this phrase are resigned to accepting whatever adversity life throws in their paths. His mother has used the phrase to try to explain how his grandfather, who started out life as a teacher, ended up as a farmer. She says that it was a waste of a good mind. Arturo thus believes that his grandfather was not strong enough to stand up to life's adversities in order to get what he wanted. He is certain that he is different and that nothing will stand in his way and keep him from achieving his goals. "I'm not going to let la vida get in my way," he says.

However, as Abuelo reads his life story to Arturo, it becomes more and more clear that Arturo and his grandfather share more than just their names. As a young man, Abuelo loved reading and writing, just as Arturo does. Abuelo studied hard and graduated from high school, despite the poverty of his family. He did not let his family's condition get in the way of his pursuit of education. Arturo, too, works hard to succeed in school. He is spending much of his summer vacation reading books so that he will be able to enroll in an advanced-placement class in the fall. Likewise, Abuelo's most valued possessions were the books the government sent him when he was the teacher in his village. Arturo reads whatever he can get his hands on and values the pile of books he must read. Most importantly, although Abuelo had to postpone his dream of being a teacher and writer because of his responsibility to his family, he never stopped pursuing his dream. He taught his children how to read and write, and now, as an old man, he is teaching his peers something about poetry. Although he is nearing the end of his life, he still works hard to accomplish his goals.

The irony arises because Arturo completely misunderstands what his *abuelo* means by the phrase "*Así es la vida*." Abuelo understands that the good times and the bad, the struggles and the joys, are *la vida* itself. Thus, the recording of the events of his life is a triumph, not a resignation. It is the realization of his dreams.

A final irony at work in the story stems from Arturo's belief that his visit to Abuelo is of benefit to his grandfather but a great inconvenience for himself. Arturo seems to believe that he is doing his grandfather a favor by honoring him with a one-hour visit. The reality of the situation, as Arturo discovers at the very end of the story, is that the visit is of far more value for him than for his grandfather. Indeed, he would like to spend time talking with his grandfather about why he made the choices he did and why his life turned out the way it has. Arturo has learned a great deal about his grandfather because of their visit, and it appears that he would like to extend the time they have together. However, when the lady in the pink jogging suit comes to take Abuelo to the rec room to read his poetry, Arturo suddenly realizes that his grandfather has other plans for the afternoon. Abuelo has only allotted one hour of his time to spend with his grandson. Arturo says, "I can't help but think that my abuelo has been timing *me*. It cracks me up."

As is often the case, when the irony of a situation becomes apparent, it is humorous. Arturo laughs because he suddenly sees the discrepancy between what he thought was true and what was really true. Cofer has stated, in an

Arthur's abuelo has many stories to tell.
(hartphotography / Shutterstock.com)

interview with Nikki Grimes appearing on the Teaching Multicultural Literature Web site, "Arturo became my favorite character [in the stories of *An Island Like You*] because I felt there was a lot of me in him: the kid who finds early on that books are extremely good friends and who thinks about situations and tends to be solitary, and also has a sense of humor." Ultimately, it is Arturo's humorous appreciation of the irony of his visit that indicates how much he has learned from his hour with Abuelo. His laughter suggests that he is able to see both his own mistaken beliefs as well as his grandfather's wisdom.

Source: Diane Andrews Henningfeld, Critical Essay on "An Hour with Abuelo," in *Short Stories for Students*, Gale, Cengage Learning, 2012.

Carmen Faymonville

In the following excerpt, Faymonville presents an argument that Cofer redefines the idea of "nation" in her writing.

> "THE STEREOTYPE THAT ORTIZ COFER ULTIMATELY SEEKS TO DISPEL IS THAT OF THE READY APPROPRIATION OF MIGRANT WRITERS INTO A NATIONALIST SCHEME UNDER THE GUISE OF MULTICULTURALISM: IN THIS SCHEME, ANY WRITER FROM ANOTHER COUNTRY MOVING TO THE UNITED STATES UNDERGOES ETHNICIZATION BY BECOMING CLASSIFIED AS A HYPHENATED AMERICAN WRITER."

A HOME BUILT OF LANGUAGE INSTEAD OF TERRITORY?

...Ortiz Cofer's politics of identity joins those who are geographically scattered into an imagined unity of identification via a new postmodern transnationalism. This transnational politics creates a placeless community of interests to be imagined by anyone who feels connected by heritage or history to a nation. *The Line of the Sun* thus succeeds in the struggle to construct counternarratives to traditional nation-space by developing new literary spaces. While on a structural level Ortiz Cofer narrates the first part of her novel in the South American style of magical realism made popular by Gabriel Garcia Marquez, Jorge Luis Borges, and Isabel Allende, the plot also makes frequent thematic allusions to witch hunts, societal impositions on female self-realization, and rebel boyhoods familiar to readers of American classics such as *The Scarlet Letter*, *The Adventures of Huckleberry Finn*, and *The Crucible*. Amalgamating these US and South American literary allusions, Ortiz Cofer creates a novel that represents itself as a hybridized form joining the conventions of American realist narratives with South American anti-realism such as magic realism and indigenous folklore.

In part through the very hybridity of her chosen literary forms, Ortiz Cofer pushes conceptions of nationhood to a re-visioning of the nature of a "nation." Yet the larger significance of Ortiz Cofer's identity politics lies in her critique of ethnification and the limits she perceives in visions of multicultural societies that enforce national stereotypes. Since the multicultural ideal is still tied to the notion of a singular nation, only identities within the nation can be contested but not the identity of the nation itself. In other words, whereas both ethnic and assimilationist identities are generally available to female migrants, non-American or transnational identities are only beginning to be possible. Questioning the longstanding rhetoric of "us" and "them," citizen and foreigner, through the lens of a transnational perspective, Ortiz Cofer's critique of nationalist orthodoxy breaks the arbitrary link underlying race, nation, and culture. In Paul Gilroy's words, Ortiz Cofer might indeed be warning us that "unless identity politics can transcend the nation, escaping the bounds of the homeland, the radicalism of the challenge to old images and narratives is critically constrained within the assumption of nationalism."

Although Ortiz Cofer respects the right of the migrant to retain cultural identity, she suggests something different from both multicultural identity and from ethnic nationalist membership in one particular diasporic group. Echoing Wemer Sollors' groundbreaking argument in *The Invention of Ethnicity*, Ortiz Cofer points to the difficulties of ethnic identification in today's postmodern consumer culture in which the maintenance of national culture is much less a matter of descent than increasingly a matter of consent or voluntary identification even if racial discrimination through "descent" still exists. In other words, as Sollors describes the complex psychology of national and ethnic affiliation, "ethnicity . . . is a matter not of content, but of the importance that individuals ascribe to it." This separation of soil from political and psychological space is nowadays necessary since community always has to be imagined. As Ortiz Cofer's novel suggests, community must go beyond immediate experience and location if it is to embrace inclusiveness rather than exclusiveness. *The Line of the Sun* effectively looks beyond boundaries and universalistic homelands to a new conception of national identity where "us" and "them" are no longer reproduced as necessarily tied to geographical spaces.

Taking this imaginative step, Ortiz Cofer breaks with the modernist nationalist imagination in which separate nations stand completely apart from each other and in which borders that distinguish between citizens and non-citizens are tightly controlled. Ortiz Cofer instead recognizes that the consciousness of national identity assumes an international context and that any nation must be imagined as a nation among other nations. It is Ortiz Cofer's achievement to conceptualize Puerto-Ricanness simultaneously as the universalization of particularism and the particularization of universalism. *The Line of the Sun* illustrates well in the end that migrant women cannot easily recover a culture of origin even if they follow the lines of the sun back to ancestral spaces. Yet for those migrants who have never lived in the actual world of island culture, recreation and transnational imagined communities can provide a lifeline that can sustain them through times of discrimination in their place of residence.

As an anti-melting-pot concept, Ortiz Cofer's transnationalism offers a way against mainstreaming and cultural homogeneity by taking note of shifting subject positions. Yet where the death of ancestral culture is justly feared, transnationalism offers perhaps only a faint hope of keeping up the ancestral in the present. What Ortiz Cofer's transnationalism stresses, however, is that the "old" culture is not found simply in memory. Whereas Antin had to kill off her memory and the past, contemporary migrants are better able to hold on to the "foreign" presence of their birth location. In today's multi-global and technologized culture, one can think of multiple cultures as co-existing, omnipresent, and not as located in the past and subordinated to a dominant culture. Ideally, since descent necessarily still defines people's lives, Ortiz Cofer envisions globalization not as an abstract force but as the concrete emergence of a very local transnational culture specific to region and migration pattern. Sadly, however, in homogenizing cultures such as the United States, the message is still melt or be excluded and segregated. Nevertheless, the United States cannot extricate itself any longer from that new transnational reality. In a globalized space of production and consumption, nations can no longer guarantee the survival and success of migrants. In part, that new situation, despite some of the drastic effects of a worldwide capitalist exploitation of workers, is positive since the migrant no longer must completely conform to existing standards found in the settler society but can live simultaneous lives.

As Ortiz Cofer's case also shows, translocation and migration help create new types of readers, readers who are capable of reading transnationally, bi-culturally, and bilingually. Thus, Ortiz Cofer's writing in itself helps to convert our understanding of national literary categories. But literatures are always linguistically specific. Thus, one of the primary places where issues of national culture and literature come together is in the location of language. A language can be "home" for people who have lost their cultural home physically. The uses of Spanish and English, respectively, help migrants to negotiate the space of cultural difference. "When I go to Puerto Rico," Ortiz Cofer complains, "I am always reminded that I sound like a gringa" (qtd. in Hernandez 101). Her linguistic dilemma reflects the migrant's situation of "never quite belonging" territorially or linguistically. "I speak English with a Spanish accent and Spanish with an American accent. I may end up with a Southern/Puerto Rican/American accent"! (Interview with Acosta Belen 89). Rather than choose constant code-switching without translation into English, Ortiz Cofer simply allows in her writing what linguists call interference.

Some reviewers of *The Line of the Sun* have actually misunderstood Ortiz Cofer's use of supposedly "faulty" English as a reflection on the writer's craft. One review, published in *Parnassus*, found Ortiz Cofer's use of the English language wanting in complexity and polish. What makes her prose seem unpolished to a mainstream English native speaker/reader is, in fact, a carefully constructed creative device in which direct translation and colloquial forms of speech, including repetition, add not only local color but also resistance to homogenization, a strategy, incidentally, which Antin and Yezierska also used and for which they were similarly chided. Unlike the reviewer from *Parnassus*, I see Ortiz Cofer's linguistic interference as a positive, conscious endeavor to infuse a dominant language with other, here Spanish, elements.

Since language is Ortiz Cofer's mechanism for widening identity choices, her Spanglish, a conjoining of interesting idioms or phrases from two languages, allows her to create a very different fabric of language. Explaining the crucial difference between her own and Nuyorican writing, Ortiz Cofer asserts that she does not do what "the Nuyoricans do when they mix Spanish and English. What I do is to use Spanish to flavor my language, but I don't switch. The context of the sentence identifies and defines the words so my language is different" (qtd. in Hernandez 101). In fact, her use of English as her main fictional language represents not "a political choice, it's a choice of expediency" (qtd. in Hernandez 102). The condition for the success of such linguistic strategies becomes apparent in the comment of one reviewer who instead praises "her blending of Spanish into the stories" as "skillful enough" so that "monolingual English speakers do not need a glossary, or even translation" (Zusman 461). This linguistically dominant position of the reviewer, who clearly regards English as primary, indicates, though, that the success of hybrid language use depends on the ability of readers to understand and to take part in that hybridization.

Given the cultural imperialism that the use of English symbolizes to many native Spanish speakers, how does this linguistic choice balance a representation of Ortiz Cofer as a transnational writer? Has the power of the English language and American imperialism not manifested itself to project a powerful influence beyond its own geographical borders and begun to push to the margins of the Spanish mother-tongue? A cautious answer would be that as a personal rhetoric of resistance, however, the "Span-gles" works at least preliminarily to signal some sort of transnational hybridization. Living in the United States where "English-only" movements increasingly gain recognition, Ortiz Cofer implicitly challenges the "English-only" rule tacitly enforced in US publishing. On the part of a bi- or multicultural author, this challenge still requires an act of translation. "When I am creating a character who speaks in Spanish," Ortiz Cofer tells Rafael Ocasio,

> that character is speaking Spanish to me in my head, and I am translating him or her.... My own creative process includes being a translator of my own work as I write. The effect that I wanted to create was that these were Spanish-speaking people, that they didn't think in the same way as American people, that their syntax was different yet readable by a mainstream American reader. ("Infinite Variety" 734)

Importantly, Ortiz Cofer's transnational repositioning through language opens up a whole new discussion as to how to categorize literatures by migrant authors. Should we consider Ortiz Cofer a Puerto Rican, a Puerto-Rican American, a Hispanic, a Latina, or simply an American author (given that the term "America" includes the whole continent, not just the United States)? Answering that question from an American ethnic perspective, in "Puerto Rican Literature in Georgia?", Ocasio describes Ortiz Cofer as a "Hispanic author resident in the United States" who tries to balance between assimilation and the expression of "unique, individual voices." Read from this perspective of a simultaneous defense of cultural authenticity and assimilation, Ortiz Cofer's identity politics appears doubly focused on the female immigrant torn between acculturation to the customs of the new country and the maintenance of cultural authenticity. Ortiz Cofer's decision to reject the either/or of nationalist ethnicity versus assimilation renders her epistemologically "homeless" in the sense of a displaced feminist subject. Reminiscent of Teresa de Lauretis's articulation of the displaced feminist in "Where You From," Ortiz Cofer speaks from a space that is unknown and risky. The risk is derived from a discursive position "from which speaking and writing are at best tentative, uncertain, unguaranteed" (de Lauretis 138). As de Lauretis's "eccentric" feminist subject, Ortiz Cofer also has "the capacity for movement or self-determined (dis)location" (137) even if she can only speak from a highly contingent, "dislocated" place within discourse (139). Further, as an eccentric subject, Ortiz Cofer cannot ignore that international borders are not natural but historically contingent boundaries. This awareness of the constructedness of borderlines and boundaries fosters a realization that, as Rosa Linda Fregoso writes, at "a time when people, media images, and information journey across the world at unprecedented rates," the existing geopolitical gap between the US and Puerto Rico "is a material but also an ideological spatial practice."

The question of belonging is, of course, a deeply personal one for any migrant writer who has to assert her right to native authenticity in the literary marketplace. Ortiz Cofer views both Puerto Rico and the United States as "transnational" home space by resisting the ideological imperative of dichotomies and by refusing imposed social strictures of monolingual identity. Hence, in response to others' doubts about her right to call herself a Puerto Rican, Ortiz Cofer repeatedly insists that "Even if I cannot be geographically in the place where I was born, I consider myself a Puerto Rican the same way that anybody living on the island is a Puerto Rican" (Interview with Acosta Belen 90). In an interview with Kallet, Ortiz Cofer explains that "Many people of my parents' generation felt that if we assimilated, if we learned to live within the culture, it would be easier for us. I can see that as an economic survival technique, but as an artist I discovered that assimilation is exactly what destroys the artistic" ("Art" 68). Ortiz Cofer's juxtaposition of the artistic against economic survival would seem to favor her mother's discourse of ethnic separatism over the father's acceptance of new cultural norms. But choosing the motherland is only possible through a complex strategy of defamiliarization and rerouting ("Art" 67–68).

The stereotype that Ortiz Cofer ultimately seeks to dispel is that of the ready appropriation of migrant writers into a nationalist scheme under the guise of multiculturalism: in this scheme, any writer from another country moving to the United States undergoes ethnicization by becoming classified as a hyphenated American writer. Instead, she asks, "How can I separate my national background from my artistic impulse? I am a Puerto Rican woman possessing knowledge of that fact in a very intimate, personal, and intrinsic way" ("Puerto Rican" 49). As Ortiz Cofer implies here, citizenship can be strategic and transnational when it is not based on ethnic belonging (through descent and birth) but is defined through civic participation. "Something that makes me different from other Latino immigrants," asserts Ortiz Cofer, "is the fact that I can go home. That affects your imagination and your perception of yourself in the world" (qtd. in Hernandez 104). Although the traditional mode of diaspora writing is closely associated with exilic nostalgia and mourning, Ortiz Cofer asserts that nostalgia for the lost paradise might, literally, be out of place.

Source: Carmen Faymonville, "New Transnational Identities in Judith Ortiz Cofer's Autobiographical Fiction," in *MELUS*, Vol. 26, No. 2, 2001, p. 129.

Rudine Sims Bishop

In the following review, Bishop concludes that the appeal of Cofer's work is that it mirrors the steps young people take on the road to adulthood.

In my view, the best of the new anthologies is *An Island Like You: Stories of the Barrio* (Orchard) by Judith Ortiz Cofer. As a collection, it benefits from the consistency of quality that comes from a single talented writer, even though she successfully adopts different voices for different stories. The stories are also all about people living in the same neighborhood in Paterson, New Jersey, and the reader comes to see the characters, some of whom appear in more than one story, as part of a community.

Cofer's writing is lively, and the characters are memorable. As in *American Eyes*, the adolescents in these stories are often reconciling two cultural traditions, and two languages, but Cofer takes that as a given and focuses on the individuals and their everyday problems and concerns. Her blending of Spanish into the stories is skillful enough that monolingual English speakers do not need a glossary, or even translation. The characters, their voices, and their experiences will seem familiar to many adolescents.

In "Bad Influence" Rita is sent to spend the summer in Puerto Rico with her grandparents because her parents fear she's about to get into trouble with boys. At first unhappy, by the end of the summer she has made a new friend and come to appreciate her grandparents and their way of life. When Arturo, in "Arturo's Flight," is teased by his classmates for liking poetry and having been asked to recite John Donne's "The Flea" in front of the class, he runs away, but only as far as the local church. A conversation with the church custodian helps him put his own troubles in perspective, and he goes home to drag Shakespeare out of the dumpster and discover the message he thinks his teacher has meant for him to find in one of the sonnets. In "Abuela Invents the Zero" Constancia feels remorse after making her grandmother feel worthless when the old woman cannot find her way back to her pew in church. In "Don Jose of La Mancha" Yolanda must learn to reconcile herself with her widowed mother's relationship with a romantic island "hick" who sings and dances and reminds her mother of her Puerto Rican home. Meantime, Yolanda holds onto the memory of her father.

The other stories, too, concern themes and experiences familiar to young adults: moving toward independence, recognizing that home can be a refuge, becoming comfortable with themselves, making choices between right and wrong and between good friends and bad, discovering the pleasure of doing something good for others, and finding out that adults have weaknesses as well as strengths, and sometimes need support and comfort.

There is humor, and poignancy as well. The voices in these stories ring true, as do the stories themselves. I hope Cofer continues to write for young people. The appeal of her collection, as in all three books, is in the mirror that they hold up to young people leaving childhood and taking tentative steps into the world of adults.

Source: Rudine Sims Bishop, Review of *An Island Like You: Stories of the Barrio*, in *Horn Book*, Vol. 71, No. 5, September/October 1995, pp. 581–83.

Nancy Vasilakis

In the following review, Vasilakis suggests that this collection of short stories offers "food for thought for all young adults."

Set in a New Jersey barrio, these twelve short stories feature Puerto Rican teenagers who speak in characteristic yet very distinct voices and appear in each others' stories the way neighbors step in and out of each others' lives. The Caribbean flavor of the tales gives them their color and freshness, but the narratives have universal resonance in the vitality, the brashness, the self-centered hopefulness, and the angst expressed by the teens as they tell of friendships formed, romances failed, and worries over work, family, and school. For Arturo, being asked to recite a poem in English class makes him the butt of jokes among the guys in the neighborhood. His despair brings him one night to the steps of the local church, where he meets the elderly janitor whose own life story provides a different, and larger, perspective. In "Catch the Moon" Luis finds no meaning in his job at his father's junkyard. His carelessness brings about much friction between him and his father until he meets a girl who seems to understand the unspoken loneliness he has felt since his mother's death. He returns to the yard in search of a hubcap for the girl's car, and finds satisfaction in the work, which has become a kind of treasure hunt now that "he knew what he was looking for." For Doris in "The One Who Watches," getting to know herself means abandoning her fascination for the exciting but troublesome Yolanda, and listening, really listening, to the songs her mother sings in her nightclub performances; Doris realizes that many of the words are meant for her. In many of the stories, it is adult authority, speaking firmly and unselfconsciously out of long tradition, that brings the troubled adolescents up short and gives them the opportunity to reconsider and alter the course of events. A milestone in multicultural publishing for children, this collection by the acclaimed author of *The Line of the Sun* and *Silent Dancing: A Partial Remembrance of a Puerto Rican Childhood* offers food for thought for all young adults.

Source: Nancy Vasilakis, Review of *An Island Like You: Stories of the Barrio*, in *Horn Book*, Vol. 71, No. 4, July/August 1995, pp. 464–65.

In the following review, a contributor to Publishers Weekly *discusses the theme of struggling to succeed that is present in the stories in this collection.*

Cofer's (*Silent Dancing: A Partial Remembrance of a Puerto Rican Childhood*) 12 consistently sparkling, sharp short stories pungently recreate the atmosphere of a Puerto Rican barrio in Paterson, N.J. A different teenager is the focus of each entry, but the characters and the settings throughout are linked, often to great effect. In the poignant "Don Jose of La Mancha," Yolanda observes both critically and sympathetically as her widowed mother gingerly approaches a new relationship—with a man Yolanda considers a clueless hick; the reader has previously met Yolanda in "The One Who Watches," in which Yolanda's friend Doris describes the fear and anger she experiences as Yolanda goes shoplifting. In the surreally horrifying "Matoa's Mirror," Kenny gets high on a mixture of drugs and then watches himself in a mirror, as if he's on TV, while he is getting beaten up outside his building. The overarching theme—the struggle to transcend one's roots but never succeeding (nor really wanting to)—is explored with enormous humanity and humor. This fine collection may draw special attention for its depictions of an ethnic group underserved by YA writers, but Cofer's strong writing warrants a close look no matter what the topic.

Source: Review of *An Island Like You: Stories of the Barrio*, in *Publishers Weekly*, Vol. 242, No. 16, April 17, 1995, p. 61.

Hazel Rochman

In the following review, Rochman lauds the sense of individuality in this collection of short stories.

"Dating is not a concept adults in our barrio really get." The contemporary teenage voices are candid, funny, weary, and irreverent in these stories about immigrant kids caught between their Puerto Rican families and the pull and push of the American dream. The young people hang out on the street in front of the tenement El Building in Paterson, New Jersey, where the radios are always turned full blast to the Spanish station and the thin walls can't hold the dramas of the real-life telenovelas. As in her autobiographical adult collection *Silent Dancing* (1990), Cofer depicts a diverse neighborhood that's warm, vital, and nurturing, and that can be hell if you don't fit in. Some of the best stories are about those who try to leave. Each piece stands alone with its own inner structure, but the stories also gain from each other, and characters reappear in major and minor roles. The teen narrators sometimes sound too articulate, their metaphors over-explained, but no neat resolutions are offered, and the metaphor can get it just right (the people next door "could be either fighting or dancing"). Between the generations, there is tenderness and anger, sometimes shame. In one story, a teenage girl despises the newcomer just arrived from the island, but to her widowed mother, the hick (jibaro) represents all she's homesick for. Raul Colon's glowing cover captures what's best about this collection: the sense of the individual in the pulsing, crowded street.

Source: Hazel Rochman, Review of *An Island Like You: Stories of the Barrio*, in *Booklist*, Vol. 91, No. 12, February 15, 1995, p. 1082.

SOURCES

Abbe, Elfrieda, "Judith Ortiz Cofer: Breaking the Mold," in *Writer*, Vol. 116, No. 1, January 2003, p. 21.

"About Us: History," in *Nuyorican Poets Café*, http://www.nuyorican.org/history.php (accessed February 27, 2011).

Acosta-Belen, Edna, "A *MELUS* Interview: Judith Ortiz Cofer," in *MELUS*, Vol. 18, No. 3, Fall 1993, pp. 83–97.

Bishop, Rudine Sims, Review of *An Island Like You: Stories of the Barrio*, in *Horn Book*, Vol. 71, No. 5, September/October 1995, pp. 581–83.

Bost, Suzanne, "Transgressing Borders: Puerto Rican and Latina *Mestizaje*," in *MELUS*, Vol. 25, No. 2, Summer 2000, pp. 187–210.

Cofer, Judith Ortiz, "An Hour with Abuelo," in *An Island Like You: Stories of the Barrio*, Penguin, 1995, pp. 66–71.

Crumpton, Margaret, "An Interview with Judith Ortiz Cofer," in *Meridians*, Vol. 3, No. 2, Spring 2003, pp. 93–109.

Gray, Pamela, "The Poetry Heritage of Puerto Rico," in *American Collection: Educator's Site*, National Council of Teachers of English, http://www.ncteamericancollection.org/aaw_poetry_essay.htm (accessed February 25, 2011).

Grimes, Nikki, "Authors and Literary Works: Talking with Judith Ortiz Cofer," in *Teaching Multicultural Literature*, http://www.learner.org/workshops/tml/workshop2/authors1c.html (accessed March 21, 2011).

Hernández, Carmen Delores, "Julia Ortiz Cofer," in *Puerto Rican Voices in English: Interviews with Writers*, Praeger, 1997, p. 99.

Hetzel, Lisa, and Annetta Smith, "The 65 Years and Over Population: 2000," in *Census 2000 Brief*, U.S. Census

Bureau, October 2001, http://www.census.gov/prod/2001pubs/c2kbr01-10.pdf (accessed March 3, 2011).

Murfin, Ross, and Supriya M. Ray, "Irony," in *The Bedford Glossary of Critical and Literary Terms*, 2nd ed., Bedford/St. Martin's Press, 2003, pp. 220–23.

Ocasio, Rafael, "The Infinite Variety of the Puerto Rican Reality: An Interview with Judith Ortiz Cofer," in *Callaloo*, Vol. 17, No. 3, Summer 1994, pp. 730–43.

———, "Puerto Rican Literature in Georgia? An Interview with Judith Ortiz Cofer," in *Kenyon Review*, Vol. 14, No. 4, Autumn 1992, pp. 43–50.

"Puerto Rico," in *CIA World Factbook*, http://www.cia.gov/library/publications/the-world-factbook-geos/rq.html (accessed January 11, 2011).

Review of *An Island Like You: Stories of the Barrio*, in *Cooperative Children's Book Center*, University of Wisconsin-Madison Web site, http://www.education.wisc.edu/ccbc/books/detailBook.asp?idBooks=1226 (accessed February 25, 2011).

Review of *An Island Like You: Stories of the Barrio*, in *Publishers Weekly*, Vol. 242, No, 16, April 17, 1995, p. 61.

Rochman, Hazel, Review of *An Island Like You: Stories of the Barrio*, in *Booklist*, Vol. 91, No. 12, February 15, 1995, p. 1082.

Rodríguez, Clara E., "Puerto Ricans: Immigrants and Migrants," in *Americans All: A National Education Program*, 1990, pp. 1–9, http://www.americansall.com/PDFs/02-americans-all/9.9.pdf (accessed March 1, 2011).

Sather, Jody, and Lauren Curtright, "Judith Ortiz Cofer," in *Voices from the Gap*, University of Minnesota Web Site, October 23, 2004, http:/voices.cla.umn.edu/artistpages/coferjudith.php (accessed February 25, 2011).

Shea, Renee H., "Attempting Perfection: An Interview with Judith Ortiz Cofer," in *Latina Writers*, edited by Ilan Stavans, Greenwood Press, 2005, pp. 94–106.

Shuman, R. Baird, "Judith Ortiz Cofer: Puerto Rican Poet, Short-Story Writer, and Memoirist," in *Great American Writers: Twentieth Century*, Vol. 9, edited by R. Baird Shuman, Cavendish, 2002, pp. 487–93.

"U.S. Population Projections," in *U.S. Census Bureau*, 2004, http://www.census.gov/population/www/projections/projectionsagesex.html (accessed March 3, 2011).

FURTHER READING

Bartkevicius, Jocelyn, "An Interview with Judith Ortiz Cofer," in *Speaking of the Short Story: Interviews with Contemporary Writers*, edited by Farhat Iftekharuddin, Mary Ruhrberger, and Maurice Angus Lee, University of Mississippi, 1997, pp. 57–74.

In this interview, Cofer and Bartkevicius discuss many of Cofer's short stories and her development process. The volume includes interviews with other Hispanic authors.

Cofer, Judith Ortiz, *Lessons from a Writer's Life: Readings and Resources for Teachers and Students*, Heinemann, 2011.

In this book, Cofer provides samples of her own poetry, essays, and stories as a means to increase students' interest in doing their own writing. Included in the volume are exercises, thoughts on writing, and prompts to help students grow in their own creative processes.

Conley, Kate A., *Puerto Rican Americans*, Lucent, 2003.

A volume in the "Immigrants in America" series, this young-adult book provides a description of what it is like to grow up in the United States as a Puerto Rican immigrant.

Pico, Fernando, *History of Puerto Rico: A Panorama of Its People*, Markus Weiner Publishing, 2006.

This book is an enjoyable and accessible history of Puerto Rico, written by a well-recognized authority on the subject.

SUGGESTED SEARCH TERMS

Judith Ortiz Cofer

An Hour with Abuelo AND Judith Ortiz Cofer

Puerto Rico

Paterson AND New Jersey

Judith Ortiz Cofer AND An Island in the Sun

Nuyorican

Judith Ann Cofer AND young-adult literature

immigrant experience

Boricua

Judith Ortiz Cofer AND short story

Impulse

CONRAD AIKEN

1934

"Impulse" is a short story by Conrad Aiken, a modernist poet and writer who was a contemporary of T. S. Eliot and Ezra Pound. Widely known for his poetry, Aiken was at the center of the modernist movement of the early twentieth century. He also published several novels, numerous critical essays, and short-story collections. "Impulse" first appeared in Aiken's 1934 collection *Among the Lost People* and can also be found in *The Short Stories of Conrad Aiken*, published in 1950. His poetry and prose work alike are intensely focused on philosophical and psychoanalytical questions that he spent his career trying to reason out. His quest to make little discoveries about what comprises the human condition and to explain his theories and findings drove his work.

In a 1968 interview in the *Paris Review*, Aiken admitted that he began experimenting with short stories in the early 1920s for a very simple reason: fiction paid better than poetry. In the process of writing fiction, however, he found another avenue to express the things he wrote about in his poetry. His fascination with Freud's theories of the subconscious and his intense search for a higher power permeate both his poems and his fiction. "Impulse," a story about a man who follows through on the very basic human desire to steal, exemplifies this perfectly. In the course of a few short pages, Aiken questions how a person's actions are defined by intrinsic moral codes and are determined by social strictures. He examines

Conrad Aiken *(The Library of Congres)*

the fickleness of relationships between lovers and friends. Most importantly, he explores the notion of self-knowledge and what makes up a life. "Impulse" can also be found in the anthology *Short Story Masterpieces*, published in 1954, edited by Robert Penn Warren and Albert Erskine.

AUTHOR BIOGRAPHY

Aiken was born in Savannah, Georgia, on August 5, 1889. When he was eleven years old, his father shot his mother and then killed himself. Young Conrad was the one to discover the bodies. This incident served as an impetus for the psychological self-exploration that guided his entire career. Aiken was ultimately sent to Cambridge, Massachusetts, to be raised by an uncle. He attended Harvard University, where he edited the *Advocate* with T. S. Eliot and began to explore the connections between the individual and the larger world.

Aiken married Canadian graduate student Jessie McDonald in 1912. He became a contributing editor to the literary magazine *Dial*, which introduced him to important editors and writers, including Ezra Pound. When the United States entered World War I, Aiken claimed that as a poet he was part of an "essential industry" in order to obtain exemption from military service. Aiken and his wife moved to Rye, Sussex, England, in 1921. Aiken returned to Rye often through the course of his life. There he met Malcolm Lowry, an English writer who sought to study under Aiken and with whom Aiken would remain close for the rest of his life.

Aiken commonly experienced periods of depression. Fearing that he had inherited the psychological problems that his father suffered from, Aiken devoted himself to self-exploration and developed an intense interest in psychoanalysis that was reflected in his work. "If we begin by understanding ourselves, as far as we can," he states in the 1932 essay "What I Believe" in the journal *Nation*, "we progress thus toward an understanding of man and his potentialities.... Let us be as conscious as possible."

In 1927, Aiken returned to the United States to accept a yearlong visiting professorship at Harvard. Aiken and McDonald divorced in 1929, and he married musician Clarissa Lorenz in 1930, the same year he won the Pulitzer Prize for Poetry for *Selected Poems*. In 1933, Aiken again relocated to Rye, where he wrote the column "London Letters" for the *New Yorker*. In 1934, Aiken released his second short-story collection, *Among the Lost People*, which includes "Impulse." After returning to the United States, he and Lorenz divorced. Aiken traveled to Mexico to join Lowry, where he met and wed the painter Mary Hoover. They moved to Rye, once again, in 1937 but returned to America with the outbreak of World War II.

Aiken and Hoover eventually settled in Massachusetts in 1947, where he wrote prolifically and continued to explore psychoanalytic techniques as a means to both understand the human condition and express himself in his writing. He served as poet laureate of the United States from 1950 to 1952. His 1952 autobiographical work *Ushant* is widely recognized as the pinnacle of his career. In 1954, he received the National Book Award in Poetry for *Collected Poems*.

Aiken returned to his hometown of Savannah, Georgia, in the early 1960s. His final book, *Thee*, was written there and addresses his lifelong spiritual and intellectual journey. He died there on August 17, 1973. During his career, Aiken wrote or edited more than fifty books, including poetry, short stories, novels, and his autobiography. In addition to receiving the Pulitzer Prize, the National Book Award, and the position of poet laureate, he was the recipient of the National Medal for Literature, the Bollingen Prize, a Guggenheim Fellowship, and the Gold Medal for Poetry from the National Institute of Arts and Letters.

PLOT SUMMARY

"Impulse" opens with a description of the protagonist, Michael Lowes, from his own point of view. Michael is looking at himself in the mirror and describing his features as he shaves. He places special emphasis on the asymmetry of his face, which amuses him. The first few opening lines give the reader much more than a simple physical description; they emphasize that Michael has two sides, distinct from each other, and that he is entertained by this observation. This lays the groundwork for the theme of the story: the struggle between two sides of human nature.

Michael's thought processes also give the reader an immediate hint as to what the conflict of the plot will be. On the one hand, he is remembering an argument with his wife, Dora, about money and dreading that there may be a similar conflict when he goes down to breakfast. He laments his life and the duties that come with being a husband and a father. On the other hand, he is happily contemplating the night of card playing he has planned with his friends. This central conflict between responsibility and amusement is laid out in the first paragraph.

Michael reveals his unreliable nature, saying that he is "always hopping about from one place to another" and intimating that he never holds down a job for very long. As he thinks about the upcoming bridge game, he introduces three minor but important characters to the reader: Hurwitz, Bryant, and Smith, the men with whom he will play cards. He calls them "cheap fellows" and "mere pick-up acquaintances." He deliberately plots out how he will tell Dora that he will be coming home late and then takes gleeful pride when he is able to sneak out of the house without her knowing. While waiting for the train to take him to work, he makes excuses for himself. He justifies his delay in paying bills, blames his inability to keep a steady job on bad luck, and decides that he is entitled to "a little night off" of drinking and card playing.

Toward the end of the workday, he calls Dora to tell her about the bridge game, and here the reader gets an obvious bit of foreshadowing. Michael says that he will be home late, and Dora asks if he is sure he will even be home at all. He passes it off as a joke, but the narrator abruptly hints at events to come: "But if he could have foreseen—!"

Michael meets Hurwitz, Bryant, and Smith at a restaurant for drinks and dinner, and they continue on to Smith's home for the bridge game. They play cards for a bit, and then during a break they have a conversation about human impulses. Hurwitz states that everyone has impulses that they do not act upon, such as spitting in the eye of an enemy or kissing an attractive girl without invitation. Eventually, the conversation turns to stealing. Hurwitz observes that everyone wants things and that only societal rules keep people from taking what does not belong to them. Only briefly do the men discuss following through on these impulses, saying that it would be "bad business."

They continue with their card game, but Michael cannot stop thinking about the conversation. He finds it "amusing," just as he found the reflection of his unbalanced face in the mirror that morning amusing. Simultaneously, he is relieved to discover that he is not alone in these desires. He recalls an incident from his childhood in which he stole a conch shell from a neighbor and then destroyed it when he feared he would be caught. When the game ends, he decides to get a hot chocolate from the drugstore while he waits for the last train home. Immediately upon entering

MEDIA ADAPTATIONS

- Audio Connoisseur released an audiobook in 2002 titled *Classic American Short Stories, Vol. I*. It contains, among other works, Aiken's "Impulse," read by Charlton Griffin.

the store, however, he realizes that the "real reason" he is there is to test whether he could successfully follow through on the impulse of which he and his companions had been speaking earlier and whether doing so would give him a feeling of satisfaction.

The narrator goes into great depth about the details of the store, the number of people in it and where they are placed, the items that are readily available to be stolen, and the exact plan Michael develops to carry out his action. Once again, Michael is amused at the idea of what he is about to do. When he finally sees the perfect object to steal, he describes it as "love at first sight." It is a gold razor set in a snakeskin box lined with red plush fabric, and Michael refers to it twice as his "victim." Michael is facing the temptation to do something that is illegal and morally wrong, but he has convinced himself that his action is not only acceptable but commendable in a way: he calls himself "a Columbus of the moral world."

Michael embarks on an elaborate ruse to hide his true intentions. He examines other objects in the store and walks among the crowd slowly, drawing out the moment. The narrator describes with great detail how Michael commits the theft, when actually "it was over in an instant." He slips the case in the pocket of his overcoat and proceeds to the counter to order his hot chocolate but quickly feels someone grab his arm. A man pulls him from the crowd and reveals himself to be a detective who witnessed the entire theft.

Michael attempts to explain away his action as a joke, the result of "a kind of bet with some friends," though the reader will recall that no such bet was ever made. He tells the men that he can prove it if they will let him call Hurwitz, Bryant, and Smith, but the detective takes him into custody. As the detective escorts him out of the store, Michael's mind races to try to find a way to talk himself out of his situation. The detective tells Michael that since the station is close, they can walk there rather than calling a car. The walk gives the narrator a chance to recount Michael's thought processes to the reader. Although horrified and frightened, Michael finds that a part of him is strangely detached and marvels at the absurdity of his situation.

He begins to recount the night's events to the detective in an attempt to explain away his actions, but even to his own ears he sounds "insincere" and "hollow," and the detective is unmoved. Michael changes tactics and says that he has a wife and kids waiting for him at home. The detective sneers at this. Michael convinces himself that it is a failing on the part of the detective that he does not believe him, saying, "You're so used to dealing with criminals that you think all mankind is criminal."

They arrive at the station, where Michael tries again to explain about the conversation during the bridge game. It is obvious to him that the police officers do not believe him, but they agree to call Hurwitz, Bryant, and Smith to ask them about it. The sergeant is able to contact Hurwitz and Bryant, who both deny that any bet had been made. Moreover, they both say that Michael is a mere acquaintance, not a friend, and Hurwitz tells the sergeant that Michael "was hard up." Outraged, Michael leaps up and shouts that they are liars. He is taken away. The narrator briefly mentions that Michael has a five-minute conversation with Dora, and her detachment frightens him.

Dora comes to see him the next morning and is "cold, detached, deliberate." When he repeats his story for her, her reaction is very similar to that of the police. Her disbelief is visible. Once again, Michael observes that his voice is "hollow and insincere." When he realizes that Dora does not believe him and will not stand beside him, he is stricken by the idea that they have become strangers. For the first time, he allows himself to see that Dora has long begrudged his irresponsibility and the consequences she has had to suffer because of it. He remembers the lies they had to tell to avoid prosecution for debt, the times she had to set aside her pride and take charity, and how she was never able to make friends because they were always moving so that Michael could look for work.

Dora tells Michael that she will get him a lawyer, but that he will need to figure out how to pay for it himself; she will not touch her savings in case she and the children need money. For the first time in the narration, Michael devotes a good deal of thought to his wife. He recalls a litany of superficial things about Dora such as her handwriting, the way she sings, and how small her feet are, but in spite of these details, he realizes that he does not truly know her. He asks Dora to speak with Hurwitz, Bryant, and Smith about appearing at the hearing. She assents and leaves him in his cell.

Michael's thoughts begin to spiral desperately as he faces the possibility that no one will come forward to stand by him. His lawyer finally appears and confirms that Hurwitz, Bryant, and

Smith have all refused to testify on Michael's behalf and said that if they were called before a judge, they would state that they did not know Michael well, that he was always broke and a little odd. Their presence at the trial, the lawyer says, "would be fatal."

For the first time, the narration is taken out of Michael's head briefly when the trial is summarized. The reader learns about the events of the trial from the point of view of the judge. The "friends" that Michael claims would prove his innocence never appear. Dora, though she testifies that Michael has never stolen before, says that "they were always living in a state of something like poverty." The judge also tells the reader that Michael has a history of skipping town without paying rent and that he is wanted for some rather large debts that he has not paid. Michael is sentenced to three months incarceration for thievery.

After the judgment is pronounced, Michael's internal narration resumes. He is in complete shock. He observes that Dora seems like a stranger to him and that she looks at him as though trying to figure out whether or not he is quite human. They do not speak again, but a week later he receives a letter from her in which she states that she is filing for divorce. She endured his inability to provide for his family but will not tolerate the disgrace of his criminal behavior. She asks him not to contest the divorce and says that she will not contact him again.

Michael briefly weeps over the loss of the children he hardly ever thought of before and bitterly proclaims that life is "a huge injustice." He decides that he cannot trust anyone and cries that he was betrayed by his wife and his "best friends." He decides that he will not contest the divorce; indeed, he is better off without all of them. He vows that when he is released from jail, he will somehow get rich and restore his reputation, but he is at a loss as to how.

As the story ends, Michael sits on the bed in his cell and remembers seemingly random incidents from his past: a childhood trip with his mother, a scene from college, breaking his leg as a teenager. He remembers again the conch shell he stole and destroyed when he was ten. Just as when he thinks of Dora and can only bring to mind superficial details, when he thinks of his past he only recalls "trivial and infinitely charming little episodes such as these." Looking only at the surface and never beneath, he tries to reassure himself that he has led a good life. The story ends, however, with his observation that "it had all come foolishly to an end."

CHARACTERS

Bryant

Bryant is one of the three bridge partners with whom Michael has the discussion about impulse. He refuses to testify on Michael's behalf.

The Detective

The detective sees Michael commit the theft in the drugstore and arrests him for it. He walks Michael to the police station. Because he will not believe anything Michael is telling him, Michael thinks of him as "lowbrow."

Hurwitz

Hurwitz is one of Michael's three bridge partners. He is described as being the only intellectual of the three men. He leads the conversation about natural human impulses that gives Michael the idea to steal. It is Hurwitz who says that "civilization is only skin-deep," which becomes a running theme in the story. He refuses to testify on Michael's behalf and tells the police that Michael is financially insecure.

The Judge

The judge at the trial is a minor but very important character. He provides information about Michael Lowes that the reader otherwise would not have known, such as the fact that he is college educated, comes from a respectable background, and has left a string of bad debts behind him.

Dora Lowes

Dora is the wife of Michael Lowes, the protagonist, and the mother of his two children. She is constantly trying to provide for the children and make up for Michael's inability to support his family. At the opening of the story, Michael is remembering an argument they had about unpaid bills, and as the story progresses it becomes clear that this is a common disagreement between them. When Michael is arrested, it is the last straw for Dora. She decides to stop relying on her husband for anything and support the children from her own finances. After Michael's incarceration, Dora files for divorce.

Michael Lowes

Michael Lowes is an irresponsible husband and father who follows through on an impulse to steal. He is unreliable and often unemployed, but he does not want to admit to doing any wrong. Instead, he makes excuses for himself constantly. Self-indulgent and thoughtless, Michael displays no care for his wife or children and thinks he is better than his only three friends. He speaks dismissively or derisively about all of the other characters in the beginning of the story. However, as the story progresses his attitude toward them changes.

During a game of bridge, Michael and his friends have a conversation about temptation and impulse. He is relieved to find that other people are also tempted to do things that they should not, and he realizes that it is only the superficial veneer of civilization that keeps people from acting on their impulses. After the bridge game, he decides to steal a razor in a snakeskin box from a drugstore. He takes great pleasure in it—far more pleasure, it seems, than he has taken in his family or his friends. He is caught and taken to jail. Along the way, he thinks to himself that he is a "thief by accident." He tries to tell everyone that the theft was only a joke, but no one believes him.

He feels betrayed by his friends because they will not testify on his behalf, even though he never showed respect or admiration for them. His wife, Dora, tells him she will not help him pay for a lawyer since she has to look out for herself and the children, and he is bitter and angry about this. During the trial, the judge reveals that Michael is college educated and comes from a very respectable background. He has also skipped town in the past without paying rent or other debts. He is sentenced to three months in jail. A week later, Dora sends him a letter saying that she is filing for divorce, and he reacts with bitterness. He feels betrayed and unfairly persecuted and vows that when he gets out of jail, he will prove to everyone by being a success that they should have stood by him.

At the end of the story, Michael thinks back on superficial incidents in his life, including an incident when he was ten in which he stole from a neighbor. He thinks that he has led a good and charmed life up to that point but that his conviction for stealing has ended it. Self-deluded until the end, Michael never realizes that he has been giving in to impulses and temptations his entire life by always taking the easy way out. His theft from the drugstore and incarceration are not an anomaly; the episode fits perfectly into the way he has always lived.

Smith

Smith is one of the three bridge partners with whom Michael has the discussion about impulse. He refuses to testify on Michael's behalf.

THEMES

Narcissism

Narcissism is a term coined by the psychoanalyst Sigmund Freud to refer to a person's sense of conceit, self-centeredness, or selfishness. Freud believed that a certain amount of narcissism is not only healthy but necessary for self-preservation; this is called primary narcissism. In contrast to this, pathologically high levels of narcissism are regarded as destructive and referred to as secondary narcissism.

In "Impulse," Michael Lowes shows an unhealthy degree of narcissistic personality traits—an inability to see his faults, unwillingness to accept blame, and a sense of superiority over others to name a few—that ultimately result in disaster for him. The narcissistic theme manifests itself not only in Michael's actions and dialogue but also in the narration of the story. Although the story is narrated in the third person, the action is portrayed almost exclusively through Michael's point of view, because to him, his is the only point of view that matters.

Although the reader can look at his actions objectively and recognize his severe character deficiencies, Michael is incapable of accepting any sort of blame. Michael's line of reasoning is constantly shifting so as to accommodate his need for blamelessness and his desperation to have the admiration of others. He cannot empathize with anyone other than himself, such as when he is bitter that Dora wants to use her savings to support the children rather than pay for his lawyer. He has no significant relationships. His "friends" are really mere acquaintances, he fully admits that he does not know his wife even after seven years of marriage, and very rarely does he even think of his children. He is self-consumed.

Although it is clear that Michael Lowes suffers from what psychologists name narcissistic personality disorder, the theme of narcissism is also evident elsewhere in the story. As previously

TOPICS FOR FURTHER STUDY

- Hurwitz says at one point, in regards to impulse, "It would be easy . . . to give in to it. . . . Temptation is too close." Michael's experiment soon runs into a number of difficulties that ultimately lead to ruination. In a community with societal norms, laws and enforcers, and a clearly defined bias toward temperance, how easy is it to give in to impulse? Together with a group, record various media influences forbidding or encouraging different forms of impulsivity. Create a blog and post the examples you have found. Examine and write about why you think certain destructive impulses, such as fast-food indulgence or frivolous spending, are encouraged, while other similar impulses are forbidden.
- Early in the story, the narrator laments, "But if he could have foreseen—!" One of the issues most difficult to resolve in ethics is the problem of foresight or lack thereof. No human can foresee all the consequences of their actions, and thus, to a degree, it can be argued that at least some of an action's virtue lies in the ignorant intention behind it. Recall a time when you or someone you know acted on impulse with unexpected results, good or bad. Write an essay examining the virtue of the action (or lack thereof) with respect to foresight and re-examining the action's virtue ex post facto (after the fact).
- Modernism is often cited as being a reactionary movement against the strict form and style found in the realism of the Age of Enlightenment. In what ways is the society of you and your peers defined by its reactions to the social actions that came before it? In what ways are you a participating member of that society? Finally, in what ways are you defined by the people or events that came before you? Create a multimedia presentation or short video documentary that clearly shows the major influences on your society and on you.
- Films such as William Wyler's *The Best Years of Our Lives* and Orson Welles's *Citizen Kane* pioneered psychological realism as a style in motion pictures. Just as in fiction, psychological realism in film continues to be a successful and applicable style today. Rodrigo Garcia's *Nine Lives* and Christopher Nolan's *Memento* are often cited as contemporary examples of the style. Watch a film that can be classified as psychological realism. What techniques in the film mirror those in literature such as internal narration, allusion, and symbolism? List five elements in the film that fit this genre, and write a paragraph on each explaining how the film achieved its goal.
- Michael Lowes's internal narration conveys the psychological drive behind the action of the story, and the ability of the reader to see his world from his point of view is vital to understanding the piece. Harper Lee's popular classroom perennial *To Kill a Mockingbird* is narrated in the first person from the point of view of six-year-old Scout Finch. Themes such as class, race, and the justice system are explored through her internal narration. In the last chapter of the book, Scout tries to imagine what life would look like through the eyes of the character Boo Radley. Read the book and pay special attention to the characters of Boo, Atticus Finch, and Tom Robinson. How would the story change if one of these characters had narrated it? Write a paper examining one of the themes mentioned above as it might have been portrayed by a narrator other than Scout.

---

mentioned, some degree of narcissism is considered healthy, and instances of this low-level narcissism appear everywhere. The detective and employees at the drugstore look at Michael with "contempt"; because he is a thief, they feel morally superior to him. His three fellow card players are far more concerned with saving themselves from scandal than helping Michael when he is arrested. They "all three refused flatly to be mixed up in the business" because "they were all afraid of the effects of the publicity." Even Dora displays a marked trait of self-preservation when she refuses to help Michael obtain a lawyer and then files for divorce after he is incarcerated. To the outside observer, their acts of narcissism may seem justified, but in Michael's point of view, his are, as well.

Psychological Realism

Fiction that emphasizes interior characterization to reveal the impetus behind the action of a narrative is classified as psychological realism. "Impulse" is a prime example of this kind of prose. The internal workings of Michael Lowes's mind are what drive the plot, rather than outside influences. The focus is on Michael's motivations and thought processes. The story is almost entirely told from his point of view, and thus it is his inner dialogue that serves to elucidate and develop the plot. If the reader were not allowed to see the psychology behind his actions, "Impulse" would be a much briefer story about a man who shaves, goes to work, plays bridge, randomly steals from a drugstore, and is inexplicably betrayed by everyone he knows. It is not enough in a story such as "Impulse" to simply know *what* happens; the author wants the reader to know *why* it is happening.

Antiheroes

An antihero is the protagonist of a story whose character runs contrary to what might typically be thought of as heroic or virtuous. Many times, an antihero lacks courage or conviction and cannot be trusted to make decisions that would be seen as admirable by conventional society. For this reason, antiheroes are often social outcasts of some kind, displaced and detached. Typically, antiheroes take some sort of pride in the exact qualities that keep them from being typical heroes in an attempt to feel more in control of themselves and their situations. In "Impulse," Michael's irresponsibility and thoughtlessness keep him from being a hero. The reader has difficulty admiring or even sympathizing with him. Although Michael does act as "his own worst enemy" and might be called the antagonist of the story, the antagonist is not the same thing as the antihero in literary terms.

Michael chose to play poker all night long.
(Val Thoermer / Shutterstock.com)

STYLE

Hamartia

Hamartia is the literary term for the event that causes the downfall of a protagonist. Within the plot of "Impulse," Michael's theft of the shaving set is the ultimate hamartia, for it is with this act that the protagonist begins his slide toward ruin. At times, it is difficult to tell the actual hamartia of a narrative. For example, one could argue that Michael's life was well on its way toward being devastated before the action of the story even begins. After all, as we find out through the course of the story, Michael has committed a series of acts that have contributed to his downfall: he has skipped town on debts, is irresponsible about paying bills, and spends his extra time and money drinking and playing cards with people he does not even call his friends. However, in order to identify the hamartia, the reader must only look at the action contained within the narrative itself. Within the limits of the narrative action of "Impulse," it is Michael's theft that begins the chain reaction that ultimately causes his downfall.

Hamartia can be a character's tragic flaw that also results in the downfall of the hero or heroine (or antihero or antiheroine). In contrast to an event or act, the tragic flaw is the main quality of the character that results in their fall. Thus, the theft is the hamartia of "Impulse," but Michael's tragic flaw is his unwillingness to live within the structure and under the rules of civilization. It is not the impulse to steal that flaws Michael. As Hurwitz illustrates, everyone has impulses. However, not everyone acts upon those impulses. It is the quality in Michael that allows him to feel justified in acting upon the impulse to steal that is his tragic flaw.

Point of View

The perspective from which an author narrates a story is called the point of view. The traditional way to see the differences in points of view is to remember that there are three "people" involved in the storytelling process. The first person is the character in the story, the second person is the reader of the story, and the third person sits outside of the story as neither character nor reader. Very rarely, a story will be narrated as if it is actually happening to the reader: "*You* hummed as *you* shaved." This is the second-person point of view. If a story is told from the perspective of one of the characters, it is then called first-person narration. The most obvious way to tell if a story is told from the first-person point of view is if the narrator refers to him- or herself as "I." If "Impulse" was a first-person point of view narrative, it might open with the line "I hummed as I shaved." Instead, it refers to the characters from an outside perspective: "Michael Lowes hummed as he shaved." Thus, it is told in the third-person point of view. Sometimes third-person narratives are told from an all-seeing, godlike perspective, which is referred to as omniscient narration, but "Impulse" is told from a limited point of view, largely Michael's, giving the reader deep insight into his thoughts and his character.

Allusion

Allusion is the technical term for a literary figure of speech that references a specific literary or historical event or figure. Different from a metaphor or a simile, which directly compare one idea or thing to another, an allusion draws upon a reader's prior knowledge in order to capitalize on the emotional connotations implicit in the reference. Many modern works are characterized by their use of allusion. One of the most famous examples is T. S. Eliot's *The Waste Land*, which is riddled with complex and intertwining allusions to well-known stories, poems, historical events, and religious myths.

In "Impulse," there are allusions to the story of the fall of Adam and Eve in the Garden of Eden from the Bible. Michael is faced with the temptation of a human impulse just as Adam and Eve are. The gold razor set in red plush and encased in snakeskin that Michael steals is an allusion to the apple from the Tree of Knowledge that Eve takes. Just as Adam and Eve are condemned by God for succumbing to temptation, Michael is condemned by society, his friends, and his wife for not resisting his own impulse. Although Aiken never directly references the story of Eden, he supplies the reader with hints such as these that evoke the story and provide a framework for the emotion and knowledge he wishes the reader to have in mind while reading "Impulse."

HISTORICAL CONTEXT

Modernism

The era of artistic experimentation in the first part of the twentieth century is generally referred to as modernism. A reaction to the realism of the Age of Enlightenment in the nineteenth century, it encouraged artists to experiment in form and style as a means of social progression. The changes in social structure, economics, industry, and societal values led many artists and intellectuals to believe that traditional concepts of philosophy and art should be left behind.

Modernism centers on the notion that the individual and society as a whole bear impact on each other in turn. Individualism is a predominant theme in modernist literature, and established authority structures such as governments and religion are thrown into question. Many modernist writers wanted to force their readers to question what they thought they knew about the world and about literature, and they did this by using techniques to draw attention to form and language. T. S. Eliot, for example, is famous for his experimental style that was created and designed to draw attention to social issues such as alienation in poems like *The Waste Land.*

In an interview in the *Paris Review*, Aiken said that he and Eliot greatly influenced one another, though their styles are often seen as quite different. The new focus on depth psychology gave writers an incredible amount of

COMPARE & CONTRAST

- **1930s:** Women are largely dependent upon their husbands both financially and socially. It is extremely difficult for women to obtain a divorce, and the stigma of being an unmarried mother carries great weight. No laws exist to enforce financial support from a divorced parent without custody.

  Today: The single mother is a common figure, and divorce is seen as an unfortunate but sometimes necessary process that carries little social stigma. Divorced spouses who do not have primary custody of children are often required by law to provide financial support, and the consequences for abandoning this responsibility can be severe, including jail time.

- **1930s:** The lack of electronic record keeping makes it somewhat simple to escape bad debts by moving and allows an easier fresh start in a new place.

  Today: Credit-reporting agencies track every financial move of citizens and maintain financial histories in a central database irrespective of location. Bad debts remain on credit reports, visible to any agency making a financial history inquiry of an individual, for sometimes as long as ten years.

- **1930s:** The theories of Freud and other psychologists are new concepts to society, and they revolutionize the way people look at human motivation and culture. Psychoanalytic concepts remain foreign to many people outside the fields of psychology or philosophy.

  Today: Psychology is a common field of study, and psychological motivators are easily recognizable to everyday people. Recent emphases on post-traumatic stress disorder, bipolar disorder, and depression bring psychological issues into public awareness. There is no longer a stigma attached to seeking psychological counseling.

---

material to plumb for their characters and poetry. The poet H. D., for instance, worked extremely closely with Sigmund Freud in the early 1930s; their respective work illustrates the profound influence they had on one another. In literature, modernist thinking changed the purposes of many poets and writers from representation of reality to interpretation of it, and entirely new techniques and forms were developed that are still in use today. Although Aiken was a modernist and his literary criticism focused heavily on modernist issues, his form was more traditional than many of his peers, and he is not often cited as a prominent figure in the movement.

Psychoanalysis

Freudian psychology proposes that psychological trauma can be analyzed through examination of the unconscious mind. Methods such as dream analysis and free association allow the analyst to bring to light conditions that the patient may not be consciously aware of. The psychoanalytic theories of Sigmund Freud exploded in popularity in the early part of the twentieth century, and terms such as *ego*, *superego*, *id*, *phobia*, *compulsion*, and *neurosis* began to appear in everything from street culture to high art. In literature, the concept led to different ways of depicting and interpreting character motivations. The presence or absence of symbols and subtext became a major focus of literary criticism. However, the application of psychoanalysis to a character was found to be more than just a way to discover the true meaning or theme of a narrative; taken one step further, psychoanalytic criticism can be used to discover truths about the author, as well.

Interwar Social Consciousness

The social impact of World War I was world changing. Not only did the war bring nations

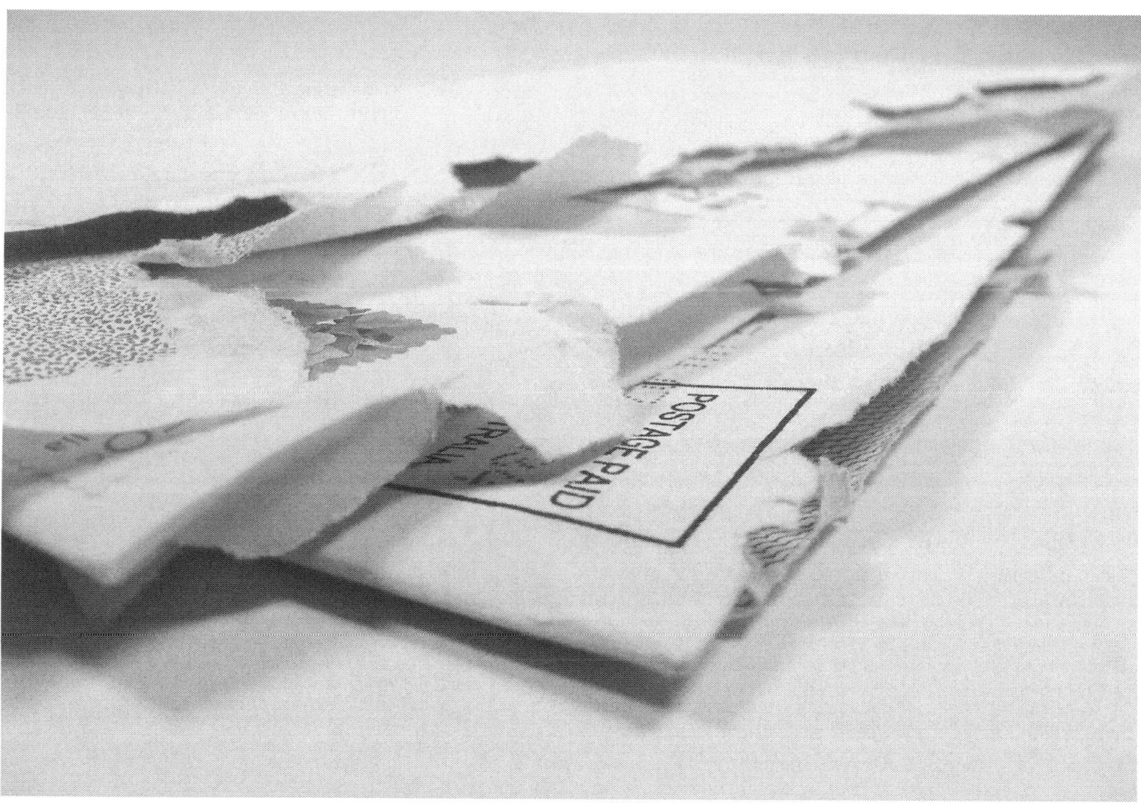

Michael used the bill money to play cards. (AJM / Shutterstock.com)

throughout Europe and the Americas together in conflict, but it also brought social classes together in arms. The previously established strict lines that divided the social hierarchy began to blur as the lower, working class and the educated middle and upper classes fought together in the trenches and dealt with the same psychological and emotional traumas upon returning home. The stock market crash of 1929, as well as the Great Depression that followed, further called social mores into question. Philosophers, politicians, and artists of all kinds struggled to make sense out of the ruins of Western society.

In addition, the rise of fascism in Europe was raising serious concerns, as the threat of a second world war loomed on the horizon. Like most every other medium of artistic expression, literature began to heavily focus on social themes. The running theme in "Impulse" of how human nature works in the confines of civilization is exemplary of interwar issues. Artists and writers alike began to appeal both to the high-minded and the lowbrow in an attempt to both reach wider audiences and bridge the gaps between classes. Like "Impulse," then, much of literature portrayed easily understood and relatable issues such as unemployment and societal frustrations with themes of philosophy, modernistic experimentation, and psychoanalysis.

CRITICAL OVERVIEW

"Impulse" was originally published in Aiken's 1934 short-story collection *Among the Lost People*. The collection, like the vast majority of Aiken's work, is a meditation on and search for the meaning of the individual within the larger constructs of civilization. Although this was a common thrust of literature in the interwar period, Aiken differed from his contemporaries in his seemingly conventional means of narration. Experimentation in form was one of the chief modernist techniques, but Aiken maintained an almost traditional adherence to structure while choosing instead to plumb both his own psychoanalytic depths and those of his characters in efforts to discover truth about life. The title of the story refers to a universal element of humanity, but specific stylistic and thematic choices enable the reader to connect with Michael Lowes on an individual level. Carolyn Handa, in her essay "'Impulse': Calculated Artistry in Conrad Aiken," calls Aiken's work a "type of stylistic and thematic genre interchange."

The theme of the story is representative of Aiken's career-long search for the place of the individual in the universal constructs of society: "civilization is only skin-deep." Beneath the disguise of civilization, all people feel impulses such as those discussed in the story. This running theme led some critics such as John R. Moore to criticize what they see as vagueness in Aiken's work. Moore observes in the *Sewanee Review* that Aiken's work tends to have too much "abstraction, and this in spite of his plentiful use of concrete detail." Still, many critics, such as Jennifer Aldrich in her essay "The Deciphered Heart: Conrad Aiken's Poetry and Prose Fiction," laud Aiken's self-defined purpose as a writer to examine the "context of human generality in which the subject is at once highly individual and slightly anonymous." Aldrich observes that Aiken uses his fiction to plumb the "general consciousness of humanity" and that it is through that process that he comes to better understand himself. Aiken's characters and worlds invite us to think about how we would react and to know ourselves better.

Although some critics vilify Michael, others, such as Bernard Winehouse in his essay in *Studies in Short Fiction*, find that Michael is to be esteemed for his honesty in throwing civilization aside and acting according to his natural impulses. He writes that the narrative style and characterization "in fact call upon the reader to make an almost total identification with Michael Lowes." Whether the reader approves of Michael or not, however, almost seems secondary. Aiken's main goal is to get the reader thinking about the human condition and the role of the individual within civilization, and "Impulse" achieves this goal.

CRITICISM

Kristy Blackmon

Blackmon is a poet, writer, and critic of literature. In the following essay, she analyzes "Impulse" through a psychoanalytic critical lens and considers how the work explores the themes of individual responsibility and narcissism in the context of social constructs at large.

"'IMPULSE' IS A STORY IN WHICH THE PROTAGONIST SUFFERS FROM A PATHOLOGICAL NARCISSISM SO DEEP THAT IT RENDERS HIM INCAPABLE OF FUNCTIONING NORMALLY WITHIN THE STRICTURES OF CIVILIZATION, BUT IT IS ALSO A COMMENTARY ON THE NARCISSISTIC TENDENCIES OF THAT CIVILIZATION ITSELF."

Conrad Aiken was a man utterly devoted to the pursuit of self-knowledge and a firm believer in the power and responsibility of literature to help people better understand themselves. He was an early follower of Freud's school of psychoanalysis, and both Aiken's poetry and prose were nearly always autobiographical in nature, dealing at least peripherally with his own psychological problems channeled through his characters. In particular, Aiken's work tended to focus on the two Freudian concepts of narcissism and the oedipal complex. This seems perfectly natural in light of the murder-suicide of Aiken's parents as a child and his subsequent lifelong quest to make psychological sense of his father's insanity and the trauma he suffered as a result.

As Ted R. Spivey points out in his chapter on Conrad Aiken in his 1986 book *Revival: Southern Writers in the Modern City*, Aiken believed that his father's narcissism was a leading cause of his violent behavior and insanity. Spivey says that Aiken concluded that "narcissism, the individual's worship of his own image, was also a cultural phenomenon and should be treated as such," and this is very evident in his work. "Impulse" is a story in which the protagonist suffers from a pathological narcissism so deep that it renders him incapable of functioning normally within the strictures of civilization, but it is also a commentary on the narcissistic tendencies of that civilization itself.

Early in his time as a student at Harvard, under the guidance of his beloved mentor the esteemed philosopher George Santayana, Aiken began to explore the connections between the

WHAT DO I READ NEXT?

- "The Lie," by T. C. Boyle, published in the *New Yorker* in 2008, tells the story of a man who, tired of his boring job and mundane existence, tells a simple lie that grows in import until it eventually ruins his life.
- William Golding's *Lord of the Flies* (1954) examines the truth of human nature and psychology through a group of children who are stranded after a shipwreck and must build a new society with minimal preconceptions of civilization. It depicts the psychology of both the individual and the culture, how the two intertwine, and how they affect each other.
- Argentine writer Jorge Luis Borges published his acclaimed short-story collection *Ficciones* in 1944. The stories deal with the philosophy inherent in the modernist movement and established Borges as perhaps the most important Latin American author of his time. The book was published in English by Grove Press in 1994.
- Aiken's second wife, Clarissa Lorenz, published the memoir *Lorelei Two: My Life with Conrad Aiken* in 1983. In it, she reveals the psychological trauma Aiken suffered early in life and chronicles his struggle with depression, including a suicide attempt.
- "Silent Snow, Secret Snow," by Aiken, is his most widely anthologized short story, first published in *The Collected Short Stories of Conrad Aiken* in 1934. It tells the story of a boy who withdraws from reality and is often cited as a work that plays heavily upon Aiken's own psychological issues.
- Aiken won the Pulitzer Prize for Poetry in 1930 for *Selected Poems of Conrad Aiken* (1929), a collection of favorites of his own work spanning over forty years. The poems are renowned for their philosophical and psychological themes.
- Karen Hesse's 1998 Newbery Award-winning young-adult novel *Out of the Dust* is written in a series of free-verse poems that represent fourteen-year-old Billie Jo's experience of living in the dust bowl of Oklahoma in the 1930s. The form of the first-person narrative gives an intimate and unique feel to Billie Jo's character and helps the reader see the action from her perspective.

---

individual and the larger world. As he states in a 1932 essay for *Nation* called "What I Believe," Aiken believed that by understanding our individual selves, we are better equipped to understand mankind as a whole. Aiken, a staunch believer in the therapeutic qualities of literature, was adamant that the role of the writer included a responsibility to, as Catharine F. Seigel phrases it in her book *The Fictive World of Conrad Aiken*, "teach a reader how to come to terms with his or her individual consciousness."

Aiken's commitment to the pursuit of self-knowledge was the driving force behind his entire oeuvre. This focus lends itself naturally to psychological realism, which—if he might be assigned a trademark style of prose—is the genre to which Aiken gravitated and of which he eventually became a master. His focus on interior characterization as the chief element of the story is evident in nearly all of his fiction. This is certainly the case with "Impulse," a story that concentrates attention so intently upon the inner workings of the main character's mind that it almost pulls off the trick of convincing the reader that the narrator is in full sympathy with Michael Lowes, the antihero of the piece. Because the narration is told almost completely through the filter of Michael's mind and from his perspective, his thought processes and inner dialogue give clues as to the intention of the author and meaning of the story. It is not enough in a story such as "Impulse" to simply know what happens; the reader must know why it is happening.

The defining characteristic of Michael's personality is his narcissism, and evidence of it appears everywhere in the story. In the opening paragraph, he is staring at himself in the mirror as he shaves, "amused by the face he saw." This sets up a mirror motif that is repeated throughout the story. The mirrors never show Michael the truth of himself, however; they only reflect back things that support his egotism.

In this opening scene, Michael is remembering an argument he and his wife, Dora, had about unpaid bills the night before, and as the story progresses it becomes clear that this is a common disagreement between them. The reader is led to believe that these are normal, almost typical financial arguments between spouses; however, it is revealed late in the story that the Lowes family is actually "living in a state of something like poverty." Michael never admits to himself the gravity of the situation, his culpability for it, or the stress it places upon Dora, choosing instead to slip out of the house that morning unnoticed by his wife or two children and making a decision to go out drinking and playing cards that night despite his lack of funds and the outstanding bills. His trivialization of their monetary ruin and his refusal to take responsibility for it are hallmark traits of pathological narcissists. In addition, the emphasis placed on money by conventional society underscores his lack of ability to function within a civilization with rather strict rules about such things as bad debts and providing for children.

Later that night at the card game, Hurwitz leads a conversation about the conflict between natural human impulses and the repression of them by society, saying that "civilization is only skin-deep." This is a theme perfectly suited to Michael, a man who never looks beyond his own surface reflection in any attempt at truly knowing himself. Michael latches on to this idea, and the admission by the other men that they, too, have been victims of temptation to give in to impulse relieves him and perhaps is a big reason why he feels justified in acting on his own desire to steal at the drugstore. Typically, he sees himself as superior to such conventions as not committing theft. It is, after all, only the superficiality of civilization that stops people from acting on impulse. The emphasis on the role of the individual within civilization is not only a favorite topic of Aiken's but also a predominant theme in modernist literature, which always seems to be questioning traditional authority structures.

The conversation turns at one point away from common desires—such as the desire to kiss a pretty girl—to impulses that may better be described as compulsions: slashing fur coats with razor blades or cutting off braids of hair. These sorts of behaviors are not ordinary or universal impulses. The brief mention of these out-of-the-ordinary desires deepens the psychological tenor of the conversation and reemphasizes Aiken's fascination with Freudian psychology. "What would be more human?" Hurwitz asks. Compulsions and impulses, he seems to be saying, are common to every individual.

Michael seems to be the only one present who does not realize that although having inappropriate impulses is common and natural, giving in to such temptations is not. Indeed, a moral struggle over whether or not to commit the theft never arises within him. He is not "in the least excited" over the prospect—he is only amused. Amusement seems to be one of the only human emotions with which Michael can identify. He deliberately refrains from self-examination of any kind, and amusement is an oft-repeated state of mind for him in the first part of the story. It is one of the only things he can feel without having to look too deeply at the causes of it.

In sharp contrast to the extremely brief accounts of his wife, children, job, and friends, the narrator spends a great deal of time showing Michael plotting out and committing his theft in the store. What else is there to think about? If Michael thinks too carefully about the possible consequences of his actions or what is waiting for him at home, he would cease to be amused, would, in fact, be forced to confront many of the hard truths he seems to spend his life avoiding. Instead, the reader gets every detail of Michael's theft from the moment he sets foot in the drugstore.

The irony of this passage, of course, is that it proves Michael is not acting on impulse at all, but with decided premeditation. When confronted by the detective in front of the manager and clerk, Michael observes that they look at him with "astonishment, shame, and contempt." These specific and somewhat contradictory descriptors illustrate the reactions not only of the employees but also of civilization at large: astonishment that someone would actually break such a certain rule of society; shame, perhaps, at the recognition of an impulse they themselves have felt; and contempt for Michael's weakness in giving in to such temptation.

The store employees' reaction is evidence of the presence of what Freud called "primary narcissism," the healthy, nonpathological form of narcissism that allows one to function within a social unit. Further examples of primary narcissism present themselves throughout the course of the story, most specifically in the self-preserving rejection of Michael by his friends and wife. Once again, Michael and society are serving as mirrors of one another, giving credence to the assertion that Aiken's focus is primarily the interchange between the individual and the world and how better knowing one will aid in gaining knowledge of the other. This also reiterates Hurwitz's assertion of the universality of temptation and impulse.

One of the most significant thoughts Michael has that shows the degree of his narcissism and his inability to accept blame of any kind is his conception of himself as a "thief by accident." This phrase clearly reiterates Michael's inability to claim responsibility for his actions. The reader is reminded of the many excuses Michael has made for himself since the beginning of the story. He blames fate for the fact that he cannot make decent friends because he must always move from place to place looking for work. He justifies not paying bills because "bad luck hounded him everywhere." Once he discovers that he is not alone in the desire to follow through on bad impulses, he feels justified in acting on those impulses. There is nothing accidental, of course, about Michael's thievery. On the contrary, he spends a great deal of time choosing what he will steal and plotting exactly how he will commit the theft. However, he panics at the idea of actually being labeled a thief, even by himself.

When Michael is arrested, it is the last straw for Dora. She decides to stop relying on her husband for anything and support the children with her own finances, an excellent example of primary narcissism. Michael's lack of character becomes even more evident as he bitterly resents the fact that women and children must come first. This is another unwritten rule of society that he feels is unfair, but he cannot bring himself to be uncivilized enough to voice his bitterness, just as he shies away from ever calling himself a thief even in his own mind.

At this point, Michael indulges in the deepest self-analysis in the story. He thinks of Dora and all of the superficial, trivial things he knows about her: her handwriting, her voice, and the familiar sight of her brushing her hair at night before the mirror. Just as the appearance of the mirror in the beginning of the story illustrates that Michael cannot see past his own superficial reflection, the reappearance of it here shows the reader that he cannot see beyond these superficial details about his wife, either. In a rare moment of clarity, he realizes that he does not truly know her: "The woman herself stood before him as opaque as a wall." The reader understands that he does not truly know himself, either. Nearly the entire story is told through narration from Michael's point of view, and not once is he ever honest with either himself or the reader about anything.

For this reason, the judge at the trial is a very important character. With his brief appearance, the narration moves outside of Michael's perspective—the only time during the story when this happens. The judge provides information about Michael Lowes that the reader otherwise would not know, such as the fact that he is college educated, comes from a respectable background, and has left a string of bad debts behind him. It is odd that in all of the praise Michael gives himself, he never reveals that he is either educated or, as the reader can deduce, that he comes from a comfortable background. This fact gives a whole other layer to Michael's personality. Remembering his past successes, perhaps, would only force him to face his failures. This new knowledge gives the reader considerable material with which to examine Michael's psychological makeup. It is appropriate that these facts are given by an impartial judge, a character otherwise removed from the action of the story, because these are the facts that tip the scales fully against Michael.

At the end of the story, Michael thinks back on seemingly trivial events in his life, including an incident when he was ten in which he stole a conch shell from a neighbor. He thinks that through his theft and imprisonment, he has ended what he is remembering as a charmed life, but the reader knows that that life never really existed. His theft in the drugstore mirrors his theft as a boy. Self-deluded until the end, Michael never realizes that he has been giving in to impulses and temptations his entire life by always taking the easy way out. Thus, the situation in which he has put himself ends nothing. It only continues a very long trend of living without thought—of acting on impulse.

Source: Kristy Blackmon, Critical Essay on "Impulse," in *Short Stories for Students*, Gale, Cengage Learning, 2012.

Michael's impulses landed him in jail. *(Lou Oates / Shutterstock.com)*

Catharine F. Seigel

In the following excerpt, Seigel follows the theme of suicide in Aiken's life and work, including the influence of Freud.

Responding to the news that his lifelong friend, Conrad Aiken, had died from heart failure, at the age of eighty-four, earlier in the day, George B. Wilbur, a noted Boston psychiatrist, wrote to his widow, Mary Hoover Aiken, "Your news tonight comes as a sort of relief. As you understand Conrad struggled all his life to avoid sharing in the fate of his father. I feared he was losing his battle for reasons I knew nothing about nor could help. So that is over." While it is true that Wilbur did not know the reasons for Aiken's most recent suicidal inclinations, he knew all too well how the trauma of Aiken's father's having murdered his mother and then killed himself had dominated the writer's life since he was eleven years old. In addition, the trauma had appeared obliquely or directly in much of Aiken's fiction and poetry. In fact, in mid-career, when Aiken was struggling with his second novel, *Great Circle*, he had written to Wilbur complaining that his mind unconsciously kept returning to his past, throwing impediments in the progress of the new novel:

> It [*Great Circle*] has come to an end, pro tem, largely because it has uncovered so many infantile blocks and such that it has momentarily paralyzed me. And very curious too to observe how my dreams have gone back many stages. Night after night I've revisited my father and mother; alternately replaced my father and accepted him; death and birth inseparably interlocked. (7 February 1931)

He continues that in one dream his grandmother asked him when he would join her in the tomb, and he had assured her "that it would be soon."

> "AS A SUICIDE SURVIVOR, HE HAD TO FIND A WAY TO SUSTAIN HIS SURVIVAL. AS A WRITER, HE FOUND A WAY TO TRANSMUTE HIS ILLNESS, TO TURN HIS SUFFERING INTO ART."

That a survivor of suicide often identifies with the deceased is thoroughly documented. Albert C. Cain, editor of *Survivors of Suicide*, concludes, "They live not merely with a conviction of but an essential resignation to their own ultimate suicide; a passive (yet at times tenacious) insistence that they are controlled by Fate, that their end has long since been irrevocably determined and utterly beyond their power to change." With varying degrees of transparency, many of Aiken's writings reflect his attempt to come to terms with those early morning pistol shots on 28 February 1901.

One would be hard pressed to name another U.S. writer of the first half of the twentieth century who so nearly satisfied T. S. Eliot's famous conditions for literary greatness: abundance, variety, and complete competence. Aiken published over fifty volumes of fiction, poetry, essays, and several books of criticism. He won almost every coveted literary award, including the Pulitzer, the Bollingen, and the National Medal for Literature. Yet Aiken never commanded the reading public he deserved. Mark Schorer, for instance, observed that about Conrad Aiken there appeared to be "a conspiracy of silence." Critic Henry Popkin's oft-repeated estimate that he was "famous for not being famous enough" points to the realities of Aiken's literary career. Although he was none too happy to have Louis Untermeyer title an article in a popular journal "Conrad Aiken: Our Best Known Unread Poet," the title unhappily reflected the truth about the readership for both his fiction and poetry. Malcolm Cowley lamented that Aiken had been more neglected than any other major writer since Herman Melville and Emily Dickinson (p. 250). Over the years literary critics have offered a host of reasons for Aiken's neglect, but one that has never been seriously considered is the extent to which Aiken's being emotionally crippled by his parents' death and, in particular, by his father's suicide affected his literary career.

Dr. William Aiken, a Harvard-educated ophthalmologist, had moved his family from their New England roots and home to Savannah, Georgia, on the advice of his physician, who felt that the more relaxed environment of the South would be beneficial to Dr. Aiken's mental health. Some ten years later the double murder occurred. The following contemporary account of the scene that dominates Conrad Aiken's entire fifty-five volume canon has never been republished in its totality since it appeared in the *Savannah Morning News* (28 February 1901). Police officer Lange, on duty in the station house the morning of the killings, told the *Morning News* that he heard the "patter of bare and boyish feet" and turned to face Conrad Aiken, Dr. Aiken's eleven-year-old son:

> "Papa has shot mama and then shot himself," said the boy.
> "Who is your father?" the policeman queried.
>
> "Dr. Aiken." With a degree of calmness and self-possession beyond his years and that under the tragic circumstances was almost weird, the lad indicated the room of his mother. Lange pushed open the door and entered. The room was in almost total darkness, as it was then scarcely broad daylight, and the shutters of the windows were closed. The policeman had a single match, and striking it, a flickering and uncertain light shed itself over the room. By its rays the grim details of the tragedy were revealed. The bed was just to the left of the policeman as he entered the room and stretched on this, lying in an easy and natural position on her left side, was the body of Mrs. Aiken. A pistol wound, ghastly and gaping, in her right temple, explained too well the cause of her death. On pillows and bedclothing, and on the walls of the room near the head of the bed, were further evidence of the short distance from which the fatal shot had been fired.
>
> On a rug at the side of the bed, face downward, was the body of Dr. Aiken, a like gaping wound in his right temple and the revolver from which the shots had been fired still clasped in his right hand. The position in which he had fallen showed that death had been instantaneous. . . .
>
> It was a scene to touch and melt the hardest heart. The eldest boy, Conrad, lingered outside the door, while the other children, Elizabeth, Kempton and Robert, the last named but 6 years old, scarce realizing the extent of the awful calamity of which they were the innocent victims and from which they would be the greatest sufferers, cowed in terror and sorrow unrestrained, in the adjoining room which they occupied.

In the following days Conrad's three siblings were sent to live with a cousin in Philadelphia. He was sent to a great aunt in New Bedford for a year and, subsequently, to an uncle in Cambridge, a librarian at Harvard College, who agreed to take "one male child." Much of Conrad Aiken's entire life (1889–1973) and art were to be shadowed by the tragedy occurring in his eleventh year.

The trauma clearly hovered ever at the edge of his consciousness and is echoed throughout his work, but it is particularly apparent in his fiction. Suicide, as a theme, first appeared in Aiken's undergraduate short story, "The Cat and the Mouse," published in the *Harvard Advocate* in 1909. In young Aiken's story a crippled jeweler wants to flee the world that has mocked him over the years: "What a world of trouble would be saved him. One sip—and everything in the visible, or the audible, would slowly pale, dim, and swirl away like vapor." He purchases his poison, locks the door of his shop, drinks the vial, and crawls behind his counter to die. "Utterly weary of life," his only regret was never having had the chance "to torture a human being" in turn for being reviled by the world. But then he does get that chance. A novice robber breaks into his shop, and the hidden jeweler first frightens him with strange moans and groans. Next the jeweler decides to take his final revenge by choking the robber, only to be denied by the robber's death from fright. Suicide and murder are likewise thematic concerns in his first three novels: *Blue Voyage* (1927), *Great Circle* (1932), and *King Coffin*

(1935), as well as in *Ushant* (1955), his "fictional" autobiography written forty-three years after "The Cat and the Mouse."

Aiken's most complete confessional work remains this strange autobiography, *Ushant*. Its importance in Aiken's life and work cannot be underestimated. Aiken's form is unique: *Ushant* is written as a third-person narrative about an author identified as "D." Aiken's works in general are thinly disguised with alternative titles: *Blue Voyage* becomes *Purple Passage*; *Great Circle* appears as *Dead Reckoning*. All of the people important in Aiken's life are here—his parents, the aunts and uncles, three wives, assorted liaisons—but they are all renamed as are Aiken's literary colleagues: T. S. Eliot is "Tsetse" and Ezra Pound, "Rabbi Ben Ezra." Although the first edition of *Ushant* was published in 1952, Aiken had been writing the autobiography over the previous nineteen years. Finally, while the seduction of death also weaves in and out of much of Aiken's poetry, the sheer mass of it (twenty-five volumes) precludes it from consideration in this essay. Then, too, Jay Martin, in *Conrad Aiken: A Life of His Art*, suggested that Aiken created fables and drew on myths in his poetry but that it was in his fiction that he turned to a confessional, self-exploitative writing in order to understand himself.

Throughout his life, Aiken wrestled time and again with his father's action until he resolved, as an adult, that his father must have suffered from insanity, but such a conclusion offered grim comfort to the writer. In their essay, "A Study of Grief: Emotional Responses to Suicide," Erich Lindemann and Ina May Greer observe,

> Death by one's own hand is so unacceptable a thought in our culture that we tend to say the suicide was insane, out of his mind. But to tell a grieving person that his loved one was crazy is not to make his burden easier. Insanity does not add to one's social status, nor does a family history of mental disease increase one's sense of security or feeling of individual worth. Moreover, it makes the dangerous threat of identification with the lost person and a copying of one of the symptoms of his last act easier.

We know that Aiken was keenly apprehensive about the presence of *petit mal* epilepsy in his family background and of the fact that his parents had been cousins. He reveals in *Ushant* that it had been a "marriage of cousins: his mother's surnames had merely, after the marriage, been reversed." And of course Aiken knew that the official explanation for his mother's murder and his father's suicide was his father's terrible fear of going insane and that, consequently, his wife would have him committed. As the *Savannah Morning News* sensationally headlined the story, "Consumed by the Mad Belief His Wife Wished to Have Him Forcibly Confined in an Asylum for the Insane, Frenzied by the Dread Nightmare Possibility of Dementia, Dr. Aiken Shot and Killed His Wife, Then Fired a Second Bullet Through His Brain—On a Single Subject He'd Been Insane a Year—Twice Attempted Suicide." The newspaper account further suggests that Dr. Aiken's father had committed suicide: "It is a mournful fact, interesting in the light of the tragic happenings of his final end, that his father was afflicted with a somewhat similar dementia to that which harassed Dr. Aiken and ended his life by shooting himself through the brain" (28 February 1901).

In addition, Elizabeth, Aiken's only sister, lived out her long life in an insane asylum. And Aiken specifically acknowledged in an interview with R. H. Wilbur for the *Paris Review* that his best-known, frequently-anthologized short story, "Silent Snow, Secret Snow," had been "a projection of my own inclination to insanity." Critic Steven E. Olson, in an essentially psychoanalytic analysis of *Great Circle*, quotes a letter to James L. Wheeler (17 January 1970) in which Aiken insists that there was no agreement between his parents about the suicide: "On my mother's part it was involuntary, it was murder, and my father was definitely insane." Clearly the life of Conrad Aiken, the first-born son, was permanently shadowed by the fear of inherited insanity and the fear of and attraction toward suicide. As a suicide survivor, he had to find a way to sustain his survival. As a writer, he found a way to transmute his illness, to turn his suffering into art.

The doctor-mentor for Aiken was to be Sigmund Freud. It was young Aiken's good fortune to be an undergraduate at Harvard when the works of the Viennese psychiatrist were first becoming available in the United States. In 1909 Aiken had his fellow student, George Wilbur, begin translating Freud for him. When, in 1934, the editors of *New Verse* asked forty poets the question, "Have you been influenced by Freud and how do you regard him?" Aiken unhesitatingly replied,

> Profoundly, but so has everybody, whether they are aware of it or not. However, I decided very early, I think as early as 1912 [Aiken was twenty-three], that Freud, and his co-workers and rivals and followers, were making the most important contribution of the century to the understanding of man and his consciousness.

Aiken read widely and appreciatively in Freud, but of particular significance to him was the importance of childhood experiences, the nature of dreams, the function of wit, and especially the relationship between art and neurosis. Freud's suggestion that art was, indeed, a product of neuroses and that it was an escape from reality for both the creator and receiver was tempered by the consequent realization that it was often therapeutic for both. In Aiken's "Preface" to his long poem, "Changing Mind" (1925), he speaks to the role of the artist as an expander of the consciousness of others through an understanding and expression of his own: "He must make his experience articulate for the benefit of others, he must be, in the evolving consciousness of man, the servant-example, and in fact he has little choice in the matter."

Freud concluded his 1924 "self-portrait," "An Autobiographical Study," with the reassurance that "the artist, like the neurotic, had withdrawn from an unsatisfying reality into this world of imagination; but, unlike the neurotic, he knew how to find a way back from it and once more to get a firm foothold in reality." While Freud carefully drew this distinction between neurotic and artist, Aiken was often tempted not to return from his temporary escape into the world of the imagination. In *Ushant*, he talks about "prescribed insulations" (frequently through alcohol) from the pain of living and concludes that

> despite these libations to the god of forgetfulness, the moment had at last supervened when such temporary rests from the vision seemed not enough and when a more famous sleep had suddenly appeared, one evening, as the ultimate, the only, desideratum. If one had learned, and dangerously, to live, should not one also learn, as dangerously, and of one's own purest volition, to die?

Freud, then, provided a convincing philosophical justification for the extreme autobiographical dimension of Aiken's writing, including the persistent fear of insanity and the corresponding seductiveness of suicide. It explained the urgent need for unabashed honesty in his narratives. It valorized the relationship between personal suffering and art. . . .

Source: Catharine F. Seigel, "Conrad Aiken and the Seduction of Suicide," in *Literature and Medicine*, Vol. 18, No. 1, 1999, pp. 82–99.

Kenneth Womack

In the following excerpt, Womack examines Aiken in terms of his adult relationships rather than his childhood experiences.

The bulk of the psychologically oriented hermeneutical study devoted to Conrad Aiken's autobiographical volume, *Ushant* (1952), consists largely of Freudian or psychoanalytic readings. Given the childhood-oriented direction of such readings, this should hardly be surprising, especially when one considers the importance these critics place on the defining moment of Aiken's tragic childhood. In February 1901, during Aiken's eleventh year, his father, a terribly jealous and paranoid husband, killed Aiken's mother in a fit of rage before turning the gun on himself. "From then on," Aiken later revealed, "they would possess me" (Lorenz 2). Few critics ever consider *Ushant* in terms of Aiken's adult experiences, opting instead to assess Aiken's work by starting with his early, devastating loss of his parents. Freudian and other psychoanalytical approaches—perhaps because of their intense focus on issues of "downstream causality" and early childhood experiences—simply neglect to consider similarly pivotal moments in adulthood, and moreover, the very nature of such methodologies does not allow critics to evaluate the important interpersonal dynamics which shaped Aiken throughout his biographical and literary life.

Examining Aiken's autobiography in terms of these adult interpersonal relationships reveals the complex system of betrayals that motivated Aiken's conduct during the course of his relationships with his three wives, as well as during his lengthy friendship with the British poet and novelist Martin Donisthorpe Armstrong. Armstrong's role in *Ushant*—as "Chapman," the older, learned friend of Aiken's alter-ego, "D."—remains unexplicated in the mélange of criticism dedicated to unraveling the vague threads of Aiken's autobiography. In this loosely fictionalized account of his life, Aiken employs a Joycean, unmediated narrative structure which allows him to record his memories in a deliberately dreamlike, atemporal manner. Along the way, Aiken offers a series of portraits of the many personalities which affected him—disguising T. S. Eliot as "Tsetse" and Malcolm Lowry as "Hambo," for example—while throughout the novel, Aiken, as D., carefully navigates the stormy waters of his life which both lead to and depart from Ushant, the name of that barren, rocky outreach off the tip of Brittany which is the final stretch of land one encounters before being enveloped by the vastness of the Atlantic Ocean.

It is within the pages of this equally vast and challenging personal portrait that Aiken reveals the intricate patterns of jealousy and betrayal which haunted him throughout his adult life, and likewise resulted in his especially disparaging portrait of Armstrong, once his treasured guide and friend. Because of the remarkably interpersonal nature of *Ushant's* subject matter, employing a family systems approach in a study of Aiken's autobiography affords critics the opportunity of identifying the interactive loops which function as connectives between individuals and their families, while at the same time allowing them to examine the motives and experiences of adult literary characters. Such an approach is particularly worthwhile in the case of *Ushant*—a narrative in which Aiken attempts to replicate fictionally his actual life experiences. Owing to its very recent infusion into the vernacular of literary study, however, the fundamental vocabulary of this new critical approach requires some additional elucidation.

With family systems, the family presupposes the individual as the matrix of identity. As Charles P. Barnard and Ramon Garrido Corrales note in *The Theory and Technique of Family Therapy* (1979), "The members of one's family are one's significant others par excellence." Similarly, in the family systems schema, the principle of "emergence"—or the notion that the whole is greater than the sum of its parts—functions as a significant factor in the life of an individual. Proponents of the family systems approach also acknowledge that the family's most important role is fraught with difficulty. The family, as an inherently open system, must at once provide support for both integration into a solid family unit as well as differentiation into relatively autonomous selves. The constructs of this mutual developmental process also produce functional and dysfunctional families. In functional families, individual members create solid selves which allow them to act, think, and feel for themselves. In dysfunctional families, however, family members develop pseudo-selves—often fostered by fear and anxiety within the system—and thus, such individuals frequently remain unable to maintain any real stasis between their inner feelings and their outward behavior.

In *The Family Crucible* (1978), Augustus Y. Napier and Carl Whitaker argue that families—both functional as well as dysfunctional—operate as singular, conglomerate persons. They also suggest that the family rigidly controls the individual members of the system through their roles in the family's structure. Families attempt to effect these control measures by preserving a state of equilibrium, or homeostatic balance, through the creation of constancy loops. Likewise, each family system functions upon a series of subsystems, beginning with the spouse-spouse dyad at the top of the hierarchy, followed by the parent-child dyad, and concluding with the sibling-sibling dyad. The entrance of a third party into the boundaries of a dyad produces the phenomenon of triangulation, with the third entity often reducing the feelings of intimacy for which the original members of the dyad continue to yearn. When a dyad expands into a triangulated form, notions of secrecy and emotional distortion infiltrate the subsystem, with devastating effects upon the entire family system as a result (Barnard and Corrales 24–28).

In Aiken's case, triangulation manifests itself within the confines of his expanded family system as a means of protection—an extension of his pseudo-self—manufactured as an implicit barrier against the inevitable feelings of loss and betrayal which often accompanied his close interpersonal relationships. Using the various precepts of family systems in interpretive study allows critics to employ highly powerful tools for explicating the fictive worlds of literary texts, and with Aiken's autobiography, this approach proves especially revelatory as a means of analyzing the larger Aiken family system. Likewise, the family systems paradigm offers cogent explanations for the complex pattern of betrayals that Aiken remained unable to shatter through the course of his biographical and literary life.

. . . Of particular interest to this study, however, is Aiken's lengthy relationship with Armstrong. In early 1911, Aiken temporarily resigned from Harvard after being named Class Poet, a position which required the shy Aiken to compose and recite a poem for graduation exercises the following spring. At once angered and terrified by the prospects of his new position, Aiken quickly fled to the safety of a lengthy sabbatical in Europe (Butscher 155). In April, he met Armstrong while touring Florence, and was immediately intrigued by the affable Briton's interests—art, music, and literature—as well as his knowledge and education. The erudite Armstrong accompanied Aiken as they visited "the great Perugino triptych, and the Michelangelo *abbozzi*, and everything else" (*Ushant* 172). Aiken later remembered their travels, especially their visit to the summit of Mount Scenario, with a special fondness. Soon the new companions were reading their poems aloud to each other, for like Aiken, Armstrong aspired to be a writer. Their reasons for travelling to Italy were similar as well; Armstrong had fled to Florence to escape an unfulfilling job in a London architect's office. A graduate of Pembroke College, Cambridge, Armstrong majored in mechanical science, a vocation he later confessed to disliking "intensely." Determined to become a writer, Armstrong travelled to Florence under the pretense of pursuing a study of pre-Renaissance and Renaissance Italian art (Womack 100).

They soon renewed their friendship in England, with Armstrong again reprising his role as the younger Aiken's learned guide while introducing him to the London literary scene (Womack 101). In the interim, Aiken's relatives convinced him to return to Harvard in the fall and graduate in 1912. With his new relationship with Armstrong reduced for the moment to the whimsy of trans-Atlantic correspondence, a rejuvenated Aiken returned to Massachusetts at the end of the summer (Butscher 168, 174). In the autumn of his first semester back at Cambridge, he met and fell in love with a brilliant young graduate student at Radcliffe, Jessie McDonald. Aiken later wrote to his old friend Grayson McCouch ("Old Bird" in *Ushant*), sharing his new feelings for Jessie: "I am at present keeping a tender thumb on my pulse (resigned at last to the belief that it will in no wise prevent there being a pulse) and hoping thereby to keep the warm realities close under my eyes as an antidote to impalpable dream.... Sentimentalism gives me an image and a philtre, and my dreams are full of the lady, and my work woven with her and I say, I am in love" (*Letters*). At 23, Aiken for the first time seemed to be surrendering himself to a committed, interpersonal relationship.

Aiken and Jessie married after his graduation from Harvard in 1912, and over the next fifteen years, their marriage followed the course of a typical family life cycle. According to Barnard and Corrales, families undergo their own particular life cycles, including the phases of courtship, marriage, children, career choices, illnesses, aging, and death—all of which serve to change and inevitably alter the balance of the family system. These same perceptions about marriages can easily be applied to close friendship as well. When such relationships inevitably pierce the boundaries of the family system, they too become powerful forces in the politics of the family's ceaseless desire for homeostasis. Such cyclical phases confront families with pivotal moments which they must adjust to in order to restore the state of equilibrium which all systems, including families, so desperately desire. In most cases, these life cycle changes simply require families to reorganize as they shift to a new level of homeostasis (Barnard and Corrales 88–90).

After a lengthy European honeymoon, the Aikens settled into their new life together back in Cambridge, where Aiken penned his first volume of poems, *Earth Triumphant and Other Tales in Verse* (1914). Their first child, John Kempton, was born in October 1913, and the following summer, with Jessie pregnant again, Aiken travelled to London with the deliberate intention of widening his literary circle and doing "much selling and self-advertising." Sadly, after Aiken's return to America, the baby died during childbirth. "It was an excellent *boy*," Aiken wrote, "Looked very like his father." After the birth in late 1917 of a daughter, Jane Kempton, the Aikens, feeling the strain of a poet's modest income, moved to the village of South Yarmouth on Cape Cod. During this period, Aiken developed the form of the long narrative, symphonic poem with which he is largely associated today, and by 1921 had published seven poetry volumes, almost 75 articles and reviews, and a volume of criticism (*Letters*).

In the autumn of 1921, the Aikens moved to England, first to Lookout Cottage in Winchelsea, and later to the historic Jeake's House in Rye. The promise of the move to England, coupled with his recent vast literary output, was a source of great excitement and anticipation for Aiken, as he wrote in *Ushant*:

> And the wonderful decade or more was to unravel itself as predestined—in the Arnault bookshop, at Soho restaurants, in the Bloomsbury tea-shops, Lyons or ABC's, and at Inglesee [Winchelsea] and Saltinge [Rye]. A time of blooming, of profusion, of hard work and endless debate; of good food, good drinks, and good living. But a time of competitive stress also, of unceasing literary *sauve-qui-peut*.... Which of them would survive? which of them wouldn't?

Survival for Aiken in his created family was indeed a problematic undertaking. The expansion of the Aiken's family system carried additional financial pressures for Aiken, still struggling under his meager poet's income, and he was likewise burdened with the necessity of promoting his fledgling literary career. Aiken's demanding vocation frequently required him to travel to London, and occasionally to the United States, leaving Jessie alone to maintain their home and care for their children, which now included the infant Joan Delano, born in September 1924 (*Letters*). These accumulating burdens on their marital relationship no doubt forced the Aikens to postpone their personal demands in favor of the needs of their family, likewise fostering an increasing underlying tension in their union. As Napier and Whitaker note, "So frightening are these tensions that the couple often cannot allow themselves to be consciously aware of them."

It was in precisely such a desultory state that Aiken travelled to New York and Boston in the fall of 1926, hoping to land a publisher for his first novel, *Blue Voyage* (1928). While visiting Cambridge, he consented to an interview with Clarissa Lorenz, then writing for the Boston *Evening Transcript*. Years later, Clarissa recalled how Aiken's "resonant voice paralyzed my reflexes." Their mutual attraction was immediate, and they spent the remainder of Aiken's time in America together. Before leaving for England, Aiken revealed his true intentions to her: "We must have each other, darling. I don't care how or when. If you don't come to England, I'll come back here. I've decided to ask Jessie for a divorce" (Lorenz 15, 45). Aiken himself, perhaps fearing the inevitable betrayals that shadowed his previous interpersonal relationships, usurped fate and exploded the "impalpable dream."

Back in England, however, Aiken found the dissolution of his marriage a troubling enterprise. As he wrote to his friend G. B. Wilbur ("Jacob" in *Ushant*): "For years I've been sure, and happy in being sure, that I would never fall in love again. And now Clarice and I look at each other for ten minutes and the whole bloody world is blown to smithereens. And nevertheless, my feeling for the children is so intense, and my compassion and fondness for Jessie, that I wonder incessantly if *that* will not present a very real and permanent obstacle to happiness" (*Letters*). Once back at Jeake's House, Aiken had rediscovered the patterns of familywide symbiosis to which he had grown accustomed. According to Napier and Whitaker, these comfortable patterns inhibit individual members from threatening the balance of the family system as a whole. In this sense, then, Aiken was fully cognizant of his dilemma—as well as of the dire possibilities that such a devastating, irrevocable life decision presents—and in *Ushant*, aptly described it as his "moment of greatest distress," his "self-inflicted wound."

Tiring of their marital struggle, Jessie agreed to a divorce in January 1927, on a single, remarkably modern, condition: that Aiken give his relationship with Clarissa a probationary period of one year before marrying her (Lorenz 45). During 1927, however, the dual triangulation of Armstrong complicated matters significantly. Aiken and Armstrong had earlier renewed their friendship when the Aikens moved to England in the early 1920s, as their correspondence attests, and Armstrong became a permanent fixture in the Aiken household—visiting the family on weekends and providing Aiken with a conduit to the London literary scene. When Aiken began his affair with Clarissa in late 1926, he placed his old friend in a most precarious position by confiding in Armstrong about his new lover, and at one point, sending him a long, detailed analysis of her sexuality (Lorenz 58). At the same time, after Aiken's return to Clarissa and a teaching position at Harvard in the fall of 1927, Armstrong began visiting Jessie and the children on weekends in Rye, now having moved himself to the nearby village of Sutton, where he was working on his latest novel (Womack 111). With their husband-wife dyad lost in a deeply troubled state of flux, Aiken and Jessie now maintained the balance of their relationship through a triangulated third-party, in this instance, the beleaguered Armstrong.

Meanwhile, again missing his family and the rigid systematic patterns they had established in Rye, Aiken met Jessie for a reconciliation in March 1928. Jessie surprised Aiken, however, when she announced her plans to divorce him and marry Armstrong. Aiken later wrote Eliot, informing him that "I was planning to return to my abandoned family in Rye, in June; but Armstrong has beaten me to it. He is going to marry Jessie" (*Letters*). Aiken continued to attempt a reconciliation, but as his daughter Joan remembers, Jessie refused to discuss the matter with him: "he wanted to try to talk her out of her decision. But she refused to see him; on hearing of his arrival she walked straight out of the house and caught a bus to the next village" (Womack 111).

Armstrong married Jessie in 1929 and his relationship with Aiken remained understandably strained thereafter. Aiken's bitterness continued to grow as Armstrong's recent novel, *St. Christopher's Day* (1928), became a financial success: "My husband in law keeps discreetly out of my way, and out of London. His book is making pots of money, and he's got himself a house in the country, which he's fixing up and furnishing for the family. I am arranging to have it bombed" (*Letters*). Despite the humorous undertones, Aiken felt horribly deceived, telling Clarissa, "It's a double betrayal." His friendship with Armstrong, well into its second decade, was unable to survive the new marriage, for their interests were at last "dividing and conflicting" (*Ushant*). Armstrong was saddened as well; as he wrote to Aiken in March 1929: "I am sorry you have gone back on the more friendly feelings towards me which you not only showed but verbally expressed when we met in January. It is a pity to repent of the one spark of goodwill you have shown me throughout the whole business" (Huntington Archives, 19 Mar. 1929). Shortly before the wedding, Aiken summoned Armstrong to his rented rooms in London for what he called "five hours of sheer candour," and Aiken concluded his evening of verbal tirades against Armstrong by vomiting (Lorenz 66). The pseudo-self which Aiken hid behind for so long was finally dismantled, and after Armstrong's marriage to Jessie—with their betrayal of him at last complete—Aiken never saw either of them again.

Having returned to America in late 1928, Aiken later married Clarissa in February 1930 in the New Jersey home of William Carlos Williams. Once again, Aiken proved that he could be unusually prolific within the bounds of the spouse-spouse dyad, and during the course of his relationship with Clarissa published three novels and seven volumes of poetry, including the Pulitzer Prize-winning *Selected Poems* (1929). Sadly, from the earliest days of their marriage, Aiken and Clarissa were rarely happy. In late 1930, the Aikens moved into the now vacant Jeake's House, and once there, Aiken began to accuse Clarissa continually of imagined infidelities with his friends, proving that he had hardly recovered from his recent experiences with Armstrong and Jessie (*Letters*). Likewise Clarissa, remarking on her marriage to Aiken and his protracted fears of betrayal, once wrote: "Conrad was never really mine. I only borrowed him." The "wonderful decade" that Aiken wrote of in *Ushant* was now emphatically over. After six years of marital difficulties with Clarissa, Aiken reprised his 1926 voyage to personal freedom by again travelling to Boston in the summer of 1936, where he met and fell in love with Mary Hoover, a young artist (*Letters*). Remarkably, after nearly a decade, Aiken rediscovered the behavioral patterns which afforded him his escape from marriage with Jessie.

Clearly from the beginning of his marriage to Lorenz, Aiken appeared bent on avoiding the betrayals that troubled him throughout his life, thus opting once again to effect the betrayal himself. As Napier and Whitaker note, "Some marriages are begun with an implicit, unconscious plan for a later divorce." They also argue that the origins of this plan often lie in problems relating to one or both of the spouse's families-of-origin, and surely the early cessation of Aiken's family-of-origin could foster such interpersonal difficulties. Aiken's parting words to Clarissa indeed evince such a conclusion. She recalls feeling "bemused" as he said: "If only you had given me a chance; you were the only woman for me. It's all your fault and you know it." In his final conscious betrayal of Clarissa, Aiken again perpetrated the "self-inflicted wound" necessary to sate his need for avoiding any of the pain which so often accompanies human relationships. Moreover, dismissing her in such a manner allowed Aiken to breathe new life into the pseudo-self that Armstrong and Jessie helped to collapse in the late 1920s. . . .

Source: Kenneth Womack, "Unmasking Another Villain in Conrad Aiken's Autobiographical Dream," in *Biography*, Vol. 19, No. 2, Spring 1996, pp. 137–57.

SOURCES

Aiken, Conrad, "Impulse," in *Short Story Masterpieces*, edited by Albert Erskine and Robert Penn Warren, Dell Publishing, 1954, pp. 1–14.

———, "What I Believe," in *Nation*, Vol. 135, No. 3499, July 27, 1932, p. 80.

Aldrich, Jennifer, "Conrad Aiken: The Deciphered Heart," in *Sewanee Review*, Vol. 75, No. 3, July 1967, pp. 486, 502.

Handa, Carolyn, "'Impulse': Calculated Artistry in Conrad Aiken," in *Studies in Short Fiction*, Vol. 12, No. 4, 1975, p. 376.

Moore, John R., "Conrad Aiken: The Egotistical Sublime?" in *Sewanee Review*, Vol. 74, No. 3, July 1966, p. 701.

Seigel, Catharine F., *The Fictive World of Conrad Aiken*, Northern Illinois University Press, 1992, pp. 2, 6.

Spivey, Ted R., *Revival: Southern Writers in the Modern City*, University Presses of Florida, 1986, pp. 89–90.

Wilber, Robert Hunter, "Conrad Aiken, The Art of Poetry No. 9," in *Paris Review*, No. 42, Winter/Spring 1968, http://www.theparisreview.org/interviews/4283/the-art-of-poetry-no-9-conrad-aiken (accessed March 8, 2011).

Winehouse, Bernard, "'Impulse': Calculated Artistry in Conrad Aiken," in *Studies in Short Fiction*, Vol. 15, No. 1, January 1978, p. 108.

FURTHER READING

Aiken, Conrad, *Selected Letters of Conrad Aiken*, edited by Joseph Killorin, Yale University Press, 1978.

Killorin's collection of letters from Aiken shows his friendships with literary figures such as Malcolm Cowley and T. S. Eliot. The letters give the reader a sense of Aiken's voice and further insight into his opinions—often harsh—of his contemporaries, their work, and criticism of the literary canon of the time.

———, *Ushant: An Essay*, Duell, Sloan and Pearce, 1952.

Widely considered Aiken's most provocative and honest work, *Ushant* explores the author's life and literary output through a self-applied psychoanalytical lens. The autobiographical work invites the reader to accompany Aiken on a journey of self-discovery and revelation. Aiken examines the trauma of his childhood, his attitude toward literature and art, and his friendships with famous literary figures with honesty and haunting beauty.

Butler, Christopher, *Modernism: A Very Short Introduction*, Oxford University Press, 2010.

Butler offers a survey of modernism across literature and art. He examines the origins of modernism, analyzes some important works, and explains different concepts and movements. The volume also addresses modernist ideas as applied to the self, society, and established structures such as politics and technology.

Freud, Sigmund, *On Narcissism: An Introduction*, edited by Peter Fonagy, Ethel Person, and Joseph Sandler, Yale University Press, 1991.

This 1914 essay by renowned psychoanalyst Sigmund Freud explores narcissism as it applies to human development, libido, and therapy. This edition by Yale University Press is part of the "Contemporary Freud" series, which includes essays from numerous scholars that help clarify different aspects of his concepts, placing his theories in modern-day applications. These volumes also contain references on new developments in psychoanalysis.

Head, Dominic, *The Modernist Short Story: A Study in Theory and Practice*, Cambridge University Press, 2009.

Head demonstrates that the short story, in particular, is a central literary form in which to study modernism. He examines the literary theories of Louis Althusser and Mikhail Bakhtin, noted thinkers of the modernist period, and uses examples from texts to illustrate modernist techniques and forms.

SUGGESTED SEARCH TERMS

Conrad Aiken

psychological realism

Conrad Aiken AND Impulse

Conrad Aiken AND psychological realism

modernism AND Conrad Aiken

On Narcissism AND Freud

psychoanalytic criticism

human condition in literature

modernism

Aiken AND T. S. Eliot

The Lucky Stone

LUCILLE CLIFTON

1979

Lucille Clifton, a poet best known for her vibrant verse celebrating womanhood, was also an award-winning author of books for children and young adults. Her illustrated volume *The Lucky Stone* (1979) lets the reader listen over the shoulder of the young Tee as she enjoys stories told by her great-grandmother, who is in her seventies, about a lucky stone that has been passed along through several pairs of hands over more than a century. The book's last chapter is narrated by Tee, who tells of emotional trials in the year she turned fourteen. Presenting snapshot images of African American life since the days of slavery—brought to life through the nuanced pencil illustrations by Dale Payson—the book is a moving read. It has been listed in the "Stories for Younger Children" section of *The Black Experience in Children's Literature*, published by the New York Public Library in 1989, and in the "Fiction for Older Readers: Family Stories" section of the seventh edition of *Best Books for Children: Preschool through Grade 6*, published by John T. Gillespie in 2002.

AUTHOR BIOGRAPHY

Clifton was born Thelma Lucille Sayles on June 27, 1936, in Depew, New York. Her father was a steelworker, and her mother was a homemaker and laborer. She was raised in the Baptist church to

Lucille Clifton *(AP Images)*

which her father belonged, and spirituality would come to play a significant role in her life. Like her own mother and her first daughter, Lucille was born with twelve fingers—a rarity superstitiously associated with witchcraft—but the extra digits were removed in her infancy. Finding herself to have a sixth sense for the sacred, as an adult she underwent mystical experiences, and her poetry reflects her intimate familiarity with the myths of the Bible. When Lucille was five, the family moved to Buffalo, New York. Inspired by her mother's poetry and her own love of words, Lucille began writing poems at the age of ten. After completing high school, she earned a scholarship to attend Howard University, in Washington, D.C., where she met future luminaries such as the literary giants Amiri Baraka (then known as LeRoi Jones) and Toni Morrison. In 1958, Sayles married Fred Clifton, and the two lived in Buffalo, having six children over the next decade. During that time—the climactic years of the civil rights movement—Lucille Clifton became absorbed in writing poetry.

Shortly after the family moved to Baltimore in 1967, Clifton looked to be published, and her poems were entered into the 1969 YW-YMCA Poetry Center Discovery Award competition on her behalf. She won the award, leading to the publication of her first collection, *Good Times* (1969), which gained national critical praise. She was also pointedly asked whether she had ever written for children; in light of her love for telling stories to her own children and the evident need for children's literature representative of African American experiences, she produced her first children's book, *Some of the Days of Everett Anderson*, in 1969. In her ensuing poetry collections through the 1970s, Clifton produced lively, effusive images of African American womanhood, feminism, and spirituality. One of her most famous poems, from the collection *Two-Headed Woman* (1980), is "homage to my hips." Clifton also wrote more than a dozen children's books in the 1970s, including *The Lucky Stone* in 1979. After publishing *Everett Anderson's Goodbye* in 1983, she focused almost exclusively on poetry through the end of the century. Her later collections shifted focus to questions of her own life cycle, self-knowledge, and mortality. She held various professorships, including positions at St. Mary's College of Maryland and Columbia University, and she especially valued showing young people how enlightening poetry can be. She collected an array of awards, including a National Book Award for *Blessing the Boats* (2000) and the Ruth Lilly Poetry Prize in 2007 for lifetime achievement. Stricken with cancer, Clifton died in Baltimore in 2010.

PLOT SUMMARY

The Lucky Stone opens with two paragraphs narrated in the first person by someone nicknamed Tee. Perhaps a young woman now, she is reminiscing about her life as a girl, when she lived with her parents and great-grandmother in a house with a nice big porch. Tee loved the stories her "Great-grand" used to tell, and they shared some favorites, like the ones about the lucky stone.

One

The story now switches to third-person narration. Tee and her great-grandmother, Mrs. Elzie F. Pickens, are sitting on the porch on a hot June morning, and Tee asks for a story. Seeing Tee's

MEDIA ADAPTATIONS

- The Connections Literary Series has archived online a video of Clifton reading from *The Lucky Stone* and chatting with the young audience at the College of Southern Maryland on December 11, 1992. The video can be found on YouTube (http://www.youtube.com/watch?v=tKiGbL2cKj0).

smile, Mrs. Pickens thinks of a lady from a long time ago named Vashti, who used to likewise sit on her porch with her mother. They both had very long fingernails and toenails, which frightened the young Elzie and their friends whenever they passed. But one day, Vashti tells Elzie she would give her a lucky stone in exchange for a cool glass of water. Elzie runs home and fetches one for her. At first, she is too scared to accept the shiny black stone with an *A* scratched into it, but Vashti confides that she has no one else to give it to, so Elzie takes it.

Mrs. Pickens continues with the story of the stone. Vashti's mother, Mandy, was a slave as a young girl. One day, after picking cotton in the hot sun, Mandy is frightened by a snake and drops and spoils her whole sackful. Scared of the beating she expects to receive, she tries to creep away—but the "bossman," or slave driver, sees her and, wielding a whip, spurs his horse after her. Mandy finds a cave to hide in. By nightfall, she is too scared to return; after three days, she hears dogs barking, and she knows she has nowhere to run.

A week later, an older slave from the plantation is driving a carriage past the cave when the horse is spooked by a thrown stone. Irritated, he tosses the stone back into the cave—but as he returns to his horse, the stone is thrown out again, now with an *A* scratched into it. Since Mandy's full name is Amanda, the driver concludes that she must be hiding inside. Thenceforth, all the local slaves take care to drop foodstuffs near the cave whenever they pass by. Weeks and months pass until, more than a year later, the slaves are at last emancipated. Mandy can finally emerge, wild-eyed and unkempt. When she grows up and has a daughter of her own, she passes along the stone—the one Vashti later gave to Elzie.

Finishing her story as the sun sets, Mrs. Pickens is helped up by Tee, who asks why the stone was lucky. Mrs. Pickens points out that it saved her life by allowing her to signal for help, and she says the stone would prove lucky for Vashti, as well.

Two

Tee and her great-grandmother sing a spiritual on the porch in the evening, which reminds Mrs. Pickens of her own mother's beautiful singing. Mrs. Pickens begins a story about when her mother was the lead singer in the church choir, after emancipation, when African Americans were free to congregate as they pleased. This church meets outside in a field, where a stage has been built, and the circuit preacher Reverend Jones comes from time to time.

One Sunday a storm is threatening, but everyone gets dressed up and gathers anyway to hear the reverend. The choir sings several songs, with Mrs. Pickens's mother singing the lead for "Jesus Keep Me Near the Cross" (the same spiritual Tee and Mrs. Pickens were just singing). One man takes up forty minutes confessing all his sins. More people proceed upon the stage one by one to testify. When it is Vashti's turn, alone up there, she breaks out into the same spiritual. Then, the string holding a pouch around her neck—with the lucky stone inside—breaks, and the pouch bounces off the stage; Vashti stops singing, and a silence engulfs everyone. At last she jumps down to retrieve the pouch, and at that very moment the storm breaks: lightning strikes the stage, which bursts into flames and burns down.

Tee agrees that the stone proved lucky for Vashti. Someday, Mrs. Pickens says, she might tell Tee about how the stone was lucky for her.

Three

One afternoon Tee brings her great-grandmother some dogwood blossoms, which reminds Mrs. Pickens of the day she met her future husband. She and Ovella Wilson, her best friend, had secretly and fancifully decided to join a circus-like show called the Silas Greene. On a nice spring day, they plait their hair, dress up, pack a sack, and go off for the show. Amid grand music and other wonders, they find a dog in a dress dancing for the crowd, and people toss pennies. Joining in the fun, Ovella tosses a pin she had earned. Elzie accidentally tosses her lucky stone—which hits the dog right on the nose, and the dog chases her all over the fairgrounds.

Just when she thinks the dog might catch her, Elzie sees the dashing Amos Pickens—"the finest fast runnin hero in the bottoms of Virginia"—following behind and twirling a lasso rodeo-style. In a moment, he ropes the dog, which he then gently coddles. They take the dog back, and he helps her find the lucky stone. Having gotten their fill, the girls walk home, and Amos trails behind to see them safe.

Tee surmises that the stone was not lucky after all that time, since it almost got her great-grandmother bitten, but Mrs. Pickens assures her, "That was the luckiest time of all," since she met Amos through this incident. Tee hopes to have "that kind of good stone luck one day," and her great-grandmother says she just might.

In the chapter's closing lines, Tee resumes narrating in the first person, to tell the story of how she acquired the stone.

Four

Tee laments that until she was fourteen she had yet to receive a single valentine in the mail. That year, her great-grandmother, who is nearly eighty, catches pneumonia, and she spends all her time lying in bed and looking toward the sun, rasping audibly. Although she prefers to be healed by the sun, Mrs. Pickens is at length convinced to let Tee's mother and father take her to the hospital. Tee tries to visit, but the nurse always turns her away, saying no visitors are allowed.

Finally, one time the nurse is absent, and Tee sneaks through to find her great-grandmother's room. Upon seeing each other, the two hug and cry. Tee then admits that she is feeling sad because she imagines she will never have a boyfriend. Her great-grandmother dismisses her worries, saying that in time, Tee will have more admirers than she wants. When the nurse finds Tee and tells her to leave, her great-grandmother tells her to look on the dresser when she gets home.

That evening, Tee goes to her great-grandmother's sweet-smelling room and looks through the pictures of unknown aunts and uncles and of her grandmother, whom she never knew. Next to her grandmother's picture, she finds an envelope addressed to her; inside is the stone. Clutching the stone, she falls asleep in her great-grandmother's chair. Her parents bring the old woman, now recovering, home that night. The very next day, Tee gets a valentine in the mail from a boy named J.D., apparently someone she has been gazing at in school. Finishing the story of how she got the stone, Tee tells the reader that someday she might tell more about how else it was lucky for her.

CHARACTERS

Bossman

The overseer, or boss, at Mandy's plantation chases after her, threatening with a whip, when he notices her sneaking away.

Daddy

Tee's father helps take Mrs. Pickens to the hospital when she has pneumonia and later helps bring her home. In focusing on the relationship between Tee and her great-grandmother, the story tells little of Tee's parents.

Driver

An old carriage driver makes Mandy's whereabouts known to the slave community so that they will bring her food, allowing her to remain safely in hiding. She gets his attention by throwing the lucky stone at his horse and then at him.

Kenford Gamble

At the church meeting, a man named Kenford Gamble takes forty minutes to confess his sins while the thunderstorm is threatening.

J.D.

The first boy to send Tee a valentine in the mail has the initials J.D. He seems to be someone Tee has been eyeing in school.

Reverend Matthew James Jones

A circuit preacher (a traveling preacher responsible for a number of churches), the Reverend Jones is so popular that the members of the Greater Glory Baptist Church—including Vashti and Mrs. Pickens's mother as a young girl—are not turned away by the threatening storm when he is in town.

Mama

Tee's mother helps take Mrs. Pickens to and from the hospital when she has pneumonia. Like Tee's father, she plays a minimal role in the story.

Mandy

Vashti's mother, whose name is short for Amanda, runs away from her plantation after she spoils a sackful of cotton and expects a beating. She stays hidden away in a cave. After a week, she is able to spook an old carriage driver's horse by tossing what proves to be the lucky stone. When the driver tosses it back, she marks it with an *A* and tosses it once more, and the driver figures out she is hiding there. Sustained by local slaves' gifts, Mandy stays in hiding and grows wild, with long fingernails and toenails. When emancipation is declared more than a year later, she can return safely to the community. Retaining her unkempt appearance, Mandy intimidates others who later meet her—including the young Elzie Pickens and their friends, who pass by Mandy and Vashti sitting on their porch.

Nurse

The nurse at the hospital never lets Tee visit her great-grandmother; only when she is absent can Tee slip in and enjoy a short visit before the nurse kicks her out.

Amos Pickens

When the dancing dog chases Elzie around the Silas Greene fairgrounds, the charming Amos comes to the rescue. He lassos the dog to end the chase, makes sure the dog is not hurt, and then helps Elzie find her lucky stone. Afterward, he trails Elzie and Ovella home in a gentlemanly manner, seeing to their safety.

Mrs. Elzie F. Pickens

Mrs. Elzie Pickens, whose middle name is Free, holds a sacred place in her great-granddaughter Tee's heart. The porch is something like their sanctuary, and for Tee, her great-grandmother's room is practically luminescent with love. Mrs. Pickens, a mesmerizing storyteller, spends endless hours regaling Tee with tales from the nearly eighty years of her own life as well as from even further in the past. The stories told here, all about the lucky stone, serve to link Tee—first as a listener and then as an actor in her own story—with earlier generations of African Americans, all the way back to the days of slavery. Mrs. Pickens, a wise, placid figure content in having lived a life worth living and telling about, embodies this essential connection with the past.

Mrs. Pickens's Mama

At the outdoor church meeting, Mrs. Pickens's mother, as a young girl, sings the lead for the spiritual "Jesus Keep Me Near the Cross."

Tee

As the narrator of the passages framing the book, as well as the main actor in the final tale, Tee is the character with whom the reader empathizes most. Her mournful reminiscence about story time with her great-grandmother in the second paragraph—"Oh, I loved it so, I loved her so!"—gives the impression that Mrs. Pickens has since passed away. Based on the chronology as presented, Tee's early teen years would take place in the 1960s or 1970s. Tee's devotion to her great-grandmother is palpable throughout the story, in her caring gestures and in her thoughtful questions about the stories. The minimal involvement of Tee's parents serves to heighten the sense that her relationship with her great-grandmother gives Tee a unique sort of emotional and spiritual nourishment. As with Mrs. Pickens, for Tee the luck of the stone comes into play with regard to love, as her receipt of the stone coincides with her first valentine from a boy.

Vashti

Vashti receives the lucky stone from her mother, Mandy. It proves lucky for her when it falls to the ground from a platform where Vashti is singing; she jumps down to retrieve it just before lightning strikes the platform. As a grown woman, Vashti lets her nails grow wild, like her mother's. Having no heirs of her own, Vashti passes the lucky stone to the young Elzie Pickens, who kindly fetches her a glass of cold water.

Ovella Wilson

The young Elzie is accompanied to the Silas Greene show by her best friend, Ovella. The two dreamily intend to run away with the show, but first they enjoy the diversions. After Ovella tosses a penny and a pin at the dancing dog, Elzie follows suit, tossing her lucky stone, causing the dog to run after her. After the big chase, Ovella and Elzie walk home together.

THEMES

Storytelling

The four distinct tales included in *The Lucky Stone* are linked through the context of the cherished storytelling sessions shared between Tee

TOPICS FOR FURTHER STUDY

- Ask your elder family members whether they are in possession of an old or antique item, whether lucky or simply cherished, that has been passed along through more than one pair of hands, or you may have such an item in your own possession. Find out whatever interesting stories there are about this item—if there are none, invent stories yourself—and write a short work of fiction, in a framework like Clifton's or a different framework, that relates the stories about the item.
- Write a research paper on how Africans' spiritual and religious practices were variously sustained intact, adapted into Christian practices, or abandoned in the course of American slavery.
- Select two other books illustrated by Dale Payson and write an analysis of her work in the three titles, considering such matters as the technical merits of the illustrations, variations and consistencies in style between the works, the relationship of the illustrative style to the narrative style in each work, and other concerns. Post your analysis on a Web page. Scan some of the illustrations and post the images to support your points.
- In a small group discussion, brainstorm notions about how the art of storytelling has been affected by the various forms of modern media. For each medium you consider—such as the telephone, television, film, cellular phones with text messaging, Web chat rooms, blogs, or social networking sites—list positive and negative effects that the medium or format has had on the art of storytelling. Come up with conclusions about each medium's effects that the whole group agrees on; be descriptive and detailed.
- Read *The Black BC's* (1970), another children's book by Clifton that delves into African American history using an alphabetic format and poetic text. Write a paper or blog post comparing the different approaches of the two books, focusing on the impressions left on the reader by the content and by the narrative style.

---

and her great-grandmother. From these stories, Tee gains a sense of the history experienced by her forebears, personal glimpses into the life lived by her great-grandmother, and an immediate emotional connection with this elder family member. Mrs. Pickens, too, strengthens the bond she shares with her great-granddaughter, and she seems to enhance her own vitality in recollecting and communicating these memories. In a sense, she is rewarded for a life honorably led with the chance to use stories of her own life, and of others she has known, to impart wisdom on her daughter.

The moments before and after the telling of the stories are critical elements of the sessions; Tee helps the elder in and out of her seat, sharing physical contact and support, and asks questions that give Mrs. Pickens the chance to guide Tee's focus and understanding to a certain perspective. For instance, with the story of meeting her future husband, Mrs. Pickens subtly teaches Tee to consider that any seeming misfortune—such as being chased by an angry dog—might turn out to be the greatest fortune one has ever known, such as meeting the love of one's life. The reader can imagine that beyond the tales told here, Tee would have learned countless such life lessons from her great-grandmother. Interestingly, while Tee's teen years can be calculated as occurring in the 1960s or 1970s, there is a timeless quality to the storytelling sessions, in that there are no modern intrusions into the intimate environs of the wraparound porch. In particular, there is no television, a bit of contemporary technology that has surely reduced the amount of time spent in many a family by grandparents and grandchildren sharing stories.

Luck

Central to each of the four stories here is the good fortune provided by the lucky stone. The stone brings luck twice in being thrown—by Mandy, alerting the driver and the greater slave community to her whereabouts, and by Elzie, beaning the dog and sparking the chase ended by Amos Pickens—and once in falling, spurring Vashti to step down from the platform and escape the lightning. Thus, the luck of the rock becomes associated with motion and action—not with stasis but with progress. For Tee, merely acquiring and holding the rock seems to bring luck, as she receives her first valentine the very next day.

Being "black as night"—a phrase that is used four times—and marked with the letter *A*, the stone might be understood to symbolize the spirit or hope of African Americans as a people or perhaps the continent of Africa itself. This might be viewed as a reconstruction of the famous device in Nathaniel Hawthorne's novel *The Scarlet Letter*, in which the Puritan Hester Prynne, judged guilty of adultery, must always wear a scarlet *A*, forever identifying her in the eyes of others with her so-called crime. Here, the *A* scrawled by Mandy—whose full name, Amanda, starts with that letter—may signify not guilt (though the slave owner certainly considers her guilty of turning fugitive) but pride, in both her identity and her incidental assertion of her freedom. Thus, each of the four African American girls, in bearing the pride and spirit of the race, allies herself with the needs and causes of her people—and meets with good luck.

African American History

The stories in *The Lucky Stone* provide the reader with a glancing survey of African American life since 1850. The opening tale presents African Americans' transplanted origins in the dark days of slavery, evoked by the dark cave in which Mandy must hide away for more than a year while awaiting the slaves' emancipation. Just as African Americans were in some cases reduced by the barbarity of slave owners to subsistence states, being forced to focus exclusively on physical survival, Mandy grows wild in the unlit confines of the cave. This motif may be a nod to the ancient Greek philosopher Plato, who in Book VII of *The Republic* uses the image of prisoners in a cave, able to see only the shadows of forms passing outside, as an allegory for the human condition without education. With

Mr. Pickens helps Elsie find her lucky stone.
(Runa / Shutterstock.com)

freedom, then, comes the light of knowledge; Mrs. Pickens points out that after emancipation, people "could learn how to read and write and most everybody was anxious to do it."

This newfound freedom also embraces the spiritual realm, as, released from slave owners' rules, African Americans become free to "have church all out in the open." The scene of peaceful worship, however, is disrupted by the thunderstorm; this might be interpreted as reflecting the period when the ideals of equality suggested during the Reconstruction era were swept away through southern whites' backlash of Redemption, when widespread segregation and inequality were reinforced. However, Clifton evokes such historic symbolism only indirectly, and she does not seek to carry an allegory of the African American experience any further. Instead of being framed in the context of the trials of segregation, Mrs. Pickens's lucky stone experience is situated in a scene of delight and revelry, at a traveling carnival that the reader can conclude (based on both the era and the illustrations) is directed and populated entirely by blacks. Thus, Clifton highlights the positive sense of community provided by such convivial aspects of segregated society. In turn, Tee's experience, rather than evoking the civil rights movement itself, highlights the sense of domestic tranquillity and the focus on love that are finally enabled by the relative absence of political and societal strife brought about by the civil rights movement's success. Thus, instead of dwelling on the traumas and conflicts of the African American experience, Clifton allows her characters to make collective progress toward the ideal domestic peace of the fulfilled American dream.

STYLE

Multiple Narratives

Clifton's story features multiple narratives embedded within one another, a technique reflective of the postmodern era in which the book was written. At one point, the stories are layered some four deep: within the framework provided by Tee's introductory and closing paragraphs, Mrs. Pickens tells a story in which Vashti tells a story that was originally related by Mandy. This technique allows Clifton—the master storyteller here—to more intricately intertwine the tales, as well as the lives, of the four African American women featured. With all four young woman appearing to be roughly the same age in the four stories, the sense that the past lives echo through the present ones—that the lives of all of these women overlap in fundamental ways—is heightened by the nested narrative framework.

African American Vernacular

Clifton, herself a native of northern New York and longtime resident of Maryland, presents this story using the speech cadences and patterns of an eighty-year-old African American woman living in Virginia. Elzie Pickens tells the tales in the first three chapters, and the reader is easily induced to hear her distinct narrative voice through lines such as "They was smilin and rockin on they porch." One interesting stylistic choice made by Clifton was to omit the apostrophe usually added when the *g* has been trimmed from a word ending in *–ing*. This omission imparts the sense that the spellings she uses are not, say, trimmed versions of the "correct" spellings but rather correct spellings in their own right, accurately reflecting the speech of a community. Modern linguistic scholars recognize that African American dialects of English are no less legitimate than other American English dialects, considered with respect to the parent British English.

HISTORICAL CONTEXT

The four stories about the lucky stone together give a patchwork impression of African American history from the mid-nineteenth century through the twentieth century. The first story is set about a year before the slaves' emancipation, which could refer to various possible times, since, while Tee's family lives in Virginia, the home state of Mandy's plantation is not specified. The Emancipation Proclamation was issued about two years into the Civil War, on January 1, 1863, freeing by law all of the slaves in the rebelling Confederate states (but not in the Union states); however, only a small fraction of the nation's four million slaves were in areas that were under Union control and thus able to be freed at that time. As the Union army advanced into new territory, slaves in those areas were liberated. Even the surrender of the Confederacy on April 9, 1865, however, did not end slavery completely, as the Northern slaveholding states would not see the institution fully banned by federal law until the passage of the Thirteenth Amendment on December 18, 1865.

Mandy's circumstances only hint at the sorts of trials experienced by African American slaves on a cotton plantation. The degree of fear typically instilled in slaves by owners is evinced by Mandy's certainty upon spoiling her load of cotton that she will be beaten. The ever-present dilemma faced by slaves—whether to endure the constant affronts to their health, dignity, and identity so as to ensure their survival, or to seek freedom at the risk of death—has already been resolved in the mind of this young girl: as the great-grandmother relates, "She hadn't never been whipped before, and she had promised herself she never would be." Thus, she runs away, hiding in a cave. Emerging more than a year later, Mandy's "wild hair and eyes" and long fingernails and toenails serve to signify the state of deprivation that so many African Americans were reduced to by white slaveholders.

COMPARE & CONTRAST

- **1860s:** With the provisions of the Fugitive Slave Law of 1850 leaving even free African Americans vulnerable to kidnappers, the mobility of African Americans is severely limited throughout the South.

  1870s: Though all enslaved African Americans have been freed, many blacks remain tied to their farmland as sharecroppers and have little hope of gaining the financial resources needed to relocate their families.

  1920s: In the course of the Great Migration, great numbers of African Americans move from the South to northern cities to escape racist violence and seek employment in the expanding industrial sector.

  Today: With migration to the North leveled out, African American populations remain concentrated in the South and urban centers, while recent population trends suggest that many African Americans have engaged in a new southern migration.

- **1860s:** Although some masters have slaves baptized, enslaved African Americans are generally restricted from practicing either their traditional religions (considered threatening and improper) or Christianity, since familiarity with biblical teachings could promote a desire for freedom.

  1870s: African Americans are able to practice religion freely, but some of the churches they establish, being prominent community centers, are targeted by white-supremacist groups, limiting blacks' practical freedom of religion.

  1920s: Under Jim Crow laws across the South, African Americans' churches are mandated to be separate from those of whites.

  Today: In the wake of the Civil Rights Act of 1964, which ended segregation, some African American religious communities are integrated with those of other races, though many established congregations change only as people move in and out of areas.

- **1860s:** With slaves' access to facilities for entertainment and recreation limited, creative communal activities such as storytelling, playing music, singing, and dancing are popular among southern African Americans.

  1870s: With slavery ended, increasing numbers of African Americans gain employment as musicians and performers, but they often must play in whites-only venues.

  1920s: Although their opportunities are limited by segregation, African Americans' socioeconomic gains allow for many blacks to own and run entertainment ventures such as clubs, theaters, and traveling shows catering to black audiences. The rise of jazz and the Harlem Renaissance provide outlets for African American creative ventures.

  Today: African Americans participate fully in all the same means of entertainment and recreation available to whites and other races. Great numbers of successful film, music, art, and theater stars are African American.

The story of Vashti and the lightning takes place not long after the end of the Civil War, during the period called Reconstruction, when African Americans gained many of the rights they were due as free citizens—though many of these rights would later be withdrawn or nullified by segregation. At the very least, Vashti's community then had the freedom to congregate, something they were surely denied during slavery. In addition to being prevented from socializing in contexts where revolt might be planned, many slaves were prevented from becoming literate, since the ability to read could quickly lead to the understanding that the Bible and the

A circus dog danced in a foreshadowing moment. *(Vitaly Titov and Maria Sidelnikova / Shutterstock.com)*

Declaration of Independence, for example, suggest that all human beings deserve to be free. Here, Clifton does not refer to holy books or scriptures, but the circuit preacher, for one—who is confirmed as African American by the illustrations—would have been literate and familiar with the Bible. The fact that this congregation is visited by this circuit preacher only every so often might suggest that, at the time of the tale, there were yet very few African Americans who had had the liberty to gain enough religious knowledge and experience to serve as preachers.

The third story occurs perhaps twenty or thirty years later, around the turn of the twentieth century. With Congress-led Reconstruction ending in 1877, conservative Democrats—the party of secession—regained control of their state governments; and after the landmark case *Plessy v. Ferguson* was decided in 1896, allowing "separate but equal" treatment for different races, state-mandated segregation became the norm throughout the South. The setting of the story—a traveling carnival that (as implied by the text and illustrations) is staffed and visited entirely by African Americans—reflects the historical reality that in this era, whites and blacks in the South did not mix socially in commercial environments. It is noteworthy that Clifton chose to address segregation obliquely, as implied through the setting, rather than more directly, as she might have by contrasting this with a whites-only establishment. As such, the story serves to celebrate the strength and joy of African American community rather than dwelling on matters of racial inequality.

The final story, about Tee as a fourteen-year-old, bears the least relation to contemporary political circumstances for African Americans. Segregation was officially ended through the Supreme Court's decision in *Brown v. Board of Education of Topeka* in 1954, while the civil rights movement brought the momentous Civil Rights Act of 1964 and Voting Rights Act of 1965, among other legislation. Tee's story would be understood to take place after all the upheaval of the movement, when, having gained long-sought political equality, African Americans were finally free to enjoy life beyond the burden of lingering legislative oppression (though some societal circumstances and collective attitudes remained unfavorable). Indeed, race is by and large irrelevant to the final story; J.D., the sender of the valentine, could very well be white, Hispanic, or of any other ethnicity.

CRITICAL OVERVIEW

With regard to her children's books, titles in Clifton's popular Everett Anderson series have received the most attention, often spurring praise for all her works for younger readers. In her essay "The Chronicling of African-American Life and Consciousness: Lucille Clifton's Everett Anderson Series," Dianne Johnson asserts:

> Fortunately for the world of young people's literature, there are those authors who broaden our realms of experience by representing and exploring African American culture. Lucille Clifton is one of the most prolific and accomplished of this number.

Though Clifton did not explicitly connect her work with the Black Arts movement of the 1960s and 1970s, her approach harmonized with the sense of African American community characteristic of that movement. As Nancy Tolson relates in *Black Children's Literature Got de Blues: The Creativity of Black Writers and Illustrators*, the Black Arts movement

> did not pass by nor escape the notice of Black children's writers. Lucille Clifton . . . and others heard the call, took pen in hand, and produced literature that contained messages of Black pride, Black love, and Black struggle.

Mary Jane Lupton, in her essay "Mirrors and Windows: Lucille Clifton's Empowering Books about African American Boys," praises the author as "a woman whose intense exploration of African American heritage has helped to shape her own psyche and has radically transformed the literature being written for Black children." Lupton notes that alongside her dozen books of poetry, Clifton wrote some twenty children's books, and "no investigation of her writing can ignore their significance." Stressing how Clifton portrayed authentically African American characters, settings, and mores, Lupton concludes, "Clifton shattered the stereotypes about African Americans that had dominated literature for children, offering Black readers not only relevant and aesthetically pleasing books but also books that infused pride in their African American ancestry."

CRITICISM

Michael Allen Holmes

Holmes is a writer and editor. In the following essay, he considers how The Lucky Stone *subtly encourages readers to allow themselves to be guided by faith.*

Luck is a notoriously difficult thing to prove. One might claim that a certain object has brought luck in various instances, but whether the positive events or opportunities would have come about in the lucky object's absence can rarely be determined, since real-life experiences cannot be replayed. With regard to the title object of Lucille Clifton's *The Lucky Stone*, the fugitive slave Mandy might have thrown any other stone from the cave with the same results. Elzie might just as well have hit the dancing dog in the nose with an eraser or button from her bag. And Tee would have surely received the valentine in the mail regardless of whether she had yet taken possession of the stone. The one instance where the stone's role is indisputable is when the pouch drops from Vashti's neck while she is singing. The only reason she wore the pouch around her neck, one may presume, was because the stone was lucky; thus, without the lucky stone, there would have been no pouch to fall. Regardless of the degree of actual luck contained in a lucky object, Clifton's story seems to communicate that the holder's belief in that luck—or, in effect, the holder's faith in fate—may be what is most essential.

The act that establishes the stone as a lucky object is its being thrown from the cave by the runaway slave girl Mandy. The text does not indicate whether or not Mandy chose the stone for the sake of its shiny black color, but among African Americans enslaved on plantations, who would have grown accustomed to speaking in coded language regarding the whereabouts of runaways, a stone of such a color would surely have been of especial significance, just as to the modern reader the color resonates with symbolic significance throughout Clifton's narrative. If Mandy did not choose the stone for this reason—if, perhaps, in the dark cave she only instinctively picked up any old stone and threw it—then she was indeed lucky to happen upon such a stone. In any case, her trusting the carriage driver to see to her survival, with nothing communicated to him but the letter *A*, is an act of significant faith. This act of faith is what endows the stone with luck.

WHAT DO I READ NEXT?

- Clifton won the 1984 Coretta Scott King Award for *Everett Anderson's Goodbye* (1983), in which her popular children's book character copes with his father's death; also, *Everett Anderson's Friend* (1976), in which the new neighbors turn out to be a family of girls, was named an honor book for the same award.
- The famed poet Paul Laurence Dunbar's collection *Little Brown Baby* (1905) is a foundational publication of children's verse written for African Americans.
- Eloise Greenfield, a contemporary of Clifton's who also focuses on African American community and pride in her children's books, won the Coretta Scott King Award for *Africa Dream* (1976), which poetically narrates the dreams enjoyed by a black child about her ancestral continent and culture.
- Virginia Hamilton won the Newbery Medal—the first received by an African American author—for *M. C. Higgins, the Great* (1975), a young-adult novel about a teenage boy living in an Appalachian mountain community in Kentucky who must reconcile tradition and superstition with modern change.
- *Tales and Stories for Black Folk* (1980), collected by the politically active African American author Toni Cade Bambara, includes works by Langston Hughes, Alice Walker, and others.
- In a psychic journey that echoes Tee's storytime journeys through past African American consciousnesses, the heroine of Paule Marshall's novel *Praisesong for the Widow* (1983) experiences visions of ancestors and connects with the Yoruba gods.
- In his nonfiction work *12 Million Black Voices: A Folk History of the Negro in the United States* (1945), the renowned author Richard Wright supplies prose to accompany a collection of captivating photographs of African Americans in their daily existence.
- *Wise Women of the Dreamtime: Aboriginal Tales of the Ancestral Powers* (1993), collected by K. Langloh Parker and edited by Johanna Lambert, includes traditional Australian Aboriginal myths revolving around magic, healing, and ancestral ways.

The line between luck and faith is blurred in the story of Vashti. The setting itself glows with spiritual imagery, as the preacher's instilling the congregation with inner harmony and the thunder's threatening from a distance together make for an electric atmosphere. The triple recurrence of the singing of "Jesus Keep Me Near the Cross"—by Mrs. Pickens and her great-granddaughter, by the choir as led by Mrs. Pickens's mother (as a girl), and by Vashti—suggests that Clifton specifically wanted that title (and even the tune itself for those who know it) to echo through the story. Directly considered, the phrase is a plea to Jesus to assist the speaker in remaining true to Christian principles; an analogous phrase might be "Let my faith remain strong." Vashti is in the middle of singing this song when the pouch drops from around her neck, and Clifton uses five sentences just to describe the immense stillness of that moment. In this pause, the words of the song may drift through the reader's mind, such that the sense of the cross is correlated with the sense of the stone. The notion that Vashti should keep the stone at hand—or that she should keep herself near the stone, so to speak—is confirmed when descending the platform to retrieve the stone saves her life.

In *Telling Tales: The Pedagogy and Promise of African American Literature for Youth*, Dianne Johnson—as cited in the essay "In Her Own Images: Lucille Clifton and the Bible," by Akasha Gloria Hull—discusses how Clifton intertwines the notions of faith and luck in this passage:

"CLIFTON CANNOT PUT A LUCKY STONE IN THE HANDS OF HER LITERARY AUDIENCE, BUT THROUGH THIS STORY SHE SHOWS THAT FAITH, WHETHER IN A FRIEND OR IN A GOD OR IN A LUCKY OBJECT OR IN THE CROSSWINDS OF FATE, MAY BE THE MOST PRECIOUS POSSESSION A PERSON CAN HAVE."

> There is little or no differentiation between the "religious" and the "superstitious" as commonly understood in everyday English.... Vashti's shiny black stone is a savior just as God himself is a deliverer. Belief in God's power is at the base of the events taking place. Yet the power of the stone is an inextricable element too. Both are part of the acknowledged order of things.

Interestingly, while the power of the stone is in one sense equated with the power of God—that is, the stone is elevated to the status of sacred object—the stone is also depicted as functioning in opposition to God's power. The great-grandmother does not frame the platform's destruction as an event in which God worked through the stone to save Vashti from the lightning. Rather, the stone in and of itself saved Vashti from "a great arm of God's lightnin." Thus, on the one hand, the scene depicts an African American congregation gaining spiritual fulfillment through the grace of God, but on the other, God in turn casts down lightning that razes the very platform that enabled the congregation to meet, and only through the stone—through faith in the luck it brings—does Vashti avoid being struck herself.

Hull addresses this apparently paradoxical situation in her essay: "Born of African cosmology and of experiences in America that often made no 'sense,' this ability to live well and happily with apparent contradiction is a notable feature of African American culture." Clifton confirmed this notion in an interview with Charles Rowell for *Callaloo*, remarking, "I say to students all the time that either/or is not an African tradition. Both/and is tradition. I don't believe in either/or. I believe in both/and." What the story of Vashti and the lightning seems to teach, then, is that whether faith is placed in God or nature or some lucky object, that faith itself, which allows one to trust in the unseen order of the world and thus be mentally at peace, is what is essential. Faith in any one deity or doctrine or energy need not be exclusive of faith in any other. As Hull proclaims, "Clifton's equipoise of contrasting doctrines can also be framed as an agile juxtaposition of folk and religious beliefs." In her writings as in her life, "she accepts phenomena usually dubbed superstition as valid reality and does so from a deep rootedness in her cultural identity as an African American woman."

Beyond the second story, organized religion plays no role, as the circumstances and concerns of the final two stories are entirely secular. Thus, the sense of the luck inherent in the stone is emphasized. With regard to faith and luck, the most significant aspect of the story of Mrs. Elzie Pickens meeting her future husband is perhaps the fact that Elzie seems to activate the stone's luck by tossing it away. Considering the stone's status as a lucky/sacred object, the reader might expect Elzie to be so consciously possessed of it as to never accidentally discard it. Of course, at the time, Elzie and her friend Ovella are being thoroughly carried away by not just the present amusement of the dancing dog but also their dream of joining the traveling show. In other words, they are lost in the moment, not clutching at present expectations but open to any and all future possibilities—to whatever fate may send their way. This openness, this temporary abandonment of her predefined ego, her sense of self, is what allows Elzie to act freely and naturally without thwarting herself; moved in the moment to toss some small item the dancing dog's way, she does not censor or restrain this action owing to her attachment to the stone. She is rewarded for this openness, as her deft tossing of the stone leads to the heroic rescue by one Amos Pickens. Thus, Elzie's faith in fate, rather than precisely her faith in luck and in the stone, is perhaps the most critical factor here, though the stone itself indeed proves that it deserves to be called lucky.

The fourth and final story has the least gravity in that Tee's circumstances are in no way threatening—with neither a slave driver's whip nor a thunderstorm on hand—and in that there is no suggestion that the particular boy who sends her a valentine is to play a notable role in her life. Yet the modern reader will perhaps empathize with Tee more readily than with any of the other bearers of the stone precisely because of the modern nature of her plight: her life is placid enough to allow her the liberty to seriously fret, as a perfectly free and healthy fourteen-year-old, over whether she will ever get attention from boys. Her great-grandmother knows that she surely does not need to worry. But somehow the question is an existential dilemma for Tee—the one thing foremost on her mind when she visits her pneumonia-stricken great-grandmother in the hospital after at least several days of unrewarded journeys. The problem, Mrs. Pickens seems to recognize, is that Tee lacks faith in fate. And if anything can instill faith in fate in a person—outside of religion, which Clifton has demonstrated ambivalence toward, or spirituality, which often does not develop until after a person has reached maturity—it would be a lucky object.

For children, especially, the luck assigned to ordinary or extraordinary objects can be as serious as the sacredness assigned to religious icons by adults. Among children playing sports, for example, if a player proclaims that a green whistle he found helps the team win games, to deface or even defame that whistle might be perceived as an act of blasphemy. If a dancer insists that she needs to kiss a lucky postcard before every performance, to disrupt that routine could indeed compromise her mental focus. In either case, whether or not the object can be legitimately called "lucky," the bearer's belief in that luck—or belief that with the lucky object on hand, fate will be kind—may be what is essential. The belief in the luck is what allows the person to perform with freedom and openness, rather than being stressed by expectations or restrained by concerns. In *The Lucky Stone*, Mrs. Pickens, seeing that her great-granddaughter lacks just such a faith in fate, decides that it is time for Tee to inherit the object known to her to be luckier than any other: the stone. Sure enough, a valentine arrives in the mail the very next day; but what the stone more surely brought was the peace of mind that allowed Tee, in the absence of the reassuring presence of her beloved elder relative, to dismiss her concerns and fall asleep curled up in her great-grandmother's chair. Clifton cannot put a lucky stone in the hands of her literary audience, but through this story she shows that faith, whether in a friend or in a god or in a lucky object or in the crosswinds of fate, may be the most precious possession a person can have.

"

CLIFTON'S POETRY, IN ITS PERVASIVE AWARENESS OF FUTURE POSSIBILITY AND OF OTHER PEOPLE, PROPHESIES AND CONJURES THE SELF, THE BODY, AND THE BIBLE."

Source: Michael Allen Holmes, Critical Essay on *The Lucky Stone*, in *Short Stories for Students*, Gale, Cengage Learning, 2012.

Eberle Kriner

In the following excerpt, Kriner analyzes Clifton's use of the Bible in her eschatology of hope.

> the world is turning in the body of Jesus and the future is possible
>
> —"spring song" by Lucille Clifton, from *Good News About the Earth*

In a 2000 interview with Michael Glaser, African-American poet and memoirist Lucille Clifton identified hope as a central function of her work. She said,

> I think that writing is a way of continuing to hope. When things sometimes feel as if they're not going to get any better, writing offers a way of trying to connect with something beyond that obvious feeling... because you know, there is hope in connecting, and so perhaps for me it is a way of remembering I am not alone. And the writing may be sending tentacles out to see if there is a response to that.

For Clifton, who wrote her first collection in the late 1960s as the Civil Rights movement began to fade, the hope that writing offers is one that transcends and resists the discouragement of the present, "that obvious feeling." It looks toward the future, a future that will "get [. . .] better" not through escape from life situations, but rather through "trying to connect" with the responses of others.

Clifton's statements linking her writing of hope to the future and to relationship suggest an eschatological framework for reading her poetry. Eschatology, the theology of hope, possesses several characteristics that make it a worthwhile critical lens. According to Jurgen Moltmann's *Theology of Hope*, eschatology properly conceived is future-oriented, resistant to the present, missional, and destabilizing to both knowledge and personal identity. That is, hope is comprised of "anticipations which show reality in its prospects and its future possibilities," a future orientation manifest within "present mission." "Hope's statements of promise," declares Moltmann, "must stand in contradiction to the reality that can at present be experienced. They [. . .] lead existing reality towards the promised and hoped-for transformation." Since the future is primarily "the thing we cannot already think out and picture for ourselves," hope in the God of the future unsettles knowledge. It "leads our modern institutions away from their own immanent tendency toward stabilization, [making] them uncertain [. . .] and open[ing] them." For the individual, committing to the theology of hope means a deferral of the "haven of identity"; the mission of hope is served through the "self-emptying" sacrifice of the hopeful person.

Clifton's poetry, widely understood as celebrating black culture and developing a vocal black female self, appears quite different when viewed as eschatological strains of self-sacrifice and performative rhetoric come to light. Clifton's *Good Times*, the first volume in *Good Woman: Poems and a Memoir, 1969–1980*, was declared by the *New York Times* to be one of the year's best books in 1969 for its "hard, angry poems." In terms of Clifton's literary context, interviewers and critics have often sought to place Clifton's early poetry within the Black Arts Movement, but the designation is one she has always resisted. She has written poems for the Black Panthers, for Malcolm X, for Eldridge Cleaver and for Bobby Seale, but she refuses to be categorized as part of the literary arm of the Black Power movement or as reflecting a Black Aesthetic. Her black aesthetic, she jokes, was the succession of children emerging from her body during the development of the 'black is beautiful' ideology. In an interview with Charles H. Rowell in *Callaloo*, Clifton asserts that the Black Power Movement's "sudden" realization and response to programmatic racial inequity seemed to her somewhat strange. She had "been knowing" the inequities, and found her poems conscious of blackness, without an obsessive need for constant repetition. Still, with her use of vernacular black speech and simple language, Clifton's work certainly converses with Black Arts poetry of Amiri Baraka and Nikki Giovanni.

The most often recognized quality in Clifton's poems is grace and affirmation. Critics read Clifton as one who affirms rather than criticizes: "her new poems continue her work in defining and affirming 'us'" (Lazer 54). People see in Clifton a poet who looks for the good, for grace, to salvage the community from contemporary confusion about what kind of knowledge and access to supernatural forces are available to contemporary seekers (Ostriker, Thyreen-Mizingou). In the light of hope, readers sense that Clifton wields power-on-behalf-of-others, deliberately dismantling self rather than empowering self in any traditional manner. This powerful self-sacrifice—as well as her poetry's commitment to the mission of bringing a better future into being—is accomplished through forms commonly associated with power for others and bringing the future to pass: prophecy and conjure.

Prophecy—that is, self-fulfilling and transformative proclamations that identify problems and act to solve them—and conjure—that is, performative mimetic ritual—cohabit within African-American cultural and religious practices, alongside and within Christian forms of practice. Prophecy issues both moral imperatives and predictive statements, indissolubly linking the two: predictions of the future profoundly announce the future of a specific reality according to the social and moral mission of the prophet. Prophecy is also active and transformative: Cornel West has argued that "[t]o be a prophetic Afro-American Christian is to negate what is and transform prevailing realities against the backdrop of present historical limits" (19–20). Prophecy and conjure overlap in Clifton's work as well, performing an anticipatory mimesis that models and reconstructs the future.

The intertwined formal structures of prophecy and conjure inform Clifton's poetic eschatology. Clifton uses prophecy and conjure to diagnose and to resist problems in the present, to anticipate the future, and to set in motion the transformation from present injustice to future possibility. Clifton's poems employ prophetic and conjuring forms in an eschatology of the black female body and the Bible; she conjures the body in order to develop an eschatological self, one that can balance a desire for future wholeness with ethical responsibility for the other by deferring stable identity. Clifton also conjures the Bible using typological mimesis in order to extend its meaning beyond its own pages into the present and future of the reader. Ultimately, the poems call forth an eschatological reader who, being conjured by the text, will bodily engage in the mission of hope....

PROPHET OF THE OTHER: CONJURING THE BIBLE

I have been arguing that Clifton's eschatological rhetoric of belief—enacted in prophecy and conjure—complicates the understanding of the black female body and self and also entails an ethics of the other. In these tasks, Clifton's work often engages the Bible as a central sourcebook. Akasha (Gloria) Hull rightly points out how Clifton makes the figures of the Bible speak in the voices of the African diaspora. More than simply adding an African flavor to the sacred text, however, Clifton's conjuring of the Bible, or use of the Bible as conjure book functions eschatologically as well. Prophecy and conjure work within the context of Clifton's biblically derived poems to specifically develop anticipatory models through figural prophecy, or typology.

Clifton centers her poetic use of the Bible on the characters of biblical history rather than the Bible's specific messages or content. In her second book, *Good News About the Earth*, fully one third of the poems refer to characters from the Old Testament through the resurrection, under the title "some jesus." Clifton has returned to the Bible later in her work on David, Samson, Naomi, Sarah, and others. Her work reads the characters as pointing toward the future, that is, as models or typological anticipations of the future. In "spring song" for instance, Clifton uses the figure of Jesus (post-resurrection, when he has seen that his purpose is to "slide down like a great dipper of stars / and lift men up,") to assert a possibility for the future:

the green of Jesus
is breaking the ground
and the sweet
smell of delicious Jesus
is opening the house and
the dance of Jesus music
has hold of the air and
the world is turning
in the body of Jesus and
the future is possible

Clifton's interest in rewriting the Bible could be read as an interest in revising history/herme neutics—to the extent that doing so specifically affects future practice. Her use, for instance, of Daniel bespeaks the prescriptions Clifton would offer to a Daniel of the latter days: "when a man / walk manly / he don't stumble." The early biblical poems in "some jesus" are indeed, as Hull and others have suggested, poems of the diaspora, but beyond asserting the inclusiveness of the diasporic community, they also speak prophetically to the community. Jonah becomes a warning of slavery and the middle passage, "Be care full of the ocean," and Cain is a reminder of the consequences of destructive violence: "my brother / don't rise up." The poems create new versions of the characters that become anti-types of the characters in the present day while also becoming themselves types and texts that expect further fulfillment. The poem "the raising of lazarus" for instance, calls for hope and a new resurrection for the dead in slavery: "stand up / even the dead shall rise."

Clifton's biblical characters are not stock Sunday-School models of perfect behavior however; especially in later poems they doubt, want to turn back, and suffer. In "naomi watches as ruth sleeps," from *The Book of Light*, Naomi's journey toward Boaz is figured as a way to get rid of Ruth and her annoying devotion. Naomi says,

she clings to me
like a shadow
when all that I wish
is to sit alone
longing for my husband,
my sons.

We know that in Naomi's case, the mourning is comforted when Boaz and Ruth produce a son that sits on Naomi's lap, a knowledge that allows us to see the poem as a moment leading toward a future that we can imagine. The characters of Clifton's biblical poems also work for a future that is better than the present. In "sarah's promise," from the same volume, Sarah's fury over the possible sacrifice of Isaac leads her to "march into the thicket" like the ram from the biblical narrative, and promise God "the children of young women, / yours for a thousand years" if God will "speak to [her] husband" and "spare [her her] one good boy." We can read the dissatisfaction and disillusionment as serving the typological function that Clifton ascribes to the characters. Clifton's biblical figures, as the biblical phrase puts it, "groan in anticipation," their lives engendering specific positive and negative possibilities for the future.

Clifton's cycle of poems on Mary, the mother of Jesus, begins with the future in "the astrologer predicts at mary's birth," and end with an epilogue of four prophetic proclamations to "the blind," "the mad," "the lame," and "the mute." Thus Clifton circumscribes Mary's life with vision and prediction. Clifton figures the astrologer, Mary's mother, and Mary herself as dreamers, visionaries who see the future.

In the poems, the moments described shimmer with possibility and potential, both positive and negative. In "a song of mary," when Mary reflects on the ordinariness of her life prior to the vision of the "winged women" and the birth of her son, she sings the past partly in nostalgia, having lost the smile and the innocence. However, we read the song knowing the story and after the orgasmic poem "holy night" which describes Jesus' spiritual conception or birth.

> somewhere it being yesterday.
> i a maiden in my mother's house.
> the animals silent outside.
> is morning.
> princes sitting on thrones in the east
> studying the incomprehensible heavens.

In part, each of the descriptions could be seen as pointing toward their future convergence in the stable, when the "animals silent outside" are lowing, and "the princes sitting on thrones in the east" are on camels laden with gifts. Yet Mary doesn't bring them together as historically causal, but instead leaves them open, "incomprehensible" as the skies that the wise men study in the east. In the context of this cycle, Mary interprets each of these moments in their possibility before the birth of the Christ—both knowing their causal outcomes and picturing those outcomes as unknowable and multiple in possibility.

Even when Mary is old and reminiscing, her thoughts about her life have a distinctly futuristic cast. She wonders about each moment's possibilities, from the moment of her own vision forward, particularly about whether she would have been able to turn down the blessings of the winged women and escape the heartache of having no son. However, she is not only concerned about the future of the past and the possibility of the present having being different, but about a future reincarnation of blessed motherhood:

> another young girl asleep
> in the plain evening.
> what song around her ear?
> what star still choosing?

Here, as in the Daniel and Lazarus poems, the poetic concern is typological. "Island mary," the Caribbean incarnation of the Middle Eastern mother of Jesus, wishes for a different past that formulates itself as a typological wish for the future, a wish that another woman could reject the angelic interruption of "the plain evening." Yet Island Mary's concern for the young girl represents precisely the mothering that Mary is destined to do through her own suffering. In the final Mary poem, Mary is seen as "shook by the / awe full affection of the saints."

As in the other poems in Clifton's eschatological grab bag, in the Marian cycle, trust in the future or a vision of the future leads to both action in the present and a sacrifice/breaking of the self for the other. Mary's mother wants to "fight this thing" with work, the "medicine / for dreams," seeing that the dreaming and looking forward will cause pain and loss. The astrologer says the crucifixion will "break" Mary's "eye" and Anna knows that continuing to dream will force her to "give" Mary "up" to the grief of her future. Mary's grasp of her own dream of "winged women [...] saying/ 'full of grace' and like" involves a push toward "a name and a blessing" which causes her to leave the "only i" to join them in their project. In the last Mary poem, the communal speaker suggests that "mary marinka" was "split by sanctified seed / into mother and mother," another instance of the breaking and giving of the self that the visionary perspective entails. Emmanuel Levinas, in *Otherwise Than Being* mentions the substitutive giving of the self that motherhood represents in its embodied proximity to the other being associated with the infinite or transcendence of totality:

> Maternity in the complete being 'for the other' which characterizes it, which is the very signifyingness of signification, is the ultimate sense of this vulnerability. This hither side of identity is not reducible to the for-itself; where, beyond its immediate identity, being recognizes it-self in its difference.

Clifton's for the other maternity figures' vulnerability more flexibly than Levinas, certainly. However, the "worrying now for / another young girl asleep" in "island mary" suggests both the vulnerability of Mary's sorrow and loss in motherhood as well as a vulnerability latent in all future mothers. Her sacrifice is ambivalent, perhaps, but still leads to prophetic embrace: it engenders blessing in poems such as "for the blind" and "for the lame," which directly follow the Marian cycle.

CONCLUSION

Clifton teaches the reader how to understand futurity and possibility in the figure of Mary (and perhaps in all her poems) by presenting a prologue to the cycle that functions as a reading guide for the group of poems; it warns the reader to be on the look out for possibility. The poem speaks directly to the reader, conjuring her—or perhaps jolting her with a quiet jeremiad—into awareness.

> the mystery that surely is present
> as the underside of the leaf
> turning to stare at you quietly
> from your hand,
> that is the mystery you have not
> looked for, and it turns
> with a silent shattering of your life
> for who knows ever after
> the proper position of things
> or what is waiting to turn from us
> even now?

This poem deals with what Moltmann would call "the element of otherness that encounters us [. . .] the thing that we cannot already think out and picture for ourselves on the basis of the given world and of the experiences we already have of that world." It indicts the reader for her perceptive failure: "you have / not looked" for the mystery of the present in its ability to turn in innumerable ways. We can read the poem of course as prophetically forecasting Mary's "shattering" since it precedes the cycle, however; the poem's direct address of its audience suggests that we also read it as forecasting and calling for our own shattering for the other. In light of this poem, the nostalgia and tragedy of Mary's victimization results from a life lived in a non-anticipatory present (it "is morning" in "a song of mary") of work ("we scrubbing scrubbing"). Her ordinary life and ordinary pleasures are not viewed with mystery or future possibility in mind. Only when the winged women come to her, shatter her "only I," and "break her eye" with a communal vision and the pain of the crucifixion does Mary's awareness of her own ability to look for and interpret possibility begin. In "[I]sland [M]ary," the Mary figure finally sees the possibility or unknowability of her experiences and begins to consider them in terms of what might have been, and what might occur in some other girl's life, pushing her experiences beyond nostalgia and reminiscence into love and meaning.

In the above cycle, particularly considering its prologue, Mary's development in awareness from innocent individuality to self-sacrificial "mother and mother for ever and ever" offers the reader a suggestion to look for the possibilities that the present offers, both for future hope and connection with others. Clifton's poetry, in its pervasive awareness of future possibility and of other people, prophesies and conjures the self, the body, and the Bible. In doing so, it seeks to move actively toward the future and the other finding in a connection to the other. It seeks to show and to provide the hope that her world desperately needs. Clifton's work conjures in the reader that awareness of the multiplicity of possibilities and futures within any epiphanic moment, calling us to connection with others and self-sacrifice—a true hope.

"

THIS POEM THUS TAKES SOME SOLACE IN THE BELIEF THAT, NO MATTER WHAT INDIGNITIES THE SLAVES SUFFERED AT THE HANDS OF THEIR MASTERS AND MISTRESSES, THEIR SOULS (SIGNIFIED BY THEIR HUMAN NAMES) WERE THEIRS AND THEIRS ALONE."

Source: Eberle Kriner, "Conjuring Hope in a Body: Lucille Clifton's Eschatology," in *Christianity and Literature*, Vol. 54, No. 2, Winter 2005, pp. 185–209.

Hilary Holladay

In the following excerpt, Holladay considers how Clifton uses names to illustrate knowledge and understanding of slave heritage.

As the daughter of a Virginian and a Georgian, the African American poet Lucille Clifton has always had the South in her blood, and the region has naturally found its way into her life and writing. Born in 1936 in Depew, New York, Clifton grew up there and later in Buffalo. Despite these northern credentials, she maintains that her upbringing was southern ("A Music in Language" 74). Her parents had come to the North during the Great Migration, but that did not mean that they had truly left the South behind. It was alive in their memories and in the stories they told their attentive daughter, who retells many of those tales in *Generations: A Memoir* (1976).

In recent years, Clifton—who won the 2000 National Book Award for Poetry for her eleventh volume of verse, *Blessing the Boats: New and Selected Poems 1988–2000*—has frequently read her poetry in the South, and she has held visiting teaching positions at Memphis State

University and Duke University. But she has lived most of her adult life in Maryland, which is in or near the South, depending on your perspective and perhaps depending on where you are in Maryland. The poet and her husband, Fred Clifton, moved to Baltimore from Buffalo early in their marriage and brought up their six children there. Clifton became poet-in-residence at Coppin State College in 1974 and served as Maryland's poet laureate for a decade beginning the following year. Widowed in 1984, she took a teaching position at the University of California at Santa Cruz but after several years returned to Maryland, where she now holds the Hilda C. Landers Chair in the Liberal Arts at St. Mary's College of Maryland. From the slight but seemingly strategic remove that Maryland affords her, Clifton is able to contemplate her ancestral South. Although she does not have the intimate knowledge of the region that her father and mother had, her feelings about the region are nevertheless complicated and passionate. The South we encounter in her poems is a conceit enabling her to address two subjects, the first concrete and the second abstract, that have been equally important to her poetry for many years: 1) slavery and its seemingly endless impact on American life, and 2) the all-powerful role of language in determining our knowledge of ourselves and others. In her poems with southern settings, we don't see much of the region's landscape, but we do see how language, especially the language of names, can either obliterate or validate one's identity. While this is true to a certain extent for all, Clifton shows how names are especially germane to our knowledge and understanding of slaves and their descendants.

In "at the cemetery, walnut grove plantation, south carolina, 1989" (*Quilting*), the silencing of slaves in their time haunts the poet in her own time:

> among the rocks
> at walnut grove
> your silence drumming
> in my bones,
> tell me your names.

The rocks are unmarked slave graves, and the narrator, confronted with this injustice, yearns to make contact with these lost souls and speak on their behalf. The slaves' silence paradoxically "drumming" within her calls to mind African drums and perhaps even the drums played during the Civil War. The drumming silence is, if not a call to arms, at least a call to speech. Significantly, the silence seems to emanate from the poet's own bones; what she doesn't know about the slaves amounts to things that she doesn't know about herself and her own ancestry.

Generations helps illuminate the emotion animating this poem. In this fifty-four-page memoir (which Toni Morrison shepherded into print at Random House), Clifton writes movingly of her great-great-grandmother Caroline, who as a young child was captured in western Africa's Dahomey region and brought to the United States as a slave. Caroline, who outlived slavery and became a prominent midwife in the community of Bedford, Virginia, helped rear Samuel Sayles, Clifton's father. Samuel's memories of the family matriarch, as recounted in *Generations*, focus alternately on her strongly vocalized strength and her mystifying silences. When Samuel asks her to reveal her African name, for instance, Caroline refuses to answer. We don't know whether she keeps the name secret because it means so much to her or because, in the country of her captivity, it means so little. One hardly dares consider the heartbreaking possibility that Caroline has forgotten her African name and hence has no answer for her great-grandson's question.

When Clifton implores the dead slaves at Walnut Grove to offer up their names, it may well be that she has her great-great-grandmother in mind, since Caroline's grave in Bedford is also unmarked. On the first page of *Generations*, Clifton writes, "Who remembers the names of the slaves? Only the children of slaves." She speaks as a slave descendant in "at the cemetery" as well as in her memoir. The fact that the stones at Walnut Grove have no names on them is no surprise, of course. It is perhaps a wonder that they are even recognizable as graves, let alone slave graves. But it is not just the stones that indicate the slaves' presence on the farm:

> nobody mentions slaves
> and yet the curious tools
> shine with your fingerprints.
> nobody mentioned slaves
> but somebody did this work
> who had no guide, no stone,
> who moulders under rock.

The tools are in plain view, yet, as recently as 1989, when Clifton paid her visit, people touring the plantation heard nothing about the slaves or the work they did ("Lucille Clifton" 87). Like the silence drumming in the speaker's bones, the evidence of a hard-working community of black people demands recognition. No matter what the plantation's present-day staff does or does not say, there is no getting around the fact that the life of this farm depended on slave labor for a very longtime. During the plantation's productive years, the farm tools, now laid out for tourists' inspection, did not magically cut wood or tan leather all on their own.

Clifton's poem challenges the received version of Walnut Grove's history and implicitly argues that such a challenge is worthy of literary as well as historical consideration. In acknowledging the palpable if invisible presence of the slaves, she responds to a phenomenon that Toni Morrison identifies in "Unspeakable Things Unspoken: The Afro-American Presence in American Literature":

> We can agree, I think, that invisible things are not necessarily 'not-there'; that a void may be empty, but is not a vacuum. In addition, certain absences are so stressed, so ornate, so planned, they call attention to themselves; arrest us with intentionality and purpose, like neighborhoods that are defined by the population held away from them. Looking at the scope of American literature, I can't help thinking that the question should never have been "Why am I, an Afro-American, absent from it?" It is not a particularly interesting query anyway. The spectacularly interesting question is "What intellectual feats had to be performed by the author or his critic to erase me from a society seething with my presence, and what effect has that performance had on the work?" What are the strategies of escape from knowledge? Of willful oblivion?

Rather than accept the willful oblivion perpetuated at Walnut Grove, Clifton speaks directly to the slaves whose presence she feels so strongly: "tell me your names, / tell me your bashful names / and i will testify" ("at the cemetery"). If the slaves' names are "bashful," it is perhaps because they have been hidden away and denied for so long. The poet will have to coax them into being by listening closely to the message-laden silence. The white space that follows this entreaty, however, symbolizes the slaves' unwillingness or inability to supply the basic information that the poet craves. This, too, conjures the memory of Caroline.

Drawing on the Christian tradition and the democratic legal system, both of which value "testifying," the poet seeks to affirm the value of the slaves' lives and experiences. She regards them with love and charity, as good Christians are supposed to regard their fellow human beings, but she is also determined to fight for their place in history books and in the history lessons taught at museums like Walnut Grove. In short, she would like to see the slaves recognized and restored to a position of dignity in our collective memory. The poem itself functions as her testimony.

In the middle of "at the cemetery," an italicized statement heaps more injustice on a pile that is already pretty high: "the inventory lists ten slaves / but only men were recognized." The slave women did not even count as possessions. The white space following the stanza once again memorializes the void. When the poet resumes speaking, she is an angry prophet crying out in the wilderness of Walnut Grove:

> among the rocks
> at walnut grove
> some of these honored dead
> were dark
> some of these dark
> were slaves
> some of these slaves
> were women
> some of them did this
> honored work.
> tell me your names
> foremothers, brothers,
> tell me your dishonored names.
> here lies
> here lies
> here lies
> here lies
> hear

The parallel structure evokes both the Bible and the preaching Clifton heard as a girl attending the Macedonia Baptist Church, a Southern Baptist church in Buffalo. But this is Clifton's own message: The women and men buried anonymously at Walnut Grove were not anonymous during their lifetimes. They worked the fields and served the household, and the plantation would not have functioned without them. They made love and bore children, and their descendants, just like those of the white slaveholders, still walk the earth. The poem makes it clear that the sins of omission—the unmarked graves, the incomplete inventories of human chattel—expose a lie even as they obscure the truth. The poem's closing lines initially seem like epigraphs lacking the names of the slaves. But the insistent repetition turns the incomplete statements into a sharp command: Hear the lies being told. Now, as Susan Somers-Willet has noted, the white space "not only actively calls attention to the absence of inscription, but also asks the reader to consider the possibilities of what such an inscription could imply" ("lucy and her girls"). It represents both the unknown names and the cover-up manifested in the incomplete and, hence, inaccurate public record. Through the complex interplay between ambiguous words and white space, the poem illustrates Ralph Ellison's observation that "The essence of the word is its ambivalence, and in fiction it is never so effective and revealing as when both potentials are operating simultaneously, as when it mirrors both good and bad, as when it blows both hot and cold in the same breath." Ellison's point is even more apt when applied to poetry, perhaps especially to the brief lyric mode that Clifton prefers.

Something similar to the compelling dynamic at work in "at the cemetery" occurs in "slave cabin, sotterly plantation, maryland, 1989." In this companion poem, which follows "at the cemetery" in *Quilting*, Clifton visits another historically preserved plantation (this one located in St. Mary's County, Maryland) and again takes exception to the portrayal of slave life. This time, a female slave is identified by a name, but the name has little to do with her. The poem starts off stealthily:

> in this little room
> note carefully
>
> aunt nanny's bench

The white space surrounding "aunt nanny's bench" helps us imagine the words of a tour guide whose knowledge of slave history begins and ends with a gesture toward a bench. Alternatively, these words might appear on a plaque that provides no further information about "aunt nanny." The white space serves to illustrate the utter lack of context provided for this tiny sliver of history.

Confronted with this void, Clifton steps into the white space and fills it with black language, a visual representation of her racial heritage. She deconstructs "aunt nanny's bench" and then envisions the flesh-and-blood woman who once sat on the bench in question:

> three words that label
> things
> aunt
> is my parent's sister
> nanny
> my grandmother
> bench
> the board at which
> i stare
> the soft curved polished
> wood
> that held her bottom
> after the long days
> without end
> without beginning
> when she aunt nanny sat
> feet dead against the dirty floor
> humming for herself humming
> her own sweet human name ("slave cabin")

Neither "aunt" nor "nanny" tells us anything about the slave woman's identity. Together, the labels are nonsensical, amounting to "aunt grandmother," an ironic gloss in itself on the thoughtless, racist habit of addressing older black women in familial—and overly familiar—ways. The name "aunt nanny" is a means of co-opting the unidentified woman's identity and subsuming her into the white family that owned her. Like the farm tools in "at the cemetery," it is the well-worn bench that still possesses something of the lost woman's body and spirit. Concentrating on the bench, the poet calls a life into being. The "soft curved polished / wood" is beautiful in an understated way; it hints at the beauty of the unknown woman who sat there. She, too, would have been soft and curved, her body worn down by years of repetitive labor.

The poem thereby shifts from a pointed condemnation of the powers conspiring to force an identity onto the slave to a sympathetic tribute to the woman's private self. Clifton can only imagine that self, and her own long reach into the past, is symbolized by the reluctant, ironic use of "aunt nanny" when she feels compelled to call the slave woman by name. White space again functions symbolically, indicating the woman's remove from the name imposed on her as well as the isolation she would inevitably have felt on a slave-holding farm. But the extra white space also invites us to behold this woman in her own space, apart from the trappings of her subjugated circumstances.

Exhausted from her labors, the woman Clifton imagines still has the energy to hum to herself. This small, private music, the most ephemeral of art forms, symbolizes the woman's core self. The wordlessness of humming is important here, for "aunt nanny" is a nameless, essentially wordless entity. Her humming enables her to define herself on her own terms. Without words, her identity eludes everyone but her. Clifton thus honors the woman, while implying that she had a life that the slaveholders knew nothing about. By labeling her "aunt nanny" her owners—and, later, those historians who saw the bench as a winsome artifact of bygone days—did her a fundamental injustice, but they also unwittingly preserved the protective space between her and them.

The last line emphasizes the woman's humanity, her life apart from whatever burdens her owners imposed on her. Her "human name" ends the poem, though there is no period signifying an endpoint. The possibilities of the woman's private life reverberate in the blank space. We can hear the subtle music in "human name," words that sound like "humming" stretched out and polished to a high gleam. This poem thus takes some solace in the belief that, no matter what indignities the slaves suffered at the hands of their masters and mistresses, their souls (signified by their human names) were theirs and theirs alone.

Both "at the cemetery" and "slave cabin" argue that the degradation of slaves continues today. Even in an age that some deride as politically correct to the point of absurdity, the historical record all too often misses the same point that it has missed for hundreds of years: the slaves were human beings who deserve our respect for all that they suffered and for all that they did for this country. As the descendant of slaves, Lucille Clifton has a personal interest in the way slaves lived and in the way their lives are represented in museums, history books, and graveyards. Slavery does not tell the whole story of the South, but the whole story cannot be told without it. A poet as sensitive and as historically aware as Clifton naturally recognizes this. Her poems ask us to imagine the black names in and around and behind the white spaces, and consider questions such as these: Who is writing the history lessons? Whose stories still go untold? Why does this country still fear the truths embodied in the lives of the slaves?

In summoning the names of the slaves, Clifton begins to answer her own implied questions. Sometimes, as in *Generations*, it is obvious that this is a very personal endeavor for her. She has given a great deal of thought to her ancestors, and she takes her place in the family line quite seriously. Because names are the signifiers of that line, they provide a natural starting point for many of her considerations of family and individual identity. She has written about every part of her birth name, Thelma Lucille Sayles, in her poems and memoir. Her first name, Thelma, was the name of her mother, an epileptic who died at forty-four when Clifton was pregnant with her first child. Lucille was the name of her paternal great-grandmother, who, according to Samuel Sayles, was the "first Black woman legally hanged in the state of Virginia" (*Generations*). The elder Lucy's crime: killing the white man who fathered her son Gene, who would grow up to be Samuel's father.

As if all of this family history were not sufficient material for poems, the surname Sayles is also notable. Clifton writes in *Generations* that 'Sale' was the name of the white family who owned Caroline's husband, so it became Caroline's surname. After Emancipation, the black Sales added a *y* to distinguish their name from that of their former owners. Clifton writes that Samuel Sayles took this notion even further: "My father had left school in the second or third grade and could barely write more than his name, but he was an avid reader. He loved books. He had changed his name to Sayles (instead of Sayle) after finding a part of a textbook in which the plural was explained. There will be more than one of me, my father thought, and he added the *s* to his name" (*Generations*). The changes in spelling are small but meaningful steps toward autonomy, yet the connection with the white Sales of Bedford remains, as Clifton points out at the beginning of her memoir: after an awkward telephone conversation with a white Sale descendant, who shares the poet's interest in genealogy, Clifton writes, "Yet she sends the history she has compiled and in it are her family's names. And our family names are thick in her family like an omen" (*Generations*)....

Source: Hilary Holladay, "Black Names in White Space: Lucille Clifton's South," in *Southern Literary Journal*, Vol. 34, No. 2, Spring 2002, pp. 120–33.

SOURCES

Clifton, Lucille, *The Lucky Stone*, illustrated by Dale Payson, Delacorte Press, 1979.

Holladay, Hilary, *Wild Blessing: The Poetry of Lucille Clifton*, Louisiana State University Press, 2004, pp. 1–13, 181–200.

Hull, Akasha Gloria, "In Her Own Images: Lucille Clifton and the Bible," in *Dwelling in Possibility: Women Poets and Critics on Poetry*, edited by Yopie Prins and Maeera Shreiber, Cornell University Press, 1997, pp. 273–95.

Johnson, Dianne, "The Chronicling of African-American Life and Consciousness: Lucille Clifton's Everett Anderson Series," in *Children's Literature Association Quarterly*, Vol. 14, No. 4, Winter 1989, pp. 174–78.

Lupton, Mary Jane, "Mirrors and Windows: Lucille Clifton's Empowering Books about African American Boys," in *Sankofa*, Vol. 6, 2007, pp. 53–64.

Patrick, John J., *The Progress of the Afro-American*, Benefic Press, 1968, pp. 30–118.

Peppers, Wallace R., "Lucille Clifton," in *Dictionary of Literary Biography*, Vol. 41, *Afro-American Poets since 1955*, edited by Trudier Harris, Gale Research, 1985, pp. 55–60.

Rowell, Charles H., "An Interview with Lucille Clifton," in *Callaloo*, Vol. 22, No. 1, 1999, pp. 56–72.

Tolson, Nancy, *Black Children's Literature Got de Blues: The Creativity of Black Writers and Illustrators*, Peter Lang, 2008, pp. 27–28.

FURTHER READING

Bambara, Toni Cade, ed., *The Black Woman: An Anthology*, Washington Square Press, 2005.

Originally published in 1970, this updated version of Bambara's collection of essays on African American womanhood, with contributions by Alice Walker, Nikki Giovanni, and others, addresses the historical relevance of Black Power and second-wave feminism.

Bishop, Rudine Sims, *Free within Ourselves: The Development of African American Children's Literature*, Greenwood Press, 2007.

Bishop's volume escorts the reader through explorations of children's publications by intellectuals such as W. E. B. Du Bois to modern award-winning titles.

Clifton, Lucille, *Good Woman: Poems and a Memoir, 1969–1980*, BOA Editions, 1987.

This collection includes Clifton's preceding four volumes of highly praised poetry as well as her memoir, *Generations* (1976), which explores in prose the lives and times of her forebears and herself.

Wright, Richard, *Black Boy*, Harper, 1945.

Wright's fictionalized autobiography portrays his childhood as lived in the shadow of southern segregation, moving on to his later development in Chicago and embrace of Communism.

SUGGESTED SEARCH TERMS

Lucille Clifton AND The Lucky Stone

Lucille Clifton AND The Luckiest Time of All

Lucille Clifton AND children's literature

Lucille Clifton AND Black Arts movement

African American history AND spirituality OR religion

spirituality AND Lucille Clifton

Lucille Clifton AND Mary OR Lucifer

National Book Award AND Lucille Clifton

African American literature AND Lucille Clifton

The Murders in the Rue Morgue

EDGAR ALLAN POE

1841

Well-known for both his poetry and his suspenseful short fiction, Edgar Allan Poe wrote several stories featuring the amateur detective C. Auguste Dupin. These stories, including "The Murders in the Rue Morgue" (1841), highlight Dupin's intellect and rationality by depicting crimes solved through his logical deductions. In "The Murders in the Rue Morgue," often regarded as the first detective story, Dupin and his companion, the narrator, gain access to the scene of a recent gruesome double murder via Dupin's prominent connections. Through his examinations of the witness statements, as reported in the local newspapers, and his analysis of the crime scene, Dupin is able to identify the murderer as an orangutan. He subsequently detains the man responsible for the animal and explains to the narrator, and to the reader, the steps he took to reveal the truth. In this story, Poe uses Dupin to explore the notion of ratiocination—the process of logical analysis Dupin employs—as well as to craft a structure he would later follow in subsequent stories of murder and detection. Critics have pointed out that, through Dupin and the narrator, Poe also examines the relationship between the intellect and the imagination. In the details of the crime scene, and in the complicity of the gentleman from whose care the orangutan escaped, Poe also examines themes of violence and moral responsibility.

"The Murders in the Rue Morgue," originally published in *Graham's Magazine* in 1841, is available in such collections as the Modern

Edgar Allan Poe

Library's *Selected Poetry and Prose of Poe* (1951), edited by T. O. Mabbott, and more recently the Modern Library's *The Murders in the Rue Morgue: The Dupin Tales* (2006), edited by Matthew Pearl.

AUTHOR BIOGRAPHY

Not long after his birth on January 19, 1809, in Boston, Massachusetts, Poe was orphaned. His father, David Poe, abandoned the family in 1810 and is believed to have died shortly after; and his mother, Elizabeth Poe, died in 1811. The Poe children were then separated. Poe's brother was raised by his paternal grandparents, while his sister Rosalie was taken in by foster parents. Poe was sent to live with John and Frances Allan. From 1815 to 1820, the young Poe traveled with his caregivers to Scotland and later to London, where Allan pursued his business interests as a tobacco merchant. The remainder of Poe's youth was spent in Richmond, Virginia, where he attended private academies. For a brief period, Poe attended the University of Virginia. Unable to afford his fees with the income allotted him by his foster father, Poe resorted to gambling and subsequently incurred debts that Allan refused to help Poe pay. Poe was forced to withdraw from the university.

In 1827, Poe left for Boston, where he enlisted in the U.S. Army. The same year, Poe anonymously published his first volume of poetry, *Tamerlane, and Other Poems* (subtitled *By a Bostonian*), at his own expense. After the death of his foster mother in 1829, Poe sought a discharge from the army and applied to West Point. He published another volume of poetry, *Al Araaf, Tamerlane, and Minor Poems*, under his own name in 1829 and entered West Point the following year. After being court-martialed in 1831, Poe left West Point and moved to Baltimore, where he lived with his grandmother and extended family, including his cousin Virginia Clemm.

In 1835 Poe moved to Richmond, where he became the editor of the *Southern Literary Messenger*. The following year, he married his cousin Virginia, who was then thirteen years old. In 1837, Poe resigned from the *Messenger*. He and his wife and aunt moved first to New York and then to Philadelphia, where they settled. Becoming the editor of *Burton's Gentleman's Magazine* in 1839, Poe continued to write and publish short stories. He maintained the editorship of the magazine after it changed owners and became *Graham's Magazine*. He published a number of his short stories in this periodical, including "The Murders in the Rue Morgue" in 1841.

Poe returned to New York in 1844 to work for the journal *Evening Mirror*. One of his best-known poems, "The Raven," was published by the *Mirror* in 1845. The same year, Poe became the editor of the *Broadway Journal*. He later bought the publication.

In 1847, Poe's wife died of tuberculosis. Poe spent the next year writing and lecturing. He became engaged to Elmira Royster Shelton in 1849. Later that year, after being found in a stupor days earlier, Poe died on October 7 in Baltimore, Maryland.

PLOT SUMMARY

As "The Murders in the Rue Morgue" opens, the unnamed narrator discourses on the nature of "analytical power." He then relates how, while in

MEDIA ADAPTATIONS

- A free downloadable MP3 file of a 2011 reading of "The Murders in the Rue Morgue" is available at http://www.archive.org/details/ruemorgue_rtx_librivox.
- "The Murders in the Rue Morgue" was produced by Tantor Media in an unabridged version available on CD or as an MP3 file in 2005. The story is read by David Case.
- The three Poe tales featuring the character of Dupin—"The Murders in the Rue Morgue," "The Mystery of Marie Roget," and "The Purloined Letter"—read by Kerry Shale, are available as an audio CD from Naxos Audiobooks, produced in 2009.
- Audible.com offers a version of "The Murders in the Rue Morgue" as a downloadable file that can be burned to a CD or uploaded to a smartphone with an Audible Audio application. This adaptation, written by Jennifer Bassett and read by Geoff Woodman, was published by the Oxford University Press Oxford Bookworms Library division in 2011.

Paris, he met and befriended C. Auguste Dupin, who is described as being a member of a well-respected family who has fallen into poverty. The narrator informs the reader that he and Dupin repeatedly encountered one another in a library frequented by both men, who were drawn to its collection of rare books. Excited by the intensity of this shared interest, the narrator confides to Dupin his feelings that to be in Dupin's company would be "a treasure beyond price." The men agree to cohabit for the remainder of the narrator's stay in Paris. Having more wealth than Dupin, the narrator rents "a time-eaten and grotesque mansion" that suits the men's common gloomy temperament.

The narrator then characterizes the routine of daily life for the men, emphasizing both their desire for seclusion and their preference for the darkness of night. During the day, they closed the shutters against the daylight and lit candles to reconstruct a feeling of evening. The men then read, and wrote, and talked until nighttime. Later, they "sallied forth into the streets, arm and arm," and continued the discussions of the daytime. The narrator marvels at the analytical abilities of his friend and recounts an incident in which the companions are walking past a prominent theater. After approximately fifteen minutes, the narrator relates, Dupin makes a comment that appears to be in response to the narrator's private thoughts. Remaking on this, the narrator questions Dupin, asking him how it is possible that Dupin knew what he was thinking. Dupin makes an extensive reply in which he traces the narrator's likely thought patterns after passing the theater.

Having demonstrated to the reader Dupin's intellectual prowess, the narrator informs the reader of a newspaper article he and Dupin encountered. In the article, the details of the violent murders of two women are delineated. The narrator offers an account of the newspaper's description of the crime, the testimonies of various witnesses, and the depositions of acquaintances of the murdered women. Many of the witnesses attest to hearing screams emanating from the house. These individuals entered the home along with a policeman after the gate to the home was forcibly opened. A number of these witnesses also claim to have heard two voices, one gruff, and the other often described as shrill. This second voice is also characterized by many of the witnesses as belonging to a foreigner, as they cannot make out what the voice is saying. The Frenchman, Henri Duval, for example, states that the second voice belonged to an Italian, while the Spaniard, Alfonzo Garcio, maintains that the second voice spoke English. The Englishman, William Bird, asserts that the second voice spoke German. As the paper reports, the two women were found in an apartment locked from the inside. The windows in the rooms were closed and locked. The chambers were in disarray. The body of Camille L'Espanaye was found in the chimney, stuffed feet first through the fireplace. An examination of the courtyard outside and below the chambers revealed the corpse of Madame L'Espanaye, who was nearly decapitated. After studying the depositions and testimonies described in the paper, and reading that the police have been perplexed by the crime, Dupin criticizes the police's handling of the investigation. As the narrator informs, a bank clerk, Adolphe Le Bon, had escorted one of the women home after she withdrew money from the bank, and he was subsequently arrested in connection with the murder. Dupin expresses his interest in investigating the case, as much for his own amusement as for the fact that he owes Le Bon a favor. Through his connections, Dupin is able to acquire access to the crime scene, where they examine the evidence firsthand.

Once the narrator and Dupin have returned to their home, Dupin informs his friend that he has solved the mystery and that he is awaiting the person associated with, though not entirely responsible for, the murders. He then explains the particular details of his examination that have led him to this conclusion. Dupin goes on to assert that an escaped orangutan has killed the two women. He shows the narrator an advertisement he has placed in a newspaper regarding the missing animal. When the advertisement serves its purpose of flushing out the orangutan's owner, Dupin questions the man, who happens to be a sailor who acquired the animal overseas. Eventually the man discloses the details of the murders, describing the way the orangutan escaped and found its way into the apartments of Madame L'Espanaye and her daughter, Camille. There, the orangutan imitated actions it had seen while watching his master shaving. Having stolen a razor from his master, the orangutan proceeded to "shave" Madame L'Espanaye. Her screams transformed the animal's "probably pacific purposes . . . into those of wrath." After nearly decapitating the woman, the orangutan turned to the daughter, who had fainted, and strangled her. Seeking to hide his misdeeds, the orangutan thrust the corpse of the daughter up the chimney and flung the body of the mother out of the window before making his escape from the scene of the crime.

The narrator, who has summarized the sailor's story, informs the reader that the orangutan was captured by its owner and sold to the Jardin des Plantes (a botanical garden in Paris that features a zoo). After Dupin shares the explanation with the police, Le Bon, the man wrongfully imprisoned, is released.

CHARACTERS

William Bird

Bird, an English tailor, is one of the individuals who enters the L'Espanaye home after hearing screams. Bird, like the other witnesses, attests to having heard two voices, one gruff, that of a Frenchman, and the other shrill, possibly that of a German. He conjectures that the shrill voice might have been that of a woman.

Pauline Dubourg

Dubourg is a laundress who, according to her deposition as recounted in the newspaper, knew the murdered women for three years.

Paul Dumas

Dumas is a physician who is called upon to examine the bodies of the deceased. His descriptions of the injuries suffered by the women aid Dupin in his investigation.

C. Auguste Dupin

Dupin is a gentleman from a reputable family who has lost his fortune. A scholar with interests similar to the narrator, Dupin possesses what the narrator describes as extraordinary analytical capabilities. Dupin and the narrator rent a residence together. Having heard about the murders of Madame and Mademoiselle L'Espanaye and the authorities' failed effort to solve the crime, Dupin seeks to investigate the mysterious deaths on his own. Dupin successfully solves the crime after reviewing the depositions of a number of individuals connected to the L'Espanaye family and exploring the crime scene firsthand. He is responsible for freeing Le Bon, the man wrongfully accused of the crime. The character of the amateur detective Dupin appears in two other Poe stories.

Henri Duval

Duval is a silversmith and a neighbor to the L'Espanayes. One of the witnesses who enters the home along with the gendarme Muset, Duval also attests to hearing two voices, one gruff and French, the other shrill and possibly Italian.

Alexandre Etienne

Etienne is a surgeon who accompanies the physician Dumas at his examination of the corpses of Madame and Mademoiselle L'Espanaye. He corroborates Dumas' findings.

Alfonzo Garcio

The Spanish undertaker Garcio is a neighbor to Madame and Mademoiselle L'Espanaye. Along with several other witnesses, he enters the house with the gendarme Muset. Like the other witnesses, Garcio claims to have heard two voices, one belonging to a gruff Frenchman. Garcio describes the other voice as shrill and that of an Englishman.

Camille L'Espanaye

Mademoiselle Camille L'Espanaye is one of the two murder victims. The daughter of Madame L'Espanaye, she lived with her mother in a fourth-floor apartment in their home on the Rue Morgue. The two were reported to be wealthy and reclusive. Mademoiselle L'Espanaye was strangled to death, and her body was thrust up the chimney.

Madame L'Espanaye

Madame L'Espanaye is the second murder victim. She lived with her daughter on the fourth floor of their Rue Morgue home. Neighbors describe Madame and her daughter as possessing some wealth but living "an exceedingly retired life." They had few visitors over the course of the several years in which they occupied the home. Madame was slain in a brutal fashion, her throat slit so deeply she was almost decapitated. Her body was found in the courtyard below her chambers, having been thrown from the window.

Adolphe Le Bon

Le Bon is a clerk working for the banker Mignaud. Prior to the murders, he accompanied Madame L'Espanaye home, carrying with him the sum she had just withdrawn. Le Bon is arrested for the murders, having been the last person to see the L'Espanaye women alive, but is subsequently freed after Dupin solves the crime.

Jules Mignaud

Mignaud is a banker who comments on the banking habits of Madame L'Espanaye. Mignaud reports that she withdrew four thousand francs in gold, which was brought to her home by the clerk, Adolphe Le Bon.

Alberto Montani

Montani, an Italian confectioner, maintains that after entering the home with Muset and the crowd, he was among the first of the witnesses to make his way up the stairs. Like the other witnesses, he claims to have heard two voices, a gruff French-speaking voice and a shrill Russian-speaking one.

Pierre Moreau

Moreau is a tobacconist who reports that he sold small amounts of tobacco and snuff to Madame L'Espanaye. Like many of the other individuals whose depositions were reported in the paper, Moreau attests that the L'Espanaye women had few visitors.

Isidore Muset

Muset is a gendarme, or French police officer, who, according to his deposition, was called to the L'Espanaye home at about three o'clock A.M. At the front gate, twenty to thirty people stood gathered, attempting to force entry, having heard screams emanating from the home. As one of the individuals who entered the home, Muset states that he heard two voices from within the women's chambers. His testimony is the first one in which, as the narrator points out, it is revealed that the two voices were markedly different, one gruff and the other shrill. Muset suggests the shrill voice may have been that of a foreigner.

Narrator

Throughout the story, the first-person narrator remains unnamed. He befriends Dupin after discovering a shared scholarly interest in rare books. Somewhat better off financially than Dupin, the narrator invites him to share a rented home, where the two men pursue their academic studies in solitude. Periodically the friends venture out at night to walk and converse. The narrator repeatedly expresses his admiration for Dupin's analytical capabilities and accompanies him on his inspection of the scene of the murders of the two L'Espanaye women. Through the narrator's observations about and questions to Dupin, Poe depicts Dupin's intellectual prowess.

Odenheimer

Odenheimer is a restaurateur. A native of Amsterdam, he gives his testimony through a translator and describes the screaming and voices he heard.

Orangutan

The orangutan, who has escaped from his owner, is the perpetrator of the murders of Madame and Mademoiselle L'Espanaye. Having watched his owner shaving, he steals the razor, and after making his way into the L'Espanaye home, attempts to mimic this act with Madame. The screams of Madame L'Espanaye confuse and enrage the animal, who subsequently murders both women and hides the bodies to the best of his ability. The animal is later captured and sold to the zoo.

Sailor

The sailor is the owner of the orangutan who has murdered Mademoiselle and Madame L'Espanaye. After the orangutan escaped from the sailor's rooms, the sailor chased the animal, who still clutched the razor with which he had been pretending to shave himself. The sailor followed the orangutan as far as he could and managed to climb a lightning rod that allowed the orangutan access to the window of Madame L'Espanaye's rooms. From this vantage point, the sailor watched the orangutan murder the women. Seeing the animal at the window with the body of Madame, the sailor slid down the lightning rod and hurried home. His confession is obtained after Dupin places an advertisement regarding the orangutan.

THEMES

Intelligence

In "The Murders in the Rue Morgue," Poe uses the unnamed narrator to highlight and applaud Dupin's analytical abilities. Throughout the story, Poe contrasts the physical with the intellectual. This mind-body dichotomy is underscored through the narrator's relationship with Dupin. While the narrator delights in his physical connection to Dupin, he observes that for his part, Dupin can often seem cold and remote. The narrator describes the "perfect *abandon*" with which he gives himself over to Dupin's "wild whims." At the same time, however, Dupin comes across to the narrator as "frigid and abstract," particularly when Dupin speaks of his "intimate knowledge" of the narrator's feelings. Such remarks give way to the narrator's representation of his awe for Dupin's particular intellectual skills. The narrator expresses both surprise at and admiration for Dupin's ability to trace the course of his unspoken thoughts. His focuses on his own feelings and on his sense of physical connection to Dupin fade as the story progresses. Though early in the story he remarks happily about walking arm in arm with Dupin through the streets of Paris, the narrator then observes Dupin's cold, analytical nature and turns to a representation of Dupin's intellectual prowess.

After reading about the murders of the L'Espanayes, the narrator regards the mystery as unsolvable. Dupin, however, scoffs at the incompetence shown by the police in their investigation and turns his mind toward his own inquiry into the violent deaths of the two women. Following his study of the crime scene and the testimonies of the witnesses, Dupin soon remarks upon the ease with which he has come to the solution of the crime. The narrator's response is "mute astonishment." Dupin explains how he came to his conclusions, commenting along the way on how early his understanding of the events developed, and condescendingly acknowledging the narrator's own observations, however inaccurate they may be. When the narrator suggests that only a madman could have committed such a violent crime with so little motive, Dupin acknowledges that in some regards, the narrator's notion "is not irrelevant." Dupin's ferreting out of the murderer (the orangutan) and apprehending the animal's owner results in the freeing of the wrongfully accused Le Bon. Yet Dupin's own motives seem simply to be the exercising of his intellect for the sake of the exercise itself. While he acknowledges that he owed Le Bon a favor, he comments that investigating the crime will provide "amusement." When he has solved it, Dupin does not care that the prefect of police makes sarcastic comments about Dupin's meddling. Rather, he states that he is contented to have "defeated him [the prefect of police] in his own castle." Throughout the tale, Poe contrasts Dupin's intellect with the narrator's own simplicity. While the two men share similar interests, the narrator is an emotional man who enjoys the physical contact of his relationship with Dupin. It is Dupin's intelligence, however, that impresses and astonishes the narrator. Through the narrator's focus on Dupin's intellect, Poe draws attention not only to the quality itself but also to the impulse to employ one's intellect in subjugating both the emotional and the physical aspects of one's life.

Violence

The detailing of the gruesomeness of the murders in "The Murders in the Rue Morgue" is a hallmark of Poe's fiction in this vein. Through the accounts of witnesses who view the rooms of Madame and Mademoiselle L'Espanaye after the murders, and particularly through Dupin's careful analysis and explanations, Poe provides the reader with a catalog of details concerning the state in which the bodies were found. Dupin draws attention to a number of elements that underscore the murderer's apparent lack of motive. He highlights the fact that despite the amount of money found in the room,

TOPICS FOR FURTHER STUDY

- Poe published three stories featuring the detective Dupin. The first was "The Murders in the Rue Morgue," published in 1841. The last, "The Purloined Letter," one of Poe's best-known stories, was published in 1845. Read and compare the two stories. In what ways, if any, does Poe's character of Dupin evolve? What are the key elements of the stories, and what are the similarities in their structures? Write a comparative essay or create a Venn diagram in which you discuss the similarities and differences between the two short stories.
- The care with which Poe plotted his fiction, particularly his detective stories, is evident in his work. With a group of classmates, write a short detective story, being sure to provide a thorough range of clues along the way. Arguably, Dupin could have solved the case of the murders of the two women in the Rue Morgue even without the piece of evidence, the orangutan hair, that Poe withholds from the reader, as the physical evidence left by the inhuman grasp around Mademoiselle L'Espanaye's neck had been inventoried. Additionally, Dupin draws the proper conclusions from the mixed testimonies regarding the second, shrill voice the witnesses heard. Evidence in your story should be intermingled with extraneous information, so that the reader must sort through all the details given to find the pertinent facts. Use Poe's own detective, Dupin, as your investigator, or create your own original amateur detective. Share your story with your class through a Web page you create, by reading it aloud, or through a print version. Invite your classmates to write a review of your story on your Web page.
- Detective fiction has evolved into a variety of subgenres since Poe's time. Modern detective fiction has even been told using the format of manga, or Japanese-based comics and graphic novels. A series of young-adult manga by Kia Asamiya, whose real name is Michitaka Kikuchi, features a group of young detectives who solve crimes perpetrated by an assortment of villains. Read Volume 1 of *Steam Detectives*, published in 1999 by VIZ Media, with a small book group. What resemblance does Asamiya's manga bear to the early examples of the detective genre, such as Poe's "The Murders in the Rue Morgue?" Consider such elements as style, structure, and tone. Would you characterize the tone of the manga as humorous, sarcastic, or suspenseful? Discuss these issues with the members of the book group and create a group blog that summarizes the book and describes your assignment. Have members post their comments and share their opinions regarding questions posed here and other topics that surface during your discussions.
- The genre of detective fiction dates back to the early nineteenth century. Using sources such as Lucy Sussex's *Women Writers and Detectives in Nineteenth-Century Crime Fiction: The Mothers of the Mystery Genre*, published in 2010 by Palgrave Macmillan, and *The Cambridge Companion to American Crime Fiction*, edited by Catherine Ross Nickerson and published in 2010 by Cambridge University Press, research the history of detective fiction. If you wish, tailor your research to focus on female authors or another group. Write a research paper in which you trace the development of the genre, or the development of the genre as it pertains to your specific subcategory. Be sure to cite all your sources.

---

and the fact that the chambers appear to have been ransacked, it appears that if anything was taken from the room, it was only a few undergarments. Dupin emphasizes the "odd disorder" of the room, the strength the murderer must have possessed, the brutish "ferocity" employed, and the "butchery

A typical French street not unlike the fictional Rue Morgue. (*Julien Bastide / Shutterstock.com*)

without motive." More than once, he discusses the peculiarities of such facts and in doing so, leads the narrator, along with the reader, to deduce that only "a madman" or "some raving maniac" could have perpetrated such acts. Poe manipulates the reader's reactions, forcing him or her to conclude that man is tragically capable of such hideous, horrific brutality. The fact that the crime was in actuality committed by an animal does not necessarily mitigate the reaction of Poe's audience, whose experience mimics that of the narrator. By the time Dupin reveals the true murderer, the reader, like the narrator, has already accepted *a* truth, if not *the* truth unveiled by Dupin—that the possibility for incomprehensibly violent barbarity exists within mankind.

STYLE

First Person Narration

In "The Murders in the Rue Morgue," Poe utilizes an unnamed first-person narrator to relate the events of the story. A first-person narrator uses "I" when referring to himself or herself. Despite the narrator's primary role in "The Murders in the Rue Morgue," and despite the close interaction between the narrator and the character of Dupin, Poe opts to leave his narrator unnamed. In creating an intimate viewpoint through the use of a first-person voice but leaving this voice unidentified, Poe creates a narrative structure through which the reader is invited to be an active participant in the story through identification with the anonymous figure of the narrator. Just as the narrator is impressed by Dupin's stunning intellectual acuity, the reader is similarly offered the same opportunity to be awestruck by Dupin's skill, witnessing it alongside the narrator. Poe furthermore employs the unnamed first-person narrator as a means of representing Dupin's character. While the narrator finds Dupin at times cold and reserved, Dupin nonetheless appears to share some moments of warm affection with the narrator, as when the two walk "arm and arm" through Paris at night.

When presented with a character such as Poe's narrator, one with obvious loyalties or prejudices (Poe's narrator is unmistakably enamored to some degree with Dupin) who is tasked with conveying observations and information to the reader, the reader is obliged to question that character's reliability. Poe makes clear, however, that his narrator in "The Murders in the Rue Morgue" is at least as much fascinated with intellectual analysis itself as he is with Dupin. The lengthy opening paragraphs to the story, in which the narrator expounds on the subtle differences between analytical power, cleverness, and ingenuity, attest to this fact. Poe's narrator may be viewed, due to this proclivity, as fairly reliable, despite his emotional biases.

Detective Fiction

As observed by James M. Hutchisson in *Poe*, his 2005 analysis of Poe's works, "The Murders in the Rue Morgue" is regarded as the first detective story. In this work of short fiction, "Poe set down the pattern of the genre for all successive mystery writers," states Hutchisson. The combination of a hyperintelligent sleuth and a slower-witted companion became a staple of the genre. Hutchisson goes on to list other genre-specific elements, including the locked room in which the crime occurs and the use of logic and scientific reasoning to solve the crime.

In Poe's crafting of the genre, he created a sleuth he would use in other stories. As a detective, Dupin is motivated by his own amusement, as he explains to the narrator. The enjoyment he derives from piecing together the puzzle outweighs any sense of ethical obligation to the victims and their families or any concerns for justice. Much is made of Dupin's analytical prowess, which he does display in "The Murders in the Rue Morgue." Yet the actual means by which Dupin deems the crime solved, the physical evidence of the orangutan hair, is withheld from the narrator and the reader by Dupin. The reader does not discover the hair along with Dupin but is presented with it as Dupin explains the way in which he solved the crime. While the reader's sense of active participation in the solving of the mystery may be thus thwarted when the evidence is later revealed, the crime is arguably solvable based on the testimonies of the voices and on other physical evidence, such as the bruise marks left on Mademoiselle L'Espanaye's neck. Until the hair is revealed, however, Poe builds a sense of dread in both the narrator and the reader. The horrific possibility of a deranged madman having brutally slain the women is given space within the story to be fully contemplated before Dupin reveals the truth. The dread Poe creates in this fashion would also become characteristic of his detective fiction.

HISTORICAL CONTEXT

Literary Philosophy in Nineteenth-Century American Fiction

At the time Poe wrote, near the middle of the nineteenth century, American fiction mirrored earlier trends in British fiction. Poe's work is distinctively in the same gothic character as that of fiction by British authors writing in the late eighteenth and early nineteenth centuries. Although inspired by the works of earlier British writers, Poe, at the same time, anticipated a later movement toward realism in American fiction. Works of gothic fiction in both America and Great Britain were primarily written to entertain through their ability to frighten the reader. Such gothic tales feature mystery, a building sense of suspense, and an imaginative or anxious protagonist. In some cases, supernatural elements are employed, or merely suggested, but just as common are tales in which the protagonist suspects horrors that are later explained by rational means. Gothicism is closely linked with the literary movement known as romanticism, which began in the mid-eighteenth century as both a literary and visual artistic movement and which focused on nature and on the individual, particularly his or her instinctive, emotional, and imaginative responses to the world. An offshoot of the gothic horror novel is the gothic romance novel, such as *The Mysteries of Udolpho*, by Ann Radcliffe, published in 1794. The gothic romance novel typically features a female protagonist who, in the gothic vein, is an imaginative girl placed in a situation in which suspicious elements inspire a sense of horror and mystery. Like the writers of gothic horror or mystery novels, gothic romance authors built a sense of psychological terror and often suggested supernatural causes for mysterious occurrences.

The common denominator of gothic fiction is, as Benjamin F. Fisher observes in "Poe and the Gothic Tradition," in the 2002 *Cambridge Companion to Edgar Allan Poe*, "an atmosphere conducive to the anxieties of the protagonist and, depending on the situation in the story, among other characters in general." In American gothic tales, writers employed American landscapes and

COMPARE & CONTRAST

- **1840s:** Detective, horror, and mystery fiction are newly emerging genres in the United States, as inspired by gothic and gothic romance fiction in England. American writers such as Nathaniel Hawthorne, William Dunlap, James Kirke Paulding, and Charles Brockden Brown have begun to write in the gothic mode and incorporate elements of mystery, horror, and psychological tension. Poe builds on these traditions and is the front-runner of American detective fiction.

  Today: Fiction in the detective, horror, and mystery genres has sparked a wide variety of offshoots. Now such genres have been dovetailed with other formats and genres, including manga and vampire fiction. The more traditional murder-mystery format is also reflected in the modern obsession with television shows known as police procedurals, which focus on the police's investigation of murder or crime scenes, including *Bones*, *Law and Order*, and the *CSI* (*Crime Scene Investigation*) series. As a literary genre, the detective story as Poe conceived it can be found in modern fiction by authors such as Sue Grafton and Martha Grimes. Likewise, Stephen King is prolific in this genre and additionally incorporates elements of horror and the supernatural.

- **1840s:** The debate over slavery is waged in America's newspapers, and prominent writers share their views on the topic. Northern abolitionist writers such as Ralph Waldo Emerson and Henry David Thoreau do so eagerly and unequivocally. Some southern authors, such as Poe, are more reluctant and are decidedly vague in the ways they express their views regarding slavery.

  Today: Although the abolitionists won their fight in 1865 when the Thirteenth Amendment was enacted, intense racial conflict was prevalent for decades after the war. Today, racial tension is still an issue in the United States according to a poll compiled by the Pew Research Center in 2009. Among the statistics included in the report on the study is that although 54 percent of whites believe the country has taken the steps necessary to ensure that blacks and whites have equal rights, only 13 percent of African Americans agree.

- **1840s:** Tuberculosis is a major health threat in the United States. Virginia Clemm Poe, wife of the prominent writer, dies of tuberculosis in 1847. The earliest records kept by the U.S. Census Bureau on death statistics by disease are from 1861, and only for Massachusetts. That year, the death rate from tuberculosis in Massachusetts is 365 deaths per 100,000 people. By comparison, a decade earlier in western Europe, tuberculosis accounts for approximately 500 deaths per 100,000 people.

  Today: Although deaths from tuberculosis have drastically declined, particularly following the development of a vaccine for tuberculosis in 1908, some deaths still occur and the incidence of tuberculosis is increasing. The U.S. Centers for Disease Control and Prevention report that in 2006, 4.4 cases per 100,000 people are reported and 0.2 deaths per 100,000 people occur.

---

scenes that served as counterpoints to the settings of earlier British fiction. Whereas British gothic tales are often set in castles and abbeys, American gothic fiction is set in aging homes or mansions. American author Nathaniel Hawthorne (1804–1864), for example, set many of his short stories in Puritan New England and used the gothic elements of witchcraft and devilry to explore the darkness of human nature. Poe himself offered a largely favorable review of Hawthorne's gothic short-story collection *Twice-Told Tales* (1842). Charles Brockden Brown (1771–1810) similarly

The women were murdered but the door was locked from inside. (aopsan / Shutterstock.com)

employed elements of horror, mystery, and psychological conflict in his novels. *Wieland*, for example, published in 1798, is commonly regarded as the first American gothic novel and features the protagonist Wieland, who, upon hearing voices, is presumed by the reader to be going insane. Wieland subsequently murders his wife and children.

Like his contemporaries and predecessors in the gothic vein, Poe also makes use of horror, psychological tension, and elements of the bizarre that often are eventually explained as products of a highly imaginative or overwrought narrator. He further develops the genre by contrasting this emotional, reactive, imaginative tone with a character devoted to rationality and reason. In this way, he incorporates a sense of realism into his mystery, horror, and detective fiction. A detached, rational character is dispatched to make observations concerning the details of a murder, for example, and while the case may build to the point where it appears as if the only explanation possible is outside the realm of logic, in the end of many of Poe's stories, such as "The Murders in the Rue Morgue," the conclusion, while not probable, is not supernatural or illogical. While realism as a literary movement developed later in the nineteenth century, well after Poe's death, Poe is often consider a forerunner of American realism. Just as American realism was becoming fully incorporated into the literature of the late nineteenth century, critics such as John Mackinnon Robertson acknowledged the realist qualities in Poe's work. Robertson states in an 1885 essay, published in 1897's *New Essays Toward a Critical Method* and later reprinted in 2008's *Edgar Allan Poe*, edited by Harold Bloom, that Poe is "essentially a realist in his method." Realism as a literary movement developed as a reaction to the romanticism of the earlier nineteenth century and featured a focus on rationality, logic, and objectivism.

The American Abolitionist Movement

When Poe published "The Murders in the Rue Morgue" in 1841, the Civil War (1861–1865) was still two decades away. Nevertheless, many of the issues that contributed to the tensions that ultimately led to the war were already brewing in America. The debate over slavery was one such issue. Abolitionism as a movement, whose purpose was eradicating slavery in America, began in the

1830s. As abolitionist sentiments began to grow among religious groups such as the Society of Friends (also known as the Quakers), reformist William Lloyd Garrison began a newspaper dedicated to the abolitionist cause. Garrison's paper, the *Liberator*, ran from 1831 through 1865. Also in 1831, the first antislavery society was established in New York City. Garrison and former slaves such as Frederick Douglass were prominent members of the organization. A political party, the Liberty Party, was founded in 1840 and dedicated to the antislavery platform. The party, however, was plagued by infighting and disagreements about the proper course of action that should be followed in legally abolishing slavery.

A number of writers spoke out on the issue of abolitionism; Ralph Waldo Emerson (1803–1882), for example, was a vocal opponent of slavery and wrote regularly for Garrison's paper, as did Walt Whitman (1819–1892), Henry David Thoreau (1817–1862), and French writer Victor Hugo (1802–1885). Poe, who was living in Richmond, Virginia, and serving as the editor of the *Southern Literary Messenger* at the time, was reluctant to speak out too strongly with his personal views on slavery, suggests J. Gerald Kennedy in "Edgar Allan Poe, 1809–1849: A Brief Biography," in *A Historical Guide to Edgar Allan Poe*. A southern journal with a national circulation, the *Messenger*, led by Poe, had to tread carefully around the slavery issue so as not to offend either its northern, abolitionist readership or its southern, largely proslavery audience. Kennedy observes that Poe's views were revealed when he praised the approach of another writer, Lucian Minor (1802–1858), who advocated a gradual end to slavery and the colonization of Liberia by former slaves.

CRITICAL OVERVIEW

Poe's short fiction received largely favorable reviews among contemporary critics. His original style and structure are especially praised by early reviewers. In an 1845 essay for the *American Review*, George Colton discusses Poe's 1845 collection *Tales* and observes that "few books have been published of late, which contain within themselves the elements of greater popularity." Colton examines the Dupin stories ("The Murders in the Rue Morgue," "The Mystery of Marie Rogêt," and "The Purloined Letter") as works that will excite the curiosity and stir the sympathy of readers. Poe's *Tales* elicited similar comments among other critics. In an 1845 review for *Graham's Magazine*, J. R. Lowell states that Poe's "style is highly finished, graceful, and truly classical. It would be hard to find a living author who had displayed such varied powers." Although a contributor to an 1847 article for *Blackwood's Magazine* claims that Poe's style "has nothing particularly commendable," P. P. Cooke, in an 1848 article for the *Southern Literary Messenger*, praises Poe's fiction as demonstrative of "the presence of a singularly adventurous, very wild, and thoroughly poetic imagination."

Later critics focus on Poe's development of the detective fiction genre and on the characterization of the narrator and Dupin. Arthur Hobson Quinn, in the 1941 volume *Edgar Allan Poe: A Critical Biography*, disputes the notion, commonly held among later critics, that Poe originated the detective fiction genre. Quinn does acknowledge that Dupin, as an analytical detective, shaped the conventions of the genre. Dupin is the focus of much of the modern critical attention the story receives. John Bryant, in *Melville and Repose: The Rhetoric of Humor in the American Renaissance* (1993), examines Dupin as "the agent of Poe's duplicity" and describes the narrator as a dull-witted facilitator of Poe's and Dupin's "scheme" to dupe the reader. Dupin is studied in terms of his professionalism as a detective in William Crisman's 1995 essay for *Studies in American Fiction*. Crisman centers his work on Dupin's motives throughout the three stories in which he appears. Tracing what he describes as a "fantasy of recovering nobility" in Dupin and in Poe's "Dupin-like" characters as well, Crisman asserts that Dupin is obsessed with reclaiming his social status as well as the money he lost in the past.

Other scholars take a thematic approach to Poe's work. Joseph Church, in a 2006 essay for the journal *ATQ* (*American Transcendental Quarterly*), argues that Poe, in "The Murders in the Rue Morgue," explores themes of misogyny (hatred of women by men) and violence against women. Among other examples, Church cites the facts that the murders of Madame and Mademoiselle L'Espanaye go unpunished; that the sailor whose orangutan kills the women is rewarded with a large sum of money from the zoo to which he sells the animal; and that Poe's story "mocks the legitimacy of Madame

L'Espanaye's wealth" as evidence that misogyny plays a prevalent role in the story.

CRITICISM

Catherine Dominic

Dominic is a novelist and a freelance writer and editor. In the following essay, Dominic explores the relationship between the first-person narrator and Dupin in "The Murders in the Rue Morgue," arguing that through the delineation of this relationship, Poe provides an otherwise clinical analysis of the crime with an emotional subtext, allowing readers to access the story both emotionally and intellectually.

Although Dupin's solving of the murders of Madame and Mademoiselle L'Espanaye functions as the main plot of Edgar Allan Poe's "The Murders in the Rue Morgue," the relationship between the narrator and Dupin provides an underlying subtext that imbues the story with a subtle emotional core. In depicting the narrator and Dupin and their personal interactions, Poe elicits from the audience emotional responses that engage the reader on a number of levels. The revelations the narrator makes about himself and the observations he makes about Dupin force the reader to compare the two men, and further to evaluate their relationship. While the story is progressing, and as the reader is processing his or her assessments regarding the story's main characters, the murders are introduced to the reader, as well as to Dupin and the narrator, via the newspaper account. As Dupin eagerly vows to solve the crime, the two characters become participants in the investigation, thus linking the subplot of the men and their relationship to the main plot of the murder investigation. The reader's responses to the murders are guided by the developing understanding of Dupin and the narrator, an understanding in the process of being cultivated when the opening scenes of the story are interrupted by news of the murders. The narrator's reactions to the violent crimes mirror the reader's responses of confusion and horror. At the same time, Dupin's logical analyses shape the reader's views regarding the possible culprits. Through such connections between the characters themselves and between the characters and the reader, Poe infuses a detective story with the drama created by personal relationships and the emotions they inspire.

" THE REVELATIONS THE NARRATOR MAKES ABOUT HIMSELF AND THE OBSERVATIONS HE MAKES ABOUT DUPIN FORCE THE READER TO COMPARE THE TWO MEN, AND FURTHER TO EVALUATE THEIR RELATIONSHIP."

As "The Murders in the Rue Morgue" opens, the narrator speaks directly to the reader and expounds on the topics of analysis, intellectual prowess, and the significance of the relationship between the imagination and logical reasoning. Poe's narrator, after discussing the differences between mere ingenuity and the higher power of the analytic mind, states that "the ingenious are always fanciful, and the *truly* imaginative never otherwise than analytic." He thereby links the notion of the analytical mind and the imagination, an idea that will surface again in the story. To illustrate his discussion, the narrator relates the story of his association with C. Auguste Dupin.

In the next five paragraphs, Poe crafts in detail the relationship forged between Dupin and the narrator. First, Dupin is introduced as being from a highly respected family. The "untoward events" that have led to Dupin's current state of poverty are left unexplained. The narrator goes on to describe the way the two men repeatedly and accidentally encountered one another as they both independently searched for a rare book. The men soon strike up conversation, and as the relationship develops, the narrator confesses how much he is impressed with the "vast extent" of Dupin's reading. Furthermore, the narrator confides to the reader the depth of his own feelings for Dupin, stating, "I felt my soul enkindled within me by the wild fervor, and the vivid freshness of his imagination." So intense are his feelings that the narrator tells Dupin that to remain in his company would be "a treasure beyond price." The men then decide to live together and take up residence in an aging mansion rented by the narrator.

Thus far, Poe has established the connection the men feel with one another, a connection largely inspired by their common interests.

WHAT DO I READ NEXT?

- *The Narrative of Arthur Gordon Pym of Nantucket*, originally published in 1838, is Poe's only novel. The work is available in a 2008 edition. The expanded volume *The Narrative of Arthur Gordon Pym of Nantucket* includes several short stories featuring themes and imagery pertinent to those Poe treats in the novel, including fantastic voyages and premature burials.
- The gothic fiction of Charles Brockden Brown served as a precursor to the detective and horror genres later developed by Poe. Brown's *Wieland; or, The Transformation: An American Tale*, published in 1798, is set in rural Pennsylvania in the 1760s and explores the psychological tension that inspires a man to murder his family. A modern edition was published in 2010.
- Arthur Conan Doyle's stories centered on the detective Sherlock Holmes were originally published between 1887 and 1927. Doyle's characters and plot structures draw upon those developed by Poe in his detective fiction. Doyle's works featuring Holmes are available in a modern collection, *The Complete Sherlock Holmes: All 4 Novels and 56 Short Stories*, originally published in 1960 and reissued in 1986.
- Young-adult mystery, detective, and horror stories featuring Latino characters are presented in the collection *You Don't Have a Clue: Latino Mystery Stories for Teens*, edited by Sarah Cortez and introduced by Dr. James Blasingame, an expert in the field of young-adult literature. The collection was published in 2011.
- Alane Ferguson's "Forensic Mystery" young-adult series combines the detective-fiction genre with the police-procedural format. The first book in the series, *Christopher Killer*, was published in 2006. The series features the seventeen-year-old daughter of a county coroner who, like Poe's Dupin, embarks upon the role of amateur detective. Like Poe's "The Murders in the Rue Morgue," Ferguson's tale features vivid, gruesome details of the crime scene.
- *The Romance of Failure: First-Person Fictions of Poe, Hawthorne, and James*, by Jonathan Auerbach, explores the relationship between the author and his first-person narrator in the works of Poe, Nathaniel Hawthorne, and Henry James. The text was published in 1989.

After the two men move in together, a more intimate relationship is suggested. The narrator comments on the utter seclusion the men enjoy, into which no outside visitors are invited. "We existed," the narrator states, "within ourselves alone." After discussing the mutual love of night the men share, the narrator reveals the way he devotes himself to Dupin, "giving myself up to his wild whims with a perfect *abandon*." Such statements have led some critics to argue that Poe constructs a homosexual relationship between Dupin and the narrator. J. A. Leo Lemay suggests this notion in the essay, "The Psychology of 'The Murders in the Rue Morgue,'" originally published in 1982 and reprinted in 1993 in *On Poe: The Best from American Literature*. Whether or not it is characterized in this manner, however, the relationship between the men clearly seems to be one involving a deep emotional connection, at least on the part of the narrator.

Given the narrator's openness in expressing his emotions—he is obviously candid with the reader and has discussed his own frankness with Dupin—it is not surprising that Dupin is able to prove "his intimate knowledge" of the narrator's heart. Yet Dupin's analysis, according to the narrator, is delivered in a manner divorced from the emotional warmth that characterizes the narrator's own comments about Dupin. The narrator describes Dupin's demeanor during these discussions as "frigid and abstract." Comforting himself with the breadth of his own knowledge, he frames his perceptions of Dupin in terms of his duality. He states that Dupin exemplifies the notion of "the Bi-Part Soul," and he proceeds to amuse himself with the notion of "a double Dupin—the creative and the resolvent." (In this context, *resolvent* may be defined as "analytical" or "logical.")

Whether or not the narrator is able to soothe the pain Dupin's cold attitude has caused remains unclear, for in the next paragraph the narrator attempts to shift the tone of his account. First, he assures the reader that despite the evidence of the preceding narration, he is not "detailing any mystery, or penning any romance." Both "mystery" and "romance" have more than one meaning, and the narrator's vague use of the terms may be intended as an effort to confuse the reader regarding the narrator's feelings for Dupin. "Mystery" could refer to the nature of his relationship with Dupin or to the story that follows, in which Dupin attempts to solve a double homicide. Both branches of the story, are in fact mysteries, so it may be surmised that through the voice of the narrator, Poe is being ironic. Similarly, "romance" could refer to his relationship with Dupin or to a story containing elements of romanticism or of the gothic romance still popular during this time. The narrator then refers coldly to Dupin as "the Frenchman" and goes on to criticize Dupin's behavior and intellect. The narrator's own change in tone, precipitated, it seems, by Dupin's cold demeanor, is significant. His use of irony and sarcasm indicate how deeply he has been hurt by what he may perceive as Dupin's failure to fully reciprocate his feelings.

This portion of the story, when the narrator perceives in Dupin a lack of warmth, affection, or the reciprocity of his own feelings, is characterized by the narrator's attempt to disguise the depth of his own emotions. The narrator further attempts to disorient the reader by revising comments he has previously made about Dupin's character. Just after the story opens, the narrator informs the reader that the story to follow, of Dupin and his facility in solving the murder, will illustrate the way the imagination and the analytic intellect are linked. After the narrator experiences what he considers to be Dupin's slighting of him, the narrator focuses on the fact that Dupin, when in a certain state, distances himself emotionally from the narrator. The description the narrator gives of Dupin at this time suggests that Dupin is possessed with a creative excitement about his own analytical abilities, underscoring what the narrator has previously stated, that the imagination and the intellect are inseparable. However, hurt as he now is by Dupin's lack of affection toward him, the narrator dissembles his true feelings by subtly attacking Dupin. The narrator now describes Dupin as divided (or doubled), and "excited," pejoratively suggesting an overwrought state. The narrator even goes so far as to suggest that Dupin's intellect is "diseased."

When he continues the story, the narrator cites another example of Dupin's strange abilities. Abandoning his regaling of the reader with details about his relationship with Dupin, and having felt the sting of unrequited affection, the narrator turns his focus to Dupin's analytical skills. For several paragraphs, the narrator details the way Dupin has astonishingly traced the unspoken thread of the narrator's thoughts. The section is prefaced with the narrator's observation that the incident is indicative of "the character of his remarks at the periods in question," that is, the times when Dupin disengages emotionally from the narrator and appears both frenetic in his pursuit of his analysis and cold in his personal responses to the narrator. When Dupin reveals the content of the narrator's own thoughts, thoughts the narrator has not spoken aloud, he outwardly expresses surprise, asking Dupin to explain how he has "been enabled to fathom my soul." To himself, the narrator admits that he "was even more startled than I would have been willing to express." These comments suggest that the narrator still feels deeply connected to Dupin, despite his attempt to convince himself and the reader otherwise. His surprise at Dupin's ability may be indicative of his excitement that Dupin sustains enough interest in him to warrant such a close reading of his thoughts. The narrator may also be unsettled by the notion that although Dupin can read him so well, he senses, based on the coldness that Dupin has demonstrated he is capable of, that Dupin does not return the warmth of his affection. Alternatively, the narrator may be feeling discomforted by Dupin's strange ability to read his thoughts because it is invasive and peculiar. Having been, in a sense, spurned by Dupin, the narrator may now be looking at Dupin in a new, harsher light.

Just after this incident, the narrator and Dupin discover the story about the murders of Madame and Mademoiselle L'Espanaye in the evening paper. They follow the story in the next evening's edition, where detailed witness accounts are documented. This section of the story represents the bulk of Poe's narrative, and the content pertains exclusively to matters related to the murders. The narrator follows Dupin to the crime scene and back to their own home, where he listens to Dupin's discussion of the evidence. When Dupin is nearing the point at which he reveals the truth about the murderer's identity, he characterizes the crime as horrific in its brutality. Throughout this section, Dupin has maintained a professional demeanor, discussing the facts of the case as he has ascertained them. Yet when he reveals his perceptions regarding the brutality of what he describes as "butchery without motive," Dupin evokes in the narrator a response that appears to be appropriately horrified in tone. The narrator feels a "creeping of the flesh" and can only surmise that a "madman" or "maniac" could have committed the crime. The narrator's horrified response as he contemplates the crime in this light stands in stark contrast to that of the aloof and logical Dupin, who has eagerly pursued the case and who has relished the crime as a puzzle to be solved. The disconnect between the two sides of Dupin's personality previously noted by the narrator seems to come into play at this point in Poe's story. Just as the narrator indicated at the beginning of the story, Dupin exemplifies the mental marriage of creative energy with logical analysis. Furthermore, just as the narrator has illustrated through his own interactions with Dupin, Dupin's intellect appears to be divorced from any hint of emotional acuity.

Following the revelation of the truth, an act shared by Dupin and the sailor, whose orangutan committed the crimes, the narrator concludes the story on an abrupt note. "I have scarcely anything to add," he states. His narration is terminated quickly, and he does not again take up the earlier thread of his story in which his relationship with Dupin was heavily featured. It is only through Poe's depiction of the narrator that the story is infused with any sense of humanity. No one mourns the deaths of Madame and Mademoiselle L'Espanaye. Dupin operates in a clinical, detached fashion as he pieces together the evidence. The witnesses themselves do not directly have voices in the story; rather, their statements are reproduced in the newspaper. Yet the narrator has deep feelings for Dupin. He is euphorically swept up in the relationship at the onset of the story but then wounded by Dupin's emotional distance. And he alone expresses a sense of horror at the violent deaths of the two women. Through the narrator, then, Poe suffuses into a detective story the emotion and drama of human relationships, which serves to keep the reader engaged regardless of the reader's own ability to analyze the clues Dupin so deftly sorts, thereby allowing the reader to access and process the story on both an emotional and an intellectual level. In this manner, through his shaping of the reader's perception of and response to the story, Poe once again serves to emphasize the synthesis of the imagination and the intellect.

The sailor shaved his face with a straight razor while the orangutan watched. *(Warren Price Photography / Shutterstock.com)*

Source: Catherine Dominic, Critical Essay on "The Murders in the Rue Morgue," in *Short Stories for Students*, Gale, Cengage Learning, 2012.

> "ONLY IN UNREALISTIC CITIES DO CRIMES OCCUR AS FANTASTICAL AS AN ESCAPED BORNEO ORANGUTAN MURDERING A MOTHER AND DAUGHTER WITH A STOLEN SHAVING RAZOR."

Paul Woolf

In the following excerpt, Woolf maintains that the story presents a fatalistic view of urban life in general.

Today, the vast Palais Royal is one of central Paris's most popular tourist attractions. At the start of literature's first detective story, Edgar Allan Poe's "The Murders in the Rue Morgue" (1841), the first demonstration of detective ability takes place within the shadow of this great building.

The story's unnamed narrator and its hero, Auguste Dupin, take one of their customary nocturnal walks "amid the wild lights and shadows of the populous city," seeking "that infinity of mental excitement" only to be found in the modern metropolis (Poe, *Tales* [*Tales of Mystery and Imagination*]). "We were strolling one night down a long dirty street, in the vicinity of the Palais Royal," the narrator says. "Being both, apparently, occupied with thought, neither of us had spoken a syllable for fifteen minutes at least." At this point, Dupin speaks and, to the narrator's astonishment, reveals that he has been mind-reading—following perfectly his companion's train of thought during this quarter hour of silence. He recounts every step in a long series of thoughts that runs from street paving to astronomy to a theater performance. Dupin explains his method: not telepathy, but a display of what the narrator calls "analytical power," consisting of intense observation and attention to detail, an apparently infallible understanding of the human psyche, an "illimitable" education, and a rigorous application of deductive logic.

The scene lays out the techniques that Dupin will use as he goes on to investigate and solve the terrible crime at the heart of "The Murders in the Rue Morgue"—the brutal murder and mutilation of a mother and daughter in the bedroom of their home. The police are without "the shadow of a clue" as to how, why, and by whom these murders were committed. Dupin alone is able to work out that the culprit is, famously, a razor-wielding orangutan, escaped from its owner, a French sailor.

Stories of criminals and detectives were, of course, a feature of newspapers and novels long before Poe, but it was in his three stories about Dupin—what he called "tales of ratiocination" (Brand 104)—that the literary genre that we recognize today as detective fiction first emerged. Poe established its fundamental formulaic elements: recurring central characters and a story structure that follows the process of detection: the introduction of the detective, the statement of an apparently insoluble problem, the investigation, and finally the detective's revelatory explanation of events. "The Murders in the Rue Morgue" has thus been described as "the founding text" of detective fiction (Nickerson 6).

Historians of detective fiction agree that the genre's rise to prominence in America and Europe during the nineteenth century was intrinsically connected to the rapid, unprecedented growth of cities. Urban crimes provided the source material, and the ever-increasing urban population offered an audience eager to consume stories that reflected its paranoia about the dangers of city life. In the proliferation of new periodicals, the urban publishing industry supplied the ideal vehicle for an episodic, popular literary form. The conventional critical view is that detective fiction achieved its enormous, enduring popularity because it put forward accounts of the new urban experience that were ultimately comforting for its largely city-dwelling audience. Intended primarily for a bourgeois, conservative readership, early detective fiction, according to the argument, offered a reassuring perspective of urban life, in which through the application of scientific reasoning—"ratiocination"—the detective renders the city knowable, its mysteries solvable, its relentlessly multiplying lower classes and immigrant populations controllable, its criminals able to be captured.

In a 1998 article, Philip Howell restates this outlook succinctly: "The force of the anxieties raised by the modern city is absorbed and repelled by the reassurance that the city can through description be known and by knowledge be controlled. This ideological claim to know the city seems to enter into the formal structure of detective fiction." Certainly, such an "ideological claim" seems subtly present when Dupin tracks his companion's thoughts at the beginning of "The Murders in the Rue Morgue." This first demonstration of Dupin's "analytical power" is staged, notably, in an exterior, public space rather than in either of the interior, private spaces in which we have previously encountered him: the "obscure library" where the narrator and Dupin first meet and the "grotesque mansion" where they live. We are invited to notice the connection between the duo's pedestrian movement along the city's streets and the process of detection, between the material geography of the metropolis and Dupin's "analytical" methods of investigation. Indeed, the narrator later describes that intellectual process in terms of walking through physical space:

> There are few persons who have not [...] amused themselves in retracing the *steps* by which particular conclusions of their own minds have been attained [...] he who attempts it for the first time is astonished by the apparently illimitable *distance* and incoherence between the starting-point and the goal. (emphasis added)

Dupin reinforces the association between a person's inner thoughts and his or her physical progress through the city streets when he uses the same word a few paragraphs later: "'I had correctly followed your *steps*'" (emphasis added). It is as if Dupin can chart the sequences of a person's thoughts and simultaneously their actions in and movements through the city: that, theoretically, to know one is to know the other. In this sense, Dupin's detective ability is presented both as mastery of other individuals' thought processes and of the "topography" of the city.

Howell goes on to show how today's detective stories often resist this kind of "ideological claim"—that it is possible for the city and its myriad individuals to be comprehended and controlled—and represent the city instead as an unknowable, irredeemably dangerous place. I want to suggest here that in "The Murders in the Rue Morgue," the very "founding text" of detective fiction, Poe too ultimately depicts the city as beyond control. Dupin may be able to trace a person's "'steps,'" literal and figurative, but such acts of intellectual brilliance do not necessarily bring order to the modern metropolis. Poe portrays an urban milieu that is characterized by a symbiotic relationship between rampant commercialism and commercialized sexual pleasure. This relationship is, as much as any murderous orangutan, responsible for the atrocious killing of the two women. Poe's vision of urban life is not entirely pessimistic; after all, through the narrator, he evinces a sense of being energized by the city. Nonetheless, in my reading, Poe wants to draw attention to dangers unleashed by the city's expanding capitalist economy and its burgeoning commercial sex industry. Significantly, these dangers are not dispelled by the seemingly successful conclusion of Dupin's investigation. Poe's inclusion of the Palais Royal at the start of "The Murders in the Rue Morgue" gives our first clue to this understanding of the story.

I have never seen an analysis of the tale that more than mentions in passing the presence of the Palais. However, as the first named and first real building in the story, it might, not unreasonably, be expected to carry some symbolic value. Certainly, the history of the building chimes with the tale in interesting ways. Constructed in the 1630s by Louis XIV, the Palais was a royal residence until 1789, when it became "the birthplace, the propaganda-centre and the barometer of revolution" where "radicals [...] declaimed speeches [...] paraded heads on pikes and organised the attack on the Bastille" (Mansel 42). In 1830, the Palais was again "the focus of riots and demonstrations" (Mansel 290). Critics have proffered numerous reasons that Poe selected Paris as the location for his three narratives of crime, disorder, and detection, among them the city's unrivaled notoriety during the early and mid-1800s as a place of rampant criminality (Kalifa 178–79), its "generally sinister atmosphere" (Méral 11), and its then very recent history of social turmoil (Irwin 340–56; Miller 327–30). Scholars have long suggested that Poe set the stories in Paris specifically to conjure up images of the bloody revolutions of 1789 and 1830 in the minds of his readers. The specific reference to the Palais is perhaps a pointer to such an interpretation. In solving the mystery of the murders, argue scholars such as John Irwin and Elise Lemire, Dupin, a "young gentleman of an excellent—indeed of an illustrious family," symbolically reverses the effects of the French Revolution. Understanding the uncontrollable orangutan as a figure for the revolutionary mob, they see Dupin reasserting aristocratic authority over a city terrified by a lower class uprising (Irwin 340–56; Lemire 177–204).

Such readings contend that Poe projects onto Paris his anxieties about American cities—specifically, about the frequent working-class riots that during the 1830s troubled Philadelphia and New York, the cities in which Poe lived while writing his detective stories. Through Dupin, Poe, who considered himself something of an aristocrat, fantasizes about restoring order to American cities.

... Readings of "The Murders in the Rue Morgue" that argue that Dupin, in solving the crime, restores order to the terrorized city are troubling. Dupin may provide the answer to the mystery of who killed the L'Espanayes, but he, in fact, does nothing to make the city safer. He does not put his time and his enormous brainpower into finding and securing the homicidal orangutan, which continues to roam free; he, instead, merely revels in uncovering its role in the killings, showing off to the narrator about the cleverness of his investigation and stagily duping the sailor. What is more, Poe's Dupin utterly absolves the sailor—the orangutan's greedy, irresponsible owner—of all culpability for bringing the animal into Paris and then allowing it to escape while he is on his "sailors' frolic." Dupin is uncharacteristically repetitive when he announces, "[Y]ou are innocent of the atrocities in the Rue Morgue," using six different phrases in one passage to affirm the sailor's guiltlessness. Dupin permits the sailor to go free to recapture and sell the orangutan, as he had always intended, and Poe seems insistent that we notice this. In other words, Poe draws attention to the fact that Dupin does nothing to interrupt, regulate, or even punish the economic and sexual activities that bring disorder to the city. He just solves the puzzle.

Dupin states that his primary motivation for investigating the case is to exercise his intellectual powers. With that goal achieved, his interest ends. But one can discern a more secretive motive. Both Leo Lemay and Graham Robb have argued that Dupin and the unnamed, presumably male narrator are more than friends, but are lovers. One could offer a plausible reading of the story that takes this a step further and interprets the relationship as one of homosexual prostitution. Here, our narrator is effectively a sex tourist in Paris, a city, as Michael Sibalis describes, that decriminalized homosexuality in 1789 and that was known for homosexual as well as heterosexual prostitution. The narrator pays for the "treasure" of Dupin's company when he bankrolls their shared home. Such a reading would argue that Dupin—once impoverished, now a kept man—is as dependent on the city's sexual commerce as the prostitutes of the Palais, and does nothing to interfere with it because it provides him too with a good living.

However, something more seems to be going on that invokes Howell's statement about the "ideological claim" of detective fiction—to show the city to be both knowable and controllable—and to the Palais Royal and Dupin's opening display of detective brilliance in its shadow. First, however, it is useful to look at Poe's claims regarding detective fiction during the writing of "The Mystery of Marie Rogêt." The history of the tale's composition has been the subject of much critical discussion, with Walsh's *Poe the Detective* (1968) and Daniel Stashower's *The Beautiful Cigar Girl* (2006) dedicated to recounting Poe's investigative work into the Mary Rogers case. The first two installments of "Rogêt" ["The Mystery of Marie Rogêt"] were published in late 1842, when the real-life Rogers murder was still a mystery to police and press alike. Poe, at this stage, declared himself confident that his narrative would actually reveal Rogers's killer and would point to useful extratextual truths about crime and detection, telling a potential publisher:

> [. . .] I believe not only have I demonstrated the fallacy of the general idea—that the girl was the victim of a gang of ruffians—but have *indicated the assassin* in a manner which will give renewed impetus to investigation. My main object, nevertheless, as you will readily understand, is an analysis of the true principles which should direct inquiry in similar cases. (*Letters* 112–13; emphasis in original)

However, at this point, new information came to light in the Rogers case that forced Poe to reconsider his planned ending. Poe delayed the third and final installment until later in 1843, ostensibly to allow him to conduct further research and amend the draft version of the story's finale. Before the last installment, Poe had laid the groundwork for Dupin's revelation that the "young naval officer" committed the murder. The new evidence, however, strongly suggested that Rogers's death was the result of a botched abortion. Poe left the conclusion more open ended to incorporate the possibility that the abortion was behind the tragedy. Poe made further amendments before the story was republished in 1845, discounting the idea that the deaths of Mary and Marie are analogous:

> [. . . L]et it not for a moment be supposed that [. . .] it is my covert design to hint at an extension of the parallel [between Mary and Marie], or even to suggest that the measures adopted in Paris for the discovery of the assassin of a *grisette,* or measures founded in any similar ratiocination, would produce any similar result. (emphasis in original)

Dana Brand has argued persuasively that Poe never seriously believed that Dupin's "method" could solve real crimes and that Poe's assertion that his tale constituted "an analysis of the true principles which should direct inquiries in similar cases"—in other words, that detective fiction could somehow solve real crimes—was, in truth, no more than a ploy to sell the story. Poe himself had said of the stories, "'[P]eople think them more ingenious than they are—on account of their method and their air of method'" and had asked of "The Murders in the Rue Morgue," "'[W]here is the ingenuity of unraveling a web which you yourself (the author) have woven for the express purpose of unraveling?'" (qtd. in Brand 104). Brand adds, "Poe understood the methods of the detective story to be a hoax, an air of method, just as the flaneurs who wrote for the magazines presumably did not believe that they could actually read a person's entire history at a glance" (104). I believe that the Dupin stories slyly acknowledge that they are, in this sense, a "hoax." And it is here that the Palais Royal again becomes important.

As I have shown, the Palais is included at the start of "The Murders in the Rue Morgue" because, with its heady, flammable cocktail of sex and commerce, it is, to some extent, a microcosm of the whole of Paris itself, in turn, the epitome of the modern city as Poe envisages it. As Poe knew from his experiences living in Baltimore, Philadelphia, Richmond, and New York, American cities were quickly becoming, or perceived to be becoming, just like Paris, that is, hotbeds of "sin and merchandise." Indeed, just a few years after "The Murders in the Rue Morgue," Poe's friend Nathaniel Willis referred to the "imminent Paris-ification of New York" in a magazine article (qtd. in Brand 76). At first glance, Poe seems to show that Paris—and, by extension, American cities—can be known, their mysteries solved, by the application of scientific reasoning such as Dupin's. After all, Dupin's first act of detection involves demonstrating mastery of the streets around the Palais, the very epicenter and embodiment of urban evils.

However, although Poe begins his story with a sense of geographical verisimilitude, placing Dupin and the narrator next to the Palais, the Paris of "The Murders in the Rue Morgue" soon becomes a semi-imaginary place as the narrative progresses. The Palais is one of only a handful of real locations named in the tale. Otherwise, as William Henry Smith noted in an 1847 review, Poe demonstrates "a disregard for accuracy" in his depiction of the French capital (Walker 221–22). "There is no want of streets and passages," Smith observes, "but no Parisian would find them, or find them in the juxtaposition he has placed them." Poe "misname[s]" or simply invents many of the streets that he mentions in the tale. Even the Rue Morgue itself is a fabrication. Smith finds it "a surprise, that one so partial to detail should not have more frequently profited by the help which a common guidebook, with its map, might have given him." Of course, Poe—an expert on Paris and a writer usually methodically consistent in his use of references—could easily have made his story topographically accurate if he had so wished. Instead, he uses real streets and buildings, such as the Palais, to draw us into believing that his is a truthful depiction of Paris. By using some genuine place-names in the stories, Poe invites the reader to compare Dupin's city to the real Paris, as Smith seems to have done. But readers who sit with a map of Paris open alongside the book containing Poe's detective stories will be frustrated if they attempt to follow the movements of the fictional characters along the "real" streets. They will soon find themselves searching for imaginary avenues and wondering why two streets that are supposed to adjoin are, on the actual map, miles apart. We learn to trust Dupin's methods in a scene in which the process of detection is systematically built into these city streets, in which the "steps" involved in tracking a person's thoughts are the same as the "steps" that one takes as one moves through the city. It is as if, by following on a map the narrator and Dupin's walk, one can also follow the twists and turns of Dupin's detective work, as if the secret of solving crimes is simply a matter of plotting a route on a map. However, Poe then asks us to notice that the appearance of geographically rearranged and fictional streets undermines the story's apparent topographical verisimilitude. Dupin's "analytical" process of detection may be imbedded into those streets, but if we cannot trust (the narrator's description of) the street layout, should we also distrust Dupin's detective work, given that even as we are learning to trust his intellectual process, we are being told that it exists only in a nonexistent city? It is, Poe seems teasingly to be telling us, as much a work of fiction as is his Paris; it is a "hoax," and we would get as lost in trying to solve a crime by following Dupin's intellectual reasoning as we would in trying to navigate Paris by following the story's "mapping" of the city.

I would suggest, then, that Poe asks us instead to recognize this Paris as an unrealistic city. Only in unrealistic cities do crimes occur as fantastical as an escaped Borneo orangutan murdering a mother and daughter with a stolen shaving razor. And only in unrealistic places can a brilliant man single-handedly solve such "outré" crimes, as Dupin calls them. What Dupin cannot do is tackle the real problems of modern urban life—problems that Poe's readers would have identified through his references to the Palais Royal, theaters and sailors. In the story, Dupin both literally and figuratively walks away from the Palais and into a world of fiction. Poe asks us to understand that Dupin's ability to solve urban crime exists only on a fictional plane. One might legitimately argue that in "The Murders in the Rue Morgue," Poe moves from describing Paris authentically and toward a more imaginary version of the city for precisely the opposite reason: It is because he wants to make this city function as a symbol of all cities, and to show that Dupin's methods are as applicable in New York and Philadelphia as in the French capital, that he must avoid leading readers to believe this is a story solely about the actual Paris. However, when Dupin makes no effort to recapture the orangutan and goes out of his way to declare the sailor innocent of all responsibility, Poe draws our attention to the fact that the real problems of modern urban life have been untouched by his hero's investigation. Even Dupin, with his incredible "analytical power" and astonishing detective logic, can do nothing to regulate the real city. Far from instigating the "ideological claim" of detective fiction that Howell describes, to demonstrate the modern city to be knowable and controllable, Poe instead makes us aware that, although a genius may be able to solve a bizarre crime in a semifictional city in a work of literature, there are much more powerful forces still operating unchecked in the real city: sex and money.

"IF THE GROWTH OF PROFESSIONALISM IS A REGULARLY CHARTED, ORGANIZATIONAL CONSTANT THROUGHOUT THE THREE TALES, THE READER WOULD EXPECT SOME SIGN OF THIS AT THE OUTSET, AND INDEED THIS SIGN IS THERE."

Source: Paul Woolf, "Prostitutes, Paris, and Poe: The Sexual Economy of Edgar Allan Poe's 'The Murders in the Rue Morgue,'" in *Clues*, Vol. 25, No. 1, Fall 2006, pp. 6–19.

William Crisman

In the following excerpt, Crisman examines detective Dupin's professional status in "The Murders in the Rue Morgue" as a psychological statement about Poe.

The reader of Poe's Dupin stories is caught between two contrary models of Dupin's professional status. On the one hand, Susan Beegel considers it "obvious" that Dupin is the "prototypical amateur detective" and thus by definition not a professional at all. Indeed, on a different level of theoretical discourse, Jacques Lacan experiences Dupin's interest in fees as a "clash with the rest" of "The Purloined Letter." On the other hand, in such neo-historicist readings as Terence Whalen's, Dupin appears so money-focused that the actual solution to his mysteries becomes unimportant, and Dupin becomes the extreme opposite of the amateur puzzle solver. Adjudicating between such views requires exploring the kind of professional Dupin is as well as Poe's motive in creating such a professional.

Dupin is, of course, not a professional investigator of the movie sort with a sign outside, a receptionist, and a regular procession of clients. He also is not, on the other hand, merely a disinterested puzzle solver, in spite of his claim in "Murders in the Rue Morgue" that his "ultimate object is only the truth." In fact, following the Dupin stories in their self-conscious sequence from "The Murders in the Rue Morgue" through "The Mystery of Marie Roget" to "The Purloined Letter" shows the development of an increasing professionalism.

Such professionalism seems only reasonable given Dupin's background. A member of "an illustrious family" who "had been reduced to such poverty that the energy of his character succumbed beneath it," Dupin would naturally be interested in making money, especially since his tastes in life include buying "very rare" books ("Rue Morgue"). Dupin does not simply exist in an atmosphere of books, as Jacques Derrida rightly points out, but in a world of books as pricey commodities.

Many readers, Richard Wilbur among them, have noted the similarity in analytical thought between Dupin and Legrande of "The Gold Bug," and the reference to Dupin's character as "succumbing" to the force of poverty also recalls the parallel social condition of Legrande. Legrande's poverty not only signals lack of money and possessions but also betokens social disgrace verging on scandal, a "mortification" that has "infected" him with near madness. Moneylessness produces a deep mental wound, explicitly in Legrande's becoming a hermit, and implicitly in informing Dupin's tastes. Himself a near hermit in at least the first two detection stories, he scorns men "who wore windows in their bosoms," literally shutters his own windows, and adopts a practice of living in near darkness illuminated by "a couple of tapers which... threw out... only the feeblest of rays." Only with the "advent of true Darkness" does he go into public to perform "quiet observation" without being himself observed ("Rue Morgue"). Such a desire is more than the "freak of fancy" that the narrator fatuously sees. It is also not as complicated as George Grella would make it, seeing the love of night as a sign from Poe that Dupin actually is the criminal he pretends to seek. Financial and social embarrassment is the motive here. As Poe emphasizes in "The Philosophy of Furniture," true aristocracy is not the "aristocracy of dollars." The aristocrat distinguishes between kinds of money. Still, if money does not define nobility, nobility is nonetheless impossible in poverty, and it is impoverishment rather than social declassifying of some other sort that wounds characters like Legrande and Dupin.

That the narrator does not consciously name embarrassment over loss of money and class as Dupin's motive in seeking darkness only signals the narrator's relative lack of insight, an obtuseness long recognized as essential to the sort of "Dr. Watson" figure the narrator represents. As a sign of obtuseness in this case, the narrator explains Dupin's desire to tell his family history as a product of his being French and hence confessional ("Rue Morgue"). The narrator does not understand Dupin's compulsive engagement with this past, mortifying fall from financial grace. As John T. Irwin ingeniously shows in his analysis of Dupin's opening "mind reading" act in "Murders in the Rue Morgue," sensitivity to lost class pervades Dupin's every thought, even where class is not at all at the forefront of Dupin's conscious discussion. The mystery stories' culmination in "The Purloined Letter" implicitly allows Dupin the social mobility to associate with kings, queens, and ministers and to regain by association the aristocratic station and fortune he has lost. Shawn Rosenheim points out the parallel between the royal figures in the plot and the face cards in the whist game the narrator celebrates in "Murders in the Rue Morgue": winning entails royalty, and by "The Purloined Letter" Dupin has insinuated himself into a royal flush.

One can trace this fantasy of recovering nobility in Poe's Dupin-like characters as well, as has already been suggested for Legrande of "The Gold Bug." It has been remarked that the night wandering narrator of "The Man of the Crowd" "assumes the role of a 'Monsieur Dupin'" when this figure discerns the pursued old man's one possibly criminal act, carrying a hidden weapon, what the narrator describes as a "diamond and a dagger." Crime in his imagination requires a jeweled poinard, and even in the most impoverished part of town the narrator imagines himself into a murder at court. Of course, Legrande and the narrator of "Man of the Crowd" may differ from Dupin in important respects, but they nevertheless seem to combine night wandering or analysis with Dupin's social characteristics, the traumatic loss of aristocracy and the imaginary attempt to regain it.

Given this obsession with recovering station and money lost, professionalism on Dupin's part is not surprising. It is not, however, as Terence Whalen would have it, a professionalism that suddenly springs up in "Mystery of Marie Roget," making Dupin a figure catastrophically lapsing from Enlightenment "free thinker to hired intellectual." As Christopher Rollason says, Dupin's evolution as professional is "gradual," starting with "Murders in the Rue Morgue," not a sudden plunge. But Rollason joins a line of readers who see the Dupin stories, in Derrida's words, as "drift[ing]" from one to another, or who more radically, like Terry Martin, see no connection between the "Dupins" of the three stories at all.

If the growth of professionalism is a regularly charted, organizational constant throughout the three tales, the reader would expect some sign of this at the outset, and indeed this sign is there. The first connection between Dupin and the narrator is billed as a monetary exchange. Finding in Dupin a "treasure beyond price," the narrator exchanges for it "the expense of renting" their rooms ("Rue Morgue"). Even the narrator's vantage for observing the stories' events is one for which Dupin implicitly barters a piece of his "treasure." Interestingly, over the course of the three stories this fungible rental property, "time eaten" and "tottering" in "Murders in the Rue Morgue," becomes a congenial place of "luxury" with a "back library" in "The Purloined Letter." Lacan misremembers when he calls the Dupin of "The Purloined Letter" a "virtual pauper." Dupin has achieved professional success, and the professional detective's office is born, from what is from the start a professional agreement between the narrator and Dupin made in response to Dupin's pain of money lost.

The implied exchange of "treasure" for "expense" seems to give Dupin unconscious incentive to pursue a model of exchange. His interest in the grisly "murders" in the Rue Morgue comes not from some abstract interest in puzzle solving but from the identity of one of the killings' incidental figures. Adolphe Le Bon, a bank clerk, had attended the elder victim to her residence "with . . . 4000 francs"; this same Le Bon, Dupin says, "once rendered me a service for which I am not ungrateful." Given Le Bon's duties the reader has to assume the "service" in question entailed giving or lending money; the investigation into the Rue Morgue murders then is on its way toward becoming detective services rendered for fees paid, though at this early stage the professional arrangement is a very hazy, informal one (service as repayment or compensation for financial favor).

Moreover, in "Murders in the Rue Morgue" Dupin seems to be receiving a lesson in fee structures. When he creates the ruse that he has caught the Corsican's killer ape, the Corsican promises "to pay a reward . . .—that is to say, any thing in reason." Later, newspapers report that on recapturing the animal the Corsican sells it to the zoo "for . . . a very large sum." Dupin always reads the newspapers. The sole form of evidence in "Mystery of Marie Roget," in "Murders in the Rue Morgue" the newspapers give Dupin a first inkling of what "any thing within reason" might mean when applied to "rewards."

As might be expected in a genuinely compact series of stories, the first tale provides the hero with learning experiences that inform the series. Burton Pollin points out as peculiar Dupin's remark in "Murders in the Rue Morgue" that observation has become only "of late, a species of necessity" for him ("Rue Morgue"). The peculiarity disappears, however, if the story is taken as an early, experimental phase in Dupin's self-education. "Observation," along with other skills and techniques, are developing "of late" as responses to "necessities" in Dupin's mental life. . . .

Source: William Crisman, "Poe's Dupin as Professional: The Dupin Stories as Serial Text," in *Studies in American Fiction*, Vol. 23, No. 2, Autumn 1995, pp. 215–29.

J. Gerald Kennedy

In the following excerpt, Kennedy considers the thematic unease between rationality and imagination in Poe's detective stories.

In a canon of fiction preponderantly devoted to terror, madness, disease, death, and revivification, Poe's tales of ratiocination provide a revealing counterpoint in their idealization of reason and sanity. During the productive years 1841–44, Poe explored the theme of rational analysis in various ways: the three adventures of C. Auguste Dupin—"The Murders in the Rue Morgue" (1841), "The Mystery of Marie Rogêt" (1842–43), and "The Purloined Letter" (1844)—established the prototype of the modern detective story by focusing on the investigative methods of a master sleuth. Ratiocination led William Legrand to buried treasure in "The Gold Bug" (1843) and enabled the narrator of "Thou Art the Man" (1844) to solve a backwoods murder; analytical operations figured less prominently in "A Descent into the Maelström" (1841) and "A Tale of the Ragged Mountains" (1844). But publication of "The Purloined Letter" marked the last of Poe's investigative fiction; none of the tales after 1844 returned to the subject of ratiocination. Two basic questions to be considered here, then, are why Poe initially became interested in the detective story, and why, after the technical achievement of "The Purloined Letter," he abandoned the genre, reverting to the familiar materials of horror and the grotesque.

"FOR A BRIEF PERIOD IN POE'S CAREER, RATIOCINATION PERHAPS OFFERED A DISTRACTION FROM THE RECURRING NIGHTMARE OF DEATH AND DISINTEGRATION."

The significance of Poe's ratiocinative phase can perhaps be best understood in the context of his broader thematic concerns. The search for the figure in Poe's fictional carpet has produced myriad interpretations: Patrick F. Quinn has termed the Doppelgänger motif the "most characteristic and persistent" of Poe's fantasies, while Edward H. Davidson states that the "central bifurcation" in Poe lies between "two sides of the self, between emotion and intellect, feeling and the mind." Harry Levin sees the essential Poe hero as an "underground man" embodying "reason in madness," while more recently, Daniel Hoffman has identified "duplicity" or "the doubleness of experience" as Poe's chief theme. Behind the evident diversity of opinion about Poe's fundamental fictional concerns looms a point of focus: the author's preoccupation with the relationship between the mind, or rational consciousness, and the sensational influence of the world beyond the self. Constantly in Poe's fiction irrational forces and inexplicable phenomena threaten "the monarch Thought's dominion." In an important sense, his serious tales return continually to the process of reason—the way in which the mind orders and interprets its perceptions. Poe's narrators repeatedly seek a clarification of experience, only to discover, in the tales of terror, that rational explanation is not possible.

The condition of terror and uncertainty does not obtain, however, in the tales of ratiocination. Joseph Wood Krutch once lapsed into the assertion that "Poe invented the detective story in order that he might not go mad." The biographical fallacy aside, however, it is true that the ratiocinative tales posit a vision of reason and order not elsewhere evident in Poe's fiction. His detective hero, engaged in "that moral activity which *disentangles*," not only restores law and order to the world of mundane human affairs; he also explains the seemingly inexplicable, thereby demonstrating the ultimate comprehensibility of the world beyond the self. While the Gothic protagonist typically succumbs to a paroxysm of fear, uncertainty, or madness, the ratiocinator discerns the causes behind effects, proving that nature's laws are accessible to the man of reason. The emergence of this man of reason and his eventual disappearance from Poe's fiction can be observed in "The Man of the Crowd" (1840) and "The Oblong Box" (1844), tales which respectively signal the beginning and end of Poe's ratiocinative cycle....

II

In "The Murders in the Rue Morgue," Dupin says of Vidocq, the French minister of police: "He erred continually by the very intensity of his investigations. He impaired his vision by holding the object too close" (V). His remark succinctly defines the shortcoming of the bedeviled detective in "The Man of the Crowd." Poe describes precisely the opposite difficulty, though, in "The Oblong Box," a parody of the ratiocinative tale. Here the analytical narrator attempts to solve from a distance the mystery of an oblong box brought aboard a ship bound for New York. With comic pertinacity, he constructs an utterly wrongheaded interpretation, reached through an abstract contemplation of events. Considerably less complex than "The Man of the Crowd," "The Oblong Box" nevertheless employs the motif of self-deception, as Poe again pokes fun at "romantic busy-bodyism" and the inclination to play detective.

At the outset, the narrator offers another version of the heightened-consciousness syndrome: "I was, just at that epoch, in one of those moody frames of mind which make a man abnormally inquisitive about trifles" (V). A puzzling circumstance arouses his curiosity: Cornelius Wyatt, an artist-friend, has reserved three staterooms for a party which apparently includes only Wyatt, his new bride, and his two sisters. The intrigued narrator confides: "I busied myself in a variety of ill-bred and preposterous conjectures about this matter of the supernumerary stateroom. It was no business of mine, to be sure; but with none the less pertinacity did I occupy myself in attempts to resolve the enigma" (V). In busying himself with the affairs of Wyatt, the narrator identifies himself as a Poesque Paul Pry, a detached spectator regarding human experience primarily as a subject for analysis.

Further developments compound the mystery of the extra stateroom. On the eve of the ship's scheduled departure, the narrator learns that Mrs. Wyatt will not board the ship until the hour of sailing, thus postponing his introduction to the artist's bride. Unexplained "circumstances" then delay the departure nearly a week, and when Wyatt finally comes aboard with a heavily-veiled woman, he fails to introduce her to the narrator. A greater source of bafflement, though, is the oblong box placed in Wyatt's stateroom rather than the ship's hold. Disregarding the coffin-like dimensions of the box—which, as we discover later, actually contains the corpse of Mrs. Wyatt—the narrator concocts a theory rife with grotesque irony:

> The box in question was, as I say, oblong. It was about six feet in length by two and a half in breadth;—I observed it attentively, and like to be precise. Now this shape was *peculiar*; and no sooner had I seen it, than I took credit to myself for the accuracy of my guessing. I had reached the conclusion, it will be remembered, that the extra baggage of my friend, the artist, would prove to be pictures, or at least a picture; for I knew he had been for several weeks in conference with Nicolino:—and now here was a box which, from its shape, *could* possibly contain nothing in the world but a copy of Leonardo's *Last Supper*; and a copy of this very *Last Supper*, done by Rubini the younger, at Florence, I had known, for some time, to be in the possession of Nicolino. This point, therefore, I considered as sufficiently settled. I chuckled excessively when I thought of my acumen. (V)

With all his "precision," the narrator manages to overlook the most obvious interpretation of the oblong box; the smug reference to his "acumen" in effect announces the satirical point of the tale.

Like the narrator of "The Man of the Crowd," the aspiring detective in "The Oblong Box" is both intrigued and deceived by minute details. He suspects, for example, that the "peculiarly disgusting odor" emanating from the box derives from the paint used to letter an address on its side; he attributes Wyatt's melancholy appearance to an unhappy marriage. The disparity between the narrator's assumptions and the actual situation reveals itself best, however, in his effort to elicit the secret of the box from the mournful artist:

> I determined to commence a series of covert insinuations, or innuendoes, about the oblong box—just to let him perceive, gradually, that I was *not* altogether the butt, or victim, of his little bit of pleasant mystification. My first observation was by way of opening a masked battery. I said something about the "peculiar shape of *that* box"; and, as I spoke the words, I smiled knowingly, winked, and touched him gently with my fore-finger in the ribs. (V)

What the narrator believes to be cleverness is of course monumental indelicacy; the encounter throws Wyatt into a swoon and the narrator into further confusion.

Other misapprehensions beset the stupefied sleuth. Twice observing the supposed Mrs. Wyatt stealing into the extra stateroom, he concludes that Wyatt and his wife are on the verge of a divorce. Not until the end of the tale does he learn that the woman was Mrs. Wyatt's former maid masquerading as the wife of the artist to conceal from superstitious passengers the fact that the ship was transporting a corpse. More perverse than the divorce theory is his comment upon hearing Wyatt pry open his oblong box: "Mr. Wyatt, no doubt, according to custom, was merely giving the rein to one of his hobbies—indulging in one of his fits of artistic enthusiasm. He had opened his oblong box, in order to feast his eyes on the pictorial treasure within" (V). The reference to the "pictorial treasure" could scarcely be more ironic, for textual evidence indicates that Mrs. Wyatt has been dead at least ten days.

Though not a major work in the Poe canon, "The Oblong Box" delivers, through the narrator's grotesque misinterpretations, a clever satiric version of the detective hero. The headnote to "The Purloined Letter" furnishes a penetrating comment on the narrator's self-deception: "Nil sapientiae odiosius acumine nimio" (There is nothing more inimical to wisdom than too much acumen, VI). His failure provides another instance of the ratiocinative process run amuck. "Truth is not always in a well," Dupin remarks in "The Murders in the Rue Morgue" (IV); neither is it found in abstract analysis divorced from that world of human realities which it proposes to explain.

III

Nearly delimiting the period of Poe's interest in ratiocination by their dates of publication, "The Man of the Crowd" and "The Oblong Box" help to clarify, by the negative example of "failed" detectives, Poe's view of the nature and scope of the ratiocinative process. Both narrators resemble the comically ineffectual Prefect of

Police in the Dupin stories, being "somewhat too cunning to be profound" (IV). Like him, they overlook the obvious and find a way "*de nier ce qui est, et d'expliquer ce qui n'est pas.*" Yet the differences between the two tales are even more significant. Initiating the ratiocinative cycle, "The Man of the Crowd" dramatizes the effort to escape the conditions of terror and hypersensitivity through a rigidly analytical system of thought. But because the narrator has not yet been delivered from the nightside experience, because the principles of ratiocination have not yet been mastered, he falls prey to the same sensational influences which distort the perceptions of Roderick Usher, William Wilson, and the narrator of "Ligeia." However, "The Oblong Box" presents the opposite extreme—a narrator so detached from the subject of his investigation, so deluded by his own intellectual pretensions, that his ratiocination achieves no resemblance to actuality. The tale portrays the *reductio ad absurdum* of rational analysis: reason dissociated from reality.

Between these two poles of experience, C. Auguste Dupin balances imaginative involvement with analytical detachment. Like his adversary in "The Purloined Letter," Dupin is both poet and mathematician. As a mathematician he understands the "Calculus of Probabilities" which ordinarily governs natural phenomena. As a poet, though, he recognizes the surprising paradoxes of human experience which make an "ordinary" case sometimes more difficult to solve than one "excessively outré." According to Poe's epistemology, the two modes of cognition are inextricably related; "the *truly* imaginative [are] never otherwise than analytic," he writes in "The Murders in the Rue Morgue." But both methods of knowing are ancillary to the kind of pure reasoning to which Dupin alludes in his remark about the letter thief: "As poet *and* mathematician, he would reason well; as mere mathematician, he could not have reasoned at all" (VI). The detective's ability to combine imagination and analysis causes the narrator of "The Murders in the Rue Morgue" to recall "the old philosophy of the Bi-Part Soul" and imagine a "double Dupin—the creative and the resolvent" (IV). In the same tale Poe reminds us that "intuition" has nothing to do with the analyst's solutions, which are obtained "by the very soul and essence of method" (IV). Dupin's method typically involves both a meticulous examination of physical evidence (involvement in the world of men) and a dispassionate consideration of the case as a whole (withdrawal to the realm of abstract thought). Out of this dialectical tension between involvement and detachment, poetry and mathematics, emerges the Truth which is the detective's goal.

Significant though Dupin's conquest of the unknown may seem in the context of Poe's artistic quest for a rational vision of experience, the fact remains that the author discarded his detective hero after "The Purloined Letter." A partial explanation comes from Poe himself, who wrote to Philip Pendleton Cooke in 1846: "These tales of ratiocination owe most of their popularity to being something in a new key. I do not mean to say that they are not ingenious—but people think them more ingenious than they are—on account of their method and *air* of method. In the 'Murders in the Rue Morgue,' for instance, where is the ingenuity of unravelling a web which you yourself (the author) have woven for the express purpose of unravelling?" That Poe came to see the detective story as a rather superficial and mechanical exercise in mystification seems evident from his comment to Cooke. That realization also appears to inform "The Oblong Box," where the narrator's failure illustrates the speciousness of an intellectual system out of touch with the problems of human fallibility and mortality. Poe's fundamental vision of the human condition, the vision which even through ratiocination he could not at last escape, saw man as the predestined victim of the Conqueror Worm. In abandoning the detective story, Poe finally acknowledged that ratiocination answers no questions of genuine importance, clarifies nothing about the hopes and fears of humankind. For a brief period in Poe's career, ratiocination perhaps offered a distraction from the recurring nightmare of death and disintegration. But he could never fully recover, through his fictional man of reason, the reassuring eighteenth-century myth of a rationally designed universe; the inescapable terrors of the imagination made that task impossible.

Source: J. Gerald Kennedy, "The Limits of Reason: Poe's Deluded Detectives," in *American Literature*, Vol. 47, No. 2, May 1975, pp. 184–96.

SOURCES

"Blacks Upbeat about Black Progress, Prospects," in *Pew Social & Demographic Trends*, http://pewsocialtrends.org/2010/01/12/blacks-upbeat-about-black-progress-prospects (accessed March 8, 2011).

"A Brief History of the American Abolitionist Movement," in *American Abolitionism*, http://americanabolitionist.liberalarts.iupui.edu/brief.htm (accessed March 8, 2011).

Bryant, John, "E. A. Poe and T. B. Thorpe: Two Models of Deceit," in *Melville and Repose: The Rhetoric of Humor in the American Renaissance*, Oxford University Press, 1993, pp. 88–99.

Carlson, Eric W., "Edgar Allan Poe," in *Dictionary of Literary Biography*, Vol. 74, *American Short-Story Writers before 1880*, edited by Bobby Ellen Kimbel, Gale Research, 1988, pp. 303–22.

Church, Joseph, "'To Make Venus Vanish': Misogyny as Motive in Poe's 'Murders in the Rue Morgue,'" in *ATQ* (*American Transcendental Quarterly*), Vol. 20, No. 2, 2006, pp. 407–19.

Colton, George, Review of *Tales by Edgar A. Poe*, in *American Review*, Vol. 2, No. 3, September 1845, pp. 306–309.

Cooke, P. P., Review of *Tales by Edgar A. Poe*, in *American Prose (1607–1865)*, edited by Walter Cochrane Bronson, University of Chicago Press, 1916, p. 689; originally published in *Southern Literary Magazine*, 1848.

Crisman, William, "Poe's Dupin as Professional, the Dupin Stories as Serial Text," in *Studies in American Fiction*, Vol. 23, No. 2, 1995, pp. 215–30.

Fisher, Benjamin F., "Poe and the Gothic Tradition," in *The Cambridge Companion to Edgar Allan Poe*, Cambridge University Press, 2002, pp. 72–91.

Hutchisson, James M., "*Graham's Magazine*, 'The Penn,' and the Red Death (1841–1843)," in *Poe*, University Press of Mississippi, 2005, pp. 108–48.

Kennedy, J. Gerald, "Edgar Allan Poe, 1809–1849: A Brief Biography," in *A Historical Guide to Edgar Allan Poe*, Oxford University Press, 2001, pp. 19–62.

Lemay, J. A. Leo, "The Psychology of 'The Murders in the Rue Morgue,'" in *On Poe: The Best from American Literature*, edited by Louis J. Budd and Edwin H. Cady, Duke University Press, 1993, pp. 223–46; originally published in *American Literature*, Vol. 54, No. 2, May 1982, pp. 165–66.

Lowell, J. R., Review of *Tales by Edgar A. Poe*, in *American Prose (1607–1865)*, edited by Walter Cochrane Bronson, University of Chicago Press, 1916, p. 689; originally published in *Graham's Magazine*, 1845.

Monnet, Agnieszka Soltysik, Introduction to *The Poetics and Politics of the American Gothic: Gender and Slavery in Nineteenth-Century American Literature*, Ashgate Publishing, 2010, pp. 1–30.

Murray, John F., "A Century of Tuberculosis," in *American Journal of Respiratory and Critical Care Medicine*, Vol. 169, 2004, pp. 1181–86, http://ajrccm.atsjournals.org/cgi/content/full/169/11/1181 (accessed March 9, 2011).

Poe, Edgar Allan, "The Murders in the Rue Morgue," in *Selected Poetry and Prose of Poe*, edited by T. O. Mabbott, Modern Library, 1951, pp. 162–92.

Quinn, Arthur Hobson, "At the Summit—The Editor of *Graham's Magazine*," in *Edgar Allan Poe: A Critical Biography*, Appleton-Century-Crofts, 1941, pp. 305–45.

Review of *Tales by Edgar A. Poe*, in *American Prose (1607–1865)*, edited by Walter Cochrane Bronson, University of Chicago Press, 1916, p. 689; originally published in *Blackwood's Magazine*, 1847.

Robertson, John Mackinnon, "Poe," in *Edgar Allan Poe*, edited by Harold Bloom, Infobase Publishing, 2008, pp. 136–43; originally published in *New Essays toward a Critical Method*, 1897.

"Tuberculosis Cases, Case Rates per 100,000 Population, Deaths and Death Rates per 100,000 Population, and Percent Change: United States, 1953–2007," in *Reported Tuberculosis in the United States, 2007*, Centers for Disease Control and Prevention Web site, 2007, p. 15, http://www.cdc.gov/tb/statistics/reports/2007/ (accessed March 9, 2011).

"Vital Statistics, Health, and Nutrition: Vital Statistics—Death Rates, Selected Causes, 1861 to 1945," in *Historical Statistics of the United States, 1789–1945*, U. S. Department of Commerce, Bureau of the Census Web site, 1949, p. 48, http://www.census.gov/compendia/statab/past_years.html (accessed March 9, 2011).

FURTHER READING

Ackroyd, Peter, *Poe: A Life Cut Short*, Nan A. Talese, 2009.

> Ackroyd explores Poe's life and writings, finding connections between the traumatic events in Poe's life, such as the premature death of his mother, and the tragic situations Poe treats in his works.

Kopley, Richard, *Edgar Allan Poe and the Dupin Mysteries*, Palgrave Macmillan, 2008.

> Kopley offers a critical examination of the three Poe stories featuring the amateur detective Dupin and discusses Poe's own sources of inspiration, as well as the influence Poe had on the later development of the genre.

Lowance, Mason, ed., *Against Slavery: An Abolitionist Reader*, Penguin Classics, 2000.

> In this collection, Lowance gathers the abolitionist writings of a number of prominent American authors and abolitionists, including William Lloyd Garrison, Frederick Douglass, and Ralph Waldo Emerson. While Poe was reticent about his own views, appearing to advocate a gradual end to slavery entailing the return of former slaves to Africa, many of his contemporaries, a number of them featured in Lowance's collection, spoke out forcefully and repeatedly against the institution of slavery.

Thomas, Ronald, *Detective Fiction and the Rise of Forensic Science*, Cambridge University Press, 2000.

Thomas explores the relationship between the nineteenth-century genesis and advancement of the genre of detective fiction and the development of the field of analysis known as forensics (scientific crime-scene investigation). The work includes discussions of the fiction of Poe, Charles Dickens, Nathaniel Hawthorne, and Arthur Conan Doyle, among others.

SUGGESTED SEARCH TERMS

Edgar Allan Poe

The Murders in the Rue Morgue

The Murders in the Rue Morgue AND Edgar Allan Poe

Poe AND detective fiction

Poe AND gothic fiction

Poe AND horror fiction

Poe AND mystery

Poe AND biography

Poe AND Dupin

Poe AND slavery

Poe AND premature death

Poe AND short story

The Night Face Up

JULIO CORTÁZAR

1956

"The Night Face Up" is a story by the twentieth-century Argentine writer Julio Cortázar. It was first published in his short-story collection *The End of the Game* in 1956. It is also available in *Blow-Up, and Other Stories*, another collection of Cortázar's, translated by Paul Blackburn.

The story is about a man who is involved in a minor accident while riding his motorcycle in a city. He is taken to the hospital and receives surgery. While under the influence of the surgery drugs and a fever, he has a nightmare in which he dreams he is a Motecan Indian being pursued by Aztec warriors many centuries ago. The warriors capture him and prepare him for sacrifice. The man wakes from the dream and then slips back into it again, and at the end of the story there is a twist that plays on the relationship between dream and reality: is the motorcyclist in the hospital dreaming of the Motecan, or is the Motecan having a strange dream about a city of the future?

The origins of the story are autobiographical. In 1952, Cortázar crashed his motorcycle in Paris when he tried to avoid a woman who was crossing the street. He was hospitalized, and the incident gave him the idea for "The Night Face Up." The story is notable not only for being a good example of the work of one of the masters of the short story but also because of the clever and ambiguous way the author plays with the relationship between dream and reality and creates a surprise ending.

Julio Cortázar *(Ulf Andersen / Getty Images)*

AUTHOR BIOGRAPHY

Cortázar was born in Brussels, Belgium, on August 26, 1914. His parents, Julio Jose Cortázar and Maria Herminia Descotte, were from Argentina, and his father was a diplomat. The family moved back to Argentina after World War I, when the young Cortázar was nearly four. Cortázar was raised in Banfield, a suburb of Buenos Aires. Beginning in 1935 he completed one year of study at the University of Buenos Aires, but then in 1937, he accepted a teaching position in a high school in a small provincial town. He made this decision to supplement the family income, since his father had left the family when Cortázar was still a child, and his mother and sister needed money.

Cortázar taught high school for five years and wrote many short stories during this time, but he made no attempt to publish them. In 1944, he moved to Mendoza, where he taught French literature at the University of Cuyo. His brief academic career ended the following year when he resigned rather than face dismissal for his political opposition to the newly elected government of Juan Perón.

For two years Cortázar was manager of the Argentine Publishing Association, and he also received certification as a translator. In 1951, he left Argentina to work in Paris as a freelance translator for the United Nations Educational, Scientific and Cultural Organization, better known as UNESCO. He retained this position and lived in Paris for most of the rest of his life.

Cortázar's first published short story appeared in an Argentine literary journal in 1946. In 1949, he published *Los Reyes* (*The Kings*), a dramatic prose poem, and in 1951, his first collection of short stories, *Bestiario*, was published. His second collection, *Final del juego* (*The End of the Game*; 1956) contains the story "La noche boca arriba" ("The Night Face Up"). Cortázar published seven more short-story collections, the last being *Deshoras* (*Bad Timing*) in 1982. He was an acknowledged master of the short story.

Cortázar was also a major novelist. His first novel, *Los premios* (*The Winners*), was published in 1960. This was followed by *Rayuela* (*Hopscotch*) in 1963; *62/modela para armar* (*62: A Model Kit*) in 1968, and *Libro de Manuel* (*A Manual for Manuel*) in 1973.

Cortázar was politically active all his life and was a socialist and human rights advocate. He supported the Cuban Revolution of 1959, which established Fidel Castro in power. Cortázar visited Cuba in 1963.

Cortázar married Aurura Bernardez in 1953. Later in life, after their divorce, his companion was Carol Dunlop, who was also a collaborator. They wrote *Los autonautas del cosmopista* (*The Autonauts of the Cosmopike*), which was published in 1983, a year after Dunlop's death. Cortázar became a French citizen in 1981. He died of leukemia and heart disease in Paris on February 12, 1984.

PLOT SUMMARY

"The Night Face Up" begins as the unnamed male protagonist leaves a city hotel and goes to collect his motorcycle from where it is stored nearby. It is early morning, and he has an appointment to keep. He sits astride the motorcycle, looking forward to the ride.

He passes some stores on the main street and then rides onto a long residential street. At a crosswalk, a woman who was standing on the corner steps out in front of him, even though he has the green light. He brakes but cannot avoid an accident. He hears the woman scream, and then he loses consciousness.

He regains consciousness as several young men pull him out from under the bike. His knee and arm hurt and he feels nauseous. He learns that the woman suffered only minor injuries. The men take him to a local pharmacy, where someone gives him some medicine to swallow.

A police ambulance arrives and takes the man to the hospital. He does not feel badly injured, and he hears that the motorcycle has not suffered much damage. He is admitted to the hospital. Although he feels fine, he is X-rayed and then taken to surgery and given an anesthetic.

He dreams. In the dream he is a Motecan Indian in Mexico, fleeing at night from Aztec warriors, sometime between the fourteenth and sixteenth centuries. He is following a trail and trying to find somewhere to hide in the forest. He checks the stone knife he carries, and then an unexpected sound makes him stand still. He is frightened. But he hears nothing more and continues his journey. He can smell something foul.

He wakes up. The patient next to him tells him he will fall off the bed if he does not keep still. It is afternoon. His arm is in a plaster cast, and he is running a fever. He stays awake and listens to the talk of the patients near him. A nurse gives him an injection, and a young doctor checks on him.

Night falls. He still has a fever, which gives him a languid, hazy kind of feeling. He eats some broth and then falls asleep again.

Once more he dreams, picking up where he left off. He is running, but he has lost the trail. He knows he is surrounded and he crouches down. He grasps the amulet around his neck and prays to the goddess. His ankles are sinking in mud. Some kind of holy war has been going on for three days, and the Aztecs have already taken many prisoners.

He hears some cries and leaps up. He sees torches approaching him, and an enemy warrior leaps on him. The hunted man stabs his attacker, but then he is captured.

He wakes up in the hospital. The man in the next bed says that his restlessness is because of the fever. He tells him to drink some water.

The man drinks some mineral water and looks around the thirty-bed ward. His fever has eased. He tries to think back to the moment of the accident, but he cannot remember it. There is only a void in his mind when he tries to remember what happened, and this angers him. It is as if the void has lasted for an eternity. He falls asleep again.

He is lying on his back on a stone slab, bound by ropes. His amulet is gone, so he cannot pray. He hears kettledrums, which he associates with a feast. He realizes he is in the underground portion of a temple, awaiting his turn.

He hears a yell, and then another one, and he realizes that the man yelling is himself. He thinks of his friends in the other dungeons and of those who have already been sacrificed. He struggles against the ropes but is unable to free himself. The door opens and the priests' men approach. They untie him and carry him down a passageway. He knows he will soon be in the open, under the stars, and be taken up stairs to the sacrificial altar.

Suddenly he is back in the hospital, looking up at the ceiling. Everyone in the ward is asleep. He tries to rid himself of the disturbing images from the nightmare. He is reassured that he is now awake and it will soon be dawn, but he is drowsy and cannot keep his eyes open. He is back in the underground passageway and is about to reach the end. He sees the moon, even though he does not want to. He wants to get back to the hospital ward. They climb the steps and he sees bonfires and the sacrificial stone with blood on it. He desperately tries to wake up but sees the priest approaching him with a knife in his hand. He closes his eyes but now realizes that he will not wake up. He is awake now and has been dreaming about a strange city with lights that burn but produce no smoke. In that dream people had also picked him up off the ground and someone had also come to him with a knife. He is sure that he is truly the sacrificial victim.

CHARACTERS

Aztec Warriors

The Aztec warriors are the men who track down and capture the Motecan man, who manages to stab one of them in the chest but is powerless against the rest. They carry him to an underground cell in the temple. The Aztec warriors are taking part in a ritual war they call the war of the blossom.

Motecan Indian

The Motecan Indian is being hunted down by Aztec warriors as part of a ritual war against their enemies. He flees through a forest and tries to hide from them, but they find and capture him. He is imprisoned in an underground cell in the Aztec temple and then led down a passageway by the priest's acolytes. When he emerges from the tunnel, he sees the priest approaching him with a knife ready to kill him as a sacrifice. It may be that the Motecan man is the true protagonist of the story and that the motorcyclist is merely an alter ego in his dream, or it may be the other way around.

Motorcyclist

The motorcyclist is on his way to a morning appointment on his motorcycle when a woman steps into his path and there is an accident. He is taken to the hospital, where he receives surgery. He is not badly injured, but he does seem to suffer from a fever. While he is still under the influence of the drugs used in surgery, he has a nightmare in which he is being pursued and then captured by Aztec warriors. In the dream, he is imprisoned and then taken out for sacrifice. It is also possible that the motorcyclist is merely an alter ego in a dream of the Motecan man.

Other Patients

There are several other patients in the same hospital ward as the injured motorcyclist. One tells him to stop bouncing around or he will fall off the bed. Another tells him he is suffering from a fever and should drink some water. In his lucid moments, the motorcyclist listens to the sounds they make, such as their breathing and whispered conversation.

Police Guard

A police guard accompanies the injured man in the police ambulance after the accident. He tells him that his motorcycle has not been badly damaged.

Priest

A priest is briefly glimpsed near the end of the story. When the Motecan man is led out of the underground tunnel, he sees the priest coming toward him with a knife. The priest is to perform the human sacrifice.

Priests' Acolytes

The priests have four acolytes, or assistants, who come to get the Motecan man when he is imprisoned in a cell in the temple. They are naked except for loincloths, and they wear feathers in their hair. They seize the Motecan man and take him along a passageway. They are taking him to the priest for sacrifice.

Surgeon

The surgeon operates on the injured motorcyclist in the hospital. He is tall and thin, and the injured man glimpses the surgical knife in his hand.

Torchbearers

The torchbearers accompany the priests' acolytes when they go to collect the Motecan man from underground in the temple. Then they lead the way as the acolytes take the man for sacrifice.

Woman

As the motorcyclist drives through the city, a female pedestrian steps out in front of him, even though the traffic light is in his favor, causing an accident.

Young Men

Four or five young men help the motorcyclist immediately after the accident. They pull him out from under the motorcycle and reassure him that he is all right and his injuries are not serious.

THEMES

Ambiguity

After absorbing the surprising twist in the final paragraph, the question that most readers will ask is whether the motorcyclist is dreaming of being the Indian (as most of the story seems clearly to describe) or the Indian is dreaming of the modern city in which the motorcyclist lives (as the last paragraph suggests). There can be no definitive answer to this question, since the story is deliberately presented in a very ambiguous way. It is as if both realities are, or could be, true. The reality of each is attested to by the vivid sensory detail in which each world—the modern and the Aztec—is presented. There are no surrealistic, implausible, or impossible elements in either world, which might brand one or the other as a dream. They are each described in a very concrete, realistic manner. In addition, after the initial situation—the description of the accident

TOPICS FOR FURTHER STUDY

- Research dreams using online and print resources. How often do people dream? Why do we dream? What are some common dreams and how can they be interpreted? The Web site Dream Moods offers an excellent introduction to dreams. You may also consult *The Dream Book: A Young Person's Guide to Understanding Dreams*, by Patricia Garfield (2002). Study the offerings on the Web site and then choose one of the many forums and make a post or two, describing and explaining one of your dreams or otherwise contributing to the forum.
- Keep a dream journal for a week or so in which you record your dreams. Can you find any meaning in those dreams? Do any of the dreams, or any of the elements in the dreams, recur? Write a short story in which you incorporate dreaming in any way you choose.
- Create a digital interactive time line about the rise, achievements, and destruction of the Aztec Empire in central Mexico. Include elements that describe the political and economic structure, religion, and culture of the people, as well as the key events in their history. Use the time line to present the information to your class.
- Read "Axolotl," another short story by Cortázar that can be found in *Blow-Up, and Other Stories*, and compare it with "The Night Face Up." What themes do the two stories share? Write your response in an essay or on a blog site and invite your teacher and classmates to comment.

and the trip to the hospital—has been set up, each world is given about equal weight, with about a page devoted to each before the narrative switches back to the other world.

Time Travel

The story suggests the fluidity of time and perhaps of space. One man, the motorcyclist, seems to cross over or travel in time to experience something from a different period in history, several hundred years earlier.

There is no specified setting for the motorcyclist's story, so it could be in Europe, perhaps Paris, where the author lived and was himself involved in a motorcycle accident. In that case, the motorcyclist would have moved in both time and space, from one century and one continent to another.

Reincarnation

Given the fluidity of time and space in this story, another possibility is that the motorcyclist is experiencing not only another time period but further himself in an earlier incarnation. Cortázar had an interest in the theory of reincarnation (also called metempsychosis or transmigration of souls), in which the souls of the dead are reborn into new physical bodies. Is the motorcyclist somehow, stimulated by medicinal drugs and fever, reliving a past life, when he was a Motecan Indian? If this is so, the motorcyclist and the Indian would therefore be one and the same man, experiencing radically different moments in his soul's journey. The question of which is the dream and which the reality would then be moot, since both would be equally real.

There are many similarities between the way the two men are presented that give weight to the suggestion that they are the same man, seen at different times. Both lie on their backs, helpless. The motorcyclist's arm is in plaster and is suspended from an apparatus with weights and pulleys, so he cannot move freely. Similarly, the Indian, after being caught, is tied down on his back. The motorcyclist is also thirsty "as though he'd been running for miles" (which the Indian has); both are at the mercy of others and are approached by individuals wielding knives. In addition, one powerful simile seems to fuse the reality of the two men. The motorcyclist notices that after the X-ray, he feels the "still-damp negative lying on his chest like a black tombstone," an ominous image that foreshadows the sacrificial death of the Motecan Indian.

One interesting detail occurs when the man in the hospital bed tries to recall the moment of the accident but cannot. As he tries to remember, he gets angry because the moment seems impenetrable: "there was a void there, an emptiness he could not manage to fill." As he continues to think about it, he experiences "the feeling that this void, this nothingness, had lasted an eternity. No, not even time, more as if, in this

The story starts with a motorcycle accident. (*Danie Nel / Shutterstock.com*)

void, he had passed across something, or had run back immense distances."

Something is going on here that is a little more complex than a simple dream; it is as if he is leaping across some invisible barrier. The void that seems to him like nothing, or like an eternity, somehow contains all of time and space—or at least as much of it as this man, given his injured condition, is able to experience. The theory of metempsychosis applied to this story also suggests, of course, that just as the man in the hospital is reliving the climactic moments of a past incarnation, the Indian he then was is getting a foretaste of a future and an as-yet unknown and mysterious incarnation.

STYLE

Sensory Detail

Certain strands of imagery serve to link the two settings of the hospital and the Aztec war. The smell in the hospital provides the sensory stimulus that leads the man to dream of the smell of the swamp in the Aztec world. The sense of smell is very prominent in that world: the smell of the swamp is followed by the "fresh composite fragrance" that belongs to the night. Then there is another odor, which the Motecan identifies as the smell of war, "that cloying incense of the war of the blossom." Later, when he is in the underground cell, he is aware of the "smell of oozing rock," and when the acolytes come for him, "the smell of the torches reached him before the light."

There are images of light or lights that also serve to link the two worlds. When the acolytes come for the Motecan, the torchbearers are there also; their lights reflect "off the sweaty torsos and off the black hair dressed with feathers." The bonfires surrounding the sacrificial altar give off smoke, as well as light. The link to the world of the motorcyclist is made clear in the final paragraph, when the Motecan believes that he was dreaming of a futuristic city "with green and red lights that burned without fire or smoke." (He is referring of course to the traffic lights.)

The final image that links the two worlds is that of the knife. In the hospital, when the surgeon comes over to the injured man he has something that "gleamed in his right hand" (a surgical knife). The Motecan carries a stone knife with him, but more significant is the knife that the priest approaches him with at the moment of sacrifice.

COMPARE & CONTRAST

- **1400s:** The Aztecs practice human sacrifice on a large scale.

  1950s: Human sacrifice is reportedly eradicated worldwide.

  Today: The British Broadcasting Corporation (BBC) reports that human sacrifice has been known to occur in African immigrant communities in the United Kingdom.

- **1400s:** The Aztecs worship many gods, including Tlaloc (a rain god), Huitzilopochtli (a war god), and Quetzalcotl (the plumed serpent god). These gods are based on the cycles of the Aztec calendar. Each god has its own temple and festival.

  1950s: In Mexico, where the Aztec empire flourished, Roman Catholicism is the dominant religion, and a cathedral stands near the ruins of the former Aztec Great Temple. About 98 percent of all Mexicans are Roman Catholic.

  Today: In Mexico, Catholicism remains the dominant religion. Nearly 90 percent of all Mexicans are Catholic.

- **1400s:** The Aztecs possess a written literature, but it is nearly all destroyed by the conquering Spanish. Some poems and myths survive.

  1950s: Carlos Fuentes, who will become one of Mexico's best-known writers, begins to publish. *La región más transparente*, considered a classic contemporary novel, is published in 1958.

  Today: Modern Mexican authors include Laura Esquivel, whose 1989 novel *Como agua para chocolate* was adapted as the 1992 film *Like Water for Chocolate*. Other noted Mexican authors are David Toscana, Cristina Rivera Garza, and Eduardo Antonio Parra. In 1990, Octavio Paz became the first Mexican author to win the Nobel Prize for Literature.

In the mind of the protagonist, then, each world clearly suggests the other one, but in different ways; one travels backward in time, the other forward; the images somehow link them together.

Alternating Points of View

The two different realities of this story—those of the man in the hospital bed and the hunted Motecan Indian—are at first kept separate, but gradually they merge and become indistinguishable. This is accomplished by variation in paragraph breaks. The transition from the world of the hospital to the world of the Aztecs is first accomplished by a new paragraph, when the man in the hospital first refers to his dream, and two paragraphs are then devoted to the Aztec world. The narrative returns to the hospital world with a snatch of dialogue and continues in that world for two paragraphs, followed by two paragraphs set in the Aztec world. These are followed by another brief piece of dialogue, which brings the reader back to the hospital world. Then, though, only one paragraph follows before the setting again switches to the Aztec world. The two worlds are getting closer, and the text reflects this. Earlier, there was a clear distinction between reality and dream, but now, in the paragraph beginning, "As he was sleeping on his back," the distinction is not at first apparent. Readers may well suppose that they are still reading about the world of the hospital and the injured man, but in fact the narrative has imperceptibly shifted to the Aztec world. After two paragraphs that remain in the Aztec world, the final paragraph mingles the two several times—hospital, Aztec, hospital, Aztec—and thus sets up the final twist in the story, in which reality and dream seem to flip, and one becomes the other.

HISTORICAL CONTEXT

The Latin American Literary Boom

In the 1950s, when Cortázar began publishing his work, the Latin American short story had already attained a significant reputation, based on several major authors. The primary figure was Cortázar's fellow Argentine Jorge Luis Borges (1899–1986), an internationally renowned figure, often credited with originating or pivotally advancing the magical realism that is associated with South American authors. Magical realism incorporates magical, surreal, or fantastic elements into otherwise realistic works. Other notable regional authors included Juan José Arreola (1918–2001), a Mexican who began publishing in the late 1940s; Juan Rulfo (1918–1986), also Mexican, whose reputation rests on a collection of short stories and a novel published in 1953 and 1955, respectively; and Juan Carlos Onetti (1909–1934), a Uruguayan novelist and short-story writer.

The 1960s, when Cortázar published many of his best-known novels and short-story collections (notably the highly influential novel *Hopscotch* in 1963), was a period in Latin American literature known as the "boom," a highly productive decade in which many high-quality works were published. The boom period was notable for its experimentation, in which writers favored nonrealistic modes such as the absurd and the fantastic, often in the form of magical realism, as well as psychoanalytical stories. One of the principal works of the boom period is *One Hundred Years of Solitude* (1967), a novel by Gabriel García Márquez. Another prominent author from this period was the Peruvian/Spanish novelist and essayist Mario Vargas Llosa (born 1938), who published *La casa verde* (*The Green House*) in 1965. Guatemalan novelist Miguel Ãngel Asturias (1899–1974) won the Nobel Prize for Literature in 1967. He had been publishing since the 1930s; his acclaimed novel *Mulata de tal* was published in 1963. Other writers associated with the boom include Carlos Fuentes (born 1928), José Donoso (1924–1996), Augusto Monterroso Bonilla (1921–2003), and Guillermo Cabrera Infante (1929–2005).

The Aztecs

The Aztec Indian civilization flourished in central Mexico from the fourteenth to the sixteenth centuries. It was destroyed by the Spanish conquest of Central and South America, which began with the excursion of Christopher Columbus in 1492. In 1521, the Spanish conquistador (conqueror) Hernán Cortés, allied with indigenous Indians who were the Aztecs' enemies, defeated the Aztecs, bringing their empire to an end. The Aztec capital of Tenochtitlán was destroyed, and the Spanish settlement of Mexico City was built on its ruins. By 1600, the Aztec population was decimated, mostly through disease.

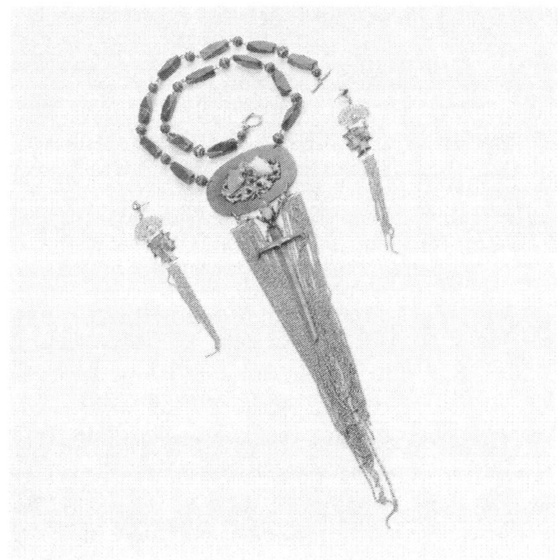

His amulet was missing when he awoke in the hospital. *(S. M. / Shutterstock.com)*

As explained in *Aztecs: Reign of Blood and Splendor*, the Aztecs were warriors who regarded war as a noble and sacred enterprise. In their view, there was no greater honor than to die on the battlefield. War was enshrined in their religion and cosmology. Every morning, the sun had to battle and kill the moon and the stars. The Aztecs believed that it was their task to assist the sun god and war god Huitzilopochtli in his daily task by offering human blood. This, they believed, would restore the god's strength. There was therefore a never-ending need for sacrificial victims (as the Motecan Indian in "The Night Face Up" knows only too well). The editors of *Aztecs* comment, "Driven by fear of the gods, particularly Huitzilopochtli, the Aztecs performed human sacrifice on a scale unknown either before or since." At the sacrificial altar in the temple, captives or slaves were placed on their backs on a slab of stone, and their hearts were cut out with stone knives. There may have been as many as twenty thousand human sacrifices carried out every year.

CRITICAL OVERVIEW

A number of critics have commented on "The Night Face Up." In *Julio Cortázar*, Terry J. Peavler groups it with many of Cortázar's early stories as an example of the fantastic, which he argues is one of four major categories in which Cortázar's short stories can be grouped. He comments that the story provides "an excellent illustration of Cortázar's ambiguity." It is not possible to choose any one interpretation regarding which aspect of the story is real and which is dream or whether both are real: "the greatest pleasure for the reader derives from accepting all of these readings as possible."

For Lida Aronne Amestoy, in "A Quest from 'Me' to 'Us': Genesis and Definition of the Pursuer Motif in Cortázar," most of the stories in *The End of the Game, and Other Stories* refer in different ways to "the basic oneness of reality," which is open to humans if they are able to "restore communication between ordinary space/time and the mythic space/time of dream, poetry and madness." Each story has a "passport" to this altered reality; in "The Night Face Up" it is the effects on the motorcyclist of "anesthesia or intense pain."

E. D. Carter, Jr., in *Julio Cortázar: Life, Work, and Criticism*, comments that the story contains the literary motif of the "double," a character who closely resembles another character, often in a disturbing kind of way. Carter's general comment on Cortázar's short fiction, as to how the stories are almost all "subject to multiple interpretations," might also serve as commentary on "The Night Face Up":

> [Cortázar] insisted upon the "open" nature of his fiction, inviting the reader to participate, to use his imagination freely, to become, in his terms, an "accomplice-reader." He does not provide answers, but makes us uncomfortable and dislodges us from our seemingly firm grasp upon reality.

CRITICISM

Bryan Aubrey

Aubrey holds a Ph.D. in English. In the following essay, he analyzes "The Night Face Up" in terms of the theme of reincarnation and Cortázar's own comments about the nature of his stories.

Most readers, no doubt, are surprised by the ending of "The Night Face Up." Even though, in retrospect, it is clear that Julio Cortázar has prepared the ground for the sudden mingling of the two worlds of the story and the apparent reversal of reality that takes place in the final paragraph, it nonetheless creates a moment of astonishment,

" CORTÁZAR PLAYS WITH THE IDEA OF REINCARNATION IN HIS STORIES, OFTEN GIVING IT AN UNUSUAL TWIST IN WHICH THE NEW LIFE TAKES PLACE NOT AFTER THE PERSON'S DEATH BUT WHILE HE OR SHE IS STILL LIVING."

as readers must suddenly realize that this engaging story is not what they had thought. The situation that had seemed clear—an injured man under the influence of anesthesia has a nightmare that is in itself an exciting story—is called into question and annihilated. The rug is pulled out from under the readers' feet, or, to switch the metaphor, reality has been turned upside down. Most readers will likely spend a minute or two after finishing the story just absorbing it, trying to reintegrate the earlier part into the new framework with which the story ends, since what is real and what is dream appear not to be what they were at the beginning. But which setting is, in truth, real—that of the motorcyclist or of the Indian? Who is dreaming of whom? Is the story a flashback or a flash-forward?

In these respects, the ambiguity of "The Night Face Up," with its two distinct worlds that are finally seen to intersect in a surprising manner, is entirely typical of Cortázar's short stories. Many of them slip from an everyday reality into another realm altogether, a dimension in which different laws of nature may apply or which in some mysterious way subverts the rational, everyday world. The two worlds may interpenetrate in some way that may make the reader uneasy, as if the usual landmarks or assumptions he or she relies upon to understand the world are being undermined. As Evelyn Picon Garfield puts it in her book, *Julio Cortázar*, "Cortázar suggests that the real, objective, palpable world about us is but one side of a coin whose other face harbors the fantastic, the subjective, and the oneiric." (*Oneiric* means relating to dreams.) It is through his exposure of the "shadow of reality" created by humanity's "imagination and subconscious," Garfield maintains, that "Cortázar reveals the complex depths of reality, one that too often ignores the 'nocturnal' side of man's life."

WHAT DO I READ NEXT?

- "The End of the Game" is one of Cortázar's best-known stories. It is about three young girls who play a game along the railroad tracks near their home. The game involves posing in such a way as to convey certain emotions or attitudes for the benefit of passengers on the train. One game involves wearing ornaments and standing like a statue. One of the girls, Letitia, is slightly disabled, but a young man who is a passenger on the train indicates in a note that he likes her performance the best. However, Letitia rejects contact with the young man. The intriguing story leaves the reader guessing as to why she acts the way she does. The story can be found in Cortázar's *Blow-Up, and Other Stories* (1967).
- *The Oxford Book of Latin American Short Stories* (1997), edited by Roberto Gonzalez Echevarria, is an anthology that contains fifty-three stories by a wide range of Latin American authors from the colonial period to the present. Authors represented, in addition to Cortázar, include Jorge Luis Borges, Alejo Carpentier, Juan Rulfo, João Guimarães Rosa, Mario Vargas Llosa, and Cristina Peri Rossi. The editor contributes an illuminating introduction to the collection.
- *Sweet Diamond Dust, and Other Stories* (1985) is the first collection of stories by noted Puerto Rican author Rosario Ferré. Originally published in Spanish and first translated into English by Ferré in 1988, it gave English-speaking readers their first chance to enjoy her critically acclaimed work. Many of the stories are set in Puerto Rico.
- *American Eyes: New Asian-American Stories for Young Adults*, edited by Lori Carlson (1995), is a collection of ten short stories in which the authors explore what it means to grow up Asian in the United States. The stories exhibit a variety of voices and racial backgrounds, including Chinese, Japanese, Vietnamese, and Filipino.
- *Life among the Aztecs* (2004), by Rachael Ramey, part of the "The Way People Live" series, includes a generous selection of black-and-white illustrations and maps exploring Aztec life and culture. There are plenty of quotations and well-presented facts in this lively narrative aimed at a young-adult readership.
- Jorges Luis Borges (1899–1986) is one of the twentieth century's most influential writers. Like Cortázar, he was from Argentina, and he was already an international figure when Cortázar began to publish. Borges's *Collected Fictions* (1999) contains all his short stories, the genre in which he produced his best-known work.

Cortázar himself wrote several essays in which he discusses the craft of the short story and his own approach to it. Some remarks in his essay "Some Aspects of the Short Story," as quoted by Garfield, offer further illumination of aspects of "The Night Face Up." Cortázar acknowledges that most of his stories belong to the category of the fantastic. These stories, he continues, were written from a certain philosophical and psychological perspective:

> They oppose that false realism that consists of believing that all things can be described and explained according to the philosophical and scientific optimism of the eighteenth century, that is, as part of a world ruled more or less harmoniously by a system of laws of principles, of cause and effect relationships and or defined psychologies, of well mapped geographies.

Cortázar outlines two principles that guided him in his literary craft that were contrary to that "false realism": first, the "suspicion of another more secret and less communicable order," and second, his interest in the work of the French writer Alfred Jarry (1873–1907), "for whom the true study of reality did not reside in laws but in exceptions to the laws."

How would these points be applied to "The Night Face Up"? To begin with, the world depicted in the first few pages of the story, before the nightmare begins, is a good example of the kind of complacent, rational optimism that Cortázar described. It is an orderly world in which everything makes sense and proceeds smoothly and efficiently. There is, granted, a motorcycle accident, but it is not a serious one. The motorcyclist is not badly injured, nor is the woman who caused the accident. Because the accident was not the man's fault, he does not have to worry about any legal consequences, and even the motorcycle is not badly damaged. All the details seem to confirm that there is nothing much to worry about in this minor disruption of the routines of daily life. The young men who pick the motorcyclist up are cheerful and efficient. The ambulance arrives within five minutes, and the injured man shares a laugh with the police guard who accompanies him. He knows he has suffered a shock, but he feels "pretty good, it had been an accident, tough luck; stay quiet a few weeks, nothing worse." When he arrives at the hospital he is treated immediately; his physical condition presents no difficulties owing to the efficiency of modern medicine and surgery. Indeed, the situation appears really quite mundane, one of the "well mapped geographies" of life that Cortázar refers to in his essay quoted above.

Unbeknownst to the motorcyclist, though, this minor disruption of the smooth texture of everyday reality—the world he takes for granted—has set up a situation in which a fissure will be opened up in his consciousness. Some other world, perhaps lurking long within him at some subterranean level, will take its opportunity to burst through in the vivid, disturbing dream of the Motecan Indian pursued by Aztec warriors. Here is a world far removed from the bright streets of the modern city in the morning sunshine. In one world, people assist each other because it is the obvious thing to do; in the other, men hunt down other men, lay them on stone slabs, and cut their hearts out. In the world of the modern city, medical science takes care of problems with clinical efficiency, but in the Aztec world, a sacred amulet worn around the neck and a prayer to a goddess are all that stand between the Indian and a gruesome death.

What secret impulses in the mind of the motorcyclist might cause him to dream of swamps and the smells of war, of dark, underground passages and a sacrificial death? And conversely, if it is not the motorcyclist but the Indian who is the dreamer, what extraordinary foreknowledge would allow him to dream of that strange city of the future in which there were "green and red lights that burned without fire or smoke" and "an enormous metal insect that whirred away between his legs"?

One interpretation would be that the motorcyclist is experiencing a past life in which he was an Indian in Mexico during the time of the Aztec Empire. It is well known that Cortázar had an interest in Buddhism and the philosophical tradition known as Vedanta, which was the core from which the Hindu religion grew. Both these traditions embrace the idea that every human soul goes through many different physical incarnations on its journey toward final liberation. After the death of one body, the soul is reborn into another one. The idea is known as reincarnation, metempsychosis, or the transmigration of souls.

Cortázar plays with the idea of reincarnation in his stories, often giving it an unusual twist in which the new life takes place not after the person's death but while he or she is still living. In "The Distances," for example, Alina, a young middle-class woman in a Latin American city, feels a strange connection with an unknown beggar woman in Budapest, Hungary, who seems to be a different version of herself. The woman is Alina's double. At the end of the story, when the two women meet, they embrace physically and seem either to become one or to exchange souls. In "A Yellow Flower," a man believes that he has met a reincarnation of himself in the form of a young boy. He explains this strange fact to be the result of "some slight imperfection in the mechanism, a crimp and doubling back of time, I mean an overlap, a re-embodiment incarnate, simultaneously instead of consecutively."

It is this crimping of time that also happens in "The Night Face Up," and it reflects Cortázar's observation about Jarry, quoted above, that the truest conception of reality consists not of laws but of exceptions to the laws. In the case of reincarnation, no one is supposed to "remember" the earlier incarnations, and yet in the mysterious process enacted in the story, the boundaries of space and time are suddenly annihilated, and a soul glimpses itself at a different stage of its evolutionary journey. As a result, the

The Aztec warriors chase the unnamed protagonist. *(Amenhotepov / Shutterstock.com)*

> "THE SHORT-STORY WRITER KNOWS HE CANNOT WORK BY ACCUMULATION, THAT TIME IS NOT ON HIS SIDE; HE CAN ONLY WORK IN DEPTH, VERTICALLY, WHETHER UPWARDS OR DOWNWARDS IN LITERARY SPACE. AND THIS, WHICH PUT THIS WAY SOUNDS LIKE A METAPHOR, EXPRESSES NONETHELESS THE CORE OF THE METHOD."

nature of human life is revealed in a more total form than is experienced in the normal, everyday, waking state of consciousness. As Cortázar puts it in "Some Aspects of the Short Story," again as quoted by Garfield, the job of the short story is to produce "that fabulous opening of the minute onto the gigantic, of that which is individual and circumscribed onto the very essence of the human condition." This story allows the protagonist, and by extension the reader, one such glimpse of true human nature.

Source: Bryan Aubrey, Critical Essay on "The Night Face Up," in *Short Stories for Students*, Gale, Cengage Learning, 2012.

Julio Cortázar

In the following excerpt, Cortázar shares his vision for building a good short story.

I find myself standing before you today in quite a paradoxical situation. An Argentine novelist makes himself available to exchange ideas on the short story, but his listeners and partners in the exchange, with few exceptions, know nothing of his work. The cultural isolation that continues to afflict our countries, added to the unjust current-day cutoff of communications with Cuba, have meant that my books, of which there are several by now, have not found their way, except here and there, into the hands of such willing and enthusiastic readers as yourselves. The problem is not just that you have had no opportunity to judge my stories, but that I feel a bit like a ghost coming to talk to you without that relatively soothing certainty of being preceded by the work one has done over the years. And this ghostly feeling I have must show, because a few days ago an Argentine lady assured me in the Hotel Riviera that I was not Julio Cortazar, and, to my stupefaction, she added that the genuine Julio Cortazar is a white-haired gentleman, a close friend of one of her relatives, and has never left Buenos Aires. Since I've been living in Paris for twelve years now, you can see how my ghostly nature has visibly intensified following this revelation. If I should suddenly disappear in midsentence, I won't be too surprised, and perhaps we will all be the better off for it.

It is said that a ghost's greatest desire is to get back at least a glimmer of substantiality, something tangible that will bring him, for a moment, back into his flesh-and-blood life. To gain a little substantiality in your eyes, I will sum up in a few words the general tendency and sense of my stories. I'm not doing this simply for the sake of information, for no abstract summary could replace the work itself; my reasons are more important. Since I'm going to be concerned with some aspects of the story as a literary genre, and it's possible some of my ideas may surprise or shock my listeners, it seems to me only fair to define the type of narrative that interests me, pointing out my special way of seeing the world. Almost all the stories I have written belong to the genre called fantastic, for lack of a better word, and are opposed to that false realism that consists of believing that everything can be described and explained, as was assumed by the optimism of nineteenth-century philosophy and science, that is, as part of a world governed more or less harmoniously by a system of laws, principles, cause-and-effect relations, well-defined psychologies, mapped-out geographies. In my case, the suspicion that there's another order, more secret and less communicable, and the seminal discovery of Alfred Jarry, for whom the true study of reality lay not in laws but in the exceptions to those laws, have been some of the guiding principles in my personal search for a literature beyond all naive realism. That's why, if in the ideas I set forth you find a predilection for everything exceptional about the short story, be it in thematics or in the forms of expression, I think this presentation of my own way of seeing the world will explain my stance and focus upon the problem. At worst, it can be said I've only spoken of the story as I write it, and yet, I don't think that's so. I feel sure that there exist certain constants, certain values that apply to all stories, fantastic or realistic, dramatic or humorous. And I think perhaps it's possible to show here those invariable elements that give a good story its particular atmosphere and qualify it as a work of art.

The opportunity to exchange ideas about the short story interests me for several reasons. I live in a country—France—where this genre has not held much of a place, though in recent years there has been a growing interest among writers and readers in this form of expression. At any rate, while critics continue to accumulate theories and maintain heated polemics about the novel, almost nobody takes an interest in the problems the short story entails. To live as a short-story writer in a country where this form of expression is almost an exotic product, forces one to seek in other literatures the sustenance lacking there. Gradually, in the original version or in translation, one gathers, almost spitefully, a vast quantity of stories past and present, and there comes the day to weigh it all in the balance, attempt an evaluative approach to this genre, so hard to define, so elusive in its many contradictory aspects, and in the last analysis so secret and turned in upon itself, a snail of language, a mysterious brother to poetry in another dimension of literary time.

But beyond this stopping-place that every author must reach at some point in his work, a discussion of the short story especially interests us because every Spanish-speaking country on the American continents is giving the short story a place of special importance that it had never enjoyed in other Latin countries like France or Spain. With us, as is only natural in young literatures, spontaneous creation almost always precedes critical examination; a good thing it is so, too. Nobody can try to say that stories should be written only after we know their laws. In the first place, there are no such laws; at most one may speak of points of view, of certain constants that structure this rather unbounded genre; in the second place, there is no reason theorists and critics should be the same people writing the stories, and they naturally would come on the scene only after there exists a body, a mass of literature that will allow for research into and clarification of its development and features. In America, in Cuba, just as in Mexico or Chile or Argentina, a great many short-story writers have been at work since the early years of the century, hardly knowing one another, at times coming across one another almost posthumously. Faced with this unwieldy panorama, where very few know one another's work well, I think it's useful to speak of the short story above and beyond particular national or international traits, because it's a genre that holds for us an ever-growing importance and vitality. One day the definitive anthologies will be drawn up—as they are in Anglo-Saxon countries, for instance—and we'll know how far we've come. For the moment it seems to me to make sense to speak of the short story in the abstract, as a literary genre. If we come up with a convincing idea of this form of literary expression, it can go toward establishing a scale of values for this ideal anthology yet to be. There's too much confusion, too many misunderstandings in this area. While writers plunge ahead with their task, it's time to speak of that task itself, leaving aside individuals and nationalities. We have to have a workable idea of what the short story is, and that's always hard because ideas tend to be abstract, to devitalize what they're about, while in turn life recoils in pain from being roped in by concepts in order to tie it down and classify it. But if we have no working idea of what a story is, our efforts will go for nothing, because a short story, in the last analysis, exists on that same human level where life and the written expression of that life wage a fraternal war, if you'll allow me the term; and the outcome of that war is the short story itself, a living synthesis and also a synthesized life, like water trembling in a crystal, a fleetingness within a permanence. Only via images can one convey that secret alchemy that explains the way a great story strikes a note deep within us, and explains as well why there are few truly great stories.

In trying to grasp the unique character of the short story, it's common practice to compare it to the novel, a much more popular genre with many precepts concerning it. It's pointed out, for example, that the novel unfolds page after page, and hence in the time it takes to read it, and need stop only when the subject matter is used up; the short story, on the other hand, starts with the idea of a limit, and first of all a physical limit, so much so that in France, when a story runs over twenty pages, it's then called a nouvelle, a genre straddling the short story and the novel proper. In this sense, the novel and the short story may be compared, using an analogy to cinema and photography, in that a film is in principle "open-ended," like a novel, while a good photograph presupposes a strict delimitation beforehand, imposed in part by the narrow field the camera covers and the aesthetic use the photographer makes of this limitation. I don't know whether you've heard a professional photographer talk about his art; I'm always surprised that it sounds so much as if it could be a short-story writer talking. Photographs as fine as Cartier-Bresson's or Brassai's define their art as an apparent paradox; that of cutting out a piece of reality, setting certain limits, but so that this piece will work as an explosion to fling open a much wider reality, like a dynamic vision that spiritually transcends the camera's field of vision. While in cinema, as in the novel, catching that broader and more multiple reality is a matter of developing an accumulation of bits, not excluding, of course, a synthesis that provides the work's climax, in a photograph or great short story it works the other way, that is, the photographer or writer has to choose and delimit an image or event that's significant, not just in and of itself, but able to work upon the viewer or reader as a sort of opening, a fermentation that moves intelligence and sensibility out toward something far beyond the visual or literary anecdote the photo or story contains. An Argentine writer, very fond of boxing, told me that in that fight that takes place between an absorbing text and its reader, the novel wins a technical victory, while the story must win by knockout. It's true, in that the novel progressively builds up its effect upon the reader, while a good story is incisive, mordant, and shows no clemency from the first lines on. This shouldn't be taken too literally, since the good story writer is a very wise boxer, and many of his first blows may seem ineffectual when he's really tearing down his opponent's most solid defenses. Take any great story you prefer and analyze the first page of it. I'd be surprised if you found any gratuitous elements just there for show. The short-story writer knows he cannot work by accumulation, that time is not on his side; he can only work in depth, vertically, whether upwards or downwards in literary space. And this, which put this way sounds like a metaphor, expresses nonetheless the core of the method. The short story's time and space must be as if condemned, subjected to a spiritual and formal pressure to achieve that "opening" I spoke of. One need only raise the question why a certain story is bad. It isn't the theme that makes it bad, because in literature there are no good or bad themes, only good or bad treatments of a theme. Nor is it bad because the characters are uninteresting, because even a stone is interesting if a Henry James or Franz Kafka turns his attention to it. A story is bad when it's written without that tension that should be there from the first words or first scenes. And so we can anticipate that the notions of meaningfulness, intensity and tension will allow us, as we'll see, to come closer to the very structure of the story.

We were saying that the short-story writer works with material we may call meaningful. The meaningful element of the story would seem to lie mainly in its theme, in the choice of a real or imagined event that possesses that mysterious ability to illuminate something beyond itself, so that a commonplace domestic episode, as is the case in so many admirable stories of a Katherine Mansfield or a Sherwood Anderson, becomes the implacable summing-up of a certain human condition or the blazing symbol of a social or historical order. A story is significant when it breaks through its own limits with that explosion of spiritual energy that throws into sudden relief something going far beyond the small and sometimes wretched anecdote it tells of. I am thinking, for example, of the theme of most of Anton Chekhov's admirable stories. What is there but the drearily everyday, mediocre conformity or pointless rebellion? What's told in these stories is almost what we, as children, in the boring gatherings we had to share with the grown-ups, heard the grandparents or aunts talking about: the petty, insignificant family chronicle with its frustrated ambitions, modest local dramas, sorrows the size of a parlor, a piano, a tea served with sweets. And yet, the stories of Katherine Mansfield or of Chekhov are meaningful; something bursts forth in them as we read and offers us a sort of breakaway from the everyday that goes well beyond the anecdote summed up therein. You have seen that this mysterious meaningfulness does not lie only in the theme of the story, because indeed most of the bad stories we've all read contain episodes similar to those treated by the authors named. The idea of meaning makes no sense unless related to intensity and tension, therefore no longer concerning just theme but the literary treatment of that theme, the technique used to develop the theme. And here is where, suddenly, there's a division between the good and the bad writer. So let's pause carefully at this parting of the ways to see a little better that strange form of life, a story that works, and see why it's alive while others, apparently like it, are no more than ink on paper, made to be forgotten. . . .

Source: Julio Cortázar, "Some Aspects of the Short Story," in *Review of Contemporary Fiction*, Vol. 19, No. 3, 1999, p. 25.

Amaryll B. Chanady

In the following excerpt, Chanady provides an in-depth retrospective of Cortázar's literary career, including discussion of the presence of the supernatural, escaping convention, and the quest for the absolute.

On February 12, 1984, one of Latin America's best known and widely read authors died in París. Most students of Hispanic literature, or Latin Americans interested in the culture of their continent, are familiar with at least part of Julio Cortázar's work, and have read and enjoyed some of his startling stories. In "Axolotl," for example, a visitor to an aquarium is transformed into a salamander. In "Carta a una señorita en París," the protagonist suffers the unusual affliction of periodically vomiting furry white rabbits. Perhaps his best known work is *Rayuela* (*Hopscotch*), a 600-page novel about a man in search of his identity, torn between two continents—South America and Europe. It is a structural and stylistic experiment that should be read, according to the author's instructions, by jumping from chapter 73 to chapter 1, and then from 2 to 116, until the reader has completed the journey of jumbled chapters in his own game of hopscotch. Praised not only for its formal innovations, *Hopscotch* was considered a cult book that expressed the emotional and intellectual preoccupations of many people, and was translated into numerous languages. Cortázar's three other novels and numerous short stories have for a long time now been read, admired and dissected in Europe and the Americas, to such an extent that for most people "Latin American literature" immediately brings to mind Cortázar, together with Jorge Luis Borges and Gabriel García Márquez. With the death of Julio Cortázar, the Western world has lost one of its most popular, eloquent and original literary figures. Cortázar started writing at a very early age. By his own account, he completed his first novel when he was nine and wrote love poems at 12. But apart from a collection of poems strongly influenced by Mallarmé that appeared in 1938 under the pseudonym Julio Denís and a "dramatic poem" brought out in 1949, Cortázar published almost nothing until 1951. Nevertheless he had been assiduously writing short stories for some time. In that year, he published his first collection of stories, *Bestiario*, which contains some of his best-known short prose. These carefully structured and polished narratives introduce two themes that reappear in his later work—the presence of the mysterious and unusual in our everyday world, and the stifling force of convention. In "Omnibus," a young girl boards a bus in which all the passengers are carrying flowers on the way to the cemetery. Since the girl, Clara, and a young stranger who sits beside her are the only people without flowers, all the other travellers stare at them with hostility. After all the passengers with flowers have left the bus, Clara and her companion are physically threatened by the driver at every stop until they escape at their destination. There they immediately buy flowers and are happy that they are like everyone else again. Read on a literal level, the story is a suspenseful narrative about an extraordinary and frightening experience, but on the symbolic level, it illustrates people's intolerance towards what is different, and depicts the distress of the outsider. "Carta a una señorita en París" can also be read on this double level. More than just a fantastic story about a man's stay in an apartment that is progressively destroyed by the rabbits he vomits at regular intervals, it is also a symbolic account of rebellion against the fastidiously tidy and well-furnished home of a financially successful friend. It is not a liberating rebellion, but one that leads to the protagonist's

> **"ACCORDING TO THE ARGENTINIAN AUTHOR, PEOPLE AND EVENTS ARE UNITED IN 'CONSTELLATIONS' OR 'FIGURES,' THAT ARE OFTEN UNKNOWN TO THE INDIVIDUALS."**

insanity and suicide. In "Lejana" ("The Distances"), a young and wealthy Buenos Aires socialite, Alina Reyes, feels that she is being suffocated by an endless round of parties and cocktails with their superficial conversations and conventional rituals. She imagines she has a double in Budapest, a beggar who shivers in the cold and leads the authentic life that is denied to the materially comfortable Alina Reyes. On a subsequent trip to Budapest, Alina meets her double, exchanges identities and casts off her former self to become the beggar. "Bestiario" is the story of a family that inexplicably keeps a tiger roaming freely through the house, while the inhabitants are careful to stay out of its way. A young relative who comes for a visit upsets this order when she lies to the family about the tiger's location and thus causes the death of her uncle. Another well-known story in the 1951 collection is "Casa tomada" ("House Taken Over") in which an elderly couple is driven out of their home by mysterious noises. In all these narratives, the supernatural and the extraordinary appear as an integral part of life. They are neither questioned nor rejected as implausible by the narrator or the characters, and are seen by the reader as a forceful expression of hidden impulses and social tensions.

In his next volume of short stories, *Final del juego* (1956), Cortázar continues to juxtapose the natural and the supernatural. "Axolotl" is the story of a man who pays daily visits to an aquarium in order to stare with fascination at the axolotl, a type of larval salamander, until he himself is transformed into one. In "El idolo de las Cícladas" ("The Idol of the Cyclades"), two men are mysteriously coerced by the statue of a pagan goddess to commit human sacrifice. In this anthology, we also see the emergence of a theme that reappears frequently in Cortázar's fiction—that of the *figure*. According to the Argentinian author, people and events are united in "constellations" or "figures," that are often unknown to the individuals. A *figure* may be created by the resemblances between two strangers, the relationship between a man and a woman, or the meeting of a group of people. In "Una flor amarilla" ("A Yellow Flower"), a middle-aged man recognizes his double in the fourteen-year-old Luc, and realizes that instead of dying, he will be reincarnated in an infinite series "of poor devils repeating the *figure* without knowing it, convinced of their liberty and free will." When Luc dies, the protagonist is happy that his unsuccessful life will not be continued by subsequent doubles. But the sight of a yellow flower suddenly reminds him of the horrible threat of nothingness, since he knows that after his death there will be no reincarnated double to appreciate the beauty of flowers. "La noche boca arriba" ("The Night Face Up") also depicts a *figure*, that of the resemblance between an injured man on a twentieth-century operating table and a sacrificial victim of the Aztecs many centuries earlier. After alternating presentations of both scenes, the modern protagonist is finally described as the sacrificial victim.

Those entertaining and stylistically sophisticated stories do not yet contain the theme of anguished search for the mystical "centre" or "absolute" that runs through much of Cortázar's later work. This theme first appears in "El perseguidor" ("The Pursuer") in 1959. The protagonist of this portrait of existential quest and tormented awareness is a brilliant jazz musician called Johnny Carter (based on the historical Charlie Parker), who submerges himself in drugs and alcohol and tries to commit suicide twice in his despair at not being able to find the elusive absolute for which he is looking. Existential searching is completed by what the author calls a "crack" in reality which permits us a glimpse of the absolute. Profoundly influenced by his readings about Zen Buddhism and the Vedanta, Cortázar frequently deplored the Western world view that restricts reality to what is logical and empirical, and divides everything in binary fashion. He believed that fantastic literature provides us with a brief view of a different reality that is obscured by our ordinary rationality. Several of Cortázar's protagonists try to break away from the sterile and stifling conventional reaction towards the world. Johnny Carter, for example, sometimes finds in his music the illumination that enables him to see a dimension of reality usually hidden to us. But he is incapable of grasping it, and finally dies of excessive drink and drugs.

One of Cortázar's most popular and humorous publications is *Historias de cronopios y de famas* (1962), which, in spite of its lighthearted tone, further develops the fundamental theme of escaping from convention. In the first selection of the volume, the world is described as a "glutinous mass" which is tedious and unchanging unless we force ourselves to see things differently.... In the final selections of the 1962 collection, Cortázar introduces the mythical famas, cronopios and esperanzas. The green and viscous cronopios with their unconventional behaviour are counterparts of the rebellious family on Humboldt street in the first part of the book. One of them invents a thermometer for measuring lives and finds out that the fama, who most resembles ordinary people, belongs to the category of "infra-life," while the professor of languages is characterized as "inter-life" ("El almuerzo," or "The Lunch").

Cortázar develops most of the themes from his earlier fiction in his major novel *Rayuela* (*Hopscotch*), published in 1963. The innovative style, experimental structure, erudite references and intellectual digressions force the reader to participate in the creation of fiction. Instead of starting on page one and passively perusing an engaging plot to its tidy conclusion, the reader must jump from chapter to chapter and constantly leave the primary plot to ponder the lengthy opinions about literary aesthetics expressed by the fictitious writer Morelli. Parallel to the author's search for authenticity in stylistic experimentation is the protagonist's search for what he calls the "kibbutz of desire" through unusual experiences. Horacio Oliveira, torn between Paris and his native Argentina, rebels against the absurdity of life by immersing himself in absurd situations. On one occasion he has a sexual encounter with a physically repulsive beggar on the bank of the Seine and is taken away by the police. On another he extends a wooden plank between two multi-storied apartment buildings so that his friend Talita can bring him some nails without having to climb up and down several fights of stairs. His unsuccessful search for the absolute and an authentic expression of his self ends in insanity and possible suicide.

Hopscotch, however, is not just the personal search of the failed writer Oliveira, who never reaches the square of the hopscotch figure that symbolizes the sky. It also contains the author's proposal for a new way of writing in which conventional categories of time, space and psychological motivation will disappear in a more authentic presentation of reality. In 1963, Cortázar published *62/modelo para armar (62: A Model Kit)*, where he put into practice the literary proposal outlined in chapter 62 of *Hopscotch.* Instead of a logical plot, the novel contains a succession of actions that are frequently absurd and unmotivated, and take place simultaneously and consecutively in London, Vienna and Paris. The characters are all connected in *figures* or "human constellations" as they travel and form groups and couples in various combinations, determined by destiny.

Many protagonists in Cortázar's fiction are dissatisfied with life and desire a more authentic existence. Inability to find it often leads to death, as in the case of Johnny Carter. The flight attendant Marini in "La isla a mediodía" ("The Island at Noon") dreams about living in idyllic seclusion on a Greek island, and finally dies there when the plane crashes. Marcelo in "Lugar Ilamado Kindberg" (*Octaedro*, 1974) drives his car into a tree when he realizes that his career as a travelling salesman robs him of freedom and spontaneity. The middle-aged couple in "Vientos aliseos" (*Alguien que anda por ahí*, 1977) commit suicide when they find out that their marriage will never be anything but a tedious ritual. Other characters search for meaning in life through political awareness and involvement. Andrés in *Libro de Manuel* (1973, translated as *A Manual for Manuel*) joins a group of Latin American revolutionaries. The protagonists of "Alguien que anda por ahí" and "La noche de Mantequilla" in *Alguien que anda por ahí* both become involved in secret missions and are killed.

In *Deshoras*, the last collection of short stories that Cortázar published before his death, the characters are no closer to reaching personal fulfilment than in the earlier narratives. Apart from the eulogy to Glenda Jackson in "Botella al mar," the stories do not paint very uplifting scenarios.... [The narrator/protagonist of "Diario para un cuento" tries unsuccessfully to write about Anabel, a woman he knew in the past. At the end of this last story, the narrator gives up in frustration when he realizes that he can only describe himself, but never the real Anabel. In a depressing conclusion he writes: "It is so sad to write about myself." He had already explained this sadness a few pages earlier. After telling us that Anabel, although ignorant in many ways, was often able to glimpse what she called "life," the narrator/protagonist admits that life for him was "a forbidden territory that only the imagination or Roberto Arlt could give him vicariously," and that the really innocent people are those, like the narrator, "with a tie and three languages." Can we draw parallels between the protagonist of "Diario para un cuento" and Cortázar himself, whose hyperintellectualism may have distanced him from what we often call "reality" and whose life consisted mainly of the reading and writing of fiction? His characters never successfully completed their quest, in spite of their anguished attempts. But Cortázar's work, although often difficult and disquieting, yet always original and stimulating, is a magnificent monument to his own quest.

Source: Amaryll B. Chanady, "Julio Cortázar's Fiction: The Unfinished Quest," in *Antigonish Review*, No. 57, Spring 1984, pp. 45–53.

Gregory Rabassa

In the following essay, Rabassa reflects on Cortázar's conception of structure in his writing.

Julio Cortázar is a writer who has thrown off the restrictions of mental Calvinism imposed by the past century and still so much with us.... [He] finds that life imitates art and that homo ludens must precede homo faber ("homo faber & faber," as he calls him in *Libro de Manuel*). This is most evident in his conception of structure. A form is of its own making, an object is defined by its use, as Ortega y Gasset has said, and the reader really creates his own novel as he goes forward. This is the starting point of *Hopscotch*, where Cortázar gives us a carefully ordered alternate version and also invites us to go to work and bring forth further variations. We have before us a rich lode of chiastic possibilities. When the novel was first published in the United States, a great many critics did not know that along with the interesting possibilities put forth to them they were also being had. Cortázar shook his head in dismay at this straitlaced interpretation and agreed that it would be awful to have to read any novel through twice, this one above all. What he did do, however, was to point out the possibilities of reality, and this can best be done and perhaps only be done by recourse to fiction, to the lie. Our wisdom is still so limited that it most often needs to be primed with a cupful of untruth in order to start pumping up new ideas and concepts. Before we can begin to write, we must unwrite, as the mononymous Morelli says in *Hopscotch* (a fine and complex pun can be essayed in Spanish with the words *escribir* and *describir*).

"OF ALL THE SPANISH AMERICAN WRITERS WHO HAVE BEEN SAID TO PRACTICE A STYLE CALLED 'MAGIC REALISM,' CORTÁZAR IS THE ONE WHO MIGHT BE CLOSEST TO THE MARK."

As we put the pieces of *Hopscotch* together we find that the puzzle is the novel itself, that we are in a sense writing it as we read it, much in the way that Aureliano Babilonia in *One Hundred Years of Solitude* lives his life to the end and can only do so as he reads the manuscript of Melquíades, which is the book we are reading too. This is also the structure of *Don Quixote*, accepted as the first novel, although Homer and, indeed, Odysseus himself have some claim through the narrative techniques of the *Odyssey*....

Cortázar's art as seen in *Hopscotch* and its sequel *62: A Model Kit* is essentially indehiscent. The conclusion is vague, real rather than factual. Life cannot end so neatly and so precisely.... Oliveira seeks truth and meaning in the accepted sense and finally comes to realize that they are elusive, that his illusions are closer to his goal. The very name of his friend Traveler is evidence that our words and labels in their assigned usage are apt ultimately to be a mockery of the very thing they are meant to represent. Oliveira's *nostos* is tragic, more like Agamemnon's than that of Odysseus, perhaps because, like the former, he is prone to accept standard definitions in spite of himself and only becomes a contriver when his mind begins to slip.

In Cortázar's perception of the truth the use of dreams and dreamlike states leads us in important directions. Much of this in *Hopscotch* is hallucinatory or a ribald caricature of surface reality, like the Berthe Trépat episode.... In *62* we meet the City, a vision shared by the characters and not really a dream. It is, rather, an epiphany which has a collective mise-en-scène. The City is, of course, a labyrinth and the hotel a labyrinth within a labyrinth. Here the direction of the elevator leads to anabasis before it turns horizontal. The coming up is frustrated, then, and the revelation incomplete, leading into difficulties on a higher level. This would bear out what has subsequently been discovered in mathematics regarding the so-called "Traveling Salesman Problem," a sort of maze puzzle which can be solved when it is in limited form but becomes insoluble when enlarged, showing that microcosmic solutions do not always obtain in the macrocosm.

It is also in *62* that the other self acquires more cohesion. In *Hopscotch* Traveler is seen as a kind of doppelgänger for Oliveira (the irony of names again: Traveler who has never left Buenos Aires, and Oliveira with the connotations of roots and staff of life, the trunk upon which the bed of Odysseus and Penelope was anchored). The idea of the double is broadened in *62*, and we have the notion of the *paredros*, the Egyptian concept of a guiding spirit, a fellow traveler, but one which here is shared and which possesses different people at different times, when that character, without being identified, is referred to simply as "my paredros." Able as she is to appear to or to influence the minds of whomsoever she chooses according to her will, Athena might well be called Odysseus's paredros.... [In] *Libro de Manuel*, Cortázar has a figure called "the one I told you," quite similar in concept to the paredros, but given an added dimension by the satanic suggestion of his title, so close to many Latin American euphemisms for the Prince of Darkness; and, of course, the name of God is never spoken in Hell except by the foul-mouthed Vanni Fucci. In classical mythology Hermes/Mercury, the messenger (*angelos*) of the gods, was given many of the mischief-making attributes later assigned to the Christian devil—Candanga, as he is known in some Asturian parts. Indeed, in Brazilian *candomblé* Exu, the messenger in the Yoruban pantheon, has often and mistakenly been coordinated with the devil.

Of all the Spanish American writers who have been said to practice a style called "magic realism," Cortázar is the one who might be closest to the mark. Straight fantasy is found more often in the short stories and is never explained. In the novels the case is more often one of creating fantasy out of the raw material of the reality at hand, as in the case of the Berthe Trépat episode in *Hopscotch* and Frau Marta in *62*. The most striking example of the creation of fantasy out of the stuff of reality is also in *62*.... As is the case with Joyce, Cortázar and many of his Latin American contemporaries delve deeply into the real and the unreal and try to separate or conjoin them according to less traditional standards.

Another holdover from realism that Cortázar has been forced to grapple with is the element of time. His approach has not been as patently self-conscious as that of another neoteric Spanish American novelist, Mario Vargas Llosa, and it is therefore much more effective and "real." Although temporal changes are more clearly discerned in some of his stories, the stuff of time has also been manipulated in the novels. The pathetic and bitter death scene of Rocamadour shows how the time of going hence differs from the banal time roundabout....

The time of the City becomes the time of Rocamadour's agony, brief and intense and existing amidst the superficiality of the other world or dimension, the one we see or see the shadows of.... In *62* it is the residue of time past in the Blutgasse of Vienna which brings Tell and Juan to relive a vampiric episode in Mozart's room. This is another version of reality which Cortázar brings out and follows much in the spirit of a recent breakthrough in mathematics which has revealed that any infinite series of numbers contains within itself an infinite quantity of other series of infinite numbers. This was the basis of Borges's story "El libro de arena" in his... collection of the same name. The paradoxical problem is that the universe (macrocosm) is finite and speckled with quanta, adding to the difficulties of finding reality or truth, if such there is. Pontius Pilate, a noble Roman who tarried too long in the Hellenistic world, has yet to receive a proper answer to his question.

Julio Cortázar is wise enough to know that there is no answer; for it is a question that can only be put to the gods, and ever since Eden and after Babel we are hard put enough to communicate with our fellows. While life as we see it in our daily rapidity has the feel of the flow of a *carmen perpetuum* about it, it is really made up of individual frames. As in the story "Blow-Up" and the subsequent film, when we examine these frames at our leisure, we see another reality, one which has come out of our own purview, however. Both aspects, then, are true, both are real; but as they are so different, can they both be such? Is Athena lying to us instead? Is our very wisdom, what we have of it, the culprit which leads us into conceptual error? The seemingly absurd becomes possible through words, but always with a mystery remaining as regards the fruition of our verbal notion.

The Cortazarian hero is, like all of us, schizophrenic in that he too is the heir to two distinct though superficially similar heroisms. Like Aeneas he is seeking his dutiful dose of *pietas* so that Rome can be built, the promised land, the *civis*, civilization; but the Odyssean element is too strong, the best he can do is preserve Ithaca and then go forth again in search of people who do not know what oars are for.... [We] can see that words are the real liars, that the truth is found in what is left unsaid, even though in English we cover those gaps with grunts while Spanish Americans use *éste* and Spaniards a rather more scabrous bit of putty. Borges has also shown us that the unsaid, the unwritten has as much significance as what has been articulated, perhaps even more, and the page of *blens* in Cabrera Infante's *Three Trapped Tigers* has more extensive meaning than can be found in the whole of *Fortunata y Jacinta*. (When will we purveyors of Spanish literature join Buñuel and celebrate *Nazarín*?) It is due time that our critical Perseuses turned and looked at the heads they have severed and shared with us the petrification we have suffered at their instance.

The approach to Cortázar's works, then, must be carried on in the same spirit as that with which they are written. We must prevaricate, we must lie to our wisdom, just as our wisdom itself lies to her peers on the Olympian level, elevated and beyond our ken. Then we will be proper readers, the kind that Cortázar pleads for and the kind that he does not always receive.

Source: Gregory Rabassa, "Lying to Athena: Cortázar and the Art of Fiction," in *Books Abroad*, Vol. 50, No. 3, Summer 1976, pp. 542–47.

Roberto Gonzalez Echevarria

In the following excerpt, Echevarria examines Cortázar's mixture of real and fantastic elements in his short fiction.

Borges said, evading my question about the new Latin American novel, that he had published Julio Cortázar's first short story ["Casa tomada"] in *Los Anales de Buenos Aires*, a magazine he edited in the forties. Borges' answer was a shrewd way of avoiding a topic he always shuns and a very Borgian way of pointing, not only to the link between Cortázar's work and his own, but also to what he probably considers Cortázar's forte—the short story.

Such an opinion, if indeed Borges' characteristically ambiguous answer could be construed as one, is probably contrary to that of most readers; for, although Cortázar has excelled in the short story genre his most resounding success to date is a novel, *Hopscotch* (1963). And *Hopscotch* is not just the high point of Cortázar's literary production (from the point of view of sales and critical acclaim); it represents a turning point in Latin American prose fiction writing.

The Boom, as the success of the Latin American novel *après Hopscotch* has come to be known, now counts among its loudest echoes Asturias' Nobel Prize. This success cannot, of course, be attributed entirely to Cortázar. But it was *Hopscotch* that set off the chain reaction with record sales in the original, prizes for its English translation and an unprecedented critical response.

[In] spite of *Hopscotch*, Cortázar has been mainly a short story writer. He not only began his career as one (if one forgets his avowedly "Mallarmean" book of sonnets, *Presencia*, published in 1938 under the pseudonym Julio Denís), but has cultivated the genre assiduously. Aside from *Hopscotch*, *The Winners* (1960) and *62: Modelo para armar*, his three novels, and three ageneric books, *Los reyes* (1949), *La vuelta al día en ochenta mundos* (1967), and *El último round* (1970), Cortázar has published five volumes of short stories: *Bestiario* (1951), *Final del juego* (1956), *Las armas secretas* (1959), *Historias de cronopios y de famas* (1962) and *Todos los fuegos el fuego* (1966). There are, in addition, a few stories published elsewhere, translations of Poe's prose works and two essays on the short story genre—"Algunos aspectos del cuento," and "Del cuento breve y sus alrededores." It is also true, as Borges seemed to indicate, that if Cortázar has been an innovator almost *ad delirium* in the novel, in the short story he has remained largely faithful to a tradition, that of the River Plate area, which boasts names such as the Uruguayan master Horacio Quiroga and, of course, Jorge Luis Borges.

Some of Cortázar's early short stories are metaphysical *jeux d'esprit* in a very Borgian vein. In "Continuity of Parks," for example, the characters of a novel, chasing one another through a forest, end up in the same room with the absorbed reader of the novel. In "Night Face Up"—a story in *Las armas secretas*—an injured motorcyclist suffers a Kafkaesque nightmare in which he is persecuted by Aztecs who want to kill him in a ritual sacrifice. At the end he realizes "that the marvelous dream had been the other, absurd as all dreams are—a dream in which he was going through the strange avenues of an astonishing city, with green and red lights that burned without fire or smoke, on an enormous metal insect that whirred away between his legs." Other stories from this early period are more 'regional' and are written in a streamlined *porteño* slang. "Torito," for example, is the rambling recollections of an old boxer in his hospital bed. The story is full of pathos and ends on an anguished note....

But it is in "Night Face Up" that one finds the mixture of the real and the fantastic that will become the trademark of Cortázar's stories—a mixture that Severo Sarduy has compared to Magritte's portrait of a perfectly normal man in which a bird cage stands in place of the head.... It is precisely this particular way of conceiving the fantastic that will be studied here through an analysis of "La autopisto del sur," the opening story of *Todos los fuegos el fuego*. This analysis is necessary because Cortázar himself has reacted somewhat negatively to the interpretation of his short fiction....[He] suggests...that there is no break between the 'real' and 'fantastic' in his stories but instead a mode of presenting the 'real' that transfers it to the level of the 'unusual' (*insólito*). This perspective put forth by Cortázar may be, in the last analysis, the most fruitful one, not only for an understanding of his peculiar way of conceiving the real, but also for a more lucid understanding of his *métier*.

As in many of his short stories, Cortázar builds "La autopista del sur" upon a single situation; a set of circumstances within which the action and the characters are framed (more on this later). In "La autopista del sur" the situation is a traffic jam on the outskirts of Paris that begins on a Sunday afternoon and lasts days, months, and perhaps even years. The people caught in the jam are forced to organize communes to pool their supplies, trade services and help one another until they can reach Paris. The story focuses on one of these communes: there is a suicide, a natural death, a burial (in a trunk of a car), a desertion, a crime against the commune (drinking water without authorization) and a love affair between the protagonist, an engineer, and the girl driving the car next to his; life, in short, is resumed within a new order. The love affair between the engineer and the girl provides a tenuous plot line that does not monopolize the action. At the end of the story, when the traffic jam finally dissolves, the bonds formed in time of fear and want are forgotten....

The plot, then, is not the whole story; the story is encased within a situation that is charged with potential meaning in itself. This technique is not, of course, original, and this is why Cortázar's definition is so valid and illuminating; it may finally lead us toward a structural understanding of the short story and away from vague criteria about length. (Even a great novel such as Cervantes' *Don Quijote* is largely built upon a single situation that is repeated over and over again, exploiting in each case its multiple potential meanings. For this reason it is relatively easy to lift episodes from Cervantes' novel without their losing meaning outside the context of the book.) The situation, then, works as a sign, charged with multiple potential meanings that emerge in the telling of the story, the 'utterance' of that sign. This is obviously the case in "Blow-up," in which the protagonist, a photographer, explores the various possible meanings that arise from a situation he has captured on film....

The situation-sign that serves as point of departure for "La autopista del sur" is both a "slice of life" (*a recorte de la realidad* in the sense given this term by Cortázar) and a blatantly literary device. The vacation schedule of many Parisians, regardless of their trade, is uniform and as a result thousands leave and return to Paris at the same time (the return is called *La Rentrée* by the French). On certain days, in August particularly, when our story takes place, access to the city is practically impossible. Traffic jams such as the one portrayed in "La autopista del sur" have been known to last literally for days, especially on the *Autoroute du Sud*, which connects the city with the *Midi*. It is quite obvious that Cortázar, who has lived in Paris for many years, saw in such a jam a portion of reality he could frame and use as the mainspring for a story. On the other hand, the device of confining heterogeneous characters in an inclosure of some kind can be traced at least as far back as Boccaccio's *Decameron* or Brandt's *Ship of Fools*. In modern times it has been used very frequently both in literature and the cinema, and Cortázar himself used it as the main prop for his first novel, *The Winners* (where the inclosure, as in Brandt, is a ship) and also in "Omnibus," a story in *Bestiario*.

The inclosure has several functions. It may serve to isolate a group of characters in order to observe their responses under unusual circumstances, as in the [Luis Buñuel] film *Bus Stop*, where the emphasis lies upon the psychological and moral behavior of the characters. It may also, as in Golding's *Lord of the Flies*, present a perfectly rounded microcosm that is a scaled down model of a macrocosm, or a model for a possible one. Here the emphasis lies not so heavily on individual responses as on the model institutions created to regulate them. This has been the function served by the inclosure in utopias from More's to Skinner's *Walden Two*. Finally, the inclosure may be an allegory.

In "La autopista del sur" Cortázar exploits all these traditional functions of the inclosure: the commune is a microcosm, an isolated society that depends only on itself for survival, institutions and customs are created to regulate the interaction of the characters and, as shall be seen, it is also a sort of *theatrum mundi*.

But in Cortázar's story the nature of the device is particularly complex because there are, in fact, two inclosures—the traffic jam and the commune created by the characters. The aperture of which Cortázar speaks in his "Algunos aspectos del cuento" produces in "La autopista del sur" a double exposure—a picture where two distinct images are superimposed. This, it must be added, is the unifying device throughout *Todos los fuegos el fuego*, where Cortázar constantly portrays split worlds, images and mirror images that clash in "El otro cielo," "La isla a mediodía," the title story itself and even on the covers of the book, where the title, the name of the author and the publishing house are printed in reverse on the back cover (and may be read, of course, if put before a mirror).... In "La autopista del sur," however, the split worlds do not offer, as shall be seen, a direct commentary upon ... general metaphysical problems. If the story does indeed refer to them, it does so only in a very devious way.

It is quite obvious that Cortázar saw in *La Rentrée* a ready-made symbol for something that has been a major theme throughout his works—modern technological society and its very precarious balance. Confined in their useless metal cages, the people in the jam are obvious examples of alienated modern man. At the end, when the jam finally dissolves, each person returns to a mechanized existence controlled by machines.... The commune, on the other hand, is a primitive, tribal world of food-gathering, rituals and folklore. The people, deprived of all the trappings of modern civilization, return to a natural state where each depends on the other directly and where bonds of solidarity form; it is almost a perfect primitive Christian society.

It could very well be concluded then, particularly in view of the slightly melodramatic ending, that Cortázar offers in "La autopista del sur" an alternative to modern civilization; that the story is an indictment against modern life. In short, that the double exposure creates a dialectic between the modern and primitive worlds present in the two images. Yet, while this interpretation may be valid and justifiable, it seems to me that the 'topicality' of the story conceals a more profound reflection, not directly about man's condition, but about fiction.

The most salient characteristic of the traffic jam is its facility as metaphor. The commune, too, is not only a standard (and today standardized) alternative to technological society but consists of a series of literary *topoi*. There is the image of the river (in this case a motionless river).... Implicit in the entire story is also the image of the highway of life, so dear to the writers of romances of chivalry and of picaresque novels. In addition, there is the suggestion that the commune is organized by a mysterious supernatural being that keeps all the cars in close formation.... And the characters of the commune form, as a group, a sort of *theatrum mundi* or medieval dance of death: there is Youth—the two boys in the Simca—; Old Age—the old couple in the ID Citroen—; the Clergy—the nuns in the 2HP—; a Soldier—the soldier in the Volkswagen; and a couple of lovers, the engineer and the girl in the Dauphine. The dance of death motif is accentuated when someone throws a sickle into the middle of the commune, another symbol of medieval vintage. Cortázar's symbols are nearly always trite and obvious. The meaning of the board the characters of *Hopscotch* use to reach from one building to another is not subtle. The photograph device in "Blow-up" is not only trite but obvious, as is the platitudinous escape-dream of Marini in "La isla a mediodía" (an island in the Aegean Sea that serves a similar function to that of the commune since it represents a primitive world). This is not due to Cortázar's lack of imagination or subtlety. The triteness and the platitudinous meaning of his symbols and devices have a very specific purpose in his works: to focus attention not on the meaning of the literary sign but on the sign itself.

Some years ago—in 1947—Cortázar suggested in one of his first publications that the contrivance of an autonomous, self-sufficient fictional world was an absolute requirement in short-story writing. . . .

The inclosure device is not merely one mode of short-story writing but an ontological characteristic of the genre; all fiction and short fiction in particular is a closed, autonomous world. Thus, the inclosures in "La autopista del sur," while projecting the obvious meanings indicated above, as well as being a 'recorte de la realidad,' are ultimately symbols of fiction itself. This is the reason why Cortázar utilizes literary signs that are so blatantly literary and also the reason for the platitudinous meanings of those signs.

This interpretation of the inclosures becomes clearer if one notices the relationship between the traffic jam and the commune at a formal level. Cortázar creates the commune before the reader, as when in the modern theater the actors themselves bring the properties onto the stage and then proceed with the representation of the play. In this respect the relationship between the commune and the traffic jam could be said to be homologous to that between the play within the play and the play itself. From the first page of the story, Cortázar begins to set off from the world outside what will become the autonomous commune. . . . Cortázar gives a meticulous phenomenological description of a self-contained world, of a complete cosmos. But the important thing is that he creates that fictitious world openly and arbitrarily, as if he were inviting the reader to analyse the elements of his fiction, the props of the set and the grease paint on the actors' faces.

The arbitrariness by which Cortázar constructs his fictional microcosm alludes to the arbitrariness of the real world. His 'utopia' points to a macrocosm that may be just as arbitrary and perhaps just as fictional. . . . In Cortázar's utopia everything has a place because he has arbitrarily created a grammar that will contain it; everything, including the characters, has a name because he has wrought a grammar that will accept it. Toward the end of "La autopista del sur" snow covers the ground—winter has set in on the people who had left for Paris on an August afternoon. But this is not a break with the syntax of Cortázar's new world. The perfectly normal man in Magritte's picture is as arbitrary in his normality as the bird cage in its abnormality. The two situation signs have become one; a fiction within a larger fiction, all fictions a fiction, all fires a fire. Cortázar's "La autopista del sur" falls within a very rich tradition of literature whose main pre-occupation is literature.

Source: Roberto Gonzalez Echevarria, "'La autopista del sur' and the Secret Weapons of Julio Cortázar's Short Narrative," in *Studies in Short Fiction*, Vol. 8, No. 1, Winter 1971, pp. 130–40.

SOURCES

Amestoy, Lida Aronne, "A Quest from 'Me' to 'Us': Genesis and Definition of the Pursuer Motif in Cortázar," in *The Final Island: The Fiction of Julio Cortázar*, edited by Jaime Alazraki and Ivar Ivask, University of Oklahoma Press, 1978, p. 155.

"Boys 'Used for Human Sacrifice,'" in *BBC News*, June 16, 2005, http://news.bbc.co.uk/2/hi/uk_news/4098172.stm (accessed February 9, 2011).

Brown, Dale, ed., *Aztecs: Reign of Blood and Splendor*, Time-Life Books, 1992, p. 82.

Carter, E. Dale, *Julio Cortázar: Life, Work, and Criticism*, York Press, 1986, p. 21.

Cortázar, Julio, "The Night Face Up," in *Blow-Up, and Other Stories*, translated by Paul Blackburn, Pantheon Books, 1967, pp. 66–76.

———, "A Yellow Flower," in *Blow-Up, and Other Stories*, translated by Paul Blackburn, 1967, p. 53.

Garfield, Evelyn Picon, *Julio Cortázar*, Frederick Ungar, 1975, pp. 12–13, 29.

Menton, Seymour, ed., *The Spanish American Short Story: A Critical Anthology*, University of California Press, 1982, pp. 255–57, 419–22.

Peavler, Terry J., *Julio Cortázar*, Twayne Publishers, 1990, p. 35.

FURTHER READING

Peden, Margaret Sayers, *The Latin American Short Story: A Critical History*, Twayne Publishers, 1983.

This historical examination provides an introduction to the Latin American short story that provides a context for Cortázar's achievement in the genre.

Schmidt-Cruz, Cynthia, *Mothers, Lovers, and Others: The Short Stories of Julio Cortázar*, State University of New York Press, 2004.

Schmidt-Cruz examines the concept of the feminine theme in the short stories of Cortázar, using feminist psychoanalytic approaches and cultural studies.

Standish, Peter, *Understanding Julio Cortázar*, University of South Carolina Press, 2001.

This introduction to Cortázar's life and work is written for the general reader. Standish analyzes Cortázar's writings as a whole and discusses the relationship between his work and his political views.

Stavans, Ilan, *Julio Cortázar: A Study of the Short Fiction*, Twayne Publishers, 1996.

Stavans focuses on the connection between Cortázar's life and his work and on how Cortázar developed his unique style. The book also reprints three essays by Cortázar, including one in which he discusses the short-story genre.

SUGGESTED SEARCH TERMS

Julio Cortázar

The Night Face Up AND Julio Cortázar

Latin American short story

Spanish American short story

magical realism AND Cortázar

fantastic genre

dreams

Aztecs

Aztec Empire

Aztec AND human sacrifice

reincarnation

metempsychosis

transmigration of souls

short stories AND Cortázar

magical realism

The Rain Came

GRACE OGOT

1968

Grace Ogot, a Kenyan from the Luo ethnic group, is recognized as one of the foremost female authors of English-language fiction from the African continent. After attending a 1962 African literature conference at Makerere University, in neighboring Uganda, at which East African work was not even on display, she was inspired to publish her writings. At that conference, Ogot read aloud her story "The Year of Sacrifice," which was subsequently published in *Black Orpheus* in 1963; this story was later reworked and retitled "The Rain Came." Ogot first learned the traditional version of this tale, about a chief's daughter who a medicine man claims must be sacrificed in order to bring rain, from her grandmother in evening family storytelling sessions in the elder's hut. She felt an affinity with the daughter, Oganda—as well as a fear that she, too, might someday be called upon to be sacrificed. As she told Oladele Taiwo, who appraises her work in *Female Novelists of Modern Africa*, she resolved as a youth, "If one day I can write, I shall write the story of Oganda so that other people can know she was sacrificed for the welfare of her people." With its traditional setting and foundation in oral history, its focus on the fate of a young woman in a patriarchal society, and its sustained life-or-death tension, "The Rain Came" is one of Ogot's most renowned stories. It can be found in her collection *Land without Thunder* (1968) as well as the anthology *Global Cultures: A Transnational Short Fiction Reader* (1994), edited by Elisabeth Young-Bruehl.

The chief must make a horrible decision to get the rain to come. *(iofoto / Shutterstock.com)*

AUTHOR BIOGRAPHY

Ogot was born as Grace Emily Akinyi on May 15, 1930, in the village of Asembo, Kenya, near Kisumu, a regional center situated on Lake Victoria, which is called Nam Lolwe by the Luo. From an early age, she was very fond of hearing folktales from her grandmother, who was an inspiring storyteller. In turn, her father, a schoolteacher, read from storybooks in English and Kiswahili—Kenya's two national languages—which he also translated into Dholuo for his children. When she could read herself, Akinyi was moved to read the Old Testament in its entirety several times. Like her father and many modern Luos, Ogot is Christian, though this is not exclusive of traditional beliefs. Captivated by fiction and starting to write her own stories while attending Butere Girls' High School, Akinyi then attended nursing school in Kampala, Uganda. She gained additional training in hospitals in London, giving her an international professional perspective on contrasts between traditional African medicine and modern Western medicine. In 1959, she married historian Bethwell Allan Ogot, who praised her letters as poetry and encouraged her to try to publish her writings.

After reading her story "The Year of Sacrifice" at the African writers' conference at Makerere University, in Uganda, in 1962, Ogot published that story in 1963 in the journal *Black Orpheus*. She then sought publication through the East African Literature Bureau but was discouraged because her stories revolved around and addressed many traditional themes rather than Christian ones, which the bureau's European manager preferred in creative fiction. Ogot nonetheless persevered, and in 1966 she published her first novel—and one of the first in English by an African woman—*The Promised Land*, about a Luo man's migration across Lake Victoria with his wife in search of wealth. Ogot reworked "The Year of Sacrifice"—trimming the introduction and changing the end—to include it as "The Rain Came" in her well-received collection *Land without Thunder* (1968).

Ogot published additional volumes both in English and, after her mother expressed how much it would mean to the Luo community to read works by her in their mother tongue, in Dholuo. Her short-story collections include *The Other Woman* (1976) and *The Island of Tears* (1980).

With her intellectual resources bolstered through the historical work of her accomplished husband, Ogot wrote a text drawing on Luo history going back as far as 97 CE, which was adapted and successfully staged as a play, *In the Beginning*, by her son Michael in 1983. In addition to writing, Ogot broadcast a weekly radio magazine for the Voice of Kenya, out of Nairobi; founded the Writers' Association of Kenya in 1975, serving as chairperson until 1980; and was a member of the Kenya Parliament and an assistant minister in the president's cabinet through the mid- to late-1980s. As of 2011, Ogot lived in the Luo village of Yala, Kenya.

PLOT SUMMARY

A village chief, Labong'o, returns from a council to be greeted by his daughter Oganda, who asks for news about when it will rain. Labong'o is cryptically speechless. Notably, with Ogot's immediate presentation of this critical concern about whether or not rain will come, the reader may at once expect that this concern will be resolved favorably; the title—and there is no evidence that it is meant ironically—assures that "the rain came." Thus, the tension raised by this concern shifts to a different question: the rain will presumably come, but at what cost? Labong'o's attitude signals that this will weigh heavily on him.

In the village, all are confusedly astir. (Traditional Luo society is polygynous, with some men having multiple wives, so a "co-wife" would be another wife to the same man.) Drought appears to be causing great hardship, as the chief has grown thin, livestock are dying, and the people fret for their children. The chief has been able to do little more than pray daily.

In his hut alone, Labong'o mourns that his daughter, who wears a glittering chain around her waist, must die. While as a chief he has committed the lives of himself and his family to the good of the Luo people, as a father, he weeps and cannot bear the thought of losing his only daughter. But he feels the spirits of the ancestors with him in the hut, allowing him no choice. Among the twenty children his five wives have blessed him with, Oganda is Labong'o's favorite. Though the other mothers are jealous, they also shower her with love, especially because she is the only girl.

But while Oganda's death would wreck Labong'o spiritually, he understands that to disobey the dictates of the ancestors could potentially mean the destruction of the entire tribe. The medicine man, Ndithi, a rainmaker, was visited in a dream by Podho, a Luo ancestor, who identified a virgin girl with a chain around her waist as the one who must be sacrificed to the lake monster, at which time rain will pour down.

Beating a drum to assemble the clan members gathered there, Labong'o sends Oganda to her grandmother's hut. He then reports to everyone else the medicine man's stunning assertion that Oganda must die. After Oganda's mother, Minya, faints, the others begin to rejoice, celebrating Oganda as lucky to be the one to save the people.

In her grandmother's hut, Oganda imagines that perhaps her impending marriage is being discussed. She would much prefer Osinda, who long ago gave her the chain around her waist and whom she loves, to either Kech or Dimo. When her grandmother appears, Oganda quickly gleans from the words being sung by the villagers and the dismayed look on the elder's face that she is in great danger; feeling like a cornered animal, she knocks her grandmother over to escape—but Labong'o awaits her. He takes her to a hut with her mother and breaks the news.

In the evening, Osinda's kin and other villagers come to congratulate her on her fate, which is considered a great honor; her name will always be remembered by the community. Minya, however, stirred to visceral remembrance of her maternal connections to her daughter, cannot rejoice. Oganda is her only child, while others have many.

As the people dance before her through the night, Oganda feels like a stranger among them; if they loved her, how could they celebrate her impending death? Seeing her peers reminds her that they will all have the chance to marry and have families of their own, while she will not. She thinks of Osinda, who remains absent. A morning feast is prepared, but she does not care to eat anything. Osinda is said to be away on a private visit; she expects to never see him again.

That afternoon, Oganda bids tearful goodbyes to her parents and finds she has nothing to say to everyone else. Anointed with sacred oil, which will protect her during the forest journey, she sets off southward toward the lake, which she must reach by sunset of the following day. (This lake is presumably the vast body of water known to the Luo as Lolwe and now known internationally as Lake Victoria.) Along the way, she comforts herself by singing a song mourning her fate; people hear her song, and all give slight solace by assuring her that she is doing what must be done. At midnight, Oganda falls asleep beneath a tree.

Waking late in the morning, Oganda walks for hours before reaching the sacred swath of land adjoining the lake, where only those in touch with the spirit world can cross. Among the crowd that gathers there—with none suggesting she save her own life, in light of the desperate need for rain—a child asks her to bring an earring to her sister, who died a week earlier and forgot to take it to the underworld. Oganda gives the girl what remains of her food and water.

Upon entering the sacred land, Oganda becomes acutely alert and inclined to flee. But she advances until reaching sand, to find that the water has retreated far from the usual shoreline. The lake monster, which her people never describe or talk about, becomes a vague but fearsome and haunting presence in her mind. Plodding ahead as the sun descends, she feels exhausted and parched, meanwhile sensing that she is being followed.

When the sun threatens to set before Oganda reaches the water, she begins to run—at which point she realizes some sort of moving bush is indeed following her. She races away, but the creature catches her, and she faints. Upon waking, she finds Osinda bent over her; at first speechless, she pleads with him to let her die in order to bring rain. But Osinda urges her to run away with him to "the unknown land" to escape the anger of the ancestors and the monster. She insists that she is cursed, that misfortune would follow her forever, but he covers her in a leafy coat like his own and assures her that it will shield her from vengeful spirits.

They flee. Crossing the sacred land, they look back to see the sun just touching the surface of the water. Oganda is fearful, but Osinda confidently urges faith. As they reach the barrier, the sun sets, and Oganda wails in dismay. But as they run, dark clouds gather, thunder resounds, and "the rain came down in torrents."

CHARACTERS

Dimo

Oganda thinks briefly about being married to Dimo, but she imagines the fierce warrior would make a cruel husband.

Grandma

Oganda's grandmother proves an empty force when she goes to her hut to break the awful news to Oganda. After flashing a warning look to her granddaughter, before she even has a chance to speak, the elder is knocked over by Oganda in the youth's attempt to escape her fate. (Oganda's calling her "Mother" signals that their relationship is as intimate as if the grandmother were another mother.) This aggressive act may be seen as foreshadowing Oganda's later rejection of the dictates of the ancestors in fleeing the lake.

Kech

Oganda briefly imagines being married to Kech, who is handsome and sweet but, unfortunately, too short.

Chief Labong'o

The chief of the village is Labong'o, who has led his people since he was a young man. (The apostrophe in his name indicates that the word is pronounced not with a hard *ng* sound, as in the word *finger*, but with a soft *ng* sound as in *ringer*.) The moral dilemma he faces after his visit to Ndithi, whether to sacrifice his only daughter for the good of society, is agonizing—and yet, it seems a foregone conclusion in his dutiful mind that the words of the medicine man must be heeded. Indeed, the common perception, voiced in the chief's thoughts, is that disobeying the ancestral spirits could literally bring about the ruin of the entire tribe; and in this time of drought, that threat must feel very real. Further, since others were present at Ndithi's announcement of his dream, Chief Labong'o could not have deceived his people about its contents. As a father, he privately mourns his daughter's fate—but a chief must not cry, and when he rejoins the villagers, he sets the sacrificial ceremonies in motion. He feels he will "never be the same chief again."

Minya

Oganda's mother has neither voice nor influence in the story. Minya faints away upon first hearing the news about Oganda and can thenceforth only sob, grief-stricken. The reader shares in her anguished thoughts over her only daughter's destiny, but within the story she does not speak. This serves to reflect the fact that, although the life of her daughter is at stake, the chief's wife has no say in the matter that he decides upon.

Ndithi

The medicine man tells Chief Labong'o of a dream he has had, in which the ancestor Podho decreed that a beautiful young woman with a chain around her waist has been selected to be sacrificed to the lake monster, such that rain may finally come. Ndithi does not appear in person in the story and accordingly is not developed as a character, but rather is described in functionary terms. He is not portrayed as needing to be persuasive; his authority is established, and his dream is understood as a communication directly from the spirits of the ancestors.

Nyabog'o

A messenger, Nyabog'o, is mentioned but does not appear in the story.

Oganda

The only daughter among the chief's twenty children is Oganda, a strikingly beautiful young woman whose name means "beans," signifying her fair skin—and perhaps her perceived value to the community when her sacrifice is called for, as she becomes not a person but little more than a handful of beans to be traded away. Being the chief's favorite, her female relatives all tend to be jealous of her, and she is secure in knowing that several young men might be acceptable mates. She places great value in the promise of future happiness with a family of her own, which makes her sacrificial fate that much more painful to bear. The villagers assure her that her name will be remembered, and some might willingly choose a glorious death to ensure such posterity; but Oganda would have preferred a long, fulfilling life.

Oganda's sense of duty, like her father's, is so strong as to virtually negate the idea of somehow thwarting fate and saving her own life. This sense has been instilled through both the foundational spirituality of the tribe's ancestral reverence and the communally accepted moral code holding that individuals must give of themselves for the good of all—sometimes unto death. Though sorrowful, Oganda is resigned to her fate, and in her extreme exhaustion, she surely would have perished at the lake, one way or another. Even when Osinda catches up with her, she tries to resist him and dash for the water anyway. But after he assures her that their coats of twigs and leaves will shield them from the ancestors' judgment, his desire—which she has inspired with her affection, symbolized by the chain she still wears—at last overpowers her duty, and she is saved. And the rain comes nevertheless.

Osinda

Described only as "the lovely one" by the adoring Oganda, the reader gains a better sentimental than physical conception of Osinda. When he finally appears as the knight in shining armor, his very armor—that is, the "leafy attire" that will protect them from not physical but spiritual assault—results in his physique remaining obscure. Osinda pays little heed to Oganda's insistence that the purported will of the ancestors be obeyed. His confidence proves strong enough for Oganda to allow herself to be led away, though she does so with great anxiety. Osinda's name was perhaps chosen to reflect his role in diverting Oganda from her prescribed fate, as, derived from the Luo verb *sindo*, the word *osinda* translates as "he hinders me."

Podho

An ancestor of the Luo, Podho visits Ndithi in a dream to identify a girl with a chain as needing to be sacrificed to bring rain.

THEMES

Love

Spurring Labong'o's and Minya's grief, Oganda's hope, and Osinda's courage is the compelling force of love. In an interview cited by Gloria Chineze Chukukere in her critical volume *Gender Voices and Choices: Redefining Women in Contemporary African Fiction*, Ogot revealed that when she heard this tale as a girl, she conceived of Oganda's plight largely in terms of love: "Now it touched me a lot... because not only was she an only daughter, she was a beautiful girl and she was ready to be married and I felt she was being denied the beauty of marriage." In other words, Ogot considers the chance to share romantic love with another to be one of the foremost blessings of earthly life. This sense is stressed through the song that Oganda sings during her lonely walk, as she laments, "My age-group are young and ripe, / Ripe for womanhood and motherhood / But Oganda must die young." The parental love felt by Labong'o and Minya makes their daughter's sacrifice virtually unbearable; in losing their daughter, they will be losing an emotional and spiritual part of themselves. Osinda, too, cannot bear the thought of losing Oganda, and so, guided by his love, he saves Oganda's life.

Moral Responsibility

Ogot's story underscores the challenging moral positions in which Chief Labong'o and Oganda find themselves, while the conclusion hinges on Osinda's own rebellious moral stance. While deeply saddened by the looming loss of his daughter, the chief sees no room for either political or parental maneuvering. He is evidently a good chief, having long served his tribe, and when he considers the vow he made before the elders, committing his own life and those of his household for the sake of the tribe, the decision he must make is clear. In turn, though she is initially spurred to a catlike attempt at escape when she realizes the perilous circumstances, upon being confronted by her father—whom she addressed as "great Chief" when he first returned, signaling a mature sense of the differentiated role her father plays

TOPICS FOR FURTHER STUDY

- Read "The Bamboo Hut" and "Land without Thunder," two additional stories in Ogot's collection *Land without Thunder*, paying particular attention to the societal ethics derived from the Luos' ancestor worship. Drawing on these two stories and "The Rain Came," write an essay discussing the effectiveness of this traditional ethical system in regulating the behavior of members of society—that is, in preventing destructive deviance—as compared with the effectiveness of the ethical system derived from your own religion or another of your choosing.
- Research the layout of a traditional Luo *dala*, or homestead, and the natural resources used to construct the huts, enclosures, and fences. Create a model presentation of such a homestead, using physical materials, such as leaves, sticks, mud, plaster, clay, and other media; perspective drawings or paintings that give views from various positions within the homestead; or a three-dimensional computer modeling program. Label the natural resources being represented or provide a legend identifying the materials you used and their real-life equivalents.
- Explore the Web site of the Ugunja Community Resource Centre (UCRC; http://www.ugunja.org), a Kenyan organization devoted to assisting farmers, entrepreneurs, students, and others at the village level in Nyanza Province, homeland of the Luos. The UCRC hosts international volunteers, who pay a fee for room and board and can stay in a traditional homestead setting. Imagine that you have the opportunity to apply for a scholarship to fund your travel to Kenya to volunteer through the UCRC for up to a year. Write a personal essay, addressed to the scholarship committee, expressing your motivations for volunteering and desired length of stay; describing any special skills, experiences, or relationships you have that could prove beneficial; and providing and explaining your top three choices for divisions within the UCRC to work through.
- Read the portions of U.S. president Barack Obama's memoir *Dreams from My Father: A Story of Race and Inheritance* that feature or discuss the president's Luo father, Barack Obama, Sr., and other relatives. The most relevant sections are Part Three, "Kenya," and the epilogue. Write a paper discussing the extent to which traditional African values seem to have been instilled in President Obama based on his memoir and on specific actions and initiatives taken during his presidency.
- Read *A Hero's Magic*, a work of young-adult fiction by the Tanzanian writer Ambani Guyi, about a young man who, following his father's death, quits school to become a fisherman and overcomes many obstacles simply to survive. Considering this work as well as Ogot's "The Rain Came," write a reflective paper in which you compare how the protagonists' circumstances force them to mature, and give them perspective on death, with how circumstances do—or fail to do—likewise for American adolescents such as you and your peers. Post your paper on a blog and invite comments from your teacher and classmates.

in the community—Oganda immediately resigns herself to his expectations. (The modern scientific notion that the sacrifice of a person cannot possibly bring rain is irrelevant in this context; to disobey the will of the ancestors from a traditional Luo perspective is as damning as mortal sin from a Christian perspective.) As a folktale, then, this story would have quite explicitly impressed in the minds of listeners the occasional necessity, and virtue, of self-sacrifice (not necessarily to the extreme of death) for the good of society. This value is held among many, if not all, societies, but would be particularly important in one where relations with neighboring peoples might be tenuous, demanding participation in warfare, and where uncooperative weather potentially means that, without enough food, the survival of all could be compromised.

While the reader may recognize the virtue of self-sacrifice, surely one's sympathy rests with Oganda; the reader is fairly enticed to hope that Osinda will come to Oganda's rescue. Finally, at the close of the tale, Osinda indeed sweeps in, driven by his love to adopt the moral perspective that no one else in the parched village could: that the innocent Oganda does not deserve to die and that her death should be prevented. Whether he could not have arrived any earlier or actively chose to wait until the last minute, Osinda was fortunate to do so, as at any point prior, the drought-stricken people would have surely prevented him from rescuing Oganda. Yet even she resists his efforts, considering herself morally obligated to carry out the sacrifice and, moreover, cursed. But he convinces her that they can, in effect, escape the ancestors' gaze with their leafy garments—a moral loophole. The ancestors as well as the living Luos, then, can believe that she has indeed been sacrificed, while she escapes with her life, Osinda with his beloved. And as if signifying the moral acceptability of this wholly benevolent arrangement, the rain pours down.

The chief had to send his daughter away to get the rain. (Volodymyr Kudryavfsev / Shutterstock.com)

Patriarchy

An underlying theme in this story is the relevance of Luo society's traditional patriarchal structure. Oganda's fate is decided not by herself but by two men: the medicine man and the chief, who is also her father. In this case, neither Ndithi nor Labong'o are understood to have willed this particular fate, since they are merely heeding the dreamed words of the ancestors. Yet throughout numerous cultures' histories, it curiously seems, young women, and especially virgins, have been more frequently victimized as sacrifices. Given a society's belief in the efficacy of sacrifice, it would be logical to avoid the deaths of adult community members on whom others are dependent; while if a society is pressured by war, the lives of potential warriors might also be privileged. But such logic merely attempts to justify a misogynistic stance that to the modern mind is simply unjustifiable, especially in the absence of scientific evidence that any such sacrifice would produce any effects beyond stirring the society's blood. In this story, Ogot highlights the senselessness of Oganda's being singled out by making her the only daughter among the chief's twenty children; in emotional terms, Oganda is in fact the least expendable of the twenty, and her death is expected to "permanently cripple Labong'o spiritually."

Though, in accord with her realist approach, Ogot does not attempt to tear down this patriarchal paradigm of virgin sacrifice, she does a masterful job of subverting it. In that Oganda is portrayed as an archetype of innocence and beauty, her ruminations on her suitors can be understood to single out the ideal matching male archetype. Her rejection of the congenial but short Kech can be read as an implied acknowledgment that a woman in a traditional setting is likely to seek strength and security in a mate—owing not to any deficits in her own physique but to the fact that she is rendered more vulnerable by the circumstances of childbearing. Yet in turn Oganda rejects the hypermasculine warrior Dimo out of the expectation that "he would make a cruel husband, always quarrelling and ready to fight." The devoted Osinda, who made his affection clear long before through his gift of the chain, is instead Oganda's choice. His physical appearance, never described, is irrelevant, while he demonstrates his physical stamina and courage in his rescue. Thus, the archetype embodied by Osinda is that of the romantic hero who considers love—rather than, say, power or even simple happiness—to be the highest guiding force. The phonetic similarity of the names *Oganda* and *Osinda* heightens the sense that they are ideologically perfect for each other. And the story's conclusion validates Oganda's preference. Surely neither the "meek" Kech nor the patriarchy-invested Dimo would have been able to undertake the audaciously romantic action through which Osinda saves Oganda. Thus, while the patriarchy yet rules the village in Ogot's story, once the sacred land has been crossed, the morality of love reigns supreme.

STYLE

Folklore

In *Keep My Words: Luo Oral Literature*, B. Onyango-Ogutu and A. A. Roscoe highlight the moral significance of a culture's folktales: "a people's stories are the treasure-boxes of their cultural heritage. Common rules and attitudes, beliefs and taboos—they are all revealed by a nation's stories." In particular, Luo folktales, "even when they are not overtly didactic... usually reveal something about Luo values and attitudes." Ogot has claimed to have presented the story of "The Rain Came" largely just as related by her grandmother, such that she reproduces the moral and spiritual lessons inherent in the tale (while perhaps subtly modifying them). Notably, as Bernth Lindfors records in *Africa Talks Back: Interviews with Anglophone African Writers*, Ogot asserted in 1976 that many Luo folktales are ascribed not to a mythic past but rather to a historical one, the oral tradition being the historical record. Such tales are considered "true stories of events that occurred in other generations in the distant past, at the beginning of our society. Oganda, the girl who was sacrificed, lived in that early era."

Ogot's folkloric approach accords with her views on the centrality of a writer's moral role in society. She asserted in the 1976 interview that modern writers, "as the custodians of our cultural heritage," have a degree of moral responsibility in producing stories for consumption by society. Regarding sensationalist fiction, especially that which is sexually forward, she remarked, "If the authors are careless and reckless, they can do untold harm to the family, to the children and to society as a whole, casting aside age-old African customs" in the name of entertainment. In present-day American society, moral tales like Aesop's fables are generally considered quaint children's literature, while among adults, indulging in sexually explicit or gratuitously violent film and literature is par for the course. In incorporating traditional folktales and moral balance into her written works, Ogot evokes in the reader precisely the sort of village-level sense of community that has all but disappeared in modern America. If one is seeking just such a sense, perhaps a local church, mosque, synagogue, or other place of worship would be the best place to look.

Realism

Critics tend to describe Ogot's work as realist, in that she conveys a very accurate sense of real-life circumstances, especially as experienced by women. Even her stories based on folktales are rooted in ordinary life as traditionally lived among the Luo of Kenya. The scholar Chukukere, in *Gender Voices and Choices*, observes that the dilemmas faced by Ogot's female characters, which often go unresolved, reflect the discord and ambiguity that Kenyan women have faced throughout tradition and continue to face in their colonialized, modernized world. Chukukere asserts that "Ogot's moral courage, therefore, deserves commendation for refusing to impose non-existent falsehoods or idealized resolutions upon existent realities." This realist approach accords with Ogot's proclaimed intents of both preserving traditional Luo stories and ways of life in literature and also shedding light on the difficulties of modern life in Kenya.

Feminism

The degree to which Ogot's work might be termed feminist has been a point of substantial discussion. The women in her stories are often entrenched in traditional positions with respect to their husbands, such that Ogot might be seen as failing to provide visions of expanded possibilities for her gender. But in thus reflecting reality, she successfully highlights the means by which Luo women must maneuver within whatever patriarchal boundaries they happen to face, whether imposed by Luo traditions or European colonialism. Ogot tellingly noted in an interview published in *Wanasema: Conversations with African Writers*, "I set out to write as a universal writer for both sexes.

But of course one must see one's society as it is." In "The Rain Came," which takes place in the mytho-historic Luo past, the women of the story, including Oganda's mother and grandmother, are palpably marginalized. Ogot's subtle feminism is perhaps evident in her revision of the story from its original version, "The Year of Sacrifice," which was presumably closer to the original folktale. In that version—which the editors of *Black Orpheus* dubbed "An East African Fairy Tale"—Oganda reaches the lake and actually does encounter the monster, which is slain by Osinda. Ogot thus replaced the damsel-in-distress ending with one in which Oganda's agency comes into play, as she nobly seeks to carry out the sacrifice despite Osinda's pleas. Only when assured that the ancestors will not be crossed does she relent. The concluding downpour, perhaps not part of the original folktale, may be read as Ogot's anti-patriarchal rebuke to the medicine man and chief: a young woman did not have to die, after all, in order for rain to come.

HISTORICAL CONTEXT

Traditional Luo Society

In presenting a legendary tale passed down orally through the generations, Ogot situates the reader in a timeless African past, unblemished by modern intrusions from the Western world. The setting is largely implicit in "The Rain Came"; that is, Ogot plunges the reader into the crux of the story—the fated sacrifice of Oganda—without dwelling on greater circumstantial or geophysical details. In fact, Ogot's earliest version of the story, "The Year of Sacrifice," opens with several pages of exposition on precisely the mytho-historic circumstances. While the literary value of the story is perhaps increased in its being narrowed to the scope of Oganda's direct involvement, the modern Western reader learns so much about traditional Luo life from reading the cut pages that one's appreciation for the tale itself thereby gains added dimensions.

The introductory paragraphs of "The Year of Sacrifice" describe the agricultural cycle experienced in Luoland, which straddles the equator. Each year, there are two dry seasons (around the equinoxes), when the sun shines strongest and rain may only come once every few weeks if at all, and two rainy seasons (around the solstices), one long and one short, when rain comes nearly every day. In the story, "the long rains" have just arrived, and the cultivated crops are growing steadily, when a veritable plague descends in the form of a massive swarm of locusts from Somaliland, which devour everything in sight over a single night. With great effort, crops are replanted as the rains continue, but next a "horde of army worms" appears, devouring everything over some ten days. These misfortunes, which, with one following the other, the villagers acknowledge to be extraordinary in nature, are very real threats that have been faced by the Luo and other subsistence farmers throughout African history.

When the rains end and a severe drought follows, Ogot highlights the potential import of the calamity in a striking manner: "The end of all things seemed to be coming." Though such a statement may strike the modern Western reader, entrenched in the infrastructure and security of a technological civilization, as hyperbole—even bearing biblical echoes—the threat of extinction of an entire tribe was no exaggeration. The Luo as a people accomplished a substantial migration some five hundred years ago, as driven by pressures that may have included warring neighbors, drought, and famine—factors that may otherwise have led the tribe to perish. They left southern Sudan to track the course of the Nile River southward to Nam Lolwe, now usually called Lake Victoria. This migration gave the tribe their name, as the word *luo* means "to follow." So closely do the Luo associate themselves with the river and the lake that, as reported in Onyango-Ogutu's *Keep My Words*, elders are given to say, "We are like water . . . which keeps flowing until it has found its own level." The Luo are understood to have arrived in modern-day Kenya's Nyanza Province sometime between 1490 and 1520. Thus, incorporating Lake Victoria as it does, "The Rain Came" can be understood to take place in the sixteenth century or later.

In the ensuing text of "The Year of Sacrifice," Ogot emphasizes the gravity of traditional ancestor worship, as the plagues are blamed on "unacceptable sacrifices" made to the ancestors at the beginning of the planting season. The ancestors are described as "senior members of the society who, though invisible, participated fully and actively in the day-to-day affairs of the community." This passage bolsters the crucial significance later attributed to Ndithi's dream of Podho, the great Luo ancestor.

COMPARE & CONTRAST

- **1600s:** In their traditional religion, the Luo worship a creator deity called Nyasaye, who may be prayed to through the spirits of deceased ancestors. The ancestors are believed to play an active role in the affairs of the living.

  1960s: With Christian missionaries having been active throughout the British colonial period, about half of Kenya's total population is Christian.

  Today: Some 90 percent of Luos are Christians, although traditional practices and beliefs remain integral parts of people's spirituality. Nyasaye is still the name of God.

- **1600s:** Luo society is polygynous, meaning men sometimes have more than one wife. The number of wives a man has typically correlates to his wealth and status in the community, as he is expected to bestow gifts of cattle on a woman's parents if seeking her hand in marriage. Each woman would have her own hut in the family's homestead.

  1960s: While many Luos have become Christian, traditional polygynous marriage arrangements continue.

  Today: Among the Luo still living in rural areas, polygyny is still prominent, but as young women become more exposed to Western notions of personal independence, fewer women are interested in such relationships. In thickly populated towns, condensed housing arrangements make polygynous arrangements less practical.

- **1600s:** Groups of clans, with each clan consisting of families descended from a single ancestor, are led by councils of elders who make decisions regarding important societal matters. Regional and clan-level councils are involved in local decision making.

  1960s: With Kenya gaining independence in 1963, the Luo politicians Oginga Odinga and Tom Mboya achieve prominent roles in the nation's governance—but Odinga resigns the vice presidency owing to differences with President Jomo Kenyatta, and Mboya is assassinated in 1969. Over the ensuing decades, the Luo will remain underrepresented in and underprivileged by the government.

  Today: In the wake of the despotic reign of President Daniel arap Moi, Odinga's son Raila Odinga gains the post of prime minister, giving the Luo a voice at the highest level of government.

Another aspect of historical tradition presented by Ogot—in a passage that immerses the reader in Luoland perhaps better than any other in the story—is communication over long distances using drums. A woman steps out of her hut before dawn to hear the pounding of distant drums; though certain it is not the "distinct terrifying rhythm" of mourning drums, she chides herself for being unable to discern the meaning, which could be of vital importance: "Drums rallied warriors for attack, summoned elders to the chief's meetings, announced the departure of a member of the community from this world, ... And those who didn't understand this drum-language were the illiterates of the traditional society." The woman's husband proceeds to interpret the rhythm as being a summons by the chief to a council; he thus dons his goatskin, drinks "a calabash of cold millet porridge," hoists his spear and club, and sets off. At the meeting, Ogot presents through Chief Labong'o, who thinks back to recent warfare, one final historical image to leave a lasting impression on the reader's mind: "During one battle against Ya-Lang'o, the battle field was strewn with the cold fine bodies of their young warriors.... The few who remained fought like wild tigers till they had driven their enemies to the mountains."

The rains finally came. *(Danaiel Petrescu / Shutterstock.com)*

Together, these mytho-historical passages from "The Year of Sacrifice" give a comprehensive impression of the plague-torn, drought-stricken, battle-hardened society that is the setting of "The Rain Came."

CRITICAL OVERVIEW

Even outside of the context of Ogot's historical literary significance, her short stories are considered the work of a master of the form. Regarding her novels, critics have pointed out that her particular realist style, in which events play out so naturally that dramatic conflict is often neutralized or avoided, leaves her longer works less absorbing and satisfying. In his review of Ogot's collection *Land without Thunder* in the *East Africa Journal* in 1969, Henry Kimbugwe begins by praising the author as not only "a gifted writer but a very rare one: a schooled, sophisticated intellectual, well aware of the changes taking place around her yet retaining a deep and close understanding of the traditional ways of thought and living of her people." He refers to "The Rain Came" as "one of her finest" stories. In light of her "unique African sensitivity," reflected in her ear for authentic speech and her understanding of the workings of people's minds, he calls her "the most *African* writer in East Africa."

In his essay "The True Fantasies of Grace Ogot, Storyteller," Peter Nazareth observes that Ogot cannot be said to have an all-encompassing ideological vision into which her works schematically fit—a fact that explains a relative dearth of criticism of her work, since there are fewer tangible thematic strands that critics can easily grasp. Yet Nazareth asserts that her "lack of *a total vision* is actually one of her strengths. It permits her to travel around and find different aspects of, and angles to, the truth." The critic concludes that an overarching sensibility can nonetheless be discerned in the cumulative effect of her writings, in that she reveals and laments how traditional moral structures are being abandoned in modern Kenyan society. Nazareth concludes that Ogot's special "achievement is to write naturalistically, whether dealing with traditional life, occurrences from real life, or imagining what could happen on the basis of what is happening."

In *Gender Voices and Choices: Redefining Women in Contemporary African Fiction*, Gloria Chineze Chukukere describes "The Rain Came" as "particularly effective," with Ogot expertly evoking the dramatic circumstances and sympathy for the characters. In bypassing the "militant Tradition of westernized feminism," Ogot "presents alternatives to female dilemma that take into account the need for continued interaction between the sexes in the universe." Chukukere concludes of Ogot, "Armed with christian morality and complimentary rural ideals, her standpoint, though a passive response to the current cry for female autonomy, is nevertheless an edifying contrast to present-day moral decadence."

In *Female Novelists of Modern Africa*, Oladele Taiwo calls Ogot "one of Africa's outstanding storytellers." Considering "The Rain Came," Taiwo notes that its value "lies partly in the way it brings out most of the characteristics of the author's style of writing," as Ogot "uses the techniques of conflict and comparison, humour and pathos to advantage. A song and an element of mystery... carry forward her artistic intentions." Overall, Taiwo concludes that Ogot has "set a high standard of artistic performance" through her "lucid and attractive" style and her genuine "verbal art."

CRITICISM

Michael Allen Holmes

Holmes is a writer and editor. In the following essay, he considers Ogot's implicit commentary on traditional Luo spirituality in "The Rain Came" in light of revisions made from the earlier version, "The Year of Sacrifice."

One might argue that the villagers in Grace Ogot's story "The Rain Came" are portrayed as insensitive and selfish in their celebrations following Oganda's appointment to be sacrificed. Oganda's thoughts reveal her disillusionment with the kinship these villagers supposedly once felt for her: "now she discovered that she was a stranger among them. If they loved her as they had always professed why were they not making any attempt to save her?" Later, as she bids goodbye to the people who have gathered just outside the sacred land, "She looked appealingly at the crowd, but there was no response.... The sooner Oganda could get to her destination the better." In discussing "The Rain Came" in *Gender Voices and Choices: Redefining Women in Contemporary African Fiction*, Gloria Chineze Chukukere goes so far as to claim, "As the victim's sorrowful song indicates, it is only a cruel and unthinking society that endorses such barbarism." Yet in her song, Oganda goes no further than to note that her peers and relations have "consented" to her sacrifice, which has been demanded by the ancestors. Moreover, consideration of Ogot's earlier version of the story, "The Year of Sacrifice," suggests that the author by no means intended to portray these villagers as barbaric, as therein she gives ample support for the premise that the Luos' traditional spirituality forms a legitimate foundation for the villagers' consent to Oganda's fate.

"FOR 'THE RAIN CAME,' OGOT DEVISED A PROVOCATIVE CONCLUSION THAT SEEMS TO BALANCE PERFECTLY BETWEEN CRITICAL REFLECTION ON SPIRITUAL TRADITION AND AFFIRMATION OF THAT TRADITION'S LEGITIMACY."

In "The Rain Came," the role played by traditional Luo spirituality is significant but not overtly dwelled on or elaborated. The story makes clear that the medicine man holds unquestioned status, by virtue of whatever mystical or spiritual experiences have led him to his post, as one who can communicate with the tribe's ancestors, as through dreams. Ndithi's authority is such that the chief and Oganda mourn but never seriously question what the ancestors have demanded through his dream. Indeed, the entire community displays evident faith that Oganda's sacrifice will bring rain. Upon hearing of the ancestors' demand, after a brief "confused murmur," everyone promptly rejoices. Surely, there is little sympathy for Oganda to be found among the villagers, whose excitement leads them to sing and dance and chant Oganda's fate even before she herself has been told. The reader understands that there is a drought, and "cattle lie dying in the fields," while the lives of the people, too, will soon be threatened. But even in light of these reported circumstances, the celebrating villagers come across as tactless at best, crass or vulgar at worst. This impression is heightened as the story

WHAT DO I READ NEXT?

- In *The Island of Tears* (1980), her third short-story collection, Ogot further treats modern Luo life as well as traditional tales, including the popular legend of Nyamgondho, whose statue can still be seen on the shore of Lake Victoria, in "The Fisherman."
- In that they both published their first novel in 1966, the Nigerian Flora Nwapa is recognized along with Ogot as one of Africa's first two female novelists writing in English. Nwapa's *Efuru* (1966) addresses progress in Ibgo society with regard to community and family life, centering on the heroine Efuru.
- Ngugi wa Thiong'o is a Kenyan who writes from a Marxist perspective about the impact Western colonization has had on his people, the Kikuyu, who live primarily in the central Kenyan highlands. His 1982 novel *Devil on the Cross* features a courageous revolutionary woman named Wariinga who signifies her people's fight against lingering colonial oppression.
- The Ugandan poet Okot p'Bitek's *Song of Lawino* (1966) is an internationally esteemed long poem narrating the perspective of a rural wife whose urban-minded husband is eager for Westernization to engulf Ugandan society.
- Elspeth Huxley was a British woman who was raised on a coffee farm in Kenya from the age of five and who came to write some thirty books. Her nonfiction volume *The Flame Trees of Thika: Memories of an African Childhood*, published in 1959, is a picturesque look at her youth.
- Buchi Emecheta is a prolific writer from Nigeria whose works are studied at the highest levels in the British educational system. Her 1972 autobiographical novel *In the Ditch* tells of the trials experienced by a Nigerian woman raising her five children in London.
- *Ripples: Short Stories by Indian Woman Writers* (2010), compiled by Prashant Karhade, features stories by twenty-six different women from India examining the intersections of tradition and modern life.
- Sharon M. Draper's young-adult novel *Copper Sun* (2006) is the story of a fifteen-year-old girl from the Ashanti tribe who is abducted to travel the Middle Passage into slavery. Aimed at mature teenagers, Draper's novel addresses emotionally challenging circumstances such as rape and its consequences.

proceeds, as the villagers overflow with cheer, while Oganda laments their evident indifference to her looming death.

In "The Year of Sacrifice," Ogot provides a much firmer social and spiritual foundation for the villagers' acceptance of Oganda's prescribed fate. To begin, even before the drought arrives—the only calamity the reader of "The Rain Came" is made aware of—the Luo are visited by two plagues, one of locusts and one of army worms, which both destroy a season's entire crop. Descriptions of the different hoes being used and of the crops' gradual growth give the reader a sense of the great time and energy invested in those crops, such that with their destruction, the reader in turn feels more sympathy for the beleaguered villagers. The men agree, "We have never seen it like this"; the double-plague tragedy is truly singular.

When the drought comes, the people's anxiety is heightened. As they watch their children play, "a sickening fear gripped them. The end of all things seemed to be coming. And a feeling of helplessness in the face of the orderings of some hostile celestial power who had not been propitiated was rampant." Indeed, if visited by such calamities, people of any theistic faith would be likely to question whether their deity might be angry for some reason. Here, the Luo identify just such a reason: "The news leaked out that *Jijimb Koth* (the rain-makers) had offered unacceptable sacrifices at the beginning of the season." Further, "Rumour also had it that the angry ancestors would hold rain indefinitely unless they were appeased," and "no one in the whole society thought it right to offend these senior members of the society." In some religions, a deity may be understood to act out of anger or to wield force unfairly, and perhaps there is nothing to be done beyond humble prayer; the deity's actions are accepted regardless of their consequences. In other religious traditions, the people may have means of actively communicating with and appeasing gods or ancestors' spirits. Such is the case with the Luo tradition as presented in this story, with the medium being the rain-maker or medicine man. Belief in this person's mystic ability is so strong that when Ndithi, who is referred to as "our father," joins the meeting called by the chief, "Every one knew that the presence of the ancestors was there with them." When the rain-maker reports his dream, describing the beautiful girl by the lake and Podho's assurance that with her sacrifice, torrential rain will come, the famished, desperate listeners are so moved that their eyes are "blurred with tears." The story then proceeds to the chief's return to his household—the point at which "The Rain Came" begins.

The cumulative effect, then, of the passages on Luo spirituality in the opening pages of "The Year of Sacrifice" is to render the villagers blameless for their seeming insensitivity to Oganda's fate. Their hardships have been extreme; the question of rain is literally one of life or death for the tribe; and the order for Oganda's sacrifice has come directly from the ancestors. In another deleted passage later, in which Chief Labong'o briefly considers going after his daughter to rescue her, the recognized extent of the ancestors' authority is made unmistakably clear: "Indeed he was the chief. But the power was not his. All power was in the hands of the ancestors. Though dead, Podho was still ruling among his people. All power was in his hands."

The reader can only hazard guesses as to Ogot's precise reasons for eliminating these passages in "The Rain Came." She may have been urged by a mentor or editor to cut to the chase, so to speak—she once spoke in an interview of being pressured by a publisher to de-emphasize traditional Luo spirituality—or she may have simply considered the background material non-essential to the story. Still, she otherwise did not rework the remainder of the story to alter the reader's perception of the villagers, and so it seems fair to conclude that she did not intend to subtract the legitimacy of their spiritual beliefs. Rather, she perhaps intended only to make the story briefer, without being able to anticipate that it might thus be construed as, in Chukukere's words, "a myth that exposes a people's blind and selfish acceptance of the concept of human sacrifice." To the contrary, the original version seems to indicate that Ogot considered the villagers' acceptance of Oganda's faith neither blind, being founded in their traditional religion, nor truly selfish, since they are celebrating not merely each's own survival but the survival of the entire tribe, if at Oganda's expense.

Ogot's revision of the ending of "The Year of Sacrifice" seems more instructive regarding her intentions. In the original version, the lake monster is discovered waiting for Oganda by the shore. After a delay, with the monster awaiting in the water, Osinda sweeps in to prevent Oganda from jumping and to slay the monster. The two then leave the scene, and the story finishes without mention of whether or not rain comes. In that version Ogot thus declines to draw any conclusions with regard to the consequences of Osinda's spiritual transgression in aborting the sacrifice. This being her first published story, she was perhaps disinclined to make any controversial commentary on Luo tradition; or perhaps she simply retold her grandmother's version of the story as accurately as possible.

For "The Rain Came," Ogot devised a provocative conclusion that seems to balance perfectly between critical reflection on spiritual tradition and affirmation of that tradition's legitimacy. Throughout the story, affirmation of tradition is implicit in the spiritual framework whereby the Luos' reverence for the ancestors and their belief in the rain-maker's powers leave them no alternative but to accept the dictates of Ndithi's dream. This framework is more fully supported in the passages cut from "The Year of Sacrifice," but the import remains in the revised version.

Now, it might seem that, unless Ogot wishes to deny the legitimacy of ancestor worship, she has to end her story with either Oganda's death or with no rain. That is, the ancestors have indicated that Oganda's sacrifice is necessary for

Many of Grace Ogot's stories are set near Lake Victoria in Africa. (Styve Reineck / Shutterstock.com)

rain. If Ogot wishes to preserve Oganda's life, the drought should have to continue; these are perhaps the implied circumstances of the original version. But in "The Rain Came," the virtuous Osinda conceives of a clever means to subvert the ancestors' authority and prioritize Oganda's life. Oganda herself resists being saved, but Osinda's decisive proclamation that the leaf-and-branch disguises will hide them not just from the lake monster but from the ancestors' eyes as well finally sways her, and she and Osinda flee—and the rain pours down anyway. In preserving Oganda's life, then, Ogot can be read as asserting that the sacrifice of a young woman was not necessary after all. Whether the reader wishes to imagine that the ancestors were successfully deceived or were simply benevolent enough to reward Oganda's faith and courage—as who is to say they cannot change their minds about what is necessary for rain, whether they tell Ndithi or not?—the spiritual presence and authority of the ancestors is not refuted by the conclusion. Thus, in Ogot's stirring finale, Osinda's religious improvisation allows for Oganda's life and their shared love to be saved; for the appeased/deceived ancestors to yet bless Luoland with rain; and for the story to conclude happily without denying the legitimacy of the Luos' traditional spirituality.

Source: Michael Allen Holmes, Critical Essay on "The Rain Came," in *Short Stories for Students*, Gale, Cengage Learning, 2012.

Florence Stratton

In the following excerpt, Stratton hopes to prove that The Promised Land *is, indeed, worthy of consideration as a "mother text."*

Like 1945 and 1958, 1966 is a significant date in African literary history. For in that year Grace Ogot's *The Promised Land*, the first novel by a woman to be published by the East African Publishing House, and Flora Nwapa's *Efuru*, the first work by a woman in the Heinemann African Writers Series, both appeared. The year 1966 can thus be said to mark the advent of a contemporary female tradition in fiction. The event has not been written into the literary records, as critics have tended to treat the publication of the two novels as a non-event. Recently, however, several feminist critics, with no reference to

Ogot's *The Promised Land*, have assigned paradigmatic status to Nwapa's text. Thus according to Susan Andrade: '*Efuru* [is] the first published novel by an African woman and the text that inaugurates an African women's literary history' (97). It is 'the "mother" text of (anglophone) African women's literature' (100). In ordering my chapters, I have given priority to Ogot, partly because she has a legitimate claim to it in that she became a published author before Nwapa, with several of her short stories appearing in journals in the early 1960s. I also hope to show that, in terms of the strategies of resistance it inscribes. *The Promised Land*, too, can be deemed a "mother text."

Ogot is the most forgotten of the women writers I examine. She also provides a particularly striking example of the invisibility of African women writers. Bernth Lindfors describes her as 'Kenya's best-known female writer' ('Interview' 57). But as his own data on the canonical status of African authors shows, the title 'best-known female writer' is an empty epithet. For Ogot's ranking on the first of Lindfors's two tests is only twenty-ninth—whereas that of Kenya's 'best-known' male writer, Ngugi, is third ('Famous Authors" 141–2); and she scores so poorly on his other test—where Ngugi moves into second place—that her name doesn't appear at all ('Teaching' 54–5).

Ogot has had a fairly productive career as a writer. She has to her credit two novels—*The Promised Land* and *The Graduate* (1980)—as well as three volumes of short stories—*Land Without Thunder* (1968), *The Other Woman* (1976), and *The Island of Tears* (1980)—in English. But the critical establishment as well as feminist critics have tended to ignore these works. Ogot has also produced a number of works in Dholuo. Of these, Oladele Taiwo states:

> The writings in Luo—*Ber Wat*, *Miaha*, *Aloo Kod Apul Apul*, *Simbi Nyaima*—may be new to many outside Kenya, but they have proved extremely popular at home. For example, a recent dramatisation of *Miaha* in Luo-speaking areas of Kenya excited the people and showed to what extent drama could be used as a medium of transmitting indigenous culture. (128)

Miaha has recently been translated into English under the title *The Strange Bride* (1989).

Ogot's stance on the language issue is not essentially different from Ngugi's. As early as 1968 she stressed the need for African writers from 'an urban environment' to attempt to bridge the 'great cultural gulf' which separates them from 'the overwhelming majority of the population who live in the villages' ('African writer' 37). And in 1983, she stated that she was prompted to start writing in her first language by her mother's remark on the publication of *The Graduate* that 'If only you could write in Luo you would serve your people well.' She also indicates that she has remained committed to writing in Dholuo so that her work can 'be read by all my people' and her language preserved and not 'swallowed up by English and Kiswahili' (Burness 60). Ogot's decision has not, however, generated any of the interest or debate Ngugi's resolve did a few years earlier to begin writing in Gikuyu. The debate has, in fact, been characterized as a wholly male affair, and Ogot's act has been negated by the absence of critical commentary on it.

Speaking to Lindfors about how she and Ngugi came to write their first novels, Ogot suggests that a kind of regional nationalism inspired them both when they were made aware at the 1962 Makerere conference on African literature of the relative 'literary barrenness' of East Africa ('Interview' 58). Ngugi's *Weep Not, Child* (1964) was much more widely reviewed than Ogot's *The Promised Land*, possibly partly because it was the first novel by an East African to be published. It was also much more favourably received than *The Promised Land*, which was condemned by the critics. Charles R. Larson reviewed both books. *Weep Not, Child* he praises highly, referring to it as one of those 'remarkable first novels' ('Things' 64). Of *The Promised Land* he says, after having criticized Ogot for her handling of theme, plot, mood, dialogue, and character, that it is 'one of the most disappointing African novels in a long time' (Review 44). As is so often the case with mainstream criticism, the condemned text is one which attempts to subvert the manichean allegory of gender, while the one which is commended valorizes it. *Weep Not, Child* is a conventional male narrative—as Taban lo Liyong inadvertently reveals in his review when he contrasts the role of the male characters, the fathers and sons of the story, with that of 'the mothers.' While the former engage in historical struggles, the latter, he observes, 'are symbolic of "mother earth": they give and preserve life and are wise' (43). Or as Elleke Boehmer says of Ngugi's characterization of women in his first two novels: 'We see here Ngugi upholding the patriarchal order by establishing archetypal roles and patterns of relationships that will continue, albeit in transmuted form, into the later novels' ('Master's dance' 12–13).

The reviews of *The Promised Land* and the commentaries on it in overviews of East African literature display many of the trends that are evident in the criticism of African women's writing. The supercilious tone Gerald Moore adopts in his review is typical of male critics' attitude toward women writers. 'Grace Ogot,' he opines, 'would be advised to return to [the short story] form, which she has handled with some skill, and to abjure all attempts to give the visions of her essentially fantastic imagination a realistic dress' (*Review* 95). Moore's review also shows evidence of a careless reading, but Douglas Killam who, in his analysis, confuses, in name at least, the main male character of Ogot's novel with its female protagonist, highlights the insensibility with which some (male) critics read women's novels (126).

From the convention they adopt in naming Ogot, it is evident that Moore and Killam, as well as Larson, were actively aware of gender when they were reading her novel. For Ogot is always either 'Grace Ogot' or 'Miss/Mrs Ogot' (there is critical dissention over her marital status), whereas Ngugi, whom Killam also mentions, is never 'Mr Ngugi,' only occasionally 'James Ngugi,' and almost always 'Ngugi.' Such namings may look innocent, devoid of significance, but they, too, uphold the patriarchal order. The semantic rule underlying the convention is what Dale Spender refers to in her analysis of sexist bias in the English language system as the rule of 'the male-as-norm' (3). Masculinity is the unmarked form, the assumption being that writing is a male activity. Hence, while on first mention or for emphasis it might be 'James Ngugi,' it is almost always simply 'Ngugi.' Femininity is the marked form. In other words, the naming is gendered—'Grace/Miss/Mrs Ogot'—to show a deviation from the norm. The convention therefore not only marks the woman writer for her gender; it also rebukes her for transgressing the norm by daring to take up the pen. Even more insidiously it names her not a writer but a woman, the implicit message encoded in the naming being that it is marriage/motherhood that is her true vocation and not writing.

The rule of the 'male-as-norm' would also seem to underlie the critics' readings of *The Promised Land.* All three critics complain of inconsistencies and improbabilities in the plot. 'But, worse than that,' according to Moore, the story lacks 'force and point' as the male protagonist, Ochola, rather than being 'a tragic figure' is 'merely a misguided one' (*Review* 94); while for Larson the story's 'end destroys the mood of what could have been an idyllic memoir of African agrarian life' (*Review* 44). But it is precisely such male literary representations as Moore and Larson evidently have in mind—Moore of the Okonkwo-type tragic hero and Larson of idealized, Mother-Africa-type evocations of the past such as Camara Laye's *The African Child*—that *The Promised Land* (the title is ironic) challenges. The problem would seem to be, then, not that Ogot's plot is improbable or pointless but that her narrative does not conform to the characteristics of the conventional male narrative.

It is, however, Maryse Conde, one of the few feminist critics to treat Ogot, who offers the most perverse reading of her writing. Conde, too, complains that Ogot's stories lack credibility:

> Grace Ogot lacks neither style nor imagination. But her talents are totally wasted. She is so blinded by her respect for the European codes of behaviour, so confused as to the place of her traditional beliefs, that her female characters possess neither coherence nor credibility.... She may believe that she is an emancipated woman 'who reads books' but what she offers her fellow-countrywomen is a dangerous picture of alienation and enslavement. One feels tempted to advise her to join some Women's Lib. Movement to see how European females question the code of values and behaviour imposed upon them, and to replace her Bible by Germaine Greer's book. (142)

In the advice she offers Ogot, Conde overlooks the cultural and historical specificity of western feminism which she represents as universal. Indeed, it would seem to be Conde herself who is 'blinded by her respect for European codes of behavior.' For at the same time as she condemns Ogot for adhering to western values (of which, in fact, as we shall see, Ogot is highly critical), she urges her to take western feminists as her model.

As Lloyd Brown observes, Conde's reading of Ogot is also skewed by the prescriptive demands of the mode of feminist analysis she employs, the images mode, which requires that writers provide a positive role model for women:

> The critic's ideal of social equality or female independence ought not to distort or obscure the degree to which a writer, any writer, succeeds in depicting the less than ideal lives of women.... Conde seems to assume that an

> uncompromising realism is incompatible with a thorough-going commitment to the ideal of women's equality.

As this excerpt suggests, Brown's own criticism is grounded in what Rita Felski calls 'a reflectionist model' (26), a mode of criticism which subscribes to the notion of representation as unmediated, and which measures a work by its ability to reproduce female experience realistically. As Felski observes, such a model is unable to account for the relation between literature, ideology, and the social domain or for the shaping influence of aesthetic structures (8–9, 28). Brown also glosses over some of the subtleties of Ogot's texts, but his analysis is, on the whole, perceptive, and I draw on it in the discussion of Ogot's short stories and novels that follows.

The main ideological function of Ogot's fiction is to undermine patriarchal ideology by means of a reversal of the initial terms of the sexual allegory. Such an inversion—female and male, good and evil, subject and object—does not resolve the problems of gender, but it is, nonetheless, a subversive manoeuvre. For it exposes the sexist bias of the male literary tradition and creates space for the female subject. As we shall see, inversion is a strategy that other women writers have also employed in their attempt to combat patriarchal manicheism.

In Ogot's writing, inversion is effected in part by the designation of the national subject as explicitly female. Thus Ogot counters both colonial and African male representations of women as passive and ahistorical, as well as providing a critique of colonialism and indigenous patriarchy. I will briefly consider how this and Ogot's other major strategy, the discrediting of the male subject, operate in a number of her short stories, as well as in *The Strange Bride*, before treating *The Promised Land* and *The Graduate* in some detail.

'The old white witch' is set during colonial times at a mission hospital where male and female nurses are being trained under the supervision of Matron Jack, the 'old white witch' of the story's title. Much to the Matron's consternation, she finds that her female charges do not conform to the colonial definition of African womanhood:

> She wished the African women folk were as obedient as their men. She had been told again and again that African men were little Caesars who treated their women like slaves. But why was it that she found the men co-operative and obedient? It was these head-strong females whom she found impossible to work with.

As Nwapa also does in *Efuru*, in this story Ogot casts men in the role of colonial collaborators and portrays women as being foremost in offering resistance to colonial domination. But she is, in this respect, even more confrontational than Nwapa. For having designated women as subjects of African nationalism, she foregrounds their defiant action in her narrative.

The conflict centres on the Matron's requirement that the female nurses conform to English hospital practice and administer bedpans, a ruling which the nurses resist as it contradicts the social conventions of their own cultural heritage which exempt women from what is quite literally the shit-work of their communities and would result, if adhered to, in their social ostracism. The Matron, however, who, in her validation of the racial allegory, epitomizes colonial society, insists that administering bedpans is the nurses' Christian duty. 'Having accepted Christ,' she says, 'you must face the challenge and lead your people who are still walking in darkness and are governed by taboos and superstitions' (10).

Although the male nurses and other African male members of the hospital staff are privately incensed with the Matron for 'treating them like little children' (20) and excluding them from administrative participation, they remain silent about their grievances and identify with the hospital authorities in the dispute. Echoing the sentiments of Matron Jack, their spokesman, the Reverend Odhuno, admonishes the nurses when they threaten to take strike action to 'return to your rooms, change into your uniforms and continue to work in the Lord's Vineyard' (11). As he puts it to the other men: 'We should give our missionaries support' (16). By contrast, the female nurses under Monica's leadership act to liberate themselves from 'the iron rule' of Matron Jack (18). Branding the men 'traitors' (9), they call a strike and decide to leave the hospital and return to their homes for its duration. For, Monica reasons: 'Is it not true that [the Europeans] give orders while we work? Then let them carry urine and faeces—they will not do it for a week. When they are desperate . . . they will call us back, on our terms' (13).

However, as is the case with Okonkwo, history is on the side of Monica's adversaries, which makes a tragic ending to her story also inevitable.

For colonial power relations do not permit the emergence of African national subjects of either gender. Monica falls ill while she is at home and her people take her to the hospital 'against her wish' (25). Having lost consciousness, the once 'headstrong' Monica is as 'co-operative and obedient' as her male colleagues have always been in the face of colonial authority. '[Y]ou can keep your Christianity,' she had once told Matron Jack (10), but the last sacrament, 'the best parting gift that a dying Christian can receive,' is administered to her while she lies helpless, the object of the Matron's ministrations. Regaining consciousness just before her death and recognizing that she has been defeated, she tells her mother to return home, for 'I am staying with the Old White Witch' (25).

In 'Elizabeth' it is post-independence patriarchal relations which reduce the story's eponymous heroine to object status. Like several of the male-authored texts discussed in the previous chapter, 'Elizabeth' is a story of 'post-colonial' disillusionment. But Ogot counters the conventional male account of post-independence experience which, as we have seen, takes the primary of the male subject for granted, with an account of women's anti-national experience. . . .

Source: Florence Stratton, "Men Fall Apart: Grace Ogot's Novels and Short Stories," in *Contemporary African Literature and the Politics of Gender*, Routledge, 1994, pp. 58–66.

SOURCES

Achufusi, Ily, "Problems of Nationhood in Grace Ogot's Fiction," in *Journal of Commonwealth Literature*, Vol. 26, No. 1, 1991, pp. 179–87.

Berrian, Brenda F., "Grace Ogot," in *Dictionary of Literary Biography*, Vol. 125, *Twentieth-Century Caribbean and Black African Writers, Second Series*, edited by Bernth Lindfors and Reinhard Sander, Gale Research, 1993, pp. 184–87.

Burness, Don, ed., "Grace Ogot," in *Wanasema: Conversations with African Writers*, Ohio University Center for International Studies, 1985.

Chukukere, Gloria Chineze, "Grace Ogot: The East African Perspective," in *Gender Voices and Choices: Redefining Women in Contemporary African Fiction*, Fourth Dimension, 1995, pp. 217–67.

Flanagan, Kathleen, "African Folk Tales as Disruptions of Narrative in the Works of Grace Ogot and Elspeth Huxley," in *Women's Studies*, Vol. 25, No. 4, June 1996, pp. 371–84.

Kimbugwe, Henry, "Grace Ogot: The African Lady," in *East Africa Journal*, Vol. 6, No. 4, April 1969, pp. 23–24.

Lindfors, Bernth, ed., "Grace Ogot," in *Africa Talks Back: Interviews with Anglophone African Writers*, Africa World Press, 2002, pp. 268–80.

Nazareth, Peter, "The True Fantasies of Grace Ogot, Storyteller," in *Meditations on African Literature*, edited by Dubem Okafor, Greenwood Press, 2001, pp. 101–18.

Ochieng', William, *People Round the Lake*, Evans Brothers, 1979, pp. 1–32.

Ogot, Grace, "The Rain Came," in *Land without Thunder*, East Africa Publishing House, 1968, pp. 159–71.

———, "The Year of Sacrifice," in *Black Orpheus*, Vol. 11, 1963, pp. 41–50.

Onyango-Ogutu, B., and A. A. Roscoe, *Keep My Words: Luo Oral Literature*, East African Publishing House, 1974, pp. 9–41.

Stratton, Florence, "Men Fall Apart: Grace Ogot's Novels and Short Stories," in *Contemporary African Literature and the Politics of Gender*, Routledge, 1994, pp. 58–79.

"The Subas and Luos," in *Mama Maria Kenya*, http://www.mamamaria.org/subas.htm (accessed February 2, 2011).

Taiwo, Oladele, "Grace Ogot," in *Female Novelists of Modern Africa*, St. Martin's Press, 1984, pp. 128–62.

FURTHER READING

Haar, Gerrieter, *How God Became African: African Spirituality and Western Secular Thought*, University of Pennsylvania Press, 2009.

This brief volume gives an accessible discussion of the myriad ways that traditional spirituality and Christianity have merged on the African continent.

Kingsolver, Barbara, *The Poisonwood Bible*, HarperPerennial, 1998.

This renowned novel is narrated by the women in the family of Nathan Price, a Baptist missionary who, in 1959, plunges his wife and four daughters into the utterly foreign world of the Belgian Congo, an experience that ultimately tears the family asunder.

Maloba, Wunyabari O., *Mau Mau and Kenya: An Analysis of a Peasant Revolt*, Indiana University Press, 1998.

Maloba's volume is an excellent overview of the movement that helped usher Kenya toward independence from British colonial rule.

Ogot, Bethwell Allan, *A History of the Luo-Speaking Peoples of Eastern Africa*, Anyange Press, 2009.

Grace Ogot's husband, Bethwell Ogot, is one of the Luos' most accomplished historians, with dozens of written and edited volumes to his credit. This publication follows up on his 1967 *History of the Southern Luo* to focus on all Luo-speaking people up to the present day.

SUGGESTED SEARCH TERMS

Grace Ogot AND The Rain Came

Grace Ogot AND The Year of Sacrifice

Ogot AND Luo AND history

Bethwell Ogot AND Kenya AND history

Luo AND Kenya

Luo AND Kenya AND independence

African women novelists

modern African literature

Grace Ogot AND African literature

Wasps' Nest

AGATHA CHRISTIE

1928

Agatha Christie's "Wasps' Nest," also known by the title "The Worst of All," was first published in the periodical *Daily Mail* in 1928. It is a short mystery story with themes of hatred, revenge, and redemption. These themes are common in many of Christie's mysteries. "Wasps' Nest" is the only story that Christie ever personally adapted for television, and it was performed live for the British Broadcasting Corporation (BBC) in 1937. The short story was first presented to her American audience in the 1961 collection *Double Sin, and Other Stories*. It can also be found in the 1974 British volume *Poirot's Early Cases*, which was released as a Google eBook in 2009.

Though Christie is critically acclaimed for her mystery novels, the initial reviews of *Double Sin, and Other Stories* were weak, despite its featuring Christie's beloved detective Hercule Poirot. The character starred in her first novel, *The Mysterious Affair at Styles*, and he remained extremely popular with her fans throughout her career. The final Poirot mystery, *Curtain*, was published in 1975. Poirot is the first literary character to have an obituary printed in the *New York Times*. Often referred to as the "Queen of Crime," Christie helped define a genre, and her work remains popular.

Agatha Christie *(The Library of Congress)*

AUTHOR BIOGRAPHY

Agatha Mary Clarissa Miller was born in 1890 at her family home of Ashfield in Torquay, Devon, England. Her father died in 1901, and she frequently traveled with her mother while they rented the family home. The future author did not have a formal education, but she did study music. She was notoriously shy, however, and could not perform in public. In 1914, she married Archibald Christie, a colonel in the Royal Flying Corps. Agatha Christie volunteered at a hospital during World War I, working as a nurse and in the dispensary. While studying for her Apothecaries Hall Examination, she learned a great deal about medications and poisons. Her daughter, Rosalind, was born shortly after the war in 1919.

Christie also began her writing career soon after World War I, a time many literary critics, such as K. D. M. Snell in an article for *Social History*, refer to as "the Golden Age" of detective fiction. Christie's first mystery novel, *The Mysterious Affair at Styles*, featuring Hercule Poirot, was published in 1920. She became a well-known author in 1926 with the publication of another Poirot novel, *The Murder of Roger Ackroyd.* She also created her equally famous female detective, Miss Marple, in 1926.

Unfortunately, Christie's mother died the same year. Her husband asked her for a divorce shortly after because he had fallen in love with another woman. The Christies temporarily reconciled for the sake of their daughter; but Christie admitted in her *Autobiography* that the reconciliation was a mistake. In December of that year she went missing for eleven days. She was found registered at the Harrogate Hydropathic Hotel under the same last name as her husband's mistress. She never spoke of the incident, and the official story was that she had amnesia. Christie and her husband divorced in 1928, the same year that "Wasps' Nest" was first published in the *Daily Mail.*

In 1930, Christie met and married archaeologist Max Mallowan, who was fourteen years younger than the author, who retained the name she had been writing under. She traveled with him on digs and took pictures of his artifacts. Many of her later novels are set in the locations she traveled to with Mallowan. She was president of the famous Detection Club, whose members included Dorothy Sayers and G. K. Chesterton. Christie never stopped writing mysteries, though she diversified her writing in later years, publishing romance novels under the name Mary Westmacott. She focused on writing for theater in the 1950s, and her play *The Mouse Trap* holds the record as the longest-running modern play. In 1971, Christie was made a dame of the British Empire. She died after a brief illness on January 12, 1976, in Cholsey, near Wallingford, England. Over the course of her career, Christie completed eighty novels and short-story collections, fourteen plays, and four nonfiction books.

PLOT SUMMARY

The omniscient narrator begins "Wasps' Nest" by describing a summer morning on which John Harrison, who is spending time in his garden, is unexpectedly visited by his old friend Hercule Poirot. Harrison is described as "big," and his face is "cadaverous." This stands in stark contrast to the vision of Hercule Poirot as "dandified," a word that means the detective keeps an immaculate appearance. Poirot is a "world

MEDIA ADAPTATIONS

- "Wasp's Nest" was adapted for the BBC television series *Agatha Christie's Poirot* by David Renwick, starring David Suchet. It originally aired January 27, 1991, and was released through AcornMedia.
- *Wasp's Nest, and Other Stories* is an audiobook published by HarperCollins Audio in 2000. Hugh Fraser, who played Captain Hastings in *Agatha Christie's Poirot* on the BBC, reads the stories.
- *The Wasp's Nest* was released as a digital audiobook by BBC Audiobooks America in 2009. This version, narrated by BBC television actor David Suchet, is unabridged.

famous detective" from Belgium. His native language is French, which explains his odd English word order. Christie has Poirot use phrases in French that would be familiar to her original audience. For example, Poirot calls Harrison *mon ami*, which means "my friend."

Harrison is initially surprised to see Poirot, but Poirot reminds Harrison that he was told to stop by if he were in the area. Harrison is hospitable to his guest, and over the course of the conversation, Poirot explains that he is visiting the small town on business. Poirot is there to investigate a murder that has not occurred yet, and he is determined to stop it before it happens. He then informs a confused Harrison that his help is needed to prevent the crime.

Harrison argues that it is impossible to know when a murder is going to happen, but Poirot immediately changes the subject to the wasps' nest in Harrison's garden. Harrison explains that Claude Langton is going to kill the wasps with petrol (the British term for gasoline) later in the day. Poirot reminds Harrison, while simultaneously informing the readers, that the other method for killing wasps is the poison cyanide potassium. He goes on to explain that Claude Langton had recently purchased some of the deadly poison, according to the "poison book" at the chemist. During this period in history, people signed poison books when buying any dangerous substance from a chemist, like cyanide potassium, in order to document the purchases. Harrison does not seem disturbed by the news, even after Poirot reminds him that his fiancée, Molly Deane, was previously engaged to Langton. When Poirot asks Harrison if he likes his former rival for Molly's affection, the reply is affirmative: "I—I—well, I mean—of course I like him."

Poirot asks if Langton likes Harrison, and Harrison insists that Langton has been a good sport about losing Molly. Poirot warns him "that a man may conceal his hate till the proper time comes." Harrison refuses to acknowledge the possibility of murder. He is adamant that people in England do not kill each other over failed romances. Poirot becomes angry at Harrison's refusal to listen. He compares the victim of the coming crime to the wasps in the nest; all are going about life without any warning of the danger to come. Harrison informs Poirot that Langton will come destroy the nest at nine o'clock. Poirot leaves and tells Harrison that he will return to watch the wasps' nest be removed.

Poirot checks his watch as he leaves and notices that he has to wait three-quarters of an hour. He is unsettled as he walks around the town. He returns a few minutes early and rushes back to the garden. At the gate, Poirot meets Claude Langton as he is leaving. Langton appears nervous and in a hurry to leave. Langton is surprised when Poirot points out that he is early, and he informs the detective that he did not touch the wasps' nest.

Poirot finds Harrison on the veranda and asks him if he is feeling well. Harrison does not respond at once. In a "queer, dazed voice," he asks Poirot what he said. Now Poirot asks Harrison if he feels "ill affects" from the washing soda. Harrison is stunned as Poirot reveals to his friend, and the readers, that he placed washing soda in Harrison's pocket earlier that morning. A bewildered Harrison listens as Poirot explains that a pickpocket once paid Poirot for proving his innocence by teaching him "the tricks of his trade."

Poirot goes on to say that he traded the contents of Harrison's pocket with washing soda. He then takes the stolen substance out of his own pocket and mixes it with water. As he does so, Harrison watches, "fascinated." Once the mixture is dissolved, Poirot walks to the wasps' nest and pours the liquid into it. He watches as the wasps crawl out and die. Harrison asks Poirot how much he knows.

Poirot confesses that he spoke with Langton shortly after seeing his name in the chemist's poison book. Langton's explanation was that Harrison asked him to buy the poison for a wasps' nest. Poirot knew that Harrison prefers to use petrol on wasps because cyanide is so dangerous, and this knowledge made him suspicious. This incident, combined with overseeing a meeting between Langton and Molly, confirmed Poirot's suspicion that Molly has left Harrison and gone back to Langton.

The real clue for Poirot, however, occurred when he saw Harrison leaving an appointment with the doctor. Poirot is familiar with the doctor, and he saw in Harrison "the face of a man under sentence of death." He also saw the hatred that Harrison felt because Harrison did not believe anyone was watching. Harrison admits that he only has two months to live. Poirot reveals that the earlier conversation was a trap for Harrison, one that confirmed Poirot's suspicion that Harrison was choosing to act on his hatred for his rival. Poirot knows that Harrison's earlier surprise about the cyanide, during their first discussion, was not genuine. He knows that Langton was supposed to meet Harrison at half past eight. Poirot was aware of this from speaking with Langton earlier.

Poirot explains Harrison's plan to his friend as well as the readers. The plan was to have Langton come over thirty minutes earlier than Poirot. Harrison would drink the cyanide while alone with Langton, and Poirot would find his body. Harrison continually asks why Poirot has come, and Poirot explains, "murder is my business." Harrison argues that he planned suicide, but Poirot quickly points out that, in reality, he planned the murder of Langton. There is evidence against Langton. His name is in the poison book, and he would have been the last to see Harrison alive. Without Poirot, Langton would have been tried for murder and hanged. His humiliation and death would have been Harrison's revenge.

Poirot explains to Harrison that he also came to prevent the suicide because Harrison is not a murderer. At the end of the story, Poirot asks Harrison if he is happy or sorry about Poirot coming. Harrison, who has complained of Poirot's arrival throughout the final scene, thanks his friend for coming.

CHARACTERS

Molly Deane

Molly Deane does not make an appearance in "Wasps' Nest," but she is central to the story. Both Harrison and Langton are in love with her. She is a beautiful woman who breaks her engagement with Langton for Harrison, but she eventually returns to Langton. Her actions provide Harrison with a motive for committing suicide and trying to frame Langton for his death.

John Harrison

John Harrison is an old friend of Hercule Poirot's. He is in love with Molly Deane, and his rival for her affection is Claude Langton. He loves his traditional English rose garden, and he is described as "a big man with a lean, cadaverous face." This is a hint at the character's health. Harrison feigns a friendship with Langton but secretly hates him. There is a wasps' nest in his garden, and he asks Langton to buy cyanide for him under the pretext of needing it to destroy the wasps. During his first conversation with Poirot, Harrison attempts to encourage the detective's suspicion of Langton by pretending not to know that Langton purchased cyanide for his wasps' nest. He pretends to be naive by emphatically denying that Langton would ever attempt to kill him.

At their second encounter, Harrison admits that he planned on killing himself with the cyanide that he asked Langton to buy for him because, due to his health, he has only two months to live and wants to commit suicide. Fueled by hatred and the need for revenge, Harrison plans to frame Langton for his murder. He thinks that his plot is successful until Poirot reveals that the cyanide he drank was really washing powder. By the end of the story, Harrison sees the error of his actions and admits that he is thankful Poirot stopped him. He ends the narrative finding his dignity and redemption.

Claude Langton

Claude Langton appears briefly in the story. He was the fiancé of Molly Deane, before Harrison, and the audience eventually learns that the two have rekindled their romance. Poirot describes him as a "nervous young fellow, good-looking with a weak mouth!" Langton is unaware that

Harrison hates him and wants to frame him for murder. He buys the cyanide to kill the wasps for Harrison without knowing that Harrison plans on using the poison to commit suicide. It is Langton who unwittingly provides Poirot with the information that allows the detective to save both Langton and Harrison.

Hercule Poirot

Poirot is described as a "dandified figure" in the story, which means that he is elegantly dressed. His appearance is the exact opposite of John Harrison. Harrison does not suspect that the short detective is a threat to his plans and instead considers Poirot to be a convenient witness. Christie does not provide a detailed description of Poirot in this story because he is already established in her novels. He is known for his large mustache and impeccable wardrobe. He typically solves crimes with his friend Captain Hastings, who is inexplicably absent from "Wasps' Nest." Christie describes the Belgian detective in her *Autobiography*: "I could see him as a tidy little man, always arranging things, liking things in pairs, liking things square instead of round. And he should be very brainy." Being Belgian, Poirot's native language is French, and he frequently uses French expressions.

Poirot informs Harrison that he is trying to prevent a murder that has not happened yet. At first, Poirot appears to be warning Harrison to be careful of Langton. He becomes annoyed when Harrison refuses to acknowledge his warnings and keeps insisting that Langton would never hurt anyone. In reality, the detective is trapping Harrison into confirming his suspicions. Poirot insists that a murder will be committed and periodically insists, "Murder is my business." At his second meeting with Harrison, Poirot lets the readers and his friend in on a secret. He has been aware of Harrison's hatred of Langton and his desire for revenge from the beginning. The detective uses intuition and observation to understand what could happen and prevent Harrison's plot from becoming reality. In the end, Poirot offers Harrison a chance for redemption.

TOPICS FOR FURTHER STUDY

- Read *A Study in Scarlet: A Sherlock Holmes Graphic Novel*, Ian Edginton's young-adult adaptation of Sir Arthur Conan Doyle's classic story. Compare the methods of detection that Holmes and Poirot use. How are they similar? How are they different? Write a short story where the two detectives work on a mystery together. Be sure to include how you think they would respond to the case and to each other.
- Research the period between World War I and World War II (1919–1939) in England using both print and online resources. Create a video or multimedia presentation of the time period that focuses on the sociological changes. Include a time line of Christie's stories in the presentation.
- Read the book *Girl in Translation* by Jean Kwok, winner of an American Library Association Alex Award, and research xenophobia in the 1920s. Create a Twitter feed, social media page, or blog for Poirot. Write messages from the detective about his experiences as a foreigner among the upper class with Kimberly, the main character of Kwok's novel.
- Research Christie's contemporary and associate Dorothy Sayers. Write a one-act play in which Christie and Sayers work together to solve a murder. How well would they work together? Ask a classmate to perform the play with you. Record the performance and post it on a Web site or blog.

THEMES

Hatred

"Wasps' Nest" explores the concept of hatred, as Harrison's hatred drives his actions in the story. Harrison hides his hatred both to keep his reputation as a good person in the village and to fool his rival. His attempts to conceal his contempt for Langton from Poirot are not successful because Poirot understands that people conceal negative emotions such as hatred from those around them. Poirot is a great detective because he pays attention to clues regarding human emotion and behavior.

Poirot explains to Harrison "that a man may conceal his hate until the proper time comes," which is exactly what Harrison does. By keeping

Poirot visits Harrison in his garden patio to warn him. (Paul Saini / Shutterstock.com)

his impending death and the end of his engagement to Molly Deane secret, Harrison is able to conceal his true feelings from people. He even fools Langton into believing that they can still be friends. Poirot, however, is able to discern Harrison's hatred. He explains a time he observed a particular look on his friend's face: "I saw hate there my friend. You did not trouble to conceal it because you thought there were none to observe." Poirot knows that people who act on their hatred commit crimes of passion and seek revenge when the time is right. Hatred is the cause of many crimes in Christie's mysteries.

Revenge

Revenge is a classic motive for murder, and it is a theme that is closely aligned with hatred, particularly in "Wasps' Nest." Harrison is driven to revenge by his hatred and despair, which sets the scene for the crime that Poirot must prevent. Poirot understands Harrison's desire for revenge. "Listen, *mon ami*, you are a dying man; you have lost the girl you loved," he explains, as he sympathizes with his friend at the end of the story. Harrison's actions are motivated by his need to take revenge against Langton for stealing Molly from him at the end of his life. Harrison's desire for revenge consumes him and overpowers his better judgment. He justifies his own behavior and ignores the severity of the crime he is plotting.

In his own mind, Harrison is not responsible for Langton's murder because he is not planning on actually killing the man. His plot for revenge is to commit suicide and incriminate Langton in his death. When Poirot describes the planned murder, Harrison exclaims, "Murder? Suicide, you mean." But Poirot does not allow his friend to believe this lie, forcing Harrison to confront how his plot for revenge would lead to Langton's death. "You die suddenly, and the cyanide is found in your glass, and Claude Langton hangs. That was your plan." Harrison's need for revenge is so great that he is willing to exact it from beyond the grave and become a murderer with his final living act.

Redemption

"Wasps' Nest" is just as much a story about redemption as it is about revenge. Harrison is saved and able to find redemption through the help of Poirot. Poirot admits that one reason for his visit is murder. It is not enough, however, to simply prevent a crime. Poirot also likes Harrison; he considers the man to be a friend. In saving Langton, Poirot also saves his friend from becoming a killer. Anne Hart notes in *The Life and Times of Hercule Poirot* that Harrison is "rescued by Poirot from a terrible deed." At first, after Poirot has undone his plot, Harrison bemoans the fact that Poirot's appearance has undone his plan. Even when Poirot confronts him with the truth that his plot is indeed murder, Harrison refuses to let go of his need for vengeance. He continues to ask, "Why did you come?"

Poirot helps Harrison realize the truth by telling him, "You are not a murderer." By pointing out what he is not, Poirot reminds Harrison of his true self and warns him of what he could become. When Poirot finally asks, "Tell me now: are you glad or sorry that I came?" Harrison visibly changes. In that moment, he realizes that he has been saved. He lets go of his hatred and his need for revenge as he finds redemption.

Xenophobia

Xenophobia is a common theme in British literature from the 1920s. It is a Greek term that means a fear of anything or anyone foreign. Xenophobia leads to negative stereotypes and a feeling that one's culture is superior to others. The xenophobic argument in "Wasps' Nest" is a statement Harrison uses to hide the truth from Poirot, ostensibly defending Langton by saying that murders by "disappointed suitors" do not happen in England. Poirot himself, in turn, makes some disparaging comments about the English. Christie's story reflects the attitudes prevalent in her time, but it also creates a sense of irony in that Harrison makes a xenophobic comment to a foreigner, while Poirot insults the nationality of the friend with whom he is conversing.

STYLE

Mystery

"Wasps' Nest" is a mystery story, like most of Christie's works. Christie and many of her contemporaries wrote detective fiction, a subset of the mystery genre. Established by Edgar Allan Poe and Arthur Conan Doyle, detective fiction revolves around a detective who solves crimes, typically with the help of a confidant. By the 1920s, because the format of the mystery story "foregrounds the puzzle element, the genre has developed rules of 'fair play' that are meant to enable the reader equal opportunity to solve the puzzle," according to Malcah Effron in the journal *Narrative.*

"Wasps' Nest" is an unorthodox mystery because a crime does not actually occur. Poirot tells Harrison, and the readers, that he is there to prevent a murder involving Harrison. This statement catches the readers' attention and keeps them looking for different clues to identify the potential murderer. Christie, like other mystery writers, attempts to mislead her readers. In "The Whodunit as Riddle: Block Elements in Agatha Christie," Eliot Singer explains that in her stories, "information and interpretation provided by characters is often accidentally or deliberately false."

Short Story

Christie is best known for her mystery novels, but she is also responsible for sixteen short-story volumes, including *Double Sin, and Other Stories*, which includes "Wasps' Nest." A true short story, like "Wasps' Nest," is a short narrative that has a distinct plot, progression, and resolution. It is also possible to finish reading a short story in one sitting. Using a short story allows Christie to focus on character development. The psychological change in Harrison is more dramatic to readers because it happens quickly.

Third-Person Omniscient Narrator

The story "Wasps' Nest" is told from the point of view of an omniscient narrator who speaks in the third person. The narrator provides clues to the readers through the imagery and descriptions of the characters. For example, when presented with the question of whether he likes Langton, Harrison's reaction is peculiar: He "started. The question somehow seemed to find him unprepared." Being omniscient, the narrator is able to explain the feelings and attitudes of the characters, making the motives of the characters easier to understand. For example, the narrator

COMPARE & CONTRAST

- **1920s:** The detective story, established by Poe and Doyle, is embraced in literary circles, leading to the "Golden Age" of mystery. Christie begins a career as a mystery writer that lasts fifty years.

  Today: Mystery stories are still popular, but modern mystery writers do not strictly adhere to the format created by Poe and Doyle. Some mystery novels are more violent, but Christie's classic work remains popular.

- **1920s:** Xenophobia and certain prejudices are socially acceptable in the 1920s. This is particularly true in the upper classes. Christie and other authors of the time show the acceptance of racial and social bias.

  Today: While prejudice still exists, it is not as socially acceptable as it used to be. Many of Christie's stories have been altered to remove offensive descriptions and terms.

- **1920s:** Members of the upper class are born into their stations at the turn of the century. The British class system begins to change after World War I as education and wealth become available to the lower classes, but the social classes rarely mix.

  Today: A social class system still exists in Britain, but it is more flexible than it used to be. Birth no longer strictly determines wealth or status, and people from different classes are not as segregated. For example, it is possible for royalty to marry someone from a lower class, as in the 2011 marriage of Prince William to Kate Middleton, whose parents are businesspeople rather than nobility (people born into the upper class).

describes a moment when Poirot is "suddenly alarmed.... He feared he knew not what."

Imagery

Imagery allows readers to see pictures in their minds. The narrator provides descriptive images in "Wasps' Nest" that help the readers better understand the characters and the motives behind their actions. For example, Harrison is described as having a "cadaverous face" at the beginning of the narrative. This image associates Harrison with death. The readers later learn that Harrison is both dying and plotting a murder.

Dialogue

"Wasps' Nest" uses dialogue extensively. Dialogue is conversation that involves two or more people. Poirot has three different conversations in "Wasps' Nest." There are two conversations with Harrison and one with Langton. Christie uses dialogue in this story to provide the necessary background for the characters and move the plot forward. The dialogue presents the reader with misinformation, but it also provides clues to unmask the potential murderer.

HISTORICAL CONTEXT

British Class System

The British class system was firmly established in the early twentieth century. Society began to change rapidly after World War I. Industry and mass production made it possible for people outside the established upper class to purchase inexpensive luxuries, and common people had greater access to education, though class divisions still remained. The 1918 Education Act granted free education for everyone under the age of fourteen. G. E. Sherington explains in "The 1918 Education Act: Origins, Aims, and Development" that the impulse behind the passing of the act was "related to the historical interest in war and the social change of twentieth century Britain." Education, however, continued to divide the classes. Upper-class or upper-middle-class families sent their children to

Poirot hints to Harrison of danger through a reference to the wasp's nest. (Kirsanov / Shutterstock.com)

private schools, and lower-class children went to public institutions. Even with the class distinctions, however, society was changing. More upper-class men had to take jobs, and many found it difficult to hold onto their former way of life.

As a member of the upper-middle class, Christie set her stories in the world in which she lived. As Joan Acocella notes in the article "Queen of Crime," Christie's characters disapprove of "housing developments and supermarkets. They complain bitterly about how heavily they are taxed and how they can no longer afford to maintain the grand houses they saw as their birthright." Her mysteries reflect the social changes between the world wars and beyond. "Wasps' Nest" was published just months before the stock-market crash of 1929.

Freudianism

Sigmund Freud was born in Austria-Hungary, and he lived in Vienna for most of his life. He studied psychiatry and developed the concept of psychoanalysis in 1896. His ideas regarding the subconscious and sexuality were popularly embraced after the horrors of World War I. Freudian theories were extremely popular in the 1920s, and Christie was familiar with the concepts. They became general topics of conversation, and elements of Freudianism can be seen in the literature of the time. Mystery stories that expose the psychological motives behind actions were particularly popular venues for Freudianism.

The late 1930s were not as kind to Freudianism. Freud's books were burned in Nazi Germany and in Russia. Being of Jewish descent, Freud was forced to flee Vienna for London after the Germans invaded. He died of throat cancer in 1939. His theories, however, are still recognized.

Golden Age of Mystery

The time between World War I and World War II is known as the "Golden Age of Mystery," according to literary critics such as Snell. Edgar Allan Poe is often credited with establishing the genre of detective stories with his 1841 short story "The Murders in the Rue Morgue," featuring the eccentric detective C. Auguste Dupin. Arthur Conan Doyle solidified the rules of mystery detectives with Sherlock Holmes, who delighted readers from 1887 to 1914. The prevalence of science at the turn of the twentieth century also helped to establish the mystery story. Mysteries were taken to a new level with the influence of psychoanalysis, as the motives and passions behind crimes became important to readers. The availability of paperback books also contributed to the success of mysteries. Mystery stories from the golden age typically include an unconventional detective with a confidant or sidekick. The detective solves a crime, usually a murder, by following the chain of evidence. Christie began writing mysteries over thirty years after Doyle, and she put her own mark on the genre by using closed settings, such as an isolated spot in the countryside, a train, or another setting that forces the suspects together. An individual at the scene solves the mysteries.

Becoming a mystery writer was not a shocking choice for Christie. Mystery stories crossed the social classes in Great Britain, and female writers such as Virginia Woolf made it easier for women to enter the literary world. Members of every social class were reading and attempting to write mystery stories. Intellectual writers such as T. S. Eliot and G. K. Chesterton wrote mysteries. Female contemporaries of Christie included Dorothy Sayers and Patricia Wentworth. Sayers created the sleuth Lord Peter Wimsey, and Wentworth was famous for Maude Silver. The classic mystery changed with the times after World War II. Christie, however, continued to create settings that remained clean and cozy, even as the genre changed around her.

CRITICAL OVERVIEW

"Wasps' Nest," the short story, was not widely reviewed when first published. American critics reviewed the volume it was part of, *Double Sin, and Other Stories*, in 1961. The initial reviews of this collection of short stories were not strong. As Dennis Sanders and Len Lovallo explain in *The Agatha Christie Companion*, her short stories were not as well received as her novels: "American critics, like their English counterparts, generally thought that these collections were not the best Christie." *New York Times* critic Anthony Boucher, whom Sanders and Lovallo quote, gives the collection a "grade B . . . or possibly B-plus."

Christie's work was widely popular in her lifetime and remains popular to this day. Critics, however, have always been divided on her work. Her first popular novel, *The Murder of Roger Ackroyd*, was criticized for breaking the rules of mystery established by Poe and Doyle. At the same time, its surprise ending helped to build her popularity as an author. Christie's writing style was criticized as well. Andrew Taylor describes the viewpoint of critics who have not appreciated her work in "Agatha Christie: The Curious Case of the Cosy Queen." He reports that critics find Christie's work to be "sub-literary, best considered as something between a trivial pursuit and a mildly shameful addiction."

Jake Kerridge sums up many of the critical arguments against Christie in a 2007 essay in the London *Telegraph*. He states that some critics "criticise her for not portraying murder realistically." Others accuse her of "artificial plots, flat prose, cardboard characters. Some complain of xenophobia, snobbishness, general fuddy-duddery." Anti-Semitic sentiment has become a main source of modern criticism. It is true that Christie's work was altered in her own lifetime to remove racial stereotypes and terms. She did, however, portray the world that she knew. Her stories, including their negative attributes, illustrate the social customs of the time. Regardless of the opinions of critics, past and present, Christie has become the best-selling novelist of all time. UNESCO has declared her the second-most translated author, and about four billion copies of her books have been sold to date.

CRITICISM

April Paris

Paris is a freelance writer who has an extensive background working with literature and educational materials. In the following essay, she argues that the purpose of "Wasps' Nest" is to explore the psychological motivations that drive a person to commit murder.

Rather than presenting the solving of a crime in "Wasps' Nest," Agatha Christie explores the psychology behind murder and what may drive a good man to kill. She also provides a glimpse into

WHAT DO I READ NEXT?

- *Skip Beat*, Volume 2, by Yoshiki Nakamura, was published in 2006. In this manga, teenage girl Kyoko gives up everything for the boy she loves, only to be rejected. This is a popular young-adult story that explores the themes of betrayal and revenge in modern Japan.
- Carol Plum-Ucci's *The Body of Christopher Creed* is a 2001 Michael L. Printz Honor book, published that year. This mystery examines ideas of social class and friendship as popular high-school student Torey Adams investigates the disappearance of Christopher Creed with the help of some unlikely friends.
- The 1927 Poirot mystery *The Murder of Roger Ackroyd* is a classic example of a Christie mystery novel. Reprinted in 1996, it illustrates her skill as a writer and shows the detection methods of the famous Hercule Poirot as he solves a murder case in a small village with the help of Dr. James Sheppard.
- *Cloud of Witnesses*, by Dorothy Sayers, published in 1926, is another example of mystery from the golden age of mystery, reprinted in 1995. Sayers shows how mystery writers at the time created unique characters within similar settings, as her famous Lord Peter Wimsey attempts to prove his brother innocent of murder.
- Patricia Wentworth's 1937 novel *The Case Is Closed* features the writer's female detective Maude Silver. A contemporary of Christie's, Wentworth's character shows similarities to and striking differences with Miss Marple. The novel is perfect for anyone interested in the golden age of mystery.
- Susan Roland's *From Agatha Christie to Ruth Rendell: British Women Writers in Detective and Crime Fiction* (2001) explores the impact of women on the mystery genre. The book carefully examines the life and times of six writers, including Sayers, Margery Allingham, Ngaio Marsh, and P. D. James, as well as the title subjects.
- John and Janet Shepherd's *1920s Britain* discusses London after World War I. Published in 2010, it examines the changes in society that took place after the war was over and provides an overview of the positive and negative events of the decade.
- *Murder at the Vicarage*, published originally in 1930 and re-released in 2006, introduces readers to Christie's famous female detective, Miss Jane Marple. In her debut mystery, Miss Marple solves the murder of the hated Colonel Prothereo.

the mind of her famous detective, Hercule Poirot. The psychology of murder is a subject that dominates many of Christie's mysteries. Poirot puts his understanding of psychology to good use in this short story. He carefully observes the emotions and motives of those around him, particularly John Harrison, to identify a potential killer and prevent a murder. The detective plays a psychological game and manipulates his friend in order to stop the crime before it is committed. As a result, Poirot saves more than one life while helping his friend, Harrison, reach a personal psychological breakthrough.

Christie's 1928 audience was most likely familiar with Freud's theories and the effects of the subconscious on human behavior. Although Christie makes it easy for an unsuspecting reader to believe that Langton is the culprit, clues regarding Harrison's true feelings and mental state appear throughout the story. For example, he makes a Freudian slip regarding his feelings toward Langton. A "Freudian slip" occurs when someone misspeaks or does something that betrays hidden thoughts or feelings. Harrison's response is positive when asked if he likes Langton, but he is surprised and stammers his answer.

> **"THE DETECTIVE PLAYS A PSYCHOLOGICAL GAME AND MANIPULATES HIS FRIEND IN ORDER TO STOP THE CRIME BEFORE IT IS COMMITTED. AS A RESULT, POIROT SAVES MORE THAN ONE LIFE WHILE HELPING HIS FRIEND, HARRISON, REACH A PERSONAL PSYCHOLOGICAL BREAKTHROUGH."**

"I—I—well, I mean—of course I like him." Harrison reinforces his rather weak response by asking why he would not like Langton. Poirot knows, and later the reader understands, that Harrison has a very good reason to dislike Langton. Poirot, aware that Molly Deane is leaving Harrison to return to Langton, further baits his friend by discussing the motive that Langton would have for disliking Harrison, as Molly was previously engaged to Langton and left him for Harrison.

Using that scenario, Poirot brings up how easy it is for rivals to hate each other. As Poirot discusses Langton's possible motive for murder, he is really describing Harrison's motives. As Richard Kellogg points out in "The Psychology of Agatha Christie," "Poirot is a student of human motivation and is usually concerned with the unconscious motives of his suspects." Harrison seems to defend Langton by insisting that the man has gone out of his way to be friends. Harrison makes another Freudian slip by describing his supposed friend as "amazingly decent." Poirot latches on to this phrase: "You use the word 'amazingly,' but you do not seem to be amazed." The idea that rivals for the same woman's affection would be close friends is amazing to Poirot, as it probably is for the reader. The detective then describes the true purpose of the friendship between Harrison and Langton: "The sportsman—the good fellow—never will they believe evil of him." By feigning a friendship, it is easier for Harrison to plot revenge without detection. It also increases the likelihood that he will avoid suspicion after revenge is taken.

While he defends Langton, Harrison actually attempts to bring him under greater suspicion. The would-be killer plays the naive friend in an effort to misdirect both the detective and the audience. He tells Poirot that Langton "fancies himself at the job" of destroying the wasps' nest, meaning that Langton thinks he's good at removing wasps' nests and has offered to do away with the one in Harrison's garden. Harrison makes it seem as though the idea is Langton's. Additionally, Harrison reacts rather calmly when he is informed that Langton purchased cyanide potassium from the chemist. He does conveniently add that Langton, "said it oughtn't to be sold for the purpose" of killing wasps and other pests. Poirot, however, already knows from an earlier conversation with Langton that Harrison asked his friend to purchase the poison for him.

Harrison comes to the conclusion that Poirot is attempting to warn him that his friendship with Langton will lead to murder. He believes that the detective suspects Langton, but Poirot does not make his warning specific. He merely nods when Harrison says, "You came here today to warn me." Once Harrison thinks that Poirot suspects Langton, he becomes adamant in his defense of his rival and overcompensates while playing the role of the trusting friend.

Harrison makes a xenophobic argument to justify his friendship with Langton and to convince Poirot that he is wrong about there being a risk of murder. "This is England. Things don't happen like that here." Harrison thus makes an illogical and prejudiced argument that people in other countries may commit murder out of jealousy, but an English gentleman would not. The statement displays Harrison's personal feelings toward foreigners, and it is another attempt to disguise his own guilt. Poirot, however, uses the other man's prejudiced point of view to his advantage, as he does in several other stories. In many of Christie's books, Poirot is dismissed or underappreciated because he is not English. Rather than fight against the stereotype, however, he embraces it. The Belgian detective finds it easier to make observations when people dismiss his importance. They are less guarded with their knowledge and their responses. The fact that Harrison does not perceive Poirot as a threat to his plan provides the detective with ample opportunity to make observations and ask questions without drawing suspicion.

Before Harrison even expresses his own xenophobic point of view, Poirot expresses his own stereotype of the English. "'The English are very stupid,' said Poirot. 'They think that they can deceive anyone, but that no one can deceive them.'" The "English" in this case is John Harrison. Poirot again complains about English stupidity when Harrison refuses to take his warning of murder seriously. Harrison believes that he is successfully deceiving Poirot and everyone else. In reality, however, Poirot is deceiving Harrison. Poirot allows Harrison to continue his self-deception in order to safeguard his own plans, protect his friend, and avert a crime.

Poirot's use of psychology extends beyond simply understanding the motives of those around him. He also "uses his expertise on non-verbal communication, or body language, in solving crimes," according to Kellogg. The motives of criminals are fairly common in Christie's mysteries. In his article for *Western Folklore*, Eliot Singer explains that the criminals are typically "husbands, wives, lovers, relatives, or others with clear cut motives of gain or vengeance." The motivation may be simple, but the clues that Poirot uses to discover these motives are the subtle reactions of his suspects, such as facial expressions and tone.

Poirot becomes aware of Harrison's plan by observing three separate scenarios. He sees Harrison's fiancée with Langton when they believe no one is watching. He also notices Harrison leaving a doctor, a specialist. In his friend's unguarded face, Poirot sees the look of a dying man and his hatred. Aware of the relationship between Langton and Molly, Poirot does not find it difficult to determine exactly whom Harrison hates. When the detective sees Langton's name in the poison book, Harrison's plot for revenge becomes clear.

The detective reveals all of his observations at the end of the story, but the reader is meant to make his or her own observations about Harrison. The omniscient narrator provides the audience with many of the non-verbal cues that the detective would notice, and the reader is expected to draw conclusions based on this evidence, which is just as important as Harrison's Freudian slips. For example, when Poirot encounters Harrison the second time, Harrison is sitting "motionless." He does not even look at Poirot. His expression is "dazed." The reader who does not pay attention to the earlier clues may confuse his careless behavior with the effect of poison, but Harrison is actually displaying the disconnected behavior of a man who believes he is committing suicide.

Poirot understands hate, which is why he allows Harrison to believe that his goal to frame Langton for murder is accomplished. Poirot knows that it is not possible to reason with Harrison in his current state. The detective gives Harrison every opportunity to confess when he explains that his reason for coming was to prevent a murder. Even when confronted with his own plan, Harrison will not change. He desperately clings to his hatred and continues to plan revenge. Poirot is familiar with the way that hatred overpowers rational thought. By switching the cyanide potassium that Harrison planned to take with some harmless washing powder, Poirot allows Harrison to believe the plot is successful. Poirot manipulates and deceives Harrison in order to save him.

Harrison and the audience are not immediately aware of Poirot's ability to pick pockets. Christie's famous detective, however, is a pragmatist. He is infamous for using unorthodox, or even criminal, methods to solve crimes. As Anne Hart points out in *The Life and Times of Hercule Poirot*, "He rejoiced in his belief that the end often justified the means." The psychology of the detective is revealed in this behavior. He does not immediately confront Harrison with what he knows, and he never warns Langton of what he suspects. He is motivated by the need to solve a mystery and protect his friend. Poirot wants to save the man from becoming a murderer as much as he wants to prevent the murder itself.

The police are not summoned in this story. It is not the only time that Poirot abstains from sharing his knowledge with law enforcement. Susan Hardesty explains in the *English Journal* that Poirot always looks for justice rather than conviction, stating, "The conflict between which is worse—procedural prosecution or personal punishment—has tormented humanity for centuries." Poirot has a certain loyalty to his friend, and he wants Harrison to end his life free from the burden of hate. Throughout the mystery, Poirot provides Harrison with two reasons for his presence. The obvious one is Poirot's motto: "Murder is my business." The second reason is the fact that Poirot likes Harrison. He feels a sense of loyalty toward his friend.

Poirot finally forces Harrison to face the truth of his actions. Harrison tries to claim that Poirot only succeeded in stopping a suicide. The man's attempted suicide, however, was really a very clever murder plot. Poirot contends that it does not matter if Harrison kills Langton or if Langton receives the death penalty for Harrison's

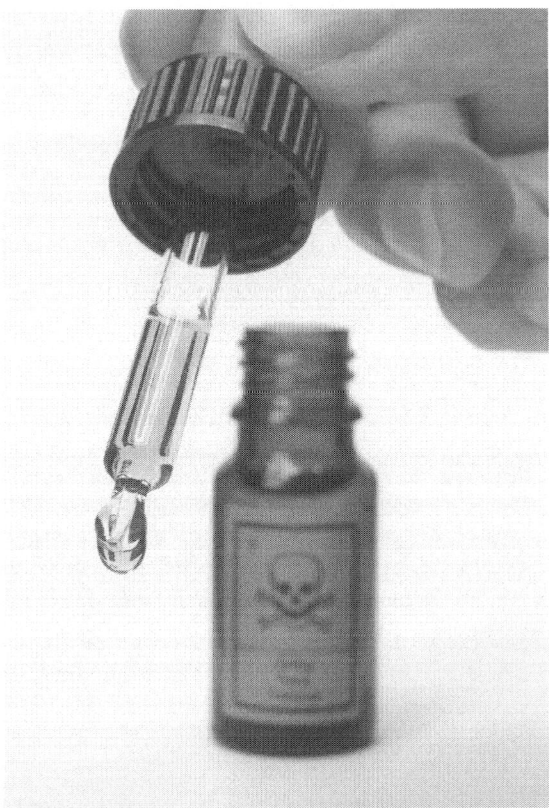

Poirot knows that Langdon bought cyanide.
(filmfoto / Shutterstock.com)

suicide. Harrison is guilty of murder if his actions are directly responsible for Langton's death. Hate and desperation cloud Harrison's better judgment. Had the detective ignored his suspicions, cleared Langton of murder, and revealed Harrison's plot, Harrison's hatred and revenge would have always been remembered. The noble actions of his life would have been forgotten. Framing Langton is out of character for Harrison, a man whom Poirot considers a friend.

By thwarting Harrison and making him see how close he came to becoming a murderer, Poirot helps the man reach a psychological breakthrough. By the end of the story, Harrison regains his control over his own life. "There was a new dignity in his face—the look of a man who has conquered his own baser self." Hate and revenge no longer consume him. He will die the way that he lived. Poirot's basic understanding of human psychology allows him to prevent a murder and save his friend from becoming a murderer.

Source: April Paris, Critical Essay on "Wasps' Nest," in *Short Stories for Students*, Gale, Cengage Learning, 2012.

"TRANSLATING THAT ART FROM THE PAGE TO THE SCREEN IS NO MEAN FEAT, THOUGH THAT HASN'T STOPPED DIRECTORS AND SCREENWRITERS FROM TRYING."

David A. Fryxell

In the following essay, Fryxell argues that Christie's works have not been successfully adapted for film.

"Everybody loves a gossip," Agatha Christie once said by way of explaining her phenomenal popularity. That's why she thought her mysteries have outsold everything but the Bible and Shakespeare: people love to snoop into other people's lives. Christie let her readers snoop into lives—and deaths—ranging from those of the tea-cozy denizens of quaint English villages to the upper crust on board the Orient Express. And what better topic for really juicy gossip than murder?

The Public Broadcasting Service knows how popular the subject of murder—especially of the Agatha Christie variety—can be, as evidenced in the popularity of its "Mystery" series. Beginning November 29, "Mystery" presents five adaptations of Christie's "Tommy and Tuppence" mysteries. James Warwick and Francesca Annis star in the London Weekend Television productions of "Partners in Crime." Tommy Beresford and Prudence "Tuppence" Crowley were two old chums who stumbled into detection and, later in their fictional careers, into matrimony. The *New York Times* called their escapades "the merriest collection of detective stories it has been our good fortune to encounter." The series begins with the couple's takeover of a detective agency, and each segment solves a different mystery. And this series only begins to tap the vast resources of Agatha Christie fiction.

Certainly, few "gossips" have been as prolific or profitable as Agatha Christie. In over fifty-five years, until her death in 1976, she penned nearly one hundred mystery novels and short-story collections, a half-dozen romantic novels under the name Mary Westmacott, twenty-one plays, and a two-volume autobiography. Her publishers claim to have long ago lost count of Christie's sales; American paperback editions of her works have easily topped half a billion books. *The Murder of Roger Ackroyd*, generally conceded to be the cream of Christie, has alone sold over a million copies. Fans have followed their beloved Agatha in more than one hundred languages.

Her play *The Mousetrap* nightly adds to its record as the longest-running production in English theatrical history. The play has outlived eight of the newspapers that originally reviewed it in 1952. Impresario Peter Saunders, who had predicted a six-month run, has since said, "Just about everybody in England has seen it except the Queen, and she thinks she's seen it."

The only media the queen of crime fiction was never quite able to crack were motion pictures and television. With a few exceptions—the Oscar-nominated *Witness for the Prosecution* and the box-office smash *Murder on the Orient Express*—Christie's works and her popularity have stubbornly resisted translation to the screen. To disappointed fans and dismayed producers, that failure remains the greatest single mystery in the career of Dame Agatha Christie.

Only Hercule Poirot could have detected the potential for greatness in this utterly conventional Englishwoman. Born Agatha Mary Clarissa Miller at a Devonshire seaside resort in 1890, she never attended school; her mother taught her at home. In 1914, Agatha showed the first clue of a taste for a life more thrilling than church fetes and tea on the lawn, marrying a dashing pioneer in the Royal Flying Corps named Archie Christie. World War I swept Archie off to the skies and Agatha to a military hospital, where she assisted in the dispensary.

Two years before, Agatha's elder sister Madge had challenged her to write a detective story. In the dispensary, surrounded by poisons, Agatha decided to take her up on it. In the years and books to come, she would knock off victims by such esoteric means as a kitchen skewer, a bronze figure of Venus, an electrified chessboard, a surgical knife, and an antique grain mill—but poison always remained her favorite. (At least one real-life poisoner modeled his crime on a Christie plot, *The Pale Horse*.) Her first poisoning was *The Mysterious Affair at Styles*, written in 1915 but not published until 1920. Therein she gave the world the inimitable Hercule Poirot.

Recalling a colony of Belgian refugees she encountered at Devonshire, she made her man a retired Belgian police detective. As a contrast to his stature—"hardly five-foot-four"—she named him for the mighty Hercules. "Poirot," she said, just popped into her head.

As far as Christie was concerned, Poirot's first case would also be his last. She'd met her sister's dare and that was that. But when the book finally saw print, it made enough money to prod her to try another. In the following six years, she published seven books and set the mystery world on its ear with the revolutionary *The Murder of Roger Ackroyd.*

That same year, 1926, Christie created a real-life mystery by vanishing without explanation for ten days. When she reappeared claiming amnesia, cynics decried it as a publicity stunt. Others have blamed a breakdown triggered by the death of her mother and the revelation of her husband's infidelity; she'd checked into a spa under the name of her husband's mistress. The mystery of those blank ten days, never unraveled, inspired a semifictional book and a 1978 movie, *Agatha*. Despite a stellar cast featuring Vanessa Redgrave and Dustin Hoffman, the film (true to Christie form) failed to shine either with critics or at the box office.

After several years of depression, Christie indulged her lifelong love of trains and an interest in ancient ruins with a jaunt to the Near East on the Orient Express. That led to a novel, *Murder on the Orient Express*, and to her second marriage, to the assistant head of the archaeological digs, Max Mallowan.

The 1930s introduced readers to Christie's second great sleuth, the spinsterish Miss Marple—inspired by Christie's grandmother—whose constant flurry of knitting needles camouflaged her true hobby, "the study of human nature." And the decade produced some of Christie's best mysteries: *The ABC Murders*, *Death on the Nile*, and *Ten Little Indians.*

She would churn out at least a book a year until her death. Christie likened her prodigious production to "a sausage machine, a perfect sausage machine"—and the readers ate it up. In 1954, the Mystery Writers of America honored her with their first Grand Master of Crime Award. The next year, *Witness for the Prosecution* won the New York Drama Critics Circle award for best foreign play, the only mystery ever to do so. (*The Mousetrap*, amazingly, had flopped on Broadway.) Though Christie was already the grande dame of mystery, the Queen made it official in 1971 by naming her a Dame of the British Empire.

Yet Dame Agatha, still an English country girl at heart, chafed under the burden of fame. "I still have that overlag of feeling that I am *pretending* to be an author," she complained. Shy with strangers, she refused to make speeches and dodged interviews. When Britain's Detection Club elected her president, she made a deputy propose all the toasts and introduce guests. Her work seemed to decline as her fame rose: Dilys Winn, founder of Manhattan's Murder Ink bookstore, rates Christie's *Elephants Can Remember* (1972) as one of the ten all-time worst mystery novels. And Christie, like Conan Doyle before her, longed to be rid of her most famous detective. She finally wrote Hercule Poirot off in 1940 in *Curtain*, but the book didn't see print until 1975.

Most agree Christie was the master plotter of the age; as reviewer Will Cuppy put it, "She's probably the best suspicion scatterer and diverter in the business." And Margaret Miller, admiring the devious scheme of *Witness for the Prosecution*, perhaps said it best for all Christie peers in the profession: "I knew she really had a twisted little mind. I wished I had thought of it."

A few carpers found Christie's elaborate plots all too bloodless, like "animated algebra." In a famous essay entitled "Who Cares Who Killed Roger Ackroyd?" Edmund Wilson railed, "You cannot read such a book, you run through it to see the problem worked out; and you cannot become interested in the characters, because they never can be allowed an existence of their own, even in a flat two dimensions, but have always to be contrived so that they can seem either reliable or sinister, depending on which quarter, at the moment, is to be baited for the reader's suspicion."

Not even Christie's most fervent partisans would lay much claim for her strictly literary ability. Asked about her writing style, Otto Penzler, owner of the Mysterious Book Shop in Manhattan, sputtered, "Writing *what?* Writing *what?* I don't think she had much of a 'writing style.' A lot of best-selling writers would have trouble getting an 'A' on a college paper, but they strike a common chord that defies explanation."

Nonetheless, Penzler made a stab at explanation. "Agatha Christie wasn't threatening to anybody. Picking up an Agatha Christie book is like putting on cuddly old slippers." Similarly, Anthony Le Jeune concluded in *The Spectator*: "The real secret of Agatha Christie . . . lies not in the carpentering of her plots, excellent though that is, but in the texture of her writing. . . . In a literary sense, she doesn't write particularly well. But there is another sense which for a writer of fiction is perhaps even more important. The ability to buttonhole a reader, to make, as Raymond Chandler put it, 'each page throw the hook for the next,' is a separate and by no means uncommon art."

Translating that art from the page to the screen is no mean feat, though that hasn't stopped directors and screenwriters from trying. They began in 1928, when both movies and Christie's reputation were young. The first Christie adaptation, like the latest, brought to life her third-string sleuths, Tommy and Tuppence. Christie introduced the happy-go-lucky pair in her second book, *The Secret Adversary* (1922), which in 1928 was made into a German film titled *Die Abenteuer Gmbh* (Adventures Inc.), not a resounding success.

The first English-language stab at a Christie film was *The Passing of Mr. Quinn*, based on a minor short story. Filmmakers finally discovered Hercule Poirot in *Alibi* (1931), the first of three movies starring Austin Trevor as the Belgian sleuth. Trevor, much too tall for Poirot, was supposedly cast because he could do a French accent. Evidently that skill was not enough; none of the British-made films was released in the United States and they've vanished since from the archives. The third, *Lord Edgeware Dies*, would be the last attempt at portraying Poirot for thirty years.

A Christie film didn't cross the Atlantic until 1937, when *Love from a Stranger* paired Ann Harding and Basil Rathbone in an adaptation of the story "Philomel Cottage." Eight more years passed before anyone tried again.

Then, at last, Christie had something of a hit. *And Then There Were None*, adapted from *Ten Little Indians*, set ten familiar stars on a remote island and bumped them off one by one. Critics and audiences liked it enough to encourage two remakes (1965 and 1975), both titled *Ten Little Indians*, though with success that dwindled over time as rapidly as the number of survivors in the plot.

But back in the postwar years, it seemed as though the Christie puzzle had been cracked. When *The Mousetrap* hit pay dirt on the London stage, Romulus Films snapped up the movie rights—accepting the stipulation that *The Mousetrap* couldn't be made until six months after the play closed. They're still waiting. In the meantime, though, *Witness for the Prosecution* went from Broadway to Hollywood under the talented direction of Billy Wilder. He assembled an impressive cast: Charles Laughton, Marlene Dietrich, Tyrone Power, and Elsa Lanchester. To further boost interest, public relations flacks hung a Secrecy Pledge outside each movie house where the film opened; everyone who bought a ticket had to swear not to reveal whodunit. The ploy drew audiences and the picture drew six Oscar nominations.

Yet the only follow-up to this success was a minor film called *The Spider's Web*, also adapted from a Christie play. Made in England in 1960, it was never even released in the United States.

Moviemakers went back to square one in 1962, trying to break the jinx with a series of five movies about (at last) Miss Marple. The draw here was not Christie as much as it was the formidable Margaret Rutherford as Miss Marple. Though utterly wrong physically for the slim, spinsterish Marple (Christie said of Rutherford, "To me, she's always looked like a bloodhound"), Rutherford brought enough verve to the role to carry it through four of the planned five films. She made *Murder, She Said*; *Murder at the Gallop*; *Murder Most Foul*; and *Murder Ahoy!* before increasing silliness and decreasing ticket sales cut the series short. Only the first derived from an actual Miss Marple novel. Two were sleuth and sex-change operations from Poirot books; an offended Christie admitted, "I get an unregenerate pleasure when I think they're not being a success." The last was an original screenplay, of which Christie clucked, "It got very bad reviews, I'm pleased to say."

The movies finally returned to the real thing—Hercule Poirot as himself—in *The Alphabet Murders* (1966, based on *The ABC Murders*). Originally intended as a Zero Mostel vehicle, the production languished for two years because Christie, from bitter experience, objected to the script. It was finally made with Tony Randall heavily made up—though not heavily enough to shield him from the critics who branded the film a slapstick travesty.

After a non-Poirot flop titled *Endless Nights* (one reviewer wrote, "This movie wasn't released—it escaped"), Poirot and Christie finally made it big on-screen with *Murder on the Orient Express* in 1974. Director Sidney Lumet spared no expense in recreating the lavish look of a bygone era, constructing his own Orient Express at Elstree Studios near London. The all-star cast of suspects—Lauren Bacall, Richard Widmark, John Gielgud, Sean Connery, Wendy Hiller, Vanessa Redgrave, Ingrid Bergman (who won an Oscar as best supporting actress)—overshadowed Albert Finney as Poirot, which was perhaps just as well. *Murder on the Orient Express* made a killing; it was the most profitable wholly British-financed film to date.

The same producers hired director John Guillermin to make more box-office magic with *Death on the Nile*. He rounded up another cast of heavyweights, substituted Peter Ustinov as Poirot, and spent seven weeks on location in Egypt. The film's New York opening coincided with ticket sales for the Metropolitan Museum's King Tut show; then *Death on the Nile* went back in the can for two months until the Tut extravaganza actually opened. With a little help from Tut, it did well enough to inspire another Ustinov outing as Poirot, *Evil under the Sun*—more posh locales, more name actors, but also more labored.

In the meantime, director Guy Hamilton had taken another crack at bringing Miss Marple to the screen, this time with Angela Lansbury in *The Mirror Crack'd*. Elizabeth Taylor and Kim Novak, as rival movie stars, turned in their best work in years.

Television has since brought a few minor Christies to life in made-for-television movies and in a series of short stories on PBS's "Mystery." Amazingly, there has never been a commercial-network series based on Christie's characters.

Otto Penzler doesn't think the mysterious record of Christie works on screen is so strange at all. "To be fair, it's very difficult to put a good detective story on screen and make a good detective movie," he observed. "Most of what happens is cerebral—observing clues, making deductions—and that's hard to portray in an exciting manner on screen. It's just a different medium. You can't translate popularity to screen necessarily, and it's a mistake to try to make analogies between the two forms. A very ordinary book can be made into a great movie, and vice versa."

Christie herself wondered why she allowed her books to be ravaged on the screen. But, for Christie's fans, hope—like murder—springs eternal. They keep tuning in, knowing that every Christie puzzle is solved eventually—isn't it?

Source: David A. Fryxell, "All about Agatha," in *Horizon*, Vol. 27, No. 9, November 1984, pp. 42–45.

"IT IS VERY CLEAR, THEN, THAT MISS CHRISTIE IS NO MORAL ABSOLUTIST WHERE MURDER IS CONCERNED."

Stewart H. Benedict

In the following essay, Benedict considers the culpability of Christie's murders, arguing that Christie may have paved the way for justifiable murders in mystery fiction.

Just as in politics the British offspring of an American mother became the symbol of Empire in a time of need, so too the most typically English mystery novels have come from the pen of an authoress who, although she can boast of almost a hundred million sales, cannot boast of one hundred percent pure U.K. blood. The lady in question is of course Agatha Christie, whose heraldry bears a transatlantic bar sinister, but who in her books has out-Harrowed the Harrovians and out-Blimped the Blimps.

Miss Christie launched her criminal career in 1920, with *The Mysterious Affair at Styles*, and, since this first case, has finished almost seventy others and has dispatched close onto two hundred fictional victims, incidentally becoming the world's best-selling authoress in the process.

Evidently fully convinced that nothing succeeds like success, Miss Christie at the start of her career relied on Sir Arthur Conan Doyle about as whole-heartedly as, say, V. I. Lenin did on Karl Marx. Her debt to the Sherlock Holmes stories can be seen in her choice of titles for novels (like *The Secret Adversary* and *The Big Four*) and short stories (like "The Adventure of the Cheap Flat," "The Tragedy at Marsdon Manor," and "The Mystery of Hunter's Lodge").

Indeed, the team of Hercule Poirot and Captain Hastings, as originally conceived, is a virtual carbon copy of Holmes and Watson. Poirot, like Holmes, is a convinced and convincing spokesman for the human rational faculty, has an unshakable faith in his own reason, uses his long-suffering Boswell as a sort of echo-chamber, and even has a mysterious and exotically named brother who works for the government. Captain Hastings, like Watson a retired military man, has much else in common with his prototype: he is a trusting, bumbling, superingenuous ex-soldier whose loyalty is touching but whose intellectual abilities, especially when turned loose on a problem of deduction, are so feeble as to be risible. Occasionally, though, the amanuensis wins applause from the master by making an observation which by its egregious stupidity illuminates some corner previously dark in the innermost recesses of the great mind.

Nor does the fumbling and ineffectual Inspector Lestrade lack a copy: Inspector Japp of the Christie novels is equally tenacious, incorruptible, and uninspired.

But the Baker Street influence permeates far deeper than these superficial features would indicate. Many scenes from Agatha's earlier works, especially those presenting conversations between the two principals, are considerably more Holmesian even than the literary collages constructed in imitation of the master by Adrian Conan Doyle and John Dickson Carr.

At the same time as she was writing by formula, Miss Christie was experimenting with a second type, in which she tried out various assorted detectives and crime-chasers, professional, semi-professional, and amateur.

In these novels she introduced a whole gallery of new sleuths: Tuppence and Tommy, Colonel Race, Superintendent Battle, Mr. Harley Quin and Mr. Satterthwaite, Parker Pyne, and Jane Marple. Some of the newcomers starred once and subsequently reappeared in supporting roles, some never moved out of short stories, while Miss Marple joined Poirot as a Christie regular.

Tuppence and Tommy Beresford, whose specialty was ferreting out espionage, made their debut in *The Secret Adversary*, showed up again in *Partners in Crime* and were resurrected in 1941 for *N or M?* Their frivolous and insouciant approach to detection, if something of a relief-giving contrast to the Holmes-Poirot methodology, nonetheless must have made them seem to their creatress too unreliable to cope with any subtle or complicated crime.

The enigmatic, laconic Colonel Race appeared first in *The Man in the Brown Suit* and sporadically thereafter. The Colonel, whose *locus operandi* was the colonies, did make it back to England for the fateful bridge party in *Cards on the Table*, but clearly his chief interest lay in shoring up the house that Rhodes built. Further, although not precisely what Miss Christie customarily refers to as "a wrong 'un," the Colonel gave the distinct impression of being willing to temporize on questions of ends and means, a point of view, we must assume, acceptable in the colonies but not in the Mother Country.

Superintendent Battle, stolid, dependable, hard-working, came onto the scene in *The Secret of Chimneys* and solved *The Seven Dials Mystery*, but his lack of color and elan must have been responsible for his being relegated to a subordinate role on later cases.

The most atypical product of the Christie imagination was the weird pair consisting of the other-worldly Harley Quin and his fussbudgety, oldmaidish "contact," Mr. Satterthwaite. The short stories in which they figured marked the authoress' closest approach to the occult.

Another unusual character who debuted during this experimental period was Parker Pyne. The ingenious Mr. Pyne specialized not in solving murders, but in manipulating the lives of others so as to bring them happiness and/or adventure. In some of these cases he was fortunate enough to have the assistance of Mrs. Ariadne Oliver, the mystery novelist. Just as it could not be proved that Willie Stark is Huey Long, so too it could not be stated flatly that Ariadne Oliver is Agatha Christie, but many of the clues seem to point in that direction. Mrs. Oliver's incessant munching on apples, her sartorial disorganization, and above all her theories on the art of the mystery novel make it difficult to avoid that conclusion.

It was in 1930, in *Murder at the Vicarage*, unquestionably the best-written Christie novel, that she first presented the character who became one of her two favorites. The attraction to Jane Marple is not hard to understand: she is one of those personified paradoxes in whom both authors and readers delight. Behind the antique, Victorian, tea-and-crumpets, crocheted-antimacassar facade, is a mind realistically aware of the frailty of all human beings and the depravity of some.

About 1935 there began to appear the third type, or what might best be called the genuine Christie novel, with its numerous unique features.

Most publicized among these features, of course, is the use of an extraordinary gimmick: in *Murder in the Calais Coach* the murder is done with the connivance of a dozen people; in *The ABC Murders*, the highly suggestible suspect believes himself guilty of a series of crimes of which he is innocent and convinces the reader of his guilt; in *And Then There Were None*, the reader is led to believe that the killer has been a victim in a series of murders.

Less discussed, but really more significant, is the Christie ability to manage what may be called (to pirate a phrase from Sarcey) "the optics of the mystery." The successful mystery novel involves a special problem: the death(s) of the victim(s) must be made of interest, but not of deep concern, to the reader. The conventional, or, by now, hackneyed, methods of developing this special attitude in the reader are two: either the prospective corpse is presented so briefly that, living, he makes no impression at all, or he is depicted as so vicious that the audience looks forward eagerly to his demise.

Miss Christie, however, has evolved a completely different formula: she arranges a situation which is implausible, if not actually impossible and into this unrealistic framework places characters who act realistically for the most realistic of motives. In *Easy to Kill*, for example, four murders are committed in a minuscule town without any suspicions being aroused; in *A Murder Is Announced* the killer advertises in advance; in *What Mrs. McGillicuddy Saw!* the witness to a murder is a passenger in a train which travels parallel to another train just long enough for Mrs. McGillicuddy to see the murder. And, of course, some of the Christie Classics, especially *Murder in the Calais Coach, And Then There Were None*, and "Witness for the Prosecution," really test the ductility of coincidence.

As for the realistic elements, in only one instance (the short story "The Face of Helen") does a murderer have recourse to a bizarre weapon; in every other case a completely pedestrian one is used: the poison bottle, the knife, the gun, the garrote, the bludgeon. The motive is always equally pedestrian: it is invariably either money or love.

The single characteristic which most stamps a whodunit as a Christie product, however, is the fate of the killer. Miss Christie sees murderers as being either good or bad individuals; the good ones dispose of evil victims, and vice versa. Further, the bad murderer is distinguished because he unvaryingly preys on people with inadequate defenses: he may be a doctor (and therefore *ipso facto* to be trusted, as contemporary folklore teaches us); or a handsome and clever lover who first uses, then kills, a woman who has been unlucky enough to fall in love with him; or an old and respected friend and confidant; or a man who selects a child, an old person, a physical or psychological cripple as a victim. This element, the victim's inadequate defenses against the criminal, puts the murderer beyond the pale—he is unsportsmanlike and consequently despicable. Over and over reference is made to the viciousness of those who betray faith and trust. Says Dr. Haydock in *Murder at the Vicarage* after he learns that the murderer has attempted to pin his crime on an innocent young curate who suffers from sleeping sickness and is not really sure of his own innocence: "The fellow's not fit to live. A defenseless chap like Hawes." In an analogous situation Hercule Poirot says to Franklin Clarke, who has actually succeeded in getting the suggestible epileptic Alexander Bonaparte Cust to believe himself a murderer: "No, Mr. Clarke, no easy death for you . . . I consider your crime not an English crime at all—not above-board—not sporting— . . ." He adds later, in analyzing the crime, "It was abominable— . . . the cruelty that condemned an unfortunate man to a living death. *To catch a fox and put him in a box and never let him go.* That is not *le sport*."

Conversely, when the victim is completely unsympathetic and the murderer a decent person, it is very possible that the culprit will be revealed to be a sufferer from a far-advanced case of some incurable disease. If he is healthy, he usually has or is presented with the opportunity to commit suicide. On rare occasions such a person escapes any punishment at the hands of the law: in *Murder in the Calais Coach*, for instance, the victim turns out to have committed an especially unsportsmanlike crime and the otherwise tenacious Hercule Poirot simply steps out of the case, leaving it unsolved.

It is very clear, then, that Miss Christie is no moral absolutist where murder is concerned. In *Mr. Parker Pyne, Detective* Ariadne Oliver, speaking, we suppose, for the authoress, asks Poirot, "Don't you think that there are people who ought to be murdered?" The view that there are indeed such people seems to be sustained in *And Then There Were None*, in which no less than ten preeminently sleazy slayers are dispatched by a retired judge who escapes legal justice through suicide. The entire tone of this book gives the strong impression that Miss Christie is not sorry to see them go. It also suggests that there is a stratification of murderers, with special punishment due those whose crimes have been particularly un-British, i.e., heinous, even though the later Miss Christie can hardly be accused of advocating unrestrained *laissez-tuer*.

Since Miss Christie's prestige among her fellow mystery writers is towering, and since she has by implication espoused the quaint theory that a sportsmanlike murder doesn't really count, it is interesting to speculate as to whether this latitudinarian attitude has in any way influenced the writers of the hard-boiled school with their philosophy that it is all right to kill a killer. Paradoxical as it may seem, perhaps the literary godmother of bone-crushing Mike Hammer is none other than genteel Jane Marple.

Source: Stewart H. Benedict, "Agatha Christie and Murder Most Unsportsmanlike," in *Claremont Quarterly*, Vol. 9, No. 2, Winter 1962, pp. 37–42.

SOURCES

Acocella, Joan, "Queen of Crime," in *New Yorker*, Vol. 86, No. 24, August 16, 2010, pp. 82–88.

"Celebrity Central: Kate Middleton," in *People.com*, http://www.people.com/people/kate_middleton/biography (accessed on April 11, 2011).

Christie, Agatha, *An Autobiography*, Dodd Mead, 1977, pp. 244, 339–40.

———, "Wasps' Nest," in *Double Sin, and Other Stories*, St. Martin's Press, 2002, pp. 27–42.

Effron, Malcah, "On the Borders of the Page, on the Borders of Genre: Artificial Paratexts in Golden Age Detective Fiction," in *Narrative*, Vol. 18, No. 2, May 2010, pp. 199–219.

Hardesty, Susan, M., "Using the 'Little Grey Cells,'" in *English Journal*, Vol. 72, No. 5, September 1983, pp. 37–40.

Hart, Ann, *The Life and Times of Hercule Poirot*, G. P. Putnam's Sons, 1990, pp. 109, 187.

"Index Translationum," in *United Nations Educational, Scientific and Cultural Organization*, http://www.unesco.org/xtrans/bsstatexp.aspx?crit1L=5&nTyp=min&topN=50 (accessed April 11, 2011).

Kellogg, Richard L., "The Psychology of Agatha Christie," in *Teaching of Psychology*, Vol. 10, No. 1, February 1983, pp. 46–47.

Kerridge, Jake, "The Crimes of Agatha Christie," in *Telegraph* (London, England), October 11, 2007, http://www.telegraph.co.uk/culture/books/non_fictionreviews/3668468/The-crimes-of-Agatha-Christie.html (accessed February 23, 2011).

"Miss Marple in Pictures: from Margaret Rutherford to Jennifer Garner," in *Telegraph* (London, England), http://www.telegraph.co.uk/culture/culturepicturegalleries/8413673/Miss-Marple-in-pictures-from-Margaret-Rutherford-to-Jennifer-Garner.html?image=9 (accessed April 11, 2011).

Sanders, Dennis, and Len Lovallo, *The Agatha Christie Companion*, Berkley Publishing Group, 1984, p. 288.

Sherington, G. E., "The 1918 Education Act: Origins, Aims, and Development," in *British Journal of Educational Studies*, Vol. 24, No. 1, February 1976, pp. 66–85.

Singer, Eliot, "The Whodunit as Riddle: Block Elements in Agatha Christie," in *Western Folklore*, Vol. 3, No. 4, July 1984, pp. 157–71.

Snell, K. D. M., "A Drop of Water from a Stagnant Pool? Inter-war Detective Fiction and the Rural Community," in *Social History*, Vol. 35, No. 1, February 2010, pp. 21–50.

Taylor, Andrew, "Agatha Christie: The Curious Case of the Cosy Queen," in *Independent* (London, England), July 23, 2010, http://www.independent.co.uk/arts-entertainment/books/features/agatha-christie-the-curious-case-of-the-cosy-queen-2032999.htm (accessed March 3, 2010).

FURTHER READING

Cade, Jared, *Agatha Christie and the Eleven Missing Days*, Peter Owen, 2006.

This is an investigative look at Christie's lost eleven days. Armed with his own theory, Cade examines the evidence from the time. It is a helpful book for anyone interested in exploring the mystery that still surrounds the author.

Curran, John, *Agatha Christie's Secret Notebooks: Fifty Years of Mysteries in the Making*, HarperCollins, 2009.

Curran's volume presents passages from Christie's notebooks that illustrate her writing process. The notebook material is presented with biographical information and criticism. Both the author's original notes and Curran's criticism are useful for an in-depth study of Christie's work.

DuBose, Martha H., *Women of Mystery: The Lives and Works of Notable Women Crime Novelists*, Minotaur Press, 2000.

This collection of essays explores the work of female mystery writers, beginning with early mystery writers and the transition to the golden age. Modern mystery authors are also included. The volume combines the study of mystery literature with feminist history.

Herbert, R., et al., eds., *The Oxford Companion to Crime and Mystery Writing*, Oxford University Press, 1999.

This reference book includes information about different types of mystery stories. Students with an interest in mystery will find this an excellent source for terms, history, and facts about the genre.

McCall, Henrietta, *The Life of Max Mallowan: Archaeology and Agatha Christie*, British Museum Press, 2001.

McCall's biography of Mallowan explores his personal life and his marriage to Christie. The book details the personal lives of both husband and wife, and it also provides information about their travels and the settings of her later books.

Oates, Jonathan, *Unsolved London Murders: The 1920s and 1930s*, Pen and Sword, 2009.

This volume contains twenty unsolved murder cases, many of which were notorious during Christie's early career. The tales of these unsolved murders provide insight into the true crimes being committed while Christie was writing her murder mysteries.

SUGGESTED SEARCH TERMS

Agatha Christie

Wasps' Nest

Hercule Poirot

Agatha Christie AND Wasps' Nest

golden age AND mystery

Agatha Christie AND biography

Hercule Poirot AND Wasps' Nest

detective fiction

Wasps' Nest AND short story

England AND 1920s

poison AND Agatha Christie

true crime AND Christie

golden age of mystery AND Agatha Christie

The White Umbrella

GISH JEN

1984

"The White Umbrella" is one of the first short stories written by noted American author Gish Jen. It was first published in the *Yale Review* in 1984 and has since been reprinted in a number of anthologies, including *Home to Stay: Asian American Women's Fiction*, edited by Sylvia Watanabe and Carol Bruchac (1990); *My Mother's Daughter: Stories by Women*, edited by Irene Zahava (1991); and *America Street: A Multicultural Anthology of Stories*, edited by Anne Mazer (1993).

Set somewhere in the greater New York City area, "The White Umbrella" is about a young Chinese American girl and what happens one day when she goes with her younger sister to the house of her piano teacher for a lesson. The story hints at the unnamed girl's awareness of herself as a Chinese American, in contrast to the all-American girl who is in the middle of her lesson when the other girls arrive. The story also involves the girls' mother, who has just started working outside the home for the first time and is uncomfortable about it. "The White Umbrella" offers insight into what it might feel like to be a member of an ethnic group in a town where almost everyone else has an American cultural background. Jen later built on stories such as "The White Umbrella" to develop the picture of Chinese American life in the novel for which she is best known, *Typical American* (1991).

Gish Jen *(Getty Images)*

AUTHOR BIOGRAPHY

Jen was born Lillian Jen on August 12, 1955, in Long Island, New York. She is the daughter of Norman and Agnes Jen, immigrants from Shanghai, China, who met in the United States in the 1940s. Jen's mother was sent to the United States to further her education, while her father was an engineer who had been employed by the U.S. Army. Both expected to return to China but were prevented from doing so by the Communist takeover of China in 1949.

As a child, Jen lived in Yonkers, New York, and she wrote her first story when she was in fifth grade. The family later moved to the Jewish suburb of Scarsdale, where Jen attended high school and read avidly in the school library. She particularly enjoyed the novels of Jane Austen. It was during this time that she acquired the nickname "Gish," after an actress with whom she shared a first name.

Jen attended Harvard University and graduated with a bachelor of arts degree in English in 1977. She enjoyed writing, but her parents expected their five children to either work in business or become doctors or lawyers. With this in mind, Jen entered Stanford University in 1979 to study business, even though she had no interest in the subject and spent most of the year writing novels and taking writing courses. The following year, she took a leave of absence and taught English in China. Returning to the United States, she enrolled in a master of fine arts program at the University of Iowa in 1981, graduating in 1983. Her parents opposed her decision, but she was convinced she wanted to become a writer, and she began to have some success. Her short story "The White Umbrella" was published in the *Yale Review* in 1984.

Jen married David O'Connor, a graduate of Harvard and Stanford Business School, and moved to California's Silicon Valley. In 1985, the couple moved to Cambridge, Massachusetts, where Jen was awarded a fellowship at Radcliffe's Bunting Institute. This enabled her to begin writing her first published novel, *Typical American*, a story about how a Chinese immigrant family gradually adapts to living in the United States. The novel was published in 1991 to much critical praise. It marked Jen's arrival as an important new voice in Asian American literature and was named a "Notable Book of the Year" by the *New York Times*. It was also a finalist for the 1991 National Book Critics Circle Award.

Jen's second novel, *Mona in the Promised Land* (1996), continues the story of the Chang family, whose lives were the subject of *Typical American*. The main character, Mona, is the same character who appears in "The White Umbrella." *Mona in the Promised Land* was named one of the ten best books of the year by the *Los Angeles Times*.

Jen's next publication was *Who's Irish? Stories* (1999), a collection of eight short stories, and in 2004 Jen published her third novel, *The Love Wife*, yet another contribution to literature about Chinese immigrants in the United States. Her fourth novel, *World and Town* (2010), is set in New England and examines the challenges faced by recent Cambodian immigrants as well as by the United States itself in the twenty-first century. As of 2011, Jen was living with her husband and two children in Cambridge, Massachusetts.

PLOT SUMMARY

"The White Umbrella" takes place in an unnamed town somewhere in New York or Connecticut, probably during the 1980s, although no date is supplied. The story is told in the first person by an unnamed twelve-year-old Chinese American girl.

The story begins with the girl and her sister Mona listening to their parents talking in the kitchen about their mother's recent decision to take a job to supplement the family income. She is doing the same thing that Mrs. Lee, a woman from the only other Chinese family in the town, started doing a year ago. Mrs. Lee took a job as a waitress, but it is not yet disclosed what job the narrator's mother has taken.

The two girls do not discuss with their mother what has happened; they seem to sense that discussion would not be welcome. If their mother comes home late, they just start cooking dinner themselves.

The girls wonder what work their mother is doing. The narrator has various ideas, thinking perhaps that their mother might be working for a florist, delivering roses. However, Mona says this is unlikely, because their mother, whose recently acquired driving skills seem not to impress her daughters, would have had a road accident by now if that were the case.

The two girls walk to their piano lesson after school. It rains, and they get wet. Their teacher, Miss Crosman, sympathizes with them. The girls sit on the couch waiting for Eugenie Roberts, who is a year older than the narrator, to finish her piano lesson. The narrator notices that Eugenie has brought with her a white umbrella.

Eugenie finishes the piece she is playing, and Miss Crosman offers her lavish praise. Mrs. Roberts arrives to pick up her daughter, and the teacher tells her that Eugenie is gifted. After the mother and daughter leave, it is Mona's turn to begin her lesson. The narrator notices that Eugenie has left her umbrella behind, but it is too late to let her know.

When Mona has finished playing her piece, Miss Crosman asks if she can call their mother and get her to bring over some dry clothes. Both girls reply that their mother will not be able to come.

While Mona resumes her lesson, the narrator stares at the umbrella, which she likes very much. She wonders if Miss Crosman will allow her to take it with her to give to Eugenie the next day at school. She considers asking her mother to get her a similar umbrella for Christmas, but she guesses her mother will say no.

When it comes to her turn, the narrator makes an effort to play extra well, and her teacher praises her. She then plays another piece that is more difficult and was not assigned to her. Miss Crosman praises her highly when she finishes but lets the girl know she is not as good as Eugenie Roberts. The narrator wants to explain to her teacher all the things she is very good at and blurts out that her mother is a concert pianist (which is not true).

The two girls wait on the steps for their mother to collect them. It has stopped raining. Twenty-five minutes go by, but their mother still has not come. It is customary for her to be late because she is working. In response to Miss Crosman's kind concern, the girls insist that their mother will be there in a moment.

It starts to rain again, and Miss Crosman tells them to come inside. Mona goes in, but the narrator insists on staying outside. Miss Crosman comes out with a blanket and the umbrella. The narrator loves holding the umbrella, and when Miss Crosman sees how much she likes it, she gives it to her. It turns out that the umbrella belongs not to Eugenie but to Miss Crosman. The girl is excited to have the umbrella and thanks her teacher profusely. She hides the umbrella in her skirt.

Their mother finally arrives. As the girls sit in the back seat of the car, their mother says that next time she will call, but she does not like to say where she is. She tells the girls that she works at the checkout in an A&P grocery store. (This gives the only clue to where the story is located, since the A&P grocery chain has stores in New York, New Jersey, and Connecticut.) Her boss had offered her a bonus if she would stay until the evening shift arrived. There is silence for a moment, and then the narrator tells her mother she should quit, but her mother replies that she has to work to bring in enough money for the family.

As they reach downtown, Mona wants to know what her sister is hiding under her skirt. Their mother stops at a traffic light, but it becomes apparent that the car is blocking a crosswalk. A man crosses the street and yells at her. The girls' mother starts to back up and hits the car behind them. They are all jolted backward and then forward.

Their mother has her eyes closed, and this frightens the narrator. She screams at her mother to wake up. Her mother opens her eyes and tells her not to yell. The girl says she thought her mother was dead, and she starts to cry.

The driver of the car behind taps on the window. Mona and her mother get out of the car. The narrator follows them, and then when no one is looking, she tosses the umbrella down a sewer.

CHARACTERS

Angry Man

The angry man is a pedestrian who crosses the street and complains that the mother's car is blocking the crosswalk. He yells at her and bangs on the hood.

Miss Crosman

Miss Crosman is an elderly piano teacher who gives lessons to the two sisters as well as Eugenie Roberts. She likes to encourage her pupils and praises their performance. She says the narrator's performance was "wonderful" and "stupendous." She is also a kind woman who is concerned about the two girls' welfare. She seems to feel sorry for them, probably because she thinks their mother does not look after them properly. When they arrive wet from the rain, she says that next time they have a lesson and it is raining, she will come and pick them up in her car. When their mother does not show up after class to collect them, Miss Crosman offers to take them home herself. Miss Crosman is a motherly figure. She tells the narrator that when she was younger, she wanted to have children, but she never married. When she sees how much the girl likes the white umbrella, she gives it to her, prompting the narrator to say that she wishes Miss Crosman were her mother.

Father

The father of the two sisters makes only a very brief appearance in the story. The narrator overhears him talking in the kitchen with his wife about the fact that she has taken a job. He agrees with her that they do not need the second income she brings in, unlike the Lee family, the only other Chinese family in town.

Mona

Mona is the younger sister of the narrator. She walks with her sister to Miss Crosman's house for their half-hour piano lessons. The narrator is not impressed with Mona's abilities at the piano. According to her, when Mona plays it sounds like a catfight. Mona and her sister have a spirited relationship in which they bicker with each other. In the car, Mona plays a game in which she tries to push her sister over every time they make a right turn.

Mother

The mother of the narrator and Mona has recently taken a job to supplement the family income. She seems to be rather ashamed of the fact that she has to work, since she does not like to talk about it. For weeks she does not even tell her daughters where she works. The girls are embarrassed about it, too, and do not like to admit to Miss Crosman that their mother works. It is revealed near the end of the story that the girls' mother works at the checkout register in a grocery store.

The girls' mother seems to be a nervous woman. She is afraid of flying. She has recently learned how to drive, and it is a running joke between her two daughters about what a bad driver she is. They seem to have good reason for thinking in this way. After she picks the girls up from their lesson, she inadvertently blocks the crosswalk with her car, and a man yells at her because of it. She then backs into the car behind her.

Narrator

The unnamed narrator of the story is a twelve-year-old Chinese American girl, Mona's elder sister. She is a very intelligent girl who is the school spelling-bee champion and a promising pianist, although she has not been playing the piano as long as Eugenie Roberts. She seems to feel that she is overshadowed by Eugenie, whom she regards as the epitome of style. She tries to sit very upright at the piano stool, just like Eugenie.

When the narrator sees the folding white umbrella, she immediately assumes, incorrectly as it turns out, that the umbrella belongs to Eugenie. She wants an umbrella just like it so she can carry it to school the way the other girls do. She wants what they all appear to have, which is not surprising perhaps, and she seems to suffer from a lack of confidence in herself, as if she lacks self-esteem or recognition from others. She seems to be conscious that some of the other girls appear to have more than she does, in terms of possessions.

She is also, unlike her sister, Mona, quite conscious of her Chinese heritage. She sees a distinction between American families, where it is common for the woman to work, and Chinese families, where, it seems, it is not. It is because of her embarrassment over the fact that her mother works that she goes to some lengths to ensure that Miss Crosman does not learn about it.

The narrator's frustration with what may be a feeling of inferiority makes her want to impress others. She thinks, for example, that if she takes the umbrella and gives it back to Eugenie the next day, Miss Crosman will be impressed with her. She also desperately wants to impress her teacher at the piano, playing a more difficult piece than she has been assigned. When her teacher lets slip that although the narrator is good, she is not as good as Eugenie Roberts, she wants to tell Miss Crosman about all the things at which she does excel. She does not want Miss Crosman to feel sorry for her. The woman's sympathy grates on her. To boost herself up in her teacher's eyes, she even lies that her mother is a concert pianist.

Eugenie Roberts

Eugenie Roberts is one grade ahead of the narrator at school. According to the narrator, there is a rumor that Eugenie has a boyfriend in high school, so she must be a very attractive girl. She has auburn hair and blue eyes and comes from an affluent family. When Mona and the narrator arrive for their piano lesson, Eugenie is still having hers. She is very talented, and Miss Crosman is full of praise for her abilities.

Mrs. Roberts

Mrs. Roberts is Eugenie's mother. She comes to collect Eugenie after the girl's piano lesson and is very proud of her daughter when Miss Crosman praises her abilities.

THEMES

Ethnic Identity

The Chinese American family that is glimpsed in the story is poised between two cultural worlds, the American and the Chinese. There is only one other Chinese family in town, the Lees, so the narrator's family might well feel isolated because of their ethnic background. At the very beginning of the story there is a hint that the narrator feels her Chinese identity quite strongly, although her younger sister Mona appears not to. When they are talking about the fact that their mother has taken a job outside the home, Mona sees nothing unusual in it, saying that lots of mothers work. The narrator replies, "Those are American people," to which her sister responds, "So what do you think we are? I can do the Pledge of Allegiance with my eyes closed."

Mona appears to think of herself as an American, pure and simple, but her sister has a more complex understanding that takes account of her Chinese heritage, for which different rules seem to apply. She is also conscious of the fact that she does not quite fit in the way that the all-American Eugenie Roberts, with her blue eyes and wealthy parents, fits in. The narrator wants to be more like the other girls she knows at school, which is why she is so fascinated by the white umbrella: all the other girls carry their umbrellas to school, and the narrator wants to imitate them.

The narrator thinks her mother will not buy her one. She has clearly heard her mother, perhaps on more than one occasion, emphasize the difference between her native Chinese culture and American culture, to the detriment of the latter. This is clear from the narrator's belief that if she were to ask for an umbrella, her mother would reply, "Things. . . . All you want is things, just like an American." This suggests that the girls' mother strongly identifies with being Chinese and has no love of what she sees as American materialism and consumerism. The incident at the end of the story, when the narrator's mother blocks the crosswalk with her car and is yelled at by the man crossing the street, is symbolic of how she does not really fit in with American culture.

However, the mother's attitude seems to lead to some inner conflict for her oldest daughter. Although this is never stated in overt terms, it seems that she feels not fully American and thus not fully appreciated for who she is. Her sense of difference or separateness eats away at her self-esteem and sense of belonging. She wants so much to impress Miss Crosman with all of her accomplishments rather than being compared adversely to Eugenie and becoming the object of Miss Crosman's sympathy. On her part, Miss Crosman's overly solicitous attitude to the narrator suggests that, her generosity and kindness notwithstanding, she also views the Chinese American girl as rather different.

In short, the narrator is growing up in two worlds, that of her home, with her Chinese mother, and the wider culture she encounters at her school and in the town. This makes her uncertain of her own identity, and this is something she will no doubt have to think about with some care as she enters her teenage years.

TOPICS FOR FURTHER STUDY

- Have you ever wanted an object the way that the narrator in the story longs for the white umbrella? Write an autobiographical essay in which you describe what that object was and why you wanted it so much. What did it represent to you? Why was it so desirable? Did you obtain it, and how? And what happened to it?
- Using online and print research, create an interactive digital time line of Chinese American history and display it in your classroom. Include at least twelve important dates and events. Make sure you include 1965, when important immigration legislation was passed. What was that legislation, and why was it significant? Post your time line on a Web site or create a presentation of it for your classmates.
- Much of Jen's work raises the question of what it means to be an American or a Chinese American. In a blog post, discuss what it means to be a "hyphenated" American, that is, someone who identifies as being, for example, Iranian American or Indian American or Italian American or Asian American or other ethnicity or race. What do people mean when they describe themselves in such a way? Who is a "real" American? Is it a matter of formal citizenship, a way of thinking, a personal history, a set of values? Invite your teacher and classmates to respond to your thoughts about the issue.
- Read *American Born Chinese*, a young-adult graphic novel by Gene Luen Yang. One of its three plots is about an Asian American middle-school student, Jin Wang, who is having a hard time fitting in with his white classmates. Write an essay in which you summarize the boy's desires and difficulties and link them to those of the narrator in "The White Umbrella." Then create a storyboard for a short-story sequel in which Jin is helped by a fellow student to fit in.

Mother-Child Relationships

The story focuses on the feelings of the young narrator and does not at first offer a great deal of information or insight into the relationship the girl has with her mother. There are some clues, however: the mother takes a job without telling her daughters and does not speak about it; the mother wants to ensure that her daughters do not become too materialistic in their attitudes; the narrator will not ask her mother for an umbrella because she fears a negative response; and the girls make a joke of their mother's poor driving skills, but, it appears, only when she is not around. What all this suggests is that mother and daughters do not, perhaps, communicate as fully as they might.

However, the incident at the end of the story shows that there is a deep, loving bond between the mother and the eldest daughter. Immediately following the car accident, the narrator gets a shock when she sees her mother with her eyes closed; she thinks she is dead and screams for her to wake up. Then, as they all get out of the car to inspect the damage that her mother's driving has caused, the narrator, without anyone seeing what she is doing, tosses the beloved white umbrella into a drain. At this moment, she knows her mother is in trouble for causing the accident, and she does not want to trouble her further by showing her the umbrella, because she guesses her mother would not approve of it. The shock of thinking for a moment that her mother was dead has sharpened her feelings about her mother. Perhaps she realizes how much she loves her and how much more important such feelings are than a mere object such as an umbrella.

Although the narrator does not speak of her feelings at this moment or explain directly why she throws the umbrella away, it is clear that she empathizes with the situation her mother is in. Her loyalty to her mother and sensitivity to her

Mona and her sister must walk to their piano lesson because of their mother's job. *(Michael Pettigrew / Shutterstock.com)*

feelings overcomes her desire for the umbrella. In this significant little moment, love for her mother overcomes love of a thing. If she ever found out, her mother would no doubt be proud of her daughter for the feelings that lay behind the choice she made.

STYLE

Point of View

The story is told by a first-person narrator, a twelve-year-old girl. This style of narration can be spotted by the frequent presence of the word "I" in narrative passages. The narrator tells the story from her point of view, as it affects her thoughts and emotions. First-person narration works well for a story with few characters and a simple structure. The narrator needs to know nothing outside her own thoughts, feelings, observations, and descriptions of events to tell the story. First-person narration means that the thoughts and emotions of the other characters are seen through the narrator's eyes only. For example, in this story, the reader is never given any direct insight into the thoughts of the narrator's mother or those of Miss Crosman. These characters reveal themselves only through their words and actions and what the narrator thinks and feels about them.

Symbols

The white umbrella seems to symbolize a lot for the narrator. In literature, a *symbol* is an object that signifies something other than itself. A rose, for example, might symbolize love.

For the narrator of this story, the umbrella is not only beautiful in itself, it is like a magical object charged with special powers; the narrator can barely take her eyes off it. When she sees the "pure white" umbrella on the blue carpet, it "glow[s] like a scepter." (A *scepter* is a staff or baton carried by a king or queen as a symbol of their authority.) When she picks it up, it seems to carry a vital energy or power:

> It sprang up by itself as if it were alive, as if that were what it wanted to do—as if it belonged in my hands, above my head. I stared up at the

> network of silver spokes, then spun the umbrella around and around and around. It was so clean and white that it seemed to glow, to illuminate everything around it.

In addition to symbolizing some secret, magical power, the umbrella also represents something else for the narrator. She wants to possess it because, she imagines, owning the umbrella will admit her to that special world shared by all the other girls at school, who all seem to have umbrellas. As she stares at the umbrella she "wanted to open it, twirl it around by its slender silver handle... to dangle it from my wrist on the way to school the way the other girls did." She longs to be like the other girls, rather than feeling different, deprived in some way. The possession of the umbrella therefore in a sense symbolizes her desire to be accepted into a particular social group—that of her classmates at school.

Metaphor

A *metaphor* occurs when one thing is identified with something else that may appear on the surface completely unlike it. The metaphor, however, brings out ways in which the two may in some way be similar. If someone says, "My love is a fire burning in my heart," for example, he or she is seeking to convey a certain feeling by the use of a metaphor: love is like a fire. It is in this sense that a metaphor occurs in "The White Umbrella."

After Miss Crosman praises the narrator's piano playing, the narrator writes, "An entire constellation rose in my heart." (A *constellation* is a certain configuration of stars.) Obviously, this statement is not to be taken literally. She is saying that the praise from her teacher produced a certain feeling in her, and she tries to convey that feeling by use of a metaphor: the happy feeling is a grand one; it makes her feel good in an expansive sort of way. Her heart expands, so the image that comes to mind is of a pattern of stars appearing in the vast night sky, so calm and beautiful and somehow beyond the usual limits that define human life. The metaphor perfectly captures in a short phrase the feeling the girl has, in a far better way than any prose explanation could manage.

HISTORICAL CONTEXT

Growth of Asian American Literature

Asian American literature began to gain recognition in the 1970s with the publication of the landmark anthology *Aiiieeeee! An Anthology of Asian-American Writers*, edited by Frank Chin, Jeffery Paul Chan, Lawson Fusao Inada, and Shawn Wong (1974). The editors of *Aiiieeeee!* wrote a strident preface in which they lambasted the racism that had kept Asian American literary voices in the shadows. They wanted in particular to promote literature written by American-born Asian American writers who wrote on American subjects for Asian Americans. The anthology included an excerpt from the first novel published by a Chinese American, Louis Chu's *Eat a Bowl of Tea* (1961), set in New York's Chinatown. The anthology also includes Chin's play *The Chickencoop Chinaman* (1971), which was performed in New York City and was the first play by a Chinese American to attract mainstream attention.

Another landmark came in 1976 with the publication of *The Woman Warrior*, a memoir by Chinese American author Maxine Hong Kingston (born in California in 1940) blending autobiography and Chinese folktales. The book became a popular success and won the National Book Critics Circle Award. It was, however, attacked by Frank Chin and Jeffery Paul Chan, both of whom had become highly influential figures in Asian American literature. They claimed that the book gave an inauthentic, distorted picture of the Chinese American experience.

During the 1980s, when Gish Jen was publishing her first short stories, literature by Asian Americans continued to break boundaries and reach across to mainstream audiences. The three years between 1989 and 1991 were remarkable for the explosion of Asian American works printed by major publishing houses.

Notable works included *M. Butterfly*, a Broadway play by Chinese American playwright David Henry Hwang (performed in 1988, published in 1989) and Amy Tan's best-selling novel *The Joy Luck Club* (1989). Japanese American writer Cynthia Kadohata (born in Chicago), like Jen, began publishing short stories in the 1980s. Her novel *The Floating World* appeared in 1989. Filipino American playwright and novelist Jessica Hagedorn, who was born in the Philippines in 1949 and moved to San Francisco in 1963, published *Dogeaters* (1990), set in Manila, the capital city of the Philippines, in the 1950s. In 1991, David Wong Louie's collection *Pangs of Love: Stories* was published by Knopf and won the First Fiction Award from the Los Angeles Times. Louie was born in New York and

COMPARE & CONTRAST

- **1980s:** Asian Americans are the fastest-growing racial ethnic group in the United States. From 1980 to 1990, their numbers increase by 96 percent to reach 6.9 million.

  Today: In 2008, the U.S. Census Bureau estimates the number of Asian Americans to be 15.5 million, making up about 5 percent of the total population.

- **1980s:** The decade becomes known by the slogan "Greed is good," a line from the movie *Wall Street*. For many, it is a time to accumulate extravagant wealth and spend lavishly on consumer goods. Many questions are raised about the ethics of those who make money on Wall Street. Some financiers, including Ivan Boesky and Michael Milken, are convicted of insider trading and fraud.

  Today: The United States is in a time of austerity. Unemployment is high, and the country is making only a slow recovery from the recession of 2008 and 2009. Many complain about excessive earnings and bonuses received by executives in the financial industry. People are more inclined to save than to spend.

- **1980s:** According to the 1990 U.S. Census, the Chinese American population is about 1.65 million out of a total U.S. population of nearly 249 million. Chinese Americans are often considered a "model minority" because of their strong work ethic and commitment to education and socioeconomic advancement.

  Today: The U.S. Census Bureau reports that there are just over three million Chinese Americans living in the United States out of a total U.S. population of over 301 million.

- **1980s:** In 1985, 71 percent of women between the ages of twenty-five and forty-four participate in the workforce in the United States. This is a dramatic increase over previous decades. However, the number of men in the workforce still exceeds the number of women by nearly 26 percent.

  Today: Women make up approximately 50 percent of the nation's workforce, the greatest percentage in American history.

graduated with a master of fine arts degree in creative writing from the University of Iowa in 1981—the same year that Jen began her creative writing studies at that university. Jen's own novel *Typical American* (1991) was part of this wave of Asian American works that reached a mainstream readership.

Over the next two decades, all of these authors helped to create a genuine Asian American literature that put to rest the old stereotypes of Asians that had been a part of American popular culture for decades. As described by Elaine H. Kim in *Asian American Literature: An Introduction to the Writings and Their Social Context*, such stereotypes depicted Asians as falling into two types: the "bad" Asian and the "good" Asian, including such figures as "the power-hungry despot, the helpless heathen, the sensuous dragon lady, the comical loyal servant, and the pudgy, de-sexed detective who talks about Confucius."

CRITICAL OVERVIEW

Because "The White Umbrella," one of Jen's earliest works, is somewhat overshadowed by her later novels, it is mentioned by critics only in passing, to point out that it is one of the several pieces by Jen, including the novels *Typical American* and *Mona in the Promised Land*, that feature the Chang family. "The White Umbrella" is typical of Jen's work in that ethnicity has some relevance to the meaning of the story, but the plot is not entirely focused on that

Mona and her sister are taking their piano lesson. *(Noam Armonn / Shutterstock.com)*

issue. Jen herself has chafed at the description of herself as an Asian American writer and insists that that is only part of who she is.

Jen's works are often viewed as assimilationist, in the sense that characters do little to preserve or discover their Chinese cultural heritage and are more concerned with fitting into American life. As Begoña Simal notes in the *Dictionary of Literary Biography*, "Ethnic issues appear in Jen's work insofar as they are significant to the delineation of her characters, rooted as they are in present-day America." Simal's conclusion about Jen's work as a whole might serve as commentary on what is present in seed form in the early story "The White Umbrella":

> Jen's fiction not only revisits traditional Chinese American paradigms, such as the stories of immigrants and second-generation Chinese Americans, but it also incorporates new ingredients into the "multicultural cauldron." Her writings constitute a clever, multilayered dissection of America and Americanness.

Jen published her first collection of stories, *Who's Irish? Stories*, twenty years after the publication of "The White Umbrella." Michiko Kakutani's comment on that collection in the *New York Times* shows how Jen's work had developed in the intervening period: "Gish Jen's characters, Chinese immigrants and their American-born children, find themselves commuting between two cultures, between familial expectations and their own yearnings for self-definition, between remembered traditions and shiny, new dreams." Readers will recognize in that description some of the elements that Jen was already considering in "The White Umbrella."

CRITICISM

Bryan Aubrey

Aubrey holds a Ph.D. in English. In the following essay, he explores the themes of identity, social class, belonging, loyalty, and love in "The White Umbrella."

Gish Jen's short story "The White Umbrella" is a fine example of a story told from the point of view of a twelve-year-old child that does not sacrifice literary elegance or subtlety of theme. The voice of the unnamed narrator rings absolutely true, and the story is illuminated by some gentle humor as it pursues its themes relating to growing up. As the narrator tells what happened at and immediately after her afternoon piano lesson, the reader understands that the young girl, without being able to articulate it, is exploring issues of identity, social class, belonging, loyalty, and love.

To begin with, the girl is extremely conscious that she is a member of a very small minority in the unnamed town in which she lives. Her parents are Chinese, possibly fairly recent immigrants, and there is only one other Chinese family in town. This means that she has probably grown up with a sense of being different from others. When her mother takes a job, the girl's younger sister, Mona, thinks nothing of it, but the narrator thinks that working outside the home is what American mothers do, which suggests that even at the age of twelve, her Chinese ethnicity is important to her—something she has no doubt learned from her parents.

Social class enters the story also. In the United States, class is usually determined by income. It is not unusual for recent immigrants to struggle for a while as they adapt to life in their new country. The fact that the narrator's mother has to take a job suggests that the family is not wealthy. Although the girl's parents, in a conversation she overhears, say they do not need a second income, it seems likely that they are implicitly conspiring to

WHAT DO I READ NEXT?

- *Typical American* (1991) is Jen's first and best-known novel, and it established her reputation as an American writer of note. The novel, which takes place over a period of two decades, examines the Chinese American experience. It is about three Chinese people who immigrate to the United States in the 1940s and gradually adapt to life in their new country, until they become like any "typical American." The novel probes deeply into what it means to become an American, dealing with issues such as personal freedom.
- *Mona in the Promised Land* (1997) is a novel by Jen that also features the Chang family that appeared in *Typical American*. Mona Chang (the same Mona who appears in "The White Umbrella") is a sixth-grader who in 1968 moves with her family to Scarsdale, a largely Jewish suburb of New York City. The novel follows her as she comes of age in the 1970s and goes through all the usual experiences of adolescence, but as an American girl of Chinese descent living amongst Jews. Mona decides to convert to Judaism, which horrifies her Chinese parents. The story is told with much wit and comedy and received excellent reviews.
- *Between Mothers and Daughters: Stories across a Generation* (2003), edited by Susan Koppelman, is a collection of twenty-four short stories by American women writers, drawn from a period extending from the 1840s to the 1990s. The stories all deal with relationships between mothers and daughters and cover a wide range of historical periods, social classes, races, religious faiths, ethnicities, ages, and experiences.
- *It's Your Rite: Girls' Coming of Age Stories* (2003), edited by Nora E. Coon and Susan Gross, is written for a young-adult readership. It is a collection of essays written by authors ranging from ages eleven to eighteen, in which they discuss important milestones in their experience of growing up. There is a lot of variety in the essays, which tend to emphasize the positive rather than negative aspects of the authors' experiences, but in ways that remain realistic and honest. There is also a chapter on how to create a coming-of-age ceremony. Fourteen-year-old editor and contributor Coon also contributes an introduction.
- *Bone* (1993) is the first novel by Chinese American writer Fae Myenne Ng. It is set in San Francisco's Chinatown and covers a period of several decades in the lives of one Chinese American family. The novel was a best seller, giving a vivid portrait of Chinese American life in San Francisco and some of the hardships that the early Chinese immigrants had to endure. The novel also shows how the younger generation, born in the United States, has different attitudes regarding self-identity and cultural heritage.
- Jen commented in an interview that she admired the work of African American author Jamaica Kincaid because Kincaid writes truthfully, without sentimentality. Kincaid's novel *Annie John* (1985) is one of her best-known works. Set on the island of Antigua, in the Caribbean Sea, it is a coming-of-age story about a young girl who finds that her previously loving relationship with her mother is turning into something different.
- *Kira-Kira* (2004), a novel by Japanese American author Cynthia Kadohata, won the Newbery Medal and the "Notable Children's Book" designation from the American Library Association in 2005. Narrated by a young girl named Katie, it is the superbly told story of a Japanese American family that moves from Iowa to Georgia in the late 1950s. Katie is forced to grow up fast because of a family tragedy.

> "THIS IS ALMOST ALWAYS AN IMPORTANT FACTOR IN THE LIFE OF AN EARLY ADOLESCENT: THE LONGING FOR PEER-GROUP APPROVAL."

be not entirely honest with each other, since if they did not need the money, the girl's mother would not have to work. It is not as if she enjoys her work as a cashier at a grocery store, which is a low-skill, low-status occupation and is also unlikely to pay well. It seems that the parents feel there is a stigma attached to a family in which the woman needs to work, and this is something they pass on to their daughters, who go to great lengths to ensure that their piano teacher, Miss Crosman, does not learn of their mother's work.

Lack of money may also be one reason why the girl's mother does not want to encourage her daughter to ask for Christmas gifts. Her daughter imagines that if she were to ask for an umbrella, her mother would dismiss her request by asking her not to think so much about acquiring things, because that is what Americans do. This suggests not only the mother's sense of being separate from the culture in which she now lives but also perhaps her knowledge that the parents do not have the means to keep their daughters supplied with the latest fashion accessories that most of the girls at the narrator's school enjoy.

The issue of class is accentuated when Eugenie Roberts is introduced into the story. She is older than the narrator, comes from a wealthier family, has greater talent as a pianist and has been playing longer, and even has a boyfriend. It appears that Eugenie is very much part of the popular crowd at school, no doubt envied by others as well as the narrator. Eugenie's status in the group serves to point to the narrator's lack of status and her longing to acquire something—the white umbrella would be perfect—that would boost her status and give her more of a sense of belonging to the group.

The dynamic that the story eventually sets up is triple-pronged. First, the narrator feels the need to establish herself among her peers, to fit in with them. This is almost always an important factor in the life of an early adolescent: the longing for peer-group approval. It is the pressure to conform to the norms of the group and to attain a sense of belonging. Second is the need to discover and affirm who she is in her own right, to form her own identity. Again, this is something that all adolescents feel. It reveals itself only briefly in this story, but it can definitely be discerned in her desire to prove her ability as a pianist—she prepares a second piece to play for Miss Crosman, beyond the piece she was assigned—and her desire to tell her teacher about all the things at which she excels. She is the spelling-bee champion and also knows about karate. These are some of the things that make her who she is and distinguish her from others. She includes the fact that she is not ticklish—a childish affirmation of her uniqueness, maybe, but one she definitely takes seriously. The third part of this three-pronged story dynamic is how she relates to her mother. Once again, all adolescents have to face up to the changing ways in which they relate to their parents as they are growing up, groping toward a sense of their own identity, and forming their own social relationships with their peers.

There is a poignant moment in the story when some of these thematic elements can be pictured in a striking visual image. After the piano lesson is over, the narrator is sitting alone on the steps of Miss Crosman's house waiting in the rain for her mother to pick her up. At first she was waiting with Mona, but Mona got fed up with being wet and cold and went inside. Here is the narrator's description at this point:

> I stared out into the empty street. The rain was pricking me all over; I was cold; I wanted to go inside. I wanted to be able to let myself go inside. If Miss Crosman came out again, I decided, I would go in.

She is very alone at this point. Her mother is very late, her sister is no help, and Miss Crosman tends to smother her with sympathy. Sitting on those steps she seems at a crossroads, an isolated figure—what direction will she take? Interestingly, in an interview with *MELUS* in 1993, Jen pinpointed this moment as containing the origin of the story. Talking about how she goes about writing, she told Yuko Matsukawa, "I start with a feeling: in the short story 'The White Umbrella,' I started with the feeling of waiting on the doorsteps for your mother to come pick you up. Then you start accumulating around that feeling and the story evolves."

In the climax of the story that soon follows, the narrator appears to take a big step in achieving the desire mentioned above as the first aspect of the triple dynamic that operates in the story: when Miss Crosman does come out again, the narrator discovers that the white umbrella belongs not to Eugenie Roberts but to Miss Crosman herself, and Miss Crosman quite unexpectedly gives it to the narrator, which sends the girl into ecstasy. She is so excited she jumps up and down in the rain. Now, not only does she possess something beautiful and magical, but she will also be able to fit in with the other girls at school, who all seem to have umbrellas.

However, the story has yet another twist at the end that dramatically draws the narrator in another direction, with regard to the third aspect of the dynamic mentioned above. In this twist, in a moment of tension and emotion, she reevaluates her relationship with her mother.

The twist happens after her mother has picked her and Mona up and is driving them home. They are involved in a minor accident when the mother inadvertently backs into another car. The girls are sitting in the backseat, and the narrator has been hiding her newly acquired umbrella inside her skirt; she does not want her mother to know she has it. When the accident happens, the narrator at first is relieved to have attention taken away from the umbrella, because Mona has been telling their mother that her sister is hiding something under her skirt. When the narrator looks at her mother, however, she gets a shock, because her mother has her eyes closed, and her head is tilted back. For one awful moment, the girl thinks that her mother is dead. She shouts at her to wake up and starts crying. She quickly discovers that her mother is not injured at all, but in that moment of terror something has shifted in the girl's emotional life. She says nothing about it directly, but she does something that seems almost inexplicable: she tosses the umbrella, the umbrella she adores and has so recently acquired, into a drain in the street.

This is another extremely poignant moment. After all, this item, this folding white umbrella, had thrilled and excited her so much. She had wanted it so badly, and it seemed like the most beautiful thing in the world to her, yet only a few minutes after she first acquired it, she tosses it away. What would cause her to do such a thing? The reader is of course free to interpret this how he or she pleases, since the story ends at that point, and no explanation is offered. It seems likely that, just for the moment at least, when the narrator is overwhelmed with concern for her mother, she realizes how much she loves her and how terrible it would be to lose her.

"THUS, BEING CHINESE IS NOT CONSTITUTED BY A SUCCESSFUL PERFORMANCE BUT BY THE INEVITABLE IMPOSSIBILITY OF EXACTLY PERFORMING CHINESE."

In her sudden, perhaps impulsive action, the narrator shows that belonging to and being accepted by the girls at school, as well as feeling pride of ownership of a beautiful object, are not as important as the loyalty and love she feels toward her mother. She does not want to do anything that might upset her, such as producing the umbrella and having to explain why and how she acquired it. In her instinctive judgment, this moment is not the right one in which to bring the subject up. The narrator is, after all, just twelve years old, a child, and at that moment what she needs most is a loving connection with her mother, not a shiny white umbrella, however desirable that object might be.

Source: Bryan Aubrey, Critical Essay on "The White Umbrella," in *Short Stories for Students*, Gale, Cengage Learning, 2012.

Fu-Jen Chen

In the following excerpt, Chen perceives evidence of postmodern subjectivity in the way Jen's characters form their identities.

In this essay, I first examine the new mode of subjectivity in the postmodern-global-capitalist era through illustrating the way characters in Gish Jen's *Mona in the Promised Land* engage in the free play of identity performance. Next I argue that their identity as a set of performances is only possible against the terrain of the Capital. In addition, the performers in the novel try to disavow class antagonism in their performance of identity of differences. The disavowal of class, however, suggests both that class secretly overdetermines other differences in political identity and that class antagonism still predominates over others in the struggle for hegemony. My final discussion, focusing on the final scene of *Mona in the Promised Land*, explores its political strategy as a mode of resistance and subversion.

Mona and her sister get wet waiting in the rain. (Black Rock Digital | Shutterstock.com)

Today's postmodern-global-capitalist regime favors a new mode of subjectivity, one characterized by an accusation of essentialist fixation and a demise of totalizing identification. The new politics of subjectivity celebrates multiple shifting identifications and free choice to identify with a proliferation of differences. The postmodern subject experiences him- or herself as an agent caught in a contingent particular context but incessantly involved in an activity of hybrid identities without constraint. Interestingly, as one asserts one's fluid identities and shifting identifications, one at the same time promotes one's particular difference(s) to indicate one's proper place within this given field. While liberating diversification is thriving and more differences are produced in late-capitalist society, one is increasingly preoccupied with differences of gender, race, culture, religion, nationality, ethnicity, and sexual orientation—various particulars and diverse lifestyles. Identity becomes performatively enacted and open to endless play of substitution: one performs and moves freely between difference(s). Yet, with no firm predetermined difference(s), one also experiences oneself as radically unsure since all identifications or performances may be reenacted. In the background of late-capitalist globalization that produces and promotes difference(s), our free choice incessantly to perform particular difference(s) aims for recognition. In fact, our demands for recognition have always already been assumed by the nexus of postmodernism, global capitalism, and multiculturalism. A multicultural society especially appeals to our demands: endlessly divided subgroups coexist, no one is excluded, all differences are tolerated, and we are all (mis)recognized.

While recognition and tolerance of multiplication of differences ground multiculturalism's politics of identity, it is assumed that all differences are equal and each carries the same weight. Inasmuch as none of the differences is privileged, class difference becomes at best one species of proliferation of new political subjectivities. Once promoted in the Marxist tradition as the determinant of social reality and human subjectivity, the politics of class difference has been referred to as essentialism, and the charge is made that class struggle can no longer overdetermine the complexity of the social reality and multiplicity of subjectivity. Today, the politics of class difference has become less fashionable and "progressively decentred by an increasing preoccupation with gender, race, ethnicity, [and] sexuality." Even class consciousness is denied because to draw clear class distinctions becomes impossible or impracticable in today's so-called classless society in which we are all middle class or working class.

Though there is a long tradition of confronting issues of class and race in Asian-American literature, Asian-American literary works shift toward investigating the possibility of a fluid, decentered identity in a postmodern era, challenging the very notion of a stable identity of sexuality, gender, and ethnicity. Even in the Asian-American critical field, new tendencies can also be observed: the lessening of cultural nationalism, the increasing feminist and deconstructivist mode, and the embrace of a postmodern subjectivity opened up to multiplicity and free play. The antiessentialist convictions are apparent in the stories of Gish Jen, a Chinese-American writer. In many interviews, Jen, a daughter of immigrant Chinese parents who grew up in Scarsdale, New York, herself advocates the concept of identity in flux, an identity performatively enacted. In addition to her antiessentialist position and highlighting the notion of performativity, Jen also devotes her attention to the politics of class.

The issue of class in Jen's stories is not obscured by such multicultural concerns as ethnic rights, inequality, racism, representation, intolerance, or immigration. Instead, her writing explores the problematic of class stratification among racial groups and "ethclasses" in our current postmodern-global-capitalist regime. While her novels *Typical American* (1991) and *Mona in the Promised Land* (1996), and her collection of short stories, *Who's Irish?* (1999), deal with immigrant experiences, they focus at heart on class. These works all attempt to examine the multicultural-capitalist-postmodern context where the characters in her stories, including "typical" Americans, Jews, Chinese, Blacks, and Irish, are all driven by the politics of class. In her stories, everyone is a "typical American," living in "the promised land," or, rather, a late-capitalist world, and the question of "Who's Irish?" is better understood as an inquiry about class—"which class?" It is class that concerns those characters most, sets their desires in motion, and drives them to act. In her writing, Jen investigates how capital functions as the field against which the performance of differences emerges.

The Cartesian notion of the subject suggests an agent of rational self-legislation and a unified being of disparate parts, mind and body, each with its own attributes. Distinguished by their opposition to this epistemological model, postmodern theories of subjectivity highlight a subject's inability to remain either stabilized or unified, thereby featuring a liberating proliferation of multiple forms of subjectivity. The radical uncertainty of any subjective position conditions the postmodern subject to experience identity as a matter of choice and an act of performance and thus to float from one contingent identification and temporary embodiment to another. The endless open practices of displacement are illuminated by Judith Butler's theories of gender performativity in which all gender and sexual configurations are performed through a process of recycling and mimicking societal markers of gender, sexuality, and desire. Because performativity, for Butler, serves as the basis of gender constitution, gender identity can only be understood as a fiction in which all members of a culture tacitly agree to act. Gender identity is not what one is, but what one does. Race or ethnicity might work in a similar vein. Butler's "racialization of gender norms" affirms de Beauvoir's statement that "one is not born but becomes woman [black/white/Asian-American]." *Mona in the Promised Land* shows to what extent the notion of an "Asian-American" identity is performatively enacted.

In the novel, which takes place in the late 1960s, almost all the characters engage in the free play of switching identities. Identity switching is extensively explored by the title character, Mona Chang, by her sister, Callie, by their parents, the Changs, and by Jewish characters of a fictional suburb in New York, Scarshill, modeled upon a mainly Jewish New York suburb, the Scarsdale of Gish Jen's youth. Opening with the Changs' relocation from Chinatown to that affluent neighborhood, the novel first pictures the fulfillment of the American dream in the economic success of the Changs, a newly prosperous immigrant family who own thriving pancake houses. Seen in Scarshill as "the New Jews," they represent "a model minority and Great American Success" in their community (*MP*).

The Changs' younger daughter, Mona, contentedly immerses herself in the Yiddish neighborhood as an adolescent and enjoys performing an identity at will. At first, in the eighth grade, Mona, like a "permanent exchange student" (*MP*), indulges in performing stereotyped, exotic, and mythic Chinese types, ones who are credited with "get[ting] pregnant with tea" (*MP*), having no body smell (*MP*), eating living monkey brains (*MP*), and inventing scalpels, tomatoes, noodles (*MP*). Boasting about her performative "Chineseness," Mona is once urged by her friend to "make a career out of it" (*MP*). Through adolescence to adulthood, Mona extends her identity switching from Chinese or Catholic to WASP or Jew. Embracing the idea that "American means being whatever you want" (*MP*) and identity performing and switching only require practice of "some rules and speeches" (*MP*), Mona converts to Judaism. She studies Jewish history, attends Jewish rituals and ceremonies, befriends Yiddish youths, and ultimately marries a Jew. At the end of the novel she changes her surname from Chang to Changowitz (*MP*). In her becoming "Mona Changowitz," her act of renaming inaugurates a new mode of subjectivity, one no longer consistent or essential, but performative and shifting.

Like Mona, other family members are obsessed with identity switching and performing. Though once sick of being Chinese (*MP*), her elder sister, Callie, becomes aware in college of the term "Asian American" coined in the late 1960s. Exploring attributes of this new subject position, Callie devotedly acts out "Chineseness." Doing so, she practices Tai Qi, eats shee-veh instead of muffin, speaks a Chinese dialect foreign to her parents' ears, wears padded Chinese jackets and cloth shoes already obsolete in China, and finally, like Mona, switches her name to "Kailan," which, to her, sounds more original and authentic. Baffled by their daughters' behavior, the parents, however, are just as "performative" as any. An overseas Chinese in Jen's first novel, *Typical American*, Ralph has become a typical American in the second novel, and Changkee—"Yankee," perhaps—is his favorite word. An owner of three pancake restaurants, Ralph is successful and his motto is "[T]here is no sure thing. I still believe make sure" (*MP*). He worries that "even our restaurant, standing there so nice, can fall down, good-bye. Forget about sure thing" (*MP*). His identity as an American (or, rather, as a WASP) is performatively enacted on the basis of capital. Similarly, Ralph's wife, Helen, clings to a subject position based on performance of class. Arranging a WASP environment for her daughters, Helen always asks them to act "properly," like WASPS, especially "in a place where people might look down on you" (*MP*). How to stand, how to sit, how to walk, and how not to drag the feet—"it's all a matter of manners," she claims (*MP*). Her own mannerisms are more obsessive: in public she always firmly holds her pocketbook (*MP*) and once cried just because her shoes did not match it (*MP*).

Many characters besides the Changs are engaged in performing multiple identities. Mona's best friend, Barbara Gugelstein, first endeavors to be a typical American teenager, which means being cool (that is, less polite than Mona) and being popular (that is, having big boobs and using a Lord and Taylor charge card). Then she abruptly announces that she is "Jewish" (*MP*) and begins to attend Jewish youth activities, to join the Temple Youth Group, and to immerse herself in Jewish rituals and traditions. She even claims that "being Jewish is great" and "there's something special about being Jewish she wouldn't want to give up" (*MP*). Yet, before long, Barbara turns to fixing her "Jewish" nose and switches back to being an American or, rather, a WASP because, as she explains to Mona, "a little Jewish is fine, but... too much is too much" (*MP*). Likewise, although Eloise Ingle, half Jewish, wavers between being a Jew and a WASP, her father, a rich and successful businessman, firmly performs what he believes: "*You've got to know how the game is played*," he insists (*MP* original emphasis). That is "the great lesson of life," he always teaches his children (*MP* original emphasis).

In the novel, the person most skilled at performing and switching is not Mona, but her boyfriend and, later, husband, Seth Mandel. Ironically, Seth is also one who insists on absolute genuineness throughout the novel, saying that "between the inside person and the outside person there should be no difference" (*MP*). Harboring antibourgeois values, Seth performs and switches identities among Jew, Japanese, Chinese, hippie, black, WASP, and Native American. He lives in a tepee, uses chopsticks, does yoga, sleeps on a tatami mat, wears dashikis, displays exquisite Zen-like melancholy, believes in a possible previous life in which he was Japanese, and endeavors to behave as "an authentic inauthentic Jew" (*MP*). At the end of the novel, having become a professor on tenure track, Seth nevertheless remains ("performs" best as) a WASP.

Identity as performatively enacted by characters in *Mona in the Promised Land* presumes some knowledge of the subject. First, a subject, denying the split within consciousness, can be fully conscious of his or her performance. Second, it assumes that identity relies on one's successful performance of difference(s). Third, it assumes that no intra-contradiction exists within a difference and that inter-relations among differences are smoothly and completely signified in language. In the novel, characters presuppose the existence of a doer who is one hundred percent conscious of what he or she is doing prior to choosing an identity to perform, an identity that is effectively constituted by their successful performance. The novel's most skilled performer, Seth, insists on being fully conscious of his deed and endeavors to maintain a radical uniformity "between the inside person and the outside person," as he claims (*MP*). Yet, staying one hundred percent conscious is impossible, and, moreover, the subject, as Slavoj Zizek maintains, is "*nothing but* the failure of symbolization, of its own symbolic representation" and "nothing 'beyond' this failure" (original emphasis). That is, identity (or, rather, subjectivity) is based not on a successful performance but its failure, not on the chain's meaning but its disruption; in other words, one's identity emerges not when identification (or disidentification) is made but when it fails to be made. One always performs more or less because one's destined failure to perform results from a sense of loss in mastering an excess of signification. An insistence on accurate performance ridicules its performer (as, for example, with Callie and Rabbi Horowitz). Thus, being Chinese is not constituted by a successful performance but by the inevitable impossibility of exactly performing Chinese. Nevertheless, in the novel, being Chinese, black, Jewish, or WASP appears as an ethnic difference that can be totally translated into a repetition of acts or a set of predetermined representations so that it can be adequately performed. But a difference without any intra-contradiction simply serves as a type, a totalized and completely rhetoricalized form that excludes a nonmimetic account of identification based on Lacan's concept of the Real. Though the subject can be signified in language, it is not purely linguistic. While a subjective position with no intra-contradiction merely functions as a representative type, to arrange differences smoothly among subjective positions orients identity to one-to-one relations (for instance, white versus black), idealizes the dominant norm, and reinforces peripheral differences. The subject is thus reduced to identification with projective models and, unable to develop into an individual being, thereby remains trapped within an essentially prescriptive discourse. . . .

> **"JEN'S CRITICISM OF ORIENTAL IDENTITY AND STEREOTYPES PROVIDES NEW MEANINGS TO CONTEMPORARY CHINESE AMERICAN AND CONTEMPORARY IMMIGRANT FICTION."**

Source: Fu-Jen Chen, "Performing Identity in Gish Jen's *Mona in the Promised Land*," in *International Fiction Review*, Vol. 34, Nos. 1–2, January 2007, pp. 56–68.

Esra Sahtiyanci Oztarhan

In the following essay, Oztarhan illustrates Jen's new approaches to nationalism, identity, multiculturalism, and assimilation in her novel.

Mona in the Promised Land is Asian American writer Gish Jen's novel about the identity quest of a Chinese American girl heroine Mona. The story takes place in early 1970s where Mona lives in a Jewish suburbia in Scarshill, NY, with her China born parents and her American born sister. The novel centers on the conversion of Mona into Judaism, thus reconstructs notions such as nationalism, assimilation, multiculturalism and identity that are the common themes of immigrant literature. Jen's novel brings new approaches to these notions by her choice of a young protagonist and her humorous style.

All the novels of Gish Jen are humorous stories about serious issues like racism and identity quest of Chinese Americans. Her first novel *Typical American* (1991) follows the lives of Ralph Chang, his sister and his sister's roommate who later becomes his wife. The novel is a satirical account of the family's various efforts of fulfilling the American dream, of becoming a "typical American" and the obstacles they face. The first line of the novel makes it clear that "it's an American story" in which the characters try to adapt to the American Dream while trying to hang on to their Chinese roots. Jen has also written a collection of short stories entitled *Who's Irish?* (1999), about the immigrant experiences of Chinese Americans, but also of Jewish Americans, African Americans, Irish Americans, etc.

Her latest book of 2004, *Love Wife*, explores similar issues such as being Chinese American in white mainstream society by portraying a racially mixed family. The family consists of Carnegie Wang, his WASP wife, whom Carnegie's mother refers to as "Blondie," their two adopted children and one biological son. Their family life is disturbed by the arrival of a Chinese cousin, who is arranged by Carnegie's mother to work as a nanny to the children. It becomes quite clear early on, however, that Carnegie's mother brings the Chinese cousin into the family with the intention of presenting "an ideal wife" for her son. The Chinese cousin not only disturbs the relations of the couple as a "love wife," she also brings with her stories and traditions of China. Thus she enables the characters', mainly Carnegie's rediscovery of his Chinese roots. Jen's novel discusses concepts like what is real, what is constructed or what is natural, which will construct the basic problematic themes in her other novels as well.

Mona in the Promised Land is the continuation of her literary tradition of exploring the Chinese American experience in contemporary United States. The novel is the story of the Chinese American family Changs (who came to America in her first novel *Typical American*) that is told through the eyes of their daughter Mona. Mona is a typical adolescent having problems with her family and her peer group, who finds herself being converted to Judaism amidst these cultural controversies. The novel is a good example of ethnic bildungsroman with a clearly defined identity search. The bildung of the novel is reached when Mona, the rebellious adolescent, comes to a final reconciliation with her mother, and by so doing with her ancestry and roots and, paradoxically enough, it is precisely through Jewish rituals and conversion that Mona comes to understand her Chineseness. It is stated in the novel as such: "Now that she is Jewish, she feels more of a Chinese than ever"; or she says: "The more Jewish you become, the more Chinese you'll be." Gish Jen therefore succeeded in portraying the pain of finding oneself in adolescence as a communal representation for the larger identity quest struggle of Chinese American immigrants as a whole. Therefore Jen defends the irresistible charm of returning to one's roots in coping with the racist and multicultural atmosphere of United States.

The novel apart from being an adolescent narrative, just like any immigrant story, reflects the in between situation of Chinese American Mona split between the Chinese and the American cultures. Jen depicts Mona's uneasiness as being like "a sore thumb . . . sticking out by herself." Being born and raised in America, she is under constant pressure from her parents who are still tied to their Chinese roots. She is also surrounded by her peer group, which pushes her to be like "an American girl." Mona has to find her own identity as opposed to her hyphenated one determined by the dominant culture, free from the identity her parents and peer group design for her. In this sense, Gish Jen's novel has so many common features with the Asian American women's fiction of 70s and 80s like Kingston, Ng and Tan's works. These works of Chinese American women [resonate] with Jen's focus on the situation of the Chinese daughters born in United States torn between their parent's world and the new world. These novels reflect the ongoing generation struggle between "the swan feather mothers" and "Coca Cola daughters" so to say.

At the same time, Jen brings a fresh insight to Asian American women literature in the 1990s to "what it means to be an Asian American girl in 70's." Her novel is quite revolutionary by portraying a purely postmodern identity model for the new immigrants. It is Mona's solution to be torn between two cultures. As Mona summarizes by saying: "American means being whatever you want, and I happened to pick being Jewish." Mona with her new chosen identity of a "Catholic Chinese Jew" differs from the hybrid characters of the earlier literary examples. In her depiction of Mona's active claiming of Judaism, Jen criticizes the American Dream in the earlier immigrant literature by choosing to portray a character who claims fluid identities. The new American experiment is about the naturalness of choices. A possible reason why Jen used conversion to Judaism in the novel is because in the United States, the Chinese are called the "New Jews." That is because they seem to be the living proof of the American Dream, the "model minority." And it is exactly what Jen criticizes in her novel.

Mona's choice of changing her identity is a practical reflection of Homi Bhabha's "third space" concept of immigrant experience. It is defined as an empowering position, which enables the subject to choose among the various possibilities. Thus, Mona being in the third space, being neither a pure Chinese nor a typical American, feels free to choose whichever she likes. Belonging to neither culture is not a disempowering situation, but an interplay of identity for Mona. She tells her friends that she [will] "just have to switch and that's all." From time to time when her exoticism attracts attention in class, she acts as if she knows Chinese and Chinese civilization. She tells her friends that: "[S]he knows karate... she can make her hands like steel by thinking hard... she knows how to get pregnant by tea... she knows Chinese." But in fact all she knows in Chinese is how to say: "Stop acting crazy. Rice gruel. Soy sauce" which becomes enough to impress her friends. And from time to time she can reject her Chinese culture and roots entirely when she felt being oppressed by Chinese traditions. Mona converts to Judaism, because she believes it to be about "ask, ask, instead of just obey, obey" which is exactly the opposite of what she always hears at home about being the oppressed minority. These identity switches are predominant throughout the whole novel in other characters as well like her Jewish friends who decide to be a WASP, and back again at their convenience. Also for example her sister decides to become more Chinese than her parents all of a sudden. Mona's boyfriend joining the black power although he is white is another example of identity switch in the novel. This postmodern sense of unfixed identity is a criticism to Orientalist discourses and essentialist theories.

Jen changes the standard notion of Americanness, Jewishness and Chineseness completely by her work. Being a Chinese American women writer herself, she deconstructs all existing stereotypes. That is to say she criticizes the model minority myth of the previous generations. Some critics like Frank Chin label the works of Kingston, Ng and Tan as a continuation of the Western myth of "the model minority," In this respect Jen unlike the previous Asian American women writers subverts this existing tradition. Gish Jen intentionally creates unconventional and unrepresentative characters in her novel to reinvent Chinese Americanness to the same extent as she reenacts her Americanness. Jen says: "This book is not a denial of my heritage, but [America] is the place where I grew up. This is my country; this is what I know. And, in this book, I lay claim to that." In the same interview of *The Asian Week*, Jen confesses that she created her own definition of American. She says: "It is not something that you come into [and] particularly does not involve abandoning where you came from. I think of Americanness as a preoccupation with identity. It is the hallmark of the New World because we live in a society where you are not only who your parents were, and you don't already know what your children will be. That is not to say that I am blond and eat apple pie, but any definition that finds me less American—well, all I can say is that something is wrong with the definition." This reaction against essentialist definitions of identity brings out one of the best examples of a protagonist with a fluid identity in *Mona in the Promised Land.*

Despite its many strengths, there are a number of small weaknesses in the novel, like the plot being a bit erratic. The coming of age story of Mona ends too quickly at the end of the novel. The final bildung of reconciliation with her mother and her marriage are mentioned at the last two or three pages of the book before we understand how she grew up that fast. However, *Mona in the Promised Land* is an important and timely novel on postmodern identity. It opens new horizons in the minds of the reader in bringing forward brand new definitions to Asian American identity. Jen's criticism of Oriental identity and stereotypes provides new meanings to contemporary Chinese American and contemporary immigrant fiction. Moreover the story of Mona—often very humorous—offers new dimensions to many concepts of American culture like assimilation and discrimination. Academicians who are interested in ethnic studies, Asian American literature, identity theory, girl studies and contemporary women's literature can find Gish Jen's *Mona in the Promised Land* worth reading to witness the experiences of the new immigrants like Mona.

Source: Esra Sahtiyanci Oztarhan, Review of *Mona in the Promised Land*, in *Interactions*, Vol. 15, No. 2, Fall 2006, pp. 165–68.

Rachel Lee

In the following essay, Lee analyzes the role of travel as a theme in Jen's work.

Engaging the topic of travel means first wrestling with the elasticity of the term. "Travel" risks trying to accomplish too much, flattening

"ONE OF THE MANY KINDS OF TRAVEL JEN ENGAGES IN HER STORIES IS THE UNSETTLING OF HOME NOT ONLY IN LITERAL LEAVE-TAKINGS OF MEMBERS FROM HOUSEHOLDS BUT ALSO IN RECONFIGURATIONS OF THE FAMILY STRUCTURE FOLLOWING INTERCULTURAL PRESSURES."

distinctions between types of migrants—between refugees and tourists, daily commuters and students on fellowship, cosmopolitan flaneurs and religious pilgrims. In this epic wrestling with the term, I follow a well-worn path. James Clifford, in his essay "Traveling Cultures," writes that the very notion that people such as Western anthropologists "are cosmopolitan (travelers) while the rest are local (natives)" reflects "the ideology of one (very powerful) traveling culture."

Asian American critics have, similarly, been concerned with the politics of naming, but from a slightly different perspective. They have inquired into the Politics of renaming Asians in the US as long-term settlers against the more common belief that they have been sojourners—perpetual aliens whose origin and destiny lie in China, Japan, Korea, Vietnam, India, Pakistan and so forth. They also have a distinct preference for terms other than the globe-trotting "traveler" to describe their subjects' immigrant, ethnic, minority and refugee experiences. Is the term "travel" elastic enough to stretch from the field of cultural anthropology to that of Asian American studies, and can we learn from those stretch marks? How fat can the term become, and can we see any gendered significance to the way those stretch marks have been configured thus far and the way they might be reconfigured in the future?

Gish Jen's exquisite comic depictions of several intercultural contact zones include not only expected places such as Manhattan and Shandong, but less cosmopolitan centers such as suburban Connecticut. *Typical American*, her first novel, explores the social mobility and decline of the immigrant Chang family, using Gatsbyesque allusions to evoke America's violent love affair with movement and speed. In her second novel, *Mona in the Promised Land*, an American-born Chinese girl becomes unsettled romantically, physically and psychically by a Japanese foreign student whose family's journey to New York is itself a testament to the wider networks of transnational capital. Taking an opposite trajectory, in Jen's latest book, the story collection *Who's Irish*, "Duncan in China" presents the pilgrimage of an "overseas Chinese" to the homeland. The title story features a Chinese immigrant matriarch's displacement from her daughter's home. And in "Birthmates," Art Woo encounters the denizens of a welfare hotel, an underclass of urban American society whose immobility makes starkly visible Woo's own contrastive business travel.

Jen's work is simultaneously a literature of travel, an Asian American portraiture and a cultural record of migration and displacement, in terms of both its transpacific production and its (multicultural) reception in diaspora-crossed venues such as New York. The rich itineraries of her fiction require us once again to wrestle with what counts as travel and to think comparatively across different textures of transit, mobility and dwelling.

Obviously, the short space of this forum does not allow me to address all of Jen's works. Allow me instead to focus on the title story from this recent collection. This story confronts a localized form of feminine displacement which, I will argue, requires us to examine the gendered presumptions of our traveling theories. It appears on the surface to be a humorous narrative of geographic displacement, but Jen hides a brutishness inside its wit.

In "Who's Irish," Jen turns to metropolitan ethnography. The field is the Shea household somewhere on the eastern seaboard of the United States (likely Boston or New York), a site of overlapping levels of migration. The plot builds toward the dramatic ouster of a Chinese matriarch from her grown daughter's house—the most localized displacement in the narrative. Notably, transpacific immigration to the US forms the larger context of this parental displacement, and transpacific as well as transatlantic migration (particularly Irish immigration to the US) set in motion the struggle over norms of femininity and maternal care that provide the ostensible rationale for the matriarch's ouster.

The unnamed first-person narrator of the story, a Chinese grandmother, lives with her daughter Natalie, vice-president of a bank, and Natalie's unemployed Irish American husband, John Shea. Struggling with the "wild" behavior of her toddlerage granddaughter, Sophie, the narrator blames the child's Irish heritage, claiming that "I am not exaggerate: millions of children in China, not one act like this." The narrator spanks Sophie, against the explicit wishes of her parents, and is asked to leave the household. She moves in with Bess Shea, John's mother, who is eager for "some female company," having been surrounded all her life by boys (she has four sons and no daughters).

Even as she renders the dramatic center of her story a struggle between a mother and a daughter (and granddaughter), Jen mines a buried intercultural history of travel, contact and labor competition between the Chinese and Irish diasporas in the United States. According to historian Robert Lee, "More than other groups, Irish workers perceived themselves directly threatened by the Chinese in California. Driven out of mining, railroad building, and agriculture, Chinese in California often displaced Irish immigrant workers in manufacturing, laundering, and domestic occupations. As Chinese entered the manufacturing labor market, employers directly and often favorably compared them to Irish immigrant workers," a comparison that Jen's narrator repeats:

> I always thought Irish people are like Chinese people, work so hard on the railroad, but now I know why the Chinese beat the Irish. Of course, not all Irish are like the Shea family... My daughter tell me I should not say Irish this, Irish that... I just happen to mention about the Shea family, an interesting fact four brothers in the family, and not one of them work.

Residues of the Irish-Chinese history of labor competition come to light also in offhand remarks, attributed to the Shea boys, wondering when Natalie's mother will be "go[ing] home" or John Shea's habit of ending arguments with his mother-in-law by suggesting she be sent "back to China."

The narrator's displacement from her daughter's home, on the one hand, allegorizes the fragility of her national status as a Chinese in America: throughout the story, Natalie's mother speaks her mind but at the risk of being deported. On the other hand, there is the risk of interpreting too strenuously the national significance of the narrator's displacement, for she is displaced not only as a Chinese but also as a Chinese woman. Jen's story compels us to interrogate what counts as travel, and what counts as the most traumatic of identificatory dislocations. What scale of territorial or communal dwelling matters most for female immigrants or for women in diaspora?

The removal of the narrator from her daughter's home—the flouting of codes of filial duty and extended family—may be in itself the most traumatic of dislocations, more violent perhaps than another transpacific crossing. It is worth recollecting that the first few sentences of the story, in which the narrator is introduced to the reader, identify the narrator in terms of her kin relations, first to her granddaughter, then to her daughter and finally to her husband. The narrator also evokes her connections to China, but here Chineseness, I would argue, signifies less a single territorial homeland than an extended familial network of customary ranks—appropriate gendered and generational behaviors. Examining longstanding transnational networks of Chinese across the Pacific, Aihwa Ong suggests that "[Chinese] subjectivity is at once deterritorialized in relation to a particular country, though highly localized in relation to family." Home is any place where one's family resides: thus dwelling in multiple countries—simultaneously, a dislocation from any one national territory—is not altogether unusual or tragic for the Chinese. The real threat is the prospect of dwelling not outside the nation but outside one's clan or extended kin. "A crazy idea," the narrator says, to "go to live with someone else's family."

The displacement of Natalie's mother is preceded by a new vocabulary of gendered familial relations. She remarks on American idioms that reconstruct social relations so that elderly mothers must take care of their grown daughters instead of the reverse: "In China, daughter take care of mother. Here it is the other way around. Mother help daughter... otherwise daughter complain mother is not supportive. I tell daughter, We do not have this word in Chinese, supportive." The narrator battles with both this one word and the restructured Chinese family it implies. Her fiercest resistance is to the maternal disrespect expressed by Sophie's acquisition of a bodily language of kicking and slinging mud at mommies. Ironically, Natalie—a mother herself—tacitly sanctions such attacks on mommies, by expelling her own mother from the household and resettling her with Bess Shea, John's mother.

A skilled adapter of classic American myths, Jen breathes new life into that timeworn melodrama of beset manhood by creating a quasi-utopian frontier of female horizontal comradeship, once the narrator's moves into Bess's household—formerly a wilderness of unemployed Irish American men. The two elderly women bond through their shared retorts to Bess's grown sons, who "hang around all the time, asking when will I go home." Bess's reply that her Chinese in-law is "a permanent resident... She isn't going anywhere" evokes an idiom of the Immigration and Naturalization Service—a state institution that regulates even as it creates new national subjects. Jen enlists the idioms of national regulation (belonging) to suggest their power to rewrite vertical, antagonistic female relations (daughters struggling against wicked mothers and grandmothers) into egalitarian sororal bonds. The narrator remarks at Bess's "talk just stick. I don't know how Bess Shea learn to use her words, but sometimes I hear what she say a long time later. Permanent resident. Not going anywhere. Over and over I hear it, the voice of Bess." These—the final words of the story—return the reader to the power of a discourse, a talk that sticks, a talk that repositions the subject in a national territory and in utopian horizontal terms.

Yet at the story's conclusion, Bess and Natalie's mother are far from floating away on a raft, new symbols of the interracial bonding that can happen once women get outside the constraints of "sivilization." The talk that sticks in the end—and which clears a space out from under the encircling demands of the boys—is that of permanent resident, of territorial rootedness, of placement and dwelling. Travel may not be the sign of freedom one expects. And it is questionable whether Bess and the narrator have conquered the deep-seated gendered divisions of labor and devaluation of domestic/maternal care. Without having addressed key gendered conundrums—why it is that the role of babysitting is assigned "naturally" to the Chinese grandmother when there is also an available parent, John Shea, to take on that job—and without having addressed the strictures of femininity (of impossible womanhood) that punish both Sophie and her grandmother for acting fierce, wild, or physically combative, the women of "Who's Irish" would seem to be stuck in, at best, a hazardous freedom as permanent residents allowed under national laws but confronted by the menace implied by the boys "surround[ing] you after a while."

The story suggests that familial bonds are not adequate to combating the fragile status of Chinese (women) in America. The narrator's biological links and cultural bonds to her daughter do not defeat the threats to expel her (to send her back). By contrast, Bess successfully rebuts her sons' suggestions that the narrator is only a sojourner by renaming her a permanent resident. The narrator is transformed by territorial modes of identification: she becomes "honorary Irish."

In answering the question of why the Irish found "a place in American society while the Chinese did not," Robert Lee calls attention to the status of the Irish as "free white persons" that made them "eligible for naturalization [thus providing] access to the legal and political systems." Becoming Irish, then, is not only a learning of the legal and political terminology of the US nation-state but also a refiguring of the rights of the immigrant laborer. When Natalie's mother adjusts to her new identity as a permanent resident, her reidentification in Irish terms, she is also no longer subject to implicit demands continually to prove herself economically useful to her hosts (working as their babysitter for nothing) in order to earn her right to dwell. Territorial identity disrupts familial identity by incorporating those who dwell in the US republic as political (national) subjects regardless of how hard they work—or so goes the liberal rhetoric of American nationalism. The good feelings produced at the conclusion of "Who's Irish" are a function of our believing in that American (national) liberalism, in the face of the entire structure of the narrative that emphasizes the Chinese woman's successive exclusions from her daughter's household. Will we be seduced by such American habits and convictions?

One of the many kinds of travel Jen engages in her stories is the unsettling of home not only in literal leave-takings of members from households but also in reconfigurations of the family structure following intercultural pressures. It may seem like an ugly stretch to call the latter "travel," but as feminist geographers have noted, unless we also take into account dwelling and placement, and the way in which mobility has far-reaching effects even for those who've never been outside their hometowns, we unwittingly sustain a focus on privileged forms of travel, the kind undertaken most often by white men, at the risk of missing how a gendered and Third World lens reformulates the kinds of questions and narratives we find appropriate to our very discussion of displacement, immigration and our modes of engagement with other cultures.

The lexicon learned in "Who's Irish" is not just that of "permanent resident" but also the vocabulary of "supportive" and "attack on mommies"—a language that simultaneously restructures relations between women and solidifies inequivalences between women and men. How do we translate terms such as "travel" to a gendered terrain? What do we do when the phrase "lady travelers" doesn't fit our Chinese matriarch's tale of being forced out of the home or when "we do not have . . . words" to speak a Chinese woman's form of displacement even as she stays in one place? These are the issues toward which Jen's fiction stretches our imagination and these are the issues around which we orbit today.

Source: Rachel Lee, "Who's Chinese? Gish Jen's Stories Explore the Gendered Terms of Our Traveling Cultures," in *Women's Review of Books*, Vol. 19, No. 5, February 2002, pp. 13–14.

SOURCES

"Asian American Populations," in *Office of Minority Health & Health Disparities*, U.S. Centers for Disease Control Web site, http://www.cdc.gov/omhd/populations/AsianAm/AsianAm.htm (accessed February 15, 2011).

"The Chinese Experience, Timeline," in *Becoming American: The Chinese Experience*, Public Broadcasting System Web site, http://www.pbs.org/becomingamerican/ce_timeline4.html (accessed February 10, 2011).

"A Century of Change: The U.S. Labor Force, 1950–2050," in *Labor Force Change, 1950–2050*, Bureau of Labor Statistics, U.S. Department of Labor Web site, http://www.bls.gov/opub/mlr/2002/05/art2full.pdf (accessed February 28, 2011).

Chin, Frank, Jeffery Paul Chan, Lawson Fusao Inada, and Shawn Wong, eds., *Aiiieeeee! An Anthology of Asian-American Writers*, Howard University Press, 1974, pp. xxii–xlviii.

Earley, Pat, "21st Century Workforce: 'The Times They Are a Changing,'" in *Huffington Post*, November 9, 2009, http://www.huffingtonpost.com/pat-earle/21st-century-workforce-th_b_351069.html (accessed February 28, 2011).

Guilder, George, "Women in the Work Force," in *Atlantic*, September 1986, http://www.theatlantic.com/magazine/archive/1986/09/women-in-the-work-force/4924/ (accessed February 28, 2011).

Jen, Gish, "The White Umbrella," in *America Street: A Multicultural Anthology of Stories*, edited by Anne Mazer, Persea Books, 1993, pp. 122–33.

Kakutani, Michiko, "Free and Confused by Infinite Possibility," in *New York Times*, June 4, 1999, http://query.nytimes.com/gst/fullpage.html?res=9A06E4DC1F30F937A35755C0A96F958260&ref=gishjen (accessed February 28, 2011).

Kim, Elaine, *Asian American Literature: An Introduction to the Writings and Their Social Context*, Temple University Press, 1982, pp. 3–4.

"*MELUS* Interview: Gish Jen," in *MELUS*, Vol. 18, No. 4, Winter 1993, pp. 111–20.

Pfeifer, Stuart, and Tom Petruno, "Michael Milken Is Still Seeking Redemption," in *Los Angeles Times*, February 3, 2009, http://articles.latimes.com/2009/feb/03/business/fi-milken3 (accessed May 31, 2011).

"Population Statistics and Demographics," in *Asian Nation*, http://www.asian-nation.org/population.shtml (accessed February 10, 2011).

"ACS Demographic and Housing Estimates," in *American FactFinder*, U.S. Census Bureau Web site, http://factfinder.census.gov/servlet/ADPTable?_bm=y&-qr_name=ACS_2009_5YR_G00_DP5YR5&-geo_id=01000US&-context=adp&-ds_name=ACS_2009_5YR_G00_&-tree id=309&-_lang=en&-_sse=on (accessed July 20, 2011).

Simal, Begoña, "Gish Jen," in *Dictionary of Literary Biography*, Vol. 312, *Asian American Writers*, edited by Deborah L. Madsen, Thomson Gale, 2005, pp. 142–54.

Wong, Sau-ling Cynthia, "Chinese American Literature," in *An Interethnic Companion to Asian American Literature*, edited by King-Kok Cheung, Cambridge University Press, 1997, pp. 39–61.

FURTHER READING

Chang, Iris, *The Chinese in America: A Narrative History*, Penguin, 2004.

Chang tells the story of the three waves of Chinese immigration to the United States, beginning in the early nineteenth century and continuing to the end of the twentieth century. Chang includes many personal stories of immigrants, which makes the book very readable.

Cheung, King-Kok, ed., *Words Matter: Conversations with Asian American Writers*, University of Hawaii Press, 2000.

This book is a collection of interviews with twentieth-century Asian American writers. Nineteen writers from a wide variety of backgrounds are interviewed. Writers featured include Jen, Jessica Hagedorn, Meena Alexander, David Wong Louie, Russell Leong, and Le Ly Hayslip.

Pearlman, Mickey, ed., *Listen to Their Voices: 20 Interviews with Women Who Write*, Mariner Books, 1994.
This book includes interviews with a wide variety of women authors, including Jen as well as Grace Paley, Fay Weldon, Jane Smiley, Sharon Olds, Jo Harjo, Cynthia Kadohata, and others.

Zia, Helen, *Asian American Dreams: The Emergence of a People*, Farrar, Straus and Giroux, 2001.
This is both a personal and a collective history. Like Gish Jen, Zia grew up in the northeast (in New Jersey) in the 1950s and 1960s. She wondered about the history of Asian Americans because no one seemed to mention them. In this book she traces the origins and development of the Asian American community from the nineteenth century to the end of the twentieth century.

SUGGESTED SEARCH TERMS

Gish Jen

The White Umbrella AND Gish Jen

Chinese American literature

Asian American literature

Chinese American

Chinatown

coming-of-age

peer group

second-generation immigrants

cultural assimilation

status symbol

The Widow and the Parrot: A True Story

VIRGINIA WOOLF

1982

Best known for her experimental novels and short stories, Virginia Woolf also dabbled in children's fiction, although only one work, "The Widow and the Parrot: A True Story," is still in existence. "The Widow and the Parrot" is a fable-like tale concerned with an elderly woman, her kindness, and her eventual financial reward. The work is believed to have been written in the early 1920s. In the story, an aged widow, lame and impoverished, discovers that her miserly brother has died and left her a sizable inheritance. Attempting to collect the money, the widow, Mrs. Gage, makes the journey to her brother's home. She finds the estate dilapidated and ultimately worthless, but additionally learns that her brother had in his possession a parrot, whom she treats kindly. With the help of the parrot, Mrs. Gage eventually, after a series of trials, discovers the treasure buried beneath the floorboards in her brother's kitchen. Woolf's tale is often taken by critics to be an ironic interpretation of more conventional children's stories. While ostensibly a story intended to entertain and instruct children, "The Widow and the Parrot" is more commonly regarded as a satirical examination of the sentimentality and nostalgia of traditional Victorian fiction in this vein.

"The Widow and the Parrot" was not published in Woolf's lifetime. It was first printed in 1982 in the July edition of *Redbook* magazine. In 1985 the story was included in the compilation *The Complete Shorter Fiction of Virginia Woolf*,

Virginia Woolf *(AP Images)*

introduced and annotated by Susan Dick. A revised edition of this work was published in 1989.

AUTHOR BIOGRAPHY

Woolf was born Virginia Stephen in 1882 in London to Leslie Stephen and Julia Prinsep Duckworth Stephen. She was the third of four children. Educated at home along with her sister while her brothers were sent to school, Virginia benefited from her parents' literary interests and expertise. Her father was a philosopher, critic, and editor, and her mother wrote children's stories. She lost her mother in 1895. That same year, the young girl suffered her first mental breakdown. Over the next several years, concerns for her health drew doctor visits and periodic halts in her lessons.

In 1897, Woolf began attending classes at King's College, in London. She later studied at the Royal Academy Schools and took lessons from private tutors. Following a period of protracted illness, her father died in 1904. In the aftermath of his death, Virginia and her siblings traveled abroad, but in May 1904, she experienced another breakdown after returning to London. During this episode, she attempted to commit suicide. She recovered, however, and moved with her siblings from their former family home in the Hyde Park Gate district of London to a more inexpensive area, Bloomsbury.

By 1905 she was writing reviews and articles for the London *Times Literary Supplement*. She also spent time discussing literature and art with her brother Thoby's group of friends from Cambridge; the group came to be known as the Bloomsburys and included Woolf's sister, Vanessa, and her husband, a prominent art critic. The group also included critic and economist Leonard Woolf, who would later become Virginia's husband.

In 1906, her brother Thoby died of typhoid fever. She then moved in with her younger brother, Adrian, and focused on her writing. Following another breakdown, she was courted by Leonard Woolf and married him in 1912, taking his last name. Together the couple founded a literary press, Hogarth Press, and published works of experimental fiction by Woolf and others. In 1913, Woolf suffered another episode of mental illness after completing the manuscript for her first novel, *The Voyage Out*, which was published in 1915. She continued to write, publish, and relapse and recover for decades. Her works, including novels and short fiction, employ an innovative, experimental style in which she explores such themes as identity and sexuality. She additionally published essays and criticism and championed the notion of a woman's right to education, independence, and her own career, in works such as 1929's *A Room of One's Own*.

After completing the manuscript for what would be her last novel, *Between the Acts*, Woolf's health began to deteriorate once again. She drowned herself in the Ouse River on March 28, 1941, near the home she shared with her husband in Rodmell, Sussex, England. *Between the Acts* was published shortly after her death, but some of her works, including "The Widow and the Parrot," remained unpublished until years later.

PLOT SUMMARY

As "The Widow and the Parrot: A True Story" opens, the reader is introduced to aging widow Mrs. Gage, the protagonist of the story. Both lame and short-sighted, Mrs. Gage is also quite poor. She receives a letter from the solicitors Mr. Beetle and Mr. Stagg in which she is informed about the death of her brother, Joseph Brand, and the inheritance he has left her, including his house, stable, property, and a sum of money. Thinking about how miserly her estranged brother had been, Mrs. Gage is unable to muster much grief at his passing. Rather, she rejoices in the wealth she now possesses. After she borrows traveling money from her minister, Reverend Tallboys, Mrs. Gage makes arrangements to have her dog, Shag, looked after and proceeds to the town in which her brother had resided. She is offered a ride with a farmer, Mr. Stacey.

Upon arriving at her brother's home, Mrs. Gage is greeted by a woman from the village, Mrs. Ford, who directs Mrs. Gage's attention to the annoyances caused by the parrot Mrs. Gage's brother had owned. After Mrs. Ford departs, Mrs. Gage feeds the parrot a lump of sugar and promises the bird—James, as Joseph called it—that she will treat him well. Mrs. Gage then surveys the property, finding it to be in extreme disrepair. Mrs. Gage consoles herself with the thought of the money still to be claimed from her brother's solicitors, and she makes arrangements with Mr. Stacey to travel to Lewes, where Joseph's bank is. The farmer warns Mrs. Gage about the dangers of attempting to cross the river at high tide. Arriving at the solicitors' office, Mrs. Gage learns that no money belonging to Joseph Brand can be found in the bank or on Mr. Brand's property. Dejected, Mrs. Gage begins the walk back to her brother's rundown home. Being lame, Mrs. Gage moves very slowly. By the time she makes it to the river, it is so dark she is unable to see the ford where the river can be safely crossed. She considers waiting until morning but is fearful she will die from the cold. As she deliberates "whether to sit or to swim, or merely to roll over in the grass, wet though it was, and sleep or freeze to death," Mrs. Gage sees a bright light illuminating the village of Rodmell, to which she is bound. Mrs. Gage soon realizes the blazing glow is a burning house. She makes her way toward her brother's house, and realizes that Joseph's home is the one burning. Nearing the house, Mrs. Gage fears for the safety of the parrot and asks bystanders if they have seen the bird. She intends to go into the burning home to seek out the parrot but is held back by the villagers, including the local minister, Reverend Hawkesford, and she is eventually led to Mrs. Ford's home to sleep for the night.

Unable to sleep, Mrs. Gage worries about the money she owes the reverend and how she will be unable to pay him, but is more distraught over the fate of her brother's parrot. She wishes she had had the opportunity to risk her life to save the bird. At this moment, she hears a tapping at the window. It is James, the parrot. He leads Mrs. Gage to the charred remains of his master's home, where he begins to pick at the floor in what was once the kitchen. Curious, Mrs. Gage investigates the area to which James is drawn and finds the bricks loose. She removes them and eventually finds the money her brother left to her, in exactly the amount stated in his will.

Mrs. Gage tells no one of her discovery and returns to her own home with her treasure and the parrot. Years later, the reader is informed, when Mrs. Gage is on her deathbed, she tells her preacher the entire story. She adds that it is her belief that James was responsible for the house being set ablaze and that through this act, he saved her from drowning in the river, and he then directed her to the money her brother had bequeathed to her. Mrs. Gage tells the preacher that she was rewarded for the kindness she has shown to animals like her dog and the parrot. James, the parrot, died moments after Mrs. Gage, several years after Mrs. Gage's dog had passed. The narrator concludes the story by mentioning that it is rumored that at the house's ruins, the parrot's tapping at the bricks can still be heard on certain moonlit nights, and some people have reported seeing an old woman kneeling on the floor in a white apron.

CHARACTERS

Mr. Benjamin Beetle

Mr. Beetle is one of the solicitors from which Mrs. Gage first receives a letter notifying her of her brother's death and of her inheritance. His partner, Mr. Stagg, informs Mrs. Gage that Mr. Beetle personally examined Mr. Brand's papers and property in search of the money he left Mrs. Gage. Mr. Beetle also reports on the "fine grey parrot," noting that his language is "very extreme."

Mr. Joseph Brand

Joseph Brand is Mrs. Gage's brother. As the story opens, she receives word that he has died.

The reader is informed that Mr. Brand did not reply to the Christmas cards Mrs. Gage sent him every year and that his miserliness was a habit "well known to her from childhood." The state of his home indicates further either Mr. Brand's reluctance to spend money or his lack of wealth, for the property is dilapidated. Mr. Brand's miserly character is further illustrated by the fact that he has buried his money, stashing it away under the bricks in the kitchen.

Mrs. Ford

Mrs. Ford is a woman who lives in the same village (Rodmell) in which Mrs. Gage's brother Joseph had resided prior to his death. Mrs. Ford admits Mrs. Gage into Mr. Brand's home when she arrives. Mrs. Ford is irritated by the parrot, who had been shrieking "Not at home!" as Mrs. Gage knocked. Mrs. Ford explains that all day long the grey parrot sits on his perch and screeches the phrase. Mrs. Ford's presence in Mr. Brand's home is unexplained. Later, when Mrs. Gage is guided to safety by the light from the burning house, Mrs. Ford takes pity on Mrs. Gage, who, in Mrs. Ford's eyes, appears crazed in her desire to enter the burning home and find the parrot. Mrs. Ford escorts Mrs. Gage back to her own cottage, where she offers Mrs. Gage a room for the night.

Mrs. Gage

Mrs. Gage is the protagonist of the story. Poor, lame, and short-sighted, Mrs. Gage receives word that her brother has passed away and has left her with property and some money. She expresses not grief over his death but joy and relief at having been left with some means of supporting herself. In contrast to her lack of affection for her brother, Mrs. Gage lovingly attends to her dog, Shag, before her departure to claim her inheritance. She shows similar kindness to James, the parrot her brother had owned. Once she discovers that not only is the property that her brother left her virtually worthless but also there is no trace of the money he supposedly bequeathed to her, Mrs. Gage bitterly recalls her childhood with her brother. As she trudges through the darkness back to Joseph's home, she thinks about what a cruel boy he was, and how he tortured insects in front of her to torment her. She even supposes he is burning in hell at that very moment. Her despair intensifies when she realizes that she cannot cross the river in the dark without risking death from drowning, nor can she remain exposed to the cold all night without risk of freezing to death. Soon, however, she is led back by the light of a burning home, the very home her brother had just left to her. Her first thought is for the parrot, but she is prevented by the villagers from entering the home to save James. When James later appears at her window, Mrs. Gage demonstrates the great faith she has in James's intelligence by following him back to the burned home, where he guides Mrs. Gage to the money buried beneath the kitchen bricks. In secret, Mrs. Gage returns with the gold first to Mrs. Ford's cottage and then home, never telling anyone about the money, which she deposits in her own bank and upon which she lives comfortably with Shag and James for years.

Reverend James Hawkesford

Reverend Hawkesford is the clergyman in Rodmell, the village where Mr. Brand lived. As Mr. Brand's house burns, Reverend Hawkesford advises Mrs. Gage not to worry about the parrot, who he suspects "was mercifully suffocated on his perch."

James, the Parrot

James is the parrot owned by Joseph Brand until Mr. Brand's death. As the property of Mr. Brand, the parrot becomes part of Mrs. Gage's inheritance. Although Mrs. Gage's first introduction to the bird is made by an annoyed Mrs. Ford, who complains of the bird's constant screeching, Mrs. Gage finds the bird beautiful, though somewhat neglected looking. Mrs. Ford informs Mrs. Gage that the bird once belonged to a sailor and learned to speak a bit roughly. She also describes to Mrs. Gage how fond of the bird Mr. Brand had been and how he spoke to him "as if he were a rational being." Mrs. Gage feeds James some sugar, wondering if he is sad or hungry. She speaks gently to the parrot and tells him that she would make sure that "he was as happy as a bird could be." Returning home from her disappointing visit to the solicitors' office to find her brother's house burning, Mrs. Gage attempts to enter the home to find James, but she is prevented from doing so by several villagers. Once she has been safely brought to Mrs. Ford's cottage, Mrs. Gage finds James tapping at her bedroom window. The parrot leads Mrs. Gage back to the remnants of the home and begins pecking at bricks in what was once the kitchen, and in doing so, he helps Mrs. Gage find the money her brother stashed away. Later, Mrs.

Gage not only credits James with revealing the treasure to her but also believes that James set the fire on purpose, in order to lead her home and guide her to the money, which she is certain could have been found in no other way. She later discovers that a kitchen stove had been built over the bricks concealing the treasure, and if the fire had not destroyed it, the treasure would never have been discovered. James dies moments after Mrs. Gage breathes her last breath.

Shag, the Dog

Shag is Mrs. Gage's dog. The reader is informed that Mrs. Gage is so devoted to him that she would rather go hungry herself than see her dog starve. Shag dies some years prior to the deaths of Mrs. Gage and James.

Mr. Stacey

Mr. Stacey is a farmer who offers to take Mrs. Gage to Rodmell with him. He likewise transports her to Lewes, the town in which the solicitors' office and bank are, and warns her about the dangers of crossing the river at high tide. On the way back to their own village, Mr. Stacey, who believes that Mrs. Gage lost all her property in the fire, offers to buy the parrot from Mrs. Gage. She staunchly refuses.

Mr. Stagg

Mr. Stagg, along with Mr. Beetle, is a solicitor who contacts Mrs. Gage regarding the death of her brother and her inheritance. Upon meeting Mrs. Gage, Mr. Stagg reports that no money could be found by his associate, Mr. Beetle, on the estate or in the bank. He furthermore advises Mrs. Gage to sell the parrot.

Reverend Samuel Tallboys

Reverend Tallboys is the village clergyman in Mrs. Gage's village of Spilsby in Yorkshire, England. He lends Mrs. Gage money to help pay her travel expenses to the neighboring town where her brother once lived.

THEMES

Kindness

In "The Widow and the Parrot," Woolf explores the theme of kindness, specifically, kindness to animals. This theme is exemplified in the character of Mrs. Gage, who is unfailingly kind to her dog Shag and to the parrot James, whom she inherits from her brother Joseph. Mrs. Gage is described as "devoted to animals." Despite her poverty, she always provides Shag sustenance, even if she must go without in order to do so. Mrs. Gage readily befriends the parrot, treating him with sugar and vowing to take care of him. She is willing to risk her own life to save the parrot's when her brother's house burns down, and she ascribes to the parrot an enormous amount of intelligence, speaking to him "as though he were a human being." No other character in the story appears to share her love of animals. Mrs. Ford is intensely annoyed with the parrot. Mr. Stagg advises her to sell the bird. Reverend Hawkesford advises Mrs. Gage not to trouble herself over the fate of the bird, whom he believes probably suffocated in the fire. Additionally, Mrs. Gage is both pitied and regarded as a bit demented for wanting to save the bird.

The kindness exchanged between the human characters in the story is contrasted with Mrs. Gage's kindness toward animals. Although Mrs. Gage treats the animals in the story with both love and respect, she exhibits little toward anyone else and is particularly uncharitable in remembering her deceased brother. However, Mrs. Gage is treated with kindness by many. She is obligingly carted from town to town by the farmer Mr. Stacey. The Reverend Tallboys lends her money. Mrs. Ford provides lodging. Despite the kindnesses shown to her, Mrs. Gage exhibits her own disdain for others in significant ways. First, she spares no kind thought to her deceased brother. She is initially joyful upon hearing of the inheritance his death brings, though she does feel grief. Later, she remembers his childish cruelty and his lifelong miserliness. Mrs. Gage goes so far as to reveal her vengeful nature: "I make no doubt he's all aflame this very moment in Hell fire," she thinks, "but what's the comfort of that to me?" When poised between the possibilities of drowning to death or freezing to death, Mrs. Gage rejoices when she sees a light that will be able to guide her home, thinking at first it might be a comet. Realizing that a house is burning, she thanks God, for it will burn long enough for her to find her way back. Disturbingly, she gives no thought to the people who could have been dying in the fire or losing all of their possessions. Arriving in the village to discover it is in fact the house she inherited from her brother, Mrs. Gage finds the villagers attempting unsuccessfully to douse the

TOPICS FOR FURTHER STUDY

- Woolf is better known for her adult fiction than for children's fiction. Select and read a short story from the 2002 collection edited by Woolf's husband, Leonard Woolf, *A Haunted House, and Other Short Stories*. Compare the story you chose with Woolf's "The Widow and the Parrot." In what ways, if any, are the stories similar? Are there resemblances in style, structure, or theme? Write an essay in which you discuss the plot, theme, style, structure, and characters of the piece you selected and then present your comparative analysis.
- Counted among Britain's modernist writers, Woolf achieved critical acclaim for her experimentation with the fictional narrative form. Like Woolf, French modernist writer Max Jacob also dabbled in stories for young readers. His modernist young-adult stories were collected in *The Story of King Kabul the First and Gawain the Kitchen Boy*, published by the University of Nebraska Press in 1994, fifty years after Jacob's death. With a small book group, read the short collection of stories by Jacob. Discuss Jacob's settings, imagery, and language. Thinking of modernism in terms of its departure from traditional storytelling methods, identify modernist elements in the works. What is unique or experimental about Jacob's language, style, and characters? How does he employ modernist techniques in ways specifically shaped toward the tastes and interests of young readers? Create a group blog where you and your classmates can discuss these issues. Describe your project and the initial responses of the group, and then allow individual members of the group to post blog entries where their dissenting opinions can be explored.
- Modernist poetry developed alongside modernist fiction, as poets likewise experimented with language, form, and technique. Kamau Brathwaite is an African Caribbean poet born in Ghana, a nation formed from the British colony of the Gold Coast. Using modernist poetic techniques, Brathwaite explores themes of race and identity. Study some of Brathwaite's poems, such as those found in his 2005 collection *Born to Slow Horses* or those in an earlier work from 1967, *Rights of Passage*, reprinted in the 1988 volume *The Arrivants: A New World Trilogy; Rights of Passage / Islands / Masks*. Select one or two poems and consider your responses to them, allowing them to inspire your own creativity. Create a work of visual art—a painting, sketch, photograph, or series of photos, for example—inspired by or related to Brathwaite's work. Alternatively, write your own poem, as inspired by Brathwaite's language, images, or style. Present your work to your class and discuss the artistic journey from Brathwaite's work to your own.
- Using print and online sources, research the history of the modernist movement in Great Britain. What political, social, and cultural events or movements helped shape British modernism? What writers were the first to be considered modernist? How were works by British modernists received by readers and by critics? Write a research paper in which you detail this history. Be sure to cite all of your sources.

---

blaze with buckets of water. Her first thought is for James, the parrot, and in asking after him her kindness toward animals is underscored, shifting the reader's attention from the hardness in her heart toward humans back to her warmth and tenderness toward animals.

Justice

Woolf treats the notion of justice in a way that reflects the conventions of the fable-like tale she has created. In this story, written with a young audience in mind, Mrs. Gage's kindness is rewarded and her brother's seemingly selfish

Mrs. Gage, the poor widow, got an inheritance from her dead brother. (DrMadra / Shutterstock.com)

intentions are thwarted. Justice is simple in the world of fables and children's stories, as children's notions of fairness are often quite stark: people should get what they deserve. In this story, they apparently do. Mrs. Gage struggles against her brother's efforts to "plague" her, even after his death. She suggests that he has led her on a chase after his fortune, believing that she would never find where he hid his money. After the parrot helps Mrs. Gage find Joseph's money, she feels vindicated, as "old Joseph's craft was defeated." In Mrs. Gage's mind, justice has been served. Her brother, she believes, is burning in Hell, and his plan to make a fool of her by leaving her money that could not be found has been foiled. In the world of absolutes in which the tale of "The Widow and the Parrot" operates, Mrs. Gage has been rewarded as she deserves, with her kindness toward animals repaid in material wealth, and her brother has been punished for his selfishness and cruelty as he deserves, with eternal damnation. The irony is that Mrs. Gage has not always been kind to humans, as her thoughts reveal, and the reader is left to contemplate whether or not justice has been served.

STYLE

Fable

Woolf's "The Widow and the Parrot" possesses a fable-like structure. Like many children's stories, it is structured around a moral lesson, and it further resembles a fable in its simple nature and in its clear depiction of hero and villain. The work features an omniscient, third-person narrator. In this type of work, a figure outside of the action tells the story and possesses a greater body of knowledge about the events than either the reader or the characters possess. In "The Widow and the Parrot," the narrator informs the reader of events that are about to happen, demonstrating her omniscient status, as when the reader is informed that "a great disappointment was in store for the poor old woman." Such statements additionally provide young readers with the sense that they are being told a story, even when they might be reading independently. To underscore the moral message in a fable or fable-like tale, writers often make stark distinctions between heroes, exemplifying goodness, and villains, who are examples of evil. Woolf does so by creating a sympathetic figure in the character of Mrs. Gage, who loves and is gentle toward animals and who is also poor and lame. Throughout the story, her willingness to sacrifice her own well-being for her dog or for the parrot is made clear. Through Mrs. Gage's recollections, Woolf emphasizes the cruel, miserly, and calculating nature of Mrs. Gage's brother. His villainous character is described by Mrs. Gage as deserving of punishment in hell.

Irony

In the literary sense, irony is the expressing of meaning in language, terms, or conventions that convey the opposite of what that language typically signifies. The fact that Woolf is better known for her adult, experimental fiction than for children's fiction has led some critics to find irony in Woolf's usage of the typical conventions of fables and children's stories and to thus examine the story for evidence of deeper purposes. In fact, the story was written for the private, family publication Woolf's nephews had begun and was described by nephew Quentin Bell as "a tease." Bell, as quoted by Ann Martin in *Red Riding Hood and the Wolf in Bed: Modernism's Fairy Tales*, goes on to state, "We had hoped vaguely for something as funny, as subversive, and as frivolous as Virginia's conversation. Knowing this, she sent us an 'improving story' with a moral, based on the very worst Victorian examples." (Bell's statements originally appeared in the 1988 Hogarth Press edition of Woolf's story.) Despite the moral lesson demonstrated by Mrs. Gage's kindness to animals, Woolf weaves an ironic undercurrent, suggesting through Mrs. Gage's vengeful thoughts about her brother that she is not as kind as she seems and, in alluding to the brother's affection for the bird, intimating that his negative qualities may be overstated by Mrs. Gage.

The subversiveness Bell expected can be seen in the way Woolf employs some of the conventions of the fable genre in an ironic fashion. Many fables, for example, feature talking animals, and Woolf's use of a talking parrot in "The Widow and the Parrot" may be seen as an ironic take on fable conventions. She has not created a fantasy world in which animals, who often reflect elements of human nature, talk to each other but rather has incorporated into her realistic world an animal who can, in reality, speak. Seen through the loving eyes of Mrs. Gage, the parrot also exhibits "more meaning in its acts than we humans know." In this way, Woolf once again calls to mind the world of fables, in which animals possess the power of speech as well as the intellect of humans. By using the elements of the fable but doing so in an ironic fashion, Woolf offers what appears to be a tale with fable-like qualities, designed to teach children that kindness to animals is a quality worthy of emulation. At the same time, Woolf's treatment of her characters and the conventions of the fable invites adult readers to question her aims.

Another example of irony in the story can be found in Woolf's employment of a subtitle. The subtitle of the "The Widow and the Parrot: A True Story" suggests to young readers that events such as those that take place in the story can and have happened to people. At the same time, adult readers, and probably many young readers as well, in all likelihood are aware that the tale is a work of fiction. Moreover, some of the events narrated entail highly improbable situations. This serves as another example of the irony Woolf employs in various aspects of the work. In some ways, Bell's assessment was accurate: his aunt's story may be regarded as "a tease," one in which she teases her audience by apparently offering a children's morality tale but incorporating enough irony to encourage readers to analyze the story more closely.

HISTORICAL CONTEXT

Late Victorian and Edwardian England and Beyond

During Woolf's lifetime, Great Britain saw several rulers ascend the British throne. Queen Victoria ruled Great Britain from 1837 through 1901. Her reign is associated with an era of progress and prosperity, during which industrialization increased and the British Empire spread across the globe. The governance of India, a British colony, for example, was transferred from a private company to Great Britain in 1857, and Queen Victoria was named Empress of India in 1877. A strong supporter of imperial expansion, Queen Victoria remained an active and visible queen even during her later years at the end of the nineteenth century. She died in 1901, at which time the crown passed to her son, Edward VI. King Edward was fifty-nine years old when he took office. With an intense interest in foreign affairs, Edward served as king until his death in 1910. He was succeeded by his son George V, who held the office through World War I, which began in 1914 and ended in 1918. Although by this time the king had limited powers, George was a significant presence among Britain's soldiers. He visited troops and military hospitals throughout the war. In the face of German aggression in continental Europe, British popular support for the war effort was rallied through the government's emphasis on the rights of small nations to their own sovereignty. In the aftermath of the war, social-reform efforts for greater equality and a more democratic nation, which had been coalescing prior to the war, finally succeeded in bringing about changes in British policy. Universal male suffrage (the right to vote) was introduced in 1918, along with limited female suffrage, as women over thirty years of age were allowed to vote. Universal suffrage for all citizens over the age of twenty-one was granted in 1927.

British Modernist Fiction

At the turn of the century and during the first two decades of the twentieth century, writers and artists responded to their dramatically changing world—a world increasingly shaped by scientific advancements, industrialization, and warfare—by questioning the traditional modes of representation and expression. The developments in the world of visual arts, including the exploration of nonrepresentational forms of expression

COMPARE & CONTRAST

- **1920s:** The modernist movement is transforming all forms of literature in Great Britain. Writers experiment with innovative forms of representation, exploring the psychological worlds of their characters; employing stream-of-consciousness narrative based on characters' inner thoughts; playing with words, language, and sound; and merging such genres as autobiography and fiction, or prose and poetry. The movement takes hold in America and Europe as well. Virginia Woolf, D. H. Lawrence, T. S. Eliot, Gertrude Stein, James Joyce, Rainier Maria Rilke, Marcel Proust, and Franz Kafka are all writers associated with the modernist movement.

  Today: Modern fiction has been influenced by the modernist movement in that modernism created new forms and modes of representation that allow many present-day writers to continue to explore innovative narrative techniques. Experimental fiction today often focuses on issues of identity and existence and questions concerning the nature of reality. Modern writers of experimental fiction include Shelley Jackson (*The Melancholy of Anatomy: Stories*, 2002), Mark Z. Danielewski (*Only Revolutions*, 2007), Ben Marcus (*Notable American Women: A Novel*, 2002), Liam Gillick (*All Books*, 2009), and Gabriel Josipovici (*Goldberg: Variations*, 2002).

- **1920s:** British culture is shaped by the recent events of World War I. In the aftermath of the war, the British enjoy the last years of the expansiveness of an empire, which soon begins to shrink as colonial territories seek independence. Social-reform movements lead to universal suffrage for British adults over the age of twenty-one. The prime minister during much of this decade is Stanley Baldwin. King George V, grandson of Queen Victoria, reigns over Great Britain during the 1920s.

  Today: British society continues to be shaped by worldwide events, including the global economic crisis of 2008, which severely affected the British economy, and wars in Iraq, Afghanistan, and Libya, to which the British sent troops to support the efforts of the United States and the United Nations. Frustrated with the liberal Labour Party's handling of such events, the British people in 2011 elected a government dominated by the Conservative Party and led by David Cameron. Queen Elizabeth II, George V's granddaughter, has reigned since 1952.

- **1920s:** British fiction for children often combines lessons in proper moral behavior for children with discreet explorations of social issues, such as class conflict, poverty, or gender inequalities within families. Popular authors of children's fiction during this early period of the twentieth century include Frances Hodgson Burnett and Edith Nesbit.

  Today: Modern British children's fiction is often created with structures similar to the works of Burnett and Nesbit in that social issues are sometimes incorporated into works ostensibly aimed at children. J. K. Rowling's "Harry Potter" series, for example, is infused with magic, mythical creatures, adventure, and explorations of identity but also contains elements of racial and social class conflicts. Angie Sage, in the "Septimus Heap" series, similarly creates a world of magic but one in which the young protagonists must find their true identities and places within a society troubled by discrimination and class tensions.

---

such as cubism (employing geometric shapes as the primary visual element) and surrealism (focusing on the visual interpretations of the unconscious mind), further influenced changes in the literary world. Paul Poplawski describes such dramatic shifts in perception and representation in his

Her brother's house burned to the ground as she returned to the village. (Vilant / Shutterstock.com)

introduction to modernism in his 2003 *Encyclopedia of Literary Modernism.* Poplawski states that the "sense of living through a period of momentous social, political and cultural upheaval can be seen as a key motivating factor in the modernist insistence on an equivalently momentous upheaval in aesthetic practice." Writers such as Virginia Woolf, James Joyce, Gertrude Stein, and T. S. Eliot all explored a variety of narrative techniques, shaping innovative modes of expression and exploring stream-of-consciousness and nonlinear narrative structures. Particularly after World War I, a sense of alienation permeates works of modernist literature, as writers sought to perceive and respond to a world irreparably damaged by the suffering caused by massive worldwide warfare.

Children's Morality Fiction

British children's fiction during the late nineteenth and early twentieth centuries often focused on conveying a moral ideal or a set of social values to children. Although a moral lesson intended for young readers remained the dominant motif of such fiction, these tales also often incorporated commentary on current social conditions—commentary aimed at adult readers. Jack David Zipes, in the 1987 volume *Victorian Fairy Tales: The Revolt of the Fairies and Elves*, looks specifically at Victorian fairy tales, observing that writers of such stories "had two ideal audiences in mind when they composed their tales—young middle-class readers whose minds and morals they wanted to influence, and adult middle-class readers whose ideas they wanted to challenge and reform." Similar observations have been made about the more realistic children's fiction of the time period, in which the conventions of Victorian family life or social and class issues of the time period were criticized. Fred Inglis, in *Women Writers of Children's Literature*, edited by Harold Bloom and published in 1998, makes such a case for children's fiction written by Frances Hodgson Burnett and Edith Nesbit, both of whom center their stories around Victorian and Edwardian social values and morality but also address concerns about gender roles, the structure of the family, and class issues. Woolf's story likewise contains a moral theme aimed at young readers: be kind to animals. At the same time, she opens up for debate among adult readers larger issues, such as the established literary conventions she had a reputation for challenging.

CRITICAL OVERVIEW

Woolf's short fiction historically has received far less critical attention than her novels. As Nena Skrbic observes in *Wild Outbursts of Freedom: Reading Virginia Woolf's Short Fiction*, Woolf's short stories, when reviewed, were often poorly received or disregarded by critics unable to interpret or categorize the works. In summarizing E. M. Forster's attempts to analyze the works, Skrbic finds that Forster characterized the works "as short, momentary post-impressionist portraits." Skrbic also analyzes the way Woolf's short stories "challenge generic classification by fusing a wide range of styles," as Woolf does with the fable and satire genres in "The Widow and the Parrot."

The humanlike qualities of the parrot, which link the story to the fable genre, are also commented on by other critics. Heather Levy, in *The Servants of Desire in Virginia Woolf's Fiction*, finds that the parrot is "forced to demonstrate extremely unlikely levels of insight in order to rescue [the widow] from her ineptness and greed." Other critics have focused on the modernism of Woolf's writing. Ann Martin, in *Red Riding Hood and the Wolf in Bed: Modernism's Fairy Tales*, claims that it is Woolf's modernism that informs her irony in "The Widow and the Parrot." She states that Woolf's tale "takes its ironic impetus from the Victorian sentimentality and pedantry that offended Woolf's modernist sensibilities."

This same sense of irony is noted by critics such as Wendy Martin. In her *New York Times* review of "The Widow and the Parrot," Martin claims that "Woolf's incisive irony undermines the conventional moralisms" in the story. She concludes that the work "does not capitulate to Victorian sentimentality as [Woolf's nephew] Quentin Bell originally thought it did. Instead, it is an amusing yet subversive story."

CRITICISM

Catherine Dominic

Dominic is a novelist and freelance writer and editor. In the following essay, she maintains that in the short children's story "The Widow and the Parrot," Woolf incorporates a distinctly modernist theme, exploring the notion of the widow's sense of isolation and alienation from human society and her attempt to restructure a new type of social identity.

Known as a modernist writer for the way her works experiment with form and reject traditional narrative styles, Virginia Woolf skillfully injected her sense of modernism into a work of short fiction written ostensibly as a children's story. "The Widow and the Parrot" is, on the surface, a moralistic tale instructing young readers about such themes as kindness toward animals. In the figure of the widow, however, Woolf captures the modernist notion of alienation. In his preface to the 2003 *Encyclopedia of Literary Modernism*, Paul Poplawski discusses modernism's "profound concern with themes of alienation, fragmentation, and the loss of shared values and meanings, and its concomitant search for alternative systems of belief in myth, mysticism, and primitivism." An examination of the apparently simple, fable-like story and an analysis of its protagonist reveals the ways in which Woolf perceived the subtleties and complexities of her world and was able to convey such observations in a format more restrictive than the short-story form with which she was experimenting. Critics have noted the ways in which Woolf exploited the short-story form to fit her own explorations with narrative technique. Nena Skrbic, for example, in *Wild Outbursts of Freedom: Reading Virginia Woolf's Short Fiction*, discusses the challenges critics have faced when contemplating her "highly unusual and original approach to the short story." When asked by her nephews to write a story, Woolf obligingly utilized the framework and conventions of the typical, didactic, fable-like tale popular during that time, although nephew Quentin Bell's comments suggest he was hoping for something "subversive" and "frivolous." (Ann Martin, in *Red Riding Hood and the Wolf in the Bed: Modernism's Fairy Tales*, relates the history of this exchange between Woolf and her nephews and quotes Bell; Bell's comments saw print in 1988, when Hogarth Press published "The Widow and the Parrot" as an illustrated children's story.) Even

WHAT DO I READ NEXT?

- Originally published in 1925, *Mrs. Dalloway* is considered one of Woolf's best, and best-known, works. Tracing a day in the life of Mrs. Dalloway, its protagonist, the novel offers detailed and often psychological portraits of its characters. An annotated version of the novel was published in 2005.
- Woolf was a prolific essayist and wrote on a variety of subjects, including the art of writing, reading, women writers, and daily life in London, among other topics. The 2008 collection *Virginia Woolf: Selected Essays* provides an expansive sampling of Woolf's work in this format.
- Just as Woolf employed elements of fable and morality stories in her children's tale "The Widow and the Parrot," a number of recent young-adult novelists have been similarly inspired by the myths, folklore, and spiritual elements of various cultures and have utilized fable-like elements in their contemporary fiction. Chitra Banerjee Divakaruni is a native of India who writes such fiction. *The Conch Bearer* (2005) is the first book in a young-adult fiction series that weaves aspects of traditional Indian tales with a modern fantasy structure.
- Few, if any, modernist novels have been written with a young-adult target audience in mind, yet several coming-of-age novels by modernist writers, in their treatment of the journey from youth to adulthood, are appropriate for young adults similarly poised to make such a transition. Rainier Maria Rilke's modernist coming-of-age novel *The Notebooks of Malte Laurids Brigge* explores the life of a young Danish poet living in Paris. Rilke's work, originally published in German in 1910, is a distinctly modernist coming-of-age story that explores issues of identity and death. An English translation was published in 2010. The challenging work may be better suited toward older or more advanced students.
- Quentin Bell, Woolf's nephew, provides an intimate portrait of his aunt in *Virginia Woolf: A Biography* (1974).
- *Leonard and Virginia Woolf, the Hogarth Press, and the Networks of Modernism*, edited by Helen Southworth and published in 2011, offers essays by a number of scholars and provides a critical overview of the Woolfs' work in shaping the modernist movement via their Hogarth Press. The critics treat the themes of modernism as well as the social and political forces that influenced the movement. They also examine the works of some of the lesser-known modernist writers published by Hogarth Press.

when confining herself to the strictures of children's fiction and fable conventions, Woolf succeeds in expressing and exploring a major theme associated with the modernist movement.

The sense of alienation endured by the widow is introduced as the story opens and is further explored as the tale proceeds. The widow, Mrs. Gage, sits alone in her cottage, mending her shoes. Her advanced age, poverty, and physical limitations are revealed. In the space of the first few sentences, Woolf paints a picture of the harsh circumstances the widow endures, alone. Upon receiving a letter notifying her of her brother Joseph's death, Mrs. Gage's first response, that her brother is "gone at last!" is suggestive of her isolation from her family. This point is emphasized as Mrs. Gage learns that Joseph has left her both property and his savings of three thousand pounds. Mrs. Gage's reaction to her brother's death is transformed from surprise, and the absence of grief, to joy when she learns that she has inherited her

"

'THE WIDOW AND THE PARROT' IS, ON THE SURFACE, A MORALISTIC TALE INSTRUCTING YOUNG READERS ABOUT SUCH THEMES AS KINDNESS TOWARD ANIMALS. IN THE FIGURE OF THE WIDOW, HOWEVER, WOOLF CAPTURES THE MODERNIST NOTION OF ALIENATION."

brother's wealth. In fact, "Mrs. Gage almost fell into the fire with joy." At this point, Mrs. Gage reflects on the recent past, recalling how Joseph was so miserly he never replied to her Christmas cards because he did not want to waste money on stamps. Much is made of this miserliness, which Mrs. Gage states was a habit of Joseph's from childhood. Although Mrs. Gage is harshly critical of her brother for not replying to her once-a-year holiday card, she makes no other mention of efforts she has made to maintain a relationship with her brother. The reader can only ascertain that Mrs. Gage at least made an effort every year to contact her brother with a Christmas card, but he perpetually failed to reply. Although Mrs. Gage will later delve further into her past relationship with her brother, through her recollections, Woolf has outlined the lonely existence Mrs. Gage experiences. This apparently friendless existence is alleviated by Mrs. Gage's dog, Shag, for whom Mrs. Gage gladly sacrifices her own meager allotment of food in order to ensure that Shag has his bone.

Before she leaves to collect her inheritance, Mrs. Gage makes certain her dog is looked after and borrows money from her clergyman to help pay her travel expenses. The financial exchange with Reverend Tallboys is characteristic of Mrs. Gage's later encounters with other people: Mrs. Gage does not have human relationships, she has transactions. Only with animals does she reveal herself or show affection, as the reader learns when Mrs. Gage first encounters the parrot, James. After taking up the farmer Mr. Stacey on his offer to drive her into the village of Rodmell in his cart (another transaction), Mrs. Gage is met at the door to her brother's dilapidated home by the villager Mrs. Ford. Having heard the screeching of James, the parrot, Mrs. Gage wonders aloud whether the bird might be unhappy or hungry. She gives him sugar and contemplates his "sadly neglected" plumage. Although Mrs. Ford replies to Mrs. Gage's concerns, discounting the bird's screeching as indicative of his "temper" rather than hunger or sadness, Mrs. Gage appears to have been talking to herself, for there is no evidence that she and Mrs. Ford are actually engaged in a mutual conversation. Mrs. Ford informs Mrs. Gage of Joseph's affection for the bird, as well as the bird's salty language, yet Mrs. Gage does not respond and is focused on attending to the parrot. After the woman leaves, however, Mrs. Gage speaks to James "in a very kind tone" and tells him how well she will care for him.

Next, Mrs. Gage once again accepts Mr. Stacey's offer of a ride, this time to Lewes, where she will meet with the solicitors of her brother's estate. On the way, Mr. Stacey shares with Mrs. Gage the dangers of the river, telling her stories of people who had died there. No reply by Mrs. Gage to Mr. Stacey is recorded. Thus far, she appears disinterested in communicating with people about anything other than business matters. Yet she responds kindly and warmly to animals. In fact, while the statements of other characters are presented, Mrs. Gage's only spoken words appear to have been either to herself or to the parrot. In the solicitors' office, things are no different. Mrs. Gage is spoken to but makes no reply. When Mr. Stagg stops speaking, Mrs. Gage perceives that he wishes her to leave, but she does not speak to him.

To this point, what initially appeared to be Mrs. Gage's solitude and likely loneliness are gradually revealed to be a deep sense of isolation from other people. Mrs. Gage appears unable to communicate with others, although she manages to muddle through business arrangements. Furthermore, this sense of disconnectedness with the rest of the world does not appear to trouble Mrs. Gage in the least. She does not seem aggrieved in any way, except when she wonders about the happiness and health of the parrot. This suggests that her alienation from society has become a natural part of her existence and has likely been ongoing for some time, perhaps since her husband's death.

When Mrs. Gage becomes stranded in the dark on the banks of the rising river, she reveals to a greater degree her isolation from her family as well as from society in general. First, she thinks of her brother and his cruel nature. Speaking to herself in the darkness, her bitterness towards Joseph is revealed in stark terms as she expresses her certainty that Joseph is burning in the fires of hell. As her situation becomes direr, the fire imagery is repeated when Mrs. Gage sees a blazing light in the distance. When she realizes it is someone's home burning, Mrs. Gage's response is relief, for houses take a long time to burn, and her path to the village will be illuminated for a long time—long enough for her to make it safely home. Mrs. Gage does not spare a moment's thought or feeling for the family whose home is burning, until she discovers it is her house—Joseph's house—that is aflame. The wish for Joseph to be burning in hell is replaced by Mrs. Gage's terror that James, the parrot, is perishing in the fire in Joseph's house. Although she values her own safety over that of the anonymous people who could have been perishing in a house fire, Mrs. Gage is now ready to risk her own life to save James. The first time she actively speaks aloud to other people in the story occurs when she cries out to ask if anyone has saved the bird.

Following this crisis, James reveals himself to Mrs. Gage, after she has been escorted by Mrs. Ford away from the burning home and to Mrs. Ford's own cottage. In the next section of the story, Mrs. Gage's sense of alienation from human society is underscored through her heightened connection to the animal world. As James knocks at her window and persuades her to follow him, Mrs. Gage observes to herself, "The creature has more meaning in its acts than we humans know." She then replies "as though he were a human being." After following James back to the charred remains of her brother's home, Mrs. Gage resolves to trust him completely and to "be guided entirely by the behaviour of the parrot James." Mrs. Gage has fully embraced a world in which her most meaningful interactions occur not with humans but with animals, specifically, James. On her deathbed she describes to the son of her former clergyman her belief that James knew of the danger she was in at the river and subsequently caused the fire that led both to her survival and to her finding the money her brother had buried.

Throughout the story, Mrs. Gage's behavior suggests her intense alienation from the rest of human society. The other characters in "The Widow and the Parrot" extend kindnesses

James, the talking parrot, was part of Mrs. Gage's inheritance. *(Eric Isselée | Shutterstock.com)*

toward Mrs. Gage, as when the villagers prevent her from entering the burning home, or when Mrs. Ford offers her shelter, or when Mr. Stacey, thinking Mrs. Gage utterly destitute, offers to buy the parrot from her. They possess the "shared values" Poplawski speaks of in his description of modernist themes, in that they universally feel compelled to aid the poor widow, whereas Mrs. Gage has lost her understanding of and connection to these values. She is disengaged from others, unresponsive to their attempts at kindness. Furthermore, Mrs. Gage's behavior illuminates another element of modernism that Poplawski has detailed, specifically, its "search for alternative systems of belief." Rather than believing in other people and in human relationships, Mrs. Gage has embraced a world in which her belief in the kindness, intelligence, and good intentions of animals guides her behavior. The connection the widow feels with animals signifies both a longing for something lost (human relationships) and a desire to build a new type of social order. In creating the character of Mrs. Gage, Woolf offers a moving portrait of the modernist's sense of alienation and isolation from traditional belief systems and from society as a whole.

Source: Catherine Dominic, Critical Essay on "The Widow and the Parrot," in *Short Stories for Students*, Gale, Cengage Learning, 2012.

"I SUBMIT THAT THIS COMBINATION OF EXCURSIONS AND JAUNTS, HIGH AND LOW ENTERTAINMENTS, SERIOUS STUDY AND PLEASURABLE READING SHAPES VIRGINIA WOOLF'S CONSCIOUSNESS, AND LEAVES A VARIEGATED TRACE ON HER ADULT WORKS."

Mia Carter

In the following excerpt, Carter argues that "Woolf's juvenilia, youthful diaries, and early fiction depict her lifelong struggle with questions of national, cultural, and ethnic inheritance."

... This article argues that Woolf's juvenilia, youthful diaries, and early fiction depict her lifelong struggle with questions of national, cultural, and ethnic inheritance. The author suggests that the peculiarities and contradictions of Woolf's familial and Victorian upbringing, and her youthful experiences of modernizing change in the social and physical landscape, permanently affected Woolf's understanding of history and historiographic impulses and attitudes.

As scholars have noted, and as the author herself frequently confessed in her writings, Virginia Woolf (née Stephen) considered herself an outsider throughout her life. Her Victorian girlhood and inability to obtain the education that was afforded her brothers initially inspired this feeling of social alienation. Experiences of domestic entrapment and enclosure are central to the conventional aspects of Woolf's childhood. However, Woolf's genius as a writer, historical observer, and critic can also be attributed to the strange contradictions of her life, and especially her childhood. The self-described outsider was steeped in English traditions and raised to pride herself in her family's heritage, and Woolf was both dubious about, and proud of, ethnic and ancestral claims of genius. The Stephen family was one of the 'extraordinary' family lines included in Sir Francis Galton's ethnological study *Hereditary Genius: An Inquiry into Its Laws and Consequences* (1870); the Victorian interest in biography and biology, in heritage and eugenics is part of Woolf's educational, familial, and cultural inheritance. Despite her depictions of her cloistered youth, the domesticated young Victorian angel was also an unusually liberated child. Woolf was given access to her father's extensive library; she was raised in a stridently agnostic household; and she was encouraged to be an artist and performer.

This article was inspired by this critic's partial resistance to Woolf's narrative of alienation, and by my desire to understand the origins of Woolf's feelings of 'outsider-ness' in a more productive way, a way that challenged Woolf's solipsism, self-pity, and her tendency to diminish and depreciate her own class and cultural privileges. Despite Woolf's declared outsider's position, her life and work reflect, instead, processes of strenuous negotiation. In a sense, Woolf wrestles with her childhood enthrallment with her own national heritage, class, and culture. Her childhood skepticism about history and the role that it plays in public and private life gradually lead her to the adult realization that the glamor of the past cannot sustain her. Woolf also recognizes that fantasy and imagination are central to cherished historical memories and the possibilities of creating a future that is not dependent on a glorified mythic past.

REPRESENTATION OF WOOLF'S CHILDHOOD

However sequestered she was in the household and family library, Woolf was free to explore and roam as a reader; she once described reading as "the removal of all restrictions." Woolf read adult books, Victorian children's penny papers like *Tit Bits*, and *Punch* magazines. She enjoyed family jaunts to parks and ponds, and interrupted serious study to attend Gilbert and Sullivan plays and other commonplace entertainments for upper-middle-class Victorian children. While much has been made of Woolf's long-term battles with mental illness and depression, her attempts at self-destruction and eventual suicide, far less attention has been paid to the vitality of her sense of humor, imagination, and sense of play. I certainly do not want to discount the seriousness of Woolf's experiences with chronic illness, or the history of her difficulties with doctors and the grotesque inadequacies of Victorian notions of mental illness and health; Woolf's valiant struggles to maintain her equilibrium have been widely analyzed and discussed. Instead of focusing on her illnesses, I submit that one of the great signs of health in Virginia Woolf's life was her ability to maintain a child's exquisite outlandishness and irreverence, a child's sense of mystery and discovery, a child's elastic sense of time and appreciation of nonsense, and a child's relative insulation from the institutionalized, disciplined, and ritualized adult world. Woolf's distrust of officialdom—official institutions and discourses—is widely apparent in her fictional works, essays, and diaries. She considered political discourse reductive and distorting. She also associated linguistic and rhetorical certainty with patriarchy and dominance. The child's sense of wonder—including anxiety and terror—and amusement at the world were privileged over thorough immersion in the political and institutional adult world.

Woolf's depictions of her childhood and past vary dramatically. Her father Leslie Stephen is represented as the Victorian traditionalist and patriarchal force that squelched her artistic sensibility; at one point in 1928 Woolf wrote: "His life would have entirely ended mine. What would have happened? No writing, no books;—inconceivable." However, the year before she shared with Vita SackvilleWest "her child's eye view" of her father in a letter about the fictional depiction of her parents as the Ramsays in *To the Lighthouse*: "Do you think it [*The Lighthouse*] sentimental? Do you think it was irreverent about him? I should like to know. I was more like him than her, I think; and therefore more critical: but he was an adorable man, and somehow, tremendous."

Woolf was quite aware of the ways in which memory erases, embellishes, and invents; the variable textures and currents of memory are topics that nearly all of her novels explore. A reader of Woolf's work and life must also attend to the inconsistencies, in and of the autobiographical narratives, she presents—not to damn her, but to understand the full complexity of the writer and her work. For example, sometimes Woolf is writing about her father, the individual person, and sometimes he becomes a Victorian Colossus, a larger than life symbol of the age she was trying to escape. The removal of Woolf from her iconic status and restoration of her human dimensions can teach us a great deal about how this one writer struggled to make sense and meaning of her childhood and her cultural environment. Woolf's frequently quoted remark about her life having been suffocated by her father's influence and presence was central to the way in which I was introduced to the writer in Women's Studies classes in the late 1970s. The author was a public and private victim of patriarchy, and her artistry was a miracle of survival and rebellion. That statement can be judged accurate and true, but Woolf was also a fabulist, as all novelists are; her positive and negative appraisals of her upbringing also seem to reflect her fluctuating periods of psychological health and distress. Woolf's autobiographical writings demand the same kinds of close reading and interpretation that are required for reading her high modernist novels.

In this article, I will be reviewing Woolf's juvenilia, early fictional works, and her later autobiographical essays. The Virginia Woolf who grew up in a dark and oppressive Victorian 'cage' should be examined alongside the exuberant teenager who adored entertaining her siblings and parents. She also fluctuated between trying to please her adult intellectual superiors while maintaining, at the same time, her own subversive vision. In her essay, "Play and Apprenticeship: The Culture of Family Magazines," Christine Alexander reads the play involved with the production of family magazines through the lens of Johan Huizinga's anthropological study of play, *Homo Ludens* (1948). She notes that:

> Appropriation of the adult world is part of... play. In the process, however, the child is not simply being colonized by the teaching adult, but is colonizing the adult world by remaking it in the image of self; and it is by this process that the child discovers the self. Insofar as children learn through imitation in the first instance, their play could be seen as a variation, a commentary on, an interpretation, or a reproduction of the world around them.

The now widely available newspaper authored by the Stephen children, *Hyde Park Gate News*, and Woolf's early journals enable us to see how the author experienced and recreated childhood, and how she came to terms with her familial and cultural Victorian inheritances. The habits of mimicry and appropriation that Alexander describes can be observed in the newspaper, and in Woolf's young adult works, well into her twenties and beyond.

WOOLF AND HERITAGE

Heritage was a lifelong obsession for Woolf. Her early novel *Night and Day* (1919) is subsumed with questions about familial, national, and cultural heritage. These concerns also run through the novels *Jacob's Room* (1922), *Orlando* (1928), *The Waves* (1931), and *The Years* (1937), and Woolf wrote several short stories about heritage and inheritance. Many of Woolf's early reviews and travel writings explore questions of heritage in ways that reveal her indebtedness to the Victorian era's eugenic discourses of race and blood; early on, she associates heritage with biology and culture. For example, the entries from the 1906 trip to Greece and Turkey (*The Passionate Apprentice*) and a later trip to Italy in 1908 (*The Passionate Apprentice*) are filled with observations about blood, physiognomy, ethnic temperaments, oriental superstitions, and essential differences. Here is an example from the Turkish entries:

> The last thing, as it is generally the first, that such superficial travelers as I am should enter into their note books is the state of a people's religion. Indeed the only remark I can make with any confidence is that no Christian, or even European, can hope to understand the Turkish point of view; you are born Christian or Mahommedans [sic] as surely as you are born black or white. The difference is in the blood that beats in the pulse. (*The Passionate Apprentice*)

Woolf's corpus reveals the writer's gradual processes of redefining heritage; the teenage and young adult Woolf is very comfortable making pronouncements about race, class, or tribe. Francis Galton's work was influenced by that of his cousin Charles Darwin; the Social Darwinists who interpreted and applied Darwin's theories of evolution and development to racial and ethnic subjects and working class citizens made supremacist views of culture a prominent and widely available common-sense social discourse. Woolf's fascination with the intersections of heritage and history, of identity and culture, enables her to examine the ways in which she, too, has been shaped by inherited ideologies, class and racial superstitions, and mythologies. This is a critical sensibility that develops in her childhood and matures with the writer as she begins to disavow some of her own Victorian inheritances. One can see the early stages of this process during a trip to visit a branch of the illustrious Stephen family in 1899; the seventeen-year-old Woolf begins to scrutinize her relatives as both relics and specimens. Rosamond Stephen's love for the rich is said to be a "startling departure from all probabilities laid down by the principles of Heredity and Physiognomy" (*The Passionate Apprentice*). As for the rest:

> The others are all Stephens without attempting to conceal the fact. They are immensely broad, long & muscular; they move awkwardly, & as though they resented the conventionalities of modern life at every step. They all bring with them the atmosphere of the lecture room; they are severe, caustic & absolutely independent & immoveable [sic]. An ordinary character would be ground to a pulp after a week's intercourse with them. They are distinct & have more character than most of the world, so for that we will bless them & thank them sincerely. (*The Passionate Apprentice*)

Childhood and adolescence served as foundations for Woolf's fictional works, aesthetic theories, and understanding of history and historiography, as well. Woolf's juvenilia gives one a multidimensional sense of the world she inhabited as a Victorian child—for example, the boom in popular entertainments (music hall shows, concerts, pantomimes, exhibitions) and public spectacles like Queen Victoria's Diamond Jubilee ("A most wonderful dreamlike sight" [*The Passionate Apprentice*]) can be observed in her diaries. Woolf's childhood diary entries frequently remark upon her generation's inherited landscape. For example, a diary entry in January 1897 describes Virginia and her older brother Thoby's excursion to the Thames Embankment, where they encountered Charles Cockerell's obelisk-shaped monument to soldiers killed at Chianwala in the Punjab (*The Passionate Apprentice*). And like many modernists, Woolf characterizes the transformation of Victorian society in terms of shock. However, her notion of shock is highlighted by the sensual and visual-photographic power of childhood memory. Leslie Stephen takes the Stephen children on frequent heritage tours; they also visit popular entertainments at which they occasionally encounter historical spectacles. On an April 1897 excursion to Brighton Pier, the fifteen-year-old Virginia describes the penny-in-the slot machine that depicted a sensational event from the recent past:

> In the morning Gerald took us and the Fishers—Emmie Boo Tom and Adeline, to the Pier. There we had the happiness of seeing the execution of Mrs Dyer—unfortunately when about three of us had had the treat, the machinery refused to work, and the back of the platform had to be opened, and some thing done to the electricity—afterwards she was hung successfully. (*The Passionate Apprentice*)

The Pier's magic and minstrel shows and carnivalesque entertainments were combined with Woolf's reading Thomas Babington Macaulay's multi-volume *The History of England* (1849–61) and a trip to the Arundel Castle. The day after the boardwalk entertainments, Woolf's father took her on a walk along the promenade and regaled her with his stories of Macaulay,

"IN FACT, WHAT 'IT' IS ABOUT IN VIRGINIA WOOLF'S SHORT FICTIONS CANNOT BE RECOGNIZED OR DISCLOSED SINCE THE MODES OF THE IMPLICIT THAT 'IT' ACTIVATES REQUIRE A THEORY OF INTERPRETATION WHICH DOES NOT IMPLY THAT SIGNIFICATION COMES PRIOR TO UTTERANCE."

with whom he had been personally acquainted (*The Passionate Apprentice*). I submit that this combination of excursions and jaunts, high and low entertainments, serious study and pleasurable reading shapes Virginia Woolf's consciousness, and leaves a variegated trace on her adult works; history is real and artificial, dioramic and malleable, and monumental and imposing. Young Virginia approaches history seriously, impatiently, and with great imaginative verve. . . .

Source: Mia Carter, "History's Child: Virginia Woolf, Heritage, and Historical Consciousness," in *Alif: Journal of Comparative Poetics*, No. 27, 2007, p. 68.

Anne Besnault-Levita

In the following essay, Besnault-Levita analyzes Woolf's use of the pronoun "it" in her short fiction.

How does "it" mean, what is "it" about and what does "it" reveal about the ethics of Virginia Woolf's poetics of the implicit, and therefore of fiction, are the three questions I would like to raise in this paper. My starting point will be the recurring use, in many short stories, of the indefinite pronoun "it," that haunting black mark on the white wall of the texts whose metalinguistic function challenges some of our common assumptions about the implicit as a linguistic and literary concept. In other words, I would like to examine the implicit theories of meaning and interpretation behind the implicit as they are put to the test by Woolf's fictional prose.

On first consideration, the use of the pronoun "it" in Virginia Woolf's short fictions has nothing to do with the notions of linguistic presupposition, cultural presupposition or pragmatic implicatures, nor does it seem to refer to the common definition of the implicit as what is suggested or understood without being stated directly. As a pronoun replacing a noun or referring to a clause, "it" first seems to call for our knowledge of language as a code and designates language as explicit. "Ah, the mark on the wall! It was a snail," the narrator of Woolf's famous short story concludes in an anti-climactic moment deflating the reader's expectations as to the nature of that "small round mark, black upon the white wall, about six or seven inches above the mantelpiece" described in the first paragraph. In what clearly reads as an ironical punch-line, "it" first anaphorically refers to the mark before cataphorically providing us with a definition—"it was a snail"—which puts an end to the thematic and imagistic meditation that it had triggered off in the first place. The deceived reader is left with the feeling that the linguistic and literary explicitness attached to the use of "it" is frustrating. But the "judicious" reader will reject explicitness as the implicit of the text to turn to implicitness as its essential mode: realizing that the mark's definition as a snail is some kind of reading lure, he will have to build up an interpretation of this short story insisting on the unsaid—this pattern of hidden, not-yet actualized signifieds—as one of its fundamental dimensions.

Thus, he may choose to read "The Mark on the Wall" as a fictional essay promoting Woolf's art of fiction as an encounter with "life itself." In this case he will foreground the text's implicit meditation on the problems of representation, a meditation opposing facts to fancy (the mark is a snail, yet "it is not the actual sight or sound that matters, but the reverberations that it makes as it travels through our minds"), comparing the Edwardian interest for "the surface with its hard separate facts" with the modernist awareness that a mirror never hides "one reflection but an almost infinite number," contrasting the hierarchical and even patriarchical order of what Woolf calls in this same story the "Whitaker's Table of Precedency" with the infinite richness of humanity as metaphorized not by the definition of the mark as a snail but by its potentially unstable nature as a referent. In the light of modernism's acknowledged self-reflexiveness and rejection of univocal determination of meaning, the reader may also conceive the story as the expression of a syntagmatic movement taking him from the illusion of significance as transparent and stable (the mark is a snail) to the revelation of signification as a paradigmatic process implying plurality and instability: "The outward sign I see and shall see for ever; but at the meaning of it I shall only guess." Inspired by a more phenomenological approach of interpretation positing the impossibility of our gaining a knowledge of the world that would remain untouched by our perception of that world, he could also probably insist on the definition "it" implicitly conveys of sight as insight, of vision as an envisioning process: objects are always the incomplete objects of our subjective perception. Now a post-modernist, if not deconstructionist, interpretation of "The Mark on the Wall" would surely underline the absence of any stabilized signified attached to "it" together with the endless circulation of unstable signifiers imparting a strong sense of the unpresentable, of the absence of a "beyond-the-text" since, indeed, "No, no nothing is proved, nothing is known. [. . .] Everything's moving, falling, slipping, vanishing. . . . "

Whatever the different and yet non-exclusive interpretations, the various signifieds explicitly referred to by the signifier "it"—"mark," "object," "hole," "nail," "snail"—all point to an implicit dimension of the text which no longer designates language as an explicit and stable code or the text as an easily deciphered riddle. In other words, Woolf's use of the implicit here implies a poetical order that should be opposed to the traditional grammatical order of language, but also to the rhetorical or pragmatic order of meaning and interpretation when the theoretical injunctions implied by those orders amount to what Jean-Jacques Lecercle, in *Interpretation as Pragmatics*, calls a "doxic" theory of interpretation and meaning. Thus, according to what could be called the metaphysical order of traditional grammar, one of those injunctions is that as a mode of grammatical ellipsis the implicit entails that 1) an elliptic sentence refers to a complete sentence 2) what is implied is always perceptible 3) the missing words define a negative form of utterance: they unmistakably refer to the intention of the speaking subject, although in a negative way. Indisputably, the way "it" works in Virginia Woolf's short fictions offers an implicit theory of language and meaning that challenges those three theoretical maxims. First and foremost, the implicit is not for Woolf a secondary phenomenon which does not, or should not, disrupt the transparency of language as its primary quality. As Woolf herself explains in an essay called "Craftsmanship" dealing with the art of fiction but also with language as a conversational tool, words always "mislead us," "fool us"; they never express "one simple statement but a thousand possibilities." The "useful meaning" of words is not, as the final line of "The Mark on the Wall" suggests, their "literal meaning," their "surface meaning." The proper way to use them is by relying on their "power of suggestion which is one of [their] most mysterious properties." "Words, English words," Woolf goes on explaining, "are full of echoes, of memories, of associations—naturally." Not only does Woolf suggest here that the implicit dimension of words—the natural vagueness and undecidability of language—comes first; she also reverses the usual hierarchy of traditional grammar and of traditional rhetorics and pragmatics according to which the implicit presupposes the existence of explicit semantic contents to which it refers as an origin. As the short story entitled "Solid Objects" suggests, the search for such an origin (whether it be of an object or of a word) is impossible, and this is partly why what is implied is not always perceptible and does not refer to any complete and originally intended form of utterance:

> It was a lump of a glass, so thick as to be almost opaque; the smoothing of the sea had completely worn off any edge or shape, so it was impossible to say whether it had been bottle, tumbler or window-pane; it was nothing but glass; it was almost a precious stone. You had only to enclose it in a rim of gold, or pierce it with a wire, and it became a jewel; part of a necklace, or a dull green light upon a finger. Perhaps after all it was really a gem; [. . .] .

In this short story, the way "it" cataphorically fails to provide us with a definition before retrospectively referring to an impossible quest for truth—"'What was the truth of it, John?' asked Charles suddenly, turning and facing him. 'What made you give it up like that all in a second?'"—is exemplary and echoes our analysis of "Mark on the Wall." But although truth (the implicit signified attached to the signifier "it" under which all the others are subsumed in this text and in Woolf's short fiction in general) is most of the time conveyed metaphorically, it cannot be approached either through traditional rhetorics when based on a definition of the rhetorical figure as transparent and "translatable." In this respect, Oswald Ducrot is right to argue that the conception of language as a code, and of rhetorics as a set of conventional categories always finally turning indirect meaning into explicit meaning is incompatible with the very notion of the implicit. The resurgence of the grammatical order of language (as defined above) in such a conception of the rhetorical order of language is obvious: it implies a positivistic account of sense based on the reductive opposition between literal and figurative meaning and argues for the view that literary interpretation is a disclosure process implying closure in the first place.

Interestingly enough, Virginia Woolf's use of the implicit challenges this view by systematically resorting to connotation at the expense of denotation, as if there could be no such thing as denoted meaning. Linguistically and literarily speaking, the mark on the wall is not a snail but a mark on a wall: just as "solid objects" are solid (i.e. clearly identifiable) in appearance only, it has no significance outside a discursive context. This is why Woolf's short fictions constantly blur our usual perception of the line between literal meaning and figurative meaning, between denotation and connotation, between the alleged transparency of the code and the alleged opacity of literature. As Jean-Jacques Lecercle points out in an essay entitled "L'écriture féminine selon Virginia Woolf," the "philosophy of the implicit" in "the feminine sentence" according to Woolf can be described in the terms of various theories of sense and discourse (he mentions Derrida, Lyotard and Deleuze), but whatever the mode of theorizing, the Woolfian truth cannot be characterized by a normative and straightforward use of "designation, signification and manifestation." Not so much because it is ultimately inaccessible or "beyond the text," as because it always exceeds ready-coded motifs, whether narrative or semiotic. In Woolf's short fictions, what we take for an explicit significance always-already implies the underdetermination of language as an implicit dimension, which accounts for the way the use of the pronoun "it" follows a circular movement from the implicit to the explicit and back again to the implicit: "But was it 'happiness'?" the narrator wonders in "Happiness." "How could she express it?" the character-focalizer asks in "A Woman's College from Outside." In both examples, "it" anaphorically refers to an implicit utterance which is cataphorically turned into an explicit signified—"happiness," "life," "the world"—before losing its explicitness through a process of metaphorization that reminds one of Gertrude Stein's conception of the use of names:

> A name is adequate or it is not. If it is adequate why go on calling it, if it is not, then calling it by its name does no good. If you feel what is inside of a thing do not call it by the name by which it is known.

"Names," "big words" as Woolf puts it, do not seem to fit "it": "No. The big word did not seem to fit it [Happiness], did not seem to refer to this state of being curled in rosy flakes around a bright light." "Big" words frozen by canonical significations, by semantic and cultural recognitions always fail in their attempt to hide the opacity of natural language behind an illusory correspondence between signifiers and signifieds, figural meaning and literal meaning:

> How could she express it—that after the dark churning of myriad ages here was light at the end of the tunnel; life; the world. Beneath her it lay—all good; all lovable. Such was her discovery.

In Virginia Woolf's short fiction, light is life is the world is truth is light. The meaning hidden behind "it," the desired epiphanic disclosure of the text, cannot but be delayed, differed and differing, Derrida would say, questioned, rendered implicit, just as the idea of a formal centre of signification releasing knowledge is itself disrupted and replaced by an infinite reserve of signifiers and therefore of "possibilities," "echoes, memories [and] associations":

> Desiring truth, awaiting it, laboriously distilling a few words, forever desiring—(a cry starts to the left, another to the right. Wheels strike divergently. Omnibuses conglomerate in conflict)—forever desiring—(the clock asseverates with twelve distinct strokes that it is midday; light sheds gold scales, children swarm)—forever desiring truth.

To understand how "it" means and what it is about therefore requires more than a positivistic account of meaning as intention and recognition. In this respect, even the traditional (Jean-Jacques Lecercle would say "doxic") pragmatic view of sense does not seem to "fit it." If Woolf would surely agree that "the interpretation of a text can be treated as an extended speech act," it seems to me that she would reject Searle's conception of meaning as intentionality (at least, her fiction does) according to which "everything that can be meant can be said," just as she would challenge Oswald Ducrot's view that implicit meaning is always added on to literal meaning which it never completely erases: "In reading we have to allow the sunken meanings to remain sunken, suggested, not stated; lapsing and pouring into each other like reeds on the bed of a river." Here again, Woolf reminds us that indirect language acts based on the use of the implicit are not secondary phenomenons. In a discursive context, the implicit has to be interpreted and constructed, not simply retrieved and reconstructed. In fact, what "it" is about in Virginia Woolf's short fictions cannot be recognized or disclosed since the modes of the implicit that "it" activates require a theory of interpretation which does not imply that signification comes prior to utterance. In this respect, the way the conventional motif of the quest in some of Woolf's famous stories ("The Mark on the Wall," "An Unwritten Novel," "A Haunted House," "Monday or Tuesday" or "The Lady in the Looking Glass") may lure the reader into a hermeneutic pattern of interpretation is a remarkable example of Woolf's subversive strategy, as the quest motif appears to orientate the writing and the reading of those texts towards the disclosure of an origin that was finally never there and therefore never lost.

"A Haunted House" is here another canonical example of the way Woolf prompts us to look at "it" as a successful, yet finally absent, centre on which the overall meaning of the story deceptively depends:

> Whatever hour you woke there was a door shutting. From room to room they went, hand in hand, lifting here, opening there, making sure—a ghostly couple. 'Here we left *it*,' she said. And he added, 'Oh, but here too!' 'It's upstairs,' she murmured, 'And in the garden,' he whispered. 'Quietly,' they said, 'or we shall wake them.'

The resort to cultural implicatures in the form of an intertextual allusion is the first mode of the implicit in this story whose title builds up a deceptive horizon of expectation for the "common reader." The convention of the gothic tale invites us to embark on a syntagmatic journey taking us from sheer absence—there is no object after the verbs "to lift" and "to open"—to the loss of the referent attached to "it"—to a discovered treasure—"the treasure yours"—to the metaphoric unveiling of the treasure's significance: "Waking, I cry 'Oh, is this your buried treasure, The light in the heart.'" However, the disclosure of the metaphorical meaning of the story's "lost" referent does not entail a recognition of its lost signified although it takes place in an epiphanic moment, announced in the rest of the passage by the shift from obscurity to light, from the past tense to the present tense. The metaphorical implicitness of the "revelation" rather challenges the traditional pattern of the quest by taking us back to the beginning of the short story rather than to a lost origin of utterance and meaning. What that obviously rapid hermeneutic analysis does not account for, among other things, is the passage from the pronoun "they"—"from room to room they went"—to the pronoun "I" in the last sentence of the text. Just as there cannot but be an unbridgeable gap between utterer's meaning and utterance meaning, between utterance meaning and interpretation, what "I" has discovered may not be what "they" have been looking for. What "it" is about is therefore not merely the infinite reserve of textual meaning; "it" is a blunt reminder of the uncontrollable implicit dimension of natural and literary language (Woolf never seems to consider literariness as a form of disruption of ordinary language or communication), which entails that authorial meaning is a partly irretrievable intention and that literary interpretation is necessarily a praxis, an "intervention" depending on a situation of enunciation and on the "determinate limits" imposed by any literary text.

I would also argue that for Woolf, it is that uncontrollable implicit dimension which renders human intercourse interesting and intense, however irrational, obscure and meaningless it may sometimes appear to be:

> Of all things, nothing is so strange as human intercourse, she thought, because of its changes, its extraordinary irrationality, her dislike being now nothing short of the most intense and rapturous love, but directly the word 'love' occurred to her, she rejected it, thinking again how obscure the mind was, with its very few words for all these astonishing perceptions, these alternations of pain and pleasure. ("Together and Apart")

> 'Yet how sad a thing is sense! How vast a renunciation it represents! Listen for a moment. Distinguish one among the voices. Now. "So cold it must seem after India. Seven years too. But habit is everything." That's sense. That's agreement. They've fixed their eyes upon something visible to each of them. They attempt no more to look upon the little spark of light, the little purple shadow which may be fruitful land on the verge of the horizon, or only a flying gleam on the water. It's all compromise—all safety, the general intercourse of human beings. Therefore we discover nothing; we cease to explore; we cease to believe that there is anything to discover. "Nonsense" you say; meaning that I shan't see your crystal globe; and I'm half ashamed to try.'

> 'Speech is an old torn net, through which the fish escape as one casts it over them. Perhaps silence is better. Let us try it. Come to the window.'

'It's an odd thing, silence. The mind becomes like a starless night; and then a meteor slides, splendid, right across the dark and is extinct. We never give sufficient thanks for this entertainment.' ("The Evening Party")

My own reading, or "praxis" of those two extracts thus makes me aware that silence, which within the modernist literary context, is often endowed with a symbolic power of attractiveness, should not be here opposed to conversation or dialogue, but to sense as "habit," "agreement," "compromise," "safety." What is valuable for Woolf in "human intercourse" is neither silence as an ideal form of communication (although such an "entertainment" might seem attractive at times) nor an impossible cooperative principle between speaker and hearer, author and reader, based on the non-proliferation of the implicit. I do not think that her characters grieve here for the loss of dialogic directness or for a prelapsarian linguistic world: natural languages would sink into the plenitude of fixed meaning if the implicit was not a fundamental linguistic category. No "discovery" would be possible, no "spark of light" would "slide" across the dark sky if there was no "little purple shadow which may be fruitful land on the verge of the horizon." As a highly political discursive mode, the implicit in Virginia Woolf's short fictions is thus inseparable from the concepts of history and society, which imply the acceptance of change, obscurity and disagreement and a distrust of "fixed" and "visible" meaning; it is inseparable from the complex and ambivalent process of subjectivation that involves both speakers and hearers, authors and readers. To take up B. C. Rosenberg's words in his analysis of the Woolfian notion of "common reader," there is a parallel between Woolf's poetics and her conception of conversation and dialogue: "dialogue, as a model for constructing knowledge, is not fluid or static, but fluid, decentered, and process-orientated. Like the common reader, dialogue is anti-authoritarian and non-didactic, unsystematic and constantly changing with each interaction [. . .]." If we agree that there are ethical implications in the way literary theory articulates the problem of how, as speaking subjects, we take into account the existence of others, then the question of the ethics of Virginia Woolf's poetics of the implicit cannot but appear to be linked with the exploration of alterity "it" stands for:

I have some restless searcher in me. Why is there not a discovery in life? Something one can lay hands on and say 'This is it'? My depression is a harassed feeling. I'm looking: but that's not it—that's not it. What is it? And shall I die before I find it?

Source: Anne Besnault-Levita, "What 'It' Is About: The Implicit in Virginia Woolf's Short Fictions," in *Journal of the Short Story in English*, No. 40, Spring 2003, pp. 135–47.

SOURCES

Dick, Susan, "Virginia Woolf," in *Dictionary of Literary Biography*, Vol. 162, *British Short-Fiction Writers, 1915–1945*, edited by John H. Rogers, Gale Research, 1996, pp. 357–71.

Fraser, Rebecca, "Overview: Britain, 1918–1945," in *British History in Depth*, British Broadcasting Corporation Web site, http://www.bbc.co.uk/history/british/britain_wwtwo/overview_britain_1918_1945_01.shtml (accessed March 18, 2011).

"History of the Monarchy," in *Official Web site of the British Monarchy*, http://www.royal.gov.uk/HistoryoftheMonarchy/HistoryoftheMonarchy.aspx (accessed March 17, 2011).

Inglis, Fred, "Frances Hodgson Burnett" and "Edith Nesbit," in *Women Writers of Children's Literature*, edited by Harold Bloom, Chelsea House, 1998, pp. 18–19, 99–101; originally published in *The Promise of Happiness: Value and Meaning in Children's Fiction*, Cambridge University Press, 1981, pp. 111–17.

Levy, Heather, "Halycon Spaces for Bliss: Heightened Class Consciousness, 1922–1926," in *The Servants of Desire in Virginia Woolf's Shorter Fiction*, Peter Lang, 2010, pp. 127–48.

Martin, Ann, "Virginia Woolf: A Slipper of One's Own," in *Red Riding Hood and the Wolf in Bed: Modernism's Fairy Tales*, University of Toronto Press, 2006, pp. 78–114.

Martin, Wendy, "Faithful James Fell Off His Perch," in *New York Times*, May 8, 1988, http://www.nytimes.com/books/00/12/17/specials/woolf-widow88.html?_r=1 (accessed March 17, 2011).

Poplawski, Paul, ed., Preface to *Encyclopedia of Literary Modernism*, Greenwood Press, 2003, pp. vii–x.

Skrbic, Nena, Introduction to *Wild Outbursts of Freedom: Reading Virginia Woolf's Short Fiction*, Praeger, 2004, pp. xi–xxiii.

"Stanley Baldwin," in *Number 10*, Official Web site of the Prime Minister's Office, http://www.number10.gov.uk/history-and-tour/prime-ministers-in-history/stanley-baldwin (accessed March 17, 2011).

Strachan, Hew, "Overview: Britain and World War One, 1901–1918," in *British History in Depth*, British Broadcasting Corporation Web site, http://www.bbc.co.uk/

history/british/britain_wwone/overview_britain_ww1_01.shtml (accessed March 17, 2011).

"United Kingdom," in *Country Profiles*, British Broadcasting Corporation Web site, http://www.news.bbc.co.uk/2/hi/europe/country_profiles/1038758.stm (accessed March 17, 2011).

Woolf, Virginia, "The Widow and the Parrot: A True Story," in *The Complete Shorter Fiction of Virginia Woolf*, 2nd ed., edited by Susan Dick, Harcourt, 1989, pp. 162–69.

Zipes, Jack David, ed., Introduction to *Victorian Fairy Tales: The Revolt of the Fairies and Elves*, Methuen, 1987, pp. xiii–xxix.

FURTHER READING

Bingham, Adrian, *Gender, Modernity, and the Popular Press in Inter-war Britain*, Oxford University Press, 2004.

In this work Bingham analyzes the treatment of gender and social issues as presented in a number of British newspapers during the years between the two world wars, thereby offering a cultural and historical context within which the works of modernist writers such as Woolf may be understood.

Eliot, T. S., *The Waste Land, and Other Writings*, Modern Library, 2002.

The long poem *The Waste Land* was originally published in 1922 and is collected here with a number of Eliot's other works. A contemporary of Woolf's, Eliot wrote modernist prose and poetry that similarly challenges traditional forms and structures and delves deeply into the inner worlds of the characters.

Ellmann, Maud, *The Nets of Modernism: Henry James, Virginia Woolf, James Joyce, and Sigmund Freud*, Cambridge University Press, 2010.

Ellmann, a literary critic, explores the relationship between psychoanalysis and modernist literature in this volume, using examples from the authors' works to offer a new perspective on the relationship between Freudian psychology and modernist writing.

Stein, Gertrude, *Tender Buttons*, Kessinger Publishing, 2010.

A contemporary of Woolf's, Stein published some of her modernist writings through Woolf's Hogarth Press. This volume of experimental poetry and prose presents Stein's reflections on the significance of everyday objects and offers a taste of her innovative experiments with language and poetic structure.

Woolf, Virginia, *Moments of Being*, Triad Books, 1978.

This series of autobiographical essays offers glimpses into Woolf's personal life, relationships, and opinions. The volumes are the only works of autobiography Woolf created for publication. Her husband eventually sold her diaries for publication years after her death.

SUGGESTED SEARCH TERMS

Virginia Woolf AND modernism

Virginia Woolf AND children's fiction

Virginia Woolf AND short fiction

Virginia Woolf AND The Widow and the Parrot

Virginia Woolf AND Leonard Woolf

Virginia Woolf AND biography

Virginia Woolf AND mental illness

Virginia Woolf AND Bloomsbury Group

Virginia Woolf AND feminism

Glossary of Literary Terms

A

Aestheticism: A literary and artistic movement of the nineteenth century. Followers of the movement believed that art should not be mixed with social, political, or moral teaching. The statement "art for art's sake" is a good summary of aestheticism. The movement had its roots in France, but it gained widespread importance in England in the last half of the nineteenth century, where it helped change the Victorian practice of including moral lessons in literature. Oscar Wilde and Edgar Allan Poe are two of the best-known "aesthetes" of the late nineteenth century.

Allegory: A narrative technique in which characters representing things or abstract ideas are used to convey a message or teach a lesson. Allegory is typically used to teach moral, ethical, or religious lessons but is sometimes used for satiric or political purposes. Many fairy tales are allegories.

Allusion: A reference to a familiar literary or historical person or event, used to make an idea more easily understood. Joyce Carol Oates's story "Where Are You Going, Where Have You Been?" exhibits several allusions to popular music.

Analogy: A comparison of two things made to explain something unfamiliar through its similarities to something familiar, or to prove one point based on the acceptance of another. Similes and metaphors are types of analogies.

Antagonist: The major character in a narrative or drama who works against the hero or protagonist. The Misfit in Flannery O'Connor's story "A Good Man Is Hard to Find" serves as the antagonist for the Grandmother.

Anthology: A collection of similar works of literature, art, or music. Zora Neale Hurston's "The Eatonville Anthology" is a collection of stories that take place in the same town.

Anthropomorphism: The presentation of animals or objects in human shape or with human characteristics. The term is derived from the Greek word for "human form." The fur necklet in Katherine Mansfield's story "Miss Brill" has anthropomorphic characteristics.

Anti-hero: A central character in a work of literature who lacks traditional heroic qualities such as courage, physical prowess, and fortitude. Anti-heroes typically distrust conventional values and are unable to commit themselves to any ideals. They generally feel helpless in a world over which they have no control. Anti-heroes usually accept, and often celebrate, their positions as social outcasts. A well-known anti-hero is Walter Mitty in James Thurber's story "The Secret Life of Walter Mitty."

Archetype: The word archetype is commonly used to describe an original pattern or model from which all other things of the same kind are made. Archetypes are the literary images that grow out of the "collective unconscious," a theory proposed by psychologist Carl Jung. They appear in literature as incidents and plots that repeat basic patterns of life. They may also appear as stereotyped characters. The "schlemiel" of Yiddish literature is an archetype.

Autobiography: A narrative in which an individual tells his or her life story. Examples include Benjamin Franklin's *Autobiography* and Amy Hempel's story "In the Cemetery Where Al Jolson Is Buried," which has autobiographical characteristics even though it is a work of fiction.

Avant-garde: A literary term that describes new writing that rejects traditional approaches to literature in favor of innovations in style or content. Twentieth-century examples of the literary avant-garde include the modernists and the minimalists.

B

Belles-lettres: A French term meaning "fine letters" or" beautiful writing." It is often used as a synonym for literature, typically referring to imaginative and artistic rather than scientific or expository writing. Current usage sometimes restricts the meaning to light or humorous writing and appreciative essays about literature. Lewis Carroll's *Alice in Wonderland* epitomizes the realm of belles-lettres.

Bildungsroman: A German word meaning "novel of development." The *bildungsroman* is a study of the maturation of a youthful character, typically brought about through a series of social or sexual encounters that lead to self-awareness. J. D. Salinger's *Catcher in the Rye* is a *bildungsroman*, and Doris Lessing's story "Through the Tunnel" exhibits characteristics of a *bildungsroman* as well.

Black Aesthetic Movement: A period of artistic and literary development among African Americans in the 1960s and early 1970s. This was the first major African-American artistic movement since the Harlem Renaissance and was closely paralleled by the civil rights and black power movements. The black aesthetic writers attempted to produce works of art that would be meaningful to the black masses. Key figures in black aesthetics included one of its founders, poet and playwright Amiri Baraka, formerly known as Le Roi Jones; poet and essayist Haki R. Madhubuti, formerly Don L. Lee; poet and playwright Sonia Sanchez; and dramatist Ed Bullins. Works representative of the Black Aesthetic Movement include Amiri Baraka's play *Dutchman,* a 1964 Obie award-winner.

Black Humor: Writing that places grotesque elements side by side with humorous ones in an attempt to shock the reader, forcing him or her to laugh at the horrifying reality of a disordered world. "Lamb to the Slaughter," by Roald Dahl, in which a placid housewife murders her husband and serves the murder weapon to the investigating policemen, is an example of black humor.

C

Catharsis: The release or purging of unwanted emotions—specifically fear and pity—brought about by exposure to art. The term was first used by the Greek philosopher Aristotle in his *Poetics* to refer to the desired effect of tragedy on spectators.

Character: Broadly speaking, a person in a literary work. The actions of characters are what constitute the plot of a story, novel, or poem. There are numerous types of characters, ranging from simple, stereotypical figures to intricate, multifaceted ones. "Characterization" is the process by which an author creates vivid, believable characters in a work of art. This may be done in a variety of ways, including (1) direct description of the character by the narrator; (2) the direct presentation of the speech, thoughts, or actions of the character; and (3) the responses of other characters to the character. The term "character" also refers to a form originated by the ancient Greek writer Theophrastus that later became popular in the seventeenth and eighteenth centuries. It is a short essay or sketch of a person who prominently displays a specific attribute or quality, such as miserliness or ambition. "Miss Brill," a story by Katherine Mansfield, is an example of a character sketch.

Classical: In its strictest definition in literary criticism, classicism refers to works of ancient Greek or Roman literature. The term may also be used to describe a literary work of recognized importance (a "classic") from any time period or literature that exhibits the traits of classicism. Examples of later works and authors now described as classical include French literature of the seventeenth century, Western novels of the nineteenth century, and American fiction of the mid-nineteenth century such as that written by James Fenimore Cooper and Mark Twain.

Climax: The turning point in a narrative, the moment when the conflict is at its most intense. Typically, the structure of stories, novels, and plays is one of rising action, in which tension builds to the climax, followed by falling action, in which tension lessens as the story moves to its conclusion.

Comedy: One of two major types of drama, the other being tragedy. Its aim is to amuse, and it typically ends happily. Comedy assumes many forms, such as farce and burlesque, and uses a variety of techniques, from parody to satire. In a restricted sense the term comedy refers only to dramatic presentations, but in general usage it is commonly applied to nondramatic works as well.

Comic Relief: The use of humor to lighten the mood of a serious or tragic story, especially in plays. The technique is very common in Elizabethan works, and can be an integral part of the plot or simply a brief event designed to break the tension of the scene.

Conflict: The conflict in a work of fiction is the issue to be resolved in the story. It usually occurs between two characters, the protagonist and the antagonist, or between the protagonist and society or the protagonist and himself or herself. The conflict in Washington Irving's story "The Devil and Tom Walker" is that the Devil wants Tom Walker's soul but Tom does not want to go to hell.

Criticism: The systematic study and evaluation of literary works, usually based on a specific method or set of principles. An important part of literary studies since ancient times, the practice of criticism has given rise to numerous theories, methods, and "schools," sometimes producing conflicting, even contradictory, interpretations of literature in general as well as of individual works. Even such basic issues as what constitutes a poem or a novel have been the subject of much criticism over the centuries. Seminal texts of literary criticism include Plato's *Republic,* Aristotle's *Poetics*, Sir Philip Sidney's *The Defence of Poesie,* and John Dryden's *Of Dramatic Poesie*. Contemporary schools of criticism include deconstruction, feminist, psychoanalytic, poststructuralist, new historicist, postcolonialist, and reader-response.

D

Deconstruction: A method of literary criticism characterized by multiple conflicting interpretations of a given work. Deconstructionists consider the impact of the language of a work and suggest that the true meaning of the work is not necessarily the meaning that the author intended.

Deduction: The process of reaching a conclusion through reasoning from general premises to a specific premise. Arthur Conan Doyle's character Sherlock Holmes often used deductive reasoning to solve mysteries.

Denotation: The definition of a word, apart from the impressions or feelings it creates in the reader. The word "apartheid" denotes a political and economic policy of segregation by race, but its connotations—oppression, slavery, inequality—are numerous.

Denouement: A French word meaning "the unknotting." In literature, it denotes the resolution of conflict in fiction or drama. The *denouement* follows the climax and provides an outcome to the primary plot situation as well as an explanation of secondary plot complications. A well-known example of *denouement* is the last scene of the play *As You Like It* by William Shakespeare, in which couples are married, an evildoer repents, the identities of two disguised characters are revealed, and a ruler is restored to power. Also known as "falling action."

Detective Story: A narrative about the solution of a mystery or the identification of a criminal. The conventions of the detective story include the detective's scrupulous use of logic in solving the mystery; incompetent or ineffectual police; a suspect who appears guilty at first but is later proved innocent; and the detective's friend or confidant—often the narrator—whose slowness in interpreting clues emphasizes by contrast the detective's brilliance. Edgar Allan Poe's "Murders in the Rue Morgue" is commonly regarded as the earliest example of this type of story. Other practitioners are Arthur Conan Doyle, Dashiell Hammett, and Agatha Christie.

Dialogue: Dialogue is conversation between people in a literary work. In its most restricted sense, it refers specifically to the speech of characters in a drama. As a specific literary genre, a "dialogue" is a composition in which characters debate an issue or idea.

Didactic: A term used to describe works of literature that aim to teach a moral, religious, political, or practical lesson. Although didactic elements are often found inartistically pleasing works, the term "didactic" usually refers to literature in which the message is more important than the form. The term may also be used to criticize a work that the critic finds "overly didactic," that is, heavy-handed in its delivery of a lesson. An example of didactic literature is John Bunyan's *Pilgrim's Progress*.

Dramatic Irony: Occurs when the reader of a work of literature knows something that a character in the work itself does not know. The irony is in the contrast between the intended meaning of the statements or actions of a character and the additional information understood by the audience.

Dystopia: An imaginary place in a work of fiction where the characters lead dehumanized, fearful lives. George Orwell's *Nineteen Eighty-four,* and Margaret Atwood's *Handmaid's Tale* portray versions of dystopia.

E

Edwardian: Describes cultural conventions identified with the period of the reign of Edward VII of England (1901–1910). Writers of the Edwardian Age typically displayed a strong reaction against the propriety and conservatism of the Victorian Age. Their work often exhibits distrust of authority in religion, politics, and art and expresses strong doubts about the soundness of conventional values. Writers of this era include E. M. Forster, H. G. Wells, and Joseph Conrad.

Empathy: A sense of shared experience, including emotional and physical feelings, with someone or something other than oneself. Empathy is often used to describe the response of a reader to a literary character.

Epilogue: A concluding statement or section of a literary work. In dramas, particularly those of the seventeenth and eighteenth centuries, the epilogue is a closing speech, often in verse, delivered by an actor at the end of a play and spoken directly to the audience.

Epiphany: A sudden revelation of truth inspired by a seemingly trivial incident. The term was widely used by James Joyce in his critical writings, and the stories in Joyce's *Dubliners* are commonly called "epiphanies."

Epistolary Novel: A novel in the form of letters. The form was particularly popular in the eighteenth century. The form can also be applied to short stories, as in Edwidge Danticat's "Children of the Sea."

Epithet: A word or phrase, often disparaging or abusive, that expresses a character trait of someone or something. "The Napoleon of crime" is an epithet applied to Professor Moriarty, arch-rival of Sherlock Holmes in Arthur Conan Doyle's series of detective stories.

Existentialism: A predominantly twentieth-century philosophy concerned with the nature and perception of human existence. There are two major strains of existentialist thought: atheistic and Christian. Followers of atheistic existentialism believe that the individual is alone in a godless universe and that the basic human condition is one of suffering and loneliness. Nevertheless, because there are no fixed values, individuals can create their own characters—indeed, they can shape themselves—through the exercise of free will. The atheistic strain culminates in and is popularly associated with the works of Jean-Paul Sartre. The Christian existentialists, on the other hand, believe that only in God may people find freedom from life's anguish. The two strains hold certain beliefs in common: that existence cannot be fully understood or described through empirical effort; that anguish is a universal element of life; that individuals must bear responsibility for their actions; and that there is no common standard of behavior or perception for religious and ethical matters. Existentialist thought figures prominently in the works of such authors as Franz Kafka, Fyodor Dostoyevsky, and Albert Camus.

Expatriatism: The practice of leaving one's country to live for an extended period in another country. Literary expatriates include Irish author James Joyce who moved to Italy and France, American writers James Baldwin, Ernest Hemingway, Gertrude Stein, and F. Scott Fitzgerald who lived and wrote in Paris, and Polish novelist Joseph Conrad in England.

Exposition: Writing intended to explain the nature of an idea, thing, or theme. Expository writing is often combined with description, narration, or argument.

Expressionism: An indistinct literary term, originally used to describe an early twentieth-century school of German painting. The term applies to almost any mode of unconventional, highly subjective writing that distorts reality in some way. Advocates of Expressionism include Federico Garcia Lorca, Eugene O'Neill, Franz Kafka, and James Joyce.

F

Fable: A prose or verse narrative intended to convey amoral. Animals or inanimate objects with human characteristics often serve as characters in fables. A famous fable is Aesop's "The Tortoise and the Hare."

Fantasy: A literary form related to mythology and folklore. Fantasy literature is typically set in non-existent realms and features supernatural beings. Notable examples of literature with elements of fantasy are Gabriel Gárcia Márquez's story "The Handsomest Drowned Man in the World" and Ursula K. Le Guin's "The Ones Who Walk Away from Omelas."

Farce: A type of comedy characterized by broad humor, outlandish incidents, and often vulgar subject matter. Much of the comedy in film and television could more accurately be described as farce.

Fiction: Any story that is the product of imagination rather than a documentation of fact. Characters and events in such narratives may be based in real life but their ultimate form and configuration is a creation of the author.

Figurative Language: A technique in which an author uses figures of speech such as hyperbole, irony, metaphor, or simile for a particular effect. Figurative language is the opposite of literal language, in which every word is truthful, accurate, and free of exaggeration or embellishment.

Flashback: A device used in literature to present action that occurred before the beginning of the story. Flashbacks are often introduced as the dreams or recollections of one or more characters.

Foil: A character in a work of literature whose physical or psychological qualities contrast strongly with, and therefore highlight, the corresponding qualities of another character. In his Sherlock Holmes stories, Arthur Conan Doyle portrayed Dr. Watson as a man of normal habits and intelligence, making him a foil for the eccentric and unusually perceptive Sherlock Holmes.

Folklore: Traditions and myths preserved in a culture or group of people. Typically, these are passed on by word of mouth in various forms—such as legends, songs, and proverbs—or preserved in customs and ceremonies. Washington Irving, in "The Devil and Tom Walker" and many of his other stories, incorporates many elements of the folklore of New England and Germany.

Folktale: A story originating in oral tradition. Folk tales fall into a variety of categories, including legends, ghost stories, fairy tales, fables, and anecdotes based on historical figures and events.

Foreshadowing: A device used in literature to create expectation or to set up an explanation of later developments. Edgar Allan Poe uses foreshadowing to create suspense in "The Fall of the House of Usher" when the narrator comments on the crumbling state of disrepair in which he finds the house.

G

Genre: A category of literary work. Genre may refer to both the content of a given work—tragedy, comedy, horror, science fiction—and to its form, such as poetry, novel, or drama.

Gilded Age: A period in American history during the 1870s and after characterized by political corruption and materialism. A number of important novels of social and political criticism were written during this time. Henry James and Kate Chopin are two writers who were prominent during the Gilded Age.

Gothicism: In literature, works characterized by a taste for medieval or morbid characters and situations. A gothic novel prominently features elements of horror, the supernatural, gloom, and violence: clanking chains, terror, ghosts, medieval castles, and unexplained phenomena. The term "gothic novel" is also applied to novels that lack elements of the traditional Gothic setting but that create a similar atmosphere of terror or dread. The term can also be applied to stories, plays, and poems. Mary Shelley's *Frankenstein* and Joyce Carol Oates's *Bellefleur* are both gothic novels.

Grotesque: In literature, a work that is characterized by exaggeration, deformity, freakishness, and disorder. The grotesque often includes an element of comic absurdity. Examples of the grotesque can be found in the works of Edgar Allan Poe, Flannery O'Connor, Joseph Heller, and Shirley Jackson.

H

Harlem Renaissance: The Harlem Renaissance of the 1920s is generally considered the first significant movement of black writers and artists in the United States. During this period, new and established black writers, many of whom lived in the region of New York City known as Harlem, published more fiction and poetry than ever before, the first influential black literary journals were established, and black authors and artists received their first widespread recognition and serious critical appraisal. Among the major writers associated with this period are Countee Cullen, Langston Hughes, Arna Bontemps, and Zora Neale Hurston.

Hero/Heroine: The principal sympathetic character in a literary work. Heroes and heroines typically exhibit admirable traits: idealism, courage, and integrity, for example. Famous heroes and heroines of literature include Charles Dickens's Oliver Twist, Margaret Mitchell's Scarlett O'Hara, and the anonymous narrator in Ralph Ellison's *Invisible Man*.

Hyperbole: Deliberate exaggeration used to achieve an effect. In William Shakespeare's *Macbeth,* Lady Macbeth hyperbolizes when she says, "All the perfumes of Arabia could not sweeten this little hand."

I

Image: A concrete representation of an object or sensory experience. Typically, such a representation helps evoke the feelings associated with the object or experience itself. Images are either "literal" or "figurative." Literal images are especially concrete and involve little or no extension of the obvious meaning of the words used to express them. Figurative images do not follow the literal meaning of the words exactly. Images in literature are usually visual, but the term "image" can also refer to the representation of any sensory experience.

Imagery: The array of images in a literary work. Also used to convey the author's overall use of figurative language in a work.

In medias res: A Latin term meaning "in the middle of things." It refers to the technique of beginning a story at its midpoint and then using various flashback devices to reveal previous action. This technique originated in such epics as Virgil's *Aeneid.*

Interior Monologue: A narrative technique in which characters' thoughts are revealed in a way that appears to be uncontrolled by the author. The interior monologue typically aims to reveal the inner self of a character. It portrays emotional experiences as they occur at both a conscious and unconscious level. One of the best-known interior monologues in English is the Molly Bloom section at the close of James Joyce's *Ulysses*. Katherine Anne Porter's "The Jilting of Granny Weatherall" is also told in the form of an interior monologue.

Irony: In literary criticism, the effect of language in which the intended meaning is the opposite of what is stated. The title of Jonathan Swift's "A Modest Proposal" is ironic because what Swift proposes in this essay is cannibalism—hardly "modest."

J

Jargon: Language that is used or understood only by a select group of people. Jargon may refer to terminology used in a certain profession, such as computer jargon, or it may refer to any nonsensical language that is not understood by most people. Anthony Burgess's *A Clockwork Orange* and James Thurber's "The Secret Life of Walter Mitty" both use jargon.

K

Knickerbocker Group: An indistinct group of New York writers of the first half of the nineteenth century. Members of the group were linked only by location and a common theme: New York life. Two famous members of the Knickerbocker Group were Washington Irving and William Cullen Bryant. The group's name derives from Irving's *Knickerbocker's History of New York.*

L

Literal Language: An author uses literal language when he or she writes without exaggerating or embellishing the subject matter and without any tools of figurative language. To say "He ran very quickly down the street" is to use literal language, whereas to say "He ran like a hare down the street" would be using figurative language.

Literature: Literature is broadly defined as any written or spoken material, but the term most often refers to creative works. Literature includes poetry, drama, fiction, and many kinds of nonfiction writing, as well as oral, dramatic, and broadcast compositions not necessarily preserved in a written format, such as films and television programs.

Lost Generation: A term first used by Gertrude Stein to describe the post-World War I generation of American writers: men and women haunted by a sense of betrayal and emptiness brought about by the destructiveness of the war. The term is commonly applied to Hart Crane, Ernest Hemingway, F. Scott Fitzgerald, and others.

M

Magic Realism: A form of literature that incorporates fantasy elements or supernatural occurrences into the narrative and accepts them as truth. Gabriel Gárcia Márquez and Laura Esquivel are two writers known for their works of magic realism.

Metaphor: A figure of speech that expresses an idea through the image of another object. Metaphors suggest the essence of the first object by identifying it with certain qualities of the second object. An example is "But soft, what light through yonder window breaks? / It is the east, and Juliet is the sun" in William Shakespeare's *Romeo and Juliet.* Here, Juliet, the first object, is identified with qualities of the second object, the sun.

Minimalism: A literary style characterized by spare, simple prose with few elaborations. In minimalism, the main theme of the work is often never discussed directly. Amy Hempel and Ernest Hemingway are two writers known for their works of minimalism.

Modernism: Modern literary practices. Also, the principles of a literary school that lasted from roughly the beginning of the twentieth century until the end of World War II. Modernism is defined by its rejection of the literary conventions of the nineteenth century and by its opposition to conventional morality, taste, traditions, and economic values. Many writers are associated with the concepts of modernism, including Albert Camus, D. H. Lawrence, Ernest Hemingway, William Faulkner, Eugene O'Neill, and James Joyce.

Monologue: A composition, written or oral, by a single individual. More specifically, a speech given by a single individual in a drama or other public entertainment. It has no set length, although it is usually several or more lines long. "I Stand Here Ironing" by Tillie Olsen is an example of a story written in the form of a monologue.

Mood: The prevailing emotions of a work or of the author in his or her creation of the work. The mood of a work is not always what might be expected based on its subject matter.

Motif: A theme, character type, image, metaphor, or other verbal element that recurs throughout a single work of literature or occurs in a number of different works over a period of time. For example, the color white in Herman Melville's *Moby Dick* is a "specific" motif, while the trials of star-crossed lovers is a "conventional" motif from the literature of all periods.

N

Narration: The telling of a series of events, real or invented. A narration may be either a simple narrative, in which the events are recounted chronologically, or a narrative with a plot, in which the account is given in a style reflecting the author's artistic concept of the story. Narration is sometimes used as a synonym for "storyline."

Narrative: A verse or prose accounting of an event or sequence of events, real or invented. The term is also used as an adjective in the sense "method of narration." For example, in literary criticism, the expression "narrative technique" usually refers to the way the author structures and presents his or her story. Different narrative forms include diaries, travelogues, novels, ballads, epics, short stories, and other fictional forms.

Narrator: The teller of a story. The narrator may be the author or a character in the story through whom the author speaks. Huckleberry Finn is the narrator of Mark Twain's *The Adventures of Huckleberry Finn.*

Novella: An Italian term meaning "story." This term has been especially used to describe fourteenth-century Italian tales, but it also refers to modern short novels. Modern novellas include Leo Tolstoy's *The Death of Ivan Ilich,* Fyodor Dostoyevsky's *Notes from the Underground,* and Joseph Conrad's *Heart of Darkness.*

O

Oedipus Complex: A son's romantic obsession with his mother. The phrase is derived from the story of the ancient Theban hero Oedipus, who unknowingly killed his father and married his mother, and was popularized by Sigmund Freud's theory of psychoanalysis. Literary occurrences of the Oedipus complex include Sophocles' *Oedipus Rex* and D. H. Lawrence's "The Rocking-Horse Winner."

Onomatopoeia: The use of words whose sounds express or suggest their meaning. In its simplest sense, onomatopoeia may be represented by words that mimic the sounds they denote such as "hiss" or "meow." At a more subtle level, the pattern and rhythm of sounds and rhymes of a line or poem may be onomatopoeic.

Oral Tradition: A process by which songs, ballads, folklore, and other material are transmitted by word of mouth. The tradition of oral transmission predates the written record systems of literate society. Oral transmission preserves material sometimes over generations, although often with variations. Memory plays a large part in the recitation and preservation of orally transmitted material. Native American myths and legends, and African folktales told by plantation slaves are examples of orally transmitted literature.

P

Parable: A story intended to teach a moral lesson or answer an ethical question. Examples of parables are the stories told by Jesus Christ in the New Testament, notably "The Prodigal Son," but parables also are used in Sufism, rabbinic literature, Hasidism, and Zen Buddhism. Isaac Bashevis Singer's story "Gimpel the Fool" exhibits characteristics of a parable.

Paradox: A statement that appears illogical or contradictory at first, but may actually point to an underlying truth. A literary example of a paradox is George Orwell's statement "All animals are equal, but some animals are more equal than others" in *Animal Farm.*

Parody: In literature, this term refers to an imitation of a serious literary work or the signature style of a particular author in a ridiculous manner. Atypical parody adopts the style of the original and applies it to an inappropriate subject for humorous effect. Parody is a form of satire and could be considered the literary equivalent of a caricature or cartoon. Henry Fielding's *Shamela* is a parody of Samuel Richardson's *Pamela.*

Persona: A Latin term meaning "mask." Personae are the characters in a fictional work of literature. The persona generally functions as a mask through which the author tells a story in a voice other than his or her own. A persona is usually either a character in a story who acts as a narrator or an "implied author," a voice created by the author to act as the narrator for himself or herself. The persona in Charlotte Perkins Gilman's story "The Yellow Wallpaper" is the unnamed young mother experiencing a mental breakdown.

Personification: A figure of speech that gives human qualities to abstract ideas, animals, and inanimate objects. To say that "the sun is smiling" is to personify the sun.

Plot: The pattern of events in a narrative or drama. In its simplest sense, the plot guides the author in composing the work and helps the reader follow the work. Typically, plots exhibit causality and unity and have a beginning, a middle, and an end. Sometimes, however, a plot may consist of a series of disconnected events, in which case it is known as an "episodic plot."

Poetic Justice: An outcome in a literary work, not necessarily a poem, in which the good are rewarded and the evil are punished, especially in ways that particularly fit their virtues or crimes. For example, a murderer may himself be murdered, or a thief will find himself penniless.

Poetic License: Distortions of fact and literary convention made by a writer—not always a poet—for the sake of the effect gained. Poetic license is closely related to the concept of "artistic freedom." An author exercises poetic license by saying that a pile of money "reaches as high as a mountain" when the pile is actually only a foot or two high.

Point of View: The narrative perspective from which a literary work is presented to the reader. There are four traditional points of view. The "third person omniscient" gives the reader a "godlike" perspective, unrestricted by time or place, from which to see actions and look into the minds of characters. This allows the author to comment openly on characters and events in the work. The "third person" point of view presents the events of the story from outside of any single character's perception, much like the omniscient point of view, but the reader must understand the action as it takes place and without any special insight into characters' minds or motivations. The "first person" or "personal" point of view relates events as they are perceived by a single character. The main character "tells" the story and may offer opinions about the action and characters which differ from those of the author. Much less common than omniscient, third person, and first person is the "second person" point of view, wherein the author tells the story as if it is happening to the reader. James Thurber employs the omniscient point of view in his short story "The Secret Life of Walter Mitty." Ernest Hemingway's "A Clean, Well-Lighted Place" is a short story told from the third person point of view. Mark Twain's novel *Huckleberry Finn* is presented from the first person viewpoint. Jay McInerney's *Bright Lights, Big City* is an example of a novel which uses the second person point of view.

Pornography: Writing intended to provoke feelings of lust in the reader. Such works are often condemned by critics and teachers, but those which can be shown to have literary value are viewed less harshly. Literary works that have been described as pornographic include D. H. Lawrence's *Lady Chatterley's Lover* and James Joyce's *Ulysses*.

Post-Aesthetic Movement: An artistic response made by African Americans to the black aesthetic movement of the 1960s and early 1970s. Writers since that time have adopted a somewhat different tone in their work, with less emphasis placed on the disparity between black and white in the United States. In the words of post-aesthetic authors such as Toni Morrison, John Edgar Wideman, and Kristin Hunter, African Americans are portrayed as looking inward for answers to their own questions, rather than always looking to the outside world. Two well-known examples of works produced as part of the post-aesthetic movement are the Pulitzer Prize–winning novels *The Color Purple* by Alice Walker and *Beloved* by Toni Morrison.

Postmodernism: Writing from the 1960s forward characterized by experimentation and application of modernist elements, which include existentialism and alienation. Postmodernists have gone a step further in the rejection of tradition begun with the modernists by also rejecting traditional forms, preferring the anti-novel over the novel and the anti-hero over the hero. Postmodern writers include Thomas Pynchon, Margaret Drabble, and Gabriel Gárcia Márquez.

Prologue: An introductory section of a literary work. It often contains information establishing the situation of the characters or presents information about the setting, time period, or action. In drama, the prologue is spoken by a chorus or by one of the principal characters.

Prose: A literary medium that attempts to mirror the language of everyday speech. It is distinguished from poetry by its use of unmetered, unrhymed language consisting of logically related sentences. Prose is usually grouped into paragraphs that form a cohesive whole such as an essay or a novel. The term is sometimes used to mean an author's general writing.

Protagonist: The central character of a story who serves as a focus for its themes and incidents and as the principal rationale for its development. The protagonist is sometimes referred to in discussions of modern literature as the hero or anti-hero. Well-known protagonists are Hamlet in William Shakespeare's *Hamlet* and Jay Gatsby in F. Scott Fitzgerald's *The Great Gatsby*.

R

Realism: A nineteenth-century European literary movement that sought to portray familiar characters, situations, and settings in a realistic manner. This was done primarily by using an objective narrative point of view and through the buildup of accurate detail. The standard for success of any realistic work depends on how faithfully it transfers common experience into fictional forms. The realistic method may be altered or extended, as in stream of consciousness writing, to record highly subjective experience. Contemporary authors who often write in a realistic way include Nadine Gordimer and Grace Paley.

Resolution: The portion of a story following the climax, in which the conflict is resolved. The resolution of Jane Austen's *Northanger Abbey* is neatly summed up in the following sentence: "Henry and Catherine were married, the bells rang and every body smiled."

Rising Action: The part of a drama where the plot becomes increasingly complicated. Rising action leads up to the climax, or turning point, of a drama. The final "chase scene" of an action film is generally the rising action which culminates in the film's climax.

Roman a clef: A French phrase meaning "novel with a key." It refers to a narrative in which real persons are portrayed under fictitious names. Jack Kerouac, for example, portrayed various friends under fictitious names in the novel *On the Road.* D. H. Lawrence based "The Rocking-Horse Winner" on a family he knew.

Romanticism: This term has two widely accepted meanings. In historical criticism, it refers to a European intellectual and artistic movement of the late eighteenth and early nineteenth centuries that sought greater freedom of personal expression than that allowed by the strict rules of literary form and logic of the eighteenth-century neoclassicists. The Romantics preferred emotional and imaginative expression to rational analysis. They considered the individual to be at the center of all experience and so placed him or her at the center of their art. The Romantics believed that the creative imagination reveals nobler truths—unique feelings and attitudes—than those that could be discovered by logic or by scientific examination. "Romanticism" is also used as a general term to refer to a type of sensibility found in all periods of literary history and usually considered to be in opposition to the principles of classicism. In this sense, Romanticism signifies any work or philosophy in which the exotic or dreamlike figure strongly, or that is devoted to individualistic expression, self-analysis, or a pursuit of a higher realm of knowledge than can be discovered by human reason. Prominent Romantics include Jean-Jacques Rousseau, William Wordsworth, John Keats, Lord Byron, and Johann Wolfgang von Goethe.

S

Satire: A work that uses ridicule, humor, and wit to criticize and provoke change in human nature and institutions. Voltaire's novella *Candide* and Jonathan Swift's essay "A Modest Proposal" are both satires. Flannery O'Connor's portrayal of the family in "A Good Man Is Hard to Find" is a satire of a modern, Southern, American family.

Science Fiction: A type of narrative based upon real or imagined scientific theories and technology. Science fiction is often peopled with alien creatures and set on other planets or in different dimensions. Popular writers of science fiction are Isaac Asimov, Karel Capek, Ray Bradbury, and Ursula K. Le Guin.

Setting: The time, place, and culture in which the action of a narrative takes place. The elements of setting may include geographic location, characters's physical and mental environments, prevailing cultural attitudes, or the historical time in which the action takes place.

Short Story: A fictional prose narrative shorter and more focused than a novella. The short story usually deals with a single episode and often a single character. The "tone," the author's attitude toward his or her subject and audience, is uniform throughout. The short story frequently also lacks *denouement*, ending instead at its climax.

Signifying Monkey: A popular trickster figure in black folklore, with hundreds of tales about this character documented since the 19th century. Henry Louis Gates Jr. examines the history of the signifying monkey in *The Signifying Monkey: Towards a Theory of Afro-American Literary Criticism,* published in 1988.

Simile: A comparison, usually using "like" or "as," of two essentially dissimilar things, as in "coffee as cold as ice" or "He sounded like a broken record." The title of Ernest Hemingway's "Hills Like White Elephants" contains a simile.

Socialist Realism: The Socialist Realism school of literary theory was proposed by Maxim Gorky and established as a dogma by the first Soviet Congress of Writers. It demanded adherence to a communist worldview in works of literature. Its doctrines required an objective viewpoint comprehensible to the working classes and themes of social struggle featuring strong proletarian heroes. Gabriel Gárcia Márquez's stories exhibit some characteristics of Socialist Realism.

Stereotype: A stereotype was originally the name for a duplication made during the printing process; this led to its modern definition as a person or thing that is (or is assumed to be) the same as all others of its type. Common stereotypical characters include the absent-minded professor, the nagging wife, the troublemaking teenager, and the kindhearted grandmother.

Stream of Consciousness: A narrative technique for rendering the inward experience of a character. This technique is designed to give the impression of an ever-changing series of thoughts, emotions, images, and memories in the spontaneous and seemingly illogical order that they occur in life. The textbook example of stream of consciousness is the last section of James Joyce's *Ulysses.*

Structure: The form taken by a piece of literature. The structure may be made obvious for ease of understanding, as in nonfiction works, or may obscured for artistic purposes, as in some poetry or seemingly "unstructured" prose.

Style: A writer's distinctive manner of arranging words to suit his or her ideas and purpose in writing. The unique imprint of the author's personality upon his or her writing, style is the product of an author's way of arranging ideas and his or her use of diction, different sentence structures, rhythm, figures of speech, rhetorical principles, and other elements of composition.

Suspense: A literary device in which the author maintains the audience's attention through the buildup of events, the outcome of which will soon be revealed. Suspense in William Shakespeare's *Hamlet* is sustained throughout by the question of whether or not the Prince will achieve what he has been instructed to do and of what he intends to do.

Symbol: Something that suggests or stands for something else without losing its original identity. In literature, symbols combine their literal meaning with the suggestion of an abstract concept. Literary symbols are of two types: those that carry complex associations of meaning no matter what their contexts, and those that derive their suggestive meaning from their functions in specific literary works. Examples of symbols are sunshine suggesting happiness, rain suggesting sorrow, and storm clouds suggesting despair.

T

Tale: A story told by a narrator with a simple plot and little character development. Tales are usually relatively short and often carry a simple message. Examples of tales can be found in the works of Saki, Anton Chekhov, Guy de Maupassant, and O. Henry.

Tall Tale: A humorous tale told in a straightforward, credible tone but relating absolutely impossible events or feats of the characters. Such tales were commonly told of frontier adventures during the settlement of the west in the United States. Literary use of tall tales can be found in Washington Irving's *History of New York,* Mark Twain's *Life on the Mississippi,* and in the German R. F. Raspe's *Baron Munchausen's Narratives of His Marvellous Travels and Campaigns in Russia.*

Theme: The main point of a work of literature. The term is used interchangeably with thesis. Many works have multiple themes. One of the themes of Nathaniel Hawthorne's "Young Goodman Brown" is loss of faith.

Tone: The author's attitude toward his or her audience maybe deduced from the tone of the work. A formal tone may create distance or convey politeness, while an informal tone may encourage a friendly, intimate, or intrusive feeling in the reader. The author's attitude toward his or her subject matter may also be deduced from the tone of the words he or she uses in discussing it. The tone of

John F. Kennedy's speech which included the appeal to "ask not what your country can do for you" was intended to instill feelings of camaraderie and national pride in listeners.

Tragedy: A drama in prose or poetry about a noble, courageous hero of excellent character who, because of some tragic character flaw, brings ruin upon him- or herself. Tragedy treats its subjects in a dignified and serious manner, using poetic language to help evoke pity and fear and bring about catharsis, a purging of these emotions. The tragic form was practiced extensively by the ancient Greeks. The classical form of tragedy was revived in the sixteenth century; it flourished especially on the Elizabethan stage. In modern times, dramatists have attempted to adapt the form to the needs of modern society by drawing their heroes from the ranks of ordinary men and women and defining the nobility of these heroes in terms of spirit rather than exalted social standing. Some contemporary works that are thought of as tragedies include *The Great Gatsby* by F. Scott Fitzgerald, and *The Sound and the Fury* by William Faulkner.

Tragic Flaw: In a tragedy, the quality within the hero or heroine which leads to his or her downfall. Examples of the tragic flaw include Othello's jealousy and Hamlet's indecisiveness, although most great tragedies defy such simple interpretation.

U

Utopia: A fictional perfect place, such as "paradise" or "heaven." An early literary utopia was described in Plato's *Republic,* and in modern literature, Ursula K. Le Guin depicts a utopia in "The Ones Who Walk Away from Omelas."

V

Victorian: Refers broadly to the reign of Queen Victoria of England (1837-1901) and to anything with qualities typical of that era. For example, the qualities of smug narrow-mindedness, bourgeois materialism, faith in social progress, and priggish morality are often considered Victorian. In literature, the Victorian Period was the great age of the English novel, and the latter part of the era saw the rise of movements such as decadence and symbolism.

Cumulative Author/Title Index

C

I

J

K

L

M

R

S

Y

Z

Cumulative Nationality/Ethnicity Index

Antiguan

Argentinian

Asian American

Australian

Austrian

Eurasian

French

German

Haitian

Hispanic American

Indian

Indonesian

Irish

Israeli

Italian

Japanese

Jewish

Spanish

Swedish

Trinidadan

Welsh

West Indian

Subject/Theme Index

L

M

N

O

P